Team Environment

W9-DHH-800

Index to Organizational ShowCASES

A multipart organizational showcase feature exposes students to communication challenges faced by real-world organizations. Part 1 opens the chapter by highlighting the feature organization's approach to the chapter's communication focus. Part 2 spotlights a key communicator in the feature organization, and Part 3 provides a critical-thinking case related to the featured organization. Part 4, an engaging web component, allows students to further analyze the organization's communication strategies.

Business Communication

14e

Carol M. Lehman

Professor of Management,
Mississippi State University

Debbie D. DuFrene

Professor of General Business,
Stephen F. Austin State University

THOMSON
SOUTH-WESTERN

Australia · Canada · Mexico · Singapore · Spain · United Kingdom · United States

THOMSON
SOUTH-WESTERN

Business Communication, 14e
Carol M. Lehman, Debbie D. DuFrene

VP/Editorial Director: Jack W. Calhoun	**Manufacturing Coordinator:** Diane Lohman	**Cover Designer:** Chris Miller/Pop Design Works
VP/Editor-in-Chief: George Werthman	**Media Production Editor:** Kelly Reid	**Cover Images:** © Getty Images
Acquisitions Editor: Jennifer L. Codner	**Design Project Manager:** Chris Miller	**Internal Designer:** Chris Miller
Developmental Editor: Taney H. Wilkins	**Photography Manager:** Deanna Ettinger & Kathryn Russell	**Photo Researcher:** Susan Van Etten
Marketing Manager: Larry Qualls	**Production House/Compositor:** DPS Associates, Inc.	**Printer:** R. R. Donnelley Willard, OH
Production Editor: Heather Mann		

For permission to use material from this text or product, contact us by
Tel (800) 730-2214
Fax (800) 730-2215
http://www.thomsonrights.com

For more information contact South-Western,
5191 Natorp Boulevard,
Mason, Ohio, 45040.
Or you can visit our Internet site at:
http://www.swlearning.com

Brief Contents

Contents

ii Communication Analysis | 79

3 Planning Spoken and Written Messages | 80

iii Communication Through Voice, Electronic, and Written Messages | 157

V Communication for Employment | 533

a Appendix A

Document Format and Layout Guide

b Appendix B

Referencing Styles

c Appendix C

Language Review and Exercises

d Appendix D

Grading Symbols and Proofreaders' Marks

r References

i Index

Preface

//preface//

Business Communication

14e

Lehman & DuFrene

Insights into Business Communication, 14e

Lehman & DuFrene

Dear *Business Communication* Colleagues:

It's a pleasure to present the 14th edition of *Business Communication*, a trusted standard and innovative trend setter that provides information and learning experiences required to prepare your students and ours for today's workplace. As you review the Illustrated Preface, the text, and wide array of electronic supplements, we believe you will agree. What's more we are convinced your students will find the cutting-edge technology and engaging exploration focus really "cool" and in touch with the way they want to learn.

Communicating our vision of the 14th edition to you as an e-newsletter rather than a traditional print document illustrates a shift in business communication. While paper documents will remain a viable medium for specific messages, today's students must also learn to speak, write, and research proficiently while using a wide array of communication technologies geared for web delivery.

Best wishes for a rewarding course as you guide your students in reaching their career potential through effective communication. Please contact us or visit us at upcoming business communication conferences to share your comments, questions, and successes as we work together to prepare our students to become powerful communicators.

Carol Lehman
Mississippi State University

Debbie DuFrene
Stephen F. Austin State University

About the Author Team

Both Carol and Debbie are professors in AACSB-accredited schools of business, each with more than twenty years' experience teaching business communication in traditional and distance classes. They are actively engaged in research and are frequent presenters at national and regional meetings of the Association for Business Communication, for which they sponsor the Meada Gibbs Outstanding Teacher Award. You are encouraged to access the "Welcome" link on the Professional Power Pak (PPP) Student CD for more detailed bios of these committed educators and authors and a movie trailer in which Carol and Debbie present the value of the PPP to your net-savvy students.

(Debbie DuFrene)   (Carol Lehman)

Business Communication, 14e is one of textbook publishing's longest-running success stories. This trusted standard has remained a best seller through constant innovation, and the 14th edition takes that practice to new heights.

While retaining the theoretical approach that made it a mainstay, *Business Communication*, 14e offers the most complete integration of traditional and cutting-edge communication content and learning tools on the market today.

Why go to such lengths to improve on a sure thing?

- To make the learning process mirror how communication functions in business today
- To respond to students' familiarity with new technologies and desire for interactivity
- To provide more coverage of voice and electronic communication, while keeping to a manageable 14 chapters
- To make the entire learning package easier to use
- To help instructors incorporate contemporary themes in an otherwise full course

Integrating "Tried and True" with "New"

Incorporating Current Issues into a Full Course

Business Communication's Strategic Forces model, a unique standard since the 12th edition, seamlessly integrates coverage of Legal and Ethical Issues, Diversity, Teams and Technology as prevailing forces in business communication today.

Chapter 1 sets the stage by explaining the importance of these issues and giving a road map of their coverage in the text, activities, course applications, and cases.

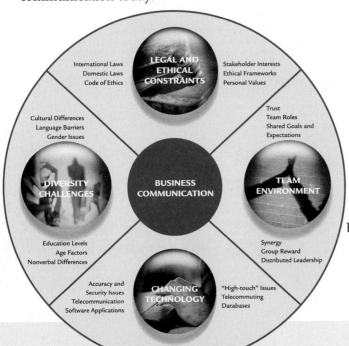

Marginal icons located throughout all 14 chapters flag sections where a particular focus area is addressed.

Model documents highlight relevant strategic forces influencing the message being studied.

Two feature boxes per chapter highlight strategic focus issues.

In addition:

- *Internet Cases* at the end of each chapter provide expanded exploration of the strategic forces.

- *ShowCASES* illustrate how real-world organizations respond to the impact of the strategic forces in their communication activities.

Adding New Content, Easier Ways to Use Learning Tools

Updated content is reflected throughout the text and ancillary package. Two new instructional elements, Electronic Café and Professional Power Pak, show students how new communication technologies are used in business today.

Electronic Café end-of-chapter sections enable professors to easily expose students to the full functionality of InfoTrac®, WebTutor™, the Text Support Site, and Professional Power Pak.

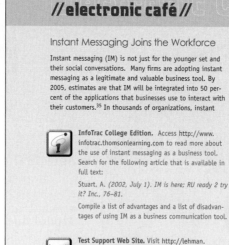

// electronic café //

Instant Messaging Joins the Workforce

Instant messaging (IM) is not just for the younger set and their social conversations. Many firms are adopting instant messaging as a legitimate and valuable business tool. By 2005, estimates are that IM will be integrated into 50 percent of the applications that businesses use to interact with their customers.[35] In thousands of organizations, instant messaging is complimenting and replacing existing media such as e-mail and voice messages. Some corporate leaders, however, have expressed concerns over productivity and security that might be jeopardized when using IM. The following electronic activities will allow you to explore the IM phenomenon in more depth:

InfoTrac College Edition. Access http://www.infotrac.thomsonlearning.com to read more about the use of instant messaging as a business tool. Search for the following article that is available in full text:

Stuart, A. (2002, July 1). IM is here; RU ready 2 try it? *Inc.*, 76–81.

Compile a list of advantages and a list of disadvantages of using IM as a business communication tool.

Test Support Web Site. Visit http://lehman.swlearning.com to learn more about instant messaging. Refer to Chapter 1's Electronic Café activity that provides links to an online article describing how instant messaging works. Be prepared to

discuss in class the features and uses of IM or follow your instructor's directions about how to use this information.

WebTutor Advantage. Your instructor will give you directions about how and when to log on to your WebTutor and participate in an online chat on the following topic:

Instant messaging can be an effective business tool if...

Professional Power Pak. Access your PPP CD for helpful tips on using instant messaging as a business communication tool.

Page 41

Café themes help students understand key topics from each chapter such as Instant Messaging, Discussion Boards, Intranets, and Personal Web Pages. (See Index in end pages for a full list.)

The Professional Power Pak Student CD includes Classroom and Professional Resources. In the classroom section, students can meet the authors, learn from Video Cases, explore Electronic Café activities, and download PowerPoint slides.

The Professional Resources section offers support for students after graduation by providing information and resources in four areas: Improving Your Global Vision, Reaching Your Career Potential, Sharpening Your Technology Skills and Speaking, Writing and Researching for Business.

Restructured *content* gives more coverage to spoken and electronic communication, providing better balance to the abundance of written documents.

Model documents show the application of effective and ineffective communication principles. Spoken, electronic and written exercises require analyzing the audience and purpose, choosing and applying an outline, and evaluating the communication.

Updating Theoretical Foundation and Critical Thinking Practice

In order to solve complex communication challenges concisely and correctly, students need a theoretical foundation and practice that encourages critical thinking. This approach, a *Business Communication* hallmark, is expanded and updated in the 14th edition.

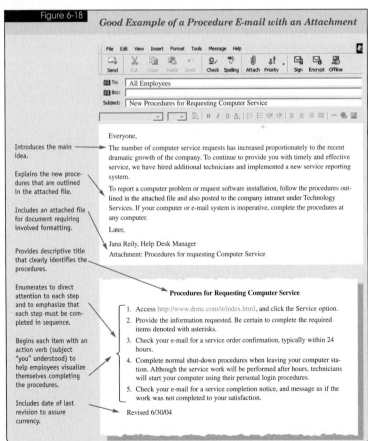

Four-part ShowCASES provide opportunities for research, analysis, and discussion of communication issues that affect real-world organizations. The fourth part of each ShowCASE is on the Web.

Page 108

Margin notes and **Digging Deeper** review require reflection and application of major points.

End-of-Chapter applications are divided into critical communication areas (Read, Think, Write, Speak and Collaborate), making it easy for instructors to build selected skills with each chapter.

Expanded **Web/e-mail** activities and applications are easy to locate (see end pages for Index of Web Enrichment activities and Web components of ShowCASES).

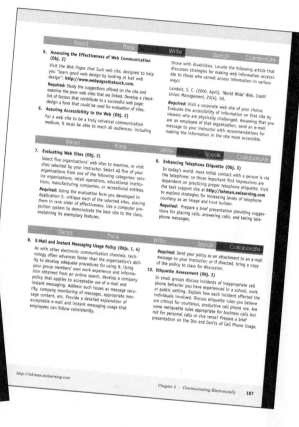

Revamping the End-of-Chapter

A new end-of-chapter organization makes it easier than ever to select activities for each class. Material is divided into *Activities* for immediate discussion or reinforcement, *Applications*, which require more thought and time, and *Cases* (Internet, Video, and ShowCASE) for extended learning. Applications are further divided by communication area to simplify and enhance assignment selection.

More emphasis is placed on **spoken** and **electronic** communication.

Cases that involve the use of different technologies allow students to apply textbook concepts, explore, make choices, and get involved in timely issues.

Organizational ShowCASES encourage exploration, analysis, and discussion. Internet cases provide a **GMAT activity** representing the type of critical thinking required in the GMAT Analytical Writing Assessments.

Hallmark Tips for Writing Business Greetings

Getting and sending greeting cards makes people feel good. But the "warm fuzzy" responses that make greeting cards so effective can also make some professional types a little nervous, especially if you are used to keeping in touch through memos, phone calls, e-mail, and other less personal types of communication. If you are uneasy about using cards to stay in touch, relax; Hallmark has some helpful suggestions to help you personalize your messages and say just the right thing.

- Visit the Hallmark web site at **http://www.hallmark.com** and read "What to Say... and How to Say It." What advantages are offered by sending greeting card messages?
- Locate "Tips on Writing Business Greetings" on the Hallmark site. What tips did you find most helpful?

Activities

Referring to the chapter, read the Strategic Forces feature on e-cards. In a class discussion, compare the roles of traditional greeting cards and e-cards in conveying business messages. Does audience impact differ; if so, how?

Part 4 of the Hallmark ShowCASE focuses on organizational communication at Hallmark and Dean Rodenbough's views on corporate communication.

Page 119

http://www.hallmark.com

Visit the text support site at **http://lehman.swlearning.com** to complete Part 4 of the Hallmark ShowCASE.

Internet Case

Can the United States Succeed Without Rewarding Rugged Individuality?

A basic element of the fabric of U.S. entrepreneurship is the faith in the ingenuity of the individual person's ability to conceive, develop, and profit from a business endeavor. The frontier spirit and triumph of the individual over looming odds have been a predominant force in the development of the United States. Such individualism has also been recognized by organizations, with reward going to those who contribute winning ideas and efforts.

The recent shift in organizational structures toward team design has caused management to reassess reward systems that focus on individual recognition and to consider rewards that are based on team performance. Some fear that removing individual incentive will lead to mediocrity and a reduction in personal effort. They argue that while the team model might work in other cultures, it is inconsistent with the U.S. way of thinking and living. According to Madelyn Hoshstein, president of DYG Inc., a New York firm that researches corporate trends, America is moving away from the model of team building in which everyone is expected to do everything and toward focusing on employees who are the best at what they do. She describes this change as a shift toward social Darwinism and away from egalitarianism, in which everyone has equal economic, political, and social rights.[37]

Team advocates say that teams are here to stay and liken those who deny that reality to the proverbial ostrich with its head in the sand. They stress the need for newly structured incentive plans to reward group effort.

Visit the text support site at **http://lehman.swlearning.com** to link to web resources related to this topic. Respond to one or more of the following activities, as directed by your instructor.

1. **GMAT** How would you respond to those with concerns about loss of individual incentive? Argue for or against the increased emphasis on team reward, using either personal examples or examples from business.

2. Structure a reward system that would recognize both individual and team performance. You may use an organization of your choice to illustrate.

3. Select a specific corporation or nation that has implemented the team model. Describe the transition away from a hierarchical structure and the consequences that have resulted from the shift, both positive and negative.

Page 44

Integrating Classroom and Boardroom

14e incorporates real-world cases from high profile companies (such as Centers for Disease Control, NASA, Hallmark, and Hewlett Packard). These cases allow students to learn about key concepts through real companies' experiences. InfoTrac and Professional Power Pak give further insights into the reality of communicating in the business world:

- *Internet Cases* are updated. (See Index in end pages for a full list).

- *Video Cases* are all new. (See Index in end pages for a full list).

- Three *ShowCASES* are new, covering extremely timely events. (The NASA case, for example, explores crisis communication surrounding the Space Shuttle Columbia disaster.) Other ShowCASES have been updated.

- *InfoTrac* gives students free access to articles in the latest issues of respected business magazines and journals.

- *Professional Power Pak* gives real-world advice for job-hunting and career building in today's competitive market.

Video Case

Renegade Animation: Animated Graphics Technology

Located in downtown Burbank, California, Renegade Animation was founded in 1992 by Ashley Quinn and Darrell Van Citters. In its first year, Renegade did $1.2 million in sales. And even though it is slightly larger in sales today, there are only four full-time employees along with 35 freelance artists. Renegade Animation does everything from low-budget public service announcements to 90-second spots that have aired on the Super Bowl.

Renegade's impressive production list (found at **http://www.renegadeanimation.com/projects.html**) includes a variety of animation projects, such as computer games and animation consulting, design, and development projects. If you enjoy animation and are using a fast Internet connection, you may want to view several of the QuickTime clips of Renegade's work at **http://www. renegadeanimation. com/movies.html**, such as "Trix Yogurt Magic Wand" and "Cheetos Stunt Double."

View the video segment about Renegade Animation and related activities on WebTutor or your Professional Power Pak CD.

Discussion Questions

1. What might be one reason that Ashley Quinn and Darrell Van Citters chose the name *Renegade Animation* for their new company, when one definition of the word "renegade" is "an individual who rejects . . . conventional behavior"?

2. What part, if any, of Ken McDonald's explanation of the animation process was new information to you? If you already knew how the animation process works before viewing this video, when and from whom did you gain your knowledge?

3. Why do you think companies such as Kraft General Foods, Midas, and Vlasic Pickles are willing to pay $120,000 to $180,000 for a 30-second animated commercial?

Integrating Spoken, Written, and Electronic Communication

Re-sequenced and expanded content throughout prepares students to communicate expertly through an ever-expanding number of channels.

Chapter 5, "**Communicating Electronically**," covers telephone, voice-mail, face-to-face/electronic presentations, e-mail, instant messaging, electronic bulletin boards, and messages exchanged at company web sites.

New coverage is included on voice mail, cell phone usage, and wireless technologies. A new Writing for the Web section explores the composition of web content.

	Written	Letters Memos
	Electronic	E-mail Instant messaging Web site
	Spoken	In person Telephone Voice mail

Model documents cover paper and electronic message delivery.

Activities, applications and cases provide practice in written, spoken, and electronic communication.

Figure 8-2

Good Example of a Sales Message Promoting a Product

Inductive Outline for Sales Messages

1. Gain the receiver's attention.
2. Introduce the product, service, or idea and arouse interest in it.
3. Present convincing evidence of the merits of the item being promoted and overcome any resistance.
4. Encourage the receiver to take the desired action (buy the product or service or accept the idea).

PearMusic ♪ **Music downloads the right way** (a division of comPear Computers)
6223 North Frontgate Road ♪ Fort Wayne, IN 46485 ♪ 219-555-4877

May 20, 2004

Ms. Jessica Lawrence
500 Louisville Street
Oxford, MS 38655

Dear Ms. Lawrence

Do you want to access the music you love and arrange the songs how YOU want to? want CD-quality songs that are easy to download? want those songs to be portable? and want the peace of mind knowing that all your downloads are sanctioned by the record company and the original recording artist? Then you want PearMusic from comPear.com.

With comPear's new online digital music store PearMusic, you can find songs from Tom Petty, Richard Marx, Harry Connick, Jr., and every other Tom, Dick, and Harry in the music world for 99 cents per song with no subscription fees. With PearMusic, you also can

♪ Load the songs onto your PearJam handheld music player and up to three comPear computers.
♪ Mix songs from various artists to make your favorite playlists.
♪ Burn a single playlist up to ten times without changes.
♪ Get a free 30-second preview for every song.
♪ Listen to CD-quality music on your computer and your PearJam.
♪ Browse the PearMusic store by genre, artist, album, composer, or song title.
♪ Access cover art for CDs and watch exclusive full-length music videos.

Visit www.comPear.com/PearMusic today and check out the collection that is growing daily. Use the enclosed authorization number to save $50 on your purchase of a PearJam (regular price $299) so that you can take your PearMusic wherever you go. Just key the authorization number into the "special offer" box on the checkout screen. The $50 savings offer expires July 31, so get your PearJam today and start making your own music choices with PearMusic.

Sincerely

Adria D. Wayne

Adria D. Wayne
Sales Manager

Enclosure

Seeks to gain attention by introducing experiences that are familiar to the receiver. Presents customized music as the as the central selling point.

Presents the "online digital music store" as a solution to the problem and reinforces the central selling point.

Uses a simple, easy-to-read bulleted list to present evidence that reflects understanding of the flexibility the receiver desires in digital music.

Keeps the focus on the receiver by use of second person, active-voice sentences.

States a specific action with reward for taking action. Makes the action easy and provides incentive for quick action.

Page 305

Integrating Content, Technology and Supplements

Now it's easier than ever to develop an optimal instructional mix for your students. In fact, with the abundance of online resources, *Business Communication* 14e makes an ideal package for your Web-based or Web-assisted course. The text and its comprehensive technology package are blended seamlessly. Supplements have been expanded and updated to fit more closely with the text.

The end-of-chapter *Electronic Café* invites use of four separate technologies to explore each topic. For example, students might be asked to download an article from InfoTrac on the café's technology theme, then discuss it live on WebTutor, take a related quiz on the Text Support Site, and view a relevant video on Professional Power Pak.

WebTutor Advantage on Web CT and Blackboard includes text-specific content created just for this edition: E-lectures, Quiz Bowl, Crossword Puzzles, Discussion Questions, and Videos.

WebTUTOR™ Advantage

The Building High-Performance Teams handbook that ships free with each copy has been expanded to include more team-building activities and team process guidelines and forms.

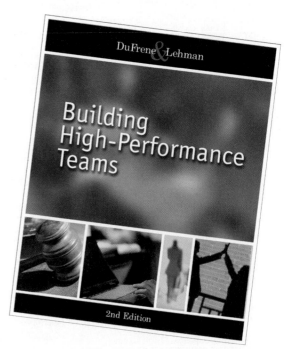

The Test Bank is totally updated, focusing on providing questions that assess students' comprehension of basic concepts as well as higher-level application and analysis.

In addition:

- The instructor's *Text Support Site* (http://lehman.swlearning.com) includes Web Enrichment activities tied to ShowCASES (one per chapter) and additional instructor's resources.

- Each chapter's *ShowCASE* presents an overview of communication issues important to a contemporary organization, a focus on the communication strategies of a Spotlight Communicator from the organization, and a research activity related to the communication focus. Then, it's onto the Web for Part 4, where students research an issue online and then participate in a threaded discussion about the ShowCASE organization.

- Guides at the end of each ShowCASE entry point reader to the next part.

- *PowerPoint downloads* are included on Power Pak, WebTutor, and the Text Support Site

- Student areas of the *Text Support Site* link to enrichment content and provide downloads for selected activities.

- Updated URLs for assignments and *Internet Cases* are provided on the Text Support Site.

- *All new Video Cases,* found on WebTutor and Professional Power Pak, include introductions, discussion, and activities, as well as full-motion video segments.

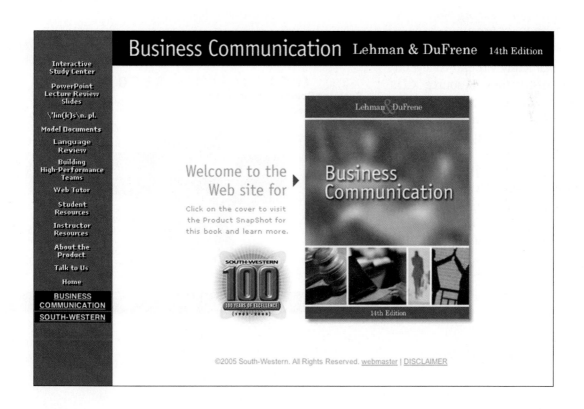

Exceptional Instructor's Resources

Instructor's Manual (ISBN 0324221371)
Prepared by Carol Lehman and Debbie DuFrene, the *Instructor's Manual* organizes each chapter by learning objectives, and includes teaching suggestions, answers to end-of-chapter activities and a list of related transparencies, PowerPoint® lecture, and resource slides.

Test Bank (ISBN 032427257X)
Prepared by Beverly Oswalt, Southern Arkansas University, the *Test Bank* is available in printed and electronic formats. A table at the beginning of each chapter classifies each question according to learning objective, type, and level of difficulty. All questions in the *Test Bank* are completely new for 14e.

ExamView Testing Software (ISBN 0324272618)
The entire *Test Bank* is available electronically via ExamView on the Instructor's Resource CD. Instructors can create custom exams by selecting questions, editing existing questions, and adding new questions. Instructors can also have questions created by calling Thomson Learning's Academic Resource Center at 1-800-423-0563 (8:30 a.m. to 6 p.m. EST.)

Transparency Acetates (0324272588)
100 color acetates are available and related to teaching suggestions in the *Instructor's Manual*. They include selected figures and key communication concepts to assist in lectures.

PowerPoint Lecture and Resource Slides (ISBN 0324272618)
Available on the Web or the Instructor's Resource CD, PowerPoint resource slides provide supplementary information, activities to reinforce key concepts, and solutions to end-of-chapter activities.

Instructor's Resource CD (ISBN 0324272618)
Includes links to the Text Support Site and WebTutor Advantage, 100 lecture PowerPoint slides, PowerPoint Resource Slides, Instructor's Manual files, Test Bank Word files, and ExamView Test Bank.

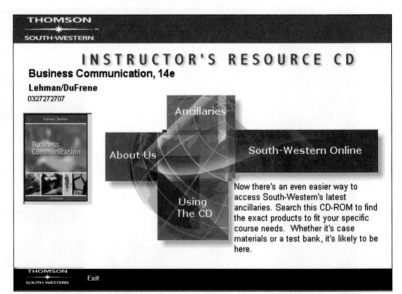

Acknowledgments

*B*usiness Communication and its numerous support tools reflect the contributions of many talented people. These appreciated individuals include our faculty colleagues, the publishing team at South-Western, and the many professional educators whose insightful reviews have been essential to the development of each edition of Business Communication. For their insights and suggestions for the 14th edition, we extend sincere thanks to the following reviewers:

Carolyn H. Ashe
University of Houston Downtown

James D. Bell
Texas State University, San Marcos

Mary Bowers
Northern Arizona University

Stuart C. Brown
New Mexico State University

Diane J. Fisher
University of Southern Mississippi

Barbara Hagler
Southern Illinois University, Carbondale

Larry R. Honl
University of Wisconsin, Eau Claire

Marcia L. James
University of Wisconsin, Whitewater

Betty A. Kleen
Nicholls State Universiey

Jeré W. Littlejohn
University of Mississippi

Donna W. Luse
University of Louisiana at Monroe

Beryl C. McEwen
North Carolina A&T State University

Beverly Oswalt
Southern Arkansas University

Jim Rucker
Fort Hays State University

Janna P. Vice
Eastern Kentucky University

William J. Wardrope
Texas State University, San Marcos

Deepest appreciation goes to the following committed and talented business communication educators who worked closely with us to plan and develop important components of the comprehensive 14e package:

Beverly Oswalt, Southern Arkansas University (*Test Bank and selected IRM and WebTutor content*)

Corinne Livesay, Bryan College (*Video Cases and select WebTutor content*)

Denise Cosper, Mississippi State University (*selected solutions and IRM and WebTutor content*)

Jeré Littlejohn, University of Mississippi (*selected solutions*).

Gratitude is also extended to our devoted spouses who have supported us through this lengthy and demanding project, as well as to our college-age children who served as a convenient focus group for content issues and technology design. Special recognition is due Stephen Lehman, whose passion for digital film editing inspired the design of the Professional Power Pak.

Additional Resources

HOW 10

(ISBN 0324178824) *by James L. Clark and Lyn R. Clark*

Since 1975, **HOW** and its subsequent editions have been a prominent reference source for business writers, office personnel, and students. With every new edition, **HOW** has kept pace with changes in language and the business environment, striving to provide a useful and easy-to-understand reference manual for all professionals involved in organizational operations. It includes detailed and precise information for writing, formatting, and transmitting communications. Unlike other reference books, **HOW 10** is tailored for the writing style, grammar, mechanics, and techniques of a business/office environment. This text can be used as a stand-alone reference or as a supplement.

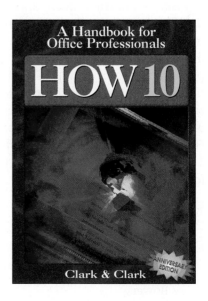

Employment Strategies for Career Success

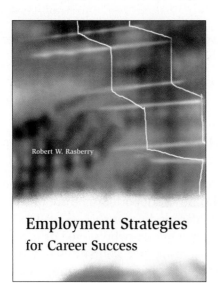

(ISBN 0324200056) *by Robert Rasberry*

Robert Rasberry's first edition of **Employment Strategies for Career Success** instructs students in managing a successful career search. This practical book covers all aspects of job-hunting, including negotiations, the case interview, and interview anxiety. It can be a useful tool for any student or executive strategically seeking career fulfillment.

Creating Dynamic Multimedia Presentations Using Microsoft® PowerPoint®, Second Edition

(ISBN 032418767X) *by Carol Lehman*

Have you ever seen a PowerPoint presentation with 10 bullets to a slide? Ideas head in all directions as words simply assemble themselves from colored fragments. The slides keep coming, too fast to read. Within this brief book by a **Business Communications** co-author, you'll never be trapped in this nightmare again! This book moves beyond the traditional manual to explore specific design techniques that lead to superior presentations. Lessons and exercises are built around Microsoft PowerPoint XP and allow students the full benefit of the latest PowerPoint functionality and features.

Writer's On-line Workshop (WOW), formerly known as PoWER

(ISBN 032401385) *by Dana Loewy and Teeanna Rizkallah*

WOW is designed to help users accurately assess their current skill level and refine their understanding of business English and business communication. Users start by taking the self-assessment to aid in diagnosing their current skills. The results of the self-assessment direct users to specific business English or business communication lessons that require further review. Modules are designed to allow users to review a concept, see an example, then practice using the concept. **WOW** also offers on-line access to a wealth of communication-based resources.

Communication Foundations

i

Establishing a Framework for Business Communication

© KEVIN HORAN/CORBIS SYGMA

Objectives *When you have completed Chapter 1, you will be able to:*

1 Define communication and describe the main purpose for communication in business.

2 Explain the communication process model and the ultimate objective of the communication process.

3 Identify the five levels of communication.

4 Discuss how information flows in an organization (formally and informally, and downward, upward, and horizontally).

5 Explain how legal and ethical constraints act as a strategic force to influence the process of business communication.

6 Explain how diversity challenges act as a strategic force to influence the process of business communication.

7 Explain how changing technology acts as a strategic force to influence the process of business communication.

8 Explain how team environment acts as a strategic force to influence the process of business communication.

COMMUNICATION CHALLENGES AT THE CDC

The events of September 11, 2001, affected every American citizen as well as the nation's business community. One agency whose mission was changed forever was the Centers for Disease Control and Prevention (CDC). The Atlanta-based federal agency whose responsibility is protecting Americans against infectious diseases and other health hazards was instantly required to retool to meet the looming threat of bioterrorism. In the fall of 2001, the agency faced the challenge of informing the public of the danger of anthrax-tainted mail. Its responsibility was further expanded to preparing for possible future attacks on Americans from anthrax or other deadly agents such as smallpox.

In its role as the lead federal agency charged with protecting public health and safety, the CDC is one of 11 federal agencies under the Department of Health and Human Services. The agency stores and controls the nation's stockpile of smallpox vaccine and leads 3,000 local public health departments in devising a plan for containing an outbreak or epidemic and administering the vaccine. It must also meld its work with national security agencies, such as the CIA, the FBI, and the Department of Homeland Security.[1]

The leadership of the CDC must balance the urgent goal of preparing for a bioterrorism emergency with the agency's fundamental mission of preventing and controlling infectious disease and other health hazards. AIDS, cigarette smoking, obesity, Type II diabetes, and asthma are among the real, long-term problems that are equally crucial to public health. And new threats, such as the West Nile virus, regularly present themselves.

According to Julie Gerberding, director of the CDC, "ultimately, our customers are the citizens of the United States, so we have to have a better understanding of what they need to improve their health—what works and what doesn't work, from their perspective."[2] She describes her agency's key communication partners as the state and local health departments who monitor citizens' health, the people who run health plans and market preventive services, and the entire business community, which has a strong interest in promoting the health of its employees. She knows the importance of effective communication with a broad audience. Such a process identifies strengths and weaknesses in programs and helps make the CDC a more credible advocate when it asks for funding to address another potential episode of bioterrorism as well as chronic health problems unrelated to terrorism. To be effective in any work setting, you will need to understand the process of communication and the dynamic environment in which it occurs.

http://www.cdc.gov

See ShowCASE, Part 2, on page 16 for Spotlight Communicator Julie Gerberding, director of the CDC.

Purposes of Communication

Objective 1

Define communication and describe the main purpose for communica- tion in business.

We communicate to satisfy needs in both our work and nonwork lives. Each of us wants to be heard, appreciated, and wanted. We also want to accomplish tasks and achieve goals. Obviously, then, a major purpose of communication is to help people feel good about themselves and about their friends, groups, and organizations. Generally people communicate for three basic purposes: to inform, to persuade, and to entertain.

What is communication? For our purposes, **communication** is the process of exchanging information and meaning between or among indi- viduals through a common system of symbols, signs, and behavior. Other words often used to describe the communication process are expressing feelings, conversing, speaking, corresponding, writing, listening, and exchanging. Studies indicate that managers typically spend 60 to 80 per- cent of their time involved in communication. In your career activities, you may communicate in a wide variety of ways, including

Critical Thinking

In what ways will communication be important in the career field you have chosen?

- attending meetings and writing reports related to strategic plans and company policy.
- presenting information to large and small groups.
- explaining and clarifying management procedures and work assign- ments.
- coordinating the work of various employees, departments, and other work groups.
- evaluating and counseling employees.
- promoting the company's products/services and image.

The Communication Process

Objective 2

Explain the communica- tion process model and the ultimate objective of the communication process.

Effective business communication is essential to success in today's work environments. A recent survey of executives documents that abilities in writing and speaking will be major determinants of career success in many fields.[3] Although essential to personal and professional success, effective business communication does not occur automatically. Your own experiences have likely taught you that a message is not inter- preted correctly just because you transmitted it. An effective communica- tor anticipates possible breakdowns in the communication process—the unlimited ways the message can be misunderstood. This mind-set pro- vides the concentration to design the initial message effectively and to be prepared to intervene at the appropriate time to ensure that the mes- sage received is on target—that is, as close as possible to what is intended.

Consider the communication process model presented in Figure 1-1. These seemingly simple steps actually represent a very complex process.

Figure 1-1

The Communication Process Model

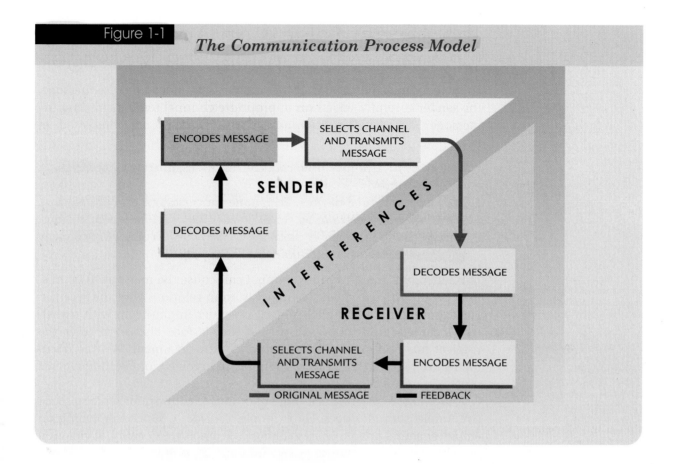

The Sender Encodes the Message

The sender carefully designs a message by selecting (1) words that clearly convey the message and (2) nonverbal signals (gestures, stance, tone of voice, and so on) that reinforce the verbal message. The process of selecting and organizing the message is referred to as *encoding*. The sender's primary objective is to encode the message in such a way that the message received is as close as possible to the message sent. Knowledge of the receiver's educational level, experience, viewpoints, and other information aids the sender in encoding the message. If information about the receiver is unavailable, the sender can put himself or herself in the receiver's position to gain fairly accurate insight for encoding the message. As you study Chapters 3 and 4, you will learn to use language effectively; Chapter 2 will assist you in refining your nonverbal communication.

Various behaviors can cause breakdowns in the communication process at the encoding stage, such as when the sender uses

- words not present in the receiver's vocabulary.
- ambiguous, nonspecific ideas that distort the message.
- nonverbal signals that contradict the verbal message.
- expressions such as "uh" or grammatical errors, mannerisms (excessive hand movements, jingling keys), or dress that distracts the receiver.

Diversity Challenges

Critical Thinking

What breakdowns in the encoding process have you experienced?

The Sender Selects an Appropriate Channel and Transmits the Message

To increase the likelihood that the receiver will understand the message, the sender carefully selects an appropriate channel for transmitting the message. Three typical communication channels are illustrated in Figure 1-2.

- *Two-way, face-to-face.* Informal conversations, interviews, oral reports, speeches, and videoconferences.
- *Two-way, not face-to-face.* Telephone conversations and online chat.
- *One-way, not face-to-face.* Written documents such as letters, memos, reports, and press releases prepared traditionally or sent electronically (electronic mail, fax, voice-mail, and web pages).

Selecting an inappropriate channel can cause the message to be misunderstood and can adversely affect human relations with the receiver. For example, for a complex subject, a sender might begin with a written document and follow up with a face-to-face discussion after the receiver has had an opportunity to study the document. Written documents are required when legal matters are involved and written records must be retained.

A face-to-face meeting is a more appropriate channel for sending sensitive, unpleasant messages. For example, consider a supervisor calling an employee into a private office to discuss the employee's continual violation of safety regulations. A face-to-face meeting provides two distinct benefits:

Critical Thinking

Which channel would be the most appropriate for communicating the following messages? Justify your answer.

- Ask a client for additional information needed to provide requested services.
- Inform a customer that an order cannot be delivered on the date specified in the contract.
- Inform the sales staff of a special sales incentive (effective six weeks from now).

Figure 1-2	*Channels of Communication*

TWO-WAY, FACE-TO-FACE
- Instant feedback
- Nonverbal signals

TWO-WAY, NOT FACE-TO-FACE
- Instant feedback
- Limited nonverbal signals

ONE-WAY, NOT FACE-TO-FACE
- No instant feedback
- Minimal nonverbal signals

- The manager can solicit immediate feedback from the receiver to clarify misunderstandings and inaccuracies in the message.
- The manager can "read" equally important nonverbal cues (tone of voice, body movements, etc.) in addition to hearing what the receiver is saying (the verbal message).

The manager may feel comfortable with the verbal message, but the nonverbal message may indicate the receiver is overamplifying the problem or is underestimating the importance of the warning. The manager's discerning choice of a channel—meeting with the employee face-to-face rather than calling or writing a disciplinary memo—marks this manager as sensitive and empathetic, qualities that foster trust and open communication.

The Receiver Decodes the Message

Diversity Challenges

The receiver is the destination of the message. The receiver's task is to interpret the sender's message, both verbal and nonverbal, with as little distortion as possible. The process of interpreting the message is referred to as *decoding*. Because words and nonverbal signals have different meanings to different people, countless problems can occur at this point in the communication process:

- The sender inadequately encodes the original message. For example, the sender may use words not present in the receiver's vocabulary; use ambiguous, nonspecific ideas that distort the message; or use nonverbal signals that distract the receiver or contradict the verbal message.
- The receiver is intimidated by the position or authority of the sender. This tension may prevent the receiver from concentrating on the message effectively enough to understand it clearly. Furthermore, an intimidated receiver may be afraid to ask for clarification because of the perceived fear that questions might be associated with incompetence.
- The receiver is unwilling to attempt to understand the message because the topic is perceived to be too difficult to understand. Regardless of the clarity of a message communicating procedures for operating a computer software program, a receiver terrified of computers may be incapable of decoding the message correctly.
- The receiver is unreceptive to new and different ideas; that is, stereotypical visions and prejudices prevent the receiver from viewing the message with an open mind.

The infinite number of breakdowns possible at each stage of the communication process makes us marvel that mutually satisfying communication ever occurs. The complexity of the communication process amplifies the importance of the next stage in the communication process—feedback to clarify misunderstandings.

The Receiver Encodes the Message to Clarify Any Misunderstandings

When the receiver responds to the sender's message, the response is called *feedback*. The feedback may prompt the sender to modify or adjust the original message to make it clearer to the receiver. Feedback may be verbal or nonverbal. A remark such as "Could you clarify . . ." or a perplexed facial expression provides clear feedback to the sender that the receiver does not yet understand the message. Conversely, a confident "Yes, I understand," and a nod of the head likely signal understanding or encouragement.

Interferences Hinder the Process

Critical Thinking

Both internal barriers *and* external barriers *make communication challenging. How?*

Diversity
Challenges

Critical Thinking

Consider a situation in which you have experienced a communication breakdown. What factor(s) was/were responsible for the miscommunication? What could have been done to assure successful communication?

Senders and receivers must learn to deal with the numerous factors that interfere with the communication process. These factors are referred to as *interferences* or *barriers* to effective communication. Previous examples have illustrated some of the interferences that may occur at various stages of the communication process. For example,

- Differences in educational level, experience, and culture and other characteristics of the sender and the receiver increase the complexity of encoding and decoding a message.
- Physical interferences occurring in the channel include a noisy environment, interruptions, and uncomfortable surroundings.
- Mental distractions such as preoccupation with other matters and developing a response rather than listening.

You can surely compile a list of other barriers that affect your ability to communicate with friends, instructors, coworkers, supervisors, and others. By being aware of them, you can make concentrated efforts to remove these interferences whenever possible.

Communicating Within Organizations

Objective 3

Identify the five levels of communication.

Organizational structure is the overall design of an organization, much like a blueprint developed to meet the company's specific needs and to enhance its ability to accomplish goals. A company's organizational structure is depicted graphically in an organization chart, as illustrated in Figure 1-3. An organizational chart helps define the scope of the organization and the division of specialized tasks among employees who work interdependently to accomplish common goals.

To be successful, organizations must create an environment that energizes and provides encouragement to employees to accomplish tasks by

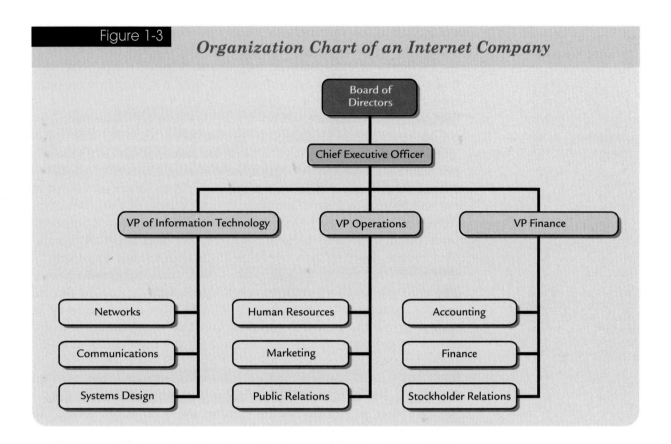

Figure 1-3 *Organization Chart of an Internet Company*

encouraging genuine openness and effective communication. *Organizational communication* is concerned with the movement of information within the company structure. Regardless of your career or level within an organization, your ability to communicate will affect not only the success of the organization but also your personal success and advancement within that organization.

Levels of Communication

Communication can involve sending messages to both large and small audiences. Some messages, *internal messages*, are intended for recipients within the organization. Other messages, *external messages*, are directed to recipients outside the organization. When considering the intended audience, communication can be described as taking place on five levels:

- *Intrapersonal communication* occurs when an individual processes information based on his or her own experiences. It is, in a sense, communication within one person. All interpretation of information ultimately takes place in the individual mind. *Self-talk* is the term used to describe conversation that takes place within a person, and it may be either positive and constructive, or negative and destructive. People's self-talk influences the communication with others that they initiate and receive, since attitudes and mind-sets have already been formed prior to the exchange of ideas between individuals. Self-talk is not considered true communication by some because it does not involve a separate sender and receiver.

Critical Thinking

Successful teams achieve both their task goal(s) and their maintenance goal(s).

- *Interpersonal communication* takes place primarily when two people are involved in the process. Their two goals are to (1) accomplish whatever task confronts them, and (2) feel better about themselves as a result of their interaction. These two goals are commonly referred to as **task goals** and **maintenance goals**, respectively, and they coexist in varying degrees in most of our daily activities. Most of your communication in business will occur in various one-to-one relationships. Understanding various behavior patterns provides supervisors valuable insights that facilitate communication with today's employees.

Critical Thinking

A corporate study by the Ford Foundation found that productivity increased in companies that show concern for employees' personal lives and needs.

- *Group communication* occurs among more than two people: a committee, a club, or all the students enrolled in a class. Groups are formed usually because the combined efforts of a number of people result in greater output than the individual efforts of the same number of people. In other words, groups can do more for the individuals than the individuals can do for themselves.

- *Organizational communication* arises when groups discover that they are unable to accomplish their goals without some kind of organization. Thus, organizations are combinations of groups formed in such a way that large tasks may be accomplished.

- *Public communication* occurs when an organization reaches out to its public to achieve its goals. Utilizing media advertising or a corporate web site are possible means for reaching a large intended audience.

Communication Flow in Organizations

Objective 4

Discuss how information flows in an organization (formally and informally, and downward, upward, and horizontally).

Communication occurs in a variety of ways in an organization; some communication flow is planned and structured; some is not. Some communication flow can be formally depicted, while some defies description.

Formal and Informal Channels

The flow of communication within an organization follows both formal and informal channels.

- *Formal communication channel.* This channel is typified by the formal organization chart, which is created by management to control individual and group behavior and to achieve the organization's goals. Essentially, the formal system is dictated by the technical, political, and economic environment of the organization. Within this system, people are required to behave in certain ways simply to get the work done.

- *Informal communication channel.* This channel develops as people interact within the formal, external system, and certain behavior patterns emerge—patterns that accommodate social and psychological needs. Because the informal channel undergoes continual changes, it cannot be depicted accurately by any graphic means.

Critical Thinking

Why do organizations tend to become more bureaucratic as they grow in size?

When employees rely almost entirely on the formal communication system as a guide to behavior, the system might be identified as a *bureaucracy*. Procedures manuals, job descriptions, organization charts, and other written materials dictate the required behavior. Communication channels are followed strictly, and red tape is abundant. Procedures are generally followed exactly; terms such as *rules* and *policies* serve as sufficient reasons for actions. Even the most formal organizations, however, cannot function long before an informal communication system emerges. As people operate within the external system, they must interact on a person-to-person basis and create an environment conducive to satisfying their personal emotions, prejudices, likes, and dislikes.

In the college classroom, for example, the student behavior required to satisfy the formal system is to attend class, take notes, read the text, and pass examinations. On the first day of class, this behavior probably is typical of almost all students, particularly if they did not know one another prior to attending the class. As the class progresses, however, the informal system emerges and overlaps the formal system. Students become acquainted, sit next to people they particularly like, talk informally, and may even plan ways to beat the external system. Cutting class and borrowing notes are examples. Soon, these behaviors become norms for class behavior. Students who do not engage in the informal system may be viewed with disdain by the others. Obviously, the informal system benefits people because it is efficient; and it affects the overall communication of the group in important ways.

The Grapevine as an Informal Communication System

Critical Thinking

Managers who ignore the grapevine have difficulty achieving organizational goals.

The **grapevine**, often called the *rumor mill*, is perhaps the best-known informal communication system. It is actually a component of the informal system. As people talk casually during coffee breaks and lunch periods, the focus usually shifts from topic to topic. One of the topics most certainly would be work—job, company, supervisor, fellow employees. Even though the formal system has definite communication channels, the grapevine tends to develop and operate within the organization.

As a communication channel, the grapevine has a reputation for being speedy but inaccurate. In the absence of alarms, the grapevine may be the most effective way to let occupants know that the building is on fire. It certainly beats sending a written memorandum or an e-mail. While the grapevine often is thought of as a channel for inaccurate communication, in reality, it is no more or less accurate than other channels. Even formal communication may become inaccurate as it passes from level to level in the organizational hierarchy. The inaccuracy of the grapevine has more to do with the message input than with the output. For example, the grapevine is noted as a carrier of rumor, primarily because it carries informal messages. If the input is rumor, and nothing more, the output obviously will be inaccurate. But the output may be an accurate description of the original rumor.

For a college student, the grapevine carries much valuable information. Even though the names of the choice instructors may not be published, students learn those names through the grapevine. How best to prepare for certain examinations, instructor attitudes on attendance and homework, and even future faculty personnel changes are messages that travel over the grapevine. In the business office, news about promotions, personnel changes, company policy changes, and annual salary adjustments often is communicated by the grapevine long before being disseminated by formal channels.

A misconception about the grapevine is that the message passes from person to person until it finally reaches a person who can't pass it on—the end of the line. Actually, the grapevine works as a network channel. Typically, one person tells two or three others, who each tell two or three others, who each tell two or three others, and so on. Thus, the message may spread to a huge number of people in a short time. Additionally, the grapevine has no single, consistent source. Messages may originate anywhere and follow various routes.

Due at least in part to widespread downsizing during the last few years, employees in many organizations are demanding to be better informed. Some companies have implemented new formal ways for disseminating information to their internal constituents, such as newsletters and intranets. Company openness with employees, including financial

Critical Thinking

Share a personal communication experience that involved the grapevine as an information source. How reliable was the message you sent or received? How time-efficient was the message transmission?

Legal & Ethical
Constraints

Team
Environment

Company openness with employees, through both formal and informal communication channels, builds trust and loyalty.

© SHOTGUN/CORBIS

information, means more information in the formal system rather than risking its miscommunication through informal channels. An employee of The Container Store—named the best company to work for in America—said that the company's willingness to divulge what it makes each year and its financial goals builds her trust in management.[4]

An informal communication system will emerge from even the most carefully designed formal system. Managers who ignore this fact are attempting to manage blindfolded. Instead of denying or condemning the grapevine, the effective manager will learn to *use* the informal communication network. The grapevine, for instance, can be useful in counteracting rumors and false information.

Directions for Communication Flow

The direction in which communication flows in an organization may be downward, upward, or horizontal, as shown in Figure 1-4. Because these three terms are used frequently in communication literature, they deserve clarification. Although the concept of flow seems simple, direction has meaning for those participating in the communication process.

Downward Communication. **Downward communication** flows from supervisor to employee, from policy makers to operating personnel, or from top to bottom on the organization chart. As messages move downward through successive levels of the organization, they seem to get larger. A simple policy statement from the top of the organization may grow into a formal plan for operation at lower levels.

Teaching people how to perform their specific tasks is an element of downward communication. Another element is orientation to a company's rules, practices, procedures, history, and goals. Employees learn about the quality of their job performance through downward communication.

Downward communication normally involves both written and spoken methods and makes use of the following guidelines:

Critical Thinking

What would be an appropriate "rule of thumb" for a manager in deciding whether to send a written or oral message to subordinates?

- People high in the organization usually have greater knowledge of the organization and its goals than do people at lower levels.
- Both spoken and written messages tend to become larger as they move downward through organizational levels. This expansion results from attempts to prevent distortion and is more noticeable in written messages.
- Spoken messages are subject to greater changes in meaning than are written messages.

When a supervisor sends a message to a lower-level employee who then asks a question or nods assent, the question and the nod are signs of feedback. Feedback may flow both downward and upward in organizational communication.

Critical Thinking

What do you believe would be the typical communication patterns of a manager working under a win/lose philosophy? Under a win/win philosophy?

Upward Communication. **Upward communication** generally is feedback to downward communication. Although necessary and valuable, upward communication does contain risks. When management requests

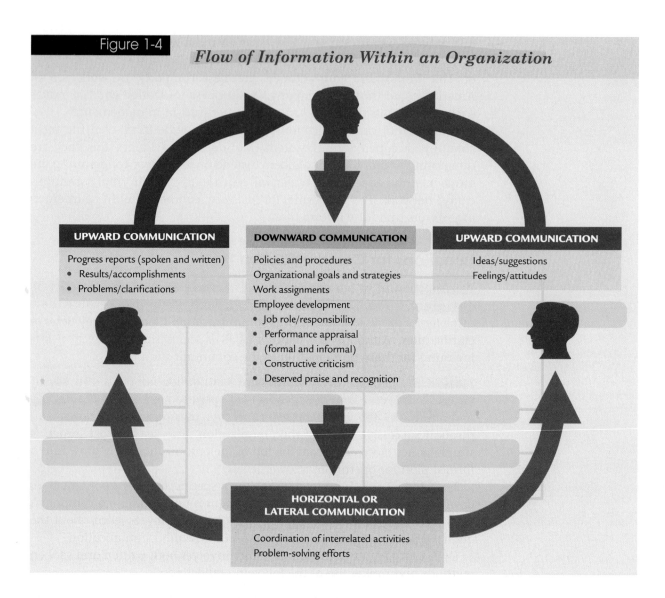

Figure 1-4 | *Flow of Information Within an Organization*

UPWARD COMMUNICATION

Progress reports (spoken and written)
- Results/accomplishments
- Problems/clarifications

DOWNWARD COMMUNICATION

Policies and procedures
Organizational goals and strategies
Work assignments
Employee development
- Job role/responsibility
- Performance appraisal
- (formal and informal)
- Constructive criticism
- Deserved praise and recognition

UPWARD COMMUNICATION

Ideas/suggestions
Feelings/attitudes

HORIZONTAL OR LATERAL COMMUNICATION

Coordination of interrelated activities
Problem-solving efforts

information from lower organizational levels, the resulting information becomes feedback to that request. Employees talk to supervisors about themselves, their fellow employees, their work and methods of doing it, and their perceptions of the organization. These comments are feedback to the downward flow transmitted in both spoken and written form by group meetings, procedures or operations manuals, company news releases, and the grapevine.

Accurate upward communication keeps management informed about the feelings of lower-level employees, taps the expertise of employees, helps management identify both difficult and potentially promotable employees, and paves the way for even more effective downward communication. Employees reporting upward are aware that their communications carry the risk of putting them on the spot or committing them to something they cannot handle.

Although employees typically appreciate and welcome genuine opportunities to send information to management, they will likely resent any superficial attempt to provide an open communication network with management. These factors, then, are important to consider when upward communication flow is involved.

- Upward communication is primarily feedback to requests and actions of supervisors.
- Upward communication may be misleading because lower-level employees often tell the superior what they think the superior wants to hear. Therefore, their messages might contradict their true observations and perceptions.
- Upward communication is based on trust in the supervisor.
- Upward communication frequently involves risk to an employee.
- Employees will reject superficial attempts by management to obtain feedback from employees.

Critical Thinking

How can a manager maximize the effectiveness of horizontal communication among subordinates?

Horizontal Communication. **Horizontal**, or **lateral**, communication describes interactions between organization units on the same hierarchical level. These interactions reveal one of the major shortcomings of organizational charts. Charts do not allow much room for horizontal communication when they depict authority relationships by placing one box higher than another and define role functions by placing titles in those boxes. Yet horizontal communication is the primary means of achieving coordination in a functional organizational structure.

Management must recognize that informal, horizontal communication takes place in any system or organization where people are available to one another. Horizontal communication serves a coordinating function in the organization. Units coordinate their activities to accomplish task goals just as adjacent workers in a production line coordinate their activities.

Team
Environment

In an organization divided into cross-functional teams, horizontal communication among the team members is extremely important to achieve individual and team goals. Total Quality Management experts emphasize that honest, open communication is the single most important factor in successfully creating a Total Quality Management environment. According to one TQM author, "if people keep talking to one another, they can work through their problems, overcome barriers, and find encouragement and support from others involved in quality efforts."[5]

Many companies are realizing that the traditional hierarchy organized around functional units is inadequate for competing in the increasingly competitive global markets. Companies utilize work teams that integrate work-flow processes rather than having specialists who deal with a single function or product. These cross-functional work teams break down the former communication barriers between isolated functional departments. Communication patterns take on varying forms to accommodate team activities.

SPOTLIGHT COMMUNICATOR
Leadership for the Times

Dr. Julie Gerberding is the first woman to lead the Centers for Disease Control and Prevention (CDC), the nation's premier public health agency, with more than 8,500 employees nationwide and a $6.8 billion budget. At the age of only 46, she was named director of the agency in 2002, arriving at a time of great opportunity and substantial challenge. The anthrax attacks brought very heightened visibility as well as new responsibility and resources.

Gerberding's background was uniquely suited to the new demands of a CDC director. A solid scientist, she had previously served for nearly two decades at the University of California, San Francisco, where she established herself as a leading expert in the treatment of AIDS. She was acting deputy director of the CDC's National Center for Infectious Diseases when the anthrax attacks began. It was during the mail-launched bioterroristic attack that Gerberding rose to national prominence as a top CDC spokeswoman, earning praise from politicians and public health groups for her straightforward style and expertise. "She is a very sensible, extraordinarily well-informed person who doesn't hide behind jargon or the idea that she has special knowledge about complicated matters that she really can't quite explain," said Dr. Julius R. Krevans, chancellor emeritus at UC San Francisco, who has known her since she was an intern.[6] Gerberding successfully combines professional talent as an infectious-disease physician with exemplary leadership and exceptional communication skills.

A firm believer in collaboration, Gerberding invites input from her staff and from medical community partners. Gerberding's solid academic background has resulted in a stronger relationship with the national health agencies, hospitals, and other medical deliverers who focus on the science, research, and treatment of diseases. She understands the importance of renowned scientists working with local healthcare providers to make sure the best information is communicated to the public. Gerberding says that as frightening as it was, the anthrax crisis paved the way for more effective communication between the CDC and its constituents: "We had the attention of most Americans, many of whom may have been hearing for the first time what the CDC really is and does. We had the attention of Congress. We had a president come to the CDC for the first time in the history of the agency. If you take that kind of attention and appreciation for what our value is, and couple it with the investments in the public health system that are being made right now, it is an incredible opportunity."[7]

© REUTERS NEWMEDIA, WC/CORBIS

Applying What You Have Learned

1. What combination of communication skills is necessary for Julie Gerberding to be an effective director of the CDC?
2. How did Gerberding use adversity as a means to strengthen internal and external communication at the CDC?

Julie Gerberding, Director, Centers for Disease Control

http://www.cdc.gov

See ShowCASE, Part 3, at the end of the chapter to expand your knowledge about communication at the CDC.

Strategic Forces Influencing Business Communication

Objective 5

Explain how legal and ethical constraints act as a strategic force to influence the process of business communication.

Critical Thinking

How would you rank the four strategic forces in terms of magnitude of importance to business communication? Why?

Legal & Ethical
Constraints

Critical Thinking

What recent events can you think of that have ethical themes?

Communication is often a complicated process. Furthermore, communication does not take place in a vacuum, but rather is influenced by a number of forces at work in the environment. The effective communicator carefully considers each of these influences and structures communication responsively. Four critical forces influence the communication process and help to determine and define the nature of the communication that occurs, as shown in Figure 1-5.

Legal and Ethical Constraints as a Strategic Force Influencing Communication

Legal and ethical constraints act as a strategic force on communication in that they set boundaries in which communication can occur. International, federal, state, and local laws affect the way that various business activities can be conducted. For instance, legislation controls can and must be stated in letters that reply to credit applications and those dealing with collection of outstanding debts. Furthermore, one's own ethical standards will often influence what he or she is willing to say in a message. A system of ethics built on honesty may require that the message provide full disclosure, for instance, rather than a shrouding of the truth. Legal responsibilities, then, are the starting point for appropriate business communication. One's ethical belief system, or personal sense of right and wrong behavior, provides further boundaries for professional activity.

The press is full of examples of unethical conduct in the business community:

- Enron was found to have improved its financial image by moving debt off its books and using other accounting tricks. As a result of the scandal, thousands of company employees lost not only their jobs but their retirement investments while the company CEO made off with millions of dollars by selling Enron stock just before the company imploded.
- Accounting misrepresentations uncovered at WorldCom included the registering of a single sale many times over, thus overinflating revenues by millions.
- Andersen Worldwide, a big-five accounting giant and consulting service, suffered financial collapse following disclosures that it failed to report pervasive and blatant fraudulent practices among its client firms. "The name Andersen is likely to live on in the popular culture as Watergate did, a shorthand way to refer to scandal."[8]
- The United States is not the only country to experience recent lapses in ethical behavior among businesses. In Japan, for example, a recent scandal occurred at the company's largest utility, Tokyo Electric Power.

Figure 1-5

Strategic Forces Influencing Business Communication

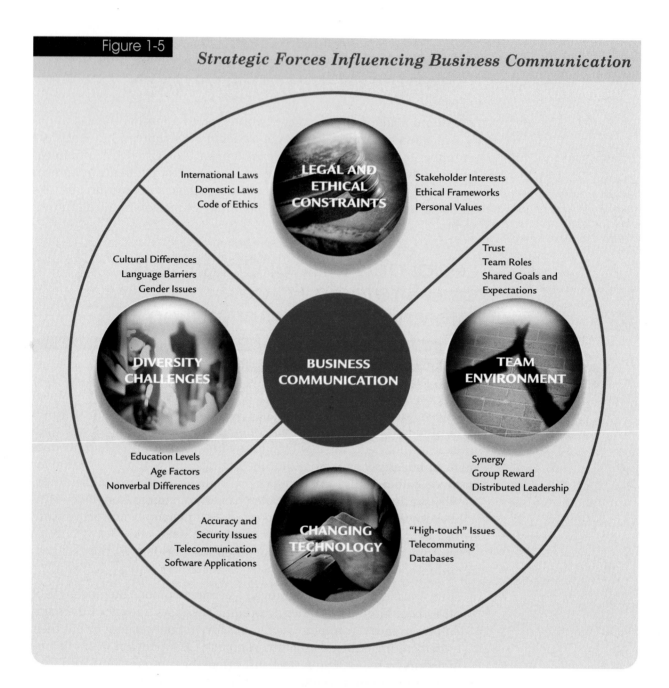

International Laws
Domestic Laws
Code of Ethics

LEGAL AND ETHICAL CONSTRAINTS

Stakeholder Interests
Ethical Frameworks
Personal Values

Cultural Differences
Language Barriers
Gender Issues

Trust
Team Roles
Shared Goals and
Expectations

DIVERSITY CHALLENGES

BUSINESS COMMUNICATION

TEAM ENVIRONMENT

Education Levels
Age Factors
Nonverbal Differences

Synergy
Group Reward
Distributed Leadership

Accuracy and
Security Issues
Telecommunication
Software Applications

CHANGING TECHNOLOGY

"High-touch" Issues
Telecommuting
Databases

Resignations of top officials followed revelations that the organization had issued falsified reports to nuclear safety regulators.[9]

Incidents such as these have far reaching consequences. Those affected by decisions, the *stakeholders*, can include people inside and outside the organization. Employees and stockholders are obvious losers when a company fails. Competitors in the same industry also suffer, since their strategies are based on what they perceive about their competition. Beyond that, financial markets as a whole suffer due to erosion of public confidence. The recovery of the U.S. economy following the terrorist attack of 2001 was further weakened because of the wounds from corporate scandals that resulted in severe drops in stock prices.

Critical Thinking

While laws represent statutory requirements for behavior, ethics are individually determined.

Business leaders, government officials, and citizens frequently express concern about the apparent erosion of ethical values in society. Even for those who want to do the right thing, matters of ethics are seldom clear-cut decisions of right versus wrong and often contain many ambiguous elements. In addition, the pressure appears to be felt most strongly by lower-level managers, often recent business school graduates, who are least experienced doing their jobs.

You can take steps now to prepare for dealing with pressure to compromise personal values:

- *Consider your personal value system.* Only if you have definite beliefs on a variety of issues and the courage to practice them will you be able to make sound ethical judgments. Putting ethical business practices first will also benefit the company for whom you work as its reputation for fairness and good judgment retains long-term clients or customers and brings in new ones.
- *Learn to analyze ethical dilemmas.* Knowing how to analyze ethical dilemmas and identify the consequences of your actions will help you make decisions that conform to your own value system. Thus, unless you know what you stand for and how to analyze ethical issues, you become a puppet, controlled by the motives of others, too weak to make a decision on your own.

The Foundation for Legal and Ethical Behavior

Although ethics is a common point of discussion, many find defining ethics challenging. Most people immediately associate ethics with standards and rules of conduct, morals, right and wrong, values, and honesty. Dr. Albert Schweitzer defined *ethics* as "the name we give to our concern for good behavior. We feel an obligation to consider not only our own personal well-being, but also that of others and of human society as a whole."[10] In other words, **ethics** refers to the principles of right and wrong that guide you in making decisions that consider the impact of your actions on others as well as yourself.

Although the recorded accounts of legal and ethical misconduct would seem to indicate that businesses are dishonest and unscrupulous, keep in mind that millions of business transactions are made daily on the basis of honesty and concern for the welfare of others. Why should a business make ethical decisions? What difference will it make? James E. Perrella, executive vice president of Ingersoll-Rand Company, gave a powerful reply to these questions:[11]

> Our question of today should be, what's the right thing to do, the right way to behave, the right way to conduct business? Don't just ask, is it legal? Have you ever considered what business would be like if we all did it? If every businessman and businesswoman followed the Golden Rule? Many people, including many business leaders, would argue that such an application of

ethics to business would adversely affect bottom-line performance. I say nay. . . . Good ethics, simply, is good business. Good ethics will attract investors. Good ethics will attract good employees.

You can do what's right. Not because of conduct codes. Not because of rules or laws. But because you know what's right.

Identifying ethical issues in typical workplace situations may be difficult, and coworkers and superiors may apply pressure for seemingly logical reasons. To illustrate, examine each of the following workplace situations for a possible ethical dilemma:

Critical Thinking

What situations have you faced as a worker or student that caused ethical dilemmas?

Changing Technology

- Corporate officers deliberately withhold information concerning a planned sellout to prevent an adverse effect on stock prices.
- A salesperson, who travels extensively, overstates car mileage to cover the cost of personal telephone calls that the company refuses to reimburse.
- To protect his job, a product engineer decides not to question a design flaw in a product that could lead to possible injuries and even deaths to consumers because the redesign would cause a delay in product introduction.
- To stay within the departmental budget, a supervisor authorizes that a software program be installed on fifty office computers when only one legal copy was actually purchased.
- Angry at a superior for an unfavorable performance appraisal, an employee leaks confidential information (e.g., trade secrets such as a recipe or product design, marketing strategies, or product development plans) to an acquaintance who works for a competitor.

Your fundamental morals and values provide the foundation for making ethical decisions. However, as the previous examples imply, even minor concessions in day-to-day decisions can gradually weaken an individual's ethical foundation.

Causes of Illegal and Unethical Behavior

Understanding the major causes of illegal and unethical behavior in the workplace will help you become sensitive to signals of escalating pressure to compromise your values. Unethical corporate behavior can have a number of causes:

- ***Excessive emphasis on profits.*** Business managers are often judged and paid on their ability to increase business profits. This emphasis on profits may send a message that the end justifies the means. According to Federal Reserve Chairman Alan Greenspan, "infectious greed" ultimately pushed companies such as Enron, Global Crossing, and WorldCom into bankruptcy.[12]
- ***Misplaced corporate loyalty.*** A misplaced sense of corporate loyalty may cause an employee to do what seems to be in the best interest of the company, even if the act is illegal or unethical.
- ***Obsession with personal advancement.*** Employees who wish to outperform their peers or are working for the next promotion may feel that

they cannot afford to fail. They may do whatever it takes to achieve the objectives assigned to them.

- *Expectation of not getting caught.* Employees who believe that the end justifies the means often believe that the illegal or unethical activity will never be discovered. Unfortunately, a great deal of improper behavior escapes detection in the business world. Believing no one will ever find out, employees are tempted to lie, steal, and perform other illegal acts.

- *Unethical tone set by top management.* If top managers are not perceived as highly ethical, lower-level managers may be less ethical as a result. Employees have little incentive to act legally and ethically if their superiors do not set an example and encourage and reward such behavior.

- *Uncertainty about whether an action is wrong.* Many times, company personnel are placed in situations in which the line between right and wrong is not clearly defined. When caught in this gray area, the perplexed employee asks, "How far is too far?"

- *Unwillingness to take a stand for what is right.* Often employees know what is right or wrong but are not willing to take the risk of challenging a wrong action. They may lack the confidence or skill needed to confront others with sensitive legal or ethical issues. They may remain silent and then justify their unwillingness to act.

Critical Thinking

"The speed of the leader is the speed of the pack" illustrates the importance of leading by example.

Framework for Analyzing Ethical Dilemmas

Determining whether an action is ethical can be difficult. Learning to analyze a dilemma from both legal and ethical perspectives will help you find a solution that conforms to your own personal values. Figure 1-6 shows the four conclusions you might reach when considering the advisability of a particular behavior.

| Figure 1-6 | *Four Dimensions of Business Behavior* |

DIMENSION 1 **Behavior that is illegal** **and unethical**	**DIMENSION 2** **Behavior that is illegal,** **yet ethical**
DIMENSION 3 **Behavior that is legal,** **yet unethical**	**DIMENSION 4** **Behavior that is both** **legal and ethical**

Critical Thinking

How can you keep up with the
legal requirements in your field?

Dimension 1: Behavior that is illegal and unethical. When considering some actions, you will reach the conclusion that they are both illegal and unethical. The law specifically outlines the "black" area—those alternatives that are clearly wrong. Your employer will expect you to become an expert in the laws that affect your particular area. When you encounter an unfamiliar area, you must investigate any possible legal implications. Obviously, obeying the law is in the best interest of all concerned: you as an individual, your company, and society. In addition, contractual agreements between the organization and another group provide explicit guidance in selecting an ethically responsible alternative. Frequently, your own individual sense of right and wrong will also confirm that the illegal action is wrong for you personally. In such situations, decisions about appropriate behavior are obvious.

Dimension 2: Behavior that is illegal, yet ethical. Occasionally, a business person may decide that even though a specific action is illegal, there is a justifiable reason to break the law. A case in point is a recent law passed in Vermont that makes it illegal for a pharmaceutical company to give any gift valued at $25 or more to doctors or their personnel.[13] Those supporting the law charge that the giving of freebies drives up medical costs by encouraging doctors to prescribe new, more expensive brand name drugs. The law's opponents contend that the gifts do not influence doctors and are merely educational tools for new products. While a pharmaceutical firm and its employees may see nothing wrong with providing gifts worth in excess of $25, they would be well advised to consider the penalty of $10,000 per violation before acting on their personal ethics. A more advised course of action probably would be to act within the law while lobbying for a change in the law.

Dimension 3: Behavior that is legal, yet unethical. If you determine that a behavior is legal and complies with relevant contractual agreements and company policy, your next step is to consult your company's or profession's **code of ethics**. This written document summarizes the company's or profession's standards of ethical conduct. Some companies refer to this document as a *credo* or *standards of ethical conduct*. If the behavior does not violate the code of ethics, then put it to the test of your own personal integrity. You may at times reject a legal action because it does not "feel right." Most Americans were appalled to learn that many leading figures in recent corporate scandals were never convicted of a single crime. While they may have acted legally, their profiting at the expense of company employees, stockholders, and the public hardly seemed ethical. You may be faced with situations in which you reject a behavior that is legal because you would not be proud for your family and community to know that you engaged in it.

Critical Thinking

Which of the ethical frameworks do
you find most appropriate for you
personally? Why?

Dimension 4: Behavior that is both legal and ethical. Decisions in this dimension are easy to make. Such actions comply with the law, company policies, and your professional and personal codes of ethics.

The Pagano Model offers a straightforward method for determining whether a proposed action is advisable.[14] For this system to work, you must answer the following six questions honestly:

Is it okay if it goes on the news? (handwritten note)

- Is the proposed action legal—the core starting point?
- What are the benefits and costs to the people involved?
- Would you want this action to be a universal standard, appropriate for everyone?
- Does the action pass the light-of-day test? That is, if your action appeared on television or others learned about it, would you be proud?
- Does the action pass the Golden Rule test? That is, would you want the same to happen to you?
- Does the action pass the ventilation test? Ask the opinion of a wise friend with no investment in the outcome. Does this friend believe the action is ethical?

Friends!!! (handwritten note)

Visit the text support site at http://lehman.swlearning.com to learn about other frameworks for examining the correctness of an action.

Diversity Challenges as a Strategic Force Influencing Communication

Objective 6

Explain how diversity challenges act as a strategic force to influence the process of business communication.

Diversity Challenges

Critical Thinking

What is the relationship between political barriers and communication barriers?

Diversity in the workplace is another strategic force influencing communication. Differences between the sender and the receiver in areas such as culture, age, gender, and education require a sensitivity on the part of both parties so that the intended message is the one that is received.

Understanding how to communicate effectively with people from other cultures has become more integral to the work environment as many U.S. companies are increasingly conducting business with international companies or becoming multinational. Successful communication must often span barriers of language and requires a person to consider differing world views resulting from societal, religious, or other cultural factors. When a person fails to consider these factors, communication suffers, and the result is often embarrassing and potentially costly.

McDonald's is an example of a large U.S. company that has expanded its operations to include most major countries in the world. To be successful on an international scale, McDonald's managers had to be aware of cultural differences and be willing to work to ensure that effective communication occurred despite these barriers.

Occasionally, however, a whopper of an intercultural communication faux pas occurs. That is what happened when McDonald's began their promotional campaign in Britain for the World Cup soccer championship. It seemed like a clever (and harmless) idea to reproduce the flags of the 24 nations participating in the event and print them on packaging—two million Happy Meal bags, to be exact. What marketing personnel failed to consider was that words from the *Koran* are printed on the Saudi flag. The idea that sacred words from Islam's holy book were mass-printed to sell a product with the knowledge that the packages would be thrown into the trash angered and offended many Muslims, who immediately complained. McDonald's apologized for the gaffe and agreed to cooperate with the Saudis in finding a solution to the problem.[15]

While NAFTA has created new business opportunities for U.S. and Mexican entities, unique problems have also occurred. After seven trips to Mexico and nine months of courtship, a U.S. firm faxed the final contract to the Mexican CEO. This action was a big mistake, since Mexican protocol calls for more formal finalizing in a face-to-face meeting.[16] These errors serve as examples of how much "homework" is involved in maintaining good relations with customers or clients from other cultures. The potential barrier of language is obvious; however, successful managers know that much more is involved in communicating with everyone—across cultures, genders, ages, abilities, and other differences.

Communication Opportunities and Challenges in Diversity

As world markets expand, U.S. employees at home and abroad will be doing business with more people from other countries. You may find yourself working abroad for a large American company, an international company with a plant in the United States, or a company with an ethnically diverse workforce. Regardless of the workplace, your **diversity skills**, that is, your ability to communicate effectively with both men and women of all ages and with people of other cultures or minority groups, will affect your success in today's culturally diverse, global economy.

Critical Thinking

How has diversity impacted the development of the United States as a world leader?

- *International issues.* Worldwide telecommunications and intense international business competition have fueled the movement of many industries into world markets. During the past four decades, U.S. firms have established facilities in Europe, Central and South America, and Asia. At many U.S. corporations, such as Dow Chemical, Gillette, and IBM, more than 40 percent of total sales in recent years has come from international operations. Over the past decade, Asians and Europeans have built plants in the United States. Many U.S. workers are now employed in manufacturing plants and facilities owned and operated by foreign interests. Understanding a person of another culture who may not speak your language well or understand your culturally based behaviors is a daily challenge faced by many. Specific guidelines for writing and speaking with an international audience are provided in later chapters.

- *Intercultural issues.* Changing demographics in the United States are requiring businesses to face ethnic diversity in the workplace. Rather than being a melting pot for people from many countries, the United States has offered an environment in which people of varying cultures could live and practice their cultural heritage. People with a common heritage generally formed their own neighborhoods and worked intently at retaining their traditional customs and language, while still sharing in the common culture. Consequently, *mosaic* seems to be a more accurate term than *melting pot* to reflect U.S. cultural diversity. As in a mosaic, small, distinct groups combine to form the pattern or design of the U.S. population and workforce. U.S. labor statistics reflect

Apparel giants such as Reebok, Nike, and Puma compete in communicating a global image for their sportswear. While celebrity endorsements cost them millions, association with successful athletes helps establish name recognition and brand desirability with consumers. Serena Williams, preferring a skintight catsuit ensemble over the traditional white tennis shirt, has become a global icon in and of herself.

© AFP/CORBIS

the declining proportion of white males in the labor force and growing proportions of minorities and women.[17] People from different backgrounds invariably bring different values, attitudes, and perceptions to the workplace.

Critical Thinking

The "graying of America" reflects the growing numbers of people who are remaining in the workforce to an older and older age.

- ***Intergenerational issues.*** While age diversity has always been present in the workplace, recent trends have made it a more important issue than ever. The so-called "graying of America" has changed the age distribution in the U.S. population. The older segment of the population is larger today than at any time previously. The maturing of the "baby-boomer" generation (those born between 1946 and 1964), a relatively low birthrate, and increasing life spans have led to a higher average age in the population. Today's workforce reflects the advancing age of the general populace. As of the year 2000, for instance, one in every three workers was 45 or older.[18] Figure 1-7 illustrates the continued trend toward an older workforce. Because of changes in laws affecting retirement benefits and better overall health, many older workers will choose to continue longer in their professional activities than in past years. Because of the broadening of the age span in the workplace, businesses will be faced with new challenges related to differences in perceptions, values, and communication styles of the generations. Chapter 3 includes a Strategic Forces focus on generational differences and their impact on workplace communication.

Figure 1-7

Changing Workforce Age Demographics

1995

Over 60
12%

60 and under
88%

2015

Over 60
40%

60 and under
60%

Source: National Council on Aging[19]

- *Gender issues.* The flood of women entering the job market has substantially changed the American workforce. Old social patterns of behavior that defined the appropriate roles for men and women do not fit in a work environment free from discrimination. While civil rights laws prohibiting sex discrimination and pay equity requirements have been in place for more than 30 years, charges continue to be filed by individuals who feel that their rights have been violated. The number of sexual harassment cases has increased in recent years, resulting from a broader-based definition of what indeed constitutes sexual harassment. Although a charge of sexual harassment may certainly be based on actions with sexual overtones, it has also been interpreted to include comments, visual images, or other conditions that create a hostile working environment. One result of the increased focus on sexual harassment in the workplace is the reluctance of some to communicate with other workers for fear that their actions or words might be misconstrued. Both men and women confront workplace communication challenges.

Critical Thinking

What other aspects of diversity can influence communication?

Workplace diversity can lead to misunderstandings and miscommunications; but it also poses opportunities to improve both workers and organizations. Managers must be prepared to communicate effectively with workers of different nationalities, genders, races, ages, abilities, and so forth.

Managing a diverse workforce effectively will require you to communicate with *everyone* and to help all employees reach their fullest potential and contribute to the company's goals. When miscommunication occurs, both sides are frustrated and often angry. To avoid such problems, increasing numbers of companies have undertaken **diversity initiatives** and are providing diversity training seminars to help workers understand and appreciate gender and age differences and the cultures of coworkers. To prepare for these communication challenges, commit the time and energy to enhance your diversity skills while you are attending classes as well as after you enter the workplace.

Culture and Communication

Critical Thinking

What are some examples in your own community of culture-oriented activities?

Managers with the *desire* and the *skill* to conduct business in new international markets and to manage a diverse workforce effectively will confront problems created by cultural differences. The way messages are decoded and encoded is not just a function of the experiences, beliefs, and assumptions of the person sending or receiving those messages but also are shaped by the society in which he or she lives.

People learn patterns of behavior from their **culture**. The *culture* of a people is the product of their living experiences within their own society. Culture could be described as "the way of life" of a people and includes a vast array of behaviors and beliefs. These patterns affect how people perceive the world, what they value, and how they act. Differing patterns can also create barriers to communication. Visit the text support site at http://lehman.swlearning.com to learn more about the characteristics of culture that shape communication.

Barriers to Intercultural Communication

Because cultures give different definitions to such basics of interaction as values and norms, people raised in two different cultures may clash. Some of the main areas in which cultures clash are explored below.

Critical Thinking

Give several examples of stereotypes that prevail concerning certain cultural groups.

- *Ethnocentrism.* Problems occur between people of different cultures primarily because people tend to assume that their own cultural norms are the right way to do things. They wrongly believe that the specific patterns of behavior desired in their own cultures are universally valued. This belief, known as **enthnocentrism**, is certainly natural; but learning about other cultures and developing sensitivity will help minimize ethnocentric reactions when dealing with other cultures.
- *Stereotypes.* One group often forms a mental picture of the main characteristics of another group, creating preformed ideas of what people in this group are like. These pictures, called **stereotypes**, influence the way members of the first group interact with members of the second. When members of the first group observe a behavior that conforms to that stereotype, the validity of the preconceived notion is reinforced. They view the other person as a representative of a class of people rather than as an individual. All cultures have stereotypes about other cultures they have encountered. These stereotypes can interfere with communication when people interact on the basis of the imagined representative and not the real individual.
- *Interpretation of time.* The study of how a culture perceives time and its use is called **chronemics**. In the United States, we have a saying that "time is money." North Americans, like some northern Europeans

who are also concerned about punctuality, make appointments, keep them, and do not waste time completing them. In some other cultures, time is the cheapest commodity and an inexhaustible resource; time represents a person's span on earth, which is only part of eternity. To these cultures, long casual conversations prior to serious discussions or negotiations is time well spent in establishing and nurturing relationships. On the other hand, the time-efficient American businessperson is likely to fret about the waste of precious time.

- *Personal space requirements.* Space operates as a language just as time does. The study of cultural space requirements is known as **proxemics**. In all cultures, the distance between people functions in communication as "personal space" or "personal territory." In the United States, for example, for intimate conversations with close friends and relatives, individuals are willing to stay within about a foot and a half of each other; for casual conversations, up to two or three feet; for job interviews and personal business, four to twelve feet; and for public occasions, more than twelve feet. However, in many cultures outside the United States, closer personal contact is accepted, or greater distance may be the norm.

Critical Thinking

Do differences exist in the nonverbal communication of people of different generations? Justify your answer.

- *Body language.* The study of body language is known as **kinesics**. Body language is not universal, but instead is learned from one's culture. Even the most basic gestures have varying cultural meanings—the familiar North American symbol for "okay" means zero in France, money in Japan, and an expression of vulgarity in Brazil. Similarly, eye contact, posture, and facial expressions carry different meanings throughout the world. Chapter 2 contains an expanded discussion of nonverbal communication.

Critical Thinking

Give some examples of words and phrases that have different meanings for speakers of British English than for speakers of American English.

- *Translation limitations.* Words in one language do not always have an equivalent meaning in other languages, and the concepts the words describe are often different as well. Translators can be helpful, but keep in mind that a translator is working with a second language and must listen to one language, mentally cast the words into another language, then speak them. This process is difficult and opens the possibility that the translator will fall victim to one or more cultural barriers. The Internet Case following Chapter 3 provides additional opportunity for you to explore translation issues.

Critical Thinking

Select a word with various synonyms. How are the meanings of each word somewhat different?

- *Lack of language training.* The following is an anecdote that speaks to the need for language training:

What do you call someone who speaks two languages? (Reply: bilingual)
What do you call someone who speaks three languages? (Reply: trilingual)
What do you call someone who speaks one language? (Reply: an American)

This tongue-in-cheek humor reinforces the language illiteracy of most U.S. citizens. Since familiarity with a second language certainly improves your competitiveness as a job applicant, be sure to exploit that ability in your résumé. In some situations, learning a second language may not be feasible—you are completing a short-term assignment, you must leave immediately, or the language is extremely difficult to learn (e.g., Japanese and Arabic). However, even if you cannot speak their language fluently, people from other cultures will appreciate simple efforts to learn a few common phrases. Other suggestions for overcoming language differences are discussed in the accompanying Strategic Forces feature, "Viva la Difference!"

Changing Technology as a Strategic Force Influencing Communication

Objective 7

Explain how changing technology acts as a strategic force to influence the process of business communication.

Changing Technology

Critical Thinking

In your opinion, what communication technology has most changed the way business is conducted?

Electronic tools have not eliminated the need for basic communication skills; and they can, in fact, create new obstacles or barriers to communication that must be overcome. These tools, however, also create opportunities, which range from the kinds of communications that are possible to the quality of the messages themselves. Electronic tools can help people in various ways, such as (1) collecting and analyzing data, (2) shaping messages to be clearer and more effective, and (3) communicating quickly and efficiently with others over long distances.

Tools for Data Collection and Analysis

Knowing how to collect information and communicate in a networked world is critical if you and your company are to be competitive. The Internet has brought vast amounts of data into our homes and businesses, and online information services provide a wide range of sources to facilitate our research. Generally, electronic communication provides researchers with two distinct advantages: (1) electronic searches of organizational databases and electronic networks can be done in a fraction of the time required to conduct manual searches of printed sources, and (2) the vast amount of information available allows researchers to develop better solutions to problems.

Internal databases enable decision makers to obtain information from their own company records quickly and accurately. Databases offer these advantages:

- *Data organization*, the ability to organize large amounts of data.
- *Data integrity*, assurance that the data will be accurate and complete.
- *Data security*, assurance that the data are secure because access to a database is controlled through several built-in data security features.

External databases (networks) allow users to access information from remote locations literally around the world and in an instant transfer that information to their own computers for further manipulation or storage. The *Internet*, a loose collection of millions of computers at thousands of sites around the world, allows users to access information of all types and share files. While the Internet was first intended to be used for academic and research purposes, the majority of the networks worldwide are registered to corporations whose primary use is electronic mail.[20]

Viva la Difference!

With so many barriers, communicating with people of other cultures can be difficult. Anyone who enters the business world today must be aware of potential trouble spots and of ways to avoid them. Application of some common-sense guidelines can help to overcome intercultural barriers.

- **Learn about that person's culture.** Many sources of useful information are available. University courses in international business communication are increasing, and experienced businesspeople have written books recounting some of the subtle but important ways that people from other cultures communicate.[21] Various Internet sites are dedicated to sharing information to help the intercultural communicator. Networking can generate the names of other businesspeople who have made successful contact with another culture. A telephone conversation or a lunch meeting may provide useful pointers on proper and improper behavior. Corporations with frequent and extensive dealings in other countries often establish workshops in which employees receive briefing and training before accepting overseas assignments.

Learning the language is an invaluable way of becoming more familiar with another culture.

- **Have patience—with yourself and the other person.** Conversing with someone from another culture, when one of you is likely to be unfamiliar with the language being used, can be difficult and time consuming. By being patient with mistakes, making sure that all questions are answered, and not hurrying, you are more likely to make the outcome of the conversation positive. You must also learn to be patient and tolerant of ambiguity. Being able to react to new, different, and unpredictable situations with little visible discomfort or irritation will prove invaluable. The author Howard Schuman writes that "a sense of humor is indispensable for dealing with the cultural mistakes and faux pas you will certainly commit."[22]

- **Get help when you need it.** If you are not sure what is being said—or why something is being said in a certain way—ask for clarification. If you feel uneasy about conversing with someone from another culture, bring along someone you trust who understands that culture. You will have a resource if you need help.

Instead of ignoring cultural factors, workers and employers can improve communication by recognizing them and by considering people as individuals rather than as members of stereotypical groups. Many companies view the implementation of a diversity initiative as a way to improve organizational communication. The goal of such a program is to increase awareness and appreciation for areas of differences among employees and to build stronger rapport by finding commonalities. Firms with successful diversity initiatives find that promoting common understanding among workers boosts morale, creativity, and productivity.

Application

Interview a person from a cultural group other than your own. Include the following questions:

1. What examples can you give of times when you experienced discrimination or isolation?

2. What information can you provide to aid other groups in understanding your cultural uniqueness?

3. What advice would you give for improving intercultural understanding?

Many people as well as organizations subscribe to an online service to assist them in using Internet resources effectively. Through membership with such an online service, subscribers can

- send electronic messages and computer files across the world.
- participate in discussion groups (forums) to get answers to questions and to benefit from the information generated by a group interested in a specific topic.
- browse occasionally through the "network news" generated by other discussion groups to read the latest discussions in these areas.
- download software available on the service.
- access vast amounts of information from a wide range of sources.

Information is available on general news, stocks, financial markets, sports, travel, weather, and a variety of publications (some of which allow you to retrieve the full text). An online encyclopedia is a standard service that is updated regularly. A clipping service that locates all articles on a specific topic from the various news services is a time-efficient way to stay abreast of important topics.

Using a modem, the appropriate communication software, and an assigned password, you can obtain information from around the world. However, knowing how to "tunnel" through the vast amount of irrelevant information to find what you want can be overwhelming. The experience can also be expensive in terms of human time spent and charges incurred for online time. Locating information from electronic sources requires that you know the search procedures and methods for constructing an effective search strategy. You will develop these skills when studying the research process in Chapter 9.

Critical Thinking

Spreadsheets provide for "if, then" analysis by allowing calculations to be modified easily by changing formula cells.

For preparing reports containing any analysis of numbers, an electronic spreadsheet is invaluable. An **electronic spreadsheet** is a forecasting and decision-making tool that can manipulate and analyze data easily. The spreadsheet's forecasting ability allows you to ask, for instance, how profits would change if costs and sales were reduced by 10 percent or increased by 5 percent. The ability to calculate quickly these variable forecasts—called "what-if" questions—is one of the main benefits of spreadsheets. Spreadsheets can transform a vast amount of numerical data into information that can be used in decision making. By condensing data into organized tables, the spreadsheet greatly assists the manager in meaningfully interpreting the data. Once it has been created, a spreadsheet can be inserted into a word processing file. To depict complex data more clearly, the manager can also quickly construct a graphic using the prepared spreadsheet.

Tools for Shaping Messages to Be Clearer and More Effective

Another significant benefit to communication offered by technology is message clarification and refinement. Documents that took days to produce during the b.c. (before computers) era can now be created in hours. Perhaps the greater benefit, however, is the advent of whole new possibilities for document preparation and presentation.

Word processing software expedites the production of a document and also improves the quality of the message. Other features that improve writing are electronic spell check, thesaurus, and writing analysis software. Using word processing, you can draft a document, store it on magnetic medium, and retrieve and revise it as many times as necessary to produce a clear, understandable document. Word processing software also allows you to format the document using print features, graphic and layout features, and various typefaces, and then print a highly professional copy.

Reports and longer documents become less tedious to produce because of features that facilitate writing and editing. Most full-feature word processing software includes a feature that generates a contents page, index, and document references automatically. This feature saves time in the initial creation of these pages and in their updating if pagination changes during editing. The mail-merge feature facilitates large-scale mailings of personalized form letters; guidelines for using this feature to personalize form letters is presented in Chapter 5.

Collaborative software assists groups in writing collaboratively. Each author marks revisions and inserts document comments in much the same way as with word processing software and then sends the computer file to the coauthor. Some collaborative software programs allow multiple authors to work on documents at the same time when they are placed on an electronic whiteboard. Drawings or information written on its surface can be displayed simultaneously on the computer monitors of others in the work team. The Strategic Force feature in Chapter 4 explores the capabilities of groupware software in greater detail.

Graphics software helps managers and other workers surpass simple word processing capabilities by using typography and design elements to create communications that are persuasive and professional looking. Using ***desktop publishing software*** and a high-quality printer, a person can create important publications such as prospectuses, annual reports, and newsletters. When printed on a laser printer, the result can be visually convincing. ***Presentation software*** allows speakers to develop dynamic multimedia presentation visuals that combine text, graphics, animation, sound, and video.

Decision makers who do not have the time to wade through pages of written text searching for key information are among the primary beneficiaries of graphic presentations. A salesperson might close a deal by incorporating into a proposal five bar graphs illustrating the superiority of a product over the competition's version. A manager may win the day by supporting a case for expansion with a highly professional slide show depicting the resulting increase in profits.

Quality graphics can be produced using a variety of software programs and are available from several sources:

- Use electronic spreadsheet and presentation graphics software to prepare charts and drawing software to generate other images such as flowcharts, pictograms, scaled drawings of products, and so on.

Team Environment

Critical Thinking

In what way has word processing software become more and more like desktop publishing software?

- Integrate clip art, photos, and sound available with full-feature software and that can be purchased from commercial sources or imported from online sources.
- Use scanners to convert images (graphics, photos, signatures, letterhead, and text) to electronic files and digital cameras to capture photographs as electronic files.

Web publishing tools facilitate the creation of web pages for posting to the Internet. Such applications allow for the integration of text and graphic elements and eliminate the need for extensive knowledge of hypertext markup language, or HTML. Hyperlinks to other documents and web sites can also be included in the page design. The formatted web pages may then be viewed using a web browser. Most organizations realize the importance of having a web presence and have devised useful web pages to provide information to their various constituents. The CDC's organization web site, shown below, offers eye-appealing access to various types of information. Additional information about web page development and maintenance is presented in Chapter 5.

Tools for Communicating Quickly and Efficiently Over Long Distances

Computer networks have placed the world at our fingertips. To exploit the possibilities, whole new channels for communication have emerged. The businessperson is no longer limited to paper-copy letters and memos, the telephone, and face-to-face meetings; rather, exciting new methods for sending and receiving messages are available:

- *Electronic mail. Electronic mail*, or *e-mail*, can be used to distribute memos, reports, and documents without sending them in a printed

An effective Internet presence is essential for the success of most businesses and organizations.

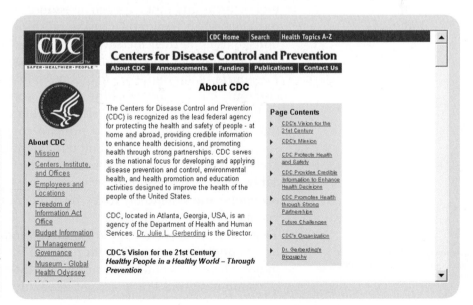

COURTESY, CENTERS FOR DISEASE CONTROL

Critical Thinking

E-mail is replacing the use of memos, telephone calls, and postal mail for many business situations.

(hard copy) form. E-mail helps solve the problem of "telephone tag." Approximately 70 percent of business telephone callers *do not* reach the person they called on the first try. The result is a game of tag, as the caller and the person called keep trying to reach the other unsuccessfully. With electronic mail, the sender keys a message and sends it to an electronic mailbox where the receiver can read the message at his or her convenience. When the message is delivered and read quickly, electronic mail can be almost as convenient and articulate as a personal conversation.

E-mail systems that operate on a company's existing computer system are relatively inexpensive. When a single message is sent to several recipients, the savings are even greater compared to the cost of traditional communication methods. More advanced corporate applications of e-mail include (a) the *forms definition feature* that allows a user to select and complete a form to be sent to a recipient, who will sign the form electronically and forward copies of the signed forms to appropriate persons, and (b) use of intelligent agents that will automatically route messages (e.g., claims of more than $10,000 will be forwarded to a senior bank officer).[23] As you study Chapter 5, you will learn more about the benefits of e-mail and acceptable practices for writing and using electronic communication appropriately.

- *Instant messaging.* **Instant messaging** is e-mail that is interactive in real time. Commonly referred to as "chat," instant messaging technology allows a varying number of people to log on to a "chat room" and exchange text dialog that can be seen by all logged in participants. While instant messaging began as a leisure application for teenagers, it is now frequently used for various business applications. The Electronic Café at the end of Chapter 1 will allow you to explore the use of instant messaging as a business communication tool.

- *Voice mail.* **Voice mail** allows you to use your telephone to dial a voice mail service and store spoken messages. Recipients can retrieve the messages when they return to the office or dial in from remote locations to listen to their messages. Voice mail provides many of the benefits of e-mail but does not require a computer.

- *Facsimile.* A **facsimile**, or **fax**, is a flexible and inexpensive form of electronic mail. A fax machine reads a document and transmits text, pictures, and graphics over telephone lines to another fax machine that receives the message and prints a copy of the document. High-speed fax machines can transmit a high-quality page in a few seconds; and because they can be programmed, the cost of transmission can be cut by sending a message in evening hours to take advantage of lower telephone rates. Sending faxes also facilitates communicating with people in different time zones.

Critical Thinking

How would telecommuting affect the social dynamics of the worker, colleagues, and family?

- *Telecommuting.* **Telecommuting** allows individuals to work in their homes and transmit work from home to the office electronically. The major advantages of telecommuting are the reduced time and expense of commuting and the increased flexibility of working hours. Rather than spending two to three hours a day commuting to work in an urban area, for example, employees use a modem, telephone lines, and a remote workstation to transmit their work electronically. Transmitting information and computing from remote locations have become prevalent because of the availability of laptop and handheld computers. These smaller computers give professionals access to computing power regardless of where they are—hotel room, airplane, taxi, client's office, and so on.

- *Cellular telephone.* **Cellular telephones**, often called *mobile phones* or *cell phones*, are cellular radios that transmit messages over airways. Cellular telephones are a powerful communication tool, especially for workers who spend several hours commuting to and from work, travel from one meeting or work site to another, or work at sites with no access to a telephone. The increased productivity resulting from the more efficient use of time justifies the cost of cellular service. Cellular telephones also help managers stay in closer contact with coworkers and with current and prospective clients and customers. Quick, courteous responses build strong interpersonal relations, which in turn lead to increased customer commitment.

Critical Thinking

Electronic conferencing has grown in popularity due to recent concerns over security as well as economic savings.

Team
Environment

- *Electronic conferencing.* **Electronic conferences** via teleconferencing and videoconferencing are alternatives to face-to-face meetings that allow several people at different locations to communicate electronically. **Teleconferencing** allows persons in different geographic locations to be on the same line at the same time. **Videoconferencing** takes advantage of all media—audio, graphics, and video. Speakers provide the audio feedback, facsimile devices send graphics, and cameras transmit the video portion of the conference in a specially equipped room. Participants engage in group discussions while observing one another's facial expressions and gestures. Using collaborative software with web camera technology, users in remote locations can see each other as they chat and "document conference," that is, share and annotate computer files and images in real time.

Electronic conferences can eliminate or reduce the high costs of face-to-face meetings: travel, hotels, food, and time lost in transit. Videoconferencing restores the nonverbal elements of interpersonal communication that are lost over the telephone, and thus, is more personal than a "disembodied" voice on the other end of a telephone line. The availability of less expensive **desktop videoconferencing systems** that allows users to hold electronic meetings across existing local area networks and telephone or cable lines has made electronic conferences more accessible to businesses of all sizes.

Legal and Ethical Implications of Technology

Legal & Ethical
Constraints

In addition to its many benefits, technology poses some challenges for the business communicator. For instance, technology raises issues of ownership, as in the case of difficulties that arise in protecting the copyright of documents transmitted over the Internet. Technology poses dilemmas over access, that is, who has the right to certain stored information pertaining to an individual or a company.

Technology threatens our individual privacy, our right to be left alone, free from surveillance or interference from other individuals or organizations. Common invasions of privacy caused by technology include collecting excessive amounts of information for decision making and maintaining too many files, monitoring the exact time employees spend on a specific task and between tasks and the exact number and length of breaks, and supervisors' or coworkers' reading of another employee's electronic mail and computer files. Integrating computer files containing information collected from more than one agency without permission is a major threat to privacy. Although an individual may have authorized the collection of the individual information, merging the information may reveal things the individual may want to remain private.[24] The privacy issue is explored further in the accompanying Strategic Forces feature, "Is Anything Private Anymore?"

Critical Thinking

Have you personally been affected by a loss of privacy because of technology? How?

Team Environment as a Strategic Force Influencing Communication

Objective  8

Explain how team environment acts as a strategic force to influence the process of business communication.

Team Environment

A team-oriented approach is replacing the traditional top-down management style in today's organizations. Firms around the world are facing problems in decreasing productivity, faltering product quality, and worker dissatisfaction. Work teams are being examined as a way to help firms remain globally competitive. Although worker involvement in the management process has long been the hallmark of Japanese business, many U.S. businesses, as well as those of other countries, are experimenting with self-directed work teams.[25] The list of companies using self-directed work teams is diverse, including such firms as Hunt-Wesson, the Internal Revenue Service, and the San Diego Zoo. Other companies using the team concept include Hewlett-Packard, Southwest Airlines, Toyota, Motorola, General Electric, and Corning.

Work Team Defined

The terms *team, work team, group, work group, cross-functional team* and *self-directed team* are often used interchangeably.[26] Whatever the title, a **team** is a small number of people with complementary skills who work together for a common purpose. Team members set their own goals, in cooperation with management, and plan how to achieve those goals and how their work is to be accomplished. The central organizing element of a team is that it has a common purpose and measurable goals for which the team can be held accountable, independent of its individual members. Employees in a self-directed work team handle a wide array of functions and work with a minimum of direct supervision.[27] Some major strengths of teams are as follows:[28]

Is Anything Private Anymore?

We all live in the Internet society, whether or not we spend any time online. For most people the convenience of e-mail, mobile phones, and voice mail has proved irresistible, but many have also begun to feel the downside of cyber vulnerability. The expanding power of electronic technology makes it possible for information to be shared globally with little effort, with or without the knowledge of the information's owner. Passage of the USA Patriot Act following the attacks of September 11, 2001, initiated new federal safety measures that many feel further endanger constitutional rights to privacy. Despite the passage of federal legislation and additional state laws designed to enhance and strengthen electronic privacy, most Americans feel they have less privacy today than ever. According to a recent Harris poll, 76 percent of Americans believe they have lost all control over personal information, and 67 percent believe that computers must be restricted in the future to preserve privacy.[29] Workplace privacy has also become an area of concern, as computer monitoring and surveillance capabilities expand.

George Orwell, in his classic novel *1984*, described what many believe to be the ultimate in privacy-shattering totalitarianism as he offered a foreboding look at future society. In his fictitious account ". . . there was of course no way of knowing whether you were being watched at any given moment. . . . It was even conceivable that they watched everybody all the time. . . . You had to live—did live—from habit that became instinct in the assumption that every sound you made was overheard, and, except in darkness, every movement scrutinized."[30] We have now advanced technologically to the point that, if desired, this kind of surveillance is easily possible, even in darkness.

An important aspect of technology is its seductive power: If a technology exists, it must be used. Where does this principle leave the individual regarding privacy needs in a highly automated world? Experts in the area of individual privacy have suggested three key aspects in the ethical management of information and protection of privacy:[31]

- **Relevance.** An inquiring party should have a clear and valid purpose for delving into the information of an individual.

- **Consent.** An individual should be given the right to withhold consent prior to any query that might violate privacy.

- **Methods.** An inquiring party should distinguish between methods of inquiry that are reasonable and customary and those that are of questionable ethical grounding.

While technology offers tremendous advantages and endless possibilities for enhancing communication, it poses challenges for both individuals and organizations in the maintenance of a proper degree of privacy. Most of us are not ready for the all-seeing eye of Orwell's "Big Brother."

Application

Read a book review of George Orwell's *1984*. In a two-page written summary, cite instances in which Orwell described futuristic technological capabilities that have been realized in recent years. How has society's response to these capabilities differed from the fictional plot?

Critical Thinking

Synergy can be mathematically defined as $1 + 1 = 3$.

- Teams make workers happier by causing them to feel that they are shaping their own jobs.
- Teams increase efficiency by eliminating layers of managers whose job was once to pass orders downward.
- Teams enable a company to draw on the skills and imagination of a whole workforce. A key element in team success is the concept of *synergy*. Synergy is defined as a situation in which the whole is greater than the sum of the parts. Teams provide a depth of expertise that is unavailable at the individual level, as illustrated in the Ziggy cartoon. Teams open

Ziggy

lines of communication that then lead to increased interaction among employees and between employees and management. The result is that teams help companies reach their goals of delivering higher-quality products and services faster and with more cost effectiveness.

Communication Differences in Work Teams

In the past most businesses were operated in a hierarchical fashion, with most decisions made at the top. Communication followed a top-down/ bottom-up or lateral pattern. Communication patterns are different in successful team environments as compared to traditional organizational structures. Trust building is the primary factor that changes the organization's communication patterns. Open meetings are an important method for enhancing communication, as they educate employees about the business while building bridges of understanding and trust. A second trust-building structure is shared leadership, which involves more direct and effective communication between management and its internal customers. Listening, problem solving, conflict resolution, negotiation, and consensus become important factors in group communication.

Communication is perhaps the single most important aspect of successful teamwork. Open lines of communication increase interaction between employees and management. Information must flow vertically up to management and down to workers, as well as horizontally among team members, other teams, and supervisors. All affected parties should be kept informed as projects progress.

Maximization of Work Team Effectiveness

Grouping employees into a team structure does not mean that they will automatically function as a team. A group must go through a developmental process to begin to function as a team. Members need training in such areas as problem solving, goal setting, and conflict resolution. Teams must be encouraged to establish the "three R's"—roles, rules, and relationships.[32]

Critical Thinking

What do you see as the three major challenges to the success of work teams?

The self-directed work team can become the basic organizational building block to best ensure success in dynamic global competition. Skills for successful participation in team environments are somewhat different from those necessary for success in old-style organizations. Effective communication skills include the ability to give and take constructive criticism, listen actively, clearly impart one's views to others, and provide meaningful feedback. Emotional barriers, such as insecurity or condescension, can limit team effectiveness. Process barriers, such as prevailing policies and procedures, can also interfere by stifling effective team functioning. Cultural barriers, such as role assignment and perceived responsibilities, can separate workers from management. Effective team communication will involve overcoming all of these barriers.[33]

Perhaps the greatest requirement for successful teams is the ability to understand the feelings and needs of coworkers. Members must feel comfortable stating their opinions and discussing the strengths and weaknesses of the team. The ability to experience this openness is largely dependent on the level of trust workers have in one another and in management. Team members must also develop leadership skills that apply to a dynamic group setting. In dynamic team leadership, which is referred to as **distributed leadership**, the role of leader may alternate among members, and more than one leadership style may be active at any given time.[34]

To improve group communication, time needs to be set aside to assess the quality of interaction. Questions to pose about the group process might include the following:

- What are our common goals?
- What roles are members playing? For instance, is one person dominating while others contribute little or nothing?
- Is the group dealing with conflict in a positive way?
- What in the group process is going well?
- What about the group process could be improved?

Diversity Challenges

Gender, cultural, and age differences among members of a team can present barriers to team communication. Knowing what behaviors may limit the group process is imperative to maximizing results. Team members may need awareness training to assist in recognizing behaviors that may hinder team performance and in overcoming barriers that may limit the effectiveness of their communication. You can explore the team model versus reward for individual effort by completing the Internet Case at the end of this chapter. *Building High-Performance Teams*, a handbook that accompanies this text, will guide you through the stages of team development and various collaborative processes as you pursue a team-based class project.

Summary

1. **Define communication and describe the main purposes for communication in business.** Communication is the process of exchanging information and meaning between or among individuals through a common system of symbols, signs, and behavior. Managers spend most of their time in communication activities.

2. **Explain the communication process model and the ultimate objective of the communication process.** People engaged in communication encode and decode messages while simultaneously serving as both senders and receivers. In the communication process, feedback helps people resolve possible misunderstandings and thus improve communication effectiveness. Feedback and the opportunity to observe nonverbal signs are always present in face-to-face communication, the most complete of the three communication levels.

3. **Identify the five levels of communication.** Communication takes place at five levels: intrapersonal (communication within one person), interpersonal (communication between two people), group (communication among more than two people), organizational (communication among combinations of groups), and public (communication from one entity to the greater public).

4. **Discuss how information flows within an organization (formally and informally, and downward, upward, and horizontally).** Both formal and informal communication systems exist in every organization. The formal system exists to accomplish tasks, and the informal system serves a personal maintenance purpose that results in people feeling better about themselves and others. Communication flows upward, downward, and horizontally or laterally. These flows often defy formal graphic description, yet each is a necessary part of the overall communication activity of the organization.

5. **Explain how legal and ethical constraints act as a strategic force to influence the process of business communication.** Communication occurs within an environment of strategic forces that includes legal and ethical constraints. Pressures to succeed often place individuals in difficult legal and ethical dilemmas. International, federal, state, and local laws impose legal boundaries for business activity. Ethical boundaries are determined by personal analysis that can be assisted by application of various frameworks for decision making.

6. **Explain how diversity challenges act as a strategic force to influence the process of business communication.** Communication occurs within an environment of strategic forces that includes diversity in nationality, culture, age, gender, and other factors. Such diversity offers challenges for the business communicator in interpretation of time, personal space requirements, body language, language translation, and lack of language training. Through diversity, the organization and the individual are provided with tremendous opportunities to maximize talent, ideas, and productivity.

7. **Explain how changing technology acts as a strategic force to influence the process of business communication.** Communication occurs within an environment of strategic forces that includes changing technology. Significant strides have occurred in the development of tools for data collection and analysis, tools for shaping messages to be clearer and more effective, and tools for communicating quickly and efficiently over long distances. The use of technology also raises various legal and ethical concerns in regard to ownership, access, and privacy.

8. **Explain how team environment acts as a strategic force to influence the process of business communication.** Communication occurs within an environment of strategic forces that includes team environment. Communicating in teams differs from communication in traditional organizational structures. Team orientation focuses on group synergy rather than on individual effort. The result of effective teams is better decisions, more creative solutions to problems, and higher worker morale.

Chapter Review

1. What are the three purposes for which people communicate? What percentage of a manager's time is spent communicating? Give examples of the types of communication managers use. (Obj. 1)

2. Describe the five stages in the communication process using the following terms: (a) sender, (b) encode, (c) channel, (d) receiver, (e) decode, (f) feedback, and (g) interferences or barriers. (Obj. 2)

3. What types of differences between sender and receiver create barriers to communication? (Obj. 2)

4. What is the difference between intrapersonal and interpersonal communication? (Obj. 3)

5. How is the formal flow of communication different from the informal flow of communication? (Obj. 4)

6. Discuss four strategic forces that influence business communication. (Objs. 5–8)

//electronic café //

Instant Messaging Joins the Workforce

Instant messaging (IM) is not just for the younger set and their social conversations. Many firms are adopting instant messaging as a legitimate and valuable business tool. By 2005, estimates are that IM will be integrated into 50 percent of the applications that businesses use to interact with their customers.[35] In thousands of organizations, instant messaging is complimenting and replacing existing media such as e-mail and voice messages. Some corporate leaders, however, have expressed concerns over productivity and security that might be jeopardized when using IM. The following electronic activities will allow you to explore the IM phenomenon in more depth:

 InfoTrac College Edition. Access http://www.infotrac.thomsonlearning.com to read more about the use of instant messaging as a business tool. Search for the following article that is available in full text:

Stuart, A. (2002, July 1). IM is here; RU ready 2 try it? Inc., 76–81.

Compile a list of advantages and a list of disadvantages of using IM as a business communication tool.

 Test Support Web Site. Visit http://lehman.swlearning.com to learn more about instant messaging. Refer to Chapter 1's Electronic Café activity that provides links to an online article describing how instant messaging works. Be prepared to

discuss in class the features and uses of IM or follow your instructor's directions about how to use this information.

 WebTutor Advantage. Your instructor will give you directions about how and when to log on to your WebTutor and participate in an online chat on the following topic:

Instant messaging can be an effective business tool if. . .

Professional Power Pak. Access your PPP CD for helpful tips on using instant messaging as a business communication tool.

---

7. Give two definitions for ethics. (Obj. 5)

8. What are some common causes of unethical behavior in the workplace? (Obj. 5)

9. What are some aspects of diversity that pose communication challenges? (Obj. 6)

10. Describe several intercultural communication barriers and how they might be overcome. (Obj. 6)

11. Describe several ways that communication technology can assist individuals and organizations. (Obj. 7)

12. What concerns are raised over the use of technology? (Obj. 7)

13. Explain the concept of synergy. (Obj. 8)

14. How does communication in work teams differ from that of traditional organizations? (Obj. 8)

15. Why has communication been identified as perhaps the single most important aspect of team work? (Obj. 8)

Digging Deeper

1. Lack of Internet access is causing some nations to be classified as information "have-nots." What international communication problems could result?

2. Considering the four strategic forces discussed, how is business communication today different from that of 30 years ago? In what ways is it easier? In what ways is it more difficult?

To check your understanding of the chapter, take the practice quizzes at **http://lehman.swlearning.com** or your WebTutor course.

Activities

1. **Shadowing a Manager's Communication Activities (Obj. 1)**

   Shadow a business manager for a day. Keep a log of his/her communication activities for the time period you are observing. Divide the communication activities into the following categories: (1) attending meetings; (2) presenting information to groups; (3) explaining procedures and work assignments; (4) coordinating the work of various employees and departments; (5) evaluating and counseling employees; (6) promoting the company's products/services and image; and (7) other activities. Calculate the percentage of time spent in each activity. Be prepared to share your results with the class.

2. **Clocking Your Own Communication Activities (Obj. 1)**

   Prepare a record of your listening, speaking, reading, and writing activities and time spent in each during the hours of 8 a.m. to 5 p.m. for the next two days. You should attempt to record the time spent doing each activity for each one-hour time block in such a way that you obtain a total time for each activity. Be prepared to share your distribution with the class.

3. **Communication Barriers (Obj. 2)**

   In groups of three, develop a list of 10 to 12 annoying habits of yours or of others that create barriers (verbal and nonverbal) to effective communication. Classify each according to the portion of the communication process it affects. For each, give at least one suggestion for improvement.

   Visit the Interactive Study Center at **http://lehman. swlearning.com** for a downloadable version of this activity.

4. **Organizational Communication Flows (Objs. 3, 4)**

   Draw an organizational chart to depict the formal system of communication within an organization with which you are familiar. How is the informal system different from the organization chart? How are the five levels of communication achieved in the organization? Be prepared to discuss these points in class.

5. **Identifying Ethical Dilemmas (Obj. 5)**

   Using an online index, locate a current newspaper or magazine article that describes an illegal or unethical act by a business organization or its employee(s). Choose an incident as closely related as possible to your intended profession. Be prepared to share details of the incident in an informal presentation to the class.

6. **Diversity Challenges as a Strategic Force (Obj. 6)**

   Conduct an online search to locate examples of intercultural communication mistakes made by U.S. companies doing business in another country. How can an organization improve its diversity awareness to avoid such problems? Be prepared to share your ideas with the class.

7. **Classroom Diversity Initiative (Obj. 6)**

   In your class, locate other students to form a "diverse" group; your diversity may include age (more than five years difference), gender, race, culture, geographic origin, etc. Discuss your areas of diversity; then identify three things the group members all have in common, excluding your school experience. Share your group experiences with the class.

8. **Changing Technology as a Strategic Force (Objs. 2, 7)**

   Indicate which of the following communication mediums would be most appropriate for sending the following messages: e-mail, fax, telephone, or face-to-face communication. Justify your answer.

   a. The company is expecting a visit from members of a committee evaluating your bid for this year's Malcolm Baldrige National Quality Award. All employees must be notified of the visit.

   b. After careful deliberation, the management of a mid-sized pharmaceutical company is convinced the only way to continue its current level of research is to sell the company to a larger one. The employees must be informed of this decision.

   c. Lincoln Enterprises is eager to receive the results of a drug test on a certain employee. The drug testing company has been asked to send the results as quickly as possible.

   d. The shipping department has located the common carrier currently holding a customer's shipment that should have been delivered yesterday. Inform the customer that the carrier has promised delivery by tomorrow morning.

   e. An employee in another division office has requested you send a spreadsheet you have prepared so he can manipulate the data to produce a report.

9. **Technology's Impact on Communication (Obj. 7)**

   In pairs, read and discuss an article from a current magazine or journal about how technology is impacting communication. Send your instructor a brief e-mail message discussing the major theme of the article. Include a complete bibliographic entry so the instructor could locate the article (refer to Appendix B for examples for formatting references). Your instructor will provide directions for setting up an e-mail account and composing and sending an e-mail message.

10. **Exploring Use of Teams in the Workplace (Obj. 8)**

    Using the Internet, locate an article that describes how a company or organization is using teams in its operation. Write a one-page abstract of the article.

Applications

Read | Think | Write | Speak | Collaborate

1. **Legal and Ethical Constraints as a Strategic Force (Obj. 5)**

   Read *The Power of Ethical Management* by Kenneth Blanchard and Norman Vincent Peale, a short, engaging story of a sales manager's attempt to make an ethical decision. Write a brief report summarizing the ethical principles presented in the book.

Read | **Think** | Write | Speak | Collaborate

2. **Analyzing an Ethical Dilemma (Obj. 5)**

   Locate the following article available in full text from InfoTrac College Edition or perhaps from another database available through your campus library: Dubinsky, J. E. (2002, October). When an employee question presents an ethical dilemma. *Payroll Manager's Report*, 1.

   After reading the article, refer to the text support site (**http://lehman.swlearning.com**) for information on other ethical frameworks. Respond to the following questions:

   a. Who are the stakeholders in the case? What does each stand to gain or lose, depending on your decision?

   b. How does the situation described in the case relate to the four-dimension model shown in Figure 1-6?

   c. What factors might influence your decision as the manager in the case?

   d. How would *you* respond to the employee in the case? Why?

Read | Think | **Write** | Speak | Collaborate

3. **Importance of Communication in Your Career Field (Objs. 1–8)**

   Conduct an online search related to communication in your chosen career field. Write a brief paper providing information such as (a) evidence of the value of communication in the profession, (b) major audiences to whom you will communicate, (c) examples of how each of the strategic forces influences communication in the field, and (d) typical communication requirements. Be prepared to share your results with the class.

Read | Think | Write | **Speak** | Collaborate

4. **Understanding Diversity Issues (Obj. 6)**

   Read the discussion of "Culture and Communication" at the text support site (**http://lehman.swlearning.com**). In groups of three, interview an international student at your institution and generate a list of English words that have no equivalents in his or her language. Find out about nonverbal communication that may differ from that used in American culture. Share your findings in a short presentation to the class.

Read | Think | Write | Speak | **Collaborate**

5. **Communication Challenges in the Future Workplace (Objs. 1–8)**

   Locate the following article through InfoTrac College Edition or another online database:

   Kaplan-Leiserson, E. (2002, July). The future of work. *T & D, 56*(7), 12(2).

   In small groups, discuss the following:

   a. What communication trends are predicted in the workplace? Are any of these surprising? Why?

   b. Which trends are likely to impact your chosen career field most significantly? In what ways?

   c. How do the predicted trends relate to the four strategic forces presented in Chapter 1?

   Select one of the resource sites provided in the article. Visit the site and prepare a brief presentation about the selected trend to be given to the class.

Communicating Internationally Looms as a CDC Challenge

Julie Gerberding, director of the CDC, has acknowledged the challenge of balancing the urgent goal of preparing for a bioterrorism emergency with the agency's fundamental mission of preventing and controlling infectious diseases and other health hazards. According to Gerberding, "HIV right now is the overwhelming global epidemic. To not put that on the front burner would simply be a sign of no credibility at all. . . . We have some programs that work and we need to get them out there."[36]

- Visit the CDC web site at **http://www.cdc.gov** and read the organization's mission statement. What aspects of the CDC's mission focus on communication?
- Locate the following article through InfoTrac College Edition (**http://www.infotrac.thomsonlearning.com**) that describes the communication strategies used in an HIV/AIDS awareness program for Ethiopia: Aids resource center to be created in Ethiopia by Johns Hopkins Center for Communication Programs with CDC support (2001,

November 15). *US Newswire*, p. 1008319n2155.

Activities
Refer to the Communication Process Model presented in Chapter 1. In a class discussion, identify some barriers that the CDC might experience in communicating its AIDS campaign to people in various countries.

Part 4 of the CDC ShowCASE focuses on positive means used by the CDC to educate the public about disease and Julie Gerberding's philosophy of collaboration.

http://www.cdc.gov

Visit the text support site at **http://lehman.swlearning.com** to complete Part 4 of the CDC ShowCASE.

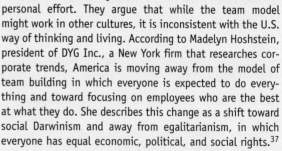

Internet Case

Can the United States Succeed Without Rewarding Rugged Individuality?

A basic element of the fabric of U.S. entrepreneurship is the faith in the ingenuity of the individual person's ability to conceive, develop, and profit from a business endeavor. The frontier spirit and triumph of the individual over looming odds have been a predominant force in the development of the United States. Such individualism has also been recognized by organizations, with reward going to those who contribute winning ideas and efforts.

The recent shift in organizational structures toward team design has caused management to reassess reward systems that focus on individual recognition and to consider rewards that are based on team performance. Some

fear that removing individual incentive will lead to mediocrity and a reduction in personal effort. They argue that while the team model might work in other cultures, it is inconsistent with the U.S. way of thinking and living. According to Madelyn Hoshstein, president of DYG Inc., a New York firm that researches corporate trends, America is moving away from the model of team building in which everyone is expected to do everything and toward focusing on employees who are the best at what they do. She describes this change as a shift toward social Darwinism and away from egalitarianism, in which everyone has equal economic, political, and social rights.[37]

Team advocates say that teams are here to stay and liken those who deny that reality to the proverbial ostrich with its head in the sand. They stress the need for newly structured incentive plans to reward group effort.

Visit the text support site at **http://lehman.swlearning.com** to link to web resources related to this topic. Respond to one or more of the following activities, as directed by your instructor.

1. **GMAT** How would you respond to those with concerns about loss of individual incentive? Argue for or against the increased emphasis on team reward, using either personal examples or examples from business.

2. Structure a reward system that would recognize both individual and team performance. You may use an organization of your choice to illustrate.

3. Select a specific corporation or nation that has implemented the team model. Describe the transition away from a hierarchical structure and the consequences that have resulted from the shift, both positive and negative.

Video Case

Altoon + Porter Architects: Global Teamwork

In 1984, Ronald Altoon and Jim Porter left a large architectural firm to build their own business, Altoon + Porter Architects, Los Angeles, California. Today they have office project locations in 10 other states and in 19 countries. The video segment begins with a description of the firm's first big project overseas—in Jakarta, the capital of Indonesia.

Employees at Altoon + Porter contribute to their firm's success by being effective team players. You will learn, if you haven't already, that having the ability to function as a team player is a key to success in nearly every area of your life—in living harmoniously with others at home, as a learner in various educational settings, as a participant of sports teams and recreational activities, and finally as a valued contributor in your place of employment.

View the video segment about Altoon + Porter Architects and accompanying activities on WebTutor or your Professional Power Pak CD.

Discussion Questions

1. What criteria does Altoon + Porter use to form teams that will result in the best team for a project? Based on what you have learned in Chapter 1 about teams, what additional criteria do you think could be used to further improve team performance?

2. What possible responses might you get from Altoon + Porter employees were you to ask them, "What are the advantages and disadvantages of having your work spaces change frequently?"

3. How do the four strategic forces influencing business communication illustrated in Figure 1-5 of your text affect the communication process at Altoon + Porter?

Activities

Locate the following article available in full text from InfoTrac College (**http://www.infotrac.thomsonlearning.com**) or perhaps from another database available through your campus library:

Rowh, M. (2001, October). "How to be a team player." *Career World*. 25–27.

After reading the article, identify the five characteristics of an effective team player and provide specific skills and behaviors that you can practice to enhance your value as a team player.

Assess your ability to resolve conflict within a team by completing the rating included in the article. After reflecting on your rate, write two to three sentences describing any new ideas you learned to help you improve your conflict resolution skills.

2

Focusing on Interpersonal and Group Communication

Objectives *When you have completed Chapter 2, you will be able to:*

1 Explain how behavioral theories about human needs, trust and disclosure, and motivation relate to business communication.

2 Describe the role of nonverbal messages in communication.

3 Identify aspects of effective listening.

4 Identify factors affecting group and team communication.

5 Discuss aspects of effective meeting management.

THE HP WAY: A WINNING PHILOSOPHY FOR HEWLETT-PACKARD

In considering new management ideas in practice, the computer industry has been characterized by flat organizations, speed, flexibility, and teams. Companies such as Hewlett-Packard and Microsoft provide an alternative organizational model to the traditional, hierarchical bureaucratic model. Hewlett-Packard's revolutionary ideas extend far beyond its organizational structure and into its practices. The HP Way, the embodiment of company philosophy, as described by company cofounder David Packard, is built around the concept of trust.

At the inception of Hewlett-Packard in 1938, William Hewlett and David Packard initiated a set of business practices, some of which had never been tried before. Central to the HP Way is the establishment of an open communication environment that allows workers to stroll into bosses' offices and offer ideas. Company power is not concentrated in its executives; employees make decisions in cases where they know best. Effective external communication is also a major hallmark of the HP Way. Customer feedback is credited for the success of HP printers.

As Hewlett-Packard climbed in its Fortune 500 ranking, the company has continued to adhere to its basic principles. The advent of new technologies has presented a continuing challenge for Hewlett-Packard: defining the company in the Internet Age while honoring the 65-year-old principles of the HP Way. The answer was "e-services," a program designed to make Hewlett-Packard's products and services conveniently available to customers over the Internet. In keeping with the company philosophy, the site allows customers to use the Internet to improve their businesses. The philosophy of the HP Way—treating customers, employees, and suppliers with respect and integrity—has defined the company throughout its history. It is a core that has remained, even through the blending corporate culture that resulted from the 2002 merger with Compaq.[1] While electronic capabilities offered new communication opportunities for Hewlett-Packard, the basic principles for success remained unchanged. Just as Hewlett-Packard uses the HP Way as a basis for its continuing success, you will need to rely on the basic principles of business communication to succeed professionally. Even in this age of instantaneous communication, the basic principles of communication are just as important—if not more important—than ever before. To be effective in any business setting, you will need to understand the process of communication and the dynamic environment in which it occurs, especially in relation to organizational communication and the forces at work in the communication environment.

http://www.hp.com

See ShowCASE, Part 2, on page 51 for Spotlight Communicator Carly Fiorina, HP CEO.

Behavioral Theories that Impact Communication

Objective 1

Explain how behavioral theories about human needs, trust and disclosure, and motivation relate to business communication.

Behavioral scientists working in the fields of sociology and psychology have strongly influenced business management by focusing on the complexities of communication in the work environment. An understanding of human needs and motivation provides a supervisor with valuable insights that facilitate effective communication with and among employees.

Recognizing Human Needs

Psychologist Abraham Maslow developed the concept of a hierarchy of needs through which people progress. In our society, most people have reasonably satisfied their two lower levels of needs: physiological needs (food and basic provision) and their security and safety needs (shelter and protection from the elements and physical danger). Beyond these two basic need levels, people progress to satisfy the three upper levels: (1) social needs for love, acceptance, and belonging; (2) ego needs to be heard, appreciated, and wanted; and (3) self-actualizing needs, including the need to achieve one's fullest potential through professional, philanthropic, political, educational, and artistic channels.

As people satisfy needs at one level, they move on to the next. The levels that have been satisfied still are present, but their importance diminishes. Effective communicators are able to identify and appeal to need

Critical Thinking

To which need level would each of the following apply: penthouse office; years of service award; expanded retirement program; employee lounge?

Southwest Airlines promotes an environment of mutual trust by empowering employees at all levels to make decisions that are vital to their effective job performance.

COURTESY, SOUTHWEST AIRLINES

levels in various individuals or groups. Advertising is designed to appeal to need levels. Luxury-car ads appeal to ego needs, teeth whitening and deodorant ads appeal to social needs, and cellular telephone and home security system ads appeal to security and safety needs. In business, efforts to help people satisfy needs are essential, since a satisfied worker is generally more productive than a dissatisfied one. In communication activities, a sender's message is more likely to appeal to the receiver if the receiver's need is accurately identified.

Stroking

People engage in communication with others in the hope that the outcome may lead to mutual trust, mutual pleasure, and psychological well being. The communication exchange is a means of sharing information about things, ideas, tasks, and selves.

Each communication interaction, whether casual or formal, provides an emotional *stroke* that may have either a positive or a negative effect on your feelings about yourself and others. Getting a pat on the back from the supervisor, receiving a congratulatory telephone call or letter, and being listened to by another person are examples of everyday positive strokes. Negative strokes might include receiving a hurtful comment, being avoided or left out of conversation, and getting reprimanded by a superior. By paying attention to the importance of strokes, managers can greatly improve communication and people's feelings about their work.

Exploring the Johari Window

Critical Thinking

Think about the types of information you (1) share freely, (2) share only with close friends, and (3) keep hidden. How do these decisions affect your interpersonal communication?

As relationships develop, the people involved continue to learn about each other and themselves, as shown by the Johari Window in Figure 2-1. Area I, the free area, represents what we know about ourselves and what others know about us. Area II, the blind area, designates those things others know about us but that we don't know about ourselves; for example, you are the only person who can't see your physical self as it really is. Things we know about ourselves but that others don't know about us occupy the hidden or secret area III. Area IV includes the unknown: things we don't know about ourselves and others don't know about us, such as our ability to handle emergency situations if we've never been faced with them.

Each of the window areas may vary in size according to the degree to which we learn about ourselves and are willing to disclose things about ourselves to others. Reciprocal sharing occurs when people develop *trust* in each other. When a confidant demonstrates that he or she can be trusted, trust is reinforced and leads to an expansion of the open area of the Johari Window. We are usually willing to tell people about various things that aren't truly personal. But we share personal thoughts, ambitions, and inner

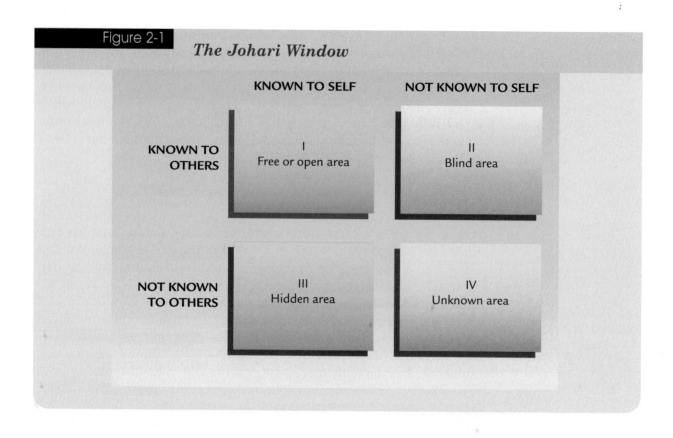

Figure 2-1

The Johari Window

	KNOWN TO SELF	NOT KNOWN TO SELF
KNOWN TO OTHERS	I Free or open area	II Blind area
NOT KNOWN TO OTHERS	III Hidden area	IV Unknown area

feelings only with selected others—those whom we have learned to trust. The relationships existing between supervisor and employee, doctor and patient, and lawyer and client are those of trust, but only in specific areas. In more intimate relationships—wife and husband, brother and sister, parent and child—deeper, personal feelings are entrusted to each other.

Critical Thinking
Trust is earned over time through consistent behaviors.

The idea that trust and openness lead to better communication between two people also applies to groups. Managers engaged in **organizational development** (OD) are concerned with developing successful organizations by building effective small groups. They believe small group effectiveness evolves mostly from a high level of mutual trust among group members. The aim of OD is to open emotional as well as task-oriented communication. To accomplish this aim, groups often become involved in encounter sessions designed to enlarge the open areas of the Johari Window.[2]

Contrasting Management Styles

Douglas McGregor, a management theorist, attempted to distinguish between the older, traditional view that workers are concerned only about satisfying lower-level needs and the more contemporary view that productivity can be enhanced by assisting workers in satisfying higher-level needs. Under the older view, management exercised strong control, emphasized the job to the exclusion of concern for the individual, and sought to motivate solely through external incentives—a job and a paycheck. McGregor

SPOTLIGHT COMMUNICATOR

Gender No Obstacle to Business Success

When Carly Fiorina was named CEO of Hewlett-Packard Co. in 1999, she became the head of the largest public corporation ever run by a female executive. Forty years after the passage of the Civil Rights Act required equal opportunity for women in employment, Fiorina is only the third woman currently holding the title of CEO at a Fortune 500 corporation. As leader of a Fortune top 20 firm, responsible for more than 123,000 employees and with $47 billion in annual revenues, she was named the most powerful woman in American business by *Fortune* Magazine.

Fiorina came to HP after serving as head of the Global Service Provider division of Lucent Technologies. Her background in management and business technology gives her the ability to bring creative problem solving to the company. Doing so, however, does not mean an abandonment of the HP Way. She espouses the long-standing HP principles of work-life balance and healthy corporate interaction while leading the company in its progression into e-services. "You have to

have fun to be successful. True, this industry requires hard work—there's no getting around that. But if you can't find joy in that work, if you can't take pleasure in teamwork, if you can't have fun in solving problems, it's not worth it."[3]

While the press has made much of her gender, Fiorina deflects attention away from it. When asked how she feels about being called the most powerful woman in corporate America, she answers, "I have never thought of myself as a woman in business; I just thought of myself as Carly who happens to be a woman who's focused on doing the best job I can. It's not a formula I plan to change. Frankly, the real challenge for me—and the reason I'm sensitive to the gender issue—is that this isn't about me as a person; this is about how to effectively and appropriately represent a business."[4]

In terms of her communication style, Fiorina isn't afraid of speaking her mind. "People sometimes interpret candor as toughness—and sometimes it's hard to tell the truth; but in the end the truth sets you

free." In offering advice for women aspiring to positions of power, Fiorina says: "All people—including women—need to stay focused on possibilities. I faced lots of doubters in my career, lots of hurdles and barriers; there were many people who didn't take me seriously, but there were also enough people who did. I would say believe in yourself, stay focused on the possibilities, seek out the people who will see what you are capable of, because talent—in whatever package it comes in—will rise to the top."[5]

Applying What You Have Learned

1. How does Carly Fiorina's leadership philosophy relate to the HP Way?
2. Explain what Fiorina means by saying that you have to have fun to be successful.

Carly Fiorina, former CEO, Hewlett-Packard Co.

http://www.hp.com

Refer to ShowCASE, Part 3, at the end of the chapter to expand your knowledge of diversity initiatives used at Hewlett-Packard.

labeled this management style Theory X. Under the contemporary style, Theory Y, management strives to balance control and individual freedom. By treating the individual as a mature person, management lessens the need for external motivation; treated as adults, people will act as adults.

The situational leadership model developed by Paul Hersey and Kenneth Blanchard does not prescribe a single leadership style, but advocates that what is appropriate in each case depends on the follower (subordinate) and the task to be performed. *Directive behavior* is characterized by the leader's giving detailed rules and instructions and monitoring closely that they are followed. The leader decides what is to be done and how. In contrast, *supportive behavior* is characterized by the leader's listening, communicating, recognizing, and encouraging. Different degrees of directive and supportive behavior can be desirable, given the situation.[6] Combining the ideas of Maslow and McGregor with those of Hersey and Blanchard leads to the conclusion that "the right job for the person" is a better philosophy than "the right person for the job."

The *Total Quality Management* movement focuses on creating a more responsible role for the worker in an organization. In a Total Quality Management environment, decision-making power is distributed to the people closest to the problem, those who usually have the best information sources and solutions. Each employee, from the president to the custodian, is expected to solve problems, participate in team-building efforts, and expand the scope of his or her role in the organization. The goal of employee empowerment is to build a work environment in which all employees take pride in their work accomplishments and begin motivating themselves from within rather than through traditional extrinsic incentives.[7] Managers of many companies understand that empowering employees to initiate continuous improvements is critical for survival. Only companies producing quality products and services will survive in today's world market.

Team Environment

Nonverbal Communication

Objective **2**

Describe the role of nonverbal messages in communication.

Managers use verbal and nonverbal messages to communicate an idea to a recipient. Verbal means "through the use of words," either written or spoken. Nonverbal means "without the use of words." Although major attention in communication study is given to verbal messages, studies show that nonverbal messages can account for over 90 percent of the total meaning.[8] Nonverbal communication includes *metacommunication* and *kinesic* messages.

Metacommunication

A metacommunication is a message that, although *not* expressed in words, accompanies a message that *is* expressed in words. For example, "Don't be

Appropriate attire sends a strong and positive nonverbal signal.

© BILL BACHMANN/PHOTOEDIT

late for work" communicates caution; yet the sentence may imply (but not express in words) such additional ideas as "You are frequently late, and I'm warning you," or "I doubt your dependability" (metacommunication). "Your solution is perfect" may also convey a metacommunication such as "You are efficient," or "I certainly like your work." Whether you are speaking or writing, you can be confident that those who receive your messages will be sensitive to the messages expressed in words and to the accompanying messages that are present but not expressed in words.

Kinesic Messages

Critical Thinking

What nonverbal messages might be conveyed by a job applicant? A customer? A salesperson?

People constantly send meaning through kinesic communication, an idea expressed through nonverbal behavior. In other words, receivers gain additional meaning from what they see and hear—the visual and the vocal:

- Visual—gestures, winks, smiles, frowns, sighs, attire, grooming, and all kinds of body movements.
- Vocal—intonation, projection, and resonance of the voice.

Some examples of kinesic messages and the meanings they may convey follow.

Action	Possible Kinesic Message
A wink or light chuckle follows a statement.	*"Don't believe what I just said."*
A manager is habitually late for staff meetings.	*"My time is more important than yours. You can wait for me."* Alternately, the action may be ordinary for a non-U.S. born manager.
A supervisor lightly links his arm around an employee's shoulders at the end of a formal disciplinary conference.	*"Everything is fine; I'm here to help you solve this problem."* Alternately, the action may be sexually motivated or paternalistic—comforting a child after necessary discipline.
An employee smokes in areas other than those designated for smoking.	*"I don't have to obey company rules that infringe on my rights. A little smoke won't hurt anyone."*
A job applicant submits a résumé containing numerous spelling and grammatical errors.	*"My spelling and grammar skills are deficient."* Alternately, *"I didn't care to do my very best."*
The supervisor looks up but then returns her attention to a current project when an employee arrives for a performance appraisal interview.	*"The performance appraisal interview is not an important process. You are interrupting more important work."*
A group leader sits at a position other than at the head of the table.	*"I want to demonstrate my equality with other members."*
An employee's clothing does not comply with company's dress code.	*"Rules are for other people; I can do what I want."* Alternately, *"I do not understand the expectations of the dress code."*
A manager hesitates when asked to justify a new rule for employees.	*"I don't have a good reason."* Alternately, *"I want to think this through to be sure I give an understandable answer."*

Understanding Nonverbal Messages

Critical Thinking

What nonverbal messages did you convey today through your attire, posture, gestures, etc?

Metacommunications and kinesic communications have characteristics that all communicators should take into account.

- **Nonverbal messages cannot be avoided. Both written and spoken words convey ideas in addition to the ideas contained in the words used.** All actions—and even the lack of action—have meaning to those who observe them.

- **Nonverbal messages may have different meanings for different people.** If a team member smiles after making a statement, one member may conclude that the speaker was trying to be funny; another may conclude that the speaker was pleased about having made such a great contribution; another may see the smile as indicating friendliness.

- **Nonverbal messages vary between and within cultures.** Not only do nonverbal messages have different meanings from culture to culture, but men and women from the same culture typically exhibit different body language. North American men make less body contact with other men than do women with women. Acceptable male body

*Diversity
Challenges*

language might include a handshake or a pat on the back, while women are afforded more flexibility in making body contact with each other. The accompanying Strategic Forces feature "Cultural Differences in Nonverbal Messages" provides more information on cultural differences in nonverbal communication.

- **Nonverbal messages may be intentional or unintentional.** "You are right about that" may be intended to mean "I agree with you" or "You are right on *this* issue, but you have been wrong on all others discussed." The sender may or may not intend to convey the latter and may or may not be aware of doing so.

Critical Thinking

Have you ever experienced a situation in which the verbal and nonverbal message did not agree? Describe it. Which message did you believe? Why?

- **Nonverbal messages can contradict the accompanying verbal message, and affect whether your message is understood or believed.** If the verbal and nonverbal messages contradict, which do you suppose the receiver will believe? The old adage "Actions speak more loudly than words" provides the answer. Picture a person who says, "I'm happy to be here," but looks at the floor, talking in a weak and halting voice, and clasping his hands together in front of his body in an inhibited "fig-leaf" posture. Because his verbal and nonverbal messages are contradictory, his audience may not trust his words. Similarly, consider the negative effect of a sloppy personal appearance by a job candidate. Favorable interviewing skills and strong job credentials would likely be overshadowed by the poor physical image projected to the interviewer.

- **Nonverbal messages may receive more attention than verbal messages.** If a supervisor rhythmically taps a pen while making a statement, the words may not register in the employee's mind. An error in basic grammar may receive much more attention than does the idea that is being transmitted.

- **Nonverbal messages provide clues about the sender's background and motives.** For example, excessive use of big words may suggest that a person reads widely or has an above-average education; it may also suggest a need for social recognition or insecurity about social background.

- **Nonverbal messages are influenced by the circumstances surrounding the communication.** Assume that two men, Ganesh and Sam, are friends who work for the same firm. When they are together on the job, Ganesh sometimes puts his hand on Sam's shoulder. To Sam, the act may mean nothing more than "We are close friends." But suppose Ganesh is a member of a committee that subsequently denies a promotion for Sam. Afterward, the same act could mean "We are still friends," but it could also arouse resentment. Because of the circumstances, the same act could now mean something like "Watch the hand that pats; it can also stab."

- **Nonverbal messages may be beneficial or harmful.** Words or actions can be accompanied by nonverbal messages that help or hurt the sender's purpose. Metacommunications and kinesic communications can convey something like "I am efficient in my business and considerate of others," or they can convey the opposite. They cannot be eliminated, but they can be made to work for communicators instead of against them.

Objective 3

Identify aspects of effective listening.

Critical Thinking

Improved listening skills can benefit you in your career advancement.

Listening as a Communication Skill

Most managers spend a major part of their day listening and speaking with supervisors, employees, customers, and a variety of business or industry colleagues and associates. Listening commonly consumes more of business employees' time than reading, writing, and speaking combined. Listening is an interpersonal skill as critical as the skill of speaking. Effective listening habits pay off in several ways:

Cultural Differences in Nonverbal Messages

Although no one can give a set of rules for interpreting nonverbal messages, being aware of their presence and impact will improve chances of encoding nonverbal messages effectively. International communication poses particular challenges for proper use of nonverbal signals. At the opening session of Bangladesh's new parliament in July 1996, legislators reacted with fury to a gesture by U.S. Shipping Minister A. S. M. Abdur Rob. "This is a dishonor not only to parliament but to the nation," said Dr. A. Q. M. Badruddoza Chowdhury, the Bangladesh Nationalist Party's deputy leader.

What Rob had done to provoke such anger was to give the thumbs up sign. In the United States, the gesture means "good going!" But in Bangladesh, it is a taunt; in other Islamic countries, it is an obscenity. This example is only one of the huge array of cross-cultural gaffes a naive U.S. businessperson could make on an overseas assignment.[9]

Becoming familiar with subtle and not-so-subtle differences in nonverbal communication in other cultures can avoid the creation of barriers to effective communication. Some cultural examples of nonverbal behavior include the following:

- The Japanese greet with a respectful bow rather than the traditional handshake. Middle Easterners may exchange kisses on the cheek as the preferred form of greeting.

- While North Americans believe that eye contact is an indicator of interest and trust, Japanese believe that lowering the eyes is a sign of respect. Asian females and many African Americans listen without direct eye contact. Extended facial gazing as is typified by the French and Brazilians is often seen by Americans as aggressive.

- The time-conscious North American can expect to be kept waiting for an appointment in Central America, the Middle East, and other countries where the North American sentiment that "time is money" is not accepted.

- North Americans, who often slap each other on the back or put an arm around the other as a sign of friendship, receive disapproval from the Japanese, who avoid physical contact. Japanese shopkeepers place change on a plastic plate to avoid physical contact with customers.[10]

Numerous research studies point out the importance of nonverbal communication in international negotiations. A 15-year study of negotiation styles in 17 cultures revealed that Japanese negotiators behaved least aggressively, typically using a polite conversation style with infrequent use of "no" and "you" as well as more silent periods. The style of French negotiators was most aggressive, including more threats and warnings, as well as interruptions, facial gazing, and frequent use of "no" and "you." Brazilians were similarly aggressive, while including more physical touching of their negotiating partners. Germans, British, and Americans fell somewhat in the middle in terms of aggressive behavior.

Removing words from a negotiation might at times give the process additional strength by avoiding many of the problems raised by verbal communication in a multicultural context. The negotiation process is the sum of such factors as the number of parties, existence of external audiences, issues to be discussed, deadlines, laws, ethics, customs, physical setting, and so on. The emphasis on nonverbal cues is often lost on American negotiators who rely on the inherent advantage provided by their mastery of global languages. Cultural awareness includes both education and sensitivity concerning behaviors, expectations, and interpretations of persons with different backgrounds and experiences.[11]

Application

Interview a person from another culture or subculture to determine how his or her expectations for nonverbal behavior differ from your own. Prepare a chart that shows three to five particular nonverbal actions and their meanings in each of the two cultures.

FRANK & EARNEST

Effective listening skills are essential to career success.

- Good listeners are liked by others because they satisfy the basic human needs of being heard and being wanted.
- People who listen well are able to separate fact from fiction, to cope effectively with false persuasion, and to avoid having others use them for personal gain. In other words, good listeners don't "get taken" very often.
- Listening opens doors for ideas and thus encourages creativity.
- Effective listeners are constantly learning—gaining knowledge and skills that lead to increased job performance, advancement, and satisfaction.
- Job satisfaction increases when people know what is going on, when they are heard, and when they participate in the mutual trust that develops from good communication.

Listening depends on your abilities to receive and decode both verbal and nonverbal messages. The best-devised messages and sophisticated communication systems will not work unless people on the receiving end of spoken messages actually listen. Senders of spoken messages must assume their receivers can and will listen, just as senders of written messages must assume their receivers can and will read.

Listening for a Specific Purpose

Individuals satisfy a variety of purposes through listening: (1) interacting socially, (2) receiving information, (3) solving problems, and (4) sharing feelings with others. Each activity may call for a different style of listening or for a combination of styles.

- *Casual listening.* Listening for pleasure, recreation, amusement, and relaxation is casual listening. Some people play music all day long to relax the brain and mask unwanted sounds during daily routines, work periods, and daily commutes. Casual listening provides relaxing breaks from more serious tasks and supports our emotional health. An interesting concept about all listening, but particularly true of casual listening, is that people are selective listeners. You listen to what you want to hear. In a crowded room in which everyone seems to be talking, you can block out

Effective listening is essential at Dell Computers, a company that has built its reputation on providing customers with custom computers based on individual needs.

© AP/WIDE WORLD PHOTOS

Critical Thinking

How have your class notes changed during your college career?

all the noise and engage in the conversation you are having with someone. Casual listening doesn't require much emotional or physical effort.

- **Listening for information.** Listening for information involves the search for data or material. In the classroom, for example, the instructor usually has a strategy for guiding the class to desired goals. The instructor will probably stress several major points and use supporting evidence to prove or to reinforce them. When engaged in this type of listening, you could become so engrossed with recording every detail that you take copious notes with no organization. Using an outlining process can help you capture main ideas and supporting subpoints in a logical way. Watch the speaker as well as listen to him or her, since most speakers exhibit a set of mannerisms composed of gestures and vocal inflections to indicate the degree of importance or seriousness they attach to portions of their presentation. Above all else, listening for information requires that you be able to separate fact from fiction, comedy from seriousness, and truth from untruth.

- **Intensive listening.** When you listen to obtain information, solve problems, or persuade or dissuade (as in arguments), you are engaged in intensive listening. Intensive listening involves greater use of your analytical ability to proceed through problem-solving steps. You should have an understanding of the problem, recognize whatever limitations are involved, and know the implications of possible solutions. You must become a good summarizer. When your turn comes to respond, trace the development of the discussion and then move from there to your own analysis. Feel free to "tailgate" on the ideas of others. Creative ideas are generated in an open discussion.

Critical Thinking

How would you score yourself as an empathetic listener? How can you improve? How will empathetic listening be important in your career?

- *Empathetic listening.* **Empathy** occurs when a person attempts to share another's feelings or emotions. Counselors attempt to use empathetic listening in dealing with their clients, and good friends listen empathetically to each other. Empathy is a valuable trait developed by people skilled in interpersonal relations. When you take the time to listen to another, the courtesy is usually returned. Poor listening is often attributed to a preoccupation with one's own problems. Talking too much and giving strong nonverbal signals of disinterest destroy employee desire to talk. Total empathy can never be achieved simply because no two people are exactly alike. However, the more similar our experiences, the better the opportunity to put ourselves in the other person's shoes. Listening with empathy involves some genuine tact along with other good listening habits. Remember that listening for feelings normally takes place in a one-to-one situation. Close friends who trust each other tend to engage in self-disclosure easily. Empathetic listening is enhanced when the participants exhibit trust and friendship.

Critical Thinking

Can empathy be carried too far? Explain.

Many people in positions of authority have developed excellent listening skills that apply to gaining information and to problem solving. However, an equal number of people have failed to develop good listening practices that work effectively in listening for feelings. An "open-door" policy does not necessarily indicate an "open ear." A supervisor's poor listening habits may interfere with problem solving and reduce employee morale.

Critical Thinking

Give other examples of situations in which combined listening is required.

Frequently you may have to combine listening intensively and listening for feelings. Performance appraisal interviews, disciplinary conferences, and other sensitive discussions between supervisors and employees require listening intensively for accurate understanding of the message and listening empathetically for feelings, preconceived points of view, and background. The interviewing process also may combine the two types of listening. Job interviewers must try to determine how someone's personality, as well as skill and knowledge, will affect job performance. Whatever the situation, good listeners stay focused on their intended purpose.

Bad Listening Habits

Physicians must first diagnose the nature of a person's medical problems before prescribing treatment. In the same way, you can't improve your listening unless you understand some of the nonphysical ailments of your own listening. Most of us have developed bad listening habits in one or more of the following areas:

- *Faking attention.* Have you ever had a parent, friend, or fellow worker ask you a question and find that you weren't listening? Have you ever left a classroom lecture and later realized that you had no idea what went on? Have you ever been introduced to someone only to realize 30 seconds later that you missed the name? If you had to answer "yes" to any of these questions, join the huge club of "fakers of attention." The club is rather large because almost all people belong. Isn't it amazing that we can look directly at a person, nod, smile, and pretend to be listening?

- ***Allowing disruptions.*** Listening properly requires both physical and emotional effort. As a result, we welcome disruptions of almost any sort when we are engaged in somewhat difficult listening. The next time someone enters your classroom or meeting room, notice how almost everyone in the room turns away from the speaker and the topic to observe the latecomer. Yielding to such disruptions begins early in life, perhaps as an expression of curiosity.

- ***Overlistening.*** Overlistening occurs when listeners attempt to record in writing or in memory so many details that they miss the speaker's major points. Overlisteners "can't see the forest for the trees." An illustration of this bad listening habit is the old story about college freshmen who, on the first day of class when the professor began with "Good morning," wrote it in their notes.

- ***Stereotyping.*** Most people use their prejudices and perceptions of others as a basis for developing stereotypes. As a result, we make spontaneous judgments about others based on their appearances, mannerisms, dress, speech delivery, and whatever other criteria play a role in our judgments. If a speaker doesn't meet our standards in any of these areas, we simply turn off our listening and assume the speaker can't have much to say.

- ***Dismissing subjects as uninteresting.*** People tend to use "uninteresting" as a rationale for not listening. Unfortunately, the decision is usually made before the topic is ever introduced. A good way to lose an instructor's respect is to ask, "Are we going to do anything important in class today?" if you have to (or want to) miss that day's class.

- ***Failing to observe nonverbal aids.*** Good listening requires use of eyes as well as ears. To listen effectively, you must observe the speaker. Facial expressions and body motions always accompany speech and contribute much to messages. Unless you watch the speaker, you may miss the meaning.

In addition to recognizing bad listening habits and the variety of barriers to effective listening, you must recognize that listening isn't easy. Many bad listening habits develop simply because the speed of spoken messages is far slower than our ability to receive and process them. Normal speaking speeds are between 100 and 150 words a minute. The human ear can actually distinguish words in speech in excess of 500 words a minute, and many people read at speeds well beyond 500 words a minute. Finally, our minds process thoughts at thousands of words a minute.

Because individuals can't speak fast enough to challenge our ability to listen, listeners have the primary responsibility for making spoken communication effective. People do seem to listen attentively to gifted speakers, but

Critical Thinking

What is your own worst listening habit? What can you do to eliminate it?

Diversity Challenges

Critical Thinking

The listener has an ethical responsibility to give full, unbiased attention to the speaker's verbal and nonverbal message.

such speakers are rare. In everyday activities, good listening requires considerable mental and emotional effort.

Suggestions for Effective Listening

Because feedback and nonverbal signs are available, you can enhance the effectiveness of your face-to-face listening by following these suggestions:

Critical Thinking

Analyze your listener response to your instructor. How can it be maximized?

- *Minimize environmental and mental distractions.* Take time to listen. Move to a quiet area where you are not distracted by noise or other conversation, close the office door, and refuse to accept telephone calls so you can concentrate on the conversation. Avoid becoming so preoccupied with thoughts of other projects or what you will say next that you fail to listen.
- *Get in touch with the speaker.* Maintain an open mind while attempting to understand the speaker's background, prejudices, and points of view. Listen for emotionally charged words and watch for body language as clues to the speaker's underlying feelings. Gestures, facial expressions, and eye movements will help you understand the speaker's point of view and emotional state.
- *Use your knowledge of speakers to your advantage.* Through experience, you will begin to recognize the unique speaking and organizing traits of particular individuals. Some people seem to run on and on with details before making the point. With this speaker, you will learn to anticipate the major point but not pay much attention to details. Other speakers give conclusions first and perhaps omit support for them. In this case, you will learn to ask questions to obtain further information.
- *Let the speaker know you are actively involved.* Show genuine interest by remaining physically and mentally involved; for example, avoid daydreaming, yawning, frequently breaking eye contact, looking at your watch or papers on your desk, whispering, or allowing numerous interruptions (phone calls, etc.). Encourage the speaker to continue by providing appropriate feedback either orally or nonverbally. A nod, smile, or encouraging grunt allows the speaker to continue and feel appreciated.
- *Do not interrupt the speaker.* Try to understand the speaker's full meaning, and wait patiently for an indication that you should enter the conversation.
- *Ask reflective questions that assess understanding.* Simply restate in your own words what you think the other person has said. This paraphrasing will reinforce what you have heard and allow the speaker to correct any misunderstanding or add clarification.
- *Use probing prompts to direct the speaker.* Use probing statements or questions to help the speaker define the issue more concretely and specifically.
- *Use lag time wisely.* Listening carefully should be your primary focus; however, you can think ahead at times as well. Thinking ahead can help you develop a sense of the speaker's logic, anticipate future points, and evaluate the validity of the speaker's ideas. Making written or mental notes allows you to provide useful feedback when the opportunity arises.

If you cannot take notes during the conversation, record important points as soon as possible so you can summarize the speaker's key points.

You can learn more about developing effective listening skills by completing the Internet Case at the end of this chapter.

Group Communication

Objective 4

Identify factors affecting group and team communication.

Team
Environment

Critical Thinking

Businesses today are streamlining their operations, often referred to as downsizing, rightsizing, or reengineering. How is this process affecting organizational charts? The communication process?

Although much of your spoken communication in business will occur in one-to-one relationships, another frequent spoken communication activity will likely occur when you participate in groups, primarily groups within the organizational work environment. The work of groups, committees, and teams has become crucial in most organizations.

Increasing Focus on Groups

Developments among U.S. businesses in recent years have shifted attention away from the employment of traditional organizational subunits as the only mechanisms for achieving organizational goals and toward the increased use of groups.

- *Flat organizational structures.* Many businesses today are downsizing and eliminating layers of management. Companies implementing Total Quality Management programs are reorganizing to distribute the decision-making power throughout the organization. The trend is to eliminate functional or departmental boundaries. Instead, work is reorganized in cross-disciplinary teams that perform broad core processes (e.g., product development and sales generation) and not narrow tasks such as forecasting market demand for a particular product.

    In a flat organizational structure, communicating across the organization chart (among the cross-disciplinary teams) becomes more important than communicating up and down in a top-heavy hierarchy. An individual may take on an expanded **role**, as important tasks are assumed. This role may involve power and authority that surpasses the individual's **status**, or formal position in the organizational chart. Much of the communication involves face-to-face meetings with team members rather than numerous, time-consuming "handoffs" as the product moves methodically from one department to another.

    The time needed to design a new card at Hallmark Cards decreased significantly when the company adopted a flat organizational structure. Team members representing the former functional areas (graphic artists, writers, marketers, and others) now work in a central area, communicating openly and frequently, solving problems and making decisions about the entire process as a card is being developed. For example, a writer struggling with a verse for a new card can solicit immediate input from the graphic artist working on the team rather than finalizing the verse and then "handing it off" to the art department.[12]

Critical Thinking

What places do competition and cooperation have in contemporary organizations?

• ***Heightened Focus on Cooperation.*** Competition has been a characteristic way of life in U.S. companies, not only externally with other businesses, but also internally. Organizations and individuals compete for a greater share of scarce resources, for a limited number of positions at the top of organizations, and for esteem in their professions. Such competition is a healthy sign of the human desire to succeed, and, in terms of economic behavior, competition is fundamental to the private enterprise system. At the same time, when excessive competition replaces the cooperation necessary for success, communication may be diminished, if not eliminated.

Just as you want to look good in the eyes of your coworkers and supervisors, units within organizations want to look good to one another. This attitude may cause behavior to take the competitive form, a "win/lose" philosophy. When excessive competition has a negative influence on the performance of the organization, everyone loses.

Although competition is appropriate and desirable in many situations, the management of many companies has taken steps through open communication and information and reward systems to reduce competition and to increase cooperation. Cooperation is more likely when the competitors (individuals or groups within an organization) have an understanding of and appreciation for others' importance and functions. This cooperative spirit is characterized as a *win/win philosophy*. One person's success is not achieved at the expense or exclusion of another. Groups identify a solution that everyone finds satisfactory and is committed to achieving. Reaching this mutual understanding requires a high degree of trust and effective interpersonal skills, particularly empathetic and intensive listening skills, and the willingness to communicate long enough to agree on an action plan that is acceptable to everyone.

Characteristics of Effective Groups

Groups form for synergistic effects; that is, through pooling their efforts, group members can achieve more collectively than they could individually. At the same time, the social nature of groups contributes to the individual goals of members. Communication in small groups leads to group decisions that are generally superior to individual decisions. The group process can motivate members, improve thinking, and assist attitude development and change. The emphasis that a particular group places on task and maintenance activities is based on several factors.

As you consider the following factors of group communication, try to visualize their relationship to some groups to which you have belonged in school, religious organizations, athletics, and social activities.

Critical Thinking

Recall a group of which you were a member. Why was the group formed? How did you achieve your group goals?

Team
Environment

• ***Common goals.*** In effective groups, participants share a common goal, interest, or benefit. This focus on goals allows members to overcome individual differences of opinion and to negotiate acceptable solutions.
• ***Role perception.*** People who are invited to join groups have perceptions of how the group should operate and what it should achieve. In

addition, each member has a self-concept that dictates how he or she will behave. Those known to be aggressive will attempt to be confrontational and forceful, and those who like to be known as moderates will behave in moderate ways by settling arguments rather than initiating them. In successful groups, members play a variety of necessary roles and seek to eliminate nonproductive ones.

- *Longevity.* Groups formed for short-term tasks such as arranging a dinner and program will spend more time on the task than on maintenance. However, groups formed for long-term assignments such as an audit of a major corporation by a team from a public accounting firm may devote much effort to maintenance goals. Maintenance includes division of duties, scheduling, record keeping, reporting, and assessing progress.

Critical Thinking

Many prefer groups with an odd number of members.

- *Size.* The smaller the group, the more its members have the opportunity to communicate with each other. Conversely, large groups often inhibit communication because the opportunity to speak and interact is limited. When broad input is desired, large groups may be good. When extensive interaction is the goal, smaller groups may be more effective. Interestingly, large groups generally divide into smaller groups for maintenance purposes, even when the large group is task oriented. Although much research has been conducted in the area of group size, no optimal number of members has been identified. Groups of five to seven members are thought to be best for decision-making and problem-solving tasks. An odd number of members is often preferred because decisions are possible without tie votes.

Critical Thinking

How can a group experience conformity without sacrificing individual expression?

- *Status.* Some group members will appear to be better qualified than others. Consider a group in which the chief executive of the organization is a member. When the chief executive speaks, members agree. When members speak, they tend to direct their remarks to the one with high status—the chief executive. People are inclined to communicate with peers as their equals, but they tend to speak upward to their supervisor and downward to lower-level employees. In general, groups require balance in status and expertise rather than homogeneity.

- *Group norms.* A **norm** is a standard or average behavior. All groups possess norms. An instructor's behavior helps establish classroom norms. If an instructor is generally late for class, students will begin to arrive late. If the instructor permits talking during lectures, the norm will be for students to talk. People conform to norms because conformity is easy and nonconformity is difficult and uncomfortable. Conformity leads to acceptance by other group members and creates communication opportunities.

- *Leadership.* The performance of groups depends on several factors, but none is more important than leadership. Some hold the mistaken view that leaders are not necessary when an organization moves to a group concept. The role of leaders changes substantially, but they still have an important part to play. The ability of a group leader to work toward task goals while contributing to the development of group and individual goals is often critical to group success. In these group activities, leadership activities may be shared among several participants. Leadership may also be rotated, formally or informally. The leader can establish norms, determine who can speak and when, encourage everyone to contribute, and provide the motivation for effective group activity.[13]

Group Roles

Critical Thinking

Which role do you view as being more destructive to group function?

*Team
Environment*

Groups are made up of members who play a variety of roles, both positive and negative. Negative roles detract from the group's purposes and include the following:

- *Isolate*—one who is physically present but fails to participate
- *Dominator*—one who speaks too often and too long
- *Free rider*—one who does not do his/her fair share of the work
- *Detractor*—one who constantly criticizes and complains
- *Digresser*—one who deviates from the group's purpose
- *Airhead*—one who is never prepared
- *Socializer*—one who pursues only the social aspect of the group

Perhaps you recognize one or more of the negative roles, based on your personal group experiences. Or perhaps your group experiences have been positive as a result of members' playing positive group roles that promote the group's purposes:

- *Facilitator* (also known as *gatekeeper*)—one who makes sure everyone gets to talk and be heard
- *Harmonizer*—one who keeps tensions low
- *Record keeper*—one who maintains records of events and activities and informs members
- *Reporter*—one who assumes responsibility for preparing materials for submission
- *Leader*—one who assumes a directive role

Critical Thinking

What group roles have you played? What were the results?

In healthy groups, members may fulfill multiple roles, which rotate as the need arises. Negative roles are extinguished as the group communicates openly about its goals, strategies, and expectations. The opinions and viewpoints of all members are encouraged and expected.

From Groups to Teams

*Team
Environment*

While some use the terms *group* and *team* interchangeably, others distinguish between them. The major distinction between a group and a team is in members' attitudes and level of commitment. A team is typified by a clear identity and a high level of commitment on the part of members. A variety of strategies have been used for organizing workers into teams. A **task force** is generally given a single goal with a limited time to achieve it. A **quality assurance team**, or quality circle, focuses on product or service quality, and projects can be either short- or long-term. A **cross-functional team** brings together employees from various departments to solve a variety of problems, such as productivity issues, contract estimations and planning, and multidepartment difficulties. A *product development team* concentrates on innovation and the development cycle of new products and is usually cross-functional in nature. Recall the organizational chart illustrated in Figure 1-3. Now consider the impact of team structures, as shown in Figure 2-2.

While chain of command is still at work in formal organizational relationships and responsibilities, team structures unite people from varying portions of the organization. Work teams are typically given the authority to act on their conclusions, although the level of authority varies, depending on the organization and the purpose of the team. Typically, the group supervisor retains some responsibilities, some decisions are made completely by the team, and the rest are made jointly.

Merely placing workers into a group does not make them a functional team. A group must go through a developmental process to begin to function as a team. The four stages of team development include *forming* (becoming acquainted with each other and the assigned task), *storming* (dealing with conflicting personalities, goals, and ideas), *norming* (developing strategies and activities that promote goal achievement), and *performing* (reaching the optimal performance level). For a variety of reasons, teams are often unable to advance through all four stages of development. Even long-term teams may never reach the optimal performing stage, settling instead for the acceptable performance of the norming stage.

Projects and activities to promote your team's successful movement through the predictable stages are provided in the *Building High-Performance Teams* handbook that accompanies this text.

Research into what makes workplace teams effective indicates that training is beneficial for participants in such areas as problem solving, goal setting, conflict resolution, risk taking, active listening, and recognizing the interests and achievement of others. Participants need to be able to satisfy one another's basic needs for belonging, personal recognition, and support. Team members at the performing stage of team development exhibit the following behaviors:[14]

- *Commitment.* They are focused on the mission, values, goals, and expectations of the team and the organization.
- *Cooperation.* They have a shared sense of purpose, mutual gain, and teamwork.
- *Communication.* They know that information must flow smoothly between top management and workers. Team members are willing to face confrontation and unpleasantness when necessary.
- *Contribution.* All members share their different backgrounds, skills, and abilities with the team.

Teams have existed for hundreds of years throughout many countries and cultures. Teams are more flexible than larger organizational groupings because they can be assembled, deployed, refocused, and disbanded more quickly, usually in ways that enhance rather than disrupt more

Critical Thinking

What are some reasons that a team may be unable to advance to the performing stage of team development?

Critical Thinking

Does position on the organizational chart indicate an employee's power in the organization? Why?

Figure 2-2

Organizational Chart with Hierarchical and Team Structures

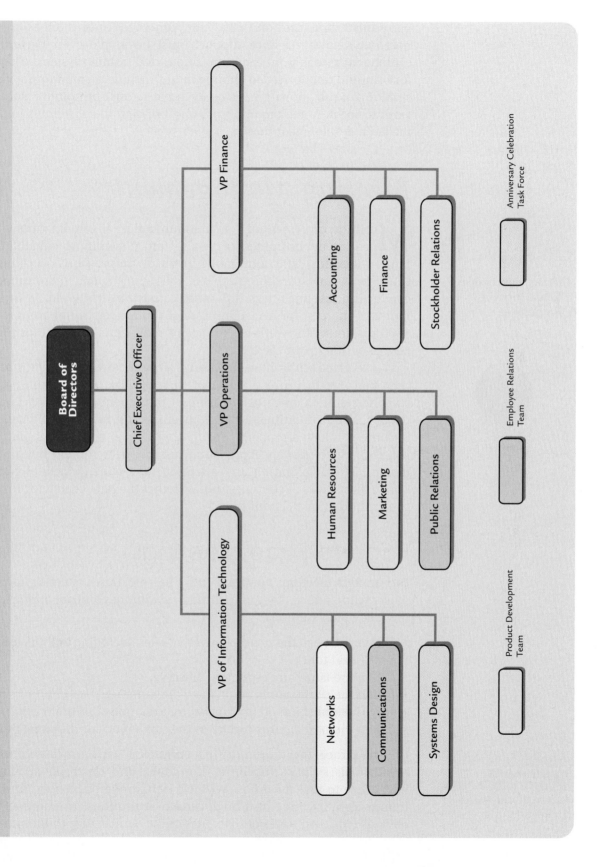

permanent structures and processes. Organizational changes are often necessary, however, since support must be in place for performance evaluation, recognition, communication, and training systems. Strategies for bringing about needed change might include arranging site visits to similar organizations that already have teams, bringing a successful team to speak to the organization, and bringing in consultants to discuss the team development process.

Meeting Management

Objective 5

Discuss aspects of effective meeting management.

Team Environment

Meetings are essential for communication in organizations. They present opportunities to acquire and disseminate valuable information, develop skills, and make favorable impressions on colleagues, supervisors, and subordinates. U.S. businesses spend more money on conducting meetings than any other country in the world. In fact, estimates of the cost for a meeting of eight managers range from $300 to $700 an hour. U.S. workers also spend more time in meetings than do people of other countries.[15]

Workers frequently have a negative attitude toward meetings because they perceive they are a waste of time. Studies support this opinion, revealing that as much as one third of time spent in meetings is unproductive. Negative attitudes toward meetings can be changed when meetings are conducted properly, giving attention to correct procedures and behavior. Successful meetings don't just happen; rather, they occur by design. Careful planning and attention to specific guidelines can help assure the success of your meetings, whether they are conducted in a face-to-face format or electronically.

Face-to-Face Meetings

Face-to-face meetings continue to be the most-used meeting format in most organizations. They offer distinct advantages and are appropriate in the following situations:[16]

- When you need the richest nonverbal cues, including body, voice, proximity, and touch.
- When the issues are especially sensitive.
- When the participants don't know one another.
- When establishing group rapport and relationships are crucial.
- When the participants can be in the same place at the same time.

Critical Thinking

Overly dominant meeting participants can be as detrimental as the isolates who do not contribute.

Face-to-face meetings may be enhanced with the use of various media tools such as flipcharts, handouts, and electronic slide shows. While face-to-face meetings provide a rich nonverbal context and direct human contact, they also have certain limitations. In addition to the obvious logistical issues of schedules and distance, face-to-face meetings may be dominated by overly vocal, quick-to-speak, and high status members. An additional potential obstacle to communication results from the differences in communication styles that men and women typically exhibit. The Strategic Forces feature "Communication Styles of Men and Women" describes how such problems can occur and what can be done to overcome possible difficulties in communicating.

Electronic Meetings

Changing Technology

A variety of technologies is available to facilitate electronic meetings. Participants may communicate with one another through telephones, personal computers, or video broadcast equipment using groupware or meeting management software applications. Electronic meetings offer certain advantages. They facilitate geographically dispersed groups, because they provide the choice of meeting at different places/same time, different places/different times, same place/same time, or same place/different times. Electronic meetings also speed up meeting follow-up activities because decisions and action items may be recorded electronically.

Electronic meetings also have certain limitations:[17]

Team Environment

- They cannot replace face-to-face contact, especially when group efforts are just beginning and when groups are trying to build group values, trust, and emotional ties.
- They may make it harder to reach consensus, because more ideas are generated and because it may be harder to interpret the strength of other members' commitment to their proposals.
- The success of same-time meetings is dependent on all participants having excellent keyboarding skills to engage in rapid-fire, in-depth discussion. This limitation may be overcome as voice input systems

Technology can facilitate electronic meetings that allow participants in various locations to communicate as a unified group.

Communication Styles of Men and Women

Research on communication patterns in mixed-gender work groups shows that the traditional behaviors of men and women may restrict the richness of discussion and limit the productivity of the group. The basic male approach to work tasks is confrontational and results oriented. By contrast, the female method of working is collaborative and oriented toward concern for individuals. The adversarial male style leads to respect, while the collaborative female style engenders rapport.[18]

Differences in male and female behavior that accentuate gender differences are often so subtle that group members may not be aware of what is happening. Here is a partial listing of those differences:[19]

- Men are more likely to control discussion through introducing topics, interrupting, and talking more than women.

- Women not only talk less, but often assume supportive rather than leadership roles in conversation and receive less attention for their ideas from the group.

- Both men and women may expect group members to follow gender stereotyped roles that can limit each individual's contributions (for example, always selecting a man as leader or a woman as note taker).

- Either women or men may use exclusionary language that reinforces gender stereotypes and that others in the group find offensive.

- Women may exhibit verbal characteristics of submissiveness (allowing sentence endings to trail off or using a shrill voice) while men communicate in ways that restrict and control a group (raising the voice or ignoring ideas generated by women).

- Men's nonverbal behavior (extended eye contact, a condescending touch, or overt gestures) may convey messages of dominance while women's nonverbal behavior (smiling, hair-twirling, or primly crossed legs) may suggest a lack of self-confidence and power.

- Men and women may sit separately, thereby limiting cross-gender interaction.

Until recently, most research on differences between the communication styles of men and women has focused on interaction in face-to-face settings. Current research has also addressed computer-mediated communication (CMC) that occurs when using electronic means such as e-mail, instant messaging, and electronic meetings. Such studies indicate differences in the communication patterns of men and women. For example, women using CMC with other women develop more disclosure and sense of community, whereas men using CMC with other men seem to ignore the socio-emotional aspects of group functioning and are more likely to use mild flaming (emotional language outbursts). Overall, men are less satisfied with the CMC experience and show lower levels of group development than do women.[20]

While caution is advised concerning stereotyping of men and women in communication situations, knowing what behaviors may limit the group process is imperative to maximizing results. Group members may need awareness training to assist in recognizing behaviors that may hinder team performance and in overcoming barriers that may limit the effectiveness of their communication. Differences can also be used to productive advantage. You will explore age-related barriers to group communication in Chapter 3.

Application

Locate an article on cross-gender communication. Compose a list of suggestions for improving cross-gender communications in the work environment. Star those that you feel would be most helpful to you in your professional activities and that you will commit to work on as part of your self-improvement.

become more prevalent. Refer to the support site at http://lehman.swlearning.com for helpful suggestions on how to maximize your performance as a member of a virtual team.

Suggestions for Effective Meetings

Whether you engage in face-to-face or electronic meetings, observing the following guidelines may help to ensure that your meetings are productive:

Team Environment

- *Limit meeting length and frequency.* Any meeting held for longer than an hour or more frequently than once a month should be scrutinized. Ask yourself whether the meeting is necessary. Perhaps the purpose can be achieved in another way, such as e-mail, instant messaging, or telephone.

- *Make satisfactory arrangements.* Select a date and time convenient for the majority of expected participants. For face-to-face meetings, plan the meeting site with consideration for appropriate seating for attendees, media equipment, temperature and lighting, and necessary supplies. For electronic meetings, check hardware and software and connectivity components.

- *Distribute the agenda well in advance.* The **agenda** is a meeting outline that includes important information: date, beginning and ending time, place, and topics to be discussed and responsibilities of those involved. Having the agenda prior to the meeting allows participants to know what is expected of them. A sample agenda is provided in the *Building High-Performance Teams* handbook.

- *Encourage participation.* While it is certainly easier for one person to make decisions, the quality of the decision making is often improved by involving the team. Rational decision making may begin with **brainstorming**, the generation of many ideas from among team members. Brainstormed ideas can then be discussed and ranked, followed by some form of voting.

- *Maintain order.* An organized democratic process assures that the will of the majority prevails, the minority is heard, and group goals are achieved as expeditiously as possible. Proper parliamentary procedure may be followed in formal meetings, as outlined in sources such as *Robert's Rules of Order* and *Jones' Parliamentary Procedure at a Glance*. For less formal meetings, a more relaxed approach may be taken to assure that everyone has an opportunity to share in the decision making.

Critical Thinking

What is the relationship between conflict and consensus?

- *Manage conflict.* In an autocratic organization, conflict may be avoided because employees are conditioned to be submissive. Such an environment, however, leads to smoldering resentment. On the other hand, conflict is a normal part of any team effort and can lead to creative discussion and superior outcomes. Maintaining focus on issues and not personalities helps assure that conflict is productive rather than destructive.

- *Seek consensus.* While unanimous agreement on decisions is an optimal outcome, total agreement cannot always be achieved. **Consensus** represents the collective opinion of the group, or the informal rule that

all team members can live with at least seventy percent of what is agreed upon.

- **Prepare thorough minutes.** Minutes provide a concise record of meeting actions, assure the tracking and followup of issues from previous meetings, and assist in the implementation of previously reached decisions. A format for meeting minutes is provided in the *Building High-Performance Teams* handbook.

Meetings are an important management tool and are useful for idea exchange. They also provide opportunities for you, as a meeting participant, to communicate impressions of power and status. Knowing how to present yourself and your ideas and exhibiting knowledge about correct meeting management will assist you in your career advancement.

Changing Technology

Other useful ideas about preparing for and conducting meetings are available at the NetMeeting web site (http://www.microsoft.com/windows/netmeeting/default.asp). You may also visit the text support site at http://lehman.swlearning.com to learn more about maximizing the effectiveness of **virtual teams**, teams that are located in more than one location. The Electronic Café located at the end of Chapter 10 will provide you with additional activities and experiences designed to make you a more effective meeting participant.

Summary

1. **Explain how behavioral theories about human needs, trust and disclosure, and motivation relate to business communication.** Behavioral theories that address human needs, trust and disclosure, and motivation are essential aspects of interpersonal communication. The needs of all individuals to be heard, appreciated, wanted, and reinforced significantly affect their interpersonal communications.

2. **Describe the role of nonverbal messages in communication.** Nonverbal communication conveys a significant portion of meaning and includes metacommunications, which are wordless messages that accompany words, and kinesic communications that are expressed through body language. The meanings of nonverbal messages are culturally derived.

3. **Identify aspects of effective listening.** Effective listening, which requires effort and discipline, is crucial to

effective interpersonal communication and leads to career success. Various types of listening require different strategies.

4. **Identify factors affecting group and team communication.** Organizations are increasingly using group structures to achieve goals. Effective group communication results from shared purpose, constructive activity and behaviors, and positive role fulfillment among members. A team is a special type of group that is typified by strong commitment among members; this commitment results in behaviors that produce synergy.

5. **Discuss aspects of effective meeting management.** Face-to-face meetings and electronic meetings each offer certain advantages and disadvantages. Effective meeting management techniques and behaviors can enhance the success of meetings.

Chapter Review

1. What is meant by stroking? How does it affect interpersonal communication in the workplace? (Obj. 1)

2. When a manager says to the sales staff, "Let's try to make budget this year," what are some of the possible metacommunications? (Obj. 2)

3. What roles do culture and gender play in nonverbal communication? (Obj. 2)

4. How is the activity of listening impacted by the particular situation? (Obj. 3)

//electronic café //

Secure E-mail Protects Corporate Information

Business organizations need secure control over incoming and outgoing e-mail. Financial services institutions are particularly aware of the need to keep their e-mail communication private. A recent study of corporate e-mail from more than 15,000 companies found that 8.7 percent of outbound mail contains sensitive financial information, and 22.8 percent of inbound e-mail contains such information.[21] Other institutions use e-mail to transmit other types of confidential and sensitive information. Various software firms offer products that help secure organizations' borders against unwanted intrusion into their e-mail. The following electronic activities will allow you to explore the topic of secure e-mail in more depth:

 InfoTrac College Edition. Access http://www.infotrac.thomsonlearning.com to read more about how Charles Schwab uses a secure electronic communications system for both its retail and institutional clients worldwide. Search for the following article that is available in full text:

Kabahar, A. (2002, March 11). Schwab to implement secure e-mail system globally. *Financial Net News*, 1-2.

 Text Support Web Site. Visit http://lehman.swlearning.com to learn more about secure e-mail systems. Refer to Chapter 2's Electronic Café activity that provides links to an online article that discusses the value of corporate e-mail policies in protecting against confidentiality breaches. Be prepared to discuss this information or use it as directed by your instructor.

 WebTutor Advantage. Your instructor will give you directions about how to use the secure e-mail provided through WebTutor. In WebTutor, e-mail your instructor or another student in your class, describing a business situation that would require a secure e-mail transaction.

 Professional Power Pak. Access your PPP CD for five lessons on e-mail security.

---

5. Discuss six bad listening habits. Which do you think is the biggest challenge for you personally? (Obj. 3)

6. What is a possible cause of most conflict between or among groups? (Obj. 4)

7. How are a group and a team different? (Obj. 4)

8. Discuss how a flat organizational structure affects communication. (Obj. 4)

9. What are some factors to consider in deciding whether to hold a face-to-face meeting or an electronic meeting? (Obj. 5)

10. Why are records such as agendas and minutes important to group success? (Obj. 5)

Digging Deeper

1. How can managers use Maslow's need levels, the Johari Window, and the management theories of McGregor and Hersey and Blanchard to improve communication with employees?

2. Why do some teams never reach the highest stage of team development? What can be done to overcome the obstacles to peak team performance?

To check your understanding of the chapter, take the practice quizzes at **http://lehman.swlearning.com** or your WebTutor course.

Activities

1. **Applying Behavioral Theories to Communication Situations (Obj. 1)**

Considering Maslow's hierarchy of needs, the Johari Window, McGregor's Theory X and Y, and Hersey and Blanchard's situational leadership theory, select one of the theories and relate it to a personal communication experience you have had. How was communication enhanced or worsened by the events and behaviors that occurred? What were the ethical implications of the situation? Prepare a brief written summary of your analysis.

2. **Understanding the Importance of Nonverbal Messages (Obj. 2)**

   In small groups, compose a list of nonverbal messages (gestures, facial expressions, etc.) that might be used by a businessperson, along with their meanings. What are some possible ways that each might be misinterpreted?

3. **Analyzing Listening Skills (Obj. 3)**

   Visit the following site and complete the listening questionnaire found there:

   http://www.highgain/SELF/index.php3

   You may link to this URL or or other updated sites from the text support site.

   Send your instructor an e-mail that summarizes your thoughts on the following: (1) How did you rate as a listener? (2) What areas did you target for improvement in your listening skills?

4. **Identifying Deterrents to Group Success (Obj. 4)**

   In small groups, discuss negative group situations in which you have participated. These groups could be related to school, organizations, sports teams, perform-

ing groups, etc. Referring to the chapter information, identify reasons for each group's lack of success. Make a list of the most common problems identified in the team. Compare your list with that of other small groups in the class.

5. **Analyzing a Meeting for Effective Behaviors (Obj. 5)**

   Attend a meeting of an organization of your choice. Compare the activities of the attended meeting with the "Suggestions for Effective Meetings" presented in the chapter. E-mail your instructor, describing the meeting attended and summarizing how well the meeting reflected the chapter suggestions and how it might have been more effective.

6. **Assessing the Professional Value of Interpersonal and Group Communication Skills (Objs. 1–5)**

   Considering your career goal, select the three concepts presented in the chapter that you feel will be most important to your professional success. Write a one-page summary, justifying and explaining your selections.

Applications

| Read | Think | Write | Speak | Collaborate |

1. **Building Teams at Saturn Corporation (Objs. 1, 4)**

   Locate the following article that describes the importance of teams at Saturn Corporation:

   Team players (1999, May). *Executive Excellence, 16*(5), 18.

   In a small group, respond to the following:

   a. What is the significance of the term "people systems"?

   b. How does Saturn assure that its employees possess skills as team players?

   c. What is the meaning of the phrase "70 percent comfortable but 100 percent supportive"?

   d. What is Saturn's philosophy concerning team diversity? How is it demonstrated?

   e. Describe Saturn's corporate philosophy. Apply the behavioral theories described in the chapter to Saturn's employer–employee interactions.

2. **Communicating Nonverbally in a Job Interview (Obj. 2)**

   Locate the following article that gives useful suggestions for assuring that your nonverbal behavior in a job interview makes a favorable impression:

   Botero, I. M. (1996, January 12). Actions often can speak louder than words. *The Business Journal (Phoenix)*, p. 41.

   Expand the list of nonverbal messages and their interpretations. Share your list with the class, complete with demonstrations, in an informal presentation.

| Read | Think | Write | Speak | Collaborate |

3. **Analyzing Limitations of Electronic Communications (Objs. 2, 3, 5)**

   Consider a distance learning conference or course in which you have participated. How were nonverbal com-

munication, listening, and other factors different from what you have experienced in traditional class settings? How do your experiences relate to the conducting of electronic meetings?

4. **Recognizing Events that Involve Metacommunication (Obj. 2)**

   Keep a journal over the next two to five days that records events that involve metacommunication. Describe how each incident influences the understanding of the verbal message involved.

   Visit the Interactive Study Center at **http://lehman. swlearning.com** for a downloadable version of this activity.

5. **Maximizing the Effectiveness of Virtual Teams (Objs. 4, 5)**

   Visit the text support site at **http://lehman.swlearning. com** to read about how to maximize the effectiveness of a virtual team. Consider the significance of this state-

ment that appears in the posting: "Certain personality types are more likely to thrive in the virtual team experience." Develop a list of personality attributes that would enable a person to work effectively as part of a virtual team. In a short written or oral report, share your list, justifying your selections with facts and references.

6. **Documenting Meeting Activities (Obj. 5)**

   Consult *Building High-Performance Teams* (your separate team handbook) for guidelines for preparing agendas and minutes. Attend a meeting of an organization of your choice. Obtain a copy of the agenda, and prepare minutes of the meeting. Submit your meeting documentation to your instructor.

7. **Locating Information on Nonverbal Communication in Other Cultures (Obj. 2)**

   Locate one or more articles in the library or over the Internet that discuss nonverbal communication in various cultures. Compile a list of gestures that have different meanings among cultures. Discuss how ignorance of these differences might affect interpersonal communication.

8. **Discussing the Impact of Flat Organizational Structure on Communication (Obj. 4)**

   Using an online database in your library, locate an article about a company that has adopted a flat organizational structure. Write a brief summary emphasizing the effect this change in organizational structure has had on the communication process.

9. **Analyzing Group and Team Experiences (Obj. 4)**

   Analyze a group or team experience you have had in the past; it might be a class project, club activity, or other situation. What were the strong factors of the group/team? What were the weak factors of the group/team? What roles, both positive and negative, were played out in the group/team? Describe your experience in a short presentation.

10. **Using Instant Messaging (Chat) to Communicate (Objs. 3, 4)**

    Following directions from your instructor, participate in an online chat with your class about one of the following topics: (a) how to overcome listening barriers, or (b) guidelines for effective group communication.

Capitalizing on Workplace Diversity at Hewlett-Packard

In 2003 only six Fortune 500 companies had female CEOs. While Carly Fiorina, CEO of Hewlett-Packard, deflects attention from her gender, other observers do not. "Whether she wants to be or not, she becomes a poster out there," says Lynn Martin, former U.S. Secretary of Labor. Despite Fiorina's credibility, Martin fears that business critics will tie her performance to her gender. "If she fails, it will be 'a woman executive failed.'"[22]

- Visit the Hewlett-Packard web site at **http://www.hp.com**. Find out the company's philosophy about diversity.
- Locate the following article that describes some success factors for workplace diversity:

  Diversity: Less than meets the eye (1997, June). *Getting Results . . . For the Hands-On Manager, 42*(6), 8.

Activities

Form a small group; identify in what ways the group is diverse. Identify a list of attitudes that promote a successful diversity initiative within an organization. Identify a list of behaviors that promote workplace diversity.

Part 4 of the Hewlett-Packard ShowCASE focuses on the efforts of major corporations to build employee trust and Carly Fiorina's candid communication style.

http://www.hp.com

Visit the text support site at **http://lehman.swlearning.com** to complete Part 4 of the Hewlett-Packard ShowCASE.

Internet Case

Is Anyone Listening?

The ability to listen effectively is consistently rated as one of the most important skills necessary for success in the workplace. A survey of North American executives reveals that 80 percent believes that listening is one of the most important skills needed in the corporate environment. The same survey participants, however, also rated the skill as one of the most lacking. Effective listening is crucial to providing quality service, facilitating groups, training staff, improving teamwork, and supervising and managing for improved performance. In times of stress and change, effective listening is the cornerstone of workplace harmony, since it furthers interpersonal and intercultural understanding. Listening is more than just hearing. It is an interactive process that takes concentration and commitment.

Although listening is critical to our daily lives, it is taught and studied far less than the other three basic communication skills: reading, writing, and speaking.

Over-reliance on television and computers also contributes to our listening problems. Much of the trouble we have communicating with others is because of poor listening skills. Studies show that we spend about 80 percent of our waking hours communicating, and at least 45 percent of that time listening. Most people can benefit from improving their listening skills. You can arrive at a fairly accurate assessment of your listening skills by thinking about your relationships with the people in your life—your boss, colleagues, best friends, family. If asked, what would they say about how well you listen? Do you often misunderstand assignments, or only vaguely remember what people have said to you? If so, you may need to improve your listening skills. These suggestions may assist you in your listening improvement:

- Become aware of biases and filters that keep you from listening effectively.
- Identify the aspects of listening that you need to improve upon.
- Get comfortable with silence.

- Monitor your body language, facial expressions, and other nonverbal signals that might appear negative.
- Listen between words for feelings.
- Give signals that you are listening.
- Take notes.
- Hear people out before cutting in with your reply.
- Don't begin answers with "I."
- Learn to ask nonaggressive questions.
- Understand that listening does not mean agreeing.

Listening skills can have a dramatic effect on your personal and professional success. By listening, you get listened to. Listening builds relationships and wins trust.[23]

Visit the text support site at **http://lehman.swlearning. com** to link to web resources related to this topic.

Respond to one or more of the following activities, as directed by your instructor.

1. **GMAT** Tell why you are either a good or poor listener. Support your conclusion with reasons and/or evidence.

2. One of the sites you visited identified a plan for improving the listening skills of a negotiator. Prepare a similar plan for a position in your chosen career field (human resources manager, auditor, salesperson, etc.), adapting the points to fit the activities and expectations of the position.

3. Outline and implement a plan for improving your own listening skills. Your plan should include the following: (1) identification of your major listening weaknesses; (2) one or more strategies for overcoming each of the stated weaknesses; (3) activities or occasions in which you applied the corrective strategies, with dates and times; and (4) outcomes of your corrective strategies. Implement your plan for one week, or some other time period as specified by your instructor. Summarize in writing the results of your self-improvement project.

Video Case

Texas Nameplate Co., Inc.: Meeting Management Skills

Texas Nameplate Co., Inc. (TNC), founded in 1946 as a small manufacturer of military identification labels, has steadily grown to be a multimillion dollar company that produces nameplates for products of all kinds, from refrigerators and computers, to high-pressure valves and oil field equipment. TNC manufactures panels and control charts, dials, scales, nameplates, information plates, labels, decals, and overlays, using processes such as chemical etching and screenprinting on materials such as aluminum, brass, polycarbonates, Mylar, stainless steel, and vinyl.

Scheduling regular meetings is an important way management can keep employees informed about what is going on at the company, seek employees' ideas on matters affecting them and their company, and contribute to an overall feeling of satisfaction on the part of employees. Accomplishing these lofty goals, however, requires expertise in meeting management skills—skills that many managers have not developed. This activity will familiarize you with an excellent Internet resource that offers advice on how to prepare and conduct effective meetings.

View the video segment about Texas Nameplate Co., Inc. on WebTutor or your Professional Power Pak.

Discussion Questions

1. *Criteria #5: Human Resource Focus* is one of the seven criteria for performance excellence by which all companies seeking to receive a Malcolm Baldrige National Quality Award are evaluated. One facet of this criterion is based on "Employee Well-Being and Satisfaction." How does TNC maintain a work environment and an employee support climate that contributes to the well-being, satisfaction, and motivation of all employees?*

2. Among the "Suggestions for Effective Meetings" at the end of Chapter 2, which two suggestions do you consider most important for TNC meetings and why?

3. How are written communication skills used in the meeting management process?

4. What spoken communication skills would be most useful to one who conducts meetings?

Activities

1. The 3M Meeting Network provides a host of useful information and tools to help those who want to get the most out of their meetings. Go to the main page of the 3M Meeting Network and acquaint yourself with the site setup and the types of information available (**http://www.3m.com/meetingnetwork/index.html**). Be sure to check out a couple of cartoons (**http://www.3m.com/meetingnetwork/cartoons/cartoon.html**), and print out your favorite.

2. Based on your interest and need, select an item featured on the "Articles & Advice" page at **http://www.3m.com/meetingnetwork/readingroom/index.html**.

Print out the article. As you read it, highlight the key points.

3. Prepare a summary sheet with your name and other course-identifying information. Write two to three paragraphs summarizing what was most relevant to you and how you plan to use the information. Submit the summary sheet, highlighted article, and cartoon to your instructor.

Criteria for Performance Excellence: Baldrige National Quality Program (Gaithersburg, MD: National Institute of Standards and Technology, 2003), p. 23.

Communication Analysis

ii

3

Planning Spoken and Written Messages

© SUSAN VAN ETTEN

Objectives *When you have completed Chapter 3, you will be able to:*

1 Identify the purpose of the message and the appropriate channel.

2 Develop clear perceptions of the audience to enhance the impact of the communication and human relations.

3 Apply techniques for adapting messages to the audience, including strategies for communicating ethically and responsibly.

4 Recognize the importance of organizing a message before writing the first draft.

5 Select the appropriate message outline (deductive or inductive) for developing messages to achieve the desired response.

HALLMARK CRAFTS MESSAGES FOR CHANGING CONSUMER MARKET

Greeting cards can be a meaningful communication tool for customers, coworkers, and important business contacts. They can provide a memorable, cost-effective way to build loyalty and increase customer retention. Hallmark Cards, Inc., located in Kansas City, Missouri, is best known for its wide assortment of greeting cards for all occasions. Hallmark has been helping people say the right things at the right time for almost 100 years, and the continued success of their cards is directly tied to effective analysis of an ever-changing audience.

As American society has become increasingly heterogeneous, Hallmark product offerings have also become more diverse. Realizing that Hispanics currently account for 11 percent of the U.S. population, the company has extended the appeal of its cards to Hispanics through its Sinceremente Hallmark line that includes more than 1,500 Spanish-language cards. Hallmark targets its African-American consumers with its Mahogany line. The Tree of Life series, meanwhile, is aimed at Jewish customers. Since women buy 80 percent of all greeting cards, Hallmark works to attract today's women, particularly women older than 45 who no longer have children at home. The Warm Wishes line is designed to provide offbeat and entertaining options for those who prefer an alternative to traditional sentiments. One of the most popular characters developed by Hallmark is senior citizen Maxine, now featured on a special collection of cards and merchandise.

Shifting cultural demographics is only one challenge faced by Hallmark. Generational changes, such as the tendency of baby boomers to purchase fewer cards than their parents did, and the current popularity of e-cards have given rise to the design of new products to entice consumers to card shop more often. A recent favorable trend in the greeting card business has been the effect of the terrorist attacks of September 11, 2001, on the way Americans communicate with each other. Since 9/11 people feel a need to stay in touch more often and to express their feelings more openly. In addition to encouraging consumers to seek greater comfort in family and friends, the 9/11 tragedy also revived patriotic feelings in many people, giving rise to Hallmark products that encompass patriotic sentiments. Expansion into international markets has shown Hallmark that message appeal is largely influenced by cultural values. The Dutch audience, for instance, tends to be more direct than Americans, while British consumers are more reserved and less direct.

Hallmark knows that building good communication with friends and family, as well as customers and business partners, means that they must design text and visual messages for consumers that effectively convey intended meanings and emotions. The company must accurately visualize its ever-changing audience in order to design appealing greeting cards. You, too, will need skills in audience analysis in order to promote effective communication in your professional activities. In this chapter you will learn various analysis skills for developing effective spoken and written messages that achieve your desired purpose.

http://www.hallmark.com

See ShowCASE, Part 2, on page 108 for Spotlight Communicator Dean Rodenbough, director of corporate communications at Hallmark Cards.

Critical Thinking

It has been said that all business messages have some persuasive intent. Do you agree or disagree?

Communication that commands attention and can be understood easily is essential for survival in today's information explosion. As an effective communicator, you will be expected to process volumes of available information and shape useful messages that respond to the needs of customers or clients, coworkers and supervisors, and other key business partners. Additionally, increased use of electronic communication for all types of messages (faxes, e-mails, instant messages, videoconferencing, etc.) will require you to be technologically savvy and capable of adapting the rules of good communication to the demands of emerging technology.

How can you learn to plan and prepare powerful business messages? The systematic analysis process as outlined in Figure 3-1 will help you develop messages that save you and your organization valuable time and money and portray you as a capable, energetic professional. A thorough analysis of the audience and your specific communication assignment will empower you to write a first draft efficiently and to revise and proofread your message for accuracy, conciseness, and appropriate tone. You will focus on the planning process in this chapter, and then learn to prepare the message in Chapter 4.

Figure 3-1

Process for Planning and Preparing Spoken and Written Business Messages

1 Determine the purpose and select an appropriate channel

2 Envision the audience

3 Adapt the message to the audience's needs and concerns

4 Organize the message

5 Prepare the first draft

6 Revise and proofread for accuracy and desired impact

Step 1: Determining the Purpose and Channel

Objective 1

Identify the purpose of the message and the appropriate channel.

If you are to speak or write effectively, you must think through what you are trying to say and understand it thoroughly before you start to communicate. This clear, logical thinking will enable you to identify the purpose of your message. Ask yourself why you are preparing the message and what you hope to accomplish. Is the purpose to get information, to answer a question, to make an announcement, to accept an offer, to deny a request, to seek support for a product or idea? Condense the answer to these questions into a brief sentence. This sentence is the purpose for writing or the central idea of your message. You will use the central idea to organize your message to achieve the results you desire.

The major purpose of many business messages is to have the receiver understand a body of information and to concentrate on the logical presentation of the content. Messages to inform are used to convey the vast amounts of information needed to complete the day-to-day operations of the business—explain instructions to employees, announce meetings and procedures, acknowledge orders, accept contracts for services, and so forth. Some messages are intended to persuade—to influence or change the attitudes or actions of the receiver. These messages include promoting a product or service and seeking support for ideas and worthy causes presented to supervisors, employees, stockholders, customers/clients, and others. You will learn to prepare messages for each of these purposes.

With your purpose in mind, you can now select an appropriate channel that will increase the likelihood that the receiver will understand and accept your message. Recall the varying degree of efficiency and effectiveness of each of the typical communication channels discussed in Chapter 1. Follow the guidelines in Figure 3-2 for selecting a communication channel that is most appropriate depending on the nature and location of the audience, formality and content of the message, and the need for feedback, written record, and privacy.

Critical Thinking

Identify the appropriate channel for (a) telling a customer damaged merchandise will be replaced, (b) notifying a sales rep of job termination, or (c) informing employees of a new Internet usage policy.

Step 2: Envisioning the Audience

Objective 2

Develop clear perceptions of the audience to enhance the impact of the communication and human relations.

Perception is the part of the communication process that involves how we look at others and the world around us. It's a natural tendency to perceive situations from our own limited viewpoint. We use our five senses to absorb and interpret the information bombarding us in unique ways; the context of a situation also affects our perception.

Individual differences in perception account for the varied and sometimes conflicting reports given by eyewitnesses to the same accident. A

Figure 3-2   *Selecting an Appropriate Communication Channel*

Channel	Recommended Use
Two-way, face-to-face	
Face-to-face conversation	Communicate an unpleasant or highly emotional message that may be subject to misinterpretation, a persuasive message, followup to a complex written message, or a personal message.
Face-to-face group meeting	Provide an optimal communication environment for discussing and reaching consensus on critical issues.
Video or teleconference	Provide an optimal communication environment for discussing and reaching consensus on critical issues when members are geographically dispersed.
Two-way, not face-to-face	
Telephone call	Deliver or obtain pleasant or routine information instantly.
Voice-mail message	Leave a message the receiver can reply to when convenient, eliminating telephone tag.
Electronic mail	Deliver the same message to a large, dispersed audience; is inappropriate for personal, confidential, or highly sensitive messages because of privacy issues.
Live chat (instant messaging)	Contact colleagues while on the telephone or provide or seek general information.
One-way, not face-to-face	
Fax	Deliver a message across time zones and international boundaries; used when speedy delivery of a written record is important.
Letter	Deliver a written record of information internally or externally.
Memorandum	Provide a written record of procedures or policy within an organization.
Report or proposal	Communicate complex information or a significant amount of data internally or externally.
Web page	Share information with external or internal audiences who are geographically dispersed and may not be individually identified (e.g., potential and existing customers, suppliers, investors, and employees).

popular television series focuses on Monk, the "defective" detective who can see things that scores of trained police workers cannot see although they've all been looking at the same crime scene. Illusions can help us understand how our senses can be tricked when there is a difference in what we expect and what really is happening. For example, ambiguous strokes on a page can produce varied interpretations from viewers. Locate an illusion on the Internet by searching with the key term "illusions" and experience this phenomenon for yourself. How does your perception affect your ability to interpret the image accurately or completely? Share the illusion with friends and see if and how their perceptions differ from your own.

Critical Thinking

What is your favorite visual illusion? Why?

Our perception of reality is also limited by previous experiences and our attitudes toward the sender of the message and ourselves. We filter messages through our own frames of reference and tend to see only things that we want to see. We support ideas that are in line with our own and decide whether to focus on the positive or the negative of a situation. At times we simply refuse to hear a message that doesn't fit into our view of the world.

Much of the confusion in communication is caused by differences in the sender and receiver's perceptions. For example, team members may clash when some members of the team perceive the task to be of greater importance than the other people involved in the work. Perceptions vary even between individuals with similar backgrounds and even more so when people from different cultures, generations, and genders communicate. You'll explore these communication challenges in later Strategic Forces features.

Critical Thinking

Differences in perception create challenges for effective communication.

Overcoming perceptual barriers is difficult but essential if you are to craft messages that meet the needs and concerns of your audience. You will need to understand your audience in order to comprehend their possible perceptions of your communication. To help you envision the audience, first focus on relevant information you know about the receiver. The more familiar you are with the receiver, the easier this task will be. When communicating with an individual, you immediately recall a clear picture of the receiver—his or her physical appearance, background (education, occupation, religion, culture), values, opinions, preferences, and so on. Most importantly, your knowledge of the receiver's reaction in similar, previous experiences will aid you in anticipating how this receiver is likely to react in the current situation. Add to your mental picture by thoughtfully considering all you know about the receiver and how this information might affect the content and style of your final message. Consider the following major areas:

Critical Thinking

What other information about your receiver might help to shape your message?

- *Age.* A letter answering an elementary-school student's request for information from your company would not be worded the same as a letter answering a similar request from an adult.
- *Economic level.* A banker's collection letter to a customer who pays promptly is not likely to be the same form letter sent to clients who have fallen behind on their payments for small loans.
- *Educational/occupational background.* The technical jargon and acronyms used in a financial proposal sent to bank loan officers may be inappropriate in a proposal sent to a group of private investors. Similarly, a message to the chief executive officer of a major corporation may differ in style and content from a message to a stockholder.
- *Needs and concerns of the receiver.* Just as successful sales personnel begin by identifying the needs of the prospective buyer, an effective manager attempts to understand the receiver's frame of reference as a basis for organizing the message and developing the content.
- *Culture.* The vast cultural differences between people (language, expressions, customs, values, religions) increase the complexity of the communication process. A memorandum containing typical American expressions (e.g., "The proposal was *shot down*," "projections are *on par*," and "*the competition is backed to the wall*") would likely confuse a manager from a different culture. Differences in values influence communication styles and message patterns. For example, Japanese readers value the beauty and flow of words and prefer an indirect writing approach, unlike Americans who prefer clarity and conciseness.[1] The Internet Case allows you to explore one of the greatest challenges related to international commerce—the ability to prepare clear, accurate translations into numerous languages.

Diversity
Challenges

- ***Rapport.*** A sensitive letter written to a long-time client may differ significantly from a letter written to a newly acquired client. The rapport created by previous dealings with this client aids understanding in this new situation.
- ***Expectations.*** Because accountants, doctors, and lawyers are expected to meet high standards, a letter from one of these professionals containing errors in grammar or spelling would likely cause a receiver to question the credibility of the source.

You may find that envisioning an audience you know well is often such a conscious action that you may not even recognize that you are doing it. On the other hand, envisioning those you do not know well requires additional effort. In these cases, simply assume an empathetic attitude toward the receiver to assist you in identifying his or her frame of reference (knowledge, feelings, emotions). In other words, project mentally how you believe you would feel or react in a similar situation and use that information to communicate understanding back to the person.

Consider the use (or lack) of empathy in the following workplace examples:

Critical Thinking

Empathy is the ability to identify another's frame of reference and to communicate understanding back to the person.

Critical Thinking

In communicating with someone of another culture, how can we effectively focus on similarities while being aware of differences?

Sample Message	Problem Analysis
Example 1: A U.S. manager's instructions to a new employee from an Asian culture:	• *Creation of confusion and intimidation caused by the acronyms and expressions peculiar to the U.S. environment.*
"Please get to work right away inputting the financial data for the Collier proposal. Oh, I need you to get this work out ASAP. Because this proposal is just a draft, why don't you just plan to give me a quick-and-dirty job. You can clean it up after we massage the stats and get final blessings from the top dog. Do you have any questions?"	• *Final open-ended question indicates the writer does not understand the importance of saving face to a person from an Asian culture. Deep cultural influences may prevent this employee from asking questions that might indicate lack of understanding.*
Example 2: An excerpt from a letter sent to Ms. Kelly Lazzara: Dear Mr. Lazarra: The desktop publishing software and the laser printer that you expressed an interest in is now available in our local stores. Both can be demonstrated at you convience. Please call your local sales representative to schedule a appointment. I remain Respectfully yours, *Hugh Washam* Hugh Washam District Manager	• *The misspelling of the receiver's name, use of Mr. to refer to a woman, and the grammatical and spelling errors are unforgivable. They confirm incompetence (or carelessness) and disrespect for the receiver.* • *The outdated closing reduces the writer's credibility further. Although the writer is claiming expertise in a technological field, the communication does not reflect modern conventions.* • *Omission of the sales representative's name and telephone number indicates the writer's failure to anticipate and adapt the message to meet the receiver's needs.*

Taking the time and effort to obtain a strong mental picture of your audience through firsthand knowledge or your empathetic attitude *before* you write will enhance your message in the following ways:

1. ***Establishes rapport and credibility needed to build long-lasting personal and business relationships.*** Your receivers will appreciate your attempting to understand their feelings, that is, your being in touch with them. A likely outcome is mutual trust, which can greatly improve communication and people's feelings about you, your ideas, and themselves (as shown in the discussion of the Johari Window in Chapter 2).

2. ***Permits you to address the receiver's needs and concerns.*** This knowledge allows you to select relevant content and to communicate in a suitable style.

3. ***Simplifies the task of organizing your message.*** From your knowledge of yourself and from your experiences with others, you can predict (with reasonable accuracy) receivers' reactions to various types of messages. To illustrate, ask yourself these questions:

   - Would I react favorably to a message saying my request is being granted or that a new client is genuinely pleased with a job I'd just completed?
   - Would I experience a feeling of disappointment when I learn that my request has been refused or that my promised pay raise is being postponed?
   - Would I need compelling arguments to convince me to purchase a new product or support a new company policy or an employer's latest suggestion for improvement?

Now, reread the questions as though you were the message recipient. Because you know *your* answers, you can predict *others'* answers with some degree of accuracy. Such predictions are possible because of commonality in human behavior.

Your commitment to identifying the needs and concerns of your audience before you communicate is invaluable in today's workplace. Companies must focus on providing quality customer service and developing work environments supportive of talented, diverse workers. Alienating valuable customers and talented employees as a result of poor audience analysis, this first important step in planning a message, is not an option in today's competitive environment. Empathy is also central to handling the challenges of communicating across the generations, as you'll learn in the accompanying Strategic Forces feature, "Bridging the Generation Gap."

Diversity Challenges

Step 3: Adapting the Message to the Audience

After you have envisioned your audience, you are ready to adapt your message to fit the specific needs of your audience. Adaptations include focusing on the receiver's point of view; communicating ethically

Bridging the Generation Gap

Age diversity is a reality in the United States workforce today, and the span of age continues to increase as older workers choose to work longer or re-enter the job market after retirement and as increasing numbers of younger workers enter the workplace. Companies committed to innovative team-based systems face the challenge of fostering teamwork between four generations spanning more than 60 years. The four generations working side by side include the following in the proportions shown in the accompanying figure.[2]

- *Matures or seniors*—Americans in their late 50s and older whose survival of hard times caused them to value hard work, sacrifice, and a strong sense of right and wrong. They like the idea of re-entering the job market after retirement or remaining there for the long haul.

- *Baby boomers*—Set squarely in middle age, they are referred to as the "Me" generation because they grew up in boom times and were indulged and encouraged by their parents to believe their opportunities were limitless. They will work longer than their parents because of greater financial strain and a limited retirement budget.

- *Generation Xers*—Members of the generation of the "latchkey" kid are fiercely independent, self-directed, and resourceful, but skeptical of authority and institutions because they entered the workforce in a time of downsizing and cutbacks.

- *Millennials (also called Generation Yers)*—The children of the boomers' children, who are just entering the workforce, are technologically savvy, active, and visually oriented due to their lifetime experience in a high tech world.

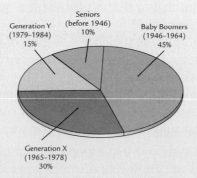

Studies indicate that generational conflict is often unfounded. For instance, baby boomer resistance to Generation X is based on an incorrect assumption that Gen Xers are slackers. Experience, however, has confirmed more positive characteristics.[3] Older workers should show trust for young workers and give them freedom to demonstrate their talents.[4] Respectively, younger workers might seek to learn from older workers and ask for coaching and mentoring.

Misconceptions such as these can cause unwarranted resistance. When properly managed, companies with a strong mix of older and younger workers have a distinct competitive edge. Each generation has something to offer; younger workers bring new ideas; older workers bring experience. Getting these workers to work together effectively requires effective communication, beginning with an appreciation for the value of diversity. Visit the text support site at **http://lehman.swlearning. com** to learn about ways to avoid clashes between the generations.

Application

1. Interview a person from a generation other than your own. Assist him/her in identifying the generation to which he/she belongs. Include the following questions in your interview:

   - Considering your own experiences with supervisors and coworkers, what type of management styles and communication patterns do you find to be most effective?

   - What guidelines can you offer to managers of older (or younger) generations for successfully communicating with persons of your generation?

2. Based on interview information and your own readings, develop a list of organizational guidelines for communicating most effectively with persons from the interviewee's generation.

Responding to a stock analyst's negative comments about Showbiz's stock price, Chuck E. Cheese, the company's large rodent icon, crafted a light-hearted response focusing on the company's fun-loving slogan, "Where a Kid Can Be a Kid!" Read Chuck E.'s letter available at the text support site (**http://lehman.swlearning.com**) and consider how the tone of the letter affected the overall impact of the message and the company's public relations efforts.

© CEC ENTERTAINMENT

and responsibly; building and protecting goodwill; using simple, contemporary language; writing concisely; and projecting a positive, tactful tone.

Focus on the Receiver's Point of View

Ideas are more interesting and appealing if they are expressed from the receiver's viewpoint. Developing a "you attitude" rather than a "me attitude" involves thinking in terms of the other person's interests and trying to see a problem from the other's point of view. A letter, memo, e-mail, or phone call reflecting a "you attitude" sends a direct signal of sincere concern for the receiver's needs and interest.

The use of the word *you* (appropriately used) conveys to receivers a feeling that messages are specifically for them. However, if the first-person pronoun *I* is used frequently, the sender may impress others as being self-centered—always talking about self. *I* used as the subject receives significant emphasis. Compare the following examples of sender-centered and receiver-centered statements:

Critical Thinking

Reword the following to show more you attitude: "I'm asking all work teams to generate a list of innovative product ideas."

I- or Sender-Centered	Receiver-Centered
<u>I</u> want to take this opportunity to offer <u>my</u> congratulations on your recent promotion to regional manager.	Congratulations on <u>your</u> recent promotion to regional manager.

We allow a 2 percent discount to customers who pay their total invoices within ten days.	Customers who pay within ten days may deduct 2 percent from their total invoice. (*You* could be the subject in a message to a customer.)
I am interested in ordering . . .	Please send me . . . (*You* is the understood subject.)

Compliments (words of deserved praise) are another effective way of increasing a receiver's receptiveness to ideas that follow. Give sincere compliments judiciously as they can do more harm than good if paid at the wrong time, in the wrong setting, in the presence of the wrong people, or for the wrong reasons. Likewise, avoid flattery (words of *un*deserved praise). Although the recipient may accept your flattery as a sincere compliment, chances are the recipient will interpret your undeserved praise as an attempt to seek to gain favor or special attention. Suspicion of your motive makes effective communication less likely.

To cultivate a "you attitude," concentrate on the following questions:

Legal & Ethical Constraints

- Does the message address the receiver's major needs and concerns?
- Would the receiver feel this message is receiver-centered? Is the receiver kept clearly in the picture?
- Will the receiver perceive the ideas to be fair, logical, and ethical?
- Are ideas expressed clearly and concisely (to avoid lost time, money, and possible embarrassment caused when messages are misunderstood)?
- Does the message serve as a vehicle for developing positive business relationships—even when the message is negative? For example, are *please*, *thank you*, and other courtesies used when appropriate? Are ideas stated tactfully and positively and in a manner that preserves the receiver's self-worth and cultivates future business?
- Is the message sent promptly to indicate courtesy?
- Does the message reflect the high standards of a business professional: quality paper, accurate formatting, quality printing, and absence of misspellings and grammatical errors?

Concentrating on these points will boost the receiver's confidence in the sender's competence and will communicate nonverbally that the receiver is valued enough to merit the sender's best effort. For people who practice courtesy and consideration, the "you attitude" is easy to incorporate into written and spoken messages.

Communicate Ethically and Responsibly

Legal & Ethical Constraints

The familiar directive "with power comes responsibility" applies especially to your use of communication skills. Because business communication affects the lives of many, you must accept responsibility for using it to uphold your own personal values and your company's standards of ethical conduct. Before speaking or writing, use the following guidelines to help you filter your message to ensure that you are communicating ethically and responsibly.

Critical Thinking

Were you ever the recipient of an unethical business practice? Describe the incident, your feelings, and the outcome.

- ***Is the information stated as truthfully, honestly, and fairly as possible?*** Good communicators recognize that ensuring a free flow of essential information is in the interest of the public and the company. The Spotlight Communicator from Hallmark shares the positive effect open, timely internal communication has had on the company's financial performance and its relationship with employees. On the other hand, withholding relevant information claimed the jobs of Harvey Pitt, the chairman of the Securities and Exchange Commission (SEC), and William Webster, the elected chairman of a new federal accounting oversight board. Although Webster told Pitt he had headed the audit committee of a company that was being investigated for fraud, Pitt chose not to tell the commission members who elected Webster to chair a committee whose purpose was to bolster the confidence of investors and consumers shaken by corporate scandals.[5]

Recognize that your honor, honesty, and credibility will build strong, long-lasting relationships and lead to the long-term success of your company. Sending complete, accurate, and timely information regardless of whether it supports your views will help you build that credibility.

Securities and Exchange Commission Chairman Harvey Pitt was forced to step down when it became known that he was aware of incriminating information about the chairman of the accounting board that he failed to disclose to other SEC commissioners.

© AFP/CORBIS

Critical Thinking

In small groups discuss the ethics of inflating a résumé to increase the chances of getting a job interview.

- ***Does the message embellish or exaggerate the facts?*** Legal guidelines related to advertising provide clear guidance for avoiding *fraud*, the misrepresentation of products or services; however, overzealous sales representatives or imaginative writers can use language skillfully to create less-than-accurate perceptions in the minds of the readers. Businesses have learned the hard way that overstating the capabilities of a product or service (promising more than can be delivered) is not good for business in the long run. Developing skill in communicating persuasively will be important throughout your profession. The persuasive techniques you will learn in this course, such as those related to writing a winning résumé and application letter, will be helpful as you begin your career; however, these techniques should *not* be used if your motive is to exploit the receiver.

- ***Are the ideas expressed clearly and understandably?*** If a message is to be classified as honest, you must be reasonably confident that the receiver can understand the message accurately. Ethical communicators select words that convey the exact meaning intended and that are within the reader's vocabulary. Consider a plumber's frustration with the following message from the Bureau of Standards: "The effect of HCL is incompatible with the metallic piping" and "We cannot assume responsibility for the production of toxic and noxious residues with HCL." Finally the Bureau sent a message the plumber could understand: "Don't use HCL. It eats the heck out of pipes!"[6] To protect consumers, some states have passed "Plain English" laws that require certain businesses and agencies to write policies, warranties, and contracts in language an average reader can understand. You can learn more about the importance of Plain English laws by completing the Internet Case at the end of Chapter 4.

Critical Thinking

How bound is a business professional to "tell the truth, the whole truth, and nothing but the truth"?

- ***Is your viewpoint supported with objective facts?*** Are facts accurately documented to allow the reader to judge the credibility of the source and to give credit where credit is due? Can opinions be clearly distinguished from facts? Have you evaluated honestly any real or perceived conflict of interest that could prevent you from preparing an unbiased message? You will learn to develop objective, well-documented written reports and presentations in Chapters 9–12.

- ***Are ideas stated with tact and consideration that preserves the receiver's self-worth?*** The metaphor, "An arrow, once it is shot, cannot be recalled," is used to describe the irrevocable damage caused by cruel or unkind words.[7] Ego-destroying criticism, excessive anger, sarcasm, hurtful nicknames, betrayed secrets, rumors, and malicious gossip pose serious ethical problems in the workplace because they can ruin reputations, humiliate, and damage a person's self-worth. Serious legal issues arise when negative statements are false, constituting defamation. Written defamatory remarks are referred to as *libel*, and similar spoken remarks are referred to as *slander*. If you choose to make negative statements about a person, be sure the facts in question are supported. Additionally, you'll hone your abilities to convey negative information and to handle sensitive situations in a constructive, timely manner rather than ignoring them until they get out of control. For considerate, fair, and civilized use of words, follow this simple rule: Communicate with and about others with the same kindness and fairness that you wish others to use when communicating with you.

- *Are graphics carefully designed to avoid distorting facts and relationships?* Communicating ethically involves reporting data as clearly and accurately as possible. Misleading graphics result either from the developers' deliberate attempt to confuse the audience or from their lack of expertise in constructing ethical graphics. You will study the principles of creating graphics that show information accurately and honestly in the Strategic Forces feature, "Presentation Software and Graphic Design Principles," in Chapter 10.

Build and Protect Goodwill

Goodwill arises when a business is worth more than its tangible assets. Things such as a good name and reputation, a desirable location, a unique product, excellent customer service, and so on, can assure earnings, and so the business has more value than simply its tangible assets. Businesses go to great lengths to build and protect goodwill and thus their future. It is no surprise that effective communication is a key strategy.

Insensitive messages—whether directed to customers, employees, or business partners—can offend and alienate and will diminish a company's goodwill. Most of us likely don't intend to be insensitive but simply may not think carefully about the impact the tone of our words may have on others. **Tone** is the way a statement sounds and conveys the writer's or speaker's attitude toward the message and the receiver. To build and protect your company's goodwill, eliminate words that are overly euphemistic, condescending, demeaning, and biased.

Use Euphemisms Cautiously

Critical Thinking

In groups, identify two more euphemisms you have heard recently. Do you believe their use is acceptable?

A **euphemism** is a kind word substituted for one that may offend or suggest something unpleasant. For example, the idea of picking up neighborhood garbage does not sound especially inviting. Someone who does such work is often referred to as a *sanitation worker*. This term has a more pleasant connotation than *garbage collector*. Choose the euphemistic terms rather than the negative terms shown in the following examples:

Negative Tone	Euphemistic Tone
disabled	physically challenged
victim	survivor
aged or elderly	senior citizen
used or secondhand	pre-owned
staff reduction	downsizing/rightsizing
resigned/fired/or laid off	voluntary severance

Critical Thinking

Using euphemisms that ridicule or mislead the recipient can undermine your trust and credibility.

Generally, you can recognize such expressions for what they are—unpleasant ideas presented with a little sugar coating. Knowing the sender was simply trying to be polite and positive, you are more likely to react favorably. Yet you should avoid euphemisms that excessively sugar-coat and those that appear to be deliberate sarcasm. For example, to refer to a janitor as a *maintenance engineer* is to risk conveying a negative meta-communication, such as "This person does not hold a very respectable position, but I did the best I could to make it sound good." To the receiver (and to the janitor), just plain *janitor* would sound better.

Also avoid using euphemisms when your motive is to ridicule or mislead. For example, a politician talking of *revenue enhancements* rather than *tax increases* or a military spokesperson speaking of *collateral damage* rather than civilians killed accidentally by the military's own weapons could lose credibility and valuable goodwill. Use euphemisms only when the purpose is to present unpleasant thoughts politely and positively.

Legal & Ethical Constraints

Avoid Condescending or Demeaning Expressions

Condescending words seem to imply that the communicator is temporarily coming down from a level of superiority to join the receiver on a level of inferiority; such words damage efforts to build and protect goodwill. Note how the reminders of inequality in the following examples hamper communication:

Ineffective Example

> Since I took a leadership role in this project, the team's performance has improved.
>
> As director of marketing, I will decide whether your product proposal has merit.
>
> You were not selected to fill our position, as we are looking for a candidate with exceptional skills.

A demeaning expression (sometimes called a *dysphemism*) makes an idea seem negative or disrespectful. Avoid demeaning expressions because they divert attention from the real message to emotional issues that have little to do with the message. Many examples can be taken as contempt for an occupation or a specific job/position (pencil pushers or bean counters for accountants; ambulance chasers for lawyers, spin doctors for politicians or public relations directors, pigs for police officers, and shrinks for psychiatrists). Like words that attack races or nationalities, words that ridicule occupations work against a communicator's purpose. Many demeaning expressions are common across regions, ages, and perhaps even cultures. Some demeaning expressions belong to a particular company; e.g., "turtles" was coined in one firm to mock first-year employees for the slow pace at which they completed their work. One software sales representative assured a group of executives that the system he was selling was no "Mickey Mouse system." The cost of using a seemingly innocent statement resulted in the loss of a very large account—Walt Disney Studios. Focus on using respectful expressions that build and protect goodwill.

BEETLE BAILEY

WWW.CARTOON.ORG

Sensitive communicators use euphemisms cautiously.

Use Connotative Tone Cautiously

Human relations can suffer when connotative words are inadvertently or intentionally used instead of denotative words. The **denotative meaning** of a word is the literal meaning that most people assign to it. The **connotative meaning** is the literal meaning plus an extra message that reveals the speaker's or writer's qualitative judgment as shown in this example:

Connotative Meaning with Negative Meaning	Denotative Meaning (Preferred)
Another <u>gripe session</u> has been scheduled for tomorrow.	Another <u>employee forum</u> has been scheduled for tomorrow.

Critical Thinking

What connotative message is conveyed in "Have you read the latest commandment from above?" How might you rewrite the sentence using the denotative meaning?

The connotative meaning of "gripe session" carries an additional message that the writer has a bias against employee forums. The connotation may needlessly introduce thoughts about whether employee forums are beneficial and distract the receiver from paying sufficient attention to statements that follow. Connotations, like metacommunications discussed in Chapter 2, involve messages that are implied. In the preceding example, the connotation seems to be more harmful than helpful.

At times, however, connotations can be helpful as seen in the following examples:

Connotative Meaning with Positive Meaning (Preferred)	Denotative Meaning
Our <u>corporate think tank</u> has developed an outstanding production process.	<u>Research and Development</u> has developed an outstanding production process.
John's likable personality <u>has made him a miracle worker</u> when he negotiates labor contracts.	John's likable personality is <u>beneficial</u> when he negotiates labor contracts.

In crafting business messages, rely mainly on denotative words or connotative words that will be interpreted in a positive manner. To be sure that your connotative words are understood and will generate goodwill, consider your audience, the context, and the timing of the message.

- *Connotative words may be more easily misinterpreted than denotative words.* Because of differences in peoples' perceptions based on their life experiences, words that are perceived positively by one person may be perceived negatively by another. In some cases, the receiver may simply not understand the connotative words; they are "clueless" to the intended message. Damaged human relations occur when managers repeatedly convey connotative messages without considering whether employees can interpret the meanings as they are intended.
- *The appropriateness of connotations varies with the audience to which they are addressed and the context in which they appear.* For example, referring to a car as a "foreign job" or "sweet" might be received differently by teenagers than by senior citizens. Such expressions are less appropriate in a research report than in a popular magazine.

Use Specific Language Appropriately

Critical Thinking

Choose precise, vigorous words that the receiver will find exciting and will remember.

To help the receiver understand your message easily, select words that paint intense, colorful word pictures. Creating clear mental images adds energy and imagination to your message, thus increasing its overall impact.

General	Specific (Preferred)
Congratulations on your <u>recent honor</u>.	Congratulations on being named <u>employee of the month</u>.
Complete the report <u>as soon as possible</u>.	Complete the report <u>by May 2</u>.
Sales <u>skyrocketed</u> this quarter.	Sales <u>increased 10 percent</u> this quarter.

Sometimes, using general statements can be useful in building and protecting goodwill. General words keep negative ideas from getting more emphasis than they deserve. In addition, senders who don't have specific information or for some reason don't want to divulge it use general words.

General (Preferred)	Specific
Thank you for the explanation of your <u>financial status</u>.	Thank you for writing me about your <u>problems with your creditors and the possibility of filing bankruptcy</u>.
Greg told me about <u>what happened last week</u>.	Greg told me about the <u>tragedy in your family</u>.

Legal & Ethical Constraints

Diversity Challenges

Critical Thinking

Sensitive communicators use bias-free language.

Use Bias-Free Language

Being responsive to individual differences requires you to make a conscious effort to use bias-free (nondiscriminatory) language. Using language that does not exclude, stereotype, or offend others permits them to focus on your message rather than to question your sensitivity. Goodwill can be damaged when biased statements are made related to gender, race or ethnicity, religion, age, or disability.

Avoid Gender Bias. The following guidelines will help you avoid gender bias:

1. ***Avoid referring to men and women in stereotyped roles and occupations.*** The use of *he* to refer to anyone in a group was once standard and accepted; however, this usage is considered insensitive and to some, offensive. Therefore, do not use the pronoun *he* when referring to a person in a group that may include women or the pronoun *she* to refer to a group that may include men. Otherwise, you may unintentionally communicate an insensitive message that only women or only men can perform certain tasks or serve in certain professions. Follow these four approaches to avoid gender bias.

Guideline	Gender-Biased	Improved
Avoid using a pronoun:	When your auditor arrives, <u>he</u> is to go . . .	Upon arrival, <u>your auditor</u> is to go . . .
Repeat the noun:	the courtesy of your guide. Ask <u>him</u> to . . .	the courtesy of your <u>guide</u>. Ask the <u>guide</u> to . . .
Use a plural noun:	A nurse must complete <u>her</u> in-service training to update her certification.	Nurses must complete <u>their</u> in-service training to update <u>their</u> certification.
Use pronouns from both genders (when necessary, but not repeatedly):	Just call the manager. <u>He</u> will in turn . . .	Just call the manager. <u>He or she</u> will in turn . . .

2. ***Use occupational titles that reflect genuine sensitivity to gender.*** Note the gender-free titles that can be easily substituted to avoid bias.

Gender-Biased	Gender-Free
waiter or waitress	server
fireman	firefighter
salesman	sales representative
businessman	executive, manager, businessperson
foreman	supervisor
working mother	working parent

Critical Thinking

Revise this statement to avoid gender bias: "Managers and their wives are invited to a weekend retreat at Lake Tahoe."

Critical Thinking

Provide other examples of gender-biased terms and appropriate gender-free alternatives.

3. ***Avoid designating an occupation by gender.*** For example, omit "woman" in "A woman doctor has initiated this research." The doctor's

profession, not the gender, is the point of the message. Similarly, avoid using the -*ess* ending to differentiate genders in an occupation:

Gender-Biased	Gender-Free
hostess	host
authoress	author
poetess	poet
actress	actor

Critical Thinking

What actions are companies taking to raise employee awareness of diversity issues?

4. ***Avoid using expressions that may be perceived to be gender-biased.*** Avoid commonly used expressions in which "man" represents all humanity, such as "To go where no man has gone before." and stereotypical characteristics, such as "man hours," "man and wife," "man-made goods," and "work of four strong men." Note the improvements made in the following examples by eliminating the potentially offensive words.

Gender-Biased	Improved
Preparing the annual report is a <u>man-sized</u> task.	Preparing the annual report is an <u>enormous</u> task.
Trey is the best <u>man</u> for the job.	Trey is the best <u>person</u> for the job.

Avoid Racial or Ethnic Bias. Include racial or ethnic identification only when relevant and avoid referring to these groups in stereotypical ways.

Racially or Ethnically Biased	Improved
Submit the request to Alfonso Perez, the <u>Spanish</u> clerk in Payroll.	Submit the request to Alfonso Perez, the clerk in Payroll.
Dan's <u>Irish</u> temper flared today.	Dan's temper flared today.

Avoid Age Bias. Include age only when relevant and avoid demeaning expressions related to age.

Critical Thinking

Give examples of words and phrases that can be used to avoid race, ethnicity, or disability bias.

Age Biased	Improved
Russ Payne, the <u>55-year-old</u> president of Norton Bank, has resigned.	Russ Payne, the president of Norton Bank, has resigned.

Avoid Disability Bias. When communicating about people with disabilities, use people-first language. That is, refer to the person first and the disability second so that focus is appropriately placed on the person's ability rather than on the disability. Also avoid words with negative or judgmental connotations, such as *handicap*, *unfortunate*, *afflicted*, and *victim*. When describing people without disabilities, use the word *typical* rather than *normal*; otherwise, you may inadvertently imply that people with disabilities are abnormal. Consider these more sensitive revisions:

Insensitive	Sensitive (People-First)
<u>Blind</u> employees receive . . .	Employees <u>with vision impairments</u> receive . . .
The elevator is for the exclusive use of <u>handicapped</u> employees and should not be used by <u>normal</u> employees.	The elevator is for the exclusive use of employees <u>with disabilities</u>.

Use Contemporary Language

Business messages should reflect correct, standard English and contemporary language used in a professional business setting. Outdated expressions and dull clichés reduce the effectiveness of a message and the credibility of a communicator.

Eliminate Outdated Expressions

Using outdated expressions will give your message a dull, stuffy, unnatural tone. Instead, substitute fresh, original expressions that reflect today's language patterns.

Outdated Expressions	Improvement
<u>Pursuant to your request</u>, the physical inventory has been scheduled for May 3.	<u>As you requested</u>, the physical inventory has been scheduled for May 3.
<u>Enclosed please find</u> a copy of my transcript.	The <u>enclosed</u> transcript should answer your questions.
<u>Very truly yours</u> (used as the complimentary close in a letter)	Sincerely

Eliminate Clichés

Critical Thinking

At what point does a word become a cliché?

Clichés, overused expressions, are common in our everyday conversations and in business messages. These handy verbal shortcuts are convenient, quick, and easy to use and often include simple metaphors and analogies that effectively communicate the most basic idea or emotion or the most complex business concept. However, writers and speakers who routinely use stale clichés may be perceived as unoriginal, unimaginative, and lazy, and perhaps even disrespectful. Less frequently used words capture the receiver's attention because they are original, fresh, and interesting.

Cliché	Improvement
Pushed (or stretched) the envelope	Took a risk or considered a new option
Eyeballs on the screen	Concentrate
Cover all the bases	Get agreement/input from everyone
Wipe the slate clean	Start again
The ball is in your court	The decision is yours
That sucks!	That's unacceptable/needs improvement

Critical Thinking

In groups, generate a list of clichés used by friends, instructors, or coworkers. How do you feel when these expressions are used frequently?

Legal & Ethical Constraints

Critical Thinking

To ensure quick and easy comprehension, use simple, informal words.

Critical Thinking

Simplify the message: "Management has become cognizant of the necessity of the elimination of undesirable vegetation surrounding the periphery of our facility."[9]

Clichés present another serious problem. Consider the scenario of shoppers standing in line at a discount store with the cashier saying to each, *Thanks for shopping with us today; please come again.* Because the last shopper has heard the words several times already, he may not consider the statement genuine. The cashier has used an expression that can be stated without thinking and possibly without meaning. A worn expression can convey messages such as "You are not special" or "For you, I won't bother to think; the phrases I use in talking with others are surely good enough for you." Original expressions convey sincerity and build strong human relations.

Increasing tolerance of profanity is an issue of concern to society as a whole and also for employers and employees as they communicate at work. You must consider the potential business liabilities and legal implications resulting from the use of profanity that may offend others or create a hostile work environment. Recognize that minimizing or eliminating profanity is another important way you must adapt your language for communicating effectively and fostering human relations in a professional setting. The accompanying Strategic Forces feature, "E-Cards Offer Greeting Alternatives," explores yet another challenge for contemporary communication, the effective use of e-cards as alternatives for traditional greetings.

Use Simple, Informal Words

Business writers prefer simple, informal words that are readily understood and less distracting than more difficult, formal words. If a receiver questions the sender's motive for using formal words, the impact of the message may be diminished. Likewise, the impact would be diminished if the receiver questioned a sender's use of simple, informal words. That distraction is unlikely, however, if the message contains good ideas that are well organized and well supported. Under these conditions, simple words enable a receiver to understand the message clearly and quickly.

To illustrate, consider the unnecessary complexity of a notice that appeared on a corporate bulletin board: "Employees impacted by the strike are encouraged to utilize the hot line number to arrange for alternative transportation to work. Should you encounter difficulties in arranging for alternative transportation to work, please contact your immediate supervisor." A simple, easy-to-read revision would be, "If you can't get to work, call the hot line or your supervisor."[8] For further illustration, note the added clarity of the following words:

Formal Words	Informal Words
terminate	end
procure	get
remunerate	pay
corroborate	support
utilize	use

Using words that have more than two or three syllables when they are the most appropriate is acceptable. However, you should avoid regular

E-Cards Offer Greeting Alternatives

They are fun and clever, and better yet, they arrive instantly. Electronic greeting cards are widely available on the Internet, many for free, and can be sent easily to individuals or groups.

Blue Mountain is the largest electronic greeting card site on the Web and has plenty of cards to choose from. Beginning as a free site, Blue Mountain now offers a limited free selection along with an extensive assortment of greetings on a subscription basis. You can add music and pick from greetings that range from sentimental to businesslike or customize your message. Another feature is the ability to send cards in several languages—a real plus in a world that is becoming ever smaller.

Many card sites allow the sender to "attach" gifts; the Hallmark web site allows customers to send free e-cards and include a gift certificate to one of nearly 300 merchants. Distinctiveness has led to the growing popularity of Regards.com. As with some other sites, you can use your own photos and images to create an original design or select one of their uniquely animated cards, some of which are so elaborate that they are very much like sending tiny cartoons. Attempting to become the number one web stop, Amazon.com also has electronic greeting cards, perhaps some of the best on the Web. Another site called Digital Greetings allows you to create a

card in a simple, step-by-step process. You pick out illustrations, headlines, and colors, with the result being a card that you created yourself.[10] Perfect Greetings is able to offer free card service because it is sustained by its business sponsors. To send a card, customers must click on one of three randomly generated ads and read about a business offering while their card processing is completed.

Of course, if you're really international, you should check out the Digital Postcard. A wide array of languages is available, including Arabic and Turkish, and cards can be customized from a database of more than 1,000 photos. You can also include a link to a web page with your card, as well as upload a music or voice file.

In response to worries about the network bandwidth that electronic greeting cards might consume, some sites sell compressed cards that load faster and take up fewer computer resources. Managers, however, are typically more concerned with lost worker productivity that may result

as more workers gain access to the Internet. Companies that offer digital greeting cards, however, maintain that these products have a place in business. For example, they can be used to inform clients of an office move or thank clients in a less costly, faster manner than with the traditional alternative of addressing and mailing company cards.[11]

Application

Visit the following greeting card sites:

http://www.bluemountain.com/

http://www.regards.com/

http://www.cards.amazon.com/

http://www.digitalgreetings.com/

http://www.perfectgreetings.com

http://www.hallmark.com

Rate the sites according to their suitability for sending business greetings. What considerations should be made when deciding whether to send an electronic greeting card rather than a traditional card or short typed message to a client or business associate?

COURTESY, HALLMARK CARDS, INC.

use of a long, infrequently used word when a simpler, more common word has the same meaning. Professionals in some fields often use specialized terminology, often referred to as **jargon**, when communicating with colleagues in the same field. In this case, the audience is likely to understand the words, and using the jargon saves time. However, when communicating with people outside the field, professionals should select simple, common words to convey messages.

You should build your vocabulary so that you can use just the right word for expressing an idea and can understand what others have said. Just remember the purpose of business messages is not to advertise a knowledge of infrequently used words but to transmit a clear and tactful message. For the informal communication practiced in business, use simple words instead of more complicated words that have the same meaning.

Communicate Concisely

Concise communication includes all relevant details in the fewest possible words. Abraham Lincoln's two-minute Gettysburg Address is a premier example of concise communication. Mark Twain alluded to the *skill* needed to write concisely when he said, "I would have written a shorter book if I had had time."

Some executives have reported that they read memos that are two paragraphs long but may only skim or discard longer ones. Yet, it's clear that this survival technique can lead to a vital message being discarded or misread. Concise writing is essential for information workers struggling to handle the avalanche of information created by technological advances and other factors. Concise messages save time and money for both the sender and the receiver. The receiver's attention is directed toward the important details and is not distracted by excessive words and details.

The following techniques will produce concise messages:

- *Eliminate redundancies.* A **redundancy** is a phrase in which one word unnecessarily repeats an idea contained in an accompanying word. "Exactly identical" and "past history" are redundant because both words have the same meaning; only "identical" and "history" are needed. To correct "3 p.m. in the afternoon," say "3 p.m." or "three o'clock in the afternoon." A few of the many redundancies in business writing are shown in the following list. Be conscious of redundancies in your speech and writing patterns.

Critical Thinking

What are other ways you can build your vocabulary?

Critical Thinking

What is the difference between conciseness and brevity?

Critical Thinking

In groups, generate a list of wordy phrases you have heard. Describe ways to simplify ideas in writing and speaking.

Redundancies to Avoid	
Needless repetition:	advance forward, it goes without saying, best ever, cash money, important essentials, each and every, dollar amount, hot water heater, looking forward to the future, pick and choose
Unneeded modifiers:	actual experience, advanced planning, brief summary, complete stop, collaborate together, disappear from sight, honest truth, trickle down, month of January, pair of twins, personal opinion, red in color, severe crisis
Repeated acronyms:	ATM Machine, PIN Number, SAT tests, SIC code

Critical Thinking

How can the effective communicator restate without being redundant?

Redundancy is not to be confused with repetition. In a sentence or paragraph, you may need to use a certain word again. When repetition serves a specific purpose, it is not an error. Redundancy serves no purpose and *is* an error.

- **Use active voice to reduce the number of words.** Passive voice typically adds unnecessary words, such as prepositional phrases. Compare the sentence length in each of these examples:

Passive Voice	Active Voice
The documentation was written by the systems analyst.	The systems analyst wrote the documentation.
The loan approval procedures were revised by the loan officer.	The loan officer revised the loan approval procedures.

- **Review the main purpose of your writing and identify relevant details needed for the receiver to understand and take necessary action.** More information is not necessarily better information. You may be so involved and perhaps so enthusiastic about your message that you believe the receiver needs to know everything that you know. Or perhaps you just need to devote more time to audience analysis and empathy.

Critical Thinking

Nonconcise letters sometimes begin with an "empty acknowledgment." Give some examples of such openings.

- **Eliminate clichés that are often wordy and not necessary to understand the message.** For example, "Thank you for your letter," "I am writing to," "May I take this opportunity," "It has come to my attention," and "We wish to inform you" only delay the major purpose of the message.

- **Do not restate ideas that are sufficiently implied.** Notice how the following sentences are improved when ideas are implied. The revised sentences are concise, yet the meaning is not affected.

Wordy	Concise
She <u>took</u> the web design course and <u>passed</u> it.	She passed the web design course.
The editor <u>checked</u> the manuscript and <u>found</u> three glaring errors.	The editor found three glaring errors in the manuscript.

Critical Thinking

Attention to careful revision of the first draft will eliminate most wordiness.

- **Shorten sentences by using suffixes or prefixes, making changes in word form, or substituting precise words for phrases.** In the following examples, the expressions on the right provide useful techniques for saving space and being concise. However, the examples in the left column are not grammatically incorrect or forbidden from use. In fact, sometimes their use provides just the right *emphasis*.

Wordy	Concise
She was a manager <u>who was courteous to others</u>.	She was a <u>courteous</u> manager.
He waited <u>in an impatient manner</u>.	He waited <u>impatiently</u>.
The production manager disregards methods considered <u>to be of no use</u>.	The production manager disregards <u>useless</u> methods.
Sales staff <u>with high energy levels</u> . . .	<u>Energetic</u> sales staff . . .
. . . arranged <u>according to the alphabet</u>	Arranged <u>alphabetically</u> . . .

- *Use a compound adjective.* By using the compound adjective, you can reduce the number of words required to express your ideas and thus save the reader a little time.

Wordy	Concise
The report that was <u>up to date</u>. . .	The <u>up-to-date</u> report . . .
B. J. Fox, <u>who holds the highest rank</u> at Neal Enterprises, is . . .	B. J. Fox, the <u>highest-ranking</u> official at Neal Enterprises, is . . .
His policy of <u>going slowly</u> was well received.	His <u>go-slow</u> policy was well received.

Project a Positive, Tactful Tone

Being adept at communicating negative information will give you the confidence you need to handle sensitive situations in a positive, constructive manner. The following suggestions reduce the sting of an unpleasant thought:

- *State ideas using positive language.* Rely mainly on positive words—words that speak of what can be done instead of what cannot be done, of the pleasant instead of the unpleasant. In each of the following pairs, both sentences are sufficiently clear, but the positive words in the improved sentences make the message more diplomatic and promote positive human relations.

Negative Tone	Positive Tone
<u>Don't forget</u> to submit your time and expense report. . . .	Remember to submit your time and expense report. . . .
We <u>cannot</u> ship your order until you send us full specifications.	You will receive your order as soon as you send us full specifications.
You <u>neglected</u> to indicate the specifications for Part No. 332-3.	Please send the complete specifications for Part No. 332-3 so your order can be finalized.

Positive words are normally preferred, but sometimes negative words are more effective in achieving the dual goals of *clarity* and positive *human relations*. For example, addition of negative words can sharpen a contrast (and thus increase clarity):

> Use an oil-based paint for this purpose; do not use latex.
>
> Final copies are to be printed using a laser printer; ink-jet print is not acceptable.

Critical Thinking

Think of examples of negative language you have heard (or used) that could easily be stated using positive words.

When pleasant, positive words have not brought desired results, negative words may be justified. For example, a supervisor may have used positive words to instruct an accounts payable clerk to verify that the unit price on the invoice matches the unit price on the purchase order. Discovering later that the clerk is not verifying the invoices correctly, the supervisor may use negative words such as "*No,* that's the *wrong way,*" demonstrate once more, and explain. If the clerk continues to complete the task incorrectly, the supervisor may feel justified in using even stronger negative words. The clerk may need the emotional jolt that negative words can provide. Thus, when the purpose is to sharpen contrast or when positive words have not evoked the desired reaction, use negative words.

- *Avoid using second person when stating negative ideas.* Avoid second person for presenting unpleasant ideas, but use second person for presenting pleasant ideas. Note the following examples:

Critical Thinking

What advice would you give a businessperson for balancing tact and assertiveness?

Pleasant idea (second person preferred)	*You* keyed a perfect copy.	*The person will appreciate the emphasis placed on his/her excellent performance.*
Unpleasant idea (third person preferred)	This page contains numerous mistakes.	*"You made numerous mistakes on this page" would direct attention to the person who made the mistakes and would not be diplomatic.*

However, use of second person with negative ideas is an acceptable technique on the rare occasions when the purpose is to jolt the receiver by emphasizing a negative.

- *Use passive voice to convey negative ideas.* Presenting an unpleasant thought emphatically (as active verbs do) makes human relations difficult. Compare the tone of the following negative thoughts written in active and passive voices:

Active Voice	Passive Voice Preferred for Negative Ideas
Saburo did not proofread this bid proposal carefully.	The bid proposal was not proofread carefully.
Saburo completed the job two months behind schedule.	The job was completed two months behind schedule.

Because the subject of each active sentence is the doer, the sentences are emphatic. Since the idea is negative, Saburo probably would appreciate being taken out of the picture. The passive voice sentences place more emphasis on the job than on who failed to complete it. When passive voice is used, the sentences retain the essential ideas, but the ideas seem less irritating. For negative ideas, use passive voice. Just as emphasis on negatives hinders human relations, emphasis on positives promotes human relations. Which sentence makes the positive idea more vivid?

Passive Voice	Active Voice Preferred for Positive Ideas
The job was completed ahead of time.	Saburo completed the job ahead of schedule.

Because "Saburo" is the subject of the active-voice sentence, the receiver can easily envision the action. Pleasant thoughts deserve emphasis. For presenting positive ideas, use active voice. Active and passive voice are discussed in greater detail in the "Write Powerful Sentences" section in Chapter 4.

Critical Thinking

Compose another sentence that uses subjunctive mood to de-emphasize a negative idea.

- **Use the subjunctive mood.** Sometimes, the tone of a message can be improved by switching to the subjunctive mood. **Subjunctive sentences** speak of a wish, necessity, doubt, or conditions contrary to fact and employ such conditional expressions as *I wish, as if, could, would, might,* and *wish*. In the following examples, the sentence in the right column conveys a negative idea in positive language, which is more diplomatic than negative language.

Negative Tone	Subjunctive Mood Conveys Positive Tone
I <u>cannot</u> approve your transfer to our overseas operation.	If positions <u>were</u> available in our overseas operation, I <u>would</u> approve your transfer.
I am <u>unable</u> to accept your invitation to speak at the November meeting.	I <u>could</u> accept your invitation to speak at the November meeting only if our scheduled speaker <u>were</u> to cancel.
I <u>cannot</u> accept the committee's recommendation.	I <u>wish</u> I <u>could</u> accept the committee's recommendation.

Legal & Ethical Constraints

Sentences in subjunctive mood often include a reason that makes the negative idea seem less objectionable, and thus improves the tone. Tone is important, but clarity is even more important. The revised sentence in each of the preceding pairs sufficiently *implies* the unpleasant idea without stating it directly. If for any reason a writer suspects the implication is not sufficiently strong, a direct statement in negative terms is preferable.

- **Include a pleasant statement in the same sentence.** A pleasant idea is included in the following examples to improve the tone:

Negative Tone	Positive Tone
Your personnel ratings for communication ability and teams skills were satisfactory.	Your personnel ratings for communication ability and teams skills were satisfactory, <u>but your rate for technical competence was excellent</u>.
Because of increased taxes and insurance, you are obligated to increase your monthly payments.	Because of increased taxes and insurance, your monthly payments will increase by $50; however, <u>your home has increased in value at the monthly rate of $150</u>.

Step 4: Organizing the Message

Objective 4

Recognize the importance of organizing a message before writing the first draft.

Legal & Ethical Constraints

After you have identified the specific ways you must adapt the message to your specific audience, you are ready to organize your message. In a discussion of communication, the word organize means "the act of dividing a topic into parts and arranging them in an appropriate sequence." Before undertaking this process, you must be convinced that the message is the right message—that it is complete, accurate, fair, reasonable, ethical, and logical. If it doesn't meet these standards, it should not be sent. Good organization and good writing or speaking cannot be expected to compensate for a bad decision.

If you organize and write simultaneously, the task seems hopelessly complicated. Writing is much easier if questions about the organization of the message are answered first: What is the purpose of the message, what is the receiver's likely reaction, and should the message begin with the main point? Once these decisions have been made, you can concentrate on expressing ideas effectively.

Outline to Benefit the Sender and the Receiver

When a topic is divided into parts, some parts will be recognized as central ideas and the others as minor ideas (details). The process of identifying these ideas and arranging them in the right sequence is known as **outlining**. Outlining *before* communicating provides numerous benefits:

- *Encourages accuracy and brevity.* Outlining reduces the chance of leaving out an essential idea or including an unessential idea.
- *Permits concentration on one phase at a time.* Having focused separately on (a) the ideas that need to be included, (b) the distinction between major and minor ideas, and (c) the sequence of ideas, total concentration can now be focused on the next challenge—expressing.
- *Saves time in structuring ideas.* With questions about which ideas to include and their proper sequence already answered, little time is lost in moving from one point to the next.

SPOTLIGHT COMMUNICATOR

Openness a "Hallmark" at Hallmark Cards, Inc.

An extensive communications audit occurred at Hallmark Cards a few years ago. Despite the fact that Hallmark was one of the top brand names in the United States for decades, greeting card sales in the early and mid-90s lagged as time-conscious consumers turned to alternative means of keeping in touch. Lower-cost long-distance telephone service, increased use of e-mail, and e-card options provided viable alternatives to traditional greeting cards. In addition, a changing retail landscape saw specialty card shops giving way to mega-retailers and deep-discount shops. Due to Hallmark's private ownership and highly competitive retail/intellectual property environment, senior management had traditionally shared little with employees in terms of company finances, business plans, and market challenges. Management's guarded approach to communication had resulted in declining trust levels among employees. Director of Corporate Communications Dean T. Rodenbough knew that changes were needed in marketing strategy and in internal communications.

With economic conditions showing that significant changes were imminent, Rodenbough and other senior managers knew they had to both prepare and rally the work force. Initial focus group research with customers, vendors, suppliers, subsidiary leadership and employees helped Hallmark identify behaviors that it wanted to integrate into its "new" corporate culture. The communication audit, which took approximately 12 months to complete, resulted in the formation of several action steps designed to assist the company in communicating openly, directly, and honestly.

One change implemented at Hallmark was to share with all employees the company's long-term vision, strategy, and financial goals. Another change was to focus more closely on internal communication tools. Publications produced primarily for external audiences had required extensive support from the editorial and design staff, limiting the resources available for key internal communication programs. As part of the transformed culture, Hallmark repositioned its long-standing *Noon News* employee newsletter to devote space to candid commentary about the communication audit and its findings. An additional change

COURTESY, HALLMARK CARDS, INC.

affected information shared over the company's intranet; now employees have access to information on monthly revenue and earnings results and other performance measures. An intranet manager and an online editor were also hired to enhance the intranet's appeal. Note the scope of valuable information communicated to employees through the Hallmark intranet and a sample issue of *Noon News* touting a shared marketing campaign with Starbucks.

Hallmark achieved its goals for operating profit during this period of cultural change. While the company's improved earnings could not be attributed completely to improved internal communication, Hallmark has a clear understanding of the vital role communication plays in the successful company performance.[12]

Dean Rodenbough, Director of Corporate Communications, Hallmark Corporation

http://www.hallmark.com

Refer to ShowCASE, Part 3, at the end of the chapter for advice from Hallmark on saying just the right thing.

Hallmark uses its intranet and employee newsletter, *Noon News*, to communicate valuable information to employees.

Critical Thinking

How can the business communicator make sure the message outline is a time saver and not a time waster?

- ***Provides a psychological lift.*** The feeling of success gained in preparing the outline increases confidence that the next step—writing or speaking—will be successful, too.
- ***Facilitates emphasis and de-emphasis.*** Although each sentence makes its contribution to the message, some sentences need to stand out more vividly in the receiver's mind than others. An effective outline ensures that important points will appear in emphatic positions.

The preceding benefits derived from outlining are sender oriented. Because a message has been well outlined, receivers benefit, too:

- The message is more concise and accurate.
- Relationships between ideas are easier to distinguish and remember.
- Reaction to the message and its sender is more likely to be positive.

A receiver's reaction to a message is strongly influenced by the sequence in which ideas are presented. A beginning sentence or an ending sentence is in an emphatic position. (Other emphasis techniques are explained later in this chapter.) Throughout this text, you will see that outlining (organizing) is important.

Sequence Ideas to Achieve Desired Goals

Objective **5**

Select the appropriate message outline (deductive or inductive) for developing messages to achieve the desired response.

When planning your communication, you should strive for an outline that will serve you in much the same way a blueprint serves a builder or an itinerary serves a traveler. Organizing your message first will ensure that your ideas are presented clearly and logically and all vital components are included. To facilitate your determining an appropriate sequence for a business document or presentation, follow the three-step process illustrated in Figure 3-3. This process involves your answering the following questions in this order:

1. *What is the central idea of the message?* Think about the *reason* you are writing or speaking—the first step in the communication process. What is your purpose—to extend a job offer, decline an invitation, or seek support for an innovative project? The purpose is the central idea of your message. You might think of it as a message condensed into a one-sentence telegram.

2. *What is the most likely receiver reaction to the message?* Ask, "If I were the one receiving the message I am preparing to send, what would *my* reaction be?" Because you would react with pleasure to good news and displeasure to bad news, you can reasonably assume a receiver's reaction would be similar. Recall the dual goals of a communicator: clarity and effective human relations. By considering anticipated receiver reaction, you build goodwill with the receiver. Almost every message will fit into one of four categories of anticipated receiver reaction: (1) pleasure, (2) displeasure, (3) interest but neither pleasure nor displeasure, or (4) no interest, as shown in Figure 3-3.

Critical Thinking

Use the deductive sequence for positive and routine messages; the inductive sequence for negative and persuasive messages.

3. *In view of the predicted receiver reaction, should the central idea be listed first in the outline; or should it be listed as one of the last items?* When a message begins with the major idea, the sequence of ideas is called **deductive**. When a message withholds the major idea until accompanying details and explanations have been presented, the sequence is called **inductive**.

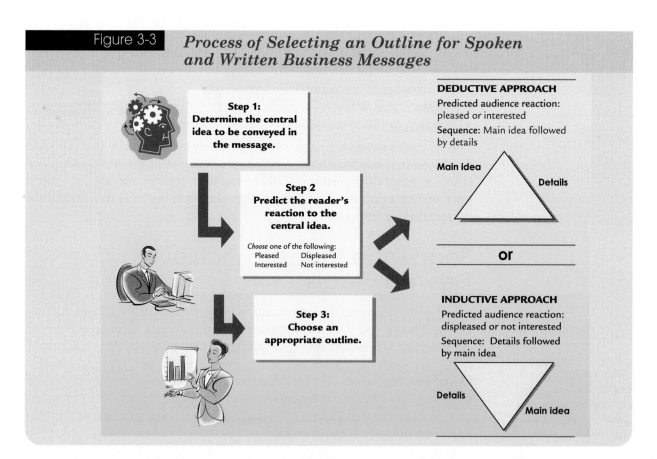

Figure 3-3

Process of Selecting an Outline for Spoken and Written Business Messages

Critical Thinking

In groups, discuss the appropriate sequence for a message (a) accepting an invitation to speak, (b) denying credit to a customer, and (c) commending an employee for exemplary performance.

Consider the receiver to determine whether to use the inductive or deductive sequence. If a receiver might be antagonized by the main idea in a deductive message, antagonism can be avoided by leading up to the main idea (making the message inductive). If a sender wants to encourage receiver involvement (to generate a little concern about where the details are leading), the inductive approach is recommended. Inductive organization can be especially effective if the main idea confirms the conclusion the receiver has drawn from the preceding details—a cause is worthy of support, an applicant should be interviewed for a job, a product/service should be selected, and so on. As you learn in later chapters about writing letters, memorandums, and e-mail messages and about planning spoken communications, you will comprehend the benefits of using the appropriate outline for each receiver reaction:

Deductive Order (main idea first)	Inductive Order (details first)
When the message will *please* the receiver	When the message will *displease* the *receiver*
When the message is *routine* (will not please nor displease)	When the receiver *may not be interested* (will need to be persuaded)

For determining the sequence of minor ideas that accompany the major idea, the following bases for idea sequence are common:

- *Time.* When writing a memo or e-mail about a series of events or a process, paragraphs proceed from the first step through the last step.
- *Space.* If a report is about geographic areas, ideas can proceed from one area to the next until all areas have been discussed.
- *Familiarity.* If a topic is complicated, the presentation can begin with a point that is known or easy to understand and proceed to progressively more difficult points.
- *Importance.* In analytical reports in which major decision-making factors are presented, the factors can be presented in order of most important to least important, or vice versa.
- *Value.* If a presentation involves major factors with monetary values, paragraphs can proceed from those with greatest values to those with least values, or vice versa.

The same organizational patterns are recommended for written and spoken communication. These patterns are applicable in memorandums, e-mail messages, and reports as well as in letters.

Summary

1. **Identify the purpose of the message and the appropriate channel.** Writing is a systematic process that begins by determining the purpose of the message (central idea) and identifying how the central idea will affect the receiver. In view of its effect on the receiver, you can determine the appropriate channel for sending a particular message (e.g., face-to-face, telephone, letter/memo, e-mail, voice mail, or fax).

2. **Develop clear perceptions of the audience to enhance the impact of the communication and human relations.** Before you compose the first draft, commit to overcoming perceptual barriers that will limit your ability to see an issue from multiple perspectives and thus plan an effective message. Then, consider all you know about the receiver, including age, economic level, educational/occupational background, culture, existing relationship, expectations, and his/her needs.

3. **Apply techniques for adapting messages to the audience, including strategies for communicating ethically and responsibly.** The insights you gain from seeking to understand your receiver will allow you to adapt the message to fit the receiver's needs. Developing concise, sensitive messages that focus on the receiver's point of view will build and protect goodwill and demand the attention of the receiver. Communicating ethically and responsibly involves stating information truthfully and tactfully, eliminating embellishments or exaggerations, supporting viewpoints with objective facts from credible sources, and designing honest graphics.

4. **Recognize the importance of organizing a message before writing the first draft.** Outlining involves identifying the appropriate sequence of pertinent ideas. Outlining encourages brevity and accuracy, permits concentration on one phase at a time, saves writing time, increases confidence to complete the task, and facilitates appropriate emphasis of ideas. From a receiver's point of view, well-organized messages are easier to understand and promote a more positive attitude toward the sender.

5. **Select the appropriate message outline (deductive or inductive) for developing messages to achieve the desired response.** A part of the outlining process is deciding whether the message should be deductive (main idea first) or inductive (explanations and details first). The main idea is presented first and details follow when the receiver is expected to be pleased by the message and the message is routine and not likely to arouse a feeling of pleasure or displeasure. When the receiver can be expected to be displeased or not initially interested, explanations and details precede the main idea.

Chapter Review

1. What is the central idea of a message? What two purposes do most business messages serve? (Obj. 1)

2. Why is selecting an appropriate communication channel important to the overall effectiveness of the message? Provide two examples. (Obj. 1)

3. How does perception and audience analysis affect the communication process? What factors about the audience should you consider? (Obj. 2)

4. What considerations should be made when deciding whether to send an electronic greeting or a more traditional paper one? (Obj. 1)

5. What differences in the ideals of the older and younger generations may explain communication clashes between these groups in the workplace? (Objs. 2, 3)

6. What value is gained from cultivating a "you attitude" in spoken and written messages? Give an example of a writer- and a reader-centered message to make your point. (Obj. 3)

7. What actions must communicators take to ensure that their messages are ethical and responsible? (Obj. 3)

8. Discuss five writing techniques that enable communicators to build and protect goodwill. (Obj. 3)

9. When is the use of a euphemism appropriate? Detrimental? Under what conditions are connotative words acceptable? Why are specific words generally preferred in business writing and speaking? In what situations would general words be preferred? (Obj. 3)

10. What techniques should be followed to make business messages simple and conversational? What value is gained from this writing style? (Obj. 3)

11. Provide five guidelines for projecting a positive, tactful tone. (Obj. 3)

12. Why is conciseness valued in business communication? Provide at least three suggestions for reducing word count without sacrificing content. (Obj. 3)

13. What is involved in "organizing a message"? (Obj. 4)

14. What primary benefits does the writer gain from outlining before writing or speaking? How does the receiver benefit? (Obj. 4)

15. What three questions assist a communicator in the decision to organize a message deductively or inductively? (Obj. 5)

Digging Deeper

1. What is empathy and how does it affect business communication? How are empathy and sympathy different?

2. Explain what is meant by writing to *express* and not to *impress*.

To check your understanding of the chapter, take the practice quizzes at **http://lehman.swlearning.com** or your WebTutor course.

Focus on the Receiver's Point of View

- Present ideas from the receiver's point of view; this "you attitude" conveys a feeling that the message is specifically for the receiver.
- Give sincere compliments.

Communicate Ethically and Responsibly

- Present information as truthfully, honestly, and fairly as possible.
  - Include all information relevant to the receiver.
  - Avoid exaggerating or embellishing facts.
  - Use objective facts to support ideas.
  - Design graphics that avoid distorting facts and relationships.
- Express ideas clearly and understandably.
- State ideas tactfully and positively to preserve the receiver's self-worth and to build future relationships.

Build and Protect Goodwill

- Use euphemisms to present unpleasant thoughts politely and positively. Avoid using euphemisms when they will be taken as excessive or sarcastic.
- Avoid using condescending or demeaning expressions.
- Rely mainly on denotative words. Use connotative words that will elicit a favorable reaction, are easily understood, and are appropriate for the setting.
- Choose vivid words that add clarity and interest to your message.
- Use bias-free language.
  - Do not use the pronoun *he* when referring to a group of people that may include women or *she* when a group may include men.
  - Avoid referring to men and women in stereotyped roles and occupations, using gender-biased occupational titles, or differentiating genders in an occupation.

- Avoid referring to groups (based on gender, race and ethnicity, age, religion, and disability) in stereotypical and insensitive ways.
- Do not emphasize race and ethnicity, age, religion, or disability when these factors are not relevant.

Convey a Positive, Tactful Tone

- Rely mainly on positive words that speak of what can be done instead of what cannot be done, of the pleasant instead of the unpleasant. Use negative words when the purpose is to sharpen contrast or when positive words have not evoked the desired reaction.
- Use second person and active voice to emphasize a pleasant idea. For better human relations, avoid using second person for presenting negative ideas. Instead, use third person and passive voice to de-emphasize the unpleasant thought.
- Consider stating an unpleasant thought in the subjunctive mood.

Use Simple, Contemporary Language

- Avoid clichés and outdated expressions that make your language seem unnatural and unoriginal.
- Use simple words for informal business messages instead of using more complicated words that have the same meaning.

Write Concisely

- Do not use redundancies—unnecessary repetition of an idea.
- Use active voice to shorten sentences.
- Avoid unnecessary details; omit ideas that can be implied.
- Shorten wordy sentences by using suffixes or prefixes, making changes in word form, or substituting precise words for phrases.

Translation Challenges

When traveling abroad, Americans expect—in fact depend on—the people in the countries they visit to speak English. Often much gets mangled in the translations. In Budapest, Hungary, for example, a sign outside a hotel elevator reports: "The lift is being fixed for the next day. During that time we regret that you will be unbearable." A Bangkok, Thailand dry cleaning establishment urges customers to "drop your trousers here for best results."[13] While humorous, such butchered translations betray a serious problem: The United States remains dependent on others knowing the English language. We are linguistically underdeveloped when compared to other nations.

 InfoTrac College Edition. Access http://www.info-trac. thomsonlearning.com to read about how to minimize language barriers and avoid miscommunication at an international convention. Search for the following article that is available in full text:

Braley, S. J. F. (1999, June). Eliminating language barriers. *Meetings & Conventions*, 30.

Write a 100-word abstract of the article, reflecting the important ideas presented.

 Text Support Web Site. Visit http://lehman. swlearning.com to explore the translation of English to Spanish. Refer to Chapter 3's Electronic Café that links you to a web site that translates words from English to Spanish, revealing the translation in print and audibly. Use the tool to translate a passage that your instructor will provide.

 WebTutor Advantage. Go to your WebTutor site; your instructor will have translated it into a language other than English. Visit the following web site that will assist you in determining what language your WebTutor is now in:

http://www.xrce.xerox.com/competencies/content-analysis/tools/guesser

Once you have determined the language in use, e-mail your instructor with the answer.

 Professional Power Pak. Access your PPP CD for a translation tool that allows you to hear and read vocabulary from a number of languages and to gain knowledge about the cultures of various countries.

Activities

1. Empathetic Attitude (Obj. 2)

Identify possible communication problems created because of a manager's lack of empathy when communicating to employees. Select a spokesperson to share your group's ideas.

a. Hurriedly as the store closed on Thursday evening, the store manager told sales clerks,

"Oh, by the way, it's time for our annual inventory. I want you here Sunday at 7 a.m. sharp and plan to stay until. . . . And one other thing. Don't bother embarrassing yourself by giving me some flimsy excuse for not being able to work. I don't want to hear it. If I don't have this job done by Monday morning, the district manager will have my head. End of conversation."

b. A manager for a U.S. firm, who has been transferred to the company's office in Japan, provides the following message to launch the marketing/production team's work on a new product:

"We really need to put our noses to the grindstone to get this new product out and onto the shelves. I've been burning the midnight oil with my people in R&D, and I have some new ideas that need to be implemented before the competition catches on and the cat's out of the bag. So everybody get to work and hit the ground running. Keep me posted on your progress, and remember, my door is always open. Everybody got it?"

c. After months of uncertainty at Ramsey, Inc., a corporate official visits an office of the national corporation with the following response to concerned questions by mostly lower-wage technical and support staff regarding layoffs and office closures:

"We are realigning our resources company-wide to be more competitive in the marketplace. Our stock has been declining at an unpromising rate, but we are taking steps to ensure future market viability. Restructuring has begun at several levels. Corporate is aware of your concerns and will continue having these meetings to provide a forum for dialogue."

d. After several trips to Mexico and nearly a year of negotiation to set up a joint venture, a U.S. partner faxed the final contract to the Mexican chief executive officer. The final contract included a request that the CEO personally guarantee the loan, a stipulation that had not been discussed previously.

2. **Appropriate Outline and Channel (Objs. 1, 2, 5)**

Complete the following analysis to determine whether a deductive or an inductive outline is appropriate for the following situations. Identify the channel you believe would be most appropriate for conveying this message; be prepared to justify your answer. Use the format shown in the following example.

Visit the Interactive Study Center at **http://lehman. swlearning.com** for a downloadable version of this activity.

- *Situation* The annual merit raise has increased to 5 percent.
- *Recommended channel* Mailed memo or e-mail message; pleasant information that should reach all employees in a timely manner.
- *Central idea* Inform employees of an increase in annual merit raise.
- *Likely receiver reaction* Pleased.
- *Appropriate outline (deductive or inductive)* Deductive.

a. To company from customer: An incorrect part ordered from a web site must be exchanged. No return instructions were provided with the invoice.

b. Quality manager to production manager: Discontinue production until a flaw just discovered in the production process has been corrected.

c. Seller to customer: Computer World is promoting a special warranty plan to its customers who recently purchased a home computer system.

d. Seller to customer: We cannot offer a refund on your laptop; however, we can repair it at our cost.

e. CEO to regional managers: Christmas bonuses will not be awarded because of sluggish Christmas sales.

f. Regional manager to employees: Christmas bonuses will not be awarded because of sluggish Christmas sales.

g. U.S. CEO to Canadian business partner: Delivery of promised shipment will be delayed due to inability to obtain raw products from a war-torn country.

h. Business to client: Ask to complete a survey instrument about the quality and type of services rendered.

i. Management to employees: A meeting to learn about the company's new stock option plan is announced.

j. Seller to customer: Refunds are being distributed to customers who purchased the Model DX laptop, which had a faulty board.

k. Seller to customer: Because of an increase in fuel cost, the company's price structure will increase beginning June 1.

l. Assistant to manager: The assistant has been asked by his manager to research an issue and respond immediately while the manager is still on the telephone with the customer.

3. **Audience Analysis (Obj. 2)**

Write a brief analysis of the audience for each of the situations presented in Activity 2.

4. **Receiver-Centered Messages (Obj. 3)**

Revise the following sentences to emphasize the reader's viewpoint and the "you" attitude.

Visit the Interactive Study Center at **http://lehman. swlearning.com** for a downloadable version of this activity.

a. We're requesting that all vacationers call us at 1-800-555-1314 on weekdays from 9:00 to 5:00 p.m. Central Standard Time to confirm reservations.

b. I think you could improve your marketability if you worked on developing your Internet skills.

c. To enable us to better serve the community, we ask that you help us understand your opinions on the parks project.

d. I give you permission to take an extra vacation day because of your performance on the Johnson account.

e. Human Resources requires all employees who work with dangerous goods or hazardous materials to have a complete physical every year.

5. **Statements that Build and Protect Goodwill (Obj. 3)**

Revise the following sentences to eliminate a tone that will damage human relations. Identify the specific weakness in each sentence.

Visit the Interactive Study Center at **http://lehman. swlearning. com** for a downloadable version of this activity.

a. Management expresses appreciation for all the maintenance engineers.

b. The senator's vote for the bill containing revenue enhancements does not violate her campaign pledge.

c. An ambulance chaser arrived at the scene moments after the crash.

d. As leader of this work team, I suggest we change our meeting time to 9 a.m.

e. The corporate watchdogs are planning a visit next week.

f. A presenter should never be surprised by the reaction of his audience.

g. Cheryl Wasson, a lady doctor, recently joined the staff at Forrest General.

h. Our quadriplegic first-shift supervisor moves around the plant in a motorized wheelchair.

i. Obviously we had reached a Mexican standoff with the negotiations.

j. Josh Williams was recognized for his efforts.

6. **Positive, Tactful Tone (Obj. 3)**

Revise the following sentences to reduce the negative tone.

Visit the Interactive Study Center at **http://lehman. swlearning.com** for a downloadable version of this activity.

a. Do not forget the staff meeting at noon tomorrow.

b. The policyholder failed to submit his forms for adding new dependents within the 30-day time period.

c. The automatic draft will not be effective until the first of the month.

d. You neglected to inform Scott and Lin Schoenholtz of the ten-day cancellation period.

e. You cannot receive benefits until after you have been with our company for three months.

7. **Conversational Language (Obj. 3)**

Substitute fresh, original expressions for each cliché or outdated expression.

Visit the Interactive Study Center at **http://lehman. swlearning.com** for a downloadable version of this activity.

a. The team is sailing into uncharted waters with this latest ad campaign.

b. The director of marketing dropped a bomb on us in yesterday morning's staff meeting.

c. Attached please find a copy of my résumé and references.

d. Pete's graphics can't hold a candle to Mary Beth's.

e. Despite her talent and obvious potential, Kelly has pursued only McJobs since her arrival here from Florida.

f. We are in receipt of your letter of July 15.

8. **Simple Words (Obj. 3)**

Revise the following sentences using shorter, simpler words.

Visit the Interactive Study Center at **http://lehman. swlearning.com** for a downloadable version of this activity.

a. Jan's dubious disappearance from the office yesterday instigated a police investigation.

b. The voluminous tome occupied the upmost shelf in the library.

c. The attendees of the convocation concurred that it should terminate at the appointed hour.

d. We utilized an innovative device to restore the computer's video display terminal.

e. Management as well as technical and administrative personnel will be remunerated for time exceeding forty hours per week.

9. **Conciseness (Obj. 3)**

Revise the following sentences to eliminate redundancies and other wordy construction.

Visit the Interactive Study Center at **http://lehman. swlearning.com** for a downloadable version of this activity.

a. The team will follow the exact same agenda as the last meeting and will conclude at 4 p.m. this afternoon.

b. Management is certain the company will overcome this serious crisis and are looking forward to coming out ahead of the competition in the future.

c. Although some damage to the building was visible to the eye, we were directed by our attorneys not to repair or change anything until the adjuster made a damage assessment.

d. Ellen's past work history includes working as a sales clerk, waiting tables in a restaurant, and stocking shelves in a bookstore.

e. Dan was instructed to note any strange and unusual transactions completed in the recent past.

10. **Adapting the Message to the Audience (Objs. 1–3)**

Revise the following sentences by adapting the message to meet the audience's needs. Identify the specific weaknesses in each sentence

Visit the Interactive Study Center at **http://lehman. swlearning.com** for a downloadable version of this activity.

a. We want all employees to be familiar with OSHA requirements as they pertain to their job.

b. Each project manager must complete the appropriate performance evaluation forms before being awarded his raise.

c. After the recent downsizing, most employees are beginning to feel like rats on a sinking ship.

d. Jim, the male nurse on the surgical floor, is responsible for recent improvements in our schedules.

e. In relation to the new policies, many people saw management as an Indian giver.

f. Please be advised that the company's new conservative business dress policy is effective on January 1.

g. Since I look a leadership role on this project, the team's performance has improved.

h. The new production manager is a real piece of work.

i. The grapevine has it that the company shrink is putting together more tests for us to take by the end of the year.

j. You failed to revise your benefits package during the annual enrollment period; therefore, we cannot honor your request at this time.

k. Through strategic alliances and by internal expansion of programs, Jefferson & Co is seeking to develop a substantial market presence as the leading provider of management consulting services in Georgia and its neighboring states.

l. The best computers we can lease through corporate channels are horribly outdated.

m. My personal opinion is that the sales and marketing divisions should merge together.

n. The supervisor asked Jerry to go back and make revisions to the final draft of the report so the data will be completely accurate.

Applications

| Read | Think | Write | Speak | Collaborate |

1. **Diversity Awareness Strategies in Real Companies (Objs. 2–3)**

   Conduct an online search to identify strategies companies have adopted to raise their employees' awareness of diversity in the workplace. In chart form, summarize the indexes you used to locate your articles, the companies you read about, and the successful strategies they have used to promote diversity.

2. **Application of Empathy in Company Strategies (Objs. 2–3)**

   Visit the web site of a company in which you are interested to explore evidence of the company's empathy for its employees and customers/clients. Alternately, you may choose a company from Fortune's Best 100 Companies to Work For or Fortune's Most Admired Companies. In a short oral report, explain the role of empathy in the strategies you identified.

3. **Ethical Communication Practices (Obj. 3)**

   Locate the following article available in full text from InfoTrac College (**http://www.infotrac.thomsonlearning.com**)

   or perhaps from another database available through your campus library:

   Williams, D. (2002, April). Un-spun: Ethical communication practices serve the public interest, *Communication World*, p. 27.

   After reading the article, respond to the following questions:

   a. What factors have contributed to the current decline in ethical and moral practices?

   b. What is meant by the statement, "Businesses communicators aren't in the hero business"?

   c. Describe briefly the code of ethics of the International Association for Business Communication.

   d. How does this professional code relate to the general guidelines for communicating ethically and responsibly presented in the text?

| Read | Think | Write | Speak | Collaborate |

4. **Choosing Communication Channels Wisely (Obj. 1)**

   Locate the following articles available in full text from InfoTrac College (**http://www.infotrac.thomsonlearning.com**) or perhaps from another database available through your campus library:

   Gilbert, J. (2002, November). Click, call, or write? With so many ways to communicate, it's tough to know what's most appropriate for each sales situation. Here's how to choose. *Sales & Marketing Management*, 25.

   After reading the article, compile a list of the advantages and recommended use for each communication channel. Refer to Figure 3–2 on page 84 for assistance in identifying channels and information for your analysis.

   Visit the Interactive Study Center at **http://lehman.swlearning.com** for a downloadable version of this activity.

5. **Building Strong Interpersonal Skills (Objs. 1–3)**

The guidelines for adapting your message to convey sensitivity for the receiver presented in this chapter are an excellent means for building relationships and strong interpersonal skills needed in today's highly competitive global market and in diverse work teams. Identify a specific situation in your work or educational experience, or school or community organizations that illustrates the negative effects of an individual who did not consider the impact of his/her message on the receiver. Send your example to your instructor as an attachment to an e-mail message. Be prepared to discuss your idea with the class or in small groups.

| Read | Think | **Write** | Speak | Collaborate |

6. **Importance of Communication in the Information Age (Objs. 1–5)**

Locate the following article that describes communication strategies at Miller Brewing Company:

Parnell, C. L. (1996). Effective business communications: It's not just for the communication department. *Executive Speeches, 11*(2), 9–13.

Consider the following questions and prepare a short summary of the article for your instructor.

a. Why is effective business communication important in today's workplace? How will the value of business communication change in the future?

b. What suggestions are offered for writing effectively in today's information age?

c. What is your response to the executive's statement, "No one in my company writes anymore. We just send e-mails"?

d. How do legal and ethical constraints, one of the four strategic forces presented in Chapter 1, affect communication at Miller Brewing?

e. What is Miller's approach to communicating with employees? How does this approach relate to the behavioral theories presented in Chapter 2?

7. **The Fax: A Blessing and a Curse (Objs. 1, 2)**

Locate the following article available in full text from InfoTrac College (**http://www.infotrac.thomsonlearning. com**) or perhaps from another database available through your campus library:

10 rules for more efficient fax use. (2002, October). *Essential Assistant*, 3.

After reading the article, prepare an engaging flier describing efficient fax use that will be distributed to staff and posted near each fax machine.

| Read | Think | Write | **Speak** | Collaborate |

8. **Cultural Barriers to Communication (Objs. 2, 3)**

Generate a list of phrases and nonverbal expressions peculiar to your culture that a person from another culture might not understand. Share your ideas with the class in a short presentation.

9. **Sensitive Language (Objs. 2, 3)**

Interview a person with a disability to find out ways to communicate acceptably using bias-free language. Share your findings with the class in a short presentation.

| Read | Think | Write | Speak | **Collaborate** |

10. **Trickery of Illusions (Obj. 2)**

In small groups, select an illusion from the links provided at the text support site (**http://lehman. swlearning.com**) or use one provided by your instructor. Allow each member to view the illusion independently and then share his or her individual interpretation with the team. Relate this experience with the concept of perception and its effect on the communication process. Be prepared to share your ideas with the class.

11. **Contemporary Language for the Workplace (Objs. 2, 3)**

In small groups generate a list of phrases peculiar to your generation that could be confusing and inappropriate for workplace communication. Refer to Merriam-Webster's list of new words for ideas if necessary (**http://merriam-webstercollegiate.com/info/new_words.htm**). Substitute an expression that would be acceptable for use in a professional setting. Prepare a transparency or slide to aid you in presenting your list to the class.

Hallmark Tips for Writing Business Greetings

Getting and sending greeting cards makes people feel good. But the "warm fuzzy" responses that make greeting cards so effective can also make some professional types a little nervous, especially if you are used to keeping in touch through memos, phone calls, e-mail, and other less personal types of communication. If you are uneasy about using cards to stay in touch, relax; Hallmark has some helpful suggestions to help you personalize your messages and say just the right thing.

- Visit the Hallmark web site at **http://www.hallmark.com** and read "What to Say . . . and How to Say It." What advantages are offered by sending greeting card messages?
- Locate "Tips on Writing Business Greetings" on the Hallmark site. What tips did you find most helpful?

Activities

Referring to the chapter, read the Strategic Forces feature on e-cards. In a class discussion, compare the roles of traditional greeting cards and e-cards in conveying business messages. Does audience impact differ; if so, how?

Part 4 of the Hallmark ShowCASE focuses on organizational communication at Hallmark and Dean Rodenbough's views on corporate communication.

http://www.hallmark.com

Visit the text support site at **http://lehman.swlearning.com** to complete Part 4 of the Hallmark ShowCASE.

It's All in the Translation

Business people frequently communicate by exchanging documents, either printed on paper or transmitted electronically. Those with overseas clients, customers, and contacts can improve their communications dramatically by using software to translate these documents automatically. Such software is used by organizations to produce documents ranging from international correspondence and invoices to complex financial and legal documents.

Growth in the use of the Internet has boosted demand for language translation dramatically, as users around the world struggle to understand pages in languages other than their own. At the end of 2000, 47 percent of Internet users were English speakers, but this figure had dropped to 32 percent by the end of 2002. Multilingual translators allow companies to open up their web sites to everyone around the globe. The software determines the country of origin of the viewer, displays the site in appropriate language, and provides a menu for selecting an alternate language if preferred. Microsoft predicts a 300 percent increase in the demand for translation services by 2005 in part because of companies' international presence on the Internet.[14]

Translation packages are typically based on two types of bilingual dictionaries, one for word-for-word translations and another for semantic and idiomatic phrases. Speed of translation is about 20,000 words per hour with a 90 percent or higher degree of accuracy. Various web-based translation systems are available. Arguably the best known online translation system is Babel Fish, which relies on Systran software to translate pages retrieved by the AltaVista search engine.[15] Language translation software is also available for handheld computers that includes interfaces for text and speech. Users enter words as text and can have the translation returned as text or speech.[16]

Unfortunately, translation systems work best when they are customized for a particular subject area; this involves analyzing typical documents and adding common words and technical terms to the system's dictionary. Using the software to translate Internet pages, which can be about anything at all, often produces dismal results. To make matters worse, most translation systems were designed for use with high quality documents, whereas many web pages, chat rooms, and e-mail messages involve slang, colloquial language, and ungrammatical constructions. Internet users, however, typically want speed of translation, rather than quality, and are more likely to accept poor results.

It is also possible to use commercial computer-based translation facilities via the telephone, using modems and fax. Messages can be translated using a message translation service for a per-word fee. Although such services may appear costly, imagine the benefit that an organization may derive from conveying an appropriately translated message to a potential client or customer.

In a technological environment that greatly simplifies language translation, some challenges still exist. The problem is often not to translate the words, but to convey ideas across cultures. A writer from the audience's culture may be employed to take translated material and write the ideas in the local language. Experienced practitioners understand the need to consider cultural as well as linguistic differences.

Visit the text support site at **http://lehman.swlearning. com** to link to web resources related to this topic. Respond to one or more of the following activities as directed by your instructor.

1. Write a one-page summary explaining the factors that have led to the need for more translation services.

2. **GMAT** Write a one-page summary explaining the difference between word translation and culture translation. Give examples of interpretation problems that result when word translation alone is used. Provide instances when word translation would be beneficial to a company.

3. Download a free online translator and translate a sample document such as your personal web page into a target language of your choice. Ask a person who speaks the target language (preferably a native speaker) to evaluate the effectiveness of the translation. Write a one-page summary explaining the quality of the translation. Work in groups if directed by your instructor.

4. Assume that you work for a company that has just entered the Japanese market. Your company wishes to translate correspondence, promotional materials, and invoices into the Japanese language. Using the sites listed above as starting points, visit four sites of organizations that offer translation and interpretation services. Prepare a two-page written report that (1) compares the services offered by each organization and the accompanying costs, and (2) recommends the one your company should use for its translation services.

5. **GMAT** Research the two software translation programs mentioned in this case. Prepare a chart that summarizes the capabilities and features available with each. Write a recommendation for the superior product.

Video Case

Black Diamond Equipment, Ltd.: Working Together

Black Diamond Equipment, Ltd., located at the base of the Wasatch Mountains in Salt Lake City, Utah, is an employee-owned company made up of climbers and backcountry skiers who work together to design and produce climbing and mountaineering equipment.

According to Black Diamond's employment web site (**http://www.bdel.com/about/working.html**), "At BD, we believe good ideas are not restricted to just the best climbers or hottest backcountry rippers; the glue that binds us together is that we live, breathe and dream these sports." Among the products Black Diamond produces are carabiners, climber-protection and belay devices, and ice equipment.

At each of the links, you will find pictures, information on getting started, equipment used for each sport, articles, and favorite trips and routes described by Black Diamond (BD) employees, who not only work together but also often climb and ski together. BD's Quality Policy, translated into 14 languages and posted throughout the company reads: "To make the best climbing and backcountry ski equipment in the world."

View the video segment about Black Diamond Equipment, Ltd., and accompanying activities on WebTutor or your Professional Power Pak CD.

Discussion Questions

1. In the way they develop products, how do BD team members illustrate the Chapter 3 communication principle "Focus on the Receiver's [Customer's] Point of View"?

2. What would you suggest are contributing factors to the successful use of teams at BD?

3. What example can you describe from your life experience—with names omitted—that illustrates the quote at the end of the video segment? ("The reason people fail at a job is usually NOT because they lack technical skills . . . They fail because they can't work as part of a team." *AT&T Resources for New Business*)

Activities

1. Complete the "Working Together" self-discovery exercise by David West at **http://www.theworkingmanager.com** —"the global community for learning about management."

2. Compare your "Results Profile" with explanations provided at this online management learning center, especially the (a) explanations of profile names and (b) roles, skills, and muscles.

3. Write a brief analysis of the insight you have gained from this self-discovery activity. Identify your team strength(s) and describe how you are similar or dissimilar to the three categories of information provided about your strength(s): (a) "What are those with your strengths like?" (b) "What are those with your strengths good at?" and (c) "What are those with your strengths not so good at?" Include a copy of your "Results Profile" with your analysis.

4

Preparing Spoken and Written Messages

Objectives *When you have completed Chapter 4, you will be able to:*

1 Apply techniques for developing effective sentences and unified and coherent paragraphs.

2 Identify factors affecting readability and revise messages to improve readability.

3 Prepare visually appealing documents that grab the receiver's attention and increase comprehension.

4 Revise and proofread a message for content, organization, and style; mechanics; and format and layout.

SECURITIES AND EXCHANGE COMMISSION PROMOTES READER-FRIENDLY DISCLOSURES

When deciding how to invest one's money, being able to accurately interpret information in a company's financial prospectus is critical. This task has not always been easy, since the concepts discussed can be quite complex and the language very complicated. In 1998, the Securities and Exchange Commission (SEC) took a giant step toward assuring readability of the all-important financial prospectus.

The SEC requirements specify the use of reader-friendly plain English in companies' investment prospectuses. An issuing company is directed to draft the prospectus with the uninformed shareholder in mind. Guidelines include the use of shorter sentences and paragraphs; concrete, everyday language; active voice; and tabular presentation of complicated information whenever possible. Bullet lists are recommended when information is embedded in paragraphs, and wider margins are specified to aid in visual appeal. The guidelines also specify the avoidance of obscure business jargon and multiple negatives. Risk factors must be presented concretely and concisely and provide enough information to allow an investor to assess the degree of risk.

Mastering the simplification of technical documents can present a significant learning curve. While the SEC's plain English requirements initially caused developmental delays for some companies, subsequent filings have typically gone much more smoothly. The general response from consumers is that prospectuses are better.

Prudential Insurance Co. of America distinguished itself as one of the first companies to comply with the SEC requirements for plain English. In addition to simplifying its prospectuses, Prudential explains the product with liberal use of graphics, colors, summaries, large type, an index, and captions. Metropolitan Life Insurance Company's overhauled report features characters from the "Peanuts" comic strip to illustrate key points. Boldface type, charts, and sidebars help make the prospectus more interesting and easier for customers to understand.[1]

A spokesperson for the SEC emphasized that writing in plain English doesn't mean writing with less substance. The Commission's intent is not for issuers to "dumb down" their prospectuses. The overall idea behind requiring plain English is to try to make prospectuses less intimidating for the average reader, with the hope that individuals making investments will be more likely to read and study shorter, more readable documents.[2] You will learn to apply specific techniques for writing reader-friendly documents as you complete this chapter. Specifically, you will focus on revising your message for vividness, clarity, conciseness, and readability and on following systematic proofreading procedures.

http://www.sec.gov

See ShowCASE, Part 2, on page 135 for Spotlight Communicator R. D. Saenz, controller of Air Transport International.

Objective 1

Apply techniques for developing effective sentences and unified and coherent paragraphs.

In Chapter 3, you read about the importance of using a systematic process to develop business messages. Figure 3-1 in the preceding chapter outlines the six steps in the development of an effective business message. You have already learned about the first four steps:

Step 1: Determine the purpose and select a channel
Step 2: Envision the audience
Step 3: Adapt the message to the audience
Step 4: Organize the message

In this chapter, you will learn about the remaining two important steps in the systematic communication process.

Step 5: Prepare the first draft
Step 6: Revise and proofread for accuracy and desired impact

Effectively capturing your ideas for various business communication situations involves skillful use of language and careful attention to accuracy and readability issues.

Prepare the First Draft

Once you have determined whether the message should be presented deductively (main idea first) or inductively (explanation and details first) and have planned the logical sequence of minor points, you are ready to begin composing the message.

Normally, writing rapidly (with intent to rewrite certain portions if necessary) is better than slow, deliberate writing (with intent to avoid any need for rewriting portions). The latter approach can be frustrating and can reduce the quality of the finished work. Time is wasted in thinking of one way to express an idea, discarding it either before or after it is written, waiting for new inspiration, and rereading preceding sentences.

Concentrating on getting your ideas down as quickly as you can is an efficient approach to writing. During this process, remember you are preparing a draft and not the final copy. If you are composing at the computer, you can quickly and easily revise your draft throughout the composition process. This seamless approach to writing allows you to continue to improve your "working draft" until the moment you are ready to print the final copy. Numerous electronic writing tools are available, and technology will continue to unfold to enhance the writing process. The accompanying Strategic Forces feature, "Writing Effectively at the Computer," will aid you in maximizing the power of these electronic tools to write effectively and efficiently.

For nearly two decades now automated speech recognition software has been promoted as a vehicle for improving the cost effectiveness of business writing with predictions that writers in the future would use the keyboard only for revising text and not for primary input. Most consumers have been disappointed with the time and energy required to "train" the product to

Critical Thinking

In groups, discuss which of these writing methods works most effectively for each of you. What habits hinder your success or enjoyment of writing? Brainstorm to identify ways to overcome them.

Changing
Technology

Writing Effectively at the Computer

A computer makes it easier for you to think and write simultaneously, become a better editor, and improve the appearance of your finished document. Despite these enhancements, you must be aware of limitations and learn to harness the full power of your software.

1. **Hone your computer skills for optimal efficiency.** Continue to learn new features that will help you accomplish tasks more easily:
   - Use the copy and paste command to move text rather than rekeying.
   - Use time-saving keystrokes for frequently used commands such as open, save, and find.
   - Draft in a font style and size that is easy to read on the screen.
   - Use commands such as *find* and *go to* when searching through a document to make changes.
   - Postpone formatting until you finish writing and revising.
   - Use automatic numbering to arrange numerical or alphabetical lists and to ensure accuracy in revising lists.
   - Use templates and model documents to save time formatting routine documents.

2. **Create the physical appearance of your document to help organize your ideas.** Use good judgment in choosing graphic features that are appropriate for the writing situation.

3. **Integrate the thinking and writing processes.** Incorporate these activities as you think, write, and revise:
   - Key points you want to make, issues these points address, supporting evidence, and any notes or sources you intend to use.
   - Continue to input and compile ideas as you think, and then develop these ideas using the appropriate approach.
   - Scroll through the document, looking for improvements in the content and transitions among ideas affected by adding, cutting, or moving text.

4. **Use the spell check, thesaurus, and grammar checker.** Use writing aids frequently as you draft and revise. Remember, though, some errors, cannot be detected electronically. Spell check will not identify miskeyings (*than* for *then*), commonly misused words (*affect* or *effect*), homophones (*principle, principal*), omitted words, enumerated items missing or out of order, and content errors. A thesaurus is useful only when you can recognize the precise meaning needed. Grammar checkers may provide suggestions inappropriate for the writing situation.

5. **Mark corrections on the printed copy.** Follow these suggestions for marking your printed copy:
   - Use standard proofreaders' marks to note simple grammatical changes or misspellings. Write simple cues to identify major revisions; e.g., insert an "X" near the error and write "Add" or "Cut," or "Reorder."
   - Input revisions, check for transitions and grammatical correctness around parts, and spell-check again.
   - Use print preview to check for placement, visual appeal, and appropriate use of headers, footers, and page numbering. Lastly, print the final copy.

Application

- Compile a list of word processing features that you have never used that would help you write more effectively. Commit a little time each day to learn these features and begin using them regularly.
- Following the guidelines provided, use the computer to write a message assigned by your instructor. Be prepared to discuss perceived changes in the quality of your writing and the efficiency with which you completed the message. Offer other suggestions for using the computer to write effectively.

Condoleezza Rice, the first-ever woman U.S. national security advisor and Secretary of State, uses her respectful but firm communication style to sharpen debates on the war and peace between powerful advisors with the goal of providing President Bush clear choices and original ideas rather than mere consensus. Her adeptness with language is also evident as she adds a seemingly minor yet significant phrase to a speech or labors to find acceptable words for a U.N. resolution.[3]

© SACHS RON/CORBIS SYGMA

Critical Thinking

Do you think keyboards will disappear from computers? Explain.

recognize their voices and the software's poor accuracy rates (e.g., garbled words and the absence of end punctuation).[4] However, recent improvements in voice activation and speech processing powering are leading to a much wider range of reliable speech-enabled applications, many of which are embedded within mobile devices such as phones and PDAs. With the convenience and safety of hands-free operation and no training time, communicators can record and hear e-mail messages, receive updates about scheduled appointments; and access many types of information from current bank balances to real-time traffic and weather updates. You will learn more in Chapter 5 about these emerging technologies that enhance workers' ability to access and disseminate information quickly and efficiently.

Craft Powerful Sentences

Well-developed sentences help the receiver understand the message clearly and react favorably to the writer or speaker. In this section, you will learn about correct sentence structure, predominant use of active voice, and emphasis of important points that affect the clarity and human relations of your message. Visit the text support site at http://lehman.swlearning.com to learn other strategies for crafting powerful messages.

Use Correct Sentence Structure

The following discussion identifies common problems and techniques business writers encounter. For a complete review of techniques for effective sentences, study Appendix C or consult an English handbook.

All sentences have at least two parts: *subject* and *verb*. In addition to a subject and a verb, a sentence may have additional words to complete the meaning. These words are called **complements**.

Subject	Verb	Complement
Sid	transferred	overseas.
Chien	transferred	to our Hong Kong office.

A group of words that is not a complete sentence is called a **phrase** or a **clause**. A phrase does not include a subject and a verb; a clause does. The phrases are underlined in the example on the left. In the clauses on the right, the subject is underlined once and the verb is underlined twice:

Phrases	Clauses
One of the workers was absent.	As the president reported this morning . . .
The people in that room have voted.	If construction is begun soon . . .
The electrician fell while replacing the socket.	Although the production schedule is incomplete . . .

Clauses are divided into two categories: dependent and independent. A **dependent clause** does not convey a complete thought. The preceding illustrations are dependent. An **independent clause** conveys a complete thought; it could be a complete sentence if presented alone.

Critical Thinking

If an independent clause could serve as a complete sentence, why not state it as a separate sentence?

Dependent Clause	Independent Clause
As the president reported this morning,	sales increased in May.

Dependent Clause	Independent Clause
If construction is begun soon,	the job can be completed by the end of the year.

The independent clause "sales increased in May" can be stated as a separate sentence. The dependent clause "As the president reported this morning" does not convey a complete thought and should not be presented without the remainder of the sentence. When a **sentence fragment** (a portion of a sentence) is presented as a separate sentence, receivers become confused and distracted.

Sentences fall into four categories: simple, compound, complex, and compound-complex.

	Independent Clause	
Simple:	The union has gone on strike.	

	Independent Clause	Independent Clause
Compound:	The union has gone on strike, and	all manufacturing lines have stopped production.

	Dependent Clause	Independent Clause
Complex:	Because contract terms cannot be reached,	the union has gone on strike.

	Dependent Clause	Independent Clause
Compound-Complex:	Because contract terms cannot be reached,	the union has gone on

Independent Clause

strike; but a settlement is expected at the end of the week.

Critical Thinking

What grammatical rules give you the most problems?

In the preceding examples, note the use of punctuation to separate one clause from another. When no punctuation or coordinating conjunction appears between the clauses, the result is a ***run-on sentence*** or ***fused sentence***. Another problem is the ***comma splice***, in which the clauses are joined only with a comma instead of a comma and coordinating conjunction or a semicolon.

Run-On or Fused Sentence	Corrected Sentence
New forms have been ordered they should be delivered next Friday.	New forms have been ordered. They should be delivered next Friday.
	New forms have been ordered, and they should be delivered next Friday.
	New forms have been ordered; they should be delivered next Friday.
	The new forms, which were ordered last week, should be delivered next Friday.
Comma Splice	**Corrected Sentence**
The number of questions has been reduced from 15 to 5, the task will require 25 percent less time.	Because the number of questions has been reduced from 15 to 5, the task will require 25 percent less time.

Rely on Active Voice

Critical Thinking

Using active voice suggests to the receiver that you are action-oriented and decisive.

Business communicators normally use active voice more heavily than passive voice because active voice conveys ideas more vividly. In sentences in which the subject is the *doer* of action, the verbs are called ***active***. In sentences in which the subject is the *receiver* of action, the verbs are called ***passive***. In the following example, the sentence in the left column uses passive voice; the right, active voice:

Passive Voice	Active Voice
Reports are transferred electronically from remote locations to the home office.	Our sales reps transfer reports electronically from remote locations to the home office.

Critical Thinking

Write several active and passive voice sentences and note the difference in the vividness of the sentences.

The active sentence invites the receiver to see the sales reps using a computer to complete a report. The passive sentence draws attention to a report.

Using active voice makes the subject the actor, which makes the idea easier to understand. Sentences written using passive voice give receivers a less-distinct picture. In the passive sentence, the receiver becomes aware that something was done to the reports, but it does not reveal who did it.

Even when a passive sentence contains additional words to reveal the doer, the imagery is less distinct than it would be if the sentence were active: *Reports compiled by our sales representatives are transferred electronically from remote locations to the home office.* "Reports" gets the most attention because it is the subject. The sentence seems to let a receiver know the *result* of action before revealing the doer; therefore, the sentence is less emphatic.

Although active voice conveys ideas more vividly, passive voice is useful

Critical Thinking

When is use of passive voice recommended?

- In concealing the doer. ("The reports have been compiled.")
- In placing more emphasis on *what* was done and what it was *done* to than on who *did* it. ("The reports have been compiled by our sales representatives.")
- In subordinating an unpleasant thought. ("The Shipping Department has not been notified of this delay" rather than "You have not notified the Shipping Department of this delay.") Review the previous discussion of using passive voice to de-emphasize negative ideas in the "Project a Positive, Tactful Tone" section of Chapter 3.

Emphasize Important Ideas

A landscape artist wants some features in a picture to stand out boldly and others to get little attention. A musician sounds some notes loudly and others softly. Likewise, a writer or speaker wants some ideas to be *emphasized* and others to be *de-emphasized*. Normally, pleasant and important ideas should be emphasized; unpleasant and insignificant ideas should be de-emphasized. Emphasis techniques include sentence structure, repetition, words that label, position, punctuation, and space and format.

Critical Thinking

Should a significant idea be placed in the dependent or independent clause? Why?

Sentence Structure. For emphasis, place an idea in a simple sentence. The simple sentence in the following examples has one independent clause. Because no other idea competes with it for attention, this idea is emphasized.

Simple Sentence Is More Emphatic	Compound Sentence Is Less Emphatic
Nicole took a job in insurance.	Nicole took a job in insurance, but she really preferred a job in accounting.

For emphasis, place an idea in an independent clause; for de-emphasis, place an idea in a dependent clause. In the following compound sentence the idea of taking a job is in an independent clause. Because an independent clause makes sense if the rest of the sentence is omitted, an independent clause is more emphatic than a dependent clause. In the complex sentence, the idea of taking a job is in a dependent clause. By itself, the clause would not make complete sense. Compared with the independent clause that follows ("Nicole really preferred . . . "), the idea in the dependent clause is de-emphasized.

Compound Sentence Is More Emphatic	Complex Sentence Is Less Emphatic
Nicole accepted a job in insurance, but she really preferred a job in accounting.	Although she accepted a job in insurance, Nicole really preferred a job in accounting.

Critical Thinking

What's the difference between repetition and redundancy?

Repetition. To emphasize a word, let it appear more than once in a sentence. For example, a clever radio ad by OfficeMax used the word *stuff* repeatedly to describe generically several types of office needs ranging from paper clips to color copies, and then ended succinctly with "OfficeMax . . . for your office stuff." Likewise, in the following example, "success" receives more emphasis when the word is repeated.

Less Emphatic	More Emphatic
The project was successful because of . . .	The project was successful; this success is attributed to . . .

Words that Label. For emphasis or de-emphasis, use words that label ideas as significant or insignificant. Note the labeling words used in the following examples to emphasize or de-emphasize an idea:

But most important of all . . .
A less significant aspect was . . .

Position. To emphasize a word or an idea, position it first or last in a sentence, clause, paragraph, or presentation. Words that appear first compete only with words that follow; words that appear last compete only with words that precede. Note the additional emphasis placed on the words *success* and *failure* in the examples in the right column because these words appear as the *first* or the *last* words in their clauses.

Less Emphatic	More Emphatic
Your efforts contributed to the <u>success</u> of the project; otherwise, <u>failure</u> would have been the result.	<u>Success</u> resulted from your efforts; <u>failure</u> would have resulted without them.
The project was <u>successful</u> because of your efforts; without them, <u>failure</u> would have been the result.	The project was a <u>success</u>; without your efforts, it would have been a <u>failure</u>.

Critical Thinking

What hidden message (metacommunication) is communicated by a message in which most paragraphs begin with I?

In paragraphs, the first and last words are in particularly emphatic positions. An idea that deserves emphasis can be placed in either position, but an idea that does not deserve emphasis can be placed in the middle of a long paragraph. The word *I*, which is frequently overused in messages, is especially noticeable if it appears as the first word. *I* is more noticeable if it appears as the first word in *every* paragraph. *However* is to be avoided as the first word in a paragraph if the preceding paragraph is neutral or positive. These words imply that the next idea will be negative. Unless the purpose is to place emphasis on negatives, such words as *denied*, *rejected*, and *disappointed* should not appear as the last words in a paragraph.

Critical Thinking

How can an effective writer restate without being redundant?

Likewise, the central idea of a written or spoken report appears in the introduction (the beginning) and the conclusion (the end). Good transition sentences synthesize ideas at the end of each major division.

Space and Format. The various divisions of a report or spoken presentation are not expected to be of equal length, but an extraordinary amount of space devoted to a topic attaches special significance to that topic. Similarly, a topic that gets an exceedingly small amount of space is de-emphasized. The manner in which information is physically arranged affects the emphasis it receives and thus, the overall impact of the document. You will learn to apply these techniques later in this chapter.

Develop Coherent Paragraphs

Critical Thinking

A deductive paragraph begins with the main idea followed by the details. How does an inductive paragraph differ?

Well-constructed sentences are combined into paragraphs that discuss a portion of the topic being discussed. To write effective paragraphs, you must learn to (a) develop deductive or inductive paragraphs consistently, (b) link ideas to achieve coherence, (c) keep paragraphs unified, and (d) vary sentence and paragraph length.

Position the Topic Sentence Appropriately

Typically, paragraphs contain one sentence that identifies the portion of the topic being discussed and presents the central idea. That sentence is commonly called a **topic sentence**. For example, consider a pamphlet written to a company that has purchased a DVD drive. The overall topic is how to get satisfactory performance from the device. One portion of that topic is installation; another portion (paragraph) discusses operation; and so forth. Within each paragraph, one sentence serves a special function. Sentences that list the steps can appear as one paragraph, perhaps with steps numbered as follows:

> To install a new DVD drive, take the following steps:
> 1. Insert . . .
> 2. Click . . .

In this illustration, the paragraphs are **deductive**; that is, the topic sentence *precedes* details. When topic sentences *follow* details, the paragraphs are called **inductive paragraphs**. As discussed previously, the receiver's likely reaction to the main idea (pleased, displeased, interested, not interested) aids in selecting the appropriate sequence.

When the subject matter is complicated and the details are numerous, paragraphs sometimes begin with a main idea, follow with details, and end with a summarizing sentence. But the main idea may not be in the first sentence; the idea may need a preliminary statement. Receivers appreciate consistency in the placement of topic sentences. Once they catch on to the writer's pattern, they know where to look for main ideas.

These suggestions seldom apply to the first and last sentences of letters, memos, and e-mail messages. Such sentences frequently appear as single-sentence paragraphs. But for reports and long paragraphs of letters, strive for paragraphs that are consistently deductive or consistently inductive. Regardless of which is selected, topic sentences are clearly linked with details that precede or follow.

Link Ideas to Achieve Coherence

Careful writers use coherence techniques to keep receivers from experiencing abrupt changes in thought. Although the word **coherence** is used sometimes to mean "clarity" or "understandability," it is used throughout this text to mean "cohesion." If writing or speaking is coherent, the sentences stick together; each sentence is in some way linked to the preceding sentences. Avoid abrupt changes in thought, and link each sentence to a preceding sentence.

The following techniques for linking sentences are common:

1. *Repeat a word that was used in the preceding sentence.* The second sentence in the following example is an obvious continuation of the idea presented in the preceding sentence.

   . . . to take responsibility for the decision. This responsibility can be shared . . .

2. *Use a pronoun that represents a noun used in the preceding sentence.* Because "it" means "responsibility," the second sentence is linked directly with the first.

   . . . to take this responsibility. It can be shared . . .

3. *Use connecting words.* Examples are *however, therefore, yet, nevertheless, consequently, also, in addition,* and so on. "However" implies "We're continuing with the same topic, just moving into a different phase." Remember, though, that good techniques can be *over*used. Unnecessary connectors are space consuming and distracting. Usually they can be spotted (and crossed out) in proofreading.

   . . . to take this responsibility. However, few are willing to . . .

Critical Thinking

What techniques are you familiar with for providing cohesion in your writing?

Just as sentences within a paragraph must link, paragraphs within a document must also link. Unless a writer (or speaker) is careful, the move from one major topic to the next will seem abrupt. A good transition sentence can bridge the gap between the two topics by summing up the preceding topic and leading a receiver to expect the next topic:

Cost factors, then, seemed prohibitive until efficiency factors were investigated.

This sentence could serve as a transition between the "Cost" division heading and the "Efficiency" division heading. Because a transition sentence comes at the end of one segment and before the next, it emphasizes the central idea of the preceding segment and confirms the relationship of the two segments.

Transition sentences are very helpful if properly used, but they can be overused. For most reports, transition sentences before major headings are sufficient. Normally, transition sentences before subheadings are unnecessary. Having encountered the previous subheading only a few lines back, a receiver should readily see its relationship to the upcoming subheading. In addition, transition sentences typically summarize, and the discussion under a subheading of a report is seldom long enough to merit summarization.

Keep Paragraphs Unified

Critical Thinking

How are unity and coherence related concepts?

Receivers expect the first paragraph of a message to introduce a topic, additional paragraphs to discuss it, and a final paragraph to tie them together. The in-between paragraphs should be arranged in a systematic sequence, and the end must be linked easily to some word or idea presented in the beginning. The effect of a message that is *not* unified is like that of an incomplete circle or a picture with one element obviously missing.

A letter or report with unity covers its topic adequately but will not include extraneous material. The document will have a beginning sentence appropriate for the expected receiver reaction, paragraphs that present the bulk of the message, and an ending sentence that is an appropriate closing for the message presented. If the sequence is logical, coherence is easy to achieve.

A report or presentation with unity begins with an introduction that identifies the topic, reveals the thesis, and previews upcoming points. The introduction may also include some background, sources of information, and the method of treating data. Between the beginning and the ending, a unified report will have paragraphs arranged in a systematic sequence. A summary or conclusion brings all major points together.

Vary Sentence and Paragraph Length

Sentences of short or average length are easy to read and preferred for communicating clearly. However, keeping *all* sentences short is undesirable because the message may sound monotonous, unrealistic, or elementary. A two-word sentence is acceptable; so is a 60-word sentence—if it is clear. Just as sentences should vary in length, they should also vary in structure. Some complex or compound sentences should be included with simple sentences.

Variety is just as desirable in paragraph length as it is in sentence length. A paragraph can be from one line in length to a dozen lines or more. However, just as average sentence length should be kept fairly short, average paragraph length also should be kept short. Paragraphs in business letters, memos, and e-mail messages are typically shorter than paragraphs in business reports. First and last paragraphs are normally short (one to four lines), and other paragraphs are normally no longer than *six lines*. A short first paragraph is more inviting to read than a long first paragraph, and a short last paragraph enables a writer to emphasize parting thoughts.

In business reports, the space between paragraphs is a welcome resting spot. Long paragraphs are difficult to read and make a page appear

Critical Thinking

Why are paragraphs in a business message typically shorter than those in a literary essay?

unattractive. Paragraph length will vary depending on the complexity of the subject matter. However, as a general rule paragraphs should be no longer than *eight to ten lines*. This length usually allows enough space to include a topic sentence and three or four supporting statements. If the topic cannot be discussed in this space, divide the topic into additional paragraphs.

To observe the effect large sections of unbroken text has on the overall appeal of a document, examine the memos in Figure 4-1 that contain identical information. Without question the memo with the short, easy-to-read paragraphs is more inviting to read than the memo with one bulky paragraph.

Although variety is a desirable quality, it should not be achieved at the expense of consistency. Using *I* in one part of a message and then without explanation switching to *we* is inadvisable. Using the past tense in one sentence and the present tense in another sentence creates variety at the expense of consistency—unless the shift is required to indicate actual changes in time. Unnecessary changes from active to passive voice (or vice versa) and from third to second person (or vice versa) are also discouraged.

Refer to the "Check Your Communication" checklist at the end of the chapter to review the guidelines for writing a first draft of the message that can be easily understood and received positively.

Figure 4-1	*Contrast the Readability and Appeal of Bulky vs. Broken Text*

RC ROSSAN CORPORATION
480 WOODSON RIDGE ROAD / CANTON, OH 44711-0480 / (206)555-8763

TO: All Employees
FROM: Victor Miranda, Manager *V.M.*
DATE: December 15, 2005
SUBJECT: EXTRA VACATION DAY

The board of directors has approved one additional vacation day for every employee. This decision is our way of expressing gratitude for the most productive and profitable year in the history of Rossan Corporation. With the approval of your department head, you may select any day between January 2 and June 30. This day of vacation is in addition to year-end bonuses you will receive soon. Thank you for all you have done to make the year successful, and best wishes for a healthy and happy new year.

RC ROSSAN CORPORATION
480 WOODSON RIDGE ROAD / CANTON, OH 44711-0480 / (206)555-8763

TO: All Employees
FROM: Victor Miranda, Manager *V.M.*
DATE: December 15, 2005
SUBJECT: EXTRA VACATION DAY

The board of directors has approved one additional vacation day for every employee.

This decision is our way of expressing gratitude for the most productive and profitable year in the history of Rossan Corporation. With the approval of your department head, you may select any day between January 2 and June 30. This day of vacation is in addition to year-end bonuses you will receive soon.

Thank you for all you have done to make the year successful, and best wishes for a healthy and happy new year.

SPOTLIGHT COMMUNICATOR

Spoken and Written Communication Skills Essential to Workplace Success

According to the Department of Labor, proficiency in verbal and written business communication skills is considered a new "key basic" in the workplace today. According to R. D. Saenz, the accounting profession is no exception. A consultant with a degree in accounting, Saenz spent nearly 20 years at Price Waterhouse, one of the top five accounting firms in the United States. Having also been employed 11 years in private industry, he knows that a college degree or advanced professional certification alone no longer meets basic required skills in the workplace.

While working as audit senior manager at Price Waterhouse, Saenz was directly involved in employee professional development. His duties involved more than developing employees technically in accounting. He worked with all facets of form evaluation, which involved written and spoken communication. He took note of strengths and weaknesses of supervisory employees. He worked with the "cream-of-the-crop" employees who had degrees from prestigious universities. Based on the employees' backgrounds, levels of intelligence, and levels of

achievement, he was sometimes appalled at their inability to communicate through writing skills. He notes, "Grammatical errors quickly detract from the credibility of the writer. Errors cast a cloud over that individual's ability or competence."

One way Saenz developed employees professionally was by focusing intently on clear writing. He regularly evaluated employees' writing and offered feedback on all documents, including intricate explanations of an exception to a policy or a resolution or a simple memo about auditing procedures for an upcoming engagement. If a written report was done incorrectly, he provided positive comments that were light-hearted but professional. He set high standards for his employees and tried to communicate his knowledge of clear, concise, correct writing to them.

Saenz finds many common connecting chords between communication and his work. Saenz believes that effective word use is fundamental to the workplace. He knows that spoken and written skills of preciseness, simplicity, parallelism, and tone must be "second nature" to an accountant. Without these

R.D. SAENZ, CEO SNEIDER COMMUNICATIONS CORPORATION

skills, employees simply will not succeed. The workplace of today has changed, he notes. "Employees must have more than the technical aptitude of accounting. They must also have proficiency in spoken and written communication skills."

Applying What You Have Learned

1. Why does Saenz consider proficiency in spoken and written communication skills basic to the accounting profession today?
2. Saenz commented that "grammatical errors quickly detract from the credibility of the writer." Explain the reason for his view.
3. Assume that you are an employee for a large accounting firm. Your duties include careful consideration of any employee's written work that leaves your office. Following Saenz's example, discuss some considerations to keep in mind when commenting about another employee's writing.

R. D. Saenz, Controller, Air Transport International

http://www.sec.gov

Refer to ShowCASE, Part 3, at the end of the chapter to learn about the efforts of health care practitioners to disclose patients' privacy rights using plain English.

Revise and Proofread

Critical Thinking

How do you draw the line between informal and sloppy?

The speed and convenience of today's electronic communication have caused many communicators to confuse informality with sloppiness. Sloppy messages contain misspellings, grammatical errors, unappealing and incorrect formats, and confusing content—all of which create a negative impression of the writer and the company and affect the receiver's ability to understand the message.

As the sender, you are responsible for evaluating the effectiveness of each message you prepare. You must not use informality as an excuse to be sloppy. Instead take one consultant's advice: "You can still be informal and not be sloppy. You can be informal and correct."[5] Roll up your sleeves and take a good hard look at the messages you prepare. Commit to adjusting the readability of your message to the audience, designing appealing documents that are easily read, and following a systematic proofreading process to assure error-free messages. This effort may save you from being embarrassed or jeopardizing your credibility.

Improve Readability

Objective *2*

Identify factors affecting readability and revise messages to improve readability.

Although sentences are arranged in a logical sequence and are written coherently, the receiver may find reading the sentences difficult. Several indexes have been developed to measure the reading difficulty of your writing. Electronic tools aid you in making computations and identifying changes that will improve readability.

Understand Readability Measures

Critical Thinking

What factors affect the readability of a message?

Leading word processing applications have readability measures built into their grammar checking features. The readability level can be calculated automatically, along with other factors. While today's communicators do not have to manually calculate reading level, understanding how such calculations are derived helps you understand how to effectively adapt text passages. A popular readability index, developed by Robert Gunning in 1968, considers the length of sentences and the difficulty of words to produce the approximate grade level a person would need to understand the material.[6] For example, a grade level of 10 indicates a person needs to be able to read at the tenth-grade level to understand the material. The desirable reading index for most business writing is in the eighth-to-eleventh-grade range.

Computer software programs calculate readability measures automatically. However, computing readability manually will help you understand how sentence length and difficulty of the words factor into the calculation.

1. **Select a passage of 100 words or more.**
   Sample business letter as shown on the next page
2. **Count the exact number of words.**
   138 words

Dear Mr. and Mrs. Lee:

[1]With <u>interest</u> rates at their lowest level in 20 years, you chose a good time to buy your first house.

[2]Choosing a fixed mortgage rate allowed you to "lock in" your 6 <u>percent</u> interest rate, <u>protect-ing</u> you from <u>potential</u> increases in <u>interest</u> rates before your closing.

[3]Had you selected a <u>variable</u> rate mortgage, you could have taken <u>advantage</u> of the recent drop in interest rates. [4]However, you would have been subject to later increases in interest rates.

[5]If <u>interest</u> rates <u>continue</u> to decline, you may want to <u>consider</u> <u>refinancing</u> your fixed rate mortgage. [6]<u>Refinancing</u> is <u>typically</u> cost effec-tive when <u>interest</u> rates are 1 percent below your current mortgage rate.

[7]Mr. and Mrs. Lee, we are glad to have been of service in your recent home purchase. [8]Please call me if you need <u>information</u> about other <u>financing</u> needs.

3. ***Count the number of sentences.***
   Count compound sentences as two sentences. Eight sentences (none of the sentences are compound). Sentences are marked with superscript numbers.
4. ***Find the average sentence length.***
   Divide the number of words by the number of sen-tences. 138 (total words) ÷ 8 (sentences) = 17 words
5. ***Count the number of difficult words.***
   A difficult word is a word with three or more syllables. Do not include (a) compound words formed from smaller words (<u>however</u> or <u>understand</u>), (b) proper nouns, or (c) verbs formed into three syllables by the addition of -<u>ed</u> or -<u>es</u> (<u>imposes</u> or <u>defended</u>). Sixteen difficult words. Difficult words are underscored. "Selected" and "increases" are not difficult words because they became three syllables by adding -ed or -es.
6. ***Find the percentage of difficult words.*** *Divide the number of difficult words by the total number of words.*
   16 (difficult words) ÷ 138 (total words) = .116 or 11.6%
7. ***Add the average sentence length and the percentage of difficult words.***
   17 (average sentence length) + 11.6 (percentage of difficult words) = 28.6
8. ***Multiply the resulting figure by 0.4.***
   28.6 × 0.4 (constant) = 11.4 (readability level)

Critical Thinking

Use simple words and short sen-tences for quick, easy reading and listening.

Critical Thinking

What value is gained from knowing the readability index of your writing?

Diversity Challenges

The reading level of this short letter is 11.4, meaning that approxi-mately 11 to 12 years of education are needed to understand it. The letter could be revised to lower the readability index to 8–11, the desired level for business writing. To lower the readability index and to make this letter easier to read, you would need to write shorter sentences and reduce the number of difficult words.

Trying to write at the exact grade level of the receiver is inadvisable. You may not know the exact grade level, and even those who have earned advanced degrees appreciate writing they can read and understand quickly and easily. Also, writing a passage with a readability index appropriate for the audience does not guarantee that the message will be understood. Despite simple language and short sentences, the message can be distorted at any stage of the communication process: imprecise words, biased lan-guage, technical jargon, translations that ignore cultural interpretations, to name just a few. The value of calculating a readability measure lies in the valuable feedback you gain. Use this information about the average length of the sentences and the difficulty of the words to identify needed revisions. Recalculate the readability index and continue revising until you feel the reading level is appropriate for the intended audience. Periodically using your word processor's grammar checking function to assess reading level will assist you in adjusting your writing level appropriately.

Use Grammar Checkers to Improve Readability

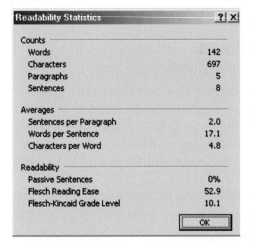

Changing Technology

Critical Thinking

How can writing-analysis software improve your writing?

Leading word processing programs have built-in grammar checkers that can help you locate grammatical errors and improve your writing style. These built-in grammar and style checkers compare the text created in a word processing program against the grammar and style principles stored in the program, highlight any text that violates the principles, and may suggest a revision. Grammar and style checkers generally highlight sentence fragments, passive verbs, jargon, wordy constructions, clichés, subject-verb disagreement, pronoun usage, language, word usage, and misspelled words. Various checking styles (casual, standard, formal, or technical) give the writer control over the strictness of the critique.

Note the helpfulness of the feedback on the sentence illustrated in the screen shown below. Using the "standard" writing style, the software displays a suggested revision and a detailed explanation of the appropriate use of active and passive voice. Because this suggestion is valid, the writer can easily click "Change" to input the recommended active-voice sentence and thus improve the style. However, the writer may overrule a suggestion inappropriate for a particular message. In this case, for example, using active voice to achieve clear, vivid images is effective. However, the writer would retain the passive-voice construction if the intention is to de-emphasize negative information by clicking "Ignore."

After the writer has responded to all suggestions the grammar checker has provided for the writing, an analysis, such as the one illustrated at the left, is displayed. These various measures guide the writer in evaluating the readability of the revised text. These analyses include (a) basic counts for words, paragraphs, and sentences, (b) averages such as sentences per paragraph, and (c) several readability measures including a grade-level index.

Those who are familiar with the principles of writing will benefit most from writing-analysis programs. Recent versions of software provide detailed explanations of writing principles with illustrations, as shown in this example highlighting the use of passive voice. Obviously, a writer

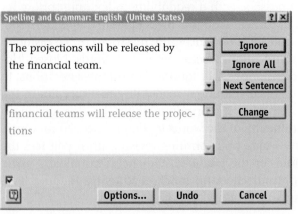

Passive Voice

For a livelier and more persuasive sentence, consider rewriting your sentence using an active verb (the subject performs the action, as in "The ball hit Catherine") rather than a passive verb (the subject receives the action, as in "Catherine was hit by the ball"). If you rewrite with an active verb, consider what the appropriate subject is—"they," "we," or a more specific noun or pronoun.

- Instead of : <u>Juanita was delighted by Michelle</u>.
- Consider: Michelle delighted Juanita.

- Instead of: Eric <u>was given</u> more work.
- Consider: The boss gave Eric more work.

- Instead of: The garbage needs to <u>be taken out</u>.
- Consider: You need to take out the garbage.

with an effective writing style will spend less time revising and be more likely to understand and benefit from the software's suggestions.

Apply Visual Enhancements to Improve Readability

Objective **3**

Prepare visually appealing documents that grab the receiver's attention and increase comprehension.

The vast amount of information created in today's competitive global market poses a challenge to you as a business writer. You must learn to create visually appealing documents that entice a receiver to read rather than discard your message. Additionally, an effective design will enable you to highlight important information for maximum attention and to transition a receiver smoothly through sections of a long, complex document. These design techniques can be performed easily using word processing software. However, be certain to add visual enhancements only when they aid in comprehension. Otherwise, your document will appear cluttered and will defeat your purpose of creating an appealing, easy-to-read document.

Critical Thinking

Visual enhancements will make your document easy to read and understand.

Enumerations. To emphasize units in a series, place a number, letter, or bullet before each element. Words preceded by numbers, bullets, or letters attract the receiver's special attention and are easier to locate when the page is reviewed.

Original	Highlighted
The human resources problems have been narrowed into three categories: absenteeism, tardiness, and pilferage.	The human resources problems have been narrowed into three categories: (1) absenteeism, (2) tardiness, and (3) pilferage.

Enumerated or Bulleted Lists. Many times writers want to save space; however, cluttered text is unappealing and difficult to read. Chunking—a desktop publishing term—is an answer to the problem. Chunking involves breaking down information into easily digestible pieces. It's the communication equivalent of Butterfinger® BBs, rather than the whole candy bar. The added white space divides the information into blocks, makes the page look more organized, and increases retention by 50 percent.[7] Specific techniques include enumerated or bulleted lists.

Enumerated or bulleted lists can be used to add even greater visual impact to items in a series. Items appear on separate lines with numerals, letters, or various types of bullets (•, ◆, ❑, ✓, and so on) at the beginning. Multiple line items often are separated by a blank line. This design creates more white space that isolates the items from other text and demands attention. Bullets are typically preferred over numerals unless the sequence of the items in the series is critical (e.g., steps in a procedure that must be completed in the correct order). In the following excerpt from a long analytical report, the four supporting reasons for a conclusion are highlighted in a bulleted list:

Original	Highlighted
For our needs, then, the most appropriate in-service training method is web-based instruction. This training is least expensive, allows employees to remain at their own workstations while improving their skills, affords constant awareness of progress, and lets employees progress at their own rates.	Web-based instruction is the most appropriate in-service training method because it • is least expensive. • allows employees to remain at their own workstations while improving their skills. • affords constant awareness of progress. • lets employees progress at their own rates.

Headings. Headings are signposts that direct the receiver from one section of the document to another. They are arranged in a hierarchy with the major headings receiving more attention than minor headings or paragraph headings. The placement of headings and the choice of typestyles and print enhancements create a hierarchy of different levels of headings. For example, a centered major heading printed in a prominent boldfaced typeface would be more emphatic than a minor heading printed at the left margin with a slightly smaller size type.

Headings are especially useful in organizing the content of a long report; however, they are also helpful in organizing résumés and complex letters and memos. Note the position and spacing of three levels of headings shown in Appendix A and the sample reports in Chapter 11.

Critical Thinking

Use talking headings to add emphasis and gain attention.

Brief headings tend to be more emphatic than long headings. Talking headings (headings that reveal the conclusions reached in the following discussion) are more emphatic than general topic headings. For example, "Costs Are Prohibitive" is more emphatic than "Cost Factors."

Tables and Graphs. Tables and graphs are used to simplify and clarify information and to add an appealing variety to long sections of dense text. The clearly labeled rows and columns in a table organize large amounts of specific numeric data and facilitate analysis. Graphics such as pie charts, line charts, and bar charts visually depict relationships within the data; they provide quick estimates rather than specific information. In Chapter 10, you will gain proficiency in selecting an appropriate graphic format for data and in designing effective and accurate tables and graphs.

Lines and Borders. Horizontal and vertical lines can be added to partition text or to focus attention on a specific line(s). For example, a thin line followed by a thick line effectively separates the identification section of a résumé from the qualifications. Placing a border around a paragraph or section of text sets that text apart; adding shading inside the box adds greater impact. For example, a shaded border might spotlight a testimonial from a satisfied customer in a sales letter, important dates to remember in a memorandum, or a section of a document that must be completed and returned.

Relevant Images. A variety of interesting shapes and lines can be used to highlight information and add appeal. Examples include creating a rectangular callout box highlighting a key idea with an arrow pointing to a specific number in a table, surrounding a title with a shaded oval for added impact, and using various shapes to illustrate the steps in a process. The applications are limited only by the writer's creativity. Clip art or photos can also be added to reinforce an idea and add visual appeal. Note the variety of drawing tools (rectangles, arrows, lines, and clip art) used in Figure 3-3 to depict the decision-making process involved in selecting an appropriate outline.

Battling to manage an avalanche of information, the recipients of your messages will appreciate your extra effort to create an easy-to-read, appealing document. These fundamental techniques will be invaluable as you enhance printed documents such as letters, memos, reports, agendas, handouts, and minutes for meetings. You'll also build on this foundation as you learn to design effective web documents and high-impact presentation visuals in later chapters.

Use Systematic Procedures for Revising and Proofreading

Objective 4

Revise and proofread a message for content, organization, and style; mechanics; and format and layout.

Errors in writing and mechanics may seem isolated, but the truth is, proofreading *is* important. You don't have to look too far to see silly typos or obvious instances of writers relying only on the computer spell check. The classifieds in a small-town newspaper advertised "fully fascinated and spade damnation puppies." The advertisement was for fully vaccinated and spayed Dalmatian puppies. These errors clearly illustrate how spell check can fail, but goofs like that are not limited to small-town newspapers, as noted in an embarrassing incident related to an honor for Brett Favre.

Not a spelling error, but a simple transposition in a telephone number created an unbelievably embarrassing situation for a telecommunications giant. AT&T customers calling to redeem points earned in a True Rewards program were connected to pay-by-the-minute erotic phone entertainment.[8] Mistakes ranging from printing ordinary typos to running entirely erroneous ads forced newspapers to refund $10.6 million to dissatisfied advertisers and to print $10.5 million in free, make-good ads.[9] Each of these actual mistakes illustrates that inattention to proofreading can be potentially embarrassing and incredibly expensive.

Critical Thinking

Share with the class negative effects of spelling errors made by other companies or organizations.

Following systematic revision procedures will help you produce error-free documents that reflect positively on the company and you. Using the procedures that follow, you will see that effective proofreading must be done several times, each time for a specific purpose. Also, using standard proofreading marks will simplify your proofreading method and will

When Brett Favre was honored as the NFL Player of the Year by *The Sporting News*, a lovely crystal trophy was ordered from Tiffany's and not unpacked until time for the presentation. The contributing editor, Dennis Dillion, realized with horror that the recipient's name had been misspelled on the trophy—Brett Farve. The ceremony went on as planned, however, and the trophy was shipped to Tiffany's for correction before being sent to Favre. Simply double-checking could have prevented this embarrassing incident.[10]

allow others who know these marks to understand your corrections easily. Study the standard proofreaders' marks shown in Appendix A and used to mark the corrections in the rough draft in Figure 4-2 on page 145.

Follow these simple procedures to produce a finished product that is free of errors in (1) content, organization, and style; (2) mechanics; and (3) format and layout:

Critical Thinking

Using a spell check is only the first step in locating all errors in a document. What types of errors can spell check help to locate?

1. ***Use the spell check to locate simple keying errors and repeated words.*** When the software cannot guess the correct spelling based on your incorrect attempt, you will need to consult a dictionary, other printed source, or online reference such as the Merriam Webster's online language center at http://m-w.com.

2. ***Print a draft copy of the document.*** Errors on a computer screen are difficult to locate; therefore, print a draft copy on plain paper and proofread carefully. Proofreading solely from the screen may be adequate for brief routine documents.

3. ***Proofread once concentrating on errors in content, organization, and style.*** To locate errors, ask the following questions:

   Content: Is the information complete? Have I included all the details the receiver needs to understand the message and to take necessary action? Is the information accurate? Have I checked the accuracy of any calculations, dates, names, addresses, and numbers? Have words been omitted?

   Organization: Is the main idea presented appropriately, based on the receiver's likely reaction (deductive or inductive organization)? Are supporting ideas presented in a logical order?

Style: Is the message clear? Will the receiver interpret the information correctly? Is the message concise and written at an appropriate level for the receiver? Does the message reflect a considerate, caring attitude? Is the message primarily focused on the receiver's needs? Does the message treat the receiver honestly and ethically?

Critical Thinking

Effective proofreading takes time that is well spent.

4. ***Proofread a second time concentrating on mechanical errors.*** You are searching for potentially damaging errors that a spell check cannot detect. These problem areas include

   - *Grammar, capitalization, punctuation, number usage, abbreviations.* Review the grammatical principles presented in Appendix C if necessary.
   - *Word substitutions.* Check the proper use of words such as *your* and *you* and words that sound alike (*there, they're*, or *their; affect* or *effect*).
   - *Parts of the document other than the body.* Proofread the entire document, including the date line, letter address, salutation, subject line, and closing lines. Errors often appear in the opening sections of letters because writers typically begin proofreading at the first paragraph.

5. ***Proofread a*** third ***time if the document is nonroutine and complex.*** Read from *right to left* to reduce your reading speed and to enable you to concentrate deliberately on each word. If a document is extremely important, you may read the document aloud, spelling names and noting capitalization and punctuation, while another person verifies the copy.

6. ***Edit for format and layout.*** Follow these steps to be certain the document adheres to appropriate business formats:
   - *Format according to a conventional format.* Compare your document to the conventional business formats shown in Appendix A and make any revisions. Are all standard parts of the document included and presented in an acceptable format? Are all necessary special letter parts (mailing notation, attention line, subject line, enclosure, and copy notations, second-page heading, and the writer's address for a personal business letter) included? Does the message begin on the correct line? Should the right margin be justified or jagged?
   - *Be sure numbered items are in correct order.* Inserting and deleting text may have changed the order of these items.
   - *Evaluate the visual impact of the document.* Could you increase the readability of long, uninterrupted blocks of texts by using enumerated or indented lists, headings, or different type styles (boldface, underlines, italics, or shadow type)? Could you increase the overall appeal by including graphics or using different fonts of various sizes and styles? Could you partition the text into logical, easy-to-read sections by using graphic lines, boxes, and borders?
   - *Be certain the document is signed or initialed (depending on the document).*

7. **Print the document on high-quality paper.** The envelope and sec-ond-page paper (if needed) should match the letterhead. The printing should read in the same direction as the watermark (the design imprinted on high-quality paper). Refer to Appendix A for paper spec-ifications and other areas related to the overall appearance of a docu-ment on the page.

The letter in Figure 4-2 has been revised for (1) content, organization, and style; (2) mechanics; and (3) format and layout. Changes are noted using proofreaders' marks, a standard, simplified way to indicate changes. The commentary makes it easy to see how revising this draft improved the doc-ument's quality. Refer to Appendix A for a handy list of proofreaders' marks.

Cultivate a Frame of Mind for Effective Revising and Proofreading

The following suggestions will guide your efforts to develop business docu-ments that achieve the purpose for which they are intended.

Diversity Challenges

- *Attempt to see things from your audience's perspective rather than from your own.* That is, have empathy for your audience. Being empathetic isn't as simple as it seems, particularly when dealing with today's diverse workforce. Erase the mind-set, "I know what *I* need to say and how *I* want to say it." Instead, ask, "How would my audience react to this message? Is this message worded so that my audience can easily understand it?"

- *Revise your documents until you cannot see any additional ways to improve them.* Resist the temptation to think of your first draft as your last draft. Instead, look for ways to improve and be willing to incorporate valid suggestions once you have completed a draft. Experienced writers believe that there is no such thing as good writing, but there is such a thing as good rewriting. Author Dorothy Parker once said, "I can't write five words that I change seven."[11] Skilled speech writers might rewrite a script 15 or 20 times. Writers in public relations firms revise brochures and advertising copy until perhaps only a comma in the final draft is recognizable from the first draft. Your diligent revising will yield out-standing dividends. Specifically, the audience (your instructor, supervi-sor, employees, or clients/customers, for example) is more likely to understand and accept your message.

Critical Thinking

Why are your own errors more diffi-cult to detect than the errors of others?

- *Be willing to allow others to make suggestions for improving your writing.* Most people consider their writing very personal. That is, they are reluctant to share what they have written with others and are easily offended if others suggest changes. This syndrome, called *writer's pride of ownership*, can needlessly prevent you from seeking assistance from expe-rienced writers—a proven method of improving communication skills. On the job, you will share your writing with the recipient (your supervi-sor, your employees, or clients/customers). Because a great deal of busi-ness writing is completed collaboratively, you will be required to subject

Figure 4-2

Rough Draft of a Letter (excerpt)

September 14, 2004

FAX Transmission

Adds mailing notation

Mr. Brent M. Weinberg
Production Manager
Worldwide Enterprises, Inc.
1635 Taylor Road
Baltimore, ~~Maryland~~ 21225-1635
MD

Uses 2-letter state abbreviation

Corrects spelling of name

Dear Mr. W~~i~~enberg:

Adds a smooth transition to next paragraph

☐ With your proven ability to produce precision-quality electronic parts, our entrance into the DVD market is certain to be successful. *We're excited about other ways our companies can benefit through sharing our expertise.*

Corrects grammatical error

is

☐ One of the objectives of our recent merger ~~are~~ to increase your competitiveness by updating your information systems. The first step of this process is to form a steering

Replaces with simple word for clarity

The committee primary

committee ~~whose rudimentary~~ function is to direct the development of the new system and to ensure that it incorporates the information needs of the user and the organization.

Divides into two sentences to enhance readability

(a)

To accomplish this goal, committee members must represent inventory control, shipping, purchasing, accounting, and marketing, ~~Further, the group must~~ consist of members from a variety of organizational levels and ~~members must~~ possess varying degrees of computer proficiency.

Enumerates list for emphasis and reduces wordiness

(b)

(c)

Recasts from receiver's viewpoint

Inserts comma to separate compound adjectives

is essential

☐ Brent, because of your knowledge of company operations, ~~we need~~ your input. Your serving on this committee will be clear, tangible evidence of management's commitment to

Eliminates cliché and includes specific action ending

let know by September 30 that

this significant change. Please ~~advise me whether or not~~ you will serve on the Information Systems Steering Committee. A meeting will be scheduled as soon as all members~~'~~ have been selected.

Eliminates redundancy

Corrects grammatical error

Organization, Content, and Style
- Add a smooth transition to ¶2.
- Eliminate cliché: "Please advise me."
- Break long sentence in ¶2 into two shorter sentences.
- Use simple words for clarity: "rudimentary."
- Eliminate redundancy: "whether or not."
- Write from the receiver's viewpoint: "Your input is essential."
- Write a specific, action-oriented ending: "by September 30."

Errors Undetectable by Spell Check
- Verify spelling of receiver's name, "Weinberg."
- Correct word substitutions: "too" for "to."

Mechanics
- Use a singular verb when "one" is the subject.
- Place comma between coordinate adjectives: "clear, tangible."
- Omit an apostrophe after plural noun: "members."

Format and Layout
- Insert mailing notation: "FAX Transmission."
- Use two-letter state abbreviation.
- Enumerate list ¶2 for emphasis.

Blondie

Seemingly small proofreading oversights can cause big problems.

Team Environment

your writing to review by others. You have nothing to lose but much to gain. Remember that the mistake hardest to detect is your own. As the "Blondie" cartoon illustrates, you have the ultimate responsibility for your document; don't simply trust that someone else will catch and correct all of your errors. The ability you've gained in following a systematic process for developing effective business messages will prove valuable as you direct your energies to sharing information and developing messages as a member of a team. The accompanying Strategic Forces feature, "Using Collaborative Technologies to Support Work Teams," will showcase exciting technologies that facilitate productive collaboration with others regardless of their location. Refer to the "Check Your Communication" checklist at the end of this chapter to review the guidelines for preparing and proofreading a rough draft.

Summary

1. **Apply techniques for developing effective sentences and unified and coherent paragraphs.** Well-written sentences and unified and coherent paragraphs will help the receiver understand the message clearly and respond favorably. To craft powerful sentences, use correct sentence structure, rely on active voice, and emphasize important points. To write effective paragraphs, develop deductive or inductive paragraphs consistently, link ideas to achieve coherence, keep paragraphs unified, and vary sentence and paragraph length.

2. **Identify factors affecting readability and revise sentences to improve readability.** The readability of a message is affected by the length of the sentences and the difficulty of the words. For quick, easy reading, use simple words and short sentences. A readability index (grade level necessary for reader to understand the material) in the eighth-to-eleventh grade range is appropriate for most business writing. Writing a message with a readability index appropriate for an audience does not guarantee

understanding but does provide feedback on the average length of the sentences and the difficulty of the words.

3. **Prepare visually appealing documents that grab the receiver's attention and increase comprehension.** Visually appealing documents entice the reader to read the document, focus attention on important ideas, and move the reader smoothly through the organization of the document without adding clutter. Techniques for preparing appealing, easy-to-read documents include enumerations, enumerated or bulleted lists, headings, tables and graphs, lines and borders, and drawing tools and clip art.

4. **Revise and proofread a message for content, organization, and style; mechanics; and format and layout.** Be willing to revise a document as many times as necessary to be certain that it conveys the message effectively and is error free. Use the spell check to locate keying errors, then follow systematic procedures for proofreading a printed copy of the document. Proofread for content, organization, and style; mechanics; and format and layout.

Using Collaborative Technologies to Support Work Teams

New systems and workgroup software are bringing team members together and allowing them to share data on a timely basis no matter where they are located. Teams are able to reach better and faster decisions because they have the necessary information and the forum to participate in discussion and idea exchange. ***Workgroup computing*** or ***collaborative computing*** are other terms used to describe this cooperative computing environment.

Leading collaboration software includes Lotus Notes and Domino software from IBM's Lotus Software Group and Microsoft Exchange Titanium.[12] Electronic collaboration tools aid effective communication, collaboration, and coordination especially in groups that are geographically dispersed. Productivity enhancements result because groupware offers the following advantages.[13]

- ***A shared work area for teams to keep track of projects.*** Up-to-date information can be accessed quickly and securely by everyone simultaneously. This "knowledge base" enables companies to respond quickly to customer needs and to new market opportunities.[14]

- ***Bulletin boards for discussing ideas, sharing and editing documents, and obtaining team member approval.*** Bulletin board comments and questions are posted, stored, routed, and organized by topic so they can be accessed and reviewed quickly when a decision must be made. Rather than call a hurried meeting to ask a question or make an important announcement, teams can access and respond to a posted message and spend the saved time completing critical tasks.

- ***Advance real-time communication.*** Participants can be linked together to read and respond to information on their computer screens, to participate in brainstorming sessions, and to vote on issues anonymously. Users in different locations can work simultaneously on the same documents on their screens and can hold a face-to-face meeting if videoconferencing technology is available.

- ***Group calendar and scheduling.*** The software identifies a convenient time for a team meeting, detects scheduling conflicts, and can even locate a member when needed. Success is dependent on the team's commitment to maintaining a complete and accurate calendar and concern for privacy.

- ***Monitoring the flow of the team's work.*** The software helps track the status of documents—who has them, who is behind schedule, and who gets the document next.

To achieve optimal results from collaborative software, employees need training in the technology, but more importantly, they must learn to work collaboratively. They need a clear understanding of their roles and responsibilities so members can reach agreement and support others in the work to be done. Employees must also be committed to sharing information, files, and resources freely, with respect for confidentiality when appropriate—a concept in direct opposition to the traditional view that "knowledge is power." Visit the text support site to learn more about ways for developing people to work with collaborative technologies.

Application

From library research or your own networking activities, identify an organization that uses workgroup software for authoring and editing documents. Conduct an interview with a member of a collaborative team within the organization that seeks the following information: (1) software product used for collaborative writing, (2) number and expertise of colleagues who typically collaborate on a single document, and (3) reactions to the use of collaborative software in terms of advantages and disadvantages. Present the results of your interview in written or spoken form, as directed by your instructor.

Powerful Sentences

- Use correct structure when writing simple, compound, complex, and compound-complex sentences. Avoid run-on sentences and comma splices.
- Use active voice to present important points or to present pleasant ideas. Use passive verbs to present less significant points or unpleasant ideas.
- Emphasize important ideas:
  - Place an idea in a simple sentence.
  - Place an idea in an independent clause; for de-emphasis, place an idea in a dependent clause.
  - Use an important word more than once in a sentence.
  - Place an important idea first or last in a sentence, paragraph, or document.
  - Use words that label ideas as significant or insignificant.
  - Use headings, graphics, and additional space to emphasize important ideas.

Coherent Paragraphs

- Write deductively if a message will likely please or at least not displease. If a message will likely displease or if understanding the major idea is dependent on prior explanations, write inductively.
- Strive for paragraphs that are consistently deductive or consistently inductive.
- Make sure compositions form a unit with an obvious beginning, middle, and ending and that in-between paragraphs are arranged in a systematic sequence.

- Avoid abrupt changes in thought, and link each sentence to a preceding sentence. Place transition sentences before major headings.
- Vary sentence and paragraph length to emphasize important ideas.
- Limit paragraphs in letters, memos, and e-mail messages to six lines and paragraphs in reports to eight to ten lines to maximize comprehension.

Readability

- Use simple words and short sentences for quick, easy reading (and listening).
- Strive for short paragraphs but vary their lengths.
- Emphasize a sentence by placing it first or last within a paragraph or by assigning it a number in a tabulated series.
- Create appealing, easy-to-read documents by
  - Preceding each unit in a series by a number, a letter, or a bullet. For stronger emphasis, place in an enumerated or bulleted list.
  - Using headings, tables and graphs, lines and borders, and images to focus attention on important information.

Systematic Proofreading

- Use the spell check to locate simple keying errors.
- Proofread once concentrating on content, organization, and style and a second time on mechanics, format, and layout.

Chapter Review

1. Is writing rapidly with intent to revise or writing slowly and deliberately more effective? Explain. (Obj. 1)

2. How has automated speech recognition software affected the preparation of business messages? What changes are predicted in the near future? (Obj. 1)

3. When is active voice preferred? When is passive voice preferred? (Obj. 1)

4. What factors affect the readability of a document? (Objs. 1, 2)

5. Discuss several strategies that will enhance the quality and efficiency of writing with a computer. (Obj. 1)

6. Explain the benefits collaborative technology provides work teams. Include several examples of the capability this technology provides. (Obj. 1)

7. What value does knowing the readability level of a document serve? What two factors should be evaluated for possible revision in an effort to reduce the readability index of a report? (Obj. 2)

// electronic café //

Intranets Expand Internal Communications

The emergence of the global marketplace has driven many organizations to find solutions that meet diverse information and communication needs. Many organizations rely on their intranets to provide restricted access to geographically dispersed employees. A single, unified structure for gathering and sharing information helps build a common organizational culture. An effective corporate intranet can meet these needs, serving as a symbol of unity for each member of the organization.

 InfoTrac College Edition. Access http://www.infotrac.thomsonlearning.com to read about several successful organizations that use their intranets to build corporate culture:

Cordasco, P. (2002, August 5). The intranet: Creating a common culture. *PR Week*, 18.

Considering the information provided about effective intranet usage, add three additional "Do" suggestions and three additional "Don't" suggestions to the list provided.

 Text Support Web Site. Visit http://lehman.swlearning.com to locate an e-journal article that describes ways that an organization can help its end users to become more self-sufficient in their computer use.

 WebTutor Advantage. Go to your WebTutor site and find out how to explore the Menu features to locate useful information.

 Professional Power Pak. Access your PPP CD to learn more about how to effectively use an intranet as a channel for organizational communication.

---

8. What are the benefits and limitations of an electronic spell check and writing-analysis software? (Objs. 3, 4)

9. Explain the importance of creating a visually appealing document, and provide four guidelines for accomplishing this objective. (Obj. 3)

10. How has instantaneous communication made possible by technology affected the proofreading stage of the writing process? (Obj. 4)

11. What are the seven steps for proofreading a document systematically to locate all errors? (Obj. 4)

12. Why is writer's pride of ownership an obstacle to good proofreading? (Obj. 4)

Digging Deeper

1. What habits hinder your success or enjoyment of writing? Identify ways to overcome them.

2. How does online writing challenge a writer's effort to develop a seamless, coherent document?

To check your understanding of the chapter, take the practice quizzes at **http://lehman.swlearning.com** or your WebTutor course.

Activities

1. Sentence Structure (Obj. 1)

Analyze the structure of the following sentences: indicate the type of sentence (i.e., simple, compound, complex, or compound-complex), mark the dependent and independent clauses, and punctuate correctly.

Visit the Interactive Study Center at **http://lehman.swlearning.com** for a downloadable version of this activity.

a. The Information Systems Department has implemented new e-mail security procedures.

b. The consultant recommended a new marketing strategy it works much better than the strategy we formerly used.

c. We need new marketing brochures, the ones we use now are out of date.

d. After analyzing the crucial issues, the manager will present an acceptable Internet usage policy for our consideration.

e. We can generate very attractive brochures in-house the new computer software makes it easy.

f. Because of the expansion of our overseas operation our current brochures no longer accurately portray our capabilities however the publications department is developing new materials.

2. **Active and Passive Voice (Obj. 1)**

Revise the following sentences using active and passive voice appropriately. Justify your decisions.

Visit the Interactive Study Center at **http://lehman. swlearning. com** for a downloadable version of this activity.

a. An exemplary job was done by the design team.

b. Elizabeth polled only the clients in the Southeast, thereby producing an inaccurate marketing report.

c. The projections will be released tomorrow by the financial team.

d. This innovative advertisement was designed by J. D. Mackay.

e. Distribution of the market survey is to be no later than May 8.

f. A proposal for consulting work for the Department of Public Works was written by Alicia.

3. **Emphasis Techniques (Obj. 1)**

Decide for each pair of sentences which one is preferred. Justify your choice.

a. (1) Our petition for promotion was denied, but we were commended for our performance.

   (2) Although the petition for promotion was denied, we were commended for our performance.

b. (1) The Lawlor account was won.

   (2) Jennifer is responsible for our winning the Lawlor account.

c. (1) Congratulations on your recent honor.

   (2) Congratulations on your receipt of the "employee of the month" award.

d. (1) We appreciate your letting us know about your concerns.

   (2) We appreciate your letting us know about the broken equipment, the outdated materials, and the poor employee morale at your branch.

e. (1) We will not be able to fund your Internet training.

   (2) We wish we could pay for your Internet training, but funds are unavailable.

4. **Emphasis and Ordering Techniques (Objs. 1–3)**

Revise the following sentences, adding emphasis to the lists.

Visit the Interactive Study Center at **http://lehman. swlearning. com** for a downloadable version of this activity.

a. Our department needs two more engineers. The workload is such that the three engineers currently on staff are out of town on site at least three days a week. Although their work is satisfactory, at this pace, it could suffer soon. Morale is also starting to become a concern. Additionally, because of the increasing workload, it has become difficult for them to attend to routine administrative tasks in a timely fashion.

b. Our company should offer employees a choice between overtime pay or compensatory time off. Many of our employees are parents and would appreciate having more time to spend with their children. Others are more interested in earning extra money. Therefore, offering a choice would improve morale and reduce employee absenteeism, leading to a more efficient, dedicated workforce.

5. **Coherence Techniques (Obj. 1)**

Link each sentence to the preceding sentence to improve coherence (avoid abrupt changes in thought).

Visit the Interactive Study Center at **http://lehman. swlearning.com** for a downloadable version of this activity.

a. The design group meets every Monday at 9 a.m. They go over plans and goals for the upcoming week. Other departments have similar meetings.

b. Diversity awareness training seems important to some employees. It is very effective in improving communication and understanding. Employees should participate in this training.

c. Our company has initiated a new overtime policy. Employees can choose between overtime pay or compensatory time off. This policy could improve morale and productivity.

d. The publications department is working on new marketing materials. Our current brochures and materials are out of date. The materials do not reflect the major corporate changes that have occurred in the past six months.

e. New computer software is being loaded onto our local area network (LAN). Personnel will be able to generate expense statements from their workstations. This will make the old paper forms obsolete.

6. **Improving Readability (Obj. 2)**

Improve readability by dividing each of the following sentences into shorter sentences.

Visit the Interactive Study Center at **http://lehman. swlearning.com** for a downloadable version of this activity.

a. Several members of our firm will be touring the manufacturing plant in Tokyo during the week of May 16, 2004, and upon return to the United States will present a slide show documenting the trip, followed by a question-and-answer session, both to be held in the banquet hall of the Ashton Hotel in Denver on Friday, May 27.

b. The accountant will be arriving on Thursday to perform the audit, and will be using the 2nd floor break room as a work area, meaning that employees should take morning and afternoon breaks in either the courtyard or the 3rd floor lounge, and employees who use the 2nd floor break room for lunch should report to the cafeteria at that time.

c. People from such different backgrounds as today's workers invariably bring different values, attitudes, and perceptions to the workplace, which can lead to misunderstandings, miscommunications, and missed opportunities to improve both the workers and the organizations.

d. Business managers have studied, completed internships, and made many sacrifices to get closer to their ultimate goals, but unless they can use electronic tools to access, assemble, and communicate information in a timely manner, however, they may find themselves lagging behind.

e. At the corporate level, the Corporate Quality Improvement Department provides guidance and recommends resources for quality improvement activities and assesses organization-wide activities, while at the branch office level, the Department assists in the collection of data, facilitates quality improvement activities, and provides education for implementing the quality improvement process.

Now suggest short, simple words to replace each of the following difficult words that raises the readability index.

f. The supervisor's deprecatory remarks demoralized the employees.

g. The applicant was poised, decorous, and articulate, making her an excellent choice for the position.

h. After a meticulous search, the committee has concurred on an epitome location for the convention.

i. Assembling the proposal required perusing voluminous stacks of files for the pertinent information.

j. Utilization of the new procedures by all personnel will contribute to the efficiency of this office.

k. We anticipate that the recently acquired computer applications will facilitate a reduction in the time currently required to generate large documents.

7. **Proofreading (Obj. 4)**

Use proofreading marks to mark spelling, grammar, punctuation, capitalization, and other errors in the following sentences.

Visit the Interactive Study Center at **http://lehman. swlearning.com** for a downloadable version of this activity.

a. We have received several suggestions and a few complaints from customers who have visited our web site, please take these into consideration as you work to improve the effectiveness of the site.

b. His advise was to listen to the clients comments.

c. The project was understaffed, the schedule was not met, has gone over budget and we apologize for any inconvenience this has caused you.

d. Austin Strong, a Project Director, will speak at the next Staff Meeting, he will address next quarters sales forecast.

e. Our trip included a conference in San Fanciso California before the larson state business council meeting in Portland OR.

f. 12 persons form our office were their to here president Bush speak at the civic center his speech was about homeland securty.

8. **Proofreading Application (Obj. 4)**

Use proofreaders' marks to correct errors in spelling, grammar, punctuation, numbers, and abbreviations in the following letter sent to Phelps Enterprise. Do not revise a sentence and state its idea in an entirely different way.

Visit the Interactive Study Center at **http://lehman. swlearning.com** for a downloadable version of this activity.

Congradulations on being selected to attend the two day seminar on effective listening. The seminar will be held in Los Angeles, California on January 3. These five guidelines for effective listening should be helpful as you begin to analyze you own listening skills.

1. Learn to block out distractions that interfere with effective listening.

2. Take notes on the material to reinforce you memory.

3. Become sincrely interested in what the speaker is saying, this procedure will help you retain information.

3. Listen to the entire message before responding to be certain that you here everything.

4. Listen with an open mind, otherwise, you may miss key points.

5. Identify your weaknesses in listening and work to improve them.

We are eager for you to this professional development seminar. When you return please be sure to share this valuable information with others at Philps Enterprises.

Applications

Read   Think   Write   Speak   Collaborate

1. Effective Professionals Must Communicate Technical Information Clearly (Objs. 1–4)

Locate the following article that offers tips on writing powerful business messages:

Rindegard, J. (1999). Use clear writing to show you mean business. *InfoWorld, 21*(47), 78.

After reading the article, respond to the following questions:

a. What does the writer's statement "information is not communication" mean?

b. Explain the writer's "bottom-line writing approach." Could you foresee exceptions to the use of this approach for all business messages? Provide examples.

c. Do you agree that front-line people should not be allowed to communicate via e-mail directly to customers? What are the pros and cons of this communication policy?

d. Summarize the hallmarks of clear, effective writing. What other "hallmarks" would you add to this list based on your study of the writing process and business experience.

2. Crafting Powerful Communication (Obj. 1)

Visit the text support site **(http://lehman.swlearning.com)** to explore other strategies for crafting powerful messages. Complete the activities that appear at the end of the document and e-mail to your instructor.

Read   Think   Write   Speak   Collaborate

3. Professional Development Is Only a Click Away (Objs. 1–4)

Some companies, facing the reality that poor writing is costly, are initiating training programs for effective writing. You can develop your own program for improving your basic communication skills (e.g., listening, speaking, and writing). Begin by studying the content at the web sites provided at **http://lehman.swlearning.com** in the Professional Resources section of your Professional Power Pak CD, and others that you locate. Then, write a brief description of at least five communication topics you will commit to study over the course of the semester. Be prepared to share your "course of study" and progress reports in the format requested by your instructor. As you prepare these assignments, bookmark useful web sites for future professional development.

http://www.mapnp.org/library/commskls/cmm_writ.htm

http://www.plainlanguage.gov/handbook/index.htm

http://www.dest.gov.au/ty/publications/plain_en/contents.htm

http://www.quintcareers.com/writing/writweb.html

4. Visual Enhancements (Obj. 3)

Evaluate the visual impact of a document that you have received or one that your instructor provides. Summarize any changes you would make and explain how the changes would improve the impact of the document. Then, as you prepare documents in this course, evaluate the need for visual enhancements that will make your document say, "Read me."

Read   Think   Write   Speak   Collaborate

5. Improving Readability (Obj. 2)

Create a substitution list of easier words for 10 to 15 difficult words. Be prepared to share your list with the class.

6. The Emergence of Speech Technology (Obj. 1)

Conduct an online search related to recent developments in speech (voice-recognition) technology. Prepare a brief written report providing information such as (a) current status of speech technology as a viable business application, including challenges that have hampered past developments and (b) examples of leading speech technology applications with related results, and (c) projections for future development of this technology. Be prepared to share your ideas with the class.

7. The Price Companies Pay for Human Errors (Obj. 4)

Using an online database or the Internet, locate an example of an error in a printed document made by an actual company. Errors might be caused by overreliance on spell check or poor proofreading for mechanical, content, or style errors. Prepare a brief presentation describing the error, specific consequences experienced as a result of the error, and actions taken to overcome negative effects.

8. Advice from Communication Students (Objs. 1-4)

Visit one of the web sites provided in Application 3 and develop a list of suggestions that you believe would help an employee prepare a clear, understandable business message. Then, in small groups, compile your suggestions into several broad categories; e.g., stages of the writing process, types of business messages, etc. Edit for completeness, consistent writing style, and appealing format so that the document is suitable for distribution to employees in print or on the company intranet.

9. Document for Analysis (Objs. 1–4)

Complete the following tasks as a group assigned by your instructor.

Visit the Interactive Study Center at **http://lehman.swlearning.com** for a downloadable version of this activity.

a. Key the following document into your word processing program.

Worldwide Enterprises is preparing to initiate a program whereby employees may participate in telecommuting. We anticipate that implementation of the program will begin sometime next quarter. To qualify for this program, an employee must secure the approval of his superior and also meet specific criteria. It has been learned that companies can realize substantial savings through the implementation of telecommuting, such as savings from reduced use of energy and other office resources, reduced need for office space and employees have less absenteeism. In order to qualify for the telecommuting program, employees must meet the following criteria: must own or be able to lease a computer compatible with those currently used in the office, complete with modem, must purchase or lease a fax machine if it is not included in computer package, must agree to work in the office a minimum of three days per week, must submit time and expense reports daily instead of weekly, and personnel must be within job grades 6 or above. Technical and administrative personnel obviously cannot participate due to the nature of their employment. Please see your supervisor if you are interested in this program. He will assist you in assessing whether telecommuting is a good option for you. Worldwide Enterprises is pleased to offer this new program to it's employees who qualify and will continue to be supportive of innovation in the workplace.

b. Complete a readability analysis using the grammar checker available to you or compute the Fog Index using the formula shown in this chapter. Note the readability index, average length of sentences, number of difficult words, number of sentences in paragraphs, average number of syllables, and other statistics provided.

c. Revise the document: (1) incorporate relevant suggestions generated by the grammar checker and (2) improve the readability by applying the principles presented in Chapters 3–4. Use the track changes feature to mark revisions.

d. Complete a readability analysis for your revision and compare with the original readability analysis. Write a brief summary that notes the areas where improvements were made.

e. Send your instructor an e-mail message with revised document attached. Print a copy so that you can quickly verify the accuracy of your team's work when your instructor reviews the corrections during class.

Plain English Requirements for Patient Privacy Disclosures

Health care providers are required by law to provide privacy notices that inform patients about how their personal information is used and how they can control their medical records. The problem, however, has been how to do this without using confusing legal and medical jargon. As of 2003, providers are required to provide such a document in plain English to patients on their first doctor visit or when signing up for health insurance. Many health care professionals worked cooperatively to develop a simplified, yet informative document.

Following the lead of food labels, the idea was to design the document so patients can easily spot the topics of interest to them.[15]

- Visit the web site of the Physicians Insurance Agency of Massachusetts to read about the information that must be included in the privacy notice: **http://www.piam.com/ compliance/HIPAATU_0601. html**
- Search the Web to find examples of privacy notices used by various medical practices or health care agencies. Prepare a short report about the challenges involved in developing a plain English document that meets the federal requirements for privacy disclosure.

Part 4 of the SEC ShowCASE further substantiates the need for impressive skills in using plain English and powerful language.

http://www.sec.gov

Visit the text support site at **http://lehman.swlearning.com** to complete Part 4 of the ShowCASE.

Internet Case

Understanding the Plain English Campaign

Effective communication is a major part of a manager's job. Yet many managers continue to bury what they want to say in pompous jargon or polysyllabic babble. Such communication fails miserably because the people to whom it is aimed either do not understand it or regard it as garbage and ignore it. A Plain English movement is gaining momentum in Great Britain and the United States. Plain English Campaign, founded in 1979, is an independent U.K.-based organization that fights to stamp out all forms of gobbledygook, a term that includes legalese, small print, and bureaucratic language. The campaign is funded by its professional services, which include editing, writing, design, and training in Plain English for a variety of companies as well as government and local authorities. The Plain English Campaign-USA, a subsidiary of the England-based campaign, is based in Miami, Florida.

Documents that achieve a good standard of clarity may qualify for endorsement with the Campaign's Crystal Mark, a widely recognized and respected symbol of clarity. The Mark can be found on over 7,000 documents around the world, and more than 1,000 organizations worldwide have received the Crystal Mark for at least one document. It is a powerful marketing tool because customers can see the Crystal Mark on documents and know they can be confident that the information is clear. The Campaign also recognizes outstanding offenders of plain English with their Golden Bull awards; criteria for selection include worst examples of gobbledygook and the negative impact of the documents on the lives of ordinary people.

Misconceptions exist concerning Plain English writing. Writing in Plain English does not mean deleting complex information to make the document easier to understand. Using Plain English assures the orderly and clear presentation of complex information so that the audience has the best possible chance of understanding; it presents information to meet its audience's needs. A Plain English document uses words economically and at a level the audience can understand. Its sentence structure is tight. Its tone is approachable and direct, and its design is visually appealing. A Plain English document is easy to read and looks as if it is meant to be read.[16]

Visit the text support site at **http://lehman.swlearning.com** to link to web resources related to this topic. As directed by your instructor, respond to one or more of the following:

1. Compile a chart that lists companies, agencies, and other organizations that have benefited from Plain English assistance and the stated results that have been realized. Arrange a telephone interview with a person representing one of the organizations to obtain firsthand information about the impact of Plain English in that organization.

2. Using links provided in the web resources for this case familiarize yourself with a recent news story that

points out the need for Plain English. Summarize the reported incident in a one-page abstract that includes the following parts: (1) bibliographic citation, (2) brief overview of the article, (3) discussion of the major points covered in the article, and (4) application section that tells who might benefit from reading the article and why.

3. **GMAT** Select an organization of your choice that could benefit from Plain English assistance; you may consult the "List of Shame" organizations or identify one on your own. Recommend a plan for implementing Plain English that includes the following: (1) reasons for implementing Plain English, (2) training courses that are available, (3) other services that can be accessed through the Plain English Campaign, and (4) the advantages of corporate membership in the Plain English Campaign.

Video Case

PaceButler Corporation: Ethics and Atmosphere

PaceButler Corporation is the recipient of the 2002 Oklahoma City Metro 50 award—an award that applauds and encourages the entrepreneurial drive and determination needed to survive and succeed in today's world of global competition. PaceButler, with about $14 million in sales last year, has specialized since 1987 in purchasing, refurbishing, and reselling computer equipment and other business assets.

Located in Edmond, Oklahoma, PaceButler employs more than 50 employees and has a state-of-the art technical center staffed by experienced technicians. PaceButler also provides equipment installation services and on-site upgrades and repairs. With a national client base, PaceButler counts some of the biggest companies in the world, including IBM, among its customers.

View the video segment about PaceButler Corporation and accompanying activities on WebTutor or your Professional Power Pak CD.

Discussion Questions

1. What factors led Tom Pace to leave his job after four months and start PaceButler Corporation—a business similar to what he had left?

2. What events led up to the employees writing an atmosphere statement at PaceButler in 1990?

3. What three statements were written after the atmosphere statement?

4. How are these four statements used in the hiring process?

Activities

1. Download the PaceButler mission statement document found at **www.pacebutler.com/about/mission.htm**.

2. Assume you are a new PaceButler employee. Based on the mission statement document, what are the standards of ethical conduct this document suggests to you?

3. CEO Tom Pace states: "My goal is to make sure that every person who comes in contact with the PaceButler Corporation benefits in a positive way." Assuming PaceButler employees treat their customers according to the guidelines suggested in the mission statement document, how might Tom's goal be realized by PaceButler's customers?

Communication Through Voice, Electronic, and Written Messages

iii

Resorts

Pick your Paradise℠

site map►

member
services & benefits

travel
& leisure services

inside
Fairfield Resorts

►Resort Search

Owner Login

Member# or Contract#

1/14/2003

Hot News & Highlights

Fairfield Resorts Acquires Kona Hawaiian Village!

Grand Opening!
Fairfield Merchandise Store

Need help making travel arrangements? Check out **Fairfield's Vacation Break Travel.**

Objectives *When you have completed Chapter 5, you will be able to:*

1 Discuss the effective use of e-mail and instant messaging in business communication.

2 Explain principles for creating, designing, publishing, maintaining, and writing effective web pages.

3 Discuss the effective use of voice and wireless technologies in business communication.

4 Identify legal and ethical implications associated with the use of communication technology.

FAIRFIELD RESORTS UTILIZES WEB TO PROVIDE OWNER SATISFACTION

From its beginnings in the late 1960s, vacation ownership has become the fastest growing segment of the U.S. travel and tourism industry. Today more than three million households have bought into vacations at nearly 4,500 resorts located in 174 countries. Timeshare resorts are found across the globe in popular vacation areas near beaches, rivers and lakes, mountains, and even major cities. By locking in the purchase price of accommodations, vacation ownership helps assure consistent pricing for future vacations. And through vacation exchange programs, timeshare owners have the flexibility to travel to popular destinations around the world.[1]

Fairfield Resorts, one of the leading resort and vacation products companies in the world, is a subentity of Cendant Corporation, owner of numerous other large companies including Century 21,

Howard Johnson, Coldwell Banker, and Avis Car Rental. Fairfield owns 65 resorts with more under development and is the first company to use a flexible points-based system successfully. The company's FairShare Plus system enables its 450,000 owners to purchase an allotment of points rather than a specific timeframe at a particular location. The points can then be used as an exchange value like currency. FairShare Plus members have the freedom to choose the resort locations, dates, unit sizes, and lengths of stay of their annual vacations.

Prior to the introduction of web-based vacation planning sites, vacation arrangements were typically made by telephone, necessitating several lengthy calls to obtain information and confirm options. FairShare Plus members have enjoyed greater communication power since the advent of Fairfield's comprehensive web-based vacation planning site. Full-service travel planning capabilities allow site visitors to

- use the site's search function to select resorts by destination, features, and amenities.
- access photos, maps, directions, resort activity calendars, local attractions, and even virtual tours of affiliated resorts.
- look up point requirements to stay at any of the Fairfield resorts and affiliates.
- make airline, hotel, and car rental reservations.
- take advantage of special cruise and package deals.
- obtain door-to-door directions and current weather reports for all Fairfield resorts.

The ability to share information effectively is a primary advantage of electronic communications. As you will see in the chapter, the primary communication challenge of technology is mastery of online dynamics.

http://www.fairfieldresorts.com

See ShowCASE, Part 2, on page 176 for Spotlight Communicator Franz Hanning, president and CEO, Fairfield Resorts.

Electronic Mail Communication

Objective 1

Discuss the effective use of e-mail and instant messaging in business communication.

A vital factor in successful global business and economic development is the effective use of knowledge and information. The audience for the communication of vital information is growing, as organizations compete on a global scale and serve a worldwide customer base. Companies must not only provide the means for their own workers to access important information and communicate it internally, but also for them to communicate with audiences who have decided to pay attention via web sites and electronic inquiries.[2] As you read in Chapter 1, the continuous evolution of technology has expanded communication options. E-mail, instant messaging, web communications, and voice and wireless technologies are important tools for accomplishing company goals.

Advantages of E-Mail

Changing Technology

Electronic mail, known as *e-mail*, has quickly become the most used communication tool in many organizations. Its ready availability, convenience, and ease of use have resulted in its skyrocketing popularity over the last decade. One company official enthusiastically states, "Because the top tier of our management is so widely dispersed, it used to take weeks to distribute the paperwork for a meeting. Now we can turn that around in a day via e-mail."[3] The advantages of e-mail are numerous:

- *It facilitates the fast, convenient flow of information among users at various locations and time zones.* Recipients receive electronic messages more quickly than printed documents, which expedites decision making and the completion of tasks. Mail service is often too slow for communicating timely information, and the telephone system is

Today's businesses are using both traditional and electronic means of sharing information. With 70 percent of communication occurring electronically, your career success will depend on the ability to exchange ideas with others and to access communication needed to complete your job.

© JOSÉ LOIS PELAEZ, INC./CORBIS

inconvenient and costly when communicating with people located in several locations and time zones. For these reasons, e-mail is especially effective when sending a single message to several recipients and when needing to communicate 24 hours a day, 365 days a year.

- *It increases efficiency.* E-mail reduces "telephone tag," and unnecessary telephone interruptions caused when delivering messages that are unlikely to require a verbal response.
- *It reduces costs.* Sending e-mail messages represents a substantial savings to companies in long-distance telephone costs and postal mail-outs.
- *It reduces paper waste.* Often an electronic message can be read and immediately discarded without the need for a printed copy.

Critical Thinking

What are some negative aspects of using e-mail?

Guidelines for Preparing E-Mail Messages

The principles of style and organization that you learned about in Chapters 3 and 4 are applicable to e-mail messages. In addition to these basic writing principles, certain techniques are specific to e-mail. All of these tools will assist you in using informal communication channels more efficiently without jeopardizing the effectiveness of your message or damaging relationships with valued coworkers and outside parties.

Standard Heading

E-mail systems automatically show a heading format that includes *To, From, Date,* and *Subject.* As the date and the sender's name are automatically entered, the sender need only provide information for the *To:* and the *Subject:* lines. Sending an e-mail message to multiple recipients simply involves inputting the e-mail address of each recipient into a distribution list (or address macro) and selecting the distribution list as the recipient.

Useful Subject Line

Critical Thinking

Write an effective subject line for a memo announcing software training classes for the upcoming month.

The subject line is a standard component of e-mail messages. It expedites the understanding of the message by (1) telling the receiver what the following message is about, (2) setting the stage for the receiver to understand the message, and (3) providing meaning when the document is referenced at a later date. Additionally, a well-written subject line in an e-mail message will help a receiver sort through an overloaded mailbox and read messages in priority order. The following suggestions should be helpful in wording subject lines.

- *Provide a useful subject line that has meaning for you and the receiver.* Identifying key words will help you develop good subject lines. Think of the five W's—Who, What, When, Where, and Why—to give you some clues for a useful subject line. Consider the following examples:

General and Ineffective	Precise and Informative
Report of Meeting	Report of June 10 Meeting on Relocation of Dublin Plant
	Provides specific information that will identify the exact purpose of the message
Product Launch or Update on Product Launch	Product Launch Snafu *Pinpoints a problem and will provoke an immediate response*
Change in Employee Benefit	New Insurance Carrier Provides Additional Benefits *Specifies exact change and indicates the change is beneficial to the receiver.*

Critical Thinking

A good subject line will be long enough to stir interest but short enough to display in one's inbox listing.

- *Restate the subject in the body of the message.* Opening sentences should not include wording such as "This is . . . " and "The above-mentioned subject . . . " The body of the message should be a complete thought and should not rely on the subject line for elaboration. A good opening sentence might be a repetition of most of the subject line. Even if the subject line was omitted, the e-mail would still be clear, logical, and complete.

SUBJECT: Budget Meeting at Crystal Bluff

Arrange your schedule to attend a day-long meeting to finalize the 2004 budget on Friday, February 24. This year we're meeting in the conference room at the Crystal Bluff Retreat and Conference Center to minimize distractions as we complete this important task.

Single Topic Directed Toward the Receiver's Needs

Be sure you understand the purpose of your writing. What do you hope to accomplish as a result of the message? Being clear in your purpose will enable you to organize and develop the content of your message to achieve your goal. Tailor your message to show how the receiver will benefit from your ideas.

Messages are generally limited to one idea rather than addressing several issues in the same message. If you address more than one topic in a single e-mail message, chances are the recipient will forget to respond to all points discussed. Additionally, discussing one topic allows you to write a descriptive subject line that will accurately describe your purpose and allow your message to compete for the receiver's attention more favorably—especially when the subject line appears in an overcrowded e-mailbox. The receiver can transfer an e-mail message to a separate mailbox folder for quick, accurate access if you don't bury multiple ideas in one e-mail message.

Lengthy messages may be divided into logical sections. Additionally, using headings to denote the divisions will alert the receiver of information that is ahead and make the information easier to comprehend.

Sequence of Ideas Based on Anticipated Reader Reaction

Critical Thinking

What place do inductive and deductive ordering have in the composition of e-mail?

Use empathy to determine a logical, efficient sequence of information and one that will respond effectively to the reaction you anticipate from the receiver. As you learned previously, ideas should be organized deductively when a message contains good news or neutral information; inductive organization is recommended when the message contains bad news or is intended to persuade. Bad-news messages are discussed in greater detail in Chapter 7 and persuasive messages in Chapter 8.

In addition, e-mail messages may use other bases for determining the sequence of ideas, for example, time (reporting events in the order in which they happened), order of importance, and geography. As a general rule of thumb, present the information in the order it is likely to be needed. For example, describe the nature and purpose of an upcoming meeting before giving the specifics (date, place, time). Otherwise, the receiver may have to reread portions of the e-mail to extract the details. You will be valued for presenting information in a logical, efficient sequence.

Careful Use of Jargon, Technical Words, and Shortened Terms

Diversity Challenges

You are more likely to use jargon and technical terms in e-mail messages than in business letters. Because people doing similar work are almost sure to know the technical terms associated with it, jargon will be understood, will not be taken as an attempt to impress, and will save time. For the same reasons, acronyms, abbreviations, and shortened forms, such as *info*, *rep*, *demo*, *pro*, and *stat*, are more useful in e-mail messages than in letters. In practicing empathy, however, consider whether the receiver will likely understand the terms. Remember that an international receiver or an external business partner you are messaging may not understand your jargon or shortened language.

Graphic Highlighting

Graphical treatment is appropriate whenever it strengthens your efforts to communicate. Enumerated or bulleted lists, tables, graphs, pictures, or other images may be either integrated into the content of the e-mail or attached as supporting material.

The e-mail message in Figure 5-1 illustrates these guidelines for using this informal communication channel effectively in a professional setting. The director of legal services begins her e-mail message to the software compliance officer with a request to research potential legal liability caused by employees downloading copyrighted music. The short paragraphs that follow include timely information and a specific request for action to be taken. The message closes by inviting the reader to instant message with updates until they can discuss this crucial issue face to face.

Figure 5-1

Good Example of an E-Mail Message

Includes a salutation and
closing to personalize the
message.

Provides a subject line that
is meaningful to the reader
and the writer.

To: Rodney Spurlin, Software Compliance Officer

From: Claire Henderson, Director of Legal Services

Subject: Legal Liability for Downloaded Music

Rodney,

Your immediate attention is needed to address the company's liability for employees' downloading copyrighted music.

The recording industry has announced its intent to prosecute organizations that allow their employees to download and store music files without proper authorization. This is not an idle threat as the recording industry has already obtained a $1 million settlement with one company whose employees violated music copyright laws.

The Recording Industry Association of America and the Motion Picture Association of America recently sent a six-page brochure to Fortune 1000 corporations that provides suggested corporate policies and sample communication to employees. We need to get a copy of this brochure and determine whether our corporation could be at risk.

Please contact me when you are ready to suggest changes to our corporate code of conduct. I'll be online all week if you want to instant message once you've seen the brochure.

Later,
Claire

Routine E-Mail Message

- Limits the message to a single idea—initiate important research.
- Uses the deductive sequence for conveying a routine request.
- Composes a short, concise message that fits on one screen. A longer message would be included in an attachment.

  Refer to Appendix A for guidelines for formatting e-mail messages.

While e-mail offers various advantages in speed and convenience, problems arise when it is used inappropriately. The following guidelines will direct you in composing effective e-mail messages. Details about the formatting of e-mail messages in accordance with acceptable electronic protocol are included in Appendix A.

Effective Use of E-Mail

Changing Technology

Established standards of online behavior have emerged to help online communicators send and receive e-mail messages that are courteous while enhancing communication effectiveness *and* productivity. Learning fundamental **netiquette**, the buzzword for proper behavior on the Internet, will assure your online success.

- ***Check mail promptly.*** Be conscientious in checking and responding to electronic messages to avoid missing important information needed to complete an assignment. Generally, a response to e-mail is expected within 24 hours. Ignoring electronic messages from coworkers can erode efforts to create an open, honest work environment. On the other hand, avoid responding every five or ten minutes so that you appear to be paying more attention to your e-mail than your job.

Critical Thinking

Which of these tips will be most helpful in managing your e-mail use?

- ***Do not contribute to e-mail overload.*** To avoid clogging the system with unnecessary messages that the receiver feels compelled to answer, send business-related messages only when necessary and only to necessary people. Follow these simple guidelines:
  - Be certain individuals need a copy of the e-mail, and forward an e-mail from another person only with the original writer's permission.
  - Never address an e-mail containing action items to more than one person to ensure a response. This practice supports the old adage "Share a task between two people, and each takes 1% responsibility."[4]
  - Avoid sending formatted documents. Messages with varying fonts, special print features (e.g., bold, italics, etc.), and clip art take longer to download, require more disk space, and may be unreadable on some computers. In addition, enhancing routine e-mail messages does not support the goals of competitive organizations, and employees and clients/customers may resent such frivolous use of time.
  - Edit the original message when you reply to an e-mail message. Returning the entire message with the reply is time-consuming for the receiver to download and to sort the reply from the original message.

Overreliance on technological channels of communication can jeopardize human relations.

DILBERT

DILBERT REPRINTED BY PERMISSION OF UNITED FEATURE SYNDICATE, INC.

Cut and paste pertinent sections within a reply that you believe will help the recipient understand your reply. You can also key brief comments in all caps below the original section.

- Follow company policy for personal use of e-mail, and obtain a private e-mail account if you are job hunting or sending many private messages to friends and relatives.

- *Use e-mail only for appropriate messages.* In addition to the factors already discussed that relate to e-mail, other issues relate specifically to e-mail:

  - Send short, direct messages that typically would be sent through printed memos. These messages usually are routine matters that need not be handled immediately and thus will reduce telephone interruptions (scheduling meetings, giving your supervisor quick updates, or other uncomplicated issues).

  - Do not send messages when you are angry. E-mail messages containing sensitive, highly emotional messages may be easily misinterpreted because of the absence of nonverbal communication (facial expressions, voice tone, and body language). Sending a **flame**, the online term used to describe a heated, sarcastic, sometimes abusive message or posting to a discussion group, may prompt a receiver to send a retaliatory response. Because of the potential damage to relationships, read e-mail messages carefully before clicking "Send." Unless a response is urgent, store a heated message for an hour while you cool off and think about the issue clearly and rationally. Then, reread the message before sending it. A possible strategy for those times when you *must* respond immediately is to acknowledge that your response is emotional and has not been thoroughly considered. Give this warning by using words such as "I need to vent my frustration for a few paragraphs" or "flame on—I'm writing in anger."[5]

- *Exercise caution against e-mail viruses and hoaxes.* An ounce of prevention can avert the problems caused by deadly **viruses** that destroy data files or annoying messages that simply waste your time while they are executing. Install an antivirus software program that will scan your hard drive each time you start the computer or access floppies, and keep backups of important files. Be suspicious of e-mail messages from people you don't know who offer free software or a screen saver as an attachment (particularly ones with an ".exe" extension). E-mail text is usually safe to open, but the attachment may contain an executable macro that can affect your files.

Additionally, be wary of **computer hoaxes**—e-mail messages that incite panic typically related to risks of computer viruses or deadly threats and urge you to forward them to as many people as possible. Forwarding a hoax can be embarrassing and causes inefficiency by overloading e-mail boxes and flooding computer security personnel with inquiries from alarmed recipients of your message. Investigate the possible hoax by visiting web sites that post virus alerts and hoax information and also provide tips for identifying a potential hoax. If a hoax is

Legal & Ethical Constraints

forwarded to you, reply to the person politely that the message is a hoax. This action allows you to help stop the spread of the malicious message and will educate one more person about the evils of hoaxes.[6]

Informative, independent web sites about computer hoaxes include the following:

- U.S. Department of Energy CIAC Internet Hoaxes Page: http://hoaxbusters.ciac.org/
- Vmyths: http://www.kumite.com/myths
- The Truth About E-Mail Viruses: http://www.gerlitz.com/virushoax
- Urban legends: http://www.urbanlegends.com

- *Develop an efficient way for handling e-mail.* Some simple organization will allow you to make better use of your e-mail capability:
  - Set up separate accounts for receiving messages that require your direct attention.
  - Keep your mailbox clean by deleting messages that you are no longer using.
  - Set up folders that organize messages you need to keep. If you receive many messages, investigate the purchase of an e-mail handler to sort and prioritize messages. Productivity is gained from having the system automatically send form letters you create as replies to messages received with a particular subject line, forward specified e-mail, and sound an alarm when you receive a message from a particular person.

Critical Thinking

Describe some other strategies for the efficient use of e-mail.

Instant Messaging

Changing Technology

Instant messaging (IM), or chat, represents a blending of e-mail with conversation. This real-time e-mail technology allows you to maintain a list of people with whom you want to interact. You can send messages to any or all of the people on your list as long as the people are online. Sending a message opens up a window in which you and your contact can type messages that you both can see immediately. The Electronic Café at the end of Chapter 1 provides opportunities for exploring the features and uses of instant messaging. Figure 5-2 illustrates a sample IM conversation that occurred as a followup to the director of legal services' e-mail message in Figure 5-1.

Business use of instant messaging has experienced phenomenal growth. Estimates are that by 2005, instant messaging will be integrated into 50 percent of the applications that businesses use to interact with their customers. Instant messaging can complement or replace existing media such as e-mail and voice.[7] The best known IM programs are free and require no special hardware and little training. With some programs, users can even exchange graphics, video clips, or voice clips.

Many of the guidelines that apply to the use of e-mail for business purposes apply also to instant messaging. With IM, however, spelling and grammar matter less when trading messages at high speed. IM users often use business shorthand for common words and phrases. Your Professional Power Pak CD contains information on using such abbreviations. IM and telephone communication also share common challenges: being sure that

Figure 5-2

Good Example of an Instant Message

Annotations

- Opens the message by "knocking" to ask if he is interrupting.
- Keeps conversation brief by limiting to a few short sentences.
- Uses a few easily recognized abbreviations and acronyms but avoids informal slang that could be confusing and detract from professional nature of the message.
- Uses instant messaging for a few quick questions but agrees to make critical decisions during a meeting.

Output Interaction Box	Users Logged On
Rodney:>>Is this a good time to talk about the issues related to music downloads?	Rodney Spurlin
Claire:>>Of course. What do you have?	Claire Henderson
Rodney:>>I reviewed the music industry's brochure—the one you spoke of during our last convo.	
Claire:>>Great. Are we at risk, in your opinion?	
Rodney:>>It's hard to tell without performing an "audit" of our computers, as suggested in the brochure.	
Claire:>>I see. What about the communication with employees?	
Rodney:>>The sample memos in the brochure are consistent with topics discussed in our quarterly corporate newsletter.	
Claire:>>Is there anything else we need to do?	
Rodney:>>We should probably look into installing software to monitor downloading activity.	
Claire:>>True. Pls. get a price quote ASAP.	
Rodney:>>I'll have the info when we meet on Friday. CU then.	

☐ Entry Chime

Enter your message below

Send URL

Quit

the sender is who he or she claims to be and that the conversation is free from eavesdropping.

Some managers worry that employees will spend too much work time using IM to chat with pals inside and outside the company. They also emphasize that IM is not the right tool for every business purpose; employees should still rely on e-mail when they need a record and use the telephone for the personal touch.

Legal & Ethical Constraints

E-Mail and the Law

Remember you are responsible for the content of an e-mail message you send. Because e-mail moves so quickly between people and often becomes

Wireless technologies have expanded communication options by overcoming location barriers. While convenient and efficient, wireless devices can be easily hacked.

© DENNIS MACDONALD/PHOTOEDIT

very informal, more like a conversation, individuals may not realize (or may forget) their responsibility. If a person denies commitments made via e-mail, someone involved may produce a printed copy of the e-mail message in question as verification.

E-mail communicators must also abide by copyright laws. Be certain to give credit for quoted material and seek permission to use copyrighted text or graphics from printed or electronic sources. Unless you inform the reader that editing has occurred, do not alter a message you are forwarding or re-posting, and be sure to ask permission before forwarding it.

The courts have established the right of companies to monitor the electronic mail of an employee because they own the facilities and intend them to be used for job-related communication only. On the other hand, employees expect that their e-mail messages should be kept private. To protect themselves against liability imposed by the *Electronic Communications Privacy Act (ECPA)*, employers simply provide a legitimate business reason for the monitoring (preventing computer crime, retrieving lost messages, regulating employee morale) and obtain written consent to intercept e-mail or at least notify employees. Employees who use the system after the notification may have given implied consent to the monitoring.[8]

Critical Thinking

What is the status of the Privacy for Consumers and Workers Act?

Federal and state laws related to employee privacy are frequently introduced for consideration. Although litigation related to present privacy issues is underway, the development of law is lagging far behind technology; nevertheless, employers can expect changes in the laws as technology continues to develop. The *Privacy for Consumers and Workers Act* has been introduced into Congress and would cover most forms of electronic surveillance, requiring employers to notify present and prospective employees of any monitoring policies and forbidding secret monitoring.[9]

The Strategic Forces feature "Legal and Ethical Implications of Technology" explores laws that affect other aspects of privacy as related to technology.

Web Page Communication

Objective *2*

Explain principles for creating, designing, publishing, maintaining, and writing effective web pages.

The World Wide Web is truly a universal communication medium, reaching a broad audience in diverse locations. The familiar web platform may be used for offering a company **intranet** to distribute various types of information to employees at numerous locations. Business partners such as vendors, suppliers, and customers can utilize the Web to access a company's **extranet**. Both intranets and extranets restrict access to those visitors with authorization such as a password. An organization can also establish a **public web presence** to extend its reach significantly and provide potential customers or clients with an always-available source of information and contact. While effective web page development is a highly specialized activity, understanding of the process will be useful to any business communicator.

Developing a Web Page

Creating Your Page

A web page is fundamentally an ordinary text or ASCII file, so special tools are not absolutely necessary, although it is easier to create web pages using editors designed for that purpose. What turns ordinary text into a web page is a web browser (such as Internet Explorer or Netscape Communicator) and instructions or tags written in HTML (hypertext markup language). The browser interprets the HTML and displays the page. Hyperlinks on a page can link to web pages or other types of files, such as sound, video, or interactive programs. Visit the text support site at http://lehman.swlearning.com for a list of sites that provide tools for creating web documents.

The official **Lord of the Rings** promotional web site at *http://www.lordoftherings.net* extends viewers' enchantment with this blockbuster epic. While engaged in creative integration of audio and graphics, fans can access insider views about the complex plot, download cool images for their desktops, and send Lord of the Rings e-cards. A "joining the ring" link opens the door for shopping and participating in thrilling online discussions with fellow fans.

© SUSAN VAN ETTEN

Designing Your Page

Critical Thinking

What are some of the annoying design features you have encountered on web sites you have visited?

Creating an effective web page is challenging because of the variety of elements that have to be combined and the artistic style needed to make everything work together. For this reason, many firms hire the talent of web page designers to manage the task of creating their web sites. One difficulty with designing a web page is that a number of technical conditions that affect the way the page looks can't be controlled—the size and type of font set by the user, number of colors displayed on a user's monitor, as well as the screen size and resolution. Size and placement may look different to users because of variations in computer hardware and software. So when designing a page, you need to think about what it will look like on different types of monitors and with different user configurations.

Some HTML tags aren't interpreted in the same way by all web browsers. For instance, comments on some web pages that say the page is optimized for Netscape or works best with Internet Explorer means that the tags used were those used by that particular browser. The worst case is that your page won't open in some browsers. Large and detailed images can also take up many bytes, which means that loading them can take a long time on your user's computer.[10]

Because of all the complexities associated with web page presentation, no substitute exists for planning and sound design. Take time to determine what you want to do and how you can best do it. Successful sites are designed around the wants and needs of specific target audiences. A web site is only as good as its content, and engaging content is what brings users back to a particular site and maintains user loyalty. The following guidelines will assist you in reaching your intended audience:

- *Design a tightly organized home page.* Be extra critical about what goes on the opening screen. After all, how many times does a picture of the corporate office building or the CEO clinch a sale? The home page often needs to include a small statement of purpose that tells newcomers what the organization does. Obviously IBM doesn't need one; but Edmund's Automobile Buyer's Guide might. Put less critical information at the bottom of the page.[11]

- *Assure a united look and feel.* Repeating certain elements of the home page on every page within the site gives a unified look and feel to the site and assures browsers that they haven't inadvertently followed a link out of your site. Unifying elements, for example, might include the use of the same band of color or a small graphic across the top of every page or the incorporation of a small logo into the repetitive design. Effective sites also often use design-redundancy—that is, several different links may direct the user to the same page.

- *Use graphics effectively.* Graphics can add order, understanding, and cohesiveness and help to reflect the image of the organization. They should, however, be functional. Edit nonessential graphics with the same critical eye you use for nonessential text. Resist the urge to offer "eye candy"—a piece of clip art or an animated graphic that offers nothing substantive. Try to limit the total size of all graphics, and make use of technology to shrink the time it takes for images to download. A list of books and web resources for web page design are located on the text support site at http://lehman.swlearning.com.

Critical Thinking

Explain why launching a web site is a process rather than an event.

- *Understand the needs of your end user.* The most important element in successful web site design is a keen understanding of your end user. You can't control the order in which people look at your pages, since users make their own experiences. You can, however, design your site for easy navigation and a comfortable look and feel that invites the user to come back. Observe the reader-centered features on the web pages illustrated in Figure 5-3.

Publishing Your Page

Critical Thinking

What are the negative consequences of placing a site on the web but failing to update it?

After proofreading and checking every element of your site for accuracy, you are ready to launch it onto the World Wide Web. Once you put your pages on a web server, you are a published author. You can announce your page by submitting it to web directories and search engines, such as Yahoo!, Excite, Alta Vista, etc. The charge for listing is usually free or quite inexpensive. These services provide you with forms to fill out including your identification, the URL for your page, and some descriptive information about the page, including the appropriate category for the listing. Depending on the workload, it may take a service several days or weeks to list your web page.[12]

Maintaining Your Page

Always put the last revision date at the bottom of your web page to let your viewers know the currentness of the information. An e-mail link back to you will allow viewers to provide feedback or ask for further information. Because of the dynamic nature of business activity, information on the web site will require constant revision, updating, and refinement. Going online with a web presence is a process, rather than a one-time achievement.

Organizations can use the Web not only to communicate with customers and clients but to interact with business partners. The Strategic Forces feature "Web Assists Interorganizational Teams" describes the role of the web in promoting team effectiveness.

Writing for the Web

Many standard rules for writing apply whether for the Web or print. However, some important differences exist between readers of paper material and web users:[13]

- Web users do not want to read. They skim, browse, and hop from one highlighted area to another trying to zero in on the word or phrase that relates to their search.
- English-speaking readers typically start scanning at the top left-hand side of the main content area. They move top to bottom, left to right. Given this pattern, it is important to put frequently accessed items close to the

Initial Screen

Content

- Provides links to major information categories.
- Includes contact link.
- Allows for topic search for specific information.

Format

- Provides one-screen viewing of content without scrolling.
- Uses quick-loading photographs.
- Provides unified feel through use of color scheme and logo repeated on every page.
- Arranges information in reader-friendly categories.

Link from Initial Screen

Content

- Refers reader to more specific information at each page level.
- Provides links to subcategories of information.

Format

- Repeats legend of major links on all pages.
- Uses small graphics to reduce load time.
- Allows for easy movement between pages.

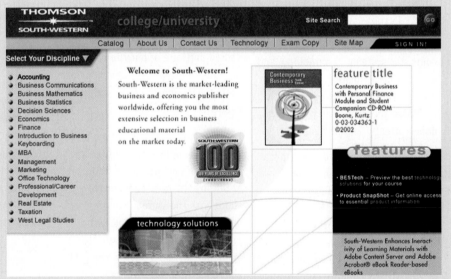

top of the content area. Information should follow the pyramid style of writing common in newspaper writing; the main idea or conclusion is presented first, and subsequent sections and pages expand upon it.

- Users can more quickly scan items in columns rather than rows, especially if they are categorized, grouped, and have headings. You can have more lists on the Web than in a typical print document.
- Users refer infrequently to directions. It is unlikely they will read little notes, sidebars, and help files, so directions must appear in simple, numbered steps.

Web Assists Inter-organizational Teams

Maintaining efficient communication is crucial in business today, especially now that more companies are working with outside vendors, rather than doing everything themselves. In product design and building projects, a project team is typically comprised of various company personnel and a variety of outside parties that provide goods and services necessary for project completion. Completion is often delayed unnecessarily by misunderstandings between different vendors or plant personnel. Compounding the problem are the differences in computer systems, terminology, and processes. Fortunately, the Web can now provide a neutral environment to bridge those gaps and get work done correctly and on time.

Web-based project software applications allow information to be viewed from any computer with Internet access, as long as the user has the proper security clearance and passwords. This means you don't necessarily have to own the same kind of system as the people with whom you are sharing data. Comfort with the familiar Internet platform means that users can be trained in a matter of minutes. The web-based software provides a quick, convenient, and controlled way to exchange information with

colleagues and vendors. Project team members have easy access regardless of their technical ability, location, application, or computer platform.[14]

A successful example of web-based project software is ActiveProject, from Framework Technologies Corp. The application, used largely for design, engineering, and manufacturing projects, comes with preformatted web site templates that allow users to set up their project management communications quickly. The integrated system uses the Web as a communication mechanism to enable a team of people to work together on a project. They don't need a shared system or shared software applications to exchange information, comment on each other's information, and proceed with the project.[15]

When a new project is planned, documents, drawings, photos, and other requirements are posted online by the host company to share with the various vendors of equipment, materials, and labor. Files on the server are instantly available to everybody on the project team. Now all of the vendors have the shop-floor drawings and can start adding information. Various members of the team can visit the site, post their information, make comments, and ask questions. Access can also be controlled, so information can be

shared with various people without opening it to everyone.

The software allows users to comment directly about various aspects of the project, either verbally or by marking up the charts and diagrams on the site. Comments and requests for information are tracked automatically, so the project manager can see all of the communication in a log form. If the manager notices that an issue is causing problems, a deadline is falling behind schedule, or a team member is not responding to requests for information, proper action can be taken to resolve the problem quickly.

Application

In small groups discuss how outside vendor projects would be handled if web-based team software were not available. How would cost, employee resources, communication, and time be impacted? What other types of business problems might be solved effectively using web-based team software?

In recognition of these Web user characteristics, writers should tailor their styles accordingly. The following tips will help you compose appropriate web content:[16]

Critical Thinking

Knowing your web audience will help you structure effective messages for your web site.

- *Be brief.* A rule of thumb is to reduce any print document by 50 percent when you put it on the Web.
- *Keep it simple.* Use short words that allow for fast reading by people of various educational backgrounds. Use mixed case, since all caps are slower to read.
- *Consider appropriate jargon.* If all your site users share a common professional language, use it. Otherwise, keep to concise yet effective word choices.
- *Use eye-catching headlines.* They may catch interest, ask a question, present the unusual, or pose a conflict.
- *Break longer documents into smaller chunks.* Provide ways to easily move through the document and return to the beginning.
- *Use attention-getting devices judiciously.* Bold, font changes, color, and graphics do attract attention but can be overdone and cause really important ideas to be lost.
- *Avoid placing critical information in graphic form only.* Many users are averse to slow-loading graphics and skip over them.

Effective web writing involves moving beyond the paper mode into the web mode of thinking. Understanding the distinctive expectations of web readers will allow you to structure your ideas effectively and efficiently.

Voice and Wireless Communication

Objective 3

Discuss the effective use of voice and wireless technologies in business communication.

We live in an age of technological miracles. Communication capabilities that were considered science fiction 20 years ago are now commonplace. Not so long ago voice communication referred to telephone usage, and using the telephone effectively is still an important skill in any profession. You can visit the text support site at http://lehman.swlearning.com for telephone etiquette tips. While the traditional telephone still plays an important role in business activity, voice communication extends to voice mail systems and cell phone usage. Both voice and data can be transmitted now using wireless communication systems.

Voice Mail Communication

Voice mail technology allows flexibility in staying in touch without the aid of a computer. Just as e-mail communication can be enhanced by adhering to some basic principles, voice mail communication can be more effective by following recommended guidelines:[17]

- Update your greeting often to reflect your schedule and leave special announcements.

SPOTLIGHT COMMUNICATOR

Vacation Planning Web Site Appeals to Today's Techno-savvy Members

In 2001, when Franz Hanning took over as President and CEO of Fairfield Resorts', Inc., he already had two decades of management experience with the growing company and had been instrumental in the creation of Fairfield's points program. Since the launch in 2000 of Fairfield Resorts' comprehensive web-based vacation planning site, members have convenient access to the information and planning flexibility they want. According to Hanning, FairShare Plus members enjoy the ability to check point balances and expiration dates online, 24 hours a day, and consider the service one of the most valuable benefits the company offers them. While personalized telephone assistance is also available, the web site is the current information delivery system of choice, with more than half of the company's 450,000 owners active online.

Fairfield Resorts' Vacation Planning web site enables members to be their own trip planners. In addition to checking point balances and expiration dates online, members can also plan their own resort reservations and exchanges online. After a secure log-in to the members-only section of the site, Fairfield owners can access their personal account data. The site's interactive Points Calculator allows members to obtain instant information on the number of points they will have available on a given travel date, even several years into the future. Additionally, the Vacation Break Travel feature offers an online solution for booking travel reservations that combines the best of e-commerce with the exceptional professional service you expect from a travel consultant. Members can also consider owners-only exclusive offers such as discounted resort condo rentals and click on links to

recommended sites for travel-related goods and services.

A glimpse of the vast travel-planning information available to Fairfield members is illustrated in the following screens. Hanning sees the Vacation Planning web site as extending the firm's commitment to offering diverse marketing channels and reaching new consumers with more product choices.

Applying What You Have Learned

1. How has the effective communication of information via Fairfield's web site empowered FairShare Plus members?

2. How does Fairfield expect to benefit from the web site?

Franz S. Hanning, President and CEO, Fairfield Resorts, Inc.

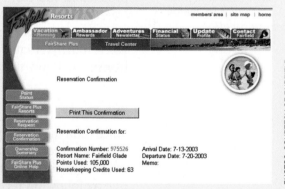

http://www.fairfieldresorts.com

Refer to ShowCASE, Part 3, at the end of the chapter to learn how Fairfield Resorts reaches out to its various constituents.

- Leave your e-mail address, fax number, or mailing address on your greeting if this information might be helpful to your callers.
- Encourage callers to leave detailed messages. If you need certain standard information from callers, use your greeting to prompt them for it. This may eliminate the need to call back to obtain the needed information.
- Instruct callers how to review their message or be transferred to an operator.
- Check your voice mail regularly, and return all voice messages within 24 hours.

When leaving a message, you can improve your communication by following these tips:[18]

- Speak slowly and clearly, and repeat your name and phone number at the beginning and end of the message.
- Spell your name for the recipient who may need the correct spelling.
- Leave a detailed message, not just your name and number. Be specific about what you want to avoid prolonged phone tag.
- Keep your message brief, typically 60 seconds or less.
- Assure that your message will be understandable. Don't call from places with distracting background noise; when using a cell phone, consider whether your connection is adequate to complete the message.

The sound of your voice makes a lasting impression on the many people who listen to your greeting or the messages you leave. To ensure that the impression you leave is a professional one, review your voice greeting before you save it. Rerecord to eliminate verbal viruses (um, uh, stumbles), flat or monotone voice, and garbled or rushed messages that are difficult to understand. Consider scripting the message to avoid long, drawn-out recitations. As you record, stand, smile, and visualize the person receiving the message; you'll hear the added energy, enthusiasm, and warmth in your voice.[19]

Remember that the voice mail message you leave should be seen as permanent. In some systems the digital files are backed up and stored for possible retrieval by managers or other company personnel. A voice mail message can also be used as evidence in a lawsuit or other legal proceeding.[20]

Cell Phone Communication

Mobile telephones, once a rarity, are now a standard accessory for many people throughout the world. In the United States, cell phones are as commonplace as landline phones, and the number continues to rise. The popularity of cell phones, however, has outstripped the development of rules for proper cell phone etiquette. Cell phone abuse causes much annoyance, and your attention to a few commonsense guidelines will help assure that you are not seen as a rude phone user.[21]

- ***Observe wireless free quiet zones.*** This obviously includes theaters, performances, and religious services, but may also include meetings, restaurants, hospitals, and other public places. Exercise judgment about silencing your ringer or turning off your phone.

Legal & Ethical Constraints

- ***Respect others in crowded places.*** Speak in low conversational tones, and consider the content of your conversation.
- ***Think safety.*** Some states and municipalities have banned the use of cell phones while driving. Others allow the use of hands-free devices only. Even if not illegal, cell phone usage does increase the risk of accident by distracting the driver.

Cell phone users should remember that the technology is not secure. Perhaps you have overheard another party's phone conversation when using your cell phone. The radio frequencies that transmit the voice signals can be picked up by other equipment. For this reason, information that is confidential or sensitive should be shared using an alternate communication channel.

Wireless Communication and the Future

With the many communication innovations that have occurred in the last 20 years, one can only wonder what the next 20 years will hold. Whatever the breakthroughs, one particular technology will figure strongly in the changes—wireless communication. For many years, wireless communication has freed us from the necessity of being literally plugged in while enabling us to communicate virtually any time anywhere. But wireless is no longer merely voice technology over a cell phone; it can now accommodate high-speed data transmission as well.

Critical Thinking

Describe a typical computer in the year 2010.

Wireless technology is driving many of the significant changes that are affecting today's business. Pocket PCs that fit in your palm offer speedy processors and full-color, full-motion displays. The next step is the full integration of hand-held devices with the mobile phone to allow extremely high-speed wireless Internet connectivity. This advance could eliminate the need for the laptop PC and the office. According to the Gartner Group, by 2007, more than 60 percent of the U.S. population between the ages of 15 and 50 will carry or wear a wireless computing and communication device at least six hours a day.[22]

The impact of wireless communication will become even more significant as voice-to-text and text-to-voice technology continues to develop. Voice-to-text and vice-versa technology offers the ability to communicate with a computer system without a keyboard. While such technology has been around for two decades, newer systems have more powerful processors, are more miniaturized, and tolerate variances in speakers' accents and inflections without sacrificing speed and accuracy. Freeing workers from being chained to a desk or office will eliminate the need for the keyboard and mouse, much the way those input devices once eliminated the need for keypunch cards. Wireless capability will increase timeliness of key business decisions, resulting in greater revenues and profitability.

However, just being able to make decisions quickly does not assure that they are the right decisions. As in the past, workers will need to have correct and timely information for making decisions. A second challenge for the wireless era will be balancing electronic communication capabilities with the need for human interaction.

Appropriate Use of Technology

While technology offers numerous advantages, a technological channel is not always the communication method of choice. Before sending a message, be certain the selected channel of communication is appropriate by considering the message's purpose, confidentiality issues, and human relations factors.

Determine the Purpose of the Message

Team Environment

If a message is straightforward and informative, chances are a technological option might be appropriate. While the use of instantaneous and efficient communication methods is quite compelling, keep in mind that written communication, printed or online, cannot replace the personal interaction so essential in today's team-based work environments. While employees floors apart or in different offices or time zones benefit from e-mail and web communications, two people sitting side by side or on the same floor shouldn't have to communicate solely by electronic means.

A second question when selecting among communication options concerns whether a permanent record of the message is needed or if a more temporary form such as a phone call or instant message would suffice.

Determine If the Information Is Personal or Confidential

Legal & Ethical Constraints

As a general guideline, keep personal correspondence off-line if you don't want it to come back and haunt you. The content of an e-mail message could have embarrassing consequences since such documents often become a part of public records and wireless communications might be unexpectedly intercepted. Your company technically "owns" your electronic communications and thus can monitor them to determine legitimate business use or potential abuse. Undeliverable e-mail messages are delivered to a mail administrator, and many networks routinely store backups of all e-mail messages that pass through them.

Even deleted messages can be "resurrected" with little effort as several public figures have discovered when investigators have retrieved archived e-mail as evidence in court cases. For sensitive situations, a face-to-face encounter may be preferred. Legal and ethical considerations may also impact your choices when considering technology, as described in the accompanying Strategic Forces feature "Legal and Ethical Implications of Technology."

Legal and Ethical Implications of Technology

Technology threatens our privacy, our right to be left alone, free from surveillance or interference from other individuals or organizations. Common invasions of privacy caused by technology include collecting excessive amounts of information for decision making and maintaining too many files, monitoring the exact time employees spend on a specific task and between tasks and the exact number and length of employee breaks, and supervisors' or coworkers' reading another employee's electronic mail and computer files. Additionally, integrating computer files containing information collected from more than one agency without permission is a major threat to privacy. Although an individual may have authorized the collection of the individual information, merging the information may reveal things the individual may want to remain private.[23]

Our right to privacy is protected primarily by the First Amendment (which guarantees freedom of speech and association), and the Fourth Amendment (which protects against unreasonable search and seizure of one's person, documents, or home, and assures due process). However, the Fair Information Practices (FIP) form the basis of 13 federal statutes that ensure the security and integrity of personal information collected by governmental and private agencies. Set forth in the FIP are conditions for handling information about individuals in such areas as credit reporting, education, financial records, newspaper records, cable communications, electronic communications, and video rentals. The FIP also holds managers responsible and liable for the reliability and security of company information systems.[24]

Recently, government response to terrorism and other security threats has resulted in further erosion of privacy for Americans. In the present climate of controversy over privacy and ownership of information, the following ethical practices are appropriate for the collection and access of information:

- Collect only information that is needed as opposed to what you would like to know.

- Develop (and use) safeguards for the security of information and instill in data handlers the values of privacy and the importance of confidentiality.

- Require employees to use passwords to gain access to the system and enforce routine changes of passwords on a periodic basis.

- Require users to "sign off" or "log out" of e-mail when they leave their computers.

- Assign user identification passwords and levels of access that limit information a person can observe and change.

- Consider the use of encryption facilities if you are sending extremely confidential information.

- Develop a clear privacy policy that complies with the law and does not unnecessarily compromise the interests of employees or employers.

Application

Stage a classroom debate with two teams of four; one team represents the right of the employer to monitor computer activities and the other team represents the right of the employee to maintain privacy in communication. Each team will study the issue and prepare its arguments. During the debate, each team will have five minutes to present its side of the issue, followed by a two-minute cross examination by the opposing team. Class members who are not participating on the debate teams will act as judges to determine which team presents the stronger case.

Decide Whether Positive Human Relations Are Sacrificed

Diversity Challenges

Be wary of using an electronic communication tool as an avoidance mechanism. Remember, too, that some people may not regularly check their e-mail or voice mail, and some have unreliable systems that are slow or prone to lose messages. Some news will be received better in person than through an electronic format that might be interpreted as cold and sterile.

Additionally, some people, especially those of certain cultures, may prefer a personal meeting even if you perceive that an electronic exchange of information would be a more efficient use of everyone's time. Choose the communication channel carefully to fit both the purpose of the message and the preference of the receiver.

Before composing electronic messages, study carefully the overall suggestions presented in Chapters 3 and 4. Then, study the specific suggestions in the "Check Your Communication" checklist at the end of this chapter. Compare your work with this checklist again after you have written a rough draft and make any corrections.

Summary

1. **Discuss the effective use of e-mail and instant messaging in business communication.** E-mail may be sent to receivers both inside and outside the organization. E-mail provides a fast, convenient way to communicate by reducing telephone tag and telephone interruptions, facilitating the transmission of a single message to multiple recipients, reducing telephone bills, eliminating time barriers, and fostering open communication among users in various locations. While general writing principles apply, acceptable e-mail formats are less formal than business letter formats. Real-time e-mail, known as instant messaging, allows two or more people to converse online. Abbreviations and on-line "shorthand" help to speed this means of rapid communication.

2. **Explain principles for creating, designing, publishing, maintaining, and writing effective web pages.** Web pages facilitate an organization's continual communication with a wide audience. Hypertext Markup Language and a web browser turn ordinary text into a web page. In designing a web page, consideration should be given to technical conditions that affect what a viewer sees on his or her computer screen. User needs should be met through tight organization, a unified look and feel, and effective use of graphics. A web page is launched on a web server and can be listed on web directories and search engines. Web maintenance involves constant revision, updating, and refinement.

3. **Discuss the effective use of voice and wireless technologies in business communication.** Voice recordings and messages should be clear and complete and considered as permanent records. While offering convenience, cell phones should be used with consideration for the receiver and the public at large. Cell phone conversations should not be viewed as secure communications. Applications and equipment to accommodate wireless communications continue to expand and offer unprecedented flexibility for transmitting voice and data. Business decisions can be improved through the appropriate use of voice and wireless technologies.

4. **Identify legal and ethical implications associated with the use of communication technology.** Legal and ethical considerations should be taken into account when communicating through technology. As you handle information, keep these legal and ethical responsibilities in mind: (a) be certain that information technology does not violate basic rights of individuals and that you abide by all laws related to the use of technology; (b) understand that e-mail is not private and can be monitored by a company; (c) develop and use procedures that protect the security of information; and (d) develop a clear and fair privacy policy.

E-Mail Messages

Organization, Content, Style, and Mechanics

- Provide a useful subject line (has meaning for the writer and receiver; will help the receiver sort through numerous e-mail messages).
- Include only one main message idea related to the receiver's needs.
- Show empathy and logic in determining sequence of ideas.
- Use jargon, technical words, and shortened terms carefully.
- Use graphical treatment such as bulleted lists, tables, graphs, or images when they strengthen communication.
- Avoid flaming and the use of overly emotional language.

Format

- Include an appropriate salutation and ending.
- Include a signature file (including writer's name, address, e-mail address, and other useful information).
- Keep message length to no longer than one screen. Use an attachment if the message must be longer.
- Keep line length the width of the screen.
- Single-space lines; leave a blank space between paragraphs; do not indent paragraphs.
- Key message using mixed-case letters. Use capital letters or quotation marks to emphasize a word or phrase.
- Omit specialized formatting (bold, italics, font changes, clip art).
- Use emoticons and abbreviations in moderation only if the receiver understands them and the message is informal.

Instant Messages

Organization, Content, Style, and Mechanics

- Consider e-mail guidelines listed above when composing instant messages.
- Choose your message participants appropriately.
- Be certain that your conversation is free from unwanted eavesdropping.

Format

- Use commonly understood shorthand and abbreviations for frequent words and phrases.
- Focus more on efficiency and less on spelling and grammar.

Web Communications

Organization, Content, Style, and Mechanics

- Consider technical conditions that may affect the page's appeal to the reader.
- Provide a tightly organized home page.
- Include functional graphics that offer substantive appeal.
- Proofread and check the accuracy of every element before publishing.
- Follow all other related checkpoints listed for e-mail messages (shown above).
- Revise, update, and refine content regularly.

Format

- Position more important information to appear at the top of the screen.
- Repeat certain elements to provide a unified look and feel to all pages on the site.
- Limit the size and complexity of graphics to reduce load time.
- Provide for easy navigation between pages.
- Provide last revision date and an e-mail link.

Voice and Wireless Communications

Voice Recordings: Organization, Content, Style, and Mechanics

- Leave your e-mail address, fax number, or mailing address on your greeting if this information might be helpful to callers.
- Encourage callers to leave detailed messages. If certain standard information is needed, use your greeting to prompt callers for it.
- Instruct callers how to review their messages or be transferred to an operator.
- Check voice mail regularly, and return all voice messages within 24 hours.

Voice Messages: Organization, Content, Style, and Mechanics

- Speak slowly and clearly.

- Repeat your name and phone number at beginning and end of the message, spelling your name if not well known to recipient.

- Leave a detailed message; be specific about what you want.

- Keep your message brief, typically 60 seconds or less.

- Assure that your message will be understandable; avoid calling from noisy environments and areas with weak signal.

Voice and Wireless Etiquette

- Exercise judgment about when to silence or turn off your phone.

- Respect others around you by speaking in low conversational tones and monitoring the content of your conversation.

- Practice safety when using wireless communication devices while driving.

Chapter Review

1. What are the advantages of sending and receiving e-mail? (Obj. 1)

2. Discuss guidelines for preparing effective e-mail messages. (Obj. 1)

3. What can you do to limit the excessive amount of e-mail that lowers productivity? (Obj. 1)

4. What practices should be followed to avoid sending a "flame"? (Obj. 1)

5. How do principles for effective e-mail use differ when applied to instant messaging? (Obj. 1)

6. Describe the legal issues related to the use of e-mail. (Obj. 1)

7. What suggestions can you offer to a business that is planning to design and launch a web site? (Obj. 2)

8. What specific principles apply to writing for the web? (Obj. 2)

9. How are interorganizational project teams using the Web to achieve goals? (Obj. 2)

10. What guidelines apply to recording an effective voice message? to leaving an effective voice message on another's phone? (Obj. 3)

11. Describe the courteous use of a cell phone. (Obj. 3)

12. How will wireless technology change the way in which work is accomplished? (Obj. 3)

13. Which communication channels are preferred when sending a message that is personal or confidential? Why? (Obj. 4)

14. How is the use of technology impacted by legal limitations and requirements? (Obj. 4)

15. Explain the factors that affect the appropriate choice of an electronic communication channel. (Obj. 4)

Digging Deeper

1. Describe three business communication situations in which a technology channel would be inappropriate for exchanging information. Explain your choices.

2. How is web communication different from other forms of business communication? How is it similar?

To check your understanding of the chapter, take the practice quizzes at **http://lehman.swlearning.com** or your WebTutor course.

Activities

1. **Useful Subject Lines (Obj. 1)**

   Write effective e-mail subject lines for the following situations.

   a. You must inform employees of the specific dates for repaving the company parking lot. Half of the normal parking spaces will be available on any given day during this process.

   b. You are part of a committee planning a reception/banquet for the company's annual alumni event. You want to give the committee a report on the menu choices available in the price range agreed on at the initial planning meeting.

   c. Notify all employees that the youth sports team (soccer, baseball, basketball) your company sponsors is playing for the league championship game.

// electronic café //

Paperless Information Exchange

In 1970 the futurist Alvin Toffler proclaimed the paperless society to be just around the corner. If he's like the rest of us, he's probably surrounded by more paper than ever before. Ever-shrinking laptops, electronic datebooks, and data-storing cell phones have all reduced our dependence on paper records. Yet while numerous technologies have emerged to

 InfoTrac College Edition. Access http://www.info-trac. thomsonlearning.com to read two contrasting views on the concept of the paperless office:

Gladwell, M. (2002, March 25). The social life of paper: Looking for method in the mess (in defense of messy desks). *The New Yorker, 78(5), 9+.*

Day, C. W. (1999, June). The paperless office. *American School & University, 71(10), 58+.*

Compile a list of advantages and disadvantages of paperless information management.

 Text Support Web site. Visit http://lehman. swlearning.com to learn how firms can use the latest technologies to move toward achieving the paperless office. Refer to Chapter 5's Electronic

help eliminate the need for paper, they tend to shift the role of paper rather than replacing it. For instance, we frequently use plenty of paper when preparing information, then throw it out once the final version is captured electronically. The following activities will allow you to explore the advantages and limitations of paperless information exchange.

Café activity that provides a link to an online article that gives tips for going paperless. Follow your instructor's directions about how to use this information.

 WebTutor Advantage. Deliver a paperless assignment to your WebTutor dropbox on the following topic or one that your instructor assigns. Write a one-page summary of how technological developments of the last 20 years have revolutionized business communication.

 Professional Power Pak. Access your PPP CD for information on effective use of a PDA for managing the security of paperless information exchange.

Provide a list of the players and encourage the employees to support the team in whatever way you believe is appropriate.

d. As a sales representative, send the production scheduler an e-mail message suggesting an alternative for managing overtime. Explain that hiring and training students to fill rush orders would be less expensive than paying excessive overtime and would avoid the sensitive issue of overtime for regular employees.

e. Encourage employees to take part in the statewide "Trash Bash" scheduled for later this month. Announce you have issued a friendly challenge to one of the company's local competitors in an effort to promote active participation in this worthy community effort.

f. Explain that a customary end-of-year employee bonus will not be possible because of declining sales. You must justify your decision without alarming the recipients.

g. Ask the human resources director if you will be able to retain your U.S. citizenship when you assume a permanent position in an international office.

2. **Document for Analysis: E-Mail Message (Obj. 2)**

Analyze the following e-mail message for content, formatting, and e-mail practices. Revise the e-mail message if directed by your instructor.

Visit the Interactive Study Center at **http://lehman. swlearning.com** for a downloadable version of this activity.

E-mail from Corie Jones-Bateman sent 12/2/2004 at 1:45 p.m.

TO: MR. NEIL MOSAL, SUPERVISOR, WHEEL ASSEMBLY DIVISION
SUBJECT: DEFECT RATES AT KREIGER ENTERPRISES
CC: Mike Larson, Jennifer Fargo, Lara Sims

DEAR NEIL

I RECOGNIZE THAT TODAY'S WORKFORCE CAN BE HARD TO MANAGE. DESPITE OUR EFFORTS TO DEVELOP SOME COMPANY LOYALTY AMONG THE WORKERS, THEY STILL SEEM CONTENT TO WORK WITH A MINIMUM EFFORT AND PRODUCE AN UNACCEPTABLE RATE OF DEFECTS. : - (

HOWEVER, LAST MONTH IN YOUR DIVISION, THE DEFECT RATE FINALLY MET COMPANY STANDARDS. WE COMMEND YOU ON THIS ACHIEVEMENT. THANK YOU FOR MAKING KRIEGER PRODUCTS BETTER THAN EVER!

BCNU,
CORIE

3. **Instant Messaging Shortcuts (Obj. 1)**

In small groups, make a list of instant messaging "short-hand"—expressions that make online chatting faster and more efficient.

4. **Web Site Effectiveness (Obj. 2)**

Using the information in the chapter, make a checklist for assessing the effectiveness of a web site. Access one of your favorite web sites and evaluate it using the checklist you developed.

5. **Writing for the Web (Obj. 2)**

Consider the following passage that is also available in downloadable form on the text support site at **http://lehman.swlearning.com**. Revise the material for posting to the home page for Green Leaf, a lawn maintenance business.

Some companies use a cookie cutter approach to lawn care. We think you deserve more than that. We know what works in another neighborhood may not be right for you. We will provide you with a service program tailored to your lawn's needs, and we include extras like our double overlap application technique to ensure even growth and thickening without unsightly streaking or spotting of your lawn. You don't have to be home during our visits. You can count on us for timely service. We will provide you with information through newsletters, notes left at the time of service, and progress reports on your lawn condition. Our web site address is **http://www.greenleafco. com** where you can get other information on yard care tips, seasonal planting, lawn disease control, lawn insect control, tree maintenance, weed control, and landscaping. You can also request a free quotation.

6. **Voice Mail Recording (Obj. 3)**

Compose scripts for the following voice mail recordings:

a. You will be away from your job as loan counselor at Hometown Bank for three days while you attend a professional conference. Fellow loan counselor, James Lumas, will be handling your calls while you are away. Compose a script of the voice mail recording you will leave on your phone prior to departing for your conference.

b. As owner and operator of Sis's Florist Shop, you close your shop on Sundays. You do, however, accept orders via your home telephone for flowers and plants to be picked up or delivered on Monday or later. Compose a message to be left on your phone when you close the shop on Saturday evenings informing customers who call in as to how to reach you for ordering.

c. You are office administrator for Medical Associates, a physicians' clinic. Compose a voice mail message that will be heard by patients and other parties who call after hours. You will need to explain how to reach

the voice mail box for the appointment desk, each physician, the insurance office, and the laboratory.

7. **Voice Mail Message (Obj. 3)**

Compose scripts for the following situations for which you would leave a voice mail message:

a. Upon returning from a meeting, you have a message on your phone from your real estate agent that says your bid on a house you wish to buy was rejected by the seller. When you call your agent to tell her you want to raise your initial offer by $2,000, you get her voice mail. What will you say in your voice mail message to her?

b. As an outside salesperson for industrial cleaning supplies, you call a client to see if you can come by his business to show him some new products. You had called him earlier in the week but did not hear back from him. You get the client's voice mail that indicates he is away from his desk. You are in the client's neighborhood now and would prefer to call on him today rather than some other time when you would have to drive back to his area. What will you say in your voice message?

c. As human resources manager, you call a job applicant to tell her she has been selected to fill a job position as sales associate. You get a voice mail message saying that she is not at home right now. What will you say in your voice mail message?

8. **Wearable Wireless Devices (Obj. 3)**

In small groups, design a perfect wearable wireless device. Describe its features and capabilities. Share your designs with the class.

9. **Appropriate Channel Choice (Obj. 4)**

Indicate one or more appropriate message channels for each of the following situations. A downloadable version of this activity is available at **http://lehman.swlearning. com**. Be prepared to discuss your choices in a class discussion.

a. Laying off an employee

b. Contacting a customer concerning late payment

c. Sending RSVP for a dinner party invitation

d. Sending a customer-requested price quote on order

e. Contacting a reference for a job applicant

f. Notifying staff of a change in work procedures

g. Recommending an action to upper management

h. Sending selected employees' test results performed by an outside laboratory or counseling clinic to human resources

i. Seeking advice from a peer regarding a challenging task

j. Announcing upcoming professional development sessions for the next quarter

10. Inappropriate Uses of Technology (Obj. 4)

In small groups, discuss situations in which you or others you know have experienced situations in which technology was inappropriately used. Possible situations might have involved breaches of privacy, misuse or loss of information, or insensitive intrusion. How was each situation resolved? How could each situation have been prevented?

Applications

Read | Think | Write | Speak | Collaborate

1. Communication Technology Success Stories (Objs. 1–4)

Conduct an electronic search to locate an article that deals with the successful use of electronic communication in a company or organization. Prepare an abstract of the article that includes the following parts: (1) article citation, (2) name of organization/company, (3) brief description of communication technique/situation, and (4) outcome(s) of the successful communication. As an alternative to locating an article, write about a successful communication situation in the organization/company for which you work.

Required: Present your abstracts as an e-mail attachment to your instructor. Refer to Appendix B for examples for formatting citations. Be prepared to give a short presentation in class.

2. E-Mail Emerges as "Evidence Mail" (Objs. 1, 4)

E-mail and other forms of electronic communication are like any other written communication in that they are subject to subpoena in court proceedings. Because e-mail is used so extensively in most businesses, it provides an ongoing record of many activities and transactions. Even deleted e-mails are frequently not really gone, as they may still exist in backup files and tapes. E-mail has become the corporate equivalent of DNA evidence, the single hair at the crime scene that turns the entire case. Using your library's databases, locate the following article that explains more about e-mail as "evidence mail":

Varchaver, N. (2003, February 3). The perils of e-mail. *Fortune 147*(3), 66(6).

You may also link to the article as follows: **http://www.fortune.com/fortune/print/0,15935,418678,00.html**

Required: Outline a plan to help an organization assure that its e-mail communications are not used as negative legal evidence.

Read | Think | Write | Speak | Collaborate

3. Critique of E-Mail Messages Produced by Real Companies (Obj. 1)

Locate a company example of both a well-written and a poorly written e-mail message. Analyze the strengths and weaknesses of each document. Be prepared to discuss your analysis in class.

4. Search for Potential Fairfield Associate. (Obj. 3)

Fairfield Resorts is continually expanding the selection of resorts available to its FairShare Plus members. One method of adding a resort is to establish an alliance with an existing, independent resort. These associate locations enable FairShare Plus members to use their points to vacation at that resort. Fairfield Communities even extends the concept of "resort" to include cruises by establishing an alliance with Carnival Cruise Lines.

Required: Use the Internet or advertisements to identify a potential associate location. Assume that Fairfield Resorts has just established an alliance with the resort. Write the script of a voice mail message that Fairfield Resorts could leave for its FairShare Plus members informing them of the new location. Provide the members with instructions for learning more about this resort by visiting the Fairfield site (**http://www.fairfieldresorts.com**).

5. Assessing the Effectiveness of Web Communication (Obj. 2)

Visit the *Web Pages that Suck* web site, designed to help you "learn good web design by looking at bad web design": **http://www.webpagesthatsuck.com.**

Required: Study the suggestions offered on the site and examine the poor web sites that are linked. Develop a checklist of factors that contribute to a successful web page; design a form that could be used for evaluation of sites.

6. Assuring Accessibility to the Web (Obj. 2)

For a web site to be a truly universal communication medium, it must be able to reach all audiences, including those with disabilities. Locate the following article that discusses strategies for making web information accessible to those who cannot access information in various ways:

Landolt, S. C. (2000, April). 'World Wide' Web. *Credit Union Management*, 23(4), 50.

Required: Visit a corporate web site of your choice. Evaluate the accessibility of information on that site by viewers who are physically challenged. Assuming that you are an employee of that organization, send an e-mail message to your instructor with recommendations for making the information in the site more accessible.

7. Evaluating Web Sites (Obj. 2)

Select five organizations' web sites to examine, or visit sites selected by your instructor. Select all five of your organizations from *one* of the following categories: service organizations, retail operations, educational institutions, manufacturing companies, or recreational entities.

Required: Using the evaluation form you developed in Application 5, critique each of the selected sites, placing them in rank order of effectiveness. Use a computer projection system to demonstrate the best site to the class, explaining its exemplary features.

8. Enhancing Telephone Etiquette (Obj. 3)

In today's world, most initial contact with a person is via the telephone, so those important first impressions are dependent on practicing proper telephone etiquette. Visit the text support site at **http://lehman.swlearning.com** to explore strategies for increasing levels of telephone courtesy as an image and trust builder.

Required: Prepare a brief presentation providing suggestions for placing calls, answering calls, and taking telephone messages.

9. E-Mail and Instant Messaging Usage Policy (Objs. 1, 4)

As with other electronic communication channels, technology often advances faster than the organization's ability to develop adequate procedures for using it. Using your group members' own work experience and information obtained from an online search, develop a company policy that applies to acceptable use of e-mail and instant messaging. Address such issues as message security, company monitoring of messages, appropriate message content, etc. Provide a detailed explanation of acceptable e-mail and instant messaging usage that employees can follow consistently.

Required: Send your policy as an attachment to an e-mail message to your instructor; or if directed, bring a copy of the policy to class for discussion.

10. Etiquette Assessment (Obj. 3)

In small groups discuss incidents of inappropriate cell phone behavior you have experienced in a school, work, or public setting. Explain how each incident affected the individuals involved. Discuss etiquette rules you believe are critical for courteous, productive cell phone use. Are some netiquette rules appropriate for business calls but not for personal calls or vice versa? Prepare a brief presentation on the Dos and Don'ts of Cell Phone Usage.

Fairfield Resorts Reaches Out to Various Constituents

The Web provides an organization with a highly interactive medium for communicating with its various stakeholders, including customers, employees, business partners, and the general public. Not only can various types of company information be presented, but the site can open the door to participation and discussion.

- Locate the following article that provides further elaboration on how organizations can avoid common web site problems to use their sites as positive communication tools:

Typos, bad links top website problem list. (2002, June 24). *PR Week*, 4.

- Visit the Fairfield Resorts web site at **http://www.fairfieldresorts. com**. Review the site options and available information.

Compose a brief report to your instructor that describes how Fairfield Resorts is using its web page to communicate with owners, potential owners, and employees. Submit to your instructor as an e-mail attachment.

Part 4 of the Fairfield ShowCASE continues exploration of effective web site development.

http://www.fairfieldresorts.com

Visit the text support site at **http://lehman.swlearning.com** to complete Part 4 of the Fairfield ShowCASE.

Internet Case

Using the Internet to Bridge the Cultural Gap

The Internet has the potential to become the primary tool for helping people of the world understand each other and view citizens of other cultures as real individuals living similar lives, while in different ways. Exploring the cultures of the world via the Internet is one step toward tolerance and acceptance of all people, regardless of race, ethnicity, religion, or national heritage.

Additionally, the Internet is a one-stop reference source for information about any country you may visit for business or pleasure. Using simple search techniques, you can use the Internet to obtain information on virtually any country in the world. One helpful site is the Central Intelligence Agency's online World Factbook, which contains a vast amount of information on every country in the world, as collected by the agency. Chat sites, such as the Yahoo! Culture Site, provide the opportunity for less formal exchange of cultural information. When planning travel outside the country, you might want to consult the U.S. State Department site's area for "Crisis Abroad." The site also includes the latest travel warnings, consular information, entry requirements, crime information, and embassy locations for the country you will visit.

If you need to know at least a little of the language of the culture you plan to visit, be sure to check the Foreign Language for Travelers site. Here you can select from among more than 80 different languages for translating. The site not only displays the words, but actually recites them for you via short audio files. And of course you will want to know what your U.S. dollars will convert to in your visited country. The Currency Converter site lets you input the number of dollars and obtain the exchanged amount for another currency. Other useful resources for improving your global vision are available in the Professional Resources section of your Professional Power Pak CD.

Armed with accurate information about a given country, you are able to understand and appreciate cultural variety. As globalization of business results in a world that grows progressively smaller, it becomes imperative for professionals to possess broad-based cultural awareness.

Visit the text support site at **http://lehman. swlearning.com** to link to web resources related to this topic. As directed by your instructor, respond to one or more of the following:

1. Select a country for study. Visit the web resources for this case and gather the following information: the country's location and size, official language(s), religion(s), customs, currency, major products, and crime statistics. Learn three phrases in the predominant language of the country. Share your information in a short oral report.

2. Locate other Internet sites that provide information about your selected country. Prepare a list of dos and don'ts for the traveler visiting that country.

3. **GMAT** Prepare a one-page essay that uses the metaphor of a bridge to describe the role of the Internet in linking cultures.

Video Case

Le Travel Store: Diversity Energizes a Workforce

In 1976 Bill and Joan Keller started what is today known as Le Travel Store. Their focus, a somewhat radical idea in 1976, was targeting the needs of independent, international travelers by offering all the travel gear, travel books, maps, and travel services needed to plan a big trip under one roof. Now in its third location—the historic Gaslamp Quarter in downtown San Diego—Le Travel Store sells a full line of travel products in its renovated 10,000-square-foot historic building, as well as online at **http://www. letravelstore.com**.

View the video segment about Le Travel Store and accompanying activities on WebTutor or your Professional Power Pak CD.

Discussion Questions

1. What benefit does Joan Keller say Le Travel Store realizes from its employee focus described by her as "we love diversity" and "I really like to mix it up"?

2. Besides the reason Joan Keller gave, what might be other benefits of having a diverse workforce in an international travel company?

3. What criteria does Joan Keller use when deciding whom to hire?

Activities

Locate the following article available in full text from InfoTrac College or from another database available through your campus library:

Strenski, J. (1994, August-September). Stress diversity in employee communications. *Public Relations Journal, 50*(7), 32–35.

1. Read the article and write a statement identifying the company that you believe best illustrates the value gained from employee diversity. Include in your statement actions the company has taken to promote diversity as well as specific communication advice given in the article. In particular, look for examples of the following diversity activities:

   a. Stressing respect for individual differences and characteristics that all employees have in common.

   b. Favoring ongoing training programs that seek not only to educate workers about ethnic, racial, and cultural differences, but also seek to change the company's culture.

   c. Finding trainers and managers with experience in diversity who are not divisive in their approach, who emphasize similarities among groups, and who stress the connection between managing diversity and competitiveness.

2. Learn about the diversity initiatives currently in place at one of the companies mentioned in the article— some ten years after the article was published. Use the links provided on WebTutor or your Professional Power Pak or sources of your choice. Companies mentioned include AT&T, Honeywell, Levi Strauss, Motorola, Mutual of New York, and Sun Microsystems, Inc.

6

Delivering Good- and Neutral-News Messages

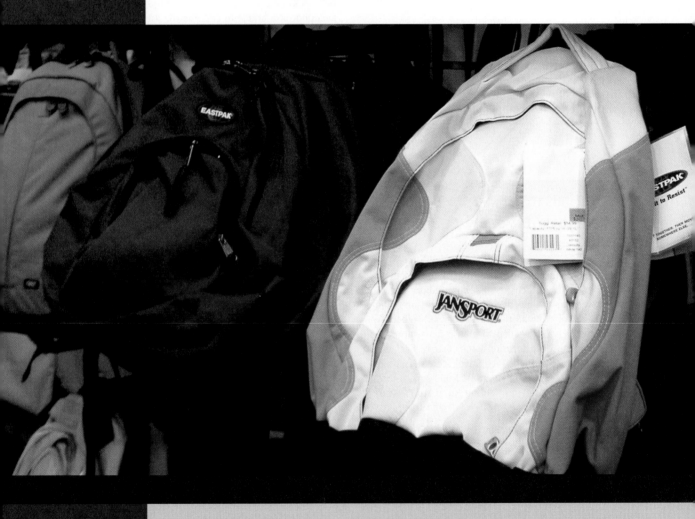

© SUSAN VAN ETTEN

Objectives *When you have completed Chapter 6, you will be able to:*

1 Identify the steps in the deductive outline for good news and routine information, and understand its uses and adaptations for specific situations and for international audiences.

2 Prepare messages that convey good news, including thank-you and appreciation messages.

3 Write messages presenting claims and making adjustments.

4 Write routine requests and favorable responses to routine requests.

5 Write messages acknowledging customer orders.

6 Compose messages providing credit information and extending credit.

7 Prepare procedural messages that ensure clear and consistent application.

JANSPORT: CUSTOMER SERVICE AT THE HEART OF ATTITUDES AND ACTIONS

"You just can't get decent service these days. Companies don't care about their customers." Such cynical observations are widely held today because far too many companies do, in fact, treat customers as though they were an afterthought. This is not the case, however, at JanSport.

Owned by VF Corp. and based in Appleton, Wisconsin, JanSport knows that its target market is the millions of middle school, high school, and college students who have made JanSport the nation's leading manufacturer of backpacks. An estimated one third of the nation's school-age citizens are hauling the company logo around on a daily basis. What makes JanSport so successful is its heritage and authenticity. "JanSport," says spokeswoman Gigi deYoung, "is the real deal, not a fad or a fashion purchase that you throw away."[1] With a wide variety of features and colors available, the backpack is an extension of personal identity, traveling not only to class, but to sporting events, recreational activities, and exotic destinations.

According to JanSport's web site, their mission is "to help you carry the stuff you need, where you need it, in the most functional, fashionable way possible." They declare a "moral obligation" to consumers to provide them not only with quality products, but to ensure that their products are made under safe, ethical, and lawful conditions. Backing its pledge with actions, JanSport offers a lifetime guarantee on all of its backpacks. From repairing a zipper to actually replacing a faulty pack, the company commits itself to assuring that a JanSport backpack will continue to serve its designed purpose as long as the user wants to carry it. And while the company's own research indicates that 72 percent of teens replace their packs every year, many units remain in use for much longer.[2]

Perhaps you will want to pass this story along whenever you hear someone say "You can't get decent service these days. Companies don't care about their customers." Skillfully communicating good news and neutral information to customers is one way to express appreciation and demonstrate a service attitude. Effective communication—whether directed to customers, employees, or business partners—reaches the intended audience, is organized to achieve the desired effect, and demonstrates an impeccable command of the language.

http://www.jansport.com

See ShowCASE, Part 2, on page 206 for Spotlight Communicator Mike Cisler, president of JanSport.

People in organizations use a number of channels to communicate with internal and external audiences. When the message is positive or neutral, a sender has numerous choices, as shown in Figure 6-1. Depending on the message, the recipient, and constraints of time and location, the best channel might be spoken or electronic, options covered in Chapter 5. In addition to the electronic and verbal tools presented in Chapter 5, (e-mail, instant messaging, web pages, and telephone) companies also use written documents such as memorandums and letters to communicate information.

The principles for preparing memorandums (commonly referred to as *memos*) are similar to those you've already applied when composing e-mail messages as both are channels for sharing information of a more informal nature. Memos provide a tangible means of sharing information with people inside an organization. Letters are more formal, because they are used to convey information to external audiences such as customers, clients, business partners, or suppliers. Regardless of whether the audience is an internal or external one, communication should be carefully structured to achieve the desired purpose.

<table>
<tr><td>Objective 1</td></tr>
</table>

Identify the steps in the deductive outline for good news and routine information, and understand its uses and adaptations for specific situations and for international audiences.

Deductive Organizational Pattern

You can organize business messages either deductively or inductively depending on your prediction of the receiver's reaction to your main idea. Learning to organize business messages according to the appropriate outline will improve your chances of preparing a document that elicits the response or action you desire.

Figure 6-1	Options for Delivering Good- and Neutral-News Messages
Written	Letters Memos
Electronic	E-mail Instant messaging Web site
Spoken	In person Telephone Voice mail

Adapting a message to the expectations and social conventions of various cultures is critical in today's diverse business environment. To ensure clarity, many companies require that a professional staff member proficient in both languages review correspondence sent to international audiences. Detailed and significant documents translated from English are reviewed carefully for possible language barriers.

Diversity Challenges

Critical Thinking

What other words can be substituted for deductive *and* inductive?

In this chapter, you will learn to compose messages that convey ideas that a receiver likely will find either *pleasing* or *neutral*. Messages that convey pleasant information are referred to as **good-news messages**. Messages that are of interest to the reader but are not likely to generate an emotional reaction are referred to as **neutral** messages. The strategies discussed for structuring good-news and neutral-news messages can be generally applied to North American audiences. Because message expectations and social conventions differ from culture to culture, the effective writer will adapt as necessary when writing for various audiences. Refer to the Strategic Forces feature "Basic Cultural Values Influence Communication Styles" that discusses international message adaptations.

Good-news or neutral messages follow a **deductive sequence**—the message begins with the main idea. To present good news and neutral information deductively, begin with the major idea, followed by supporting details as depicted in Figure 6-2. In both outlines, the third point (closing thought) may be omitted without seriously impairing effectiveness; however, including it unifies the message and avoids abruptness.

Figure 6-2

Deductive Pattern Used in Good-News and Neutral-News Messages

Good News

- States the pleasant idea.
- Provides details and explanation.
- Reminds receiver of the good news or includes a future-oriented closing thought.

Neutral News

- States the main idea.
- Provides details and explanation.
- Reminds receiver of the main idea or includes a future-oriented closing thought.

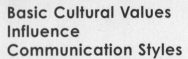

Basic Cultural Values Influence Communication Styles

Message patterns vary from culture to culture and are largely the product of the values held by each society. Differences in societal values influence social behavior, etiquette, communication styles, and business transactions. U.S. businesspeople are typically aware of basic differences in the business behaviors and practices of popular trade partners, but they may fail to recognize and understand the underlying values that shape behavior. For instance, values accepted in Japanese culture that differ from those held in U.S. culture include the following:

- U.S. corporations value independence in the workplace, whereas Japanese corporations value dependence.

- U.S. corporations value honesty in business practices; if someone says he or she can do something, it means just that. Japanese corporations, on the other hand, value "saving face," and to admit they can't produce what you are asking for is an embarrassment. The Japanese would sooner tell you they can do something while knowing they cannot than bear the shame of admitting they can't do it.[3]

- The Japanese value building business partnerships for life, while Americans often focus on short-term transactions. The Japanese prefer to develop a business relationship through a business courtship—typically beginning the business relationship by placing a small trial order, to see "how things go." If the customer is satisfied, more orders follow and continue to grow with the relationship.[4]

- In negotiating situations, the Japanese are likely more comfortable when in the buyer position than the seller position, since buyers have higher status than do sellers in the Japanese culture.

- The fact that Japanese businesspeople tend to make decisions much more slowly than do their U.S. counterparts has at least two explanations that stem from culture. Time is valued differently in Japan than in the United States; and group decisions, which are not known for their expediency, are valued over individual decisions that can be made more quickly.

Understanding such value differences can aid the business communicator in understanding variations in message patterns. When writing for intercultural audiences, keep these suggestions in mind:

- *Write naturally but avoid abbreviations, slang, acronyms, technical jargon, sports and military analogies, and other devices.* Such expressions help you clarify an idea and personalize your messages; however, they may be confusing to those unfamiliar with North American usage. Those speaking English as a second language learned it from a textbook; therefore, they may have difficulty understanding "ASAP" (as soon as possible) or "WYSIWYG" (what you see is what you get). They may be mystified when you reject bid proposals that are "out of the ball park" or "way off target," recruit job applicants who are "sharp as brass tacks," or refer to the supervisor as "the top gun."

- *Avoid words that trigger emotional responses such as anger, fear, or suspicion.* Such words are often referred to as red flag words because they elicit the same response as a *red flag* waved in front of a raging bull. Using *hot buttons*—terms that make political judgments, show condescension, or make cultural judgments, for example—is a sure way to shut a reader's mind to your message.

(continued)

- *Use simple terms but attempt to be specific as well.* Some of the simplest words must be interpreted within the context of each situation in which they are used (e.g., *fast* has several meanings). Likewise, avoid use of superlatives such as *fantastic* and *terrific* because they may be misinterpreted as overly dramatic or insincere. Also avoid overly formal and difficult words and expressions that may be confusing or considered pompous; for example, *pursuant to your request, ostentatious*, or *nebulous.*

- *Consider the subtle differences in the ways specific cultures organize messages.* Asians, for example, typically use indirect patterns of writing, even when writing about good news; they avoid negative messages or camouflage them so expertly that the reader might not recognize them. On the other hand, Germans tend to be more direct than North Americans, even with bad news.

- *Use graphics, visual aids, and forms whenever possible because they simplify the message.* When language barriers can be minimized through visual means, the opportunity for confusion is reduced.

- *Use figures for expressing numbers to avoid confusion with an international audience.* Be aware, however, of differences in the way numbers and dates are written. As a general rule, use figures for numbers, and keep in mind that most people in the world use the metric system. Note the following example:

U.S.	Other Countries
$2,400.00	2400,00
January 29, 2005	29 January 2005

- *Write out the name of the month in international correspondence to avoid misunderstandings.* When using a number to represent the month, many countries state the day before the month as shown in the following examples:

U.S.	Other Countries
2/10/05	10.2 2005 or 10.2.05
March 26, 2005	26th of March 2005

- *Become familiar with the traditional format of letters in the country of the person to whom you are writing and adapt your format as much as possible.* Note differences in the formality of the salutation and complimentary close. The Germans, who prefer a formal salutation such as "Very Honored Mr. Professor Jones," might be offended by your choice of an informal "Dear Jim," a salutation you believed was appropriate because you had met and done prior business with Professor Jones. You will also want to check the position of various letter parts such as the letter address and the writer's name and title. For example, in German letters the company name follows the complimentary close and the typed signature block is omitted, leaving the reader responsible for deciphering the writer's signature.[5]

Application

While the Japanese tend to write in a more indirect manner, even when conveying good news, Germans tend to prefer the direct message pattern for both positive and negative messages. Research the German culture to determine value differences that might account for the directness in communication. Write a one-page summary of your explanation.

The Internet provides a wealth of up-to-date information that enables communicators to understand the people of the world. A person preparing to conduct business in China would benefit from visiting the World Factbook, a helpful site provided by the Central Intelligence Agency. Clicking a country of your choice displays a current map and links to important topics such as people, geography, government, transnational issues, and more. Visit the World Factbook at **http://www.odci.gov/cia/ publications/factbook/geos/ ch.html**

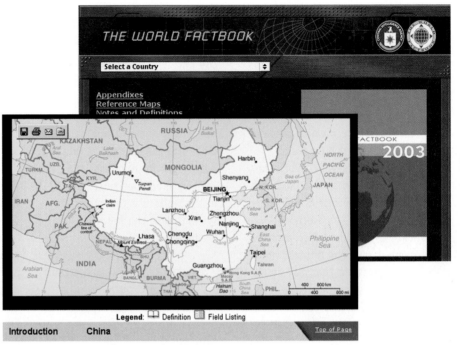

Critical Thinking

Will all deductive messages have at least three paragraphs? Explain.

The deductive pattern has several advantages:

- The first sentence is easy to write. After it is written, the details follow easily.
- The first sentence gets the attention it deserves in this emphatic position.
- Encountering good news in the first sentence puts receivers in a pleasant frame of mind, and they are receptive to the details that follow.
- The arrangement may save receivers some time. Once they understand the important idea, they can move rapidly through the supporting details.

As you study sample deductive messages in this chapter, note the *ineffective example notation* that clearly marks the examples of poor writing. Detailed comments highlight important writing strategies that have been applied or violated. While gaining experience in developing effective messages, you will also learn to recognize standard business formats. Fully formatted messages are shown as printed documents (letters on company letterhead or paper memos) or as electronic formats (e-mail messages or online input screens). Details about formatting letters, memos, and e-mail messages are included in Appendix A.

Objective *2*

Prepare messages that convey good news, including thank-you and appreciation messages.

Good-News Messages

Messages delivering good news are organized deductively according to the three-step plan illustrated in Figure 6-2. For illustration, you'll study examples of messages that convey positive news as well as thank-you and appreciation messages that generate goodwill.

Positive News

The memo sent to all employees in Figure 6-3 begins directly with the main idea, the approval of a business casual dress policy. The discussion that follows includes a brief review of the policy and ends positively by encouraging employees to seek additional information from the company web site or contact the writer.

Thank-You and Appreciation Messages

Critical Thinking

What are some other ways that business people can build lasting relationships with customers or clients?

Empathetic managers take advantage of occasions to write goodwill messages that build strong, lasting relationships among employees, clients, customers, and various other groups. People usually are not reluctant to say, "Thank you," "What a great performance," "You have certainly helped me," and so on. Despite good intentions, however, often people don't get around to sending thank yous and appreciations. Because of their rarity, written appreciation messages are especially meaningful—even treasured. A sincere written apology is needed when regrettable situations occur in order to preserve relationships. Visit the text support site at http://lehman.swlearning.com for tips for handling apologies.

Thank-You Messages

After receiving a gift, being a guest, or attending an interview, or after any of the great variety of circumstances in which a follow-up letter of thanks might be desirable, a thoughtful person will take the time to send a written message. A simple handwritten note is sufficient for some social situations. However, when written in a business office to respond to a business situation, the message may be printed on letterhead or sent electronically. Your message should be written deductively and reflect your sincere feelings of gratitude. The following thank-you messages (a) identify the circumstances for which the writer is grateful and (b) provide specific reasons the action is appreciated.

To express thanks for a gift

After conducting your in-service seminar, I was pleasantly surprised to receive the desk calendar. The convenience of being able to plan my week at a glance is an unexpected by-product of my work with your company. Thanks for your kindness and for this useful gift.

To extend thanks for hospitality

Ray and I thoroughly enjoyed the weekend excursion you hosted at Lake Douglas for our work team. Since we moved here from Savannah, sailing has become a rare pleasure. You were kind to invite us. Thanks again for a delightful time.

Figure 6-3

Good Example of a Good-News Message

Deductive Outline for Good-News Memos

1. Begin with good news.

2. Include necessary details.

3. May omit a goodwill ending when communicating a positive idea to a receiver in the company and a statement is not necessary to build unity at the end.

INTEROFFICE MEMORANDUM

TO: All Employees
FROM: Gloria Martinello, Human Resources Manager *G.M.*
DATE: May 15, 2004
SUBJECT: Casual Dress Policy Takes Effect July 1

Announces the approval of the new dress policy.

I am pleased to announce that a casual dress policy has been approved for First National Bank and will be effective July 1. As most of us agree, casual attire in the banking industry generally means "dressy casual," since virtually all of us interact with our clientele regularly throughout the day.

Provides clear explanation to ensure policy is understood. Formats as a table for quick, easy reference for specific details.

To maintain our traditional professional image while enjoying more relaxed attire, please follow these guidelines:

Men	**Women**
Sport or polo shirt, with collars	Pant suit
Khakis or corduroys	Sweater or blouse with pants or skirt
Loafers with socks	Loafers with socks
	Low heels with hosiery

Continues with additional discussion of the policy.

Tennis shoes, open-toed shoes, sandals, jogging suits, shorts, jeans, sweatpants and sweatshirts are inappropriate. Formal business attire should be worn when meeting with clients outside the office.

Encourages readers to ask questions or view additional information on the company intranet.

Please visit the HR web site for the complete casual attire policy and illustrations of appropriate casual attire. If you have questions as you begin making changes in your wardrobe, please call me at ext. 59.

Format Pointers

- Uses "Memorandum Expert," a word processing template, for efficient production. Standard memo headings transmit the memo. See Figure A-9 in the Appendix to review the format.
- Includes writer's initials after printed name and title.
- Uses single-spaced block paragraphs with a double space between paragraphs for easy readability.

Appreciation Messages

An appreciation message is intended to recognize, reward, and encourage the receiver; however, the sender also gains happiness from commending a deserving person. Such positive thinking can be a favorable influence on the sender's own attitude and performance. In appropriate situations you may wish to address an appreciation message to an individual's supervisor and send a copy of the document to the individual to ensure that he or she is aware of your positive comments. An appreciation message should be sent to commend deserving people and not for possible self-gain.

Critical Thinking

How effective is e-mail for sending appreciation messages?

To gain the full potential value to the sender and the receiver, the message should

- *Be sent in a timely manner.* Sending the appreciation message within a few days of the circumstance will emphasize the genuineness of your efforts. Appreciation letters sent long overdue may arouse questions about the sender's motive.
- *Avoid exaggerated, strong language that is hardly believable.* The sender of the message may believe the exaggerated statements to be true, but the recipient may find them unbelievable and insincere. Strong language with unsupported statements arouses questions about the sender's motive for the message.
- *Contain specific comments about the outstanding qualities or performance.* The following cold, mechanical message may have only minimal value to a speaker who has worked hard preparing and who has not been paid. While the sender cared enough to say thank you, the message could have been given to any speaker, even if its sender had slept through the entire speech. Similarly, a note closed with *sincerely* does not necessarily make the ideas seem sincere. Including specific remarks about the sender's understanding and application of the speaker's main points makes the original message meaningful and sincere.

Original:	Your speech to the Lincoln Jaycees was very much appreciated. You are an excellent speaker, and you have good ideas. Thank you.
Improved:	This past week I have found myself applying some of the time management principles discussed at the seminar you conducted last week for the Association of Business Professionals.
	Prioritizing my tasks really helped me keep my perspective. When I performed the time analysis, I easily identified some areas I can manage more effectively. Thank you for an informative and useful seminar.

The appreciation in Figure 6-4 sent from a manager to the facilitator of a ropes course that employees recently completed conveys a warmer, more sincere compliment than a generic, exaggerated message. The net effects of this message are positive: the sender feels good for having passed on a deserved compliment and the facilitator is encouraged by the client's satisfaction with her team development program.

Figure 6-4

Good Example of an Appreciation Message

Deductive Outline for an Appreciation Message

1. Begin with a statement of praise or appreciation.

2. Include specific comments about the outstanding qualities or performance being high-lighted to convey a sincere tone. Avoid strong language and exaggerations that the receiver will not believe.

3. Close with a warm statement that looks to the future.

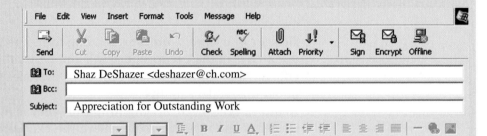

Extends appreciation for the company's providing quality opportunities for team growth.

Provides specific evidence of the worth of the experience without exaggerating or using overly strong language or mechanical statements.

Assures the writer of tangible benefits to be gained from this experiential teambuilding activity.

| File | Edit | View | Insert | Format | Tools | Message | Help |

Send | Cut | Copy | Paste | Undo | Check | Spelling | Attach | Priority | Sign | Encrypt | Offline

To: Shaz DeShazer <deshazer@ch.com>
Bcc:
Subject: Appreciation for Outstanding Work

Shaz,

Completing the ropes course at Camp Horizon was a memorable and life-changing experience for every member of our office staff.

Your facilitators were masterful in allowing our teams to take risks while ensuring their safety. The course provided a diverse series of activities that enabled each staff member to participate, regardless of our physical limitations. It was interesting for us to identify the real leaders in our office.

In the words of one colleague, "The ropes course has shown me I can do more than I have come to expect of myself." Thank you for helping us see our potential.

Best wishes,
Jana Sullivan

Format Pointers

- Uses short lines, mixed case; omits special formatting such as emoticons and e-mail abbreviations for improved readability.

- Reflects other format considerations covered in Appendix A. A .sig file appears on a printed copy of the e-mail.

Routine Claims

A *claim* is a request for an adjustment. When business communicators ask for something to which they think they are entitled (such as a refund, replacement, exchange, or payment for damages), the message is called a *claim message*.

Claim Message

Write messages present-ing claims and making adjustments.

Critical Thinking

Think of routine claims situations you have encountered. What distin-guished them from persuasive claims? How was your claim resolved?

On a corporate web site, the presence of e-mail links, chat rooms, and bulletin boards fos-ters dialogue that leads to strong relationships. With this 24-hour, 7-day a week focus group, companies gather insights about customer prefer-ences, listen and respond to concerns and questions, and give customers a reason to visit their sites frequently. If these individuals are invited to talk, communicators must be pre-pared to respond with timely, effective messages.

Requests for adjustments can be divided into two groups: ***routine claims*** and ***persuasive claims***. Persuasive claims, which are discussed in Chapter 8, assume that a request will be granted only after explanations and per-suasive arguments have been presented. Routine claims (possibly because of guarantees, warranties, or other contractual conditions) assume that a request will be granted quickly and willingly, without persuasion. Because you expect routine claims to be granted willingly, a forceful, accusatory tone is inappropriate.

When the claim is routine, the deductive pattern shown in Figure 6-2 will be followed. Let's consider a technology specialist who seeks a service pack to correct errors in a new release of an audit software program. Surely the software company intended to issue a new release free of bugs; otherwise, the company would not have sold the new release. Because the existence of the bugs appears to be obvious, the software company can be expected to correct the problem without persuasion. Thus, the technology specialist can ask for the adjustment *before* providing an explanation. Note, however, that the letter in Figure 6-5 is written *inductively*—the details are presented before the main idea, and the tone is unnecessarily forceful.

The writer is confident that his routine request for an adjustment will be granted. Therefore, in the revision (Figure 6-6) he simply states the request in the first sentence and follows with the details without showing anger, disgust, suspicion, or disappointment. Beginning with the request for an adjustment gives it the emphasis it deserves.

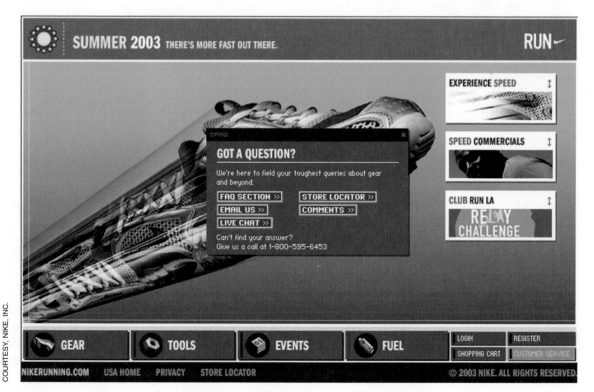

Figure 6-5

Poor Example of a Routine Claim

Ineffective Example **X**

Uses a writer-centered, forceful tone to convey details the receiver already knows.

Continues discussion of the problem but shows no empathy for the receiver.

Uses second person and negative language that emphasize the receiver is at fault.

Presents a reason for requesting the adjustment.

States the claim that should have appeared in the first paragraph and continues forceful tone damaging to human relations.

Ms. Haney:

Our company recently purchased the upgrade of your Audit Partner 7.0 software. We have used the 6.2 release in the past and were interested in the new features promoted in your advertisements. However, your new software version does not work.

When our computer technology advisory group tested the new version, we discovered several bugs, especially in the reporting modules. The attached logs and error messages prove, and your technical support staff agree, that these problems were caused by the software.

We are not willing to distribute the upgrade to our audit staff unless these errors are corrected. Please modify the program or refund our money.

Favorable Response to a Claim Message

Businesses *want* their customers to write when merchandise or service is not satisfactory. They want to learn of ways in which goods and services can be improved, and they want their customers to receive value for the money they spend. With considerable confidence, they can assume that writers of claim letters think their claims are valid. By responding fairly to legitimate requests in **adjustment messages**, businesses can gain a reputation for standing behind their goods and services. A loyal customer may become even more loyal after a business has demonstrated its integrity.

Ordinarily, a response to a written message is also a written message. Sometimes, people communicate to confirm ideas they have already discussed on the telephone. When the response to a claim letter is favorable,

Critical Thinking

What is meant by resale and sales promotional material? How are they different from sales messages?

Figure 6-6

Good Example of a Routine Claim

Deductive Outline for Routine Claim

1. Request action (refund, replacement, credit on your account, free repairs, etc.).
2. Explain the details supporting the request objectively.
3. Remind recipient of the action requested with an expression of appreciation for taking the action.

Provides a subject line that is meaningful to the reader and the writer.

Emphasizes the main idea (request for adjustment) by placing it in the first sentence.

Provides the explanation.

Ends on a positive note, reminding reader that the company can begin using the software and the user documentation.

To: Kelly Haney <khaney@qcs.com>
Bcc:
Subject: Service Pack Needed for Audit Partner Software

Ms. Haney,

Please send us a service pack that will correct the errors in the recent release of your Audit Partner software.

Our computer technology advisory group puts new software through extensive testing before we distribute software to our staff and begin our training programs. After just a short time working with Audit Partner 7.0, it became clear that this version contains numerous bugs, especially in the reporting modules. Please examine the attached logs and error messages generated by our computer technology advisory group. Their conversations with your technical support staff confirm our evaluation of this version of your audit software.

Our audit personnel are eagerly awaiting the new version of your software for implementation in our training program tentatively scheduled for next month. We're anxious to receive a service pack that will correct the errors and enable this version to operate as effectively as version 6.2.

Later,

Patrick Byrd
Technology Specialist

Format Pointers

- Limits the message to a single idea—the claim request.
- Composes a short, concise message that fits on one screen.
- Includes a salutation and closing to personalize the message.
- Reflects other formatting guidelines covered in Appendix A.

present ideas in the deductive sequence. Although the word *grant* is acceptable when talking about claims, its use in adjustment messages is discouraged. An expression such as "Your claim is being granted" unnecessarily implies that the sender is in a position of power.

Because the subject of an adjustment is related to the goods or services provided, the message can include a brief sales idea. With only a little extra space, the message can include resale or sales promotional material. **Resale** refers to a discussion of goods or services already bought. It reminds customers and clients that they made a good choice in selecting a company with which to do business, or it reminds them of the good qualities of their purchase. **Sales promotional material** refers to statements made about related merchandise or service. For example, a message about a company's office furniture might also mention its work-space design team. Mentioning the design team is using sales promotional material. Subtle sales messages that are included in adjustments have a good chance of being read, but direct sales letters may not be read at all.

Critical Thinking

What wording would you suggest in order to avoid "granting" a customer's request?

Let's evaluate the reply Patrick Byrd received to his claim reporting the errors in the new software. How would the message in Figure 6-7 affect his impression of the company's commitment to stand behind its software?

Eager to learn if (and when) he will receive the software service pack, Patrick will resent having to read through the obvious facts in the first three sentences. The vague explanation with no specific assurance that the service pack is being prepared may anger him further. Finally the last paragraph sheds considerable doubt on the integrity of the entire program.

Notice the deductive outline and the explanation in the revision in Figure 6-8. The writer knows that Patrick will be pleased the service pack

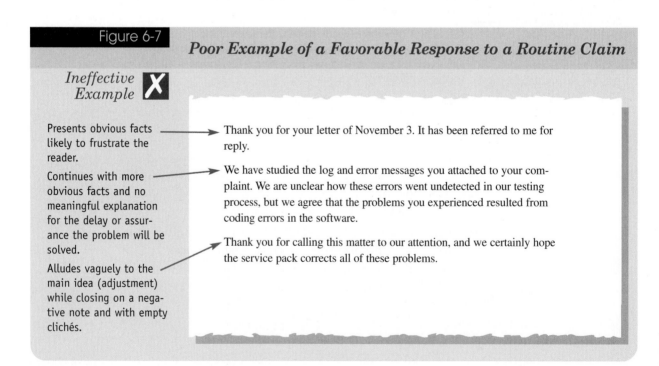

| Figure 6-7 | *Poor Example of a Favorable Response to a Routine Claim* |

Ineffective Example X

Presents obvious facts likely to frustrate the reader. → Thank you for your letter of November 3. It has been referred to me for reply.

Continues with more obvious facts and no meaningful explanation for the delay or assurance the problem will be solved. → We have studied the log and error messages you attached to your complaint. We are unclear how these errors went undetected in our testing process, but we agree that the problems you experienced resulted from coding errors in the software.

Alludes vaguely to the main idea (adjustment) while closing on a negative note and with empty clichés. → Thank you for calling this matter to our attention, and we certainly hope the service pack corrects all of these problems.

Figure 6-8

Good Example of a Favorable Response to a Routine Claim

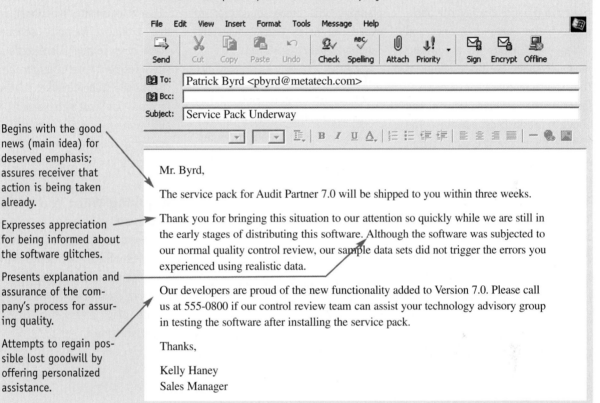

Deductive Outline for a Favorable Response to a Routine Claim

1. Approve the customer's claim in the first sentence (good news).
2. Explain the circumstances without placing blame. Include resale to assure customer of a wise choice.
3. Close on a pleasant, forward-looking note that attempts to regain the customer's confidence in the product/service and the company.

File   Edit   View   Insert   Format   Tools   Message   Help

Send   Cut   Copy   Paste   Undo   Check   Spelling   Attach   Priority   Sign   Encrypt   Offline

To: Patrick Byrd <pbyrd@metatech.com>

Bcc:

Subject: Service Pack Underway

Mr. Byrd,

The service pack for Audit Partner 7.0 will be shipped to you within three weeks.

Thank you for bringing this situation to our attention so quickly while we are still in the early stages of distributing this software. Although the software was subjected to our normal quality control review, our sample data sets did not trigger the errors you experienced using realistic data.

Our developers are proud of the new functionality added to Version 7.0. Please call us at 555-0800 if our control review team can assist your technology advisory group in testing the software after installing the service pack.

Thanks,

Kelly Haney
Sales Manager

Begins with the good news (main idea) for deserved emphasis; assures receiver that action is being taken already.

Expresses appreciation for being informed about the software glitches.

Presents explanation and assurance of the company's process for assuring quality.

Attempts to regain possible lost goodwill by offering personalized assistance.

will be sent with only a brief delay. Therefore, she conveys this good news in the first sentence. The details and closing sentence follow naturally and easily showing no reluctance for correcting the problem.

Routine Requests

Objective 4

Write routine requests and favorable responses to routine requests.

Like claims, requests are divided into two groups: ***routine requests*** and ***persuasive requests***. Persuasive requests, which are discussed in Chapter 8, assume that action will be taken after persuasive arguments are presented. Routine requests and favorable responses to them follow the deductive sequence.

SPOTLIGHT COMMUNICATOR
Customer Relations Key to Success

JanSport President Mike Cisler knows his primary job is to make sure his company continues to produce the favorite backpack brand among teens and college-aged adults. As a constant reminder about the fickle nature of today's young consumer, Michael P. Cisler keeps a small sign tacked above his desk: "Most ads suck." The point is blunt, but it is expressed in a manner in which young people speak. And young people, more than anyone else, are who Cisler wants to keep focused upon. Cisler is the first to admit he will fail in his leadership role if he ever takes his eyes off his youth target.

"In our business, the obsolescence factor is high," Cisler says. "If you're out of fashion, you're in big trouble. What's cool changes quickly, and staying on top of that is very difficult." Cisler bases these observations on years of experience, having assumed the presidency of JanSport after spending 24 years with the company, including positions in operations, information systems, marketing, finance, and strategic planning. His broad foundation of experience helps Cisler understand JanSport's young customers.

Cisler promotes JanSport's near-obsessive attention to contemporary youth culture through focus groups, panel discussions, an Internet-based advisory board, test markets, and other outlets. Reflecting current consumer interest in safety and comfort, JanSport's "Airlift" system uses patented gelastic gellycomb in pack shoulder straps. Cisler explains the JanSport advantage by saying, "We pretty much eat, drink, and sleep backpacks."[6]

Though JanSport produces day packs, fanny packs, duffel bags, travel packs, and luggage, their functional backpacks have been their most successful products. For over 30 years, the name JanSport has been synonymous with quality and durability, and the company's warranty policy is based on the understanding that customers value a legitimate, functional, credible product. Warranty service is made easy through JanSport's web site. President Mike Cisler recognizes that as the student market continues to grow, JanSport's convenient, reliable warranty service is one way to assure a longstanding relationship with customers.[7]

Applying What You Have Learned

1. How does JanSport promote the development of longstanding consumer relationships?
2. What part does JanSport's web site play in assuring customer satisfaction?

http://www.jansport.com

Refer to ShowCASE, Part 3, at the end of the chapter to learn how JanSport has simplified the handling of routine claims.

Routine Request

Most businesspeople request information about people, prices, products, and services. Because the request is a door opener for future business, receivers accept it optimistically. At the same time, they arrive at an opinion about the sender based on the quality of the message. Follow the points in the deductive outline for preparing effective requests you are confident will be fulfilled.

The e-mail link at Central Reservations' web page provided a quick, convenient channel for a national sales manager to obtain specific information essential for planning the company's national sales meeting in this famous mountain resort. Because the e-mail message in Figure 6-9 is vague, the sales manager is unlikely to receive information that will prove useful.

Critical Thinking

What can you do to make sure your routine requests don't just seem "routine"?

Note that the revision in Figure 6-10 starts with a direct request for specific information. Then as much detail as necessary is presented to enable the receiver to answer specifically. The revision ends confidently with appreciation for the action requested. The message is short, but because it conveys enough information and has a tone of politeness, it is effective.

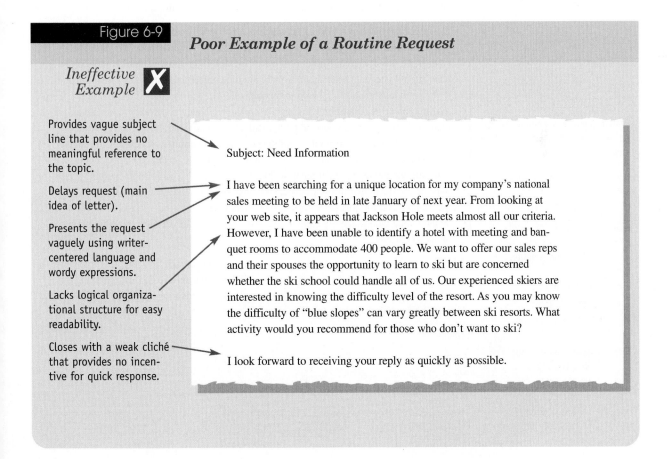

| Figure 6-9 | *Poor Example of a Routine Request* |

Ineffective Example **X**

Provides vague subject line that provides no meaningful reference to the topic.

Delays request (main idea of letter).

Presents the request vaguely using writer-centered language and wordy expressions.

Lacks logical organizational structure for easy readability.

Closes with a weak cliché that provides no incentive for quick response.

Subject: Need Information

I have been searching for a unique location for my company's national sales meeting to be held in late January of next year. From looking at your web site, it appears that Jackson Hole meets almost all our criteria. However, I have been unable to identify a hotel with meeting and banquet rooms to accommodate 400 people. We want to offer our sales reps and their spouses the opportunity to learn to ski but are concerned whether the ski school could handle all of us. Our experienced skiers are interested in knowing the difficulty level of the resort. As you may know the difficulty of "blue slopes" can vary greatly between ski resorts. What activity would you recommend for those who don't want to ski?

I look forward to receiving your reply as quickly as possible.

Figure 6-10

Good Example of a Routine Request

Deductive Outline for a Routine Request

1. State the major request in the first sentence.
2. Follow with the details that will make the request clear. Use a numbered or bulleted list for added emphasis, if possible.
3. Close with a forward look to the receiver's next step.

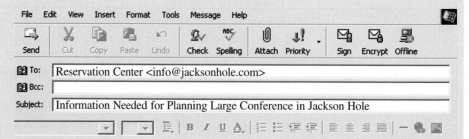

| File | Edit | View | Insert | Format | Tools | Message | Help |

To: Reservation Center <info@jacksonhole.com>
Bcc:
Subject: Information Needed for Planning Large Conference in Jackson Hole

Attn Reservation Center:

States a request plainly.

The excellent information on your web site describing the breathtaking winter scenery and legendary slopes suggests that Jackson Hole could be an ideal location for Hutton Enterprises' five-day national sales meeting. To assist us in selecting a site for this event scheduled for late January 2005, please provide the following information:

Asks specific questions with necessary explanation; uses a list for emphasis.

- Do any of the hotel(s) provide a convention center with space for a general session and meal functions for 400 attendees and a minimum of 10 concurrent breakout sessions? Can this conference hotel provide a block of 400 rooms, preferably at a conference rate? If adequate space is unavailable in the conference hotel, please recommend several suitable hotels near the conference hotel.
- Do your ski schools at SnowKing and Teton Village have the capacity to handle as many as 200 beginning skiers or snowboarders on a single day? To minimize time employees spend away from the conference, could you arrange all equipment rentals prior to our arrival and secure a private clubhouse for an on-site hospitality center?
- What are the ratings for each level of skiing (green/blue/black) for both resorts? We must be confident that the slopes will challenge our most experienced skiers, while providing a comfortable place for our beginners to learn.
- What unique indoor activity can you recommend as an alternative to downhill skiing or snowboarding?

Expresses appreciation and alludes to benefits of quick action.

Opens the door for a personal dialogue by providing a telephone number.

The information you provide could likely confirm our expectation that Jackson Hole can meet our conference needs. At that point, you will be contacted to assist us in making the many necessary reservations. Should you wish to talk with me directly, please call (630) 555-3910, Ext. 132.

Thanks,

Michael Stroug
National Sales Manager
Hutton Industries

Format Pointers

- Provides a salutation appropriate for the company.
- Includes needed .sig file identification below the writer's name in messages created at another company's web site.

Favorable Response to a Routine Request

The message in Figure 6-11 responds favorably to an online request for detailed information related to accommodations and recreation in a Wyoming mountain resort. However, it conveys the decision without much enthusiasm. With a little planning and consideration for the executive planning a major event, the message in Figure 6-12 could have been written just as quickly. Note the specific answers to the sales manager's questions and the helpful, sincere tone.

Favorable Response to a Favor Request

Occasionally, as a business professional, you will be asked special favors. You may receive invitations to speak at various civic or education groups,

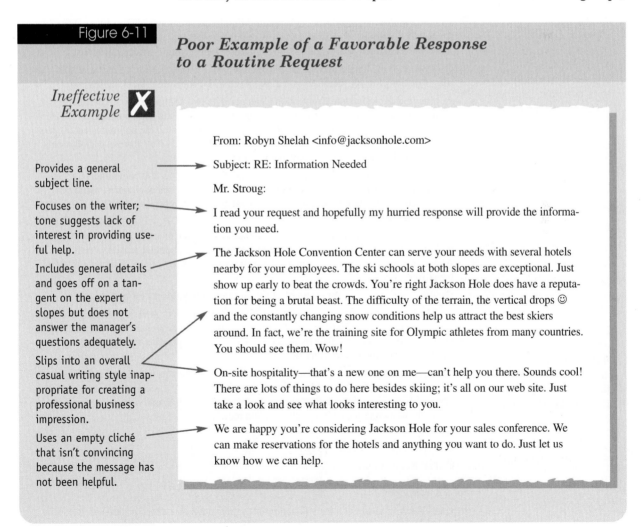

Figure 6-11

Poor Example of a Favorable Response to a Routine Request

Ineffective Example **X**

Provides a general subject line.

Focuses on the writer; tone suggests lack of interest in providing useful help.

Includes general details and goes off on a tangent on the expert slopes but does not answer the manager's questions adequately.

Slips into an overall casual writing style inappropriate for creating a professional business impression.

Uses an empty cliché that isn't convincing because the message has not been helpful.

From: Robyn Shelah <info@jacksonhole.com>

Subject: RE: Information Needed

Mr. Stroug:

I read your request and hopefully my hurried response will provide the information you need.

The Jackson Hole Convention Center can serve your needs with several hotels nearby for your employees. The ski schools at both slopes are exceptional. Just show up early to beat the crowds. You're right Jackson Hole does have a reputation for being a brutal beast. The difficulty of the terrain, the vertical drops ☺ and the constantly changing snow conditions help us attract the best skiers around. In fact, we're the training site for Olympic athletes from many countries. You should see them. Wow!

On-site hospitality—that's a new one on me—can't help you there. Sounds cool! There are lots of things to do here besides skiing; it's all on our web site. Just take a look and see what looks interesting to you.

We are happy you're considering Jackson Hole for your sales conference. We can make reservations for the hotels and anything you want to do. Just let us know how we can help.

Figure 6-12

Good Example of a Favorable Response to a Routine Request

Deductive Outline for a Favorable Reply to a Routine Request

1. State the positive request to the receiver's request.
2. Continue with details or explanation.
3. Close with a forward look to build strong human relations with the receiver.

Revises the subject line after clicking "reply" to communicate enthusiasm for providing exceptional personalized service.

Shows sincere interest in the request and the person.

Highlights specific answers to the recipient's questions using an articulate and concise writing style.

Encourages a direct call and provides more useful information that communicates a genuine interest in the person and the event.

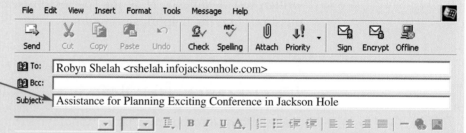

| File | Edit | View | Insert | Format | Tools | Message | Help |

Send · Cut · Copy · Paste · Undo · Check · Spelling · Attach · Priority · Sign · Encrypt · Offline

To: Robyn Shelah <rshelah.infojacksonhole.com>
Bcc:
Subject: Assistance for Planning Exciting Conference in Jackson Hole

Mr. Stroug:

Jackson Hole is the ideal location for Hutton Enterprise's national sales meeting. At Central Reservations, we can assist you with all your lodging and entertainment reservations. For easy reference, you'll find my responses below your e-mailed questions:

Q: Do any of the hotel(s) provide a convention center with space for a general session and meal functions for 400 attendees and a minimum of 10 concurrent breakout sessions?

A: The new Jackson Hole Convention Center and its two adjoining hotels can easily accommodate your meeting. The Teton Mountains ballroom can accommodate a formal dinner for 600 people, and the 12 conference rooms surrounding the ballroom seat 50 people in a presentation arrangement. The Waverly and Majestic hotels have over 500 rooms with covered walkways to the convention center.

Q: Do your ski schools have the capacity to handle as many as 200 beginning skiers or snowboarders on a single day? To minimize time away from the conference, could you arrange all equipment rentals prior to our arrival and secure a private clubhouse for an on-site hospitality center?

A: With two weeks advanced reservations, the ski schools can easily provide for 200 beginners daily. The ski schools provide fast, convenient equipment rentals slopeside. Although a private clubhouse is unavailable, the spacious Elk Lounge provides a relaxing break from the slopes.

Q: What are the ratings for each level of skiing (green/blue/black) for both resorts?

A: The beginner (green) slopes comprise 25% of the ski resort. A variety of trails provide safe environments for first-time skiers while providing a modest challenge to skiers preparing to advance to intermediate (blue) slopes. Despite our reputation for high challenge, plenty of slopes are designed for beginners.

I'm eager to help you organize a sales conference as dynamic as the natural beauty of Jackson Hole, and the Teton Mountains. Please call me at my direct line (307) 555-6180 after you've reviewed this information. You can also sign up at our web site to begin receiving snow reports, current activities, and more.

Thanks,

Robyn Shelah, Hospitality Agent
Central Reservations

Format Pointer

• Uses Q&A format to enhance readability of the response to a series of detailed questions.

Making Voice Mail Messages Work for You

Voice mail has both simplified and complicated our ability to communicate. While it provides another option for exchanging information, it can also result in partial or broken communication. You can do several things to assure that voice messaging is effective.

When preparing a voice message to leave on your phone system:[8]

- Keep menu choices to a minimum to avoid confusion and annoyance.

- Make sure callers are able to get through to a human party by pressing a button or waiting briefly.

- Keep your messages up-to-date and change them regularly.

- Check the quality of your voice system by pretending you don't know your direct line or extension number and placing a call to yourself. How many menus did you have to go through? How long were you on hold? What kind of music or messages were you forced to listen through?

- Set aside time each day to return calls. If you do not wish to talk extensively to a person, time your call when the party is away and leave your return message on voice mail. If you are not interested in what the person has to offer, leave a message saying so and that you wish to be removed from the call list.

Chances are greater that you will be leaving a message rather than talking to someone on most business phone calls. When leaving a voice message for another person:[9]

- Prepare for your call. Write out key points before you call to organize your thoughts for the message you will leave or for the conversation with a live person.

- If you suffer a mental block at the sound of the tone, hang up, organize your thoughts, and call back. This action is preferable to leaving a rambling, incoherent message.

- Start your message by greeting the person. Then identify yourself by name, affiliation, and phone number.

- Write the phone number as you state it to slow yourself down to the pace of the listener's writing speed. If the party does not know you, write each letter of your name as you speak it.

- State the purpose of your call candidly and concisely. Provide enough information for the person to meet your request by leaving a message on your phone if necessary.

- Do not leave personal information or emotionally charged verbiage in your message, as it could be an embarrassment if played back on speaker phone or forwarded to someone else.

- Close your message with directions on how to respond and times when you will be available.

Voice mail can simplify the process of giving and receiving information. Paying close attention to your messaging techniques can promote your image as an effective communicator.

Application

Assume you have moved to a new town and desire to open a bank checking account. To aid you in obtaining comparison information from local banks, outline what you will ask in a phone conversation or leave as a message if you are transferred to the new accounts voice mail system.

spearhead fund-raising and other service projects, or offer your expertise in other ways. If you say, "Yes," you might as well say it enthusiastically. Sending an unplanned, stereotyped acceptance suggests that the contribution will be similar.

In the letter in Figure 6-13, the TV production manager of a local public relations firm graciously accepts an invitation to emcee an awards banquet for the Chamber of Commerce. His polite request for specific information assures the Chamber director that this busy manager is committed to doing an outstanding job as emcee. His closing remarks reinforce the enthusiasm evident throughout the letter.

If you find yourself responding to invitations frequently, a letter such as the one shown in Figure 6-13 can be stored in a computer file to be opened and revised when responding to the next invitation. Individualized form letters produced using computer-based technology enable businesses to communicate quickly and efficiently with clients or customers.

Critical Thinking

Think of examples of favors that may be asked of you in your chosen career field.

Form Letters for Routine Responses

Changing
Technology

Form letters are a fast and efficient way of transmitting frequently recurring messages to which receiver reaction is likely favorable or neutral. Inputting the customer's name and address and other variables (information that differs for each receiver) personalizes each letter to meet the needs of its receiver. Companies may use form paragraphs that have been stored in separate word processing files. Perhaps as many as five versions of a paragraph related to a typical request are available for use in a routine request letter. The originator selects the appropriate paragraph according to the receiver's request. After assembling the selected files on the computer screen, the originator inputs any variables (e.g., name and address). A copy of the personalized letter is printed on letterhead and sent to the receiver as illustrated in Figure 6-14.

Form letters have earned a negative connotation because of their tendency to be impersonal. Many people simply refuse to read such letters for that reason. Personalizing a form letter can circumvent this problem. To make a form letter more personal,

Critical Thinking

Why do form letters have such a bad image? How can the weaknesses of a form letter be overcome?

- Add more variables to the standard text to tailor the message to the individual.
- Use personalized envelopes instead of mass-produced mailing labels.
- Be sure to spell names correctly.
- Produce a higher-quality document by using a good grade of paper and high-quality printer.

Figure 6-13

Good Example of a Favorable Response to a Request for a Favor (Invitation)

Deductive Outline for Favorable Response to an Invitation

1. Accept the invitation; confirm the date, time, and place.
2. Provide necessary details.
3. Close with a forward look to the receiver's next step.

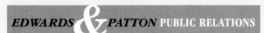

135 Copeland Street
Atlanta, GA 30304-0135
(404) 555-3000 Fax: (404) 555-1450

October 8, 2004

Mr. Conrad Eastland, President
Chamber of Commerce
642 Sixth Avenue
Atlanta, GA 30304-0908

Dear Conrad:

Yes, I will be honored to emcee the annual Chamber of Commerce banquet beginning at 6 p.m. on November 13 in the City Auditorium.

The format you described with a brief motivational speech followed by the service award presentations is an excellent change for this year's program. As soon as you have secured the speaker, please send me a detailed profile so that I can prepare an appropriate introduction. A brief description of each award and the person presenting it would help me plan smooth transitions between each award. Please send a tentative copy of the program when it is complete.

Conrad, I am eager to help the Chamber of Commerce celebrate another banner year on November 13. Let me know if I can help in any other way as plans develop.

Sincerely,

Marc

Marc Heineck, Director

Accepts immediately; therefore, the receiver is relieved no one else will have to be asked. Confirms the time, date, and place.

Uses a *you* attitude to confirm the change in format.

Outlines specific requests to ensure a highly organized, professional affair.

Uses the receiver's name to personalize the letter and involve the reader; closes by restating enthusiasm and commitment for the project.

Format Pointers

- Signs first name only in the written signature because he knows the reader well.
- Avoids right margin justification to improve comprehension and to convey the idea the letter was not methodically generated by a computer.

Figure 6-14

Using the Mail Merge Feature to Produce Personalized Form Letters

Step 1: Design a form letter including numerous variables in the body to meet the needs of the receiver.

Step 2: Input variables for each receiver.

January 11, 2005

<<recipient>>
<<street>>
<<city_state_zip>>

<<title>> <<name>>:

Thank you for registering your mortgage automatic payment service. Your monthly <<amount>> is scheduled to be deducted account beginning with the <<date>> pay each month to deduct the payment amour account by the date of the automatic payr

Adding an additional amount to each pay thousands of dollars interest. Visit us at w learn more about accelerate

Sincerely,

Katrina Magro
Sales Manager

Enclosures

recipient	street	city_state_zip	title	name	amount	date
Ms. Margaret Lowery	Washington Square	Boston, MA 02158-2628	Ms.	Lowery	$1,510	January 30
Mr. Bradley R. Zuccaro	81 West Leland Road	Allentown, PA 18184-0013	Mr.	Zuccaro	$2,194	February 1
Ms. Helen Webster	3931 Roane Drive	Boston, MA 02158-3931	Ms.	Webster	$1,957	February 15

CMC Continental Mortgage Company

1342 Harbor Drive ▪ Katy, TX 77449 ▪ (713) 555-2399 ▪ Fax: (713) 555-9319

January 11, 2005

Ms. Margaret Lowery
Watson Communication
Washington Square
Boston, MA 02158-2628

Dear Ms. Lowery:

Thank you for registering your mortgage to be paid with our automatic payment service. Your monthly payment of $1,510 is scheduled to be deducted from your bank account beginning with the January 30 payment. Please be sure each month to deduct the payment amount from your bank account by the date of the automatic payment.

Adding an additional amount to each payment can save you thousands of dollars interest. Visit us at www.EasyPay.com to learn more about accelerated payment options.

Sincerely,

Katrina Magro

Katrina Magro
Sales Manager

Enclosures

Step 3: Merge the variables list into the form letter and print each on high-quality paper.

Routine Messages About Orders and Credit

Objective 5

Write messages acknowledging customer orders.

Routine messages, such as customer order acknowledgments, are written deductively. Normally, credit information is requested and transmitted electronically from the national credit reporting agencies to companies requesting credit references. However, when companies choose to request information directly from other businesses, individual credit requests and responses must be written.

Acknowledging Customer Orders

Critical Thinking

How can a company encourage future orders by sending customer order acknowledgments?

When customers place orders for merchandise, they expect to get exactly what they ordered as quickly as possible. Most orders can be acknowledged by shipping the order; no message is necessary. For an initial order and for an order that cannot be filled quickly and precisely, companies send an ***acknowledgment message***, a document that indicates the order has been received and is being processed. Typically, acknowledgment messages are preprinted letters or copies of the sales order. An immediate e-mail message acknowledges an order placed online and confirms the expected date of shipment as shown in Figure 6-15. Individualized letters are not cost effective and will not reach the customer in a timely manner. Although the form message is impersonal, customers appreciate the company's acknowledging the order and giving them an idea of when the order will arrive.

Critical Thinking

What purposes does an individualized acknowledgment serve?

Nonroutine orders, such as initial orders, custom orders, and delayed orders, require individualized acknowledgment messages. Although initial orders can be acknowledged through form letters, the letters are more effective if individually written. When well-written, these messages not only acknowledge the order but also create customer goodwill and encourage the customer to place additional orders. Because saying "Yes" is easy, writers may develop the habit of using clichés and selecting words that make messages sound cold and mechanical. The acknowledgment letter in Figure 6-16 confirms shipment of goods in the first sentence, includes concrete resale on the product and company, and is sincere and original.

Objective 6

Compose messages providing credit information and extending credit.

Providing Credit Information

Replies to requests for credit information usually are simple—just fill in the blanks and return the document. If the request does not include a form, follow a deductive plan in writing the reply: the major idea first followed by supporting details.

Figure 6-15

Good Example of an Online Order Confirmation

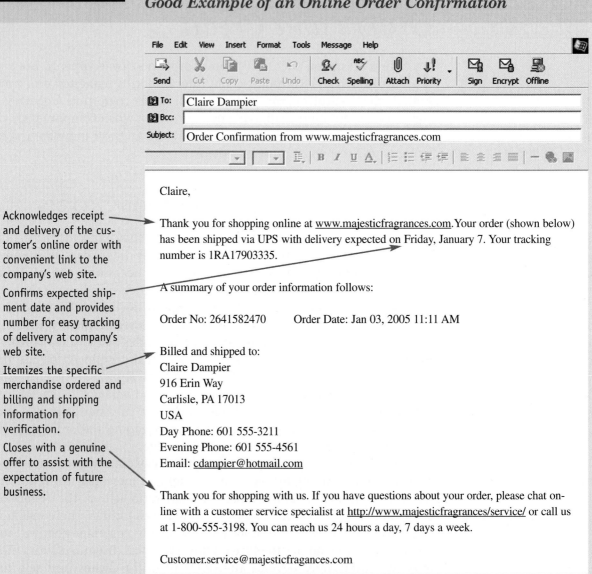

File   Edit   View   Insert   Format   Tools   Message   Help

Send | Cut | Copy | Paste | Undo | Check | Spelling | Attach | Priority | Sign | Encrypt | Offline

To: Claire Dampier

Bcc:

Subject: Order Confirmation from www.majesticfragrances.com

Claire,

Thank you for shopping online at www.majesticfragrances.com. Your order (shown below) has been shipped via UPS with delivery expected on Friday, January 7. Your tracking number is 1RA17903335.

A summary of your order information follows:

Order No: 2641582470   Order Date: Jan 03, 2005 11:11 AM

Billed and shipped to:
Claire Dampier
916 Erin Way
Carlisle, PA 17013
USA
Day Phone: 601 555-3211
Evening Phone: 601 555-4561
Email: cdampier@hotmail.com

Thank you for shopping with us. If you have questions about your order, please chat on-line with a customer service specialist at http://www.majesticfragrances/service/ or call us at 1-800-555-3198. You can reach us 24 hours a day, 7 days a week.

Customer.service@majesticfragances.com

Acknowledges receipt and delivery of the customer's online order with convenient link to the company's web site.

Confirms expected shipment date and provides number for easy tracking of delivery at company's web site.

Itemizes the specific merchandise ordered and billing and shipping information for verification.

Closes with a genuine offer to assist with the expectation of future business.

Legal & Ethical Constraints

Critical Thinking

What are the legal implications of credit information letters?

When providing credit information, you have an ethical and legal obligation to yourself, the credit applicant, and the business from whom credit is requested. You must be able to document any statement you make to defend yourself against a defamation charge. Thus, good advice is to stick with facts; omit any opinions. "I'm sure he will pay promptly" is an opinion that should be omitted, but include the documentable fact that "His payments are always prompt." Can you safely say a customer is a good credit risk when all you know is that he/she had a good credit record when he/she purchased from you?

Figure 6-16

Good Example of an Individualized Order Acknowledgement

Deductive Outline for Acknowledging a Customer Order

1. Confirm shipment of order and verify specific items ordered.
2. Include resale on the merchandise ordered and sales promotional material on related items to encourage future business.
3. Close with a positive remark that indicates future business.

Majestic Fragrances   9000 Carver Station   Atlanta, GA 30301-9000   (404) 555-4800   Fax: (404) 555-4801

November 3, 2004

Ms. Lesia Devauld
The Store
1986 Promenade Center
Orange, CA 92568-1986

Dear Lesia:

Your Majestic Fragrances starter display and first order of fragrances have been shipped and should reach you in approximately five days. Both items were shipped by UPS earlier today.

Your starter display includes an attractive display unit, 12 cases of the latest 6 decorative fragrances, 6 cases of oil for refurbishing the fragrance, and an assortment of scented candles. You might want to display several different fragrances in attractive containers throughout your store. Some of our customers have indicated they enjoy the different aromas and beautiful textures of our new Harvest Splendor products. Additionally, as an account holder, you will receive a case of our new fragrances each month.

Another new offering is our line of luxurious bath oils and body fragrances for both men and women. This new specialty item will be ideal for your clientele. With Valentine's Day approaching, these new items would make excellent gifts for a special sweetheart. The enclosed brochure details all of our fragrances.

If you have any questions after you receive your starter display, please call me. I'll be glad to assist you in selecting just the right products for your exclusive store.

Sincerely,

Sven Curtis

Sven Curtis
Marketing Manager

SC/lm

Enclosure

Implies sufficiently that order has been received and filled. Refers to specific merchandise shipped and reveals method of shipment.

Points out specific qualities of the merchandise (uses resale).

Mentions related merchandise (uses sales promotional) to encourage future business.

Closes with a genuine offer to assist with the expectation of future business.

Format Pointer

- Includes reference initials of composer and typist to show multiple party participation in the preparation of the document.

- Uses an enclosure notation to alert the receiver that something other than the letter is included.

Extending Credit

Critical Thinking

What legal requirements apply to letters extending credit?

Legal & Ethical Constraints

A timely response is preferable for any business document, but it is especially important when communicating about credit. The Equal Credit Opportunity Act (ECOA) requires that a credit applicant be notified of the credit decision within 30 days of receipt of the request or application. The party granting the credit must also disclose the terms of the credit agreement, such as the address for sending or making payments, due dates for payments, and the interest rate charged. You will learn more about other legal implications related to credit when you study credit denials in Chapter 7.

When extending credit, follow these guidelines as you write deductively:

1. ***Open by extending credit and acknowledging shipment of an order.*** Because of its importance, the credit aspect is emphasized more than the acknowledgment of the order. In other cases (in which the order is for cash or the credit terms are already clearly understood), the primary purpose of writing may be to acknowledge an order.

Critical Thinking

Why should you discuss the basis for extending credit and the credit terms?

2. ***Indicate the basis for the decision to extend credit and explain the credit terms.*** Indicating that you are extending credit on the basis of an applicant's prompt-paying habits with present creditors may encourage this new customer to continue these habits with you.

3. ***Present credit policies.*** Explain policies (e.g, credit terms, authorized discounts, payment dates). Include any legally required disclosure documents.

4. ***Communicate a genuine desire to build a strong business relationship.*** Include resale, sales promotional material, and comments that remind the customer of the benefits of doing business with you and encourage additional orders.

The letter in Figure 6-17 was written to a retailer; however, the same principles apply when writing to a consumer. Each letter should be addressed in terms of individual interests. Dealers are concerned about markup, marketability, and display; consumers are concerned about price, appearance, and durability. Consumers may require a more detailed explanation of credit terms.

Companies receive so many requests for credit that the costs of individualized letters are prohibitive; therefore, most favorable replies to credit requests are form letters. To personalize the letter, however, the writer should merge the customer's name, address, amount of loan, and terms into the computer file containing the form letter information. Typically, form messages read something like this:

> Dear [TITLE] [LAST NAME]
>
> Worldwide Industries is pleased to extend credit privileges to you. Initially, you may purchase up to [CREDIT LIMIT] worth of merchandise. Our credit terms are [TERMS]. We welcome you as a credit customer at Worldwide Industries and look forward to serving your needs for fine imported goods from around the world.

Figure 6-17

Good Example of Letter Extending Credit

Deductive Outline for Extending Credit

1. Begin by saying credit terms have been arranged. If an order has been placed, say the order has been shipped, implying the credit has been extended.
2. Indicate the foundation upon which the credit extension is based.
3. Present and explain the credit policies (e.g., credit terms, authorized discounts, payment dates).
4. Include resale or sales promotional material and encourage future business.

Acknowledges customer's electronic access to product and implies the credit extension.

Recognizes the dealer for earning the credit privilege and gives a reason for the credit extension. Introduces the credit terms and encourages taking advantage of the discount in terms of profits for the dealer.

Presents resale to remind of product benefits and to encourage future business.

Includes sales promotion for repeat business; assumes satisfaction with initial order and looks confidently for future orders.

Legal Issue
Sends letter extending credit within the required time frame (within 30 days of receipt of request) and mentions the terms of credit that will be provided, as required by law.

Format Pointer
Uses simplified block format to eliminate the need for a salutation in this letter addressed to a company. Learn more about this efficient format in Appendix A.

Century Images
985 Hunter Avenue
Boston, MA 02194
614-555-6790

July 20, 2004

Lincoln Technologies
Order Department
461 Beech Street
Fort Lauderdale, FL 33310-0461

Welcome to the most contemporary library of photographs available on the Internet. Our expert photographers are continually touring every region of the world, supplying our library with over 400 new photographs every day.

Because of your favorable current credit rating, we are pleased to provide you with a $25,000 credit line subject to our standard 2/10, n/30 terms. By paying your invoice within ten days, you can save two percent on your photograph purchases.

You can access our exclusive PhotoSearch system using the login name NelsonPublishing and the password JU12x34V. Use PhotoSearch to search our extensive photograph library by topic and date. After making your selections, your photograph files will be sent to you instantly as e-mail attachments to your invoice. To ensure your photographs will not appear in any other publication, your selections are removed from the library.

The best photographs for your publications are available to you right now, and they are just a click away.

Craig Wynne

Craig Wynne
Credit Manager

Enclosure

Although such form messages are effective for informing the customer that credit is being extended, they do little to promote sales and goodwill. Whether to say "yes" by form letter or by individualized letter is an issue that each credit manager must settle. If the list of credit customers is relatively short and few names are being added, individualized letters may be practical.

Objective 7

Prepare procedural messages that ensure clear and consistent application.

Critical Thinking

What types of procedural messages will you be writing in your career field?

Procedural Messages

Memos or e-mail messages are the most frequently used methods of communicating standard operating procedures and other instructions, changes related to personnel or the organization, and other internal matters for which a written record is needed.

Instructions to employees must be conveyed clearly and accurately to facilitate the day-to-day operations of business and to prevent negative feelings that occur when mistakes are made and work must be redone. Managers must take special care in writing standard operating procedures to ensure that all employees complete the procedures accurately and consistently.

Before writing instructions, walk through each step to understand it and to locate potential trouble spots. Then attempt to determine how much employees already know about the process and to anticipate any questions or problems. Then, as you write instructions that require more than a few simple steps, follow these guidelines:

1. *Begin each step with an action statement to create a vivid picture of the employee completing the task.* Using an action verb and the understood subject *you* is more vivid than a sentence written in passive voice. For example, a loan officer attempting to learn new procedures for evaluating new venture loans can understand "*identify* assets available to collateralize the loan" more easily than "assets available to collateralize the loan should be identified."

2. *Itemize each step on a separate line to add emphasis and to simplify reading.* Number each step to indicate that the procedures should be completed in a particular order. If the order is not important, use bullets to draw attention to each step.

3. *Consider preparing a flow chart depicting the procedures.* The cost and effort involved in creating a sophisticated flow chart may be merited for extremely important and complex procedures. For example, take a look at the flow chart in Figure 10-15, which simplifies the steps involved in processing a telephone order in an effort to minimize errors.

4. *Complete the procedure by following your instructions step-by-step.* Correct any errors you locate.

5. *Ask a colleague or employee to walk through the procedures.* This walk-through will allow you to identify ambiguous statements, omissions of relevant information, and other sources of potential problems.

Consider the seemingly simple task of reporting a computer problem. The help-desk manager might quickly respond, "No need for written instructions; just report your problem any way you wish." The process of writing step-by-step procedures may alert a manager to potential problems that clear, consistent procedures can eliminate. For example, this manager's ambiguous and inconsistent verbal instructions (reported in haste) would likely lead to inefficient service and foster mistrust regarding the priority of work completed. After anticipating potential problems and walking through a draft of these procedures, the manager sent employees an e-mail attachment that provided clear, consistent procedures for reporting computer problems as shown in Figure 6-18. For easy reference, the procedures are posted to the company intranet.

Before writing a pleasant or routine message, study carefully the overall suggestions in the "General Writing Guidelines." After you have written a rough draft, compare your work with the "Check Your Communication" checklist at the end of this chapter and make any revisions.

Summary

1. **Identify the steps in the deductive outline for good news and routine information, and understand its uses and adaptations for specific situations and for international audiences.** When the receiver can be expected to be *pleased* by the message, the main idea is presented first and details follow. Likewise, when the message is *routine* and not likely to arouse a feeling of pleasure or displeasure, the main idea is presented first (as illustrated in the messages in this chapter). The deductive approach is appropriate for positive news and thank-you and appreciation messages, routine claims, routine requests and responses to routine requests, routine messages and responses about credit and orders. Cultural differences of international audiences may necessitate adjustments in writing style and to the typical deductive pattern for good and neutral messages.

2. **Prepare messages that convey good news, including thank you and appreciation messages.** Use the deductive approach for letters, memos, and e-mail messages that contain positive news as the central idea. Thank-you messages express appreciation for a kindness or special assistance and should reflect sincere feelings of gratitude. Appreciation messages highlight exceptional performance and should avoid exaggerations and strong, unsupported statements that the receiver may not believe.

3. **Write messages presenting claims and making adjustments.** A routine claim requests the adjustment in the first sentence because you assume the company will make the adjustment without persuasion. Continue with an

explanation of the problem to support the request and an expression of appreciation for taking the action. An adjustment extends the adjustment in the first sentence and explains the circumstances related to correcting the problem. The closing may include sales promotional material or other futuristic comments indicating your confidence that the customer will continue doing business with a company that has a reputation for fairness.

4. **Write routine requests and favorable responses to routine requests.** A routine request begins with the major request, includes details that will clarify the request, and alludes to the receiver's response. A response to a routine request provides the information requested, provides necessary details, and closes with a personal, courteous ending.

5. **Write messages acknowledging customer orders.** Form or computer-generated acknowledgment messages or e-mail messages assure customers that orders will be filled quickly. An individualized acknowledgment that confirms shipment and includes resale on the product and the company generates goodwill and future business.

6. **Compose messages providing credit information and extending credit.** When providing credit information, provide only verifiable facts to avoid possible litigation. A letter extending credit begins with an approval of credit, indicates the basis for the decision, and explains credit terms. The closing may include sales promotional material or other futuristic comments. Credit extension letters must adhere to legal guidelines related to credit.

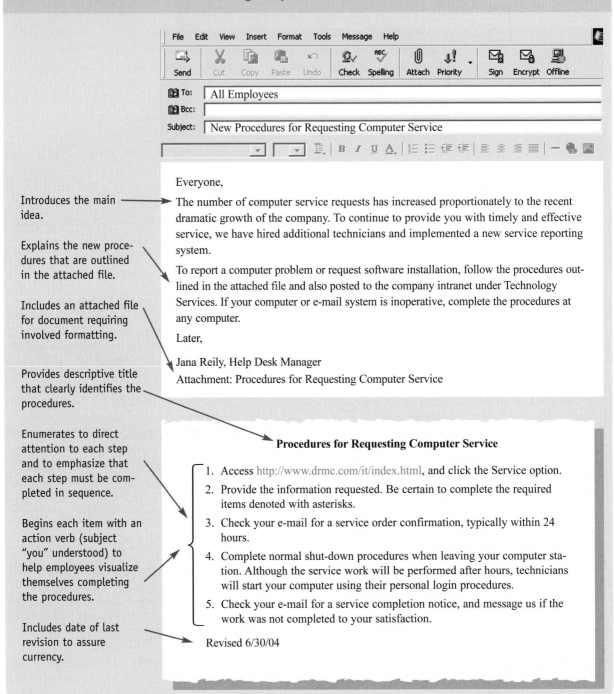

Figure 6-18

Good Example of a Procedure E-mail with an Attachment

File   Edit   View   Insert   Format   Tools   Message   Help

Send   Cut   Copy   Paste   Undo   Check   Spelling   Attach   Priority   Sign   Encrypt   Offline

To: All Employees
Bcc:
Subject: New Procedures for Requesting Computer Service

Everyone,

Introduces the main idea.

The number of computer service requests has increased proportionately to the recent dramatic growth of the company. To continue to provide you with timely and effective service, we have hired additional technicians and implemented a new service reporting system.

Explains the new procedures that are outlined in the attached file.

To report a computer problem or request software installation, follow the procedures outlined in the attached file and also posted to the company intranet under Technology Services. If your computer or e-mail system is inoperative, complete the procedures at any computer.

Includes an attached file for document requiring involved formatting.

Later,

Jana Reily, Help Desk Manager
Attachment: Procedures for Requesting Computer Service

Provides descriptive title that clearly identifies the procedures.

Procedures for Requesting Computer Service

Enumerates to direct attention to each step and to emphasize that each step must be completed in sequence.

1. Access http://www.drmc.com/it/index.html, and click the Service option.
2. Provide the information requested. Be certain to complete the required items denoted with asterisks.
3. Check your e-mail for a service order confirmation, typically within 24 hours.

Begins each item with an action verb (subject "you" understood) to help employees visualize themselves completing the procedures.

4. Complete normal shut-down procedures when leaving your computer station. Although the service work will be performed after hours, technicians will start your computer using their personal login procedures.
5. Check your e-mail for a service completion notice, and message us if the work was not completed to your satisfaction.

Includes date of last revision to assure currency.

Revised 6/30/04

7. **Prepare procedural messages that ensure clear and consistent application.** When preparing instructions, highlight the steps in a bulleted or numbered list or a flow chart and begin each step with an action state-ment. Check the accuracy and completeness of the document and incorporate changes identified by following the instructions to complete the task and asking another person to do likewise.

Content

- Identify clearly the principal idea (pleasant or routine idea).
- Present sufficient supporting detail in a logical sequence.
- Assure accuracy of facts or figures.
- Structure message to meet ethical and legal requirements.

Organization

- Place major idea in the first sentence.
- Present supporting details in a logical sequence.
- Include a final idea that is courteous and indicates a continuing relationship with the receiver; may include sales promotional material.

Style

- Assure that the message is clear and concise (e.g., words will be readily understood).
- Use active voice predominantly.
- Use first person sparingly.
- Make ideas cohere by avoiding abrupt changes in thought.
- Use relatively short sentences that vary in length and structure.
- Emphasize significant thoughts (e.g., position and sentence structure).
- Keep paragraphs relatively short.
- Use original expression (sentences are not copied directly from the definition of the problem or from sample message in text). Omit clichés.

Mechanics

- Assure that keyboarding, spelling, grammar, and punctuation are perfect.

Format

- Use a correct document format.
- Assure the document is appropriately positioned.
- Include standard document parts in appropriate position.
- Include special parts if necessary (subject line, enclosure, copy, etc.).

International Adaptations

- Avoid abbreviations, slang, acronyms, technical jargon, sports and military analogies, and other devices peculiar to the United States.

- Avoid words that trigger emotional responses.
- Use simple terms but attempt to be specific.
- Consider the communication style of the culture when selecting an organizational pattern.
- Use graphics, visual aids, and forms when possible to simplify the message.
- Use figures for expressing numbers to avoid confusion.
- Be aware of differences in the way numbers and dates are written.
- Write out the name of the month to avoid confusion.
- Adapt the document format to the traditional format of the recipient's country.

Thank-You Messages

- Begin with a statement of thanks.
- Be specific about that which is appreciated.
- Reflect a sincere feeling of gratitude.

Appreciation Messages

- Write for the right purpose (intent).
- Follow a deductive outline.
- Reflect a sincere tone by presenting specific facts and avoiding overly strong language.

Apologies

- Include the apology only once in the message.
- Avoid being overly critical.
- Avoid describing a mistake too vividly.
- Include a possible solution to the situation, if possible.

Confirmation Memos

- Serve as a written record of a telephone call or conversation that may be needed for later discussion of the topic.
- May be sent to the person involved for verification or addressed "to the file" and placed in a file for future reference.
- Provides legally defensible evidence of action taken in the event of litigation.

Follow these guidelines when composing messages for the activities, applications, and cases in this and all remaining chapters:

1. **Study the related chapter (5–8) before composing electronic, spoken, and written messages.** Look for principles that can be applied, not for expressions or sentences to paraphrase or use in your message.

2. **Study the problem until you understand the facts.**

3. **Assume that you are the person facing the writing problem.**

4. **Anticipate the receiver's reaction, and prepare an outline for your message.**

5. **Compose rapidly without looking at the definition of the problem and without looking at sample documents from the text.** A sentence written to *define* a writing problem may not be appropriate in a document designed to *solve* the problem. Concentrate on planning and expressing ideas to achieve clarity and to promote good human relations.

6. **Refer to the assignment for names, addresses, and amounts before keying the message.** The receiver's name and address appear at the end of each activity and application. Unless otherwise instructed, key your name as the sender.

7. **Consider the implications of the strategic forces influencing your message.**
   - **Legal and ethical constraints.** Consider the following guidelines:
     - Investigate the problem to identify possible legal requirements and consider any ethical implications related to the message you are writing.
     - Be certain that you have expressed ideas clearly, stated unpleasant ideas tactfully and positively, included complete, accurate information, supported your ideas with objective facts, avoided embellishing or exaggerating facts, and designed graphs to depict information honestly.
     - Exercise discretion by identifying information the receiver actually needs to respond to your message. Consider the confidentiality of the information you reveal.
   - **Diversity Challenges.** Adapt your messages so that they can be understood and received positively by receivers regardless of their ethnicity, age, and gender.
   - **Changing Technology.** Use appropriate technological tools to collect and analyze data, write and present information in a highly professional manner, and to transmit the message to the receiver efficiently and effectively.
   - **Team Environment.** Work collectively to compose a dynamic message that reflects the synergistic influence of an effective team.

8. **Review the document carefully for the use of acceptable business format.** Unless otherwise instructed, key a document according to the formatting instructions provided in Appendix A. Study formats, two-letter postal abbreviations, word-division rules, abbreviation rules, keyboarding rules, and proofreaders' marks in Appendix A.

9. **Refer to the "Check Your Communication" checklist (positioned near the summary in each chapter) before submitting an assignment.** By comparing your message with the list, you will (1) gain confidence that your message meets high standards and (2) identify any changes that need to be made.

Thoughtful use of the checklist can improve your grade on an assignment as well as indelibly stamp in your mind the four qualities that your writing should have:

- **Content:** The *right* ideas with sufficient support.

- **Organization:** The best *sequence* of ideas for clear understanding and human relations.

- **Style:** The most appropriate ways to *express* ideas in words and sentences.

- **Mechanics:** High *standards* in electronic, spoken, and written communication—keyboarding, spelling, and grammar.

// electronic café //

Expressing Yourself Through a Personal Web Page

As the number of people with access to the Internet increases exponentially, so does the number of personal web pages. Using personal web pages, individuals suddenly have access to powerful tools for the mass dissemination of information for leisure and professional purposes. But not every personal web page achieves its desired purpose. What makes a good home page? The following electronic activities will assist you in learning more about the development of an effective personal web page.

 InfoTrac College Edition. Access http://www.info-trac.thomsonlearning.com to read more about how to develop an effective personal web page. Search for the following article available in full text:

O'Connor, J. (2001, September). Make room for yourself online with a personal web page. *Chatelaine, 74(9),* 12.

Develop a list of resources for web page development, along with their accompanying web addresses. Visit selected sites as directed by your instructor.

 Text Support Web Site. Visit http://lehman.swlearning.com to learn more about what makes a good home page. Refer to Chapter 6's Electronic Café activity that provides a link to an online article that includes guidelines for home page development. Be prepared to discuss this information in class.

 WebTutor Advantage. Log on to WebTutor to develop your own personal web page.

 Professional Power Pak. Access your PPP CD for helpful tips and resources for developing dynamic web pages.

Chapter Review

1. List the steps in the deductive outline recommended for good and neutral news messages. (Obj. 1)

2. Discuss guidelines for communicating with an international audience. (Obj. 1)

3. What suggestions will contribute to a warm, genuine tone in a thank-you or appreciation letter? (Obj. 2)

4. Explain how claim messages and responses to requests both use the deductive message pattern. (Objs. 3, 4)

5. What is the difference between resale and sales promotional material? Provide an example of each. Why should resale and sales promotional material be included in an adjustment letter? (Obj. 3)

6. When is the word *grant* appropriate in communicating about a claim? Suggest an appropriate word substitution. (Obj. 3)

7. Distinguish between the two major types of request messages, and specify the outline preferable for each type. (Obj. 4)

8. What technique can be used to ensure that details within a routine request are clear and easy to read? (Obj. 4)

9. Discuss several ways form messages can be used to respond effectively to routine requests. (Obj. 4)

10. Describe the procedure typically used by companies to acknowledge orders. (Obj. 5)

11. Provide three situations when sending an individualized order acknowledgment would be appropriate and explain why. (Obj. 5)

12. Provide suggestions for writing a legally defensible credit information letter. (Obj. 6)

13. What information should be included in a letter extending credit? (Obj. 6).

14. Provide guidelines for writing instructions that can be understood and followed consistently. (Obj. 7)

15. How do enumerations (bulleted or numbered lists) impact the effectiveness of a message that explains a procedure or gives instructions? When should numbers versus bullets be used to mark each step? (Obj. 7)

Digging Deeper

1. What criteria should be used in determining whether a good- or neutral-news message would best be communicated on paper, electronically, or verbally?

2. What considerations should be given to a message recipient's culture when planning a good-news or neutral-news message?

To check your understanding of the chapter, take the practice quizzes at **http://lehman.swlearning.com** or your WebTutor course.

Activities

1. **Deductive Openings (Objs. 1–7)**

   Revise the following openings so that they are deductive.

   a. As you know, recommendations for promotions are evaluated and voted upon by the management committee semiannually. Your promotion to department manager was approved in the last meeting.

   b. In last week's budget meeting, the controller underscored that budgets are lean this quarter. However, she has approved your request for computer upgrades for personnel in your department.

   c. The Crown Club is a service organization that has always been held in high esteem within the automobile industry. Our membership is honored to extend an invitation for you to join us as we help the industry move forward.

   d. As you are already aware, Meerkat Software is the leading manufacturer of file compression software in the West. However, we would be happy to ship software to your office in Key West and provide the technical support you may require.

   e. It is rare that we receive a claim regarding a defect in our high-quality facsimile machines, especially in one that has only been in use for seven months. However, because of our belief in our product, we will ship you a replacement machine upon receipt of your current model.

   f. This letter is in response to your application for credit dated June 30; your application has now been reviewed.

2. **Document for Analysis: Thank You (Obj. 2)**

   Analyze the following letter. Pinpoint its strengths and weaknesses, and then revise the letter as directed by your instructor.

   Visit the Interactive Study Center at **http://lehman. swlearning.com** for a downloadable version of this activity.

   Dear Mr. Borris:

   Thank you for taking the time from your busy schedule to talk to our class. Your talk was outstanding. Without your help, I would not have known how to even start writing a resume.

   Again, I really appreciate your coming to talk to us about this important topic.

3. **Document for Analysis: Claim Request (Obj. 3)**

   Analyze the following letter. Pinpoint its strengths and weaknesses, and then revise the letter as directed by your instructor.

   Visit the Interactive Study Center at **http://lehman. swlearning.com** for a downloadable version of this activity.

   Dear Mr. Peck:

   When I ordered my Golden Hamster treadmill last month, you assured me that it was the best product for cardiovascular fitness. After viewing the videotape you sent, I believed in your product and your company and soon placed my order. I received the treadmill on January 12.

   The product was easy to set up, and after watching the instructional video and reading the manual, I was ready to work out on the Golden Hamster. However, I cannot seem to use the unit as shown on the instructional tape, and believe my machine may be defective.

   I have read and followed all the instructions, yet the machine's spin-wheel system produces resistance, which propels me off the front.

   I would like this problem solved, either through a new machine being sent to me free of charge, or a refund after I return this machine.

   Please contact me at 706-555-3800 and advise me how I should proceed in this matter.

4. Document for Analysis: Routine Request (Obj. 4)

Analyze the following letter. Pinpoint its strengths and weaknesses, and then revise the letter as directed by your instructor.

Visit the Interactive Study Center at **http://lehman. swlearning.com** for a downloadable version of this activity.

Dear Ms. Morgan:

I am the Vice President of Operations for Jemison Corporation, a manufacturer of golf ball components. We have operated plants across the Midwest for thirty years, and we are contemplating opening a facility in the South within the next two years.

As we evaluate our operational needs and requirements, we are collecting data from various locations we think may provide a site that will generate the maximum benefit for both Jemison and the locale under consideration. Therefore, I would appreciate it if you could send me some information about Paradise and its surrounding area, including information on population demographics and major employers, as well as geographic description of the area. I'd also like to know about the weather, education and cultural opportunities in the area, and, of course, the cost of living.

Thank you for your assistance, and I look forward to your response.

5. Document for Analysis: Procedures Message (Obj. 7)

Analyze the following section of a procedures memo intended to communicate procedures for replacing a damaged badge. Pinpoint its strengths and weaknesses, and then revise the memo as directed by your instructor.

Visit the Interactive Study Center at **http://lehman. swlearning.com** for a downloadable version of this activity.

E-mail from Shanell Gillotte, sent 1/3/2004 at 1:45 p.m.

TO: Line Supervisors
SUBJECT: Damaged Badge Readers

We have designed a form (PR-17) your employees must complete when they report faulty badges. After receiving this form from the employee, Gena Kaminski in the Payroll Office will prepare a new badge and send it to you with the completed form. You should give the new badge to the employee with instructions not to use the new badge until the next day. Have employees report their departing time directly to you; record the time on Form PR-17 and return to Gena in the Payroll Office. Requests received after 10 a.m. cannot be processed in one day.

6. Thank-You Message: Thanks for a Favor (Objs. 1, 2)

A number of individuals have been especially helpful as you have pursued your degree, and you want to express your appreciation. Your choices might include writing to an instructor who served as a job reference or advised you to complete an internship program that has now led to a full-time position, a cooperative education supervisor who provided an exceptional experience, or a speaker in a class or student organization meeting who has become a mentor.

Required: Compose an e-mail message or letter expressing thanks to one of these individuals. Alternately, your instructor may direct you to prepare an outline of a telephone conversation or the script of a voice mail message conveying your appreciation.

Applications

Read	Think	Write	Speak	Collaborate

1. Communication Success Stories (Objs. 1–7)

Conduct an electronic search to locate an article that deals with successful communication in a company or organization. Prepare an abstract of the article that includes the following parts: (1) article citation, (2) name of organization/company, (3) brief description of communication technique/situation, (4) and outcome(s) of the successful communication. As an alternative to locating an article, write about a successful communication situation in the organization or company for which you work.

Required: Present your abstract in a memo. Refer to Appendix B for examples for formatting citations. Be prepared to give a short presentation in class.

2. Interactive Potential of Electronic Communication (Objs. 1-7)

Designing corporate web sites that tap the interactive potential of electronic communication can help management build strong relationships with its public—customers, investors, and employees. The focus of business communication changes radically as organizations begin communicating *with* these individuals in chat rooms and bulletin boards rather than *to* them through formal documents or static web postings. Using your library's databases, locate the following article that explains more about using the World Wide Web as a medium for building relationships.

Cooley, T. (1999). Interactive communication—Public relations on the web. *Public Relations Quarterly, 44*(2), 41–42.

Required: Prepare a memo that summarizes benefits gained from adding interactive media such as chat rooms and discussion boards to a corporate web site, and guidelines to be followed by organizations choosing to create open dialogue with their public. Use the knowledge gained from this reading to evaluate the interactive electronic communication available at a web site of your choice or one selected by your instructor. Use a computer projection system to demonstrate the site to the class, explaining its merits.

3. **Real-World Example: Handling Apologies (Objs. 1, 2)**

Professional apologies are inevitable for companies if they wish to prevent unfortunate situations from undermining even the strongest relationships with customers, clients, and employees. Visit the text support site at **http://lehman.swlearning.com** to explore strategies for handling apologies effectively. Then use an online database to locate the following articles that provide additional information and examples of apologies made by companies or individuals. Consider how each apology was handled and improvements you'd recommend.

Lyon, C. (2002, December 19). Best apologies are quick and forthright. *Contra Costa Times.* Retrieved February 22, 2003, from InfoTrac database.

Gitomer, J. (2002, March 25). The secret formula is react, respond, recover, and "plus 1." *Budapest Business Journal, 10*(16), 25.

Required: In teams of three or four, prepare a presentation on the topic of written business apologies. If directed by your instructor, prepare a sample written apology a team member might send for missing an important team meeting.

Read	Think	Write	Speak	Collaborate

4. **Critique of Good-News and Routine Messages Produced by Real Companies (Objs. 1–7)**

Find an example of both a well-written and a poorly written good-news or routine memo, e-mail message, or letter. Analyze the strengths and weaknesses of each document. Be prepared to discuss them in class.

5. **Routine Request: Information Needed (Objs. 1, 4)**

You have special interest in a product or service that you have been researching on the Internet. If you had appropriate answers to certain questions, you might order the product or secure the service.

Required: Prepare the message you would send via e-mail in a vendor's or service provider's web site requesting answers to at least three questions. Consider using an enumerated list to emphasize the questions.

6. **Reply to Routine Request: Approval to Investigate Employee Suggestion (Objs. 1, 4)**

Thomas Harris, a college intern working in the human resources department, sent the following e-mail to the firm's suggestion box:

> At last week's management meeting, the executive board encouraged us to develop innovative, yet cost effective ways of rewarding employees who earn the employee-of-the-month award. My idea would require the company to invest $120,000 in a resort condominium in Destin. Each employee of the month would receive a free week at the resort. Other employees could rent the condominium for less than market rates, which would still enable the company to pay the $200 monthly maintenance fee while earning a return on its investment. It's a win-win situation.

Required: As the chief executive officer, write a memo or e-mail message to Thomas Harris requesting more detailed cost estimates (e.g., number of weeks to be rented, market rate, and estimated fee to employees). To complete the analysis, Thomas should assume the company strives to earn a 10 percent return on its investments.

7. **Procedural Message: Instructions for a Computer Task (Objs. 1, 7)**

As the director of computer resources, you have begun a "Tip of the Week" e-mailing for the purpose of expanding employees' use of computer technology. Your weekly message provides simple instructions for completing new computer tasks such as copying or creating folders in Windows Explorer, organizing e-mail folders in WebTutor or your e-mail program, or printing your name or displaying column headings at the top of multiple pages of a spreadsheet. To ensure accuracy and clarity, follow each step in your instructions and ask a person unfamiliar with the procedure to do the same. Incorporate any changes in a revised draft.

Required: Prepare an e-mail announcing the latest tip of the week and providing a brief description of its usefulness in completing work-related tasks. Send the procedure for the computer task of your choice as an attachment to the e-mail. Your instructor may ask you to submit a rough draft and final copy. Be prepared to discuss the types of changes required as a result of "walking through" your procedures.

8. **Positive News: Personal Employment Information a Click Away (Objs. 1, 2)**

Woodruff & Company is scheduled to launch a personal information web site for employees on May 15 with all access-related problems being handled by the Technology Help Desk. This web site will provide employees their payroll history such as past pay stubs including deductions for benefits and withholdings, personal leave information, detailed benefit information such as insurance coverage and retirement plans, etc. Access will be provided through a preassigned user identification number and a password that must be changed by May 30.

Required: As human resources director, prepare a memo informing employees of the availability of the personal information web site. Describe the benefits employees can gain from the availability of this online system, location on the company's intranet, and secure procedures for accessing information.

9. **Appreciation Message: A Job Well Done (Objs. 1, 2)**

Last year your company, Magnolia Manufacturing, hired NetSite Associates to create a B2B web site to support the ordering of component parts from your suppliers. You selected NetSite based partly on its promise to provide a quick response to technical problems. During a recent storm, lightning struck the building containing your computer operations, causing significant damage to your computers and communication lines. Within 24 hours Marsha Rackley, senior consultant for NetSite, and her team were on the scene and worked 24/7 until the site was operational.

Required: Write Marsha a letter of appreciation for her team's dedication. Her address is 121 Technology Lane, Suite 2500, Fort Wayne, IN 46808-2500.

10. **Claim Letter: Parking Issue Affects Company Interns (Objs. 1, 3)**

Patrick Industries owns several condominiums used to house its interns during their short-term assignments. In your position as a human resources manager, you received the following e-mail from one of the interns:

> Could you please assist us with a problem we are having at the condominium? The condominium next to us is being rented by four college students. Because each student has his own car, they are constantly parking in the two parking spots assigned to our unit. With a limited number of visitor spots available in the complex, we often must park in the shopping center across the 4-lane highway. We have repeatedly asked the complex manager to address the problem. Her response has been that she can't control the number of cars renters have. Because the company owns the condominium, I am hoping you are in a stronger position to resolve the issue.

Required: As the human resource manager, write an e-mail to Emma Murrell, apartment complex manager, requesting a solution to the parking problem. Alternately, your instructor may direct you to prepare a voice script of a telephone conversation with Emma.

11. **Routine Request: Availability of Facilities (Objs. 1, 4)**

Your CPA firm, Barnett & Company, recently tripled in size since its acquisition of several former Andersen partners together with their staff and clients. To help develop a cohesive culture among the firm's 240 employees, the managing partner has directed you to organize a retreat at an out-of-town resort to be held within the next three to six months. The retreat is to begin on Thursday afternoon with a golf scramble followed by a private dinner and social time. Friday will consist of a series of concurrent sessions designed for 30 participants per session. Each meal on Friday will be highlighted by a motivational speaker. Employees will depart after an informal breakfast on Saturday.

Required: Prepare a script of a voice mail message you'd leave for the sales manager at the resort where you hope to schedule the retreat. The message should inquire whether the resort has the facilities and availability for holding the retreat. Use the Internet or advertisements to identify a potential location.

12. **Routine Request: Internet Privacy Concerns (Objs. 1, 4)**

While surfing the Internet, you discovered a company selling music from the 60s and 70s remixed and recorded on CD and memory sticks. You would like to purchase several of their recordings. However, while entering your order information, the company asked you for your social security number, place of employment, and annual income. Although you canceled your order, you might reconsider entering an order if you understood the reason the company needed this information.

Required: Prepare the message you would submit on the company's web site asking the purpose for information collection.

13. **Routine Request: How Are We Doing? (Objs. 1, 4)**

Global Electronics sells video cameras and accessories via its web site. When the sale is shipped via National Parcel Service (NPS), the customer immediately receives a tracking number via e-mail. By entering the tracking number on NPS's Internet tracking system, the customer can identify the location and expected delivery date of the shipment.

Global's shipping manager recently received an e-mail from NPS asking him to comment on the quality of the company's shipments. The number of shipping-related inquiries received by Global's customer service department during the past quarter has declined, falling from over 6 to fewer than 4 inquiries per thousand. The most common complaint appears to relate from customers' inability to locate their shipments on the NPS tracking system. The shipping manager has noted that customers report that the NPS system is often "down" when they attempt to track a package.

Required: As the shipping manager, write an e-mail responding to NPS's request for feedback on its customer service.

14. Routine Response Telephone Message: Returning JanSport Backpacks (Objs. 1, 4)

Typically customers experiencing problems with a JanSport backpack call the company's toll-free number. Operators give them information about the lifetime warranty against defects in parts and workmanship, along with instructions to ship a defective backpack to the Warranty Service Center with a card that includes a description of the problem and customer identification information (name, address, telephone number, e-mail address).

Required: As Dana Miller, warranty service manager, develop a telephone script explaining procedures for requesting an adjustment on a defective or damaged backpack. Include variables in the body to personalize the message. Locate the address of the Warranty Service Center at the JanSport web site at **http://www. jansport.com**.

15. Routine Response Message: Caring for Elderly Adults (Objs. 1, 4)

Forest View Hospital provides senior citizens with a daytime program of assisted living and rehabilitation services. Similar to childcare centers, Forest View offers working families a safe place to leave their elderly loved ones during the business day.

As the administrator of the facility, write a form letter that can be sent to families interested in your adult day care services. Provide several examples of how individuals could benefit from your services (e.g. assistance to physically impaired adults, supervision, and socialization for older adults and relief to caregivers), specific programs offered (e.g., nutritious meals, transportation to medical appointments), hours of operation, and telephone number. Encourage the families to read the brochure you're enclosing and take a look at your web site. Invite them to schedule an appointment to visit the facility.

Required: Address your form letter to Russell Armstrong, 76 Everett Street, Harrisburg, PA 17105.

16. Favorable Response Message: Accepting an Invitation to Perform a Civic Duty (Objs. 1, 4)

You have been employed for several years in your career field. Today you were asked to assist in an activity sponsored by a civic organization in your area. Depending on your interest and expertise, provide the exact nature of this activity. For example, a financial planner might have been asked to discuss mutual funds at a monthly meeting; an accountant, to prepare tax returns as a service project for seniors; and a computer programmer, to assist an organization in automating its membership records or designing a web page.

Required: Accept the request and include any details needed to make arrangements for your participation in this activity. Alternately, your instructor may ask you to accept an invitation to perform a service for a student organization or community group in which you are involved.

17. Credit Approval and Customer Order Acknowledgment: New Golf Course Tees Off (Objs. 1, 5)

As the marketing manager for Pacific Golf Supply Co. (PCS), you have just approved a credit account for Pine Lake Golf Club, a new golf course in northern California. Send Kevin Dexter, the golf pro, a letter stating that you have approved his club for a $5,000 initial credit line. PCA offers its customers 2/10, n/30 payment terms and charges interest at an 18 percent annual rate on overdue accounts. Each quarter PCS reviews its outstanding accounts and offers an increase in the credit line to any customer having a current account. The letter should confirm that the initial order of golf balls, clubs, and accessories has been shipped via UPS ground (expected delivery time, 10 days). Encourage Kevin to use his remaining $2,400 credit line to invest in quality display units. Explain that experience demonstrates that sales increase by 25 percent when the product is displayed using your display units.

Required: Write the credit approval/order acknowledgment letter to Kevin at 2500 Country Club Drive, Klamath, CA 95548-1200.

18. Donor Acknowledgment: Heifer Project International (Objs. 1, 5)

Heifer Project International (HPI) strives to end world hunger by giving livestock and training needed to empower impoverished families to become more self-reliant. HPI accepts donations from individuals and from religious and civic organizations to help fund its activities. You can learn more about the activities of HPI by visiting its web site at **http://www.heifer.org**.

Required: Ms. Rebecca Hawbecker's sixth grade class at Washington Elementary School has contributed $240, enough to purchase two goats. As an HPI staff member, prepare a letter that acknowledges the donation and highlights the benefits the class's contribution will provide a needy family. Send the letter to 125 Washington Street, Auburn, NE 68305.

19. Procedural Message: Earning a Recruitment Bonus (Objs. 1, 7)

The rapid growth at Southern Communications has strained its ability to attract an adequate supply of qualified accounting, computer, and communication professionals. In response, management has adopted a policy rewarding employees for recruiting and outlined specific procedures for implementing this policy. An employee who recruits an individual to fill a position listed on the company's "Most Wanted" list receives a $2,500 cash bonus. To earn the bonus, the employee must have completed a Recruitment Bonus Request before any communication occurs between the recruit and the company. The form identifies important information, such as the recruit's name, current position, and qualifications. After being signed by the employee, the recruit, and the recruiting director, the completed form is submitted to the human resources department. The recruiting director updates the "Most Wanted" list on a weekly basis.

Required: Prepare a memo or e-mail to announce the policy to the employees and to identify the procedures to be followed to earn a bonus.

20. Confirmation Memo: Procedural Message as Record of Golf Outing (Objs. 1, 7)

Janice Graham, public relations director for Coleman Industries, organizes an annual golf outing for the company's major customers as a means of developing customer loyalty. This year the event is being held at Golden Mountain Golf Club. Janice recently returned from a meeting with David Sharp, the PGA professional, where the details of the event were discussed. David reserved the course from 8 a.m. to 2 p.m. on Saturday, May 29. A $10,000 fee includes greens fees, range balls, and golf carts for the 90 golfers. The club will staff two refreshment carts and make the club pro available for instruction during the one-hour practice session. Markers will be provided for two longest drives and two closest-to-the-pin holes with $250 gift certificates to be awarded to the winners. Approximately 50 door prizes will be selected from merchandise sold in the pro shop, with a total value of $2,000. Finally, the club will provide tables and chairs under the club pavilion for the lunch being catered by Little Dan's Deli.

Required: Visit the text support site at **http://lehman. swlearning.com** to learn how to prepare a confirmation memo, a procedural message used to provide a record of an event for later reference. Prepare a confirmation memo from Janice Graham to David Sharp confirming the arrangements for the golf outing.

Read	Think	Write	Speak	Collaborate

21. Analyzing International Business Messages (Objs. 1–7)

Obtain a copy of a business letter written by someone from another culture. Identify the major differences between this letter and a traditional U.S. letter. Include information about cultural differences that might be reflected in the message style. Create a visual of your letter and share your analysis with the class as directed by your instructor.

22. Critique of Form Letters Produced by Real Companies (Objs. 1–7)

Locate an example of a form letter you have received or have generated on your job. In small groups, discuss the appropriateness of each letter. Does the form letter accurately address the recipient's problem? Does the form letter generically address numerous situations, or is

it tailored to fit the specific needs of the recipients? What changes would you suggest for personalizing the form letter? Make a brief team presentation to the class about your analysis.

23. Information Message: We're Moving (Objs. 1, 2)

Prepare an innovative message informing customers and key partners that your company is moving. Provide your new address and any change in e-mail, fax, etc. in a clever e-card, creative postcard, or upbeat e-mail message.

Required: Place your message on an acetate or slide and share your design with the class. Refer to the Strategic Forces Feature on e-cards in Chapter 3 to learn more about the use of e-cards for business messages and a list of greeting card sites.

Read	Think	Write	Speak	Collaborate

24. Information Message: Internet Usage Policy Announced (Objs. 1, 2)

Concerns have been raised over the increasing numbers of employees listening to Internet radio on the job. While current company policy prohibits listening to the radio while on the job, Internet radio is distracting

workers in adjacent cubicles and affecting overall productivity. Related problems include employee time spent managing investment portfolios, researching vacations, keeping up with favorite sports teams, shopping, and visiting other questionable sites. New procedures are necessary to address these new technology capabilities.

An director of human resources, you have been authorized to develop an appropriate internet usage policy for your company. Using your group members' own work experience and information obtained from an online search, develop a policy that applies to acceptable Internet usage. Provide a detailed explanation of acceptable behavior that employees can follow consistently. The policy will go into effect on September 1.

Required: Send your policy as an attachment to an e-mail message to your instructor; or if directed, bring a copy of the policy to class for discussion.

25. Information Memo: Addressing Behavioral Issues (Objs. 1, 2)

As a manager you may become aware of problems requiring you to address sensitive behavioral issues. The use of profanity in the workplace, the internal distribution of rude jokes or cartoons, or improper attire are a sample of problems that, if not addressed, can undermine corporate culture and potentially lead to charges of sexual and racial discrimination.

Required: In groups of three or four, select one of these issues or one assigned by your instructor. After conducting necessary research, prepare a memo to your supervisor presenting a discussion of the issue and outlining recommendations for your company.

26. Reply to Request: Something New in the Air (Objs. 1, 3)

In groups of three or four serving as a company's product development team, develop a form letter to be sent to customers who have written asking for a specific change in your product or service. Use your team's own experiences and available consumer research to identify and support an innovative change of your choice. Consider including an incentive to entice customers to try the new product/service. For example, the Zip Crisp bag, a stand-up resealable bag, was introduced to keep Ore-Ida french fries crispier and tastier than those in standard pillow packs and to enhance customer convenience.

Required: Address your letter to Lauren Batchelder, 890 South Brodnax Drive, The Woodlands, TX 77382.

27. Reply to Routine Request: Feedback from Chat Room Requires Action (Objs. 1, 3)

You are employed by Audio Specialties, a company that sells and services a wide array of audio and sound equipment. Some time ago your team convinced management to add a live chat forum to your corporate web site to increase traffic to the site and to gather valuable feedback from customers. The chat room moderator talked to you today about a frequently recurring issue in the forum: Customers are complaining that homemade recordable CDs with adhesive labels are getting stuck in their vehicles' CD changers. This situation is exactly what you had in mind when you lobbied for this innovative communication tool. You can easily resolve this issue and thereby improve customer satisfaction—now that you're aware of the problem. Customers need a reminder of the proper usage of the changer.

Required: In groups of three or four, develop a creative message communicating the company's response to this valuable feedback. You may choose to post a new question to your frequently asked questions (FAQ) page on the web site, design a creative flyer to be mailed to customers, or write a letter or e-mail message as directed by your instructor.

JanSport Simplifies Routine Claims

A contemporary means of customer contact is the sharing of targeted information via an organization's web site. Consumer questions that previously would have necessitated a letter or telephone call to the company are often anticipated and answered through the frequently asked questions (FAQs) section of the site. JanSport uses this capability by providing answers to FAQs related to its products and warranty. Visit the JanSport web site and find out more about its FAQs. Compare the FAQ method for obtaining product information to the more traditional method illustrated in Figure 6-10. Compare the overall effect achieved by the two approaches.

Part 4 of the JanSport ShowCASE focuses on community relations at JanSport.

http://www.jansport.com

Visit the text support site at **http://lehman.swlearning.com** to complete Part 4 of the JanSport ShowCASE.

Internet Case

Snoop Proof Your PC

Protecting the security of data files and computer activities is high priority for individuals and businesses alike. However, your PC is ready and able to reveal not only your data but what you've been doing with your computer. Within a few hours, a snoop can determine and find the incoming and outgoing mail you deleted, web sites you visited, data you've entered on web forms, and even phrases you deleted from documents. Fortunately, you can take steps to protect yourself.

Using effective password protection is a simple first step. Lock important files by using carefully chosen passwords. The best passwords aren't real words or dates; they use a combination of letters, numbers, and punctuation. Knowing how to truly rid your computer of deleted and trashed files is another important security step. Regularly clearing temporary menus and files, as well as history listings, will assure that your recent file activities are not recorded for the would-be snoop to peruse.

An obvious way to protect your information is to encrypt sensitive information. Good encryption and locking solutions are increasingly user friendly and inexpensive. Numerous products are available, with the most effective tools encrypting both file contents and passwords used to access them. Encryption usually defeats casual efforts at intrusion and complicates even advanced snooping attempts.

Cookies can also provide information from your computer to remote third parties. Cookies are short pieces of data used by web servers to help identify the user and possibly to track a user's browsing habits. Cookies can tell a web server that you have been there before and can pass short bits of information from your computer to the server. If you are concerned about being identified or about having your activities traced, set your browser to not accept cookies or use one of the new cookie blocking packages. Remember, though, that blocking all cookies prevents some online services from working.

Another potential PC leak that is often overlooked is the discarded hard drive. About 150,000 hard drives are retired each year, but many find their way back onto the market. Stories occasionally surface about personal and corporate information turning up on used hard drives, raising concerns about privacy and danger of identity theft. In 1997, a Nevada woman bought a used computer and discovered it contained prescription records on 2,000 customers of an Arizona pharmacy.[10] On most operating systems, simply deleting a file and even emptying it from the trash folder does not necessarily make the information irretrievable. The information can live on until it is overwritten by new files. Even reformatting a drive may not eradicate all data.

The most common breaches of computer privacy are committed by those who have the most opportunity: coworkers, friends, and family members. But nameless, faceless hackers can also invade your computer via your Internet connection. Installing a firewall can help protect you from unauthorized access, possible file damage, and even identity theft.

Visit the text support site at **http://www.lehman. swlearning.com** for links to several articles that provide

helpful information about how to snoop proof your computer. As directed by your instructor, complete one or more of the following:

1. Locate other articles that discuss ways to protect your computer files and activities. Prepare an oral presentation about your findings.
2. **GMAT** Mark Twain once said, "There is no security in life—only opportunity." How does this philosophy relate to the use of computers in an environment of inherent security risks? Prepare a one-page essay that explains your reasoning.
3. Make a chart that summarizes the major snoop risks on your PC and actions that can be taken to minimize each risk.

UroCor, Inc.: Effective Written Communication Builds Business

UroCor, Inc. **(http://www.urocor.com)** provides a host of diagnostic services to assist in detecting, diagnosing, treating, and managing complex urological disorders. With over one third of the 7,500 office-based urologists in the U.S. using UroCor Labs, the UroCor team analyzes more than 400,000 urological cases per year. UroCor expedites lab results by arranging pickup of samples at physicians' offices and patients' homes and making rapid results available via the Internet for immediate retrieval or by fax and mail. UroCor uses direct mail to promote its services to healthcare providers who would benefit from partnering to meet their diagnostic needs.

View the video segment about UroCor, Inc. and related activities on WebTutor or your Professional Power Pak CD.

Discussion Questions

1. What criteria should the writer use, according to John Wargo, to decide which is better—a personalized salutation, such as "Dear Mr. Grantham" or a generic salutation, such as "Dear Club Member"?
2. According to John Wargo, what determines whether individuals keep or discard mail? What can business communicators learn from this principle?
3. What advice does John Wargo give about using a postscript in direct mail letters?

Activities

Locate the following article available in full text from InfoTrac College or perhaps from another database available through your campus library:

Rieck, D. (2001, April). 10 basics for writing better letters. *Direct Marketing*, 52.

Even though this article focuses on writing sales letters (a topic to be covered in Chapter 8), it covers general letter-writing principles as well. To help you identify the general principles as you read the article, answer the following questions and include a general letter-writing principle that you can derive from your answer.

1. In what situation is it appropriate to include headlines or pictures in a letter? exclude headlines or pictures?
2. What type salutations are recommended for business letters?
3. What are the characteristics of a good direct letter opening?
4. What is the benefit of cutting a sentence in two at the bottom of a page?
5. What main objective should the writer seek to accomplish in the body of the letter?
6. What are options for the content of a postscript?

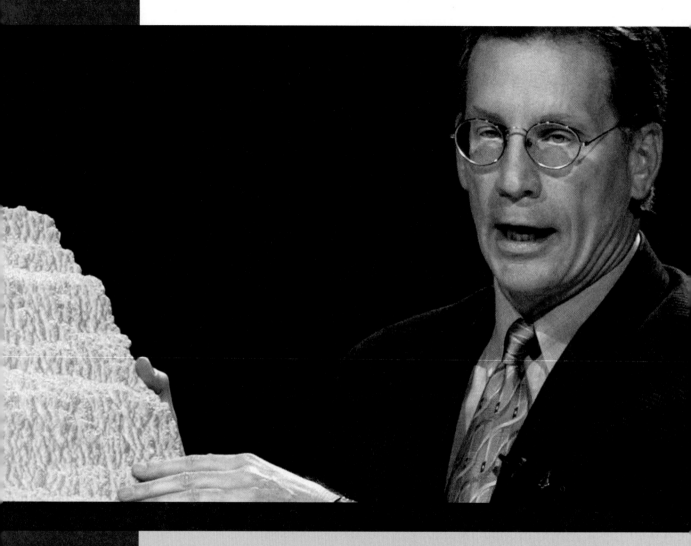

© AFP/CORBIS

7 Delivering Bad-News Messages

Objectives *When you have completed Chapter 7, you will be able to:*

1. Explain the steps in the inductive outline and the importance of selecting an appropriate communication channel for bad news.

2. Identify exceptions to using the inductive approach to communicate bad news.

3. Discuss strategies for developing the five components of a bad-news message.

4. Prepare messages refusing requests.

5. Prepare messages denying claims.

6. Prepare messages handling problems with customers' orders.

7. Prepare messages denying credit.

8. Prepare messages providing constructive criticism.

9. Prepare messages communicating negative organizational news.

NASA DEVELOPS APPLAUDED CRISIS COMMUNICATIONS PLAN

When the space shuttle Columbia disaster occurred February 1, 2003, the National Aeronautics and Space Administration (NASA) was faced once again with investigating a shuttle tragedy. NASA had learned a lot about how not to behave from the Challenger investigation in 1986. This time they had a plan in place for how to deal with a catastrophic accident and an investigation team to propose what the NASA administration would do. As a result, the public knew far more in the early stages of the investigation compared to what it knew of the Challenger explosion that occurred 17 years earlier.

"We had the press center open within 14 minutes of the loss of the shuttle," says Robert Mirelson, NASA news chief, whose position did not even exist in 1986. The first press release was issued 45 minutes later, and national broadcast and electronic media were prioritized to get the word out as widely and as quickly as possible. NASA released satellite transponder information so the media could uplink to its broadcasts, the first of which occurred only four hours after the tragedy.

Another communication network that NASA didn't have the benefit of in 1986 was the Department of Homeland Security. This time "we had one group to go to for help with the Federal Emergency Management Agency, the Coast Guard, Department of Defense, local authorities, and others," says Mirelson. With potentially hazardous and valuable pieces of the shuttle plummeting across several states, the public had to be informed about the importance of staying away from them. The Environmental Protection Agency had communicators on location at the NASA press center, issuing releases and warnings to local and national media, including print, broadcast, radio, and Internet.

According to those who had covered the Challenger explosion, NASA exhibited a dramatic improvement in response and management of the Columbia disaster. NASA's earlier reputation for being defensive and tight with information was replaced in 2003 with an image of being forthcoming and responsive.

When the Columbia Accident Investigation Board cited NASA's culture for being to blame for the shuttle disaster, NASA chief Sean O'Keefe vowed to lead a complete overhaul of the space agency, responding fully to the communication problems and bureaucratic practices that led to the tragedy. "The return to flight will not be business as usual—it cannot be, it will not be at this center," said Kennedy Space Center director Jim Kennedy. "We understand things have to change and . . . we understand that for the safety of flight and for the future of astronauts who fly on the shuttle, we must do business differently."[1]

The ability to communicate about and respond to sad events with tact, concern, and honesty is important to agencies such as NASA and to managers in every phase of business activity.

http://www.nasa.gov

See ShowCASE, Part 2, on page 268 for Spotlight Communicator Ron Dittemore, former NASA space shuttle program manager.

Objective **1**

Explain the steps in the inductive outline and the importance of selecting an appropriate communication channel for bad news.

Critical Thinking

How does empathy assist in conveying bad news?

Choosing an Appropriate Channel and Organizational Pattern

As illustrated in the NASA example, loyalty of customers and the public at large is closely tied to an organization's ability to handle difficult situations with tact and empathy. A skilled communicator will attempt to deliver bad news in such a way that the recipient supports the decision and is willing to continue a positive relationship. To accomplish these goals, allow empathy for the receiver to direct your choice of an appropriate channel and an outline for presenting a logical discussion of the facts and the unpleasant idea. Then, tactful and effective language will aid you in developing a clear, but sensitive, message.

Channel Choice and Commitment to Tact

Personal delivery of bad news has been the preferred medium for delivering bad news because it signals the importance of the news and shows empathy for the recipient. Face-to-face delivery also provides the benefit of nonverbal communication and immediate feedback that minimize the misinterpretation of these highly sensitive messages. Personal delivery, however, does carry a level of discomfort and the potential for escalation

The increased use of electronic communication is leading to the cautious use of e-mail for delivering some negative messages. Employees who are geographically dispersed and those who tend to distort or avoid sharing negative information face to face can benefit from communicating electronically.

© DIGITAL VISION/GETTY IMAGES

of emotion. The voice on the telephone triggers the same discomfort as a face-to-face meeting, and the increased difficulty of interpreting the intensity of nonverbal cues over the telephone only adds to the natural discomfort associated with delivering negative information.

The increasing widespread use of electronic media for organizational communication and studies related to the interaction dynamics of various communication media may challenge the current practice of delivering bad news in person. A recent study by the Institute for Operations Research concluded that negative messages delivered by e-mail rather than personally or by telephone are more honest and accurate and cause less discomfort for the sender. While inappropriate for extremely personal or potentially legal situations, such as firing an employee, e-mail can be a viable communication channel for facilitating the delivery of bad news when face-to-face interaction is not possible due to geographical separation. Furthermore, the straight talk fostered by e-mail may also improve upward communication and thus the performance of the company as even the most reluctant employees feel more comfortable relaying unpopular news to their superiors.[2]

You must be cautious should you elect to deliver bad news electronically, by e-mail or electronic bulletin board postings. While you may feel more comfortable avoiding the discomfort of facing the recipient, the impersonal nature of the computer may lead to careless writing that is tactless and unempathetic and perhaps even defamatory. Stay focused and follow the same communication strategies you would apply if you were speaking face to face or writing a more formal letter or memo. Regardless of the medium, your objective is to help the audience understand and accept your message, and these goals require empathy and tact.

Effective message organization varies among cultures because of values held by each society. While U.S. businesspeople prefer the indirect style for delivering bad news Germans, for instance, prefer the direct pattern for positive and negative messages. Asians and Latinos may avoid saying "no" or give qualified "no's" in order to save face. Understanding value differences can aid in interpreting messages from people of other cultures.

© DEX IMAGES, INC./CORBIS

Tactfulness may also be a problem when your personal response fails to soothe negative feelings and ensure a harmonious relationship with a customer, client, or employee. You may find it difficult to show tact when you doubt the legitimacy of the request or simply don't have the time to prepare an effective bad-news message. When this conflict exists, you must remember that your message written on behalf of the company is a direct reflection of the company's image. This important truth is illustrated in the story of a man who carried in his jacket pocket a job refusal letter he'd received years ago. Frequently he showed this superbly written letter to others and commented, "I'd accept a job from this company any day because this letter made me feel good about myself even though the company couldn't hire me." Obviously, this letter was not an impersonal form letter or hurriedly written e-mail that conveyed no tact or genuine empathy for the recipient.

Critical Thinking

Can you relay similar incidents when you had either a positive or a negative feeling for a person or company who gave you unpleasant news? Contrast the approaches used in the situations.

Use of the Inductive Approach to Build Goodwill

Just as good news is accompanied with details, bad news is accompanied with supporting details (reasons, explanations). If the bad news is presented in the first sentence, the reaction is likely to be negative: "They never gave me a fair chance"; "That's unfair"; "This just can't be." Having made a value judgment on reading the first sentence, receivers are naturally reluctant to change their minds before the last sentence—even though the intervening sentences present a valid basis for doing so. Once disappointed by the idea contained in the first sentence, receivers are tempted to concentrate on *refuting* (instead of *understanding*) supporting details.

When U.S. television networks went to wall-to-wall coverage of the war in Iraq, many advertisers pulled their ads to rethink strategy. In somber times, humorous or exuberant advertisements might be seen by customers as insincere or inappropriate.[3]

© AFP/CORBIS

From the communicator's point of view, details that support a refusal are very important. If the supporting details are understood and believed, the message may be readily accepted and good business relationships preserved. Because the reasons behind the bad news are so important, the communicator needs to organize the message in such a way as to emphasize the reasons.

Critical Thinking

What are the consequences if bad news is shared too early? Too late?

The chances of getting the receiver to understand the reasons are much better *before* the bad news is presented than *after* the bad news is presented. If the bad news precedes the reasons, (1) the message might be discarded before this important portion is even read, or (2) the disappointment experienced when reading the bad news might interfere with the receiver's ability to comprehend or accept the supporting explanation.

The five-step outline shown in Figure 7-1 simplifies the process of organizing bad-news messages. These five steps are applied in messages illustrated in this chapter.

Although the outline has five points, a bad-news message may or may not have five paragraphs. More than one paragraph may be necessary for conveying supporting reasons. In the illustrations in this chapter (as well as examples in Appendix A), note that first and final paragraphs are seldom longer than two sentences. In fact, one-sentence paragraphs (as beginnings) look inviting to read.

The inductive sequence of ideas has the following advantages:

- It sufficiently identifies the subject of the letter without first turning the receiver off.
- It presents the reasons *before* the refusal, where they are more likely to be understood and will receive appropriate emphasis.
- It avoids a negative reaction. By the time the reasons are read, they seem sensible, and the refusal is foreseen. Because it is expected, the statement of refusal does not come as a shock.
- It de-emphasizes the refusal by closing on a neutral or pleasant note. By showing a willingness to cooperate in some other way, the writer conveys a desire to be helpful.

Figure 7-1	*Inductive Sequence Used in Bad-News Messages*

BAD-NEWS MESSAGE

- Begins with the neutral idea that leads to the reasons for the refusal or bad news.
- Presents the facts, analysis, and reasons for the refusal.
- States the refusal or bad news using positive tone and de-emphasis techniques.
- Includes a counterproposal or "silver lining" idea.
- Closes with an idea that shifts emphasis away from the refusal or bad news and indicates a continuing relationship with the receiver.

Critical Thinking

Which is less desirable: an angry or an impatient reader? What can you do to minimize the delay in presenting the bad news?

You may speculate that receivers may become impatient when a message is inductive. Concise, well-written explanations are not likely to make a receiver impatient. They relate to the receiver's problem, present information not already known, and help the receiver understand. However, if a receiver becomes impatient while reading a well-written explanation, that impatience is less damaging to understanding than would be the anger or disgust that often results from encountering bad news in the first sentence.

Exceptions to the Inductive Approach

Objective 2

Identify exceptions to using the inductive approach to communicate bad news.

Normally, the writer's purpose is to convey a clear message and retain the recipient's goodwill; thus, the inductive outline is appropriate. In the rare circumstances in which a choice must be made between the two, clarity is the better choice. When the deductive approach will serve a communicator's purpose better, it should be used. For example, if you submit a clear and tactful refusal and the receiver resubmits the request, a deductive presentation may be justified in the second refusal. Apparently, the refusal needs the emphasis provided by a deductive outline. Placing a refusal in the first sentence can be justified when one or more of the following circumstances exists:

Critical Thinking

When would a deductive approach be appropriate for presenting bad news? Provide examples of your own.

- The message is the second response to a repeated request.
- A very small, insignificant matter is involved.
- A request is obviously ridiculous, immoral, unethical, illegal, or dangerous.
- A sender's intent is to "shake" the receiver.
- A sender-recipient relationship is so close and longstanding that satisfactory human relations can be taken for granted.
- The sender *wants* to demonstrate authority.

In most situations, the preceding circumstances do not exist. When they do, a sender's goals may be accomplished by stating bad news in the first sentence.

Developing a Bad-News Message

Objective 3

Discuss strategies for developing the five components of a bad-news message.

Developing a bad-news message following the inductive outline is challenging. The following suggestions will aid you in writing the (a) introductory paragraph, (b) explanation, (c) bad-news statement, and (d) closing paragraph.

Writing the Introductory Paragraph

The introductory paragraph in the bad-news message should accomplish the following objectives: (1) provide a buffer to cushion the bad news that will follow, (2) let the receiver know what the message is about without stating

Critical Thinking

Consider a situation where you might be called on to deliver bad news. How would you word your introductory "buffer" paragraph?

the obvious, and (3) serve as a transition into the discussion of reasons without revealing the bad news or leading the receiver to expect good news. If these objectives can be accomplished in one sentence, that sentence can be the first paragraph. Avoid the following weaknesses when writing the introductory paragraph:

- *Avoid empty acknowledgments of the obvious.* Omit obvious statements such as *"I am writing in response to your letter requesting . . . "* or *"Your letter of the 14th has been given to me for reply"* to shorten the message and avoid using space to present points that aren't important. Beginning with *I* signals the message may be writer centered.
- *Avoid tipping off the bad news too early.* *"Although the refund requested in your letter of May 1 cannot be approved, . . . "* may cause an immediate emotional reaction resulting in the message being discarded or interfering with understanding the explanations that follow. The neutral statement *"Your request for an adjustment has been considered. However, . . . "* does not reveal whether the answer is "Yes" or "No," but the use of "however," signals the answer is "No" before the reasons are presented. Such a beginning has about the same effect as an outright "No" beginning.
- *Avoid starting too positively so as to build false hopes.* Empathetic statements such as *"I can understand how you felt when you were asked to pay an extra $54"* may lead the receiver to expect good news. When a preceding statement has implied that an affirmative decision will follow, a negative decision is all the more disappointing.

Study the following examples that achieve the desired purposes. To illustrate transition/cohesion, the first words of the second paragraph are also presented, and transition words are shown in quotations marks for added emphasis.

Effective Introductory Paragraph	Explanation
The double-indemnity feature of your policy has two provisions. In each the words are "natural causes" and "accidental."	*Reveals the topic as a response to policy-holder's insurance claim. Uses "In each" to relate the second sentence to the first and "natural causes" to transition from the introductory paragraph to the second paragraph.*
"Natural causes" are defined as . . .	
Your application was reviewed separately by two loan officers.	*Reveals the subject as a response to the recipient's loan application. Uses "officer" to transition from the first to the second sentence. Discusses the officers' review to satisfy an expectation presented in the first sentence.*
Each officer considered . . .	
Following your request for permission to pick up leftover potatoes, we reviewed our experiences of recent years.	*Reveals the subject of the message as the reply to a humanitarian organization's request to be allowed to field and harvest potatoes left by mechanical pickers. Uses "year" to tie the second paragraph to the first and transitions into a discussion of the "experiences" mentioned in the first paragraph.*
Last year, two incidents . . .	

Here are several ideas that can be incorporated into effective beginning paragraphs:

Critical Thinking

Can you think of other ideas for effective opening paragraphs?

- *Compliment.* A letter denying a customer's request could begin by recognizing that customer's promptness in making payments.
- *Point of agreement.* If the message you are answering made a statement with which you can agree, a sentence that reveals agreement could get the message off to a positive discussion of other points.
- *Good news.* When a message contains a request that must be refused and another that is being answered favorably, beginning with the favorable answer can be effective.
- *Resale.* If the subject of correspondence is a product that was purchased, a refusal could begin with some favorable statement about the product.
- *A review.* Refusal of a current request could be introduced by referring to the initial transaction or by reviewing certain circumstances that preceded the transaction.
- *Gratitude.* Although an unjustified request may have been made, the receiver may have done or said something for which you are grateful. An expression of gratitude could be used as a positive beginning.

Presenting the Facts, Analysis, and Reasons

The reasons section of the bad-news message is extremely important because people who are refused want to know why. To them (and to the person doing the refusing) the reasons are vital. When people say "No" they usually do so because they think "No" is the better answer for all concerned. They can see how recipients will ultimately benefit from the refusal. If a message is based on a sound decision, and if it has been well written, recipients will understand and accept the reasons and the forthcoming refusal statement as valid.

To accomplish this goal, begin with a well-written first paragraph that transitions the receiver smoothly into the reasons section. Then, develop the reasons section following these guidelines:

Critical Thinking

If you were sharing news with a customer concerning a price increase, what would be a good reason from the customer's perspective?

- *Provide a smooth transition from the opening paragraph to the explanation.* The buffer should help set the stage for a logical movement into the discussion of the reasons.
- *Include a concise discussion of one or more reasons that are logical to the reader.* Read the section aloud to identify flaws in logic or the need for additional explanation.
- *Show reader benefit and/or consideration.* Emphasize how the receiver will benefit from the decision. Avoid insincere, empty statements such as "To improve our service to you, ..."
- *Avoid using "company policy" as the reason.* Disclose the reason behind the policy, which likely will include benefits to the receiver. For

example, a customer is more likely to understand and accept a 15 percent restocking fee if the policy is not presented as the "reason" for the refusal. Note the letter in Figure 7-7 on page 258 presents specific benefits to the receiver for the company's restocking policy.

The principles for developing the reasons section are illustrated in Figure 7-2, a letter written by an accounting firm refusing to accept a financial audit engagement. The introductory paragraph presents a statement that both the client and prospective auditor can agree on (the positive impact of a financial statement audit). The buffer also reveals the subject of the letter (the company's request for an auditor) and provides a smooth transition between the buffer and the reasons (accounting rules require auditor independence). The reasons section presents a logical discussion of the reason for refusal. The authoritative rule is presented, followed by a direct application of the rule to the situation. The refusal is stated positively and clearly using a complex sentence and positive language.

Figure 7-2

Developing the Components of a Bad-News Message

Begins with a statement with which both can agree. Sets the stage for the reasons by presenting the importance of a quality audit.

Reveals the subject of the letter (company's selection of an auditor) and transitions into the reasons.

Provides a rule from the authoritative literature to support the refusal and clearly applies the rule to the situation.

States the refusal positively and clearly using a complex sentence and positive language.

Includes a counterproposal as an alternative.

Closes with sales promotion for other services indicating an expectation that the business relationship will continue.

> Audited financial statements will improve your ability to negotiate contracts with suppliers, banks, and customers, as well as provide your stockholders with confidence regarding their investment. For this reason, the auditor you select must be capable of providing quality audit services.
>
> To eliminate the appearance of a conflict of interest, Rule 101 of the AICPA Code of Professional Conduct requires auditors to be independent of their clients. One of our audit partners, Patrick Rackley, is a significant stockholder in the First National Bank, which currently has loaned a large amount of money to your company. Because of this indirect financial interest, we recommend that you seek another firm to perform the 2004 financial statement audit.
>
> Since the independence rule applies only to audits of financial statements, we are available to provide other professional services. Our tax accountants are ready to assist you in finding methods to reduce your income tax liability. Please call me at 501-555-1245 to discuss these services.

Writing the Bad-News Statement

Critical Thinking

Can you relate to the value of balancing negative feedback with a few positives when your performance on the job or in class is being critiqued? How does the balanced approach affect your feeling toward the sender and the task at hand? Give examples.

In a sense, a paragraph that presents the reasoning behind a refusal at least partially conveys the refusal before it is stated directly or indirectly. Yet one sentence needs to convey (directly or by implication) the conclusion to which the preceding details have been leading. A refusal (bad news) needs to be clear; however, you can subordinate the refusal so that the reasoning for the refusal gets the deserved emphasis. The following techniques will help you achieve this goal.

- *Position the bad-news statement strategically.* Using the inductive outline positions the bad-news statement in a less important position—sandwiched between an opening buffer statement and a positive closing. Additionally, the refusal statement should be included in the same paragraph as the reasons, since placing it in a paragraph by itself would place too much emphasis on the bad news. Because the preceding explanation is tactful and seems valid, the sentence that states the bad news may cause little or no resentment. Positioning the bad-news statement in the dependent clause of a complex sentence will also cushion the bad news. This technique places the bad news in a less visible position, the dependent clause. In the sentence, *"Although our current personnel shortage prevents us from lending you an executive, we do want to support your worthy project,"* the emphasis is directed toward a promise of help in some other form.
- *Use passive voice, general terms, and abstract nouns.* Review the *emphasis techniques* that you studied in Chapter 3 as you consider methods for presenting bad news with human relations in mind.
- *Use positive language to accentuate the positive.* Simply focus on the good instead of the bad, the pleasant instead of the unpleasant, what can be done instead of what cannot be done. Compared with a negative idea presented in negative terms, a negative idea presented in positive terms is more likely to be accepted. When you are tempted to use the following terms, search instead for words or ideas that sound more positive:

chagrined	failure	lied	overlooked
complaint	ignorant	misinformed	regrettable
disappointed	ignored	mistake	ridiculous
disgusted	inexcusable	neglect	underhanded
disregard	insinuation	nonsense	upset
error	irresponsible	obnoxious	wrong

Critical Thinking

Think of other words that could be added to the list of negative words and the list of positive words that follow.

To businesspeople who conscientiously practice empathy, such terms may not even come to mind when communicating the unpleasant. Words in the preceding list evoke negative feelings that contrast sharply with the positive feelings evoked by words such as:

accurate	cordial	freedom	pretty
approval	correct	generous	productive
assist	durable	gratitude	prosper
cheerful	energetic	happy	recommendation
commend	enthusiasm	health	respect
concise	fragrance	peace	true

Critical Thinking

Compose a sentence that implies management's refusal to adopt a company casual dress policy. Contrast that sentence to a direct statement of refusal.

To increase the number of pleasant-sounding words in your messages, practice thinking positively. Strive to see the good in situations and in others. Will Rogers professed to being able to see *some* good in every person he met.

- *Imply the refusal when the receiver can understand the message without a definite statement of the bad news.* By *implying* the "No" answer, the response achieves several purposes: (1) uses positive language, (2) conveys reasons or at least a positive attitude, and (3) seems more respectful. For example, during the noon hour one employee says to another, "Will you go with me to see this afternoon's baseball game?" "No, I won't" communicates a negative response, but it seems unnecessarily direct and harsh. The same message (invitation is rejected) can be clearly stated in an *indirect* way (by implication) by saying "I must get my work done," or even, "I'm a football fan." Note the positive tone of the following implied refusals:

Implied Refusal	Explanation
I wish I could.	*Other responsibilities forbid, but the recipient would like to accept.*
Had you selected the variable mortgage rate, you could have taken advantage of the recent drop in interest rates.	*States a condition under which the answer would have been "Yes" instead of "No." Note use of the subjunctive words "if" and "would."*
By accepting the arrangement, Donahoo Industries would have tripled its insurance costs.	*States the obviously unacceptable results of complying with a request.*

Can you identify which of the suggested techniques were used to cushion the bad-news statement in the following example?

Although the Trammell Road property was selected as the building site, nearness to the railroad was considered a plus for the Drapala property.

1. States what was done rather than what was *not* done.
2. Includes a positive idea (*nearness to the railroad*) to accentuate a positive idea and thus cushion the bad news.
3. Uses passive voice (*property was selected*) to depersonalize the message.
4. Places the bad news in the dependent clause of a complex sentence ("although the Trammell property was selected"). The positive idea in the independent clause (*nearness to the railroad*) will receive more attention.

These de-emphasis techniques are illustrated in the messages that follow. The Strategic Forces feature on page 252, "Assessing Template Documents Available with Word Processing Software," addresses the advisability of using template letters available with major word processing software, especially those that convey bad news.

Offering a Counterproposal or "Silver Lining" Idea

Critical Thinking

What counterproposal could you offer in a "No, thank you" letter to a job applicant?

Following the negative news with an alternative action, referred to as a *counterproposal*, will assist in preserving future relationships with the receiver. Because it states what you can do, including a counterproposal may eliminate the need to state the refusal directly. The counterproposal can follow a refusal stated in a tactful, sensitive manner. For example, in a letter refusing to lower the interest rates on a loan with a fixed mortgage rate, a loan officer might suggest refinancing the loan as soon as interest rates fall a recommended percentage below the borrowers' current mortgage rate.

While the counterproposal may represent a tangible benefit, at times it is more intangible in nature. For instance, in a letter that informs a job applicant that he or she was not selected to fill the vacant position, the counterproposal might be an offer to reconsider the applicant's résumé when other appropriate positions become available. Any counterproposal extended must, of course, be reasonable. For instance, when informing a customer of an inability to meet a promised delivery deadline, an unreasonable counterproposal would be to offer the merchandise at no charge. A reasonable counterproposal might be to include some additional items at no charge or to offer a discount certificate good on the customer's next order.

When no reasonable counterproposal is apparent, the sender may be able to offer a "silver lining" thought that turns the discussion back into the positive direction. For instance, a statement to tenants announcing an increase in rent might be followed by a description of improved lighting that will be installed in the parking lot of the apartment complex. When offering a counterproposal or silver lining statement, care must be taken to assure that the idea does not seem superficial or minimize the recipient's situation.

Closing Positively

Critical Thinking

Why should a reference to the refusal not be included in the final paragraph?

After presenting valid reasons and a tactful refusal followed with a counterproposal or silver lining, a closing paragraph should demonstrate empathy without further reference to the bad news. A pleasant closing paragraph should close with an empathetic tone and achieve the following goals:

• **De-emphasize the unpleasant part of the message.** It should end on a positive note that takes the emphasis away from the bad news previously presented. If the writing were strictly inductive, the refusal statement would be last. Placing a statement of refusal (or bad news) in the last sentence or paragraph, however, would have the effect of placing too much emphasis on it. Preferably, *reasons* (instead of bad news) should remain uppermost in the receiver's mind. Placing bad news last would make the ending seem cold and abrupt.

Critical Thinking

What feeling do you hope to create for your reader as you end your communication?

- *Add a unifying quality to the message.* The final sentence should seem like an *appropriate* closing; that is, it should bring a unifying quality to the whole message. Repetition of a word (or reference to some positive idea) that appears early in the message serves this purpose well. Restatement of the refusal (or direct reference to it) would only serve to emphasize it. This paragraph is usually shorter than the preceding explanatory paragraphs. Sometimes, a one-sentence closing is enough; other messages may require two or three sentences.

- *Include a positive, forward-looking idea.* This idea might include a reference to some pleasant aspect of the preceding discussion or a future aspect of the business relationship, resale or sales promotion, or an offer to help in some way. Consider the following closures that apply these suggestions:

Reference to some pleasant aspect of the preceding discussion:
"Your addition of the home mortgage rider to your policy last year was certainly a wise decision." Home mortgage and other provisions had been mentioned in the early part of a letter to a client who was refused a double-indemnity settlement.

Use of resale or sales promotional material:
- *"According to a recent survey, a four-headed VCR produces sound qualities that are far superior; it was an ideal choice."* A reminder that the VCR has a superior feature will assist in regaining goodwill after a customer's request for free repair has been refused.
- *"Mini-sized compacts and adapters are now available; see the enclosed folder."* A letter refusing a request for free repair of a VCR could also include sales promotional material for a related product.

An expression of willingness to assist in some *other* way:
Specifically, you may offer an alternative solution to the receiver's problem or useful information that could not be presented logically with the bad news.
- *"Our representative will show you some samples during next week's sales call."* The samples are being proposed as a possible solution to the receiver's problem.
- *"If you would like to see the orientation film we show to management trainees, you would be welcome."* The writer seeks to show a good attitude by offering to do something other than grant the requested permission to interview certain employees on the job.

Avoid including the following types of statements in the closing paragraph:

- *Trite statements that may seem shallow and superficial.* The well-worn statement, *"Thank you for your interest,"* is often used thoughtlessly. Some refusals are addressed to people who have apparently *not* been interested enough to listen, read, or remember; otherwise, they would not have made the requests. For them, the sentence is inappropriate. For others, it may seem shallow and superficial. *"When we can be of further help, please do not hesitate to call or write"* is also well worn and negative. *Further* help may seem especially inappropriate to someone who has just read a denial. The sender may see the *explanations* as helpful, but the receiver may think the *denial* is being labeled as "helpful."

- *Statements that could undermine the validity of your refusal.* The statement *"We trust this explanation is satisfactory"* or *"We hope you will understand our position"* could be taken as a confession of doubt about the validity of the decision. Use of *position* seems to heighten controversy; positions are expected to be defended. Saying *"We are sorry to disappoint you"* risks a negative reply: "If it made you feel so bad, why did you do it?" It can also be interpreted as an apology for the action taken. If a decision merits an apology, its validity may be questionable.

- *Statements that encourage future controversy.* Statements such as *"If you have questions, please do not hesitate to let us know"* could also be perceived as doubt and possibly communicate a willingness to change the decision. If the decision is firm, including this type closing could result in the writer having to communicate the negative message a second time.

Note the closing paragraph in Figure 7-2, on page 245 is a positive, forward-looking statement that includes sales promotion of other services the accounting firm can offer. This statement implies confidence that the decision, although disappointing, is in the best interest of the client. The firm, therefore, can expect that the client will wish to continue doing business with a fair, and in this case, ethical organization.

Critical Thinking

Recall an incident where you received or communicated a disappointing message. Did the sender apply the principles presented in this chapter? Can you suggest ways the message could have been improved?

Refusing a Request

Objective 4

Prepare messages refusing requests.

To minimize disappointment and to maintain a positive relationship, it's a good idea to use the inductive (reasons-before-refusal) for refusing requests for a favor, an action, or even a donation. Present clear, understandable reasons in a way that minimizes the receiver's disappointment.

You can examine a company's refusal to provide an executive to work for a community organization in Figure 7-3. To buffer the refusal that will follow, the director begins with a compliment for the outstanding work of the organization that provides a natural connection to the introductory statement in the explanation section (*the success of this project depends on a good project director*). The reasons section includes specific reasons that communicate careful thought rather than a hurried, insincere response that says simply and coldly "I'm too busy. Go away." The refusal is implied

Figure 7-3

Good Example of a Refusal for a Favor

Inductive Outline for Refusing a Favor

1. Begin with a neutral or factual sentence that leads to the reasons behind the refusal.
2. Present the reasons and explanations.
3. Present the refusal in an unemphatic manner.
4. Offer a counterproposal that represents what you *can* do.
5. Close with a thought related to the message or to the business relationship but which does not re-address the refusal.

HILSTROM
INDUSTRIES

2700 Ridgeway • Cambridge, MA 02139-2700 • Phone: 617 555-8700 • 617 555-7961

March 18, 2004

Mr. John David Koch
Naperville Historical Society
9835 Devon Building
Richmond, VA 23261-9835

Dear John David

You are to be commended for your commitment to restore Naperville's historical downtown shopping district. In this age of megamalls and Internet shopping, the culture of a traditional main street lined with home-owned and operated shops needs to be preserved.

The success of this project depends on a good project director. The organizational, leadership, and public relations activities you described demand an individual with upper-level managerial experience. During the last year, Hilstrom has decentralized its organization, reducing the number of upper-level managers to the minimal level needed. Although our current personnel shortage prevents us from lending you an executive, we do want to support your worthy project.

Al Denny in our senior executive corps has a keen interest in historical preservation, having served on the board of a similar organization while living in Vermont. If you can benefit from his services, call him at 555-8700, extension 142.

Sincerely

Alex

Alex Weathersby
Director

Annotations (left margin):

Introduces the subject without revealing whether the answer will be "Yes" or "No."

Gives reasons that will seem logical to the reader.

Subordinates the refusal by placing it in the dependent clause of a complex sentence. Alludes to help in another form.

Closes on a positive note by offering a counterproposal. Summarizing the executive's responsibilities and providing his telephone number increase the genuineness of the offer.

Format Pointer

Signs first name only because the writer knows the receiver well.

Assessing Template Documents Available with Word Processing Software

Template letters are a common feature of leading word processing programs. To use such standard templates, the writer selects a type of letter from the menu, such as "Request." The screen then displays a form letter for request situations that the writer can modify to fit the situation at hand. The illustrated template complaint letter to a landlord shown below can be quickly modified to fit a tenant's specific circumstances.

This feature appears, at first, to be a great time saver for the busy writer. Unfortunately, however, such template examples frequently do not reflect the elements indicated for effective

inductive, deductive, or persuasive messages. The careful writer will recognize such shortcomings of the templates and use them cautiously.

Application

Select a word processing program that includes template letters. Select a document type that should reflect the deductive (good-news or neutral-news) pattern. Using the checklist at the end of Chapter 5, evaluate how well the template document follows

the recommended development pattern for deductive messages. Note in what areas the template deviates from the recommendations. Then choose a template document type that should reflect the inductive (bad-news) pattern. Using the checklist at the end of this chapter, evaluate how well the template document follows the recommended development pattern for inductive messages. Note how the template deviates from recommendations.

Arnold Ace
Ace Real Estate Associates
1234 Main Street
Anytown, U.S.A. 12345

Dear Landlord:

I am writing to you about some problems we are having with our store space at 567 Enterprise Drive.

As you know, paragraph 12 of our lease specifically says that Ace Real Estate Associates will maintain the heating and air conditioning system and keep it in good repair. I have called your office twice this week and left word that the air conditioning is not working. No one has come to fix it or given us a date when the work will be done. Our customers have complained, and on Tuesday we had to close early.

Also, under paragraph 14 of our lease, the Landlord agreed to replace the broken floor tiles in the entry area within two weeks after we took possession. We have been here for six weeks now and nothing has been done about the tiles. The broken tiles are hazardous.

These are serious violations of our lease. I am requesting that you immediately repair the air conditioning and promptly replace the broken floor tiles. We cannot operate without the air conditioning during this hot weather. Its inoperability has already caused us to lose substantial revenue and has damaged customer relationships.

If you do not take care of these matters within five days, I plan to have the work done myself and to deduct the cost from next month's rent.

If the cost of fixing the air conditioning is excessive, I may choose to terminate the lease and to sue your company for damages caused by your breaching the lease, including moving expenses and lost profits.

I hope that this will not be necessary. Please proceed at once to make the repairs as required by the lease.

Sincerely,

Peter Olsen

Peter Olsen

Templates

| General | Direct Mail Manager | Legal Pleadings | Letters & Faxes |
| Other Documents | Publications | Reports | Web Pages |

External Analysis - ...
First Collection Letter
Internal Analysis - S...
Internet Services Q...

IRC 1244 Resolution
Letter of Complaint...
Letter of Intent t...
Letter Requesting...

Letter Revoking...
Management Audit
Management Evaluation
Market Segm...

by providing an offer of a viable alternative. The director avoids stating the refusal directly (*No, we cannot lend you an executive to direct a major community effort*) by offering a **counterproposal**, an alternative to the action requested. The closing provides helpful details about the alternative (offers the services of a member of the company's senior executive corps), which conveys a genuine concern to be of help.

The letter in Figure 7-3—which is a *response* to prior correspondence— uses the same principles of sequence and style that are recommended for letters that *initiate* communication about unpleasant topics. The same principles apply whether the communication is a letter, memo, e-mail, or spoken message sent to an employee within a company.

Companies have learned that building employee relationships is just as important as developing customer goodwill. Refusing employees' requests requires sensitivity and complete honest explanations, qualities not included in the poor e-mail in Figure 7-4. The transportation manager's hasty response to a valued employee's request to install CD players in the company's fleet of trucks uses a direct, blunt approach. The explanation is vague and incomplete, and the tone is insensitive and condescending.

In the revision illustrated in Figure 7-5, the transportation manager takes the time to think about the impact his message would have on Carie, one of the company's most valued drivers. The manager recalls that several of Carie's previous suggestions have led to significant improvements in productivity, Carie has become a role model for many

Critical Thinking

Recall a time when you lost goodwill for a company or organization. What caused your reaction? Was your goodwill ever restored?

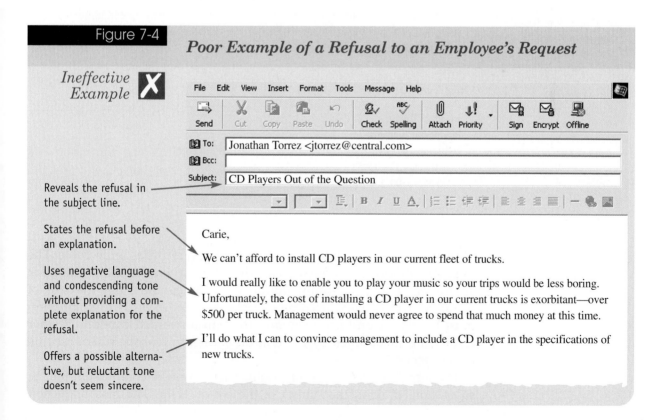

Figure 7-4

Poor Example of a Refusal to an Employee's Request

Ineffective Example **X**

Reveals the refusal in the subject line.

States the refusal before an explanation.

Uses negative language and condescending tone without providing a complete explanation for the refusal.

Offers a possible alternative, but reluctant tone doesn't seem sincere.

To: Jonathan Torrez <jtorrez@central.com>
Bcc:
Subject: CD Players Out of the Question

Carie,

We can't afford to install CD players in our current fleet of trucks.

I would really like to enable you to play your music so your trips would be less boring. Unfortunately, the cost of installing a CD player in our current trucks is exorbitant—over $500 per truck. Management would never agree to spend that much money at this time.

I'll do what I can to convince management to include a CD player in the specifications of new trucks.

Figure 7-5

Good Example of a Refusal to an Employee's Request

File   Edit   View   Insert   Format   Tools   Message   Help

Send   Cut   Copy   Paste   Undo   Check   Spelling   Attach   Priority   Sign   Encrypt   Offline

To: | Carie Monahan
Bcc: |
Subject: | Request to Install CD Players in Truck Fleet

B *I* U A ≡ ≡ ≡ ≡ | ≡ ≡ ≡ ≡ | — 🔗 🖼

Sends message by e-mail, the medium preferred by the recipient.

Cushions the bad news with a sincere compliment for the suggestion.

Transitions to the reasons and provides a complete explanation for the refusal.

Restates reason for saying "No" to de-emphasize the refusal.

Includes a logical alternative and closes with a positive look to future enjoyment when the plan is implemented.

Format Pointer
Includes a .sig file to identify the writer that appears on a printed copy of the e-mail.

Carie,

There is no better way to shorten a long haul than to truck down the highway listening to your favorite music. The company is committed to assuring that our drivers have a pleasant and productive work environment. Thank you for your suggestion to improve your work environment by installing CD players in our current fleet of trucks.

Installing a quality sound system in any vehicle can be a surprisingly complex and expensive task. The cost of installing a CD player in one of our current trucks is estimated at over $500. Because of the significant cost, installing CD players in our current trucks isn't a cost effective solution. In contrast, however, having a CD player installed as original equipment on a new truck adds only $75 to the truck's cost, a much more realistic expenditure for the company.

Carie, I'll prepare a proposal seeking approval for a change in the specifications for new trucks to include a CD player. With the normal frequency that trucks are rotated within the fleet, you should be trucking down the highway soon with your favorite CD playing in the background.

Later,

Jon

Jonathan Torrez
Production Manager
2650 Imperial Blvd.
Los Angeles, CA 90053
(213) 555-6300, Ext. 256 Fax (213) 555-6306

of the less-experienced drivers, and her driving record is impeccable. The manager thinks the suggestion is an excellent way to make the work environment more pleasant during those long hauls, but the cost of installing CD players in current trucks is prohibitive. His explanation must be logical and complete and the refusal worded carefully so that Carie isn't discouraged by the refusal. Is there a realistic alternative he could suggest?

The introductory paragraph begins with a sincere compliment for the suggestion, making the subject of the e-mail clear. The reasons section presents a complete, logical discussion of the reason for the refusal and leads to the obvious conclusion that installing CD players in current trucks just doesn't make good business sense. The closing offers a genuine offer to pursue a realistic alternative that eventually will lead to the improvements that Carie had envisioned.

Denying a Claim

Companies face a challenging task of refusing claims from customers while maintaining goodwill and developing customer loyalty. Claim refusals are necessary when a warranty does not apply or has expired or a customer has misused the product. Companies must also write refusals when customers ask for something that a company simply can't do. For example, many retailers charge customers a $25–$40 fee on returned checks. A retailer who receives a customer's request to waive the charge must refuse because the claim is inconsistent with the retailer's policies and objectives.

The inductive approach is helpful in communicating this disappointing news to customers. Presenting the explanation for the refusal first leads customers through the reasoning behind the decision and helps them *understand* the claim is unjustified by the time the refusal is presented. Tone is especially important when denying claims. Present the reasons objectively and positively without casting blame or judgment on

Critical Thinking

"The customer is always right" is a motto followed by many businesses. How do you justify that philosophy in a situation in which the customer is clearly wrong?

Companies typically deny claims that do not fall within established policies. At times, however, policy requirements are waived, as in the case of life insurance companies who paid claims for the survivors of 9/11 victims, even though death certificates could not be produced.

© REUTERS NEWMEDIA, INC./CORBIS

the customer for the problem. Avoid lecturing a customer on the actions he or she should have taken to have avoided the problem. (*The warning was printed in bold print in the User's Manual, and the toll-free operator informed you of this stipulation when you called.*) Finally, close the message with resale or sales promotional material that indicates you expect future business. Although disappointed with your decision, customers continue doing business with companies who make fair, objective decisions and communicate the *reasons* for those decisions in a positive, respectful manner.

Critical Thinking

What reasons for denying a claim will likely be satisfactory from the reader's perspective?

Assume a manufacturer of ski equipment receives the following e-mail from a customer.

> Please issue a credit to my account for $365.25. Although you accepted $2,435 of skis I returned, you only credited my account for $2,069.75. Because I could find no explanation for the discrepancy, I assume an error has been made.

The company's return policy allows customers to return unsold merchandise at the end of the winter ski season, subject to a 15 percent restocking charge. The return policy is printed clearly on the inside cover of its catalog and in bold print at the bottom of both the printed and Internet order forms. Telephone operators explain the restocking charge to customers placing orders via the company's toll-free number.

The customer's inquiry shows a lack of understanding of the return policy. Although a frustrated company representative may question why the customer can't read the return policy, the response must be more tactful than that illustrated in Figure 7-6. The revision in Figure 7-7 reveals the subject of the letter in the first sentence and leads into a discussion of the reasons. Reasons for the restocking fee, including benefits to the customer, precede the refusal. The tone is positive and respectful. The refusal statement uses several de-emphasis techniques to cushion its impact, the final sentence turns the discussion away from the refusal with reference to future business with the customer.

Critical Thinking

What advice can you give for being tactful, respectful, and positive when stating a refusal?

Refusing an Order

Objective 6

Prepare messages handling problems with customers' orders.

For various reasons, a company may not be able to send merchandise that people have ordered. The company

- May only be able to send it following a waiting period. (At such times, you would acknowledge the order and send a message saying "Yes, you will receive the . . . by . . . ")
- May not sell directly to consumers. (You would tell the customer where to buy the merchandise.)
- May not have what the customer ordered but may have something that will serve his or her needs better. (You would wait to fill the order until you have made the customer understand that you have something better.)

Figure 7-6

Poor Example of a Claim Denial

Ineffective Example ✗

Begins with an obvious idea (receipt of the request could be implied).

Includes an unnecessary apology for a justified decision and provides the refusal before the reasons.

Uses a patronizing tone that may offend the receiver.

Presents an explanation that focuses on the writer and is too brief to be understood.

Uses clichés that may undermine the decision and may lead to unnecessary correspondence.

> Your message questioning your statement has been received. I am sorry but we cannot adjust your account as you requested. Clearly, the statement is correct.
>
> Each of the order forms you have completed states that returns are subject to a 15 percent restocking charge. Surely you saw this information printed in **bold** print on the order forms, and our telephone operators also explain our return policy thoroughly when customers place orders. I am sure you can appreciate the cost and effort we incur to restock merchandise after the winter ski season is over.
>
> Thank you for doing business with us. If you have any further questions, please do not hesitate to call or message us.

Critical Thinking

Why should resale and sales promotional material be included in an order refusal?

When handling problems with orders, use the inductive approach to minimize the customer's disappointment related to problems with orders. Additionally, incorporate resale and sales promotional material to make customers' desire for the merchandise or service so strong that they will be willing to wait for it, purchase it through conventional merchandising outlets, or change the order as the writer recommends—whatever the problem might be.

Companies may prepare form letters or e-mails for repeated requests and problems with orders that involve inexpensive merchandise that do not represent a major disappointment to the customer. If you choose to follow the timely, economical path of sending a form letter, follow the guidelines you learned in Chapter 5. Your personalized letter or e-mail message should address the customer's specific problem and avoid the cold, indifferent tone communicated in the form letter on page 259. The writer states bluntly that the company doesn't sell to consumers, rather than presenting the advantages customers receive from the company's policy to distribute merchandise through dealers and thus build goodwill for the company and its products.

Figure 7-7

Good Example of a Claim Denial

Inductive Outline for Denying an Adjustment

1. Begin with a neutral or factual sentence that leads to the reasons behind the refusal.
2. Present the reasons and explanations.
3. Present the refusal in an unemphatic manner.
4. Provide a counterproposal that expresses what you are able to do.
5. Close with a thought related to the message or to the business relationship that does not address the refusal.

Legal and Ethical Constraints

Avoids corrective language that might insult, belittle, or offend.

Uses a subject line that provides the subject of the letter without revealing the refusal.

Uses resale to cushion the bad news and lead into the explanation.

Presents a clear explanation of the reasons behind the restocking policy with emphasis on ways the reader benefits from the policy.

Implies the refusal by stating the amount of the enclosed check.

Shifts emphasis away from the refusal by presenting a silver-lining sales promotion on next season's merchandise.

Format Pointers

- Uses simplified block format because the writer does not know the gender of the receiver. The courtesy title is omitted to avoid possible embarrassment.
- Specifies enclosure to emphasize the importance of the exact items.

NEWPORT LEISURE INDUSTRIES

860 MONMOUTH STREET
NEWPORT, KY 41071-6218

TELEPHONE: 800-424-6000
FAX: 800-424-0583

June 14, 2004

Lindsey Gauvin
Snowcap Limited
905 Southhaven Street
Santa Fe, NM 87501-7313

Restocking of Returned Merchandise

The HighFly skis you stocked this past season are skillfully crafted and made from the most innovative materials available. Maintaining a wide selection of quality skiing products is an excellent strategy for developing customer loyalty and maximizing your sales.

Our refund policies provide you the opportunity to keep a fully stocked inventory at the lowest possible cost. You receive full refunds for merchandise returned within 10 days of receipt. For unsold merchandise returned after the primary selling season, a modest 15 percent restocking fee is charged to cover our costs of holding this merchandise until next season. The enclosed check for $2,069.76 covers merchandise you returned at the end of February.

While relaxing from another great skiing season, take a look at our new HighFly skis and other items available in the enclosed catalog for the 2005 season. You can save 10 percent by ordering premium ski products before May 10.

Leigh Weseli

Leigh Weseli
Credit Manager

Enclosures: Check and catalog

We have your recent request that we ship you a **[ITEM]**. Unfortunately, we do not sell directly to consumers. Your nearest dealer is **[DEALER]** whose address is **[ADDRESS]**. May we suggest that you place your order there. Thank you for your interest in our merchandise.

Let's consider an example of customers who order one item when they can more profitably use another. The contractor for an exclusive country club has ordered a wet sprinkler system not recommended for cold climates. Filling the order as submitted would be a mistake, and the customer could incur significant water damage if the water pipes froze. Although the form letter in Figure 7-8 may achieve the desired results (convince the recipient that the wrong sprinkler system was ordered), the revised letter in Figure 7-9 is more effective. Note the empathetic tone and complete explanation presented in terms of the benefit to the receiver and the helpful offer to work with the architect to redesign the plan. The resale and the sales promotional material in this individualized letter did not cost anything—the company had to communicate with the customer anyway. The receiver is almost sure to read this material—something that cannot be said of the many sales messages that are instantly discarded.

Critical Thinking

Have you ever received a refusal or cancellation of an order you placed? What was the reason?

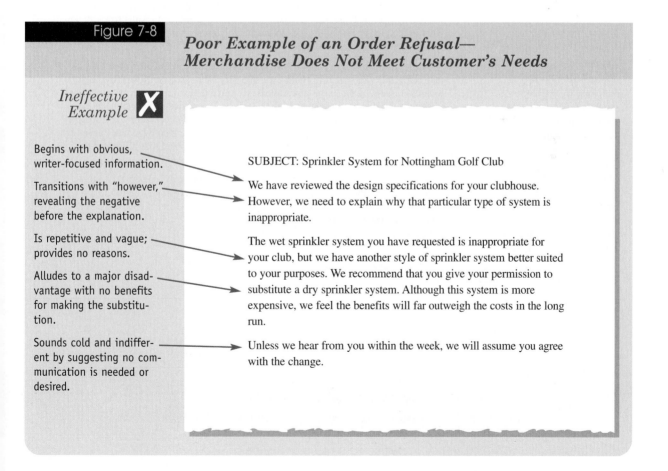

Figure 7-8

Poor Example of an Order Refusal—Merchandise Does Not Meet Customer's Needs

Ineffective Example **X**

Begins with obvious, writer-focused information.

Transitions with "however," revealing the negative before the explanation.

Is repetitive and vague; provides no reasons.

Alludes to a major disadvantage with no benefits for making the substitution.

Sounds cold and indifferent by suggesting no communication is needed or desired.

SUBJECT: Sprinkler System for Nottingham Golf Club

We have reviewed the design specifications for your clubhouse. However, we need to explain why that particular type of system is inappropriate.

The wet sprinkler system you have requested is inappropriate for your club, but we have another style of sprinkler system better suited to your purposes. We recommend that you give your permission to substitute a dry sprinkler system. Although this system is more expensive, we feel the benefits will far outweigh the costs in the long run.

Unless we hear from you within the week, we will assume you agree with the change.

Figure 7-9

Good Example of an Order Refusal—Merchandise Does Not Meet Customer's Needs

Acknowledges order but is noncommittal about shipment. Compliments clubhouse, which leads to need for alternative sprinkler system.

Continues with explanation by providing specific details about the receiver's needs.

Offsets higher cost of alternative by providing several advantages from reader's viewpoint. De-emphasizes negative point by placing it in a dependent clause of the complex sentence.

Includes an enclosure to present more details and to reinforce ideas in the letter.

Seeks permission to talk with architect to make the arrangement for alternative system easy.

HARRISON PLUMBING
2930 MAIN STREET/ LAUREL, MS 93440-0742 / PHONE: (606) 555-1900 / FAX: (606) 555-1763

September 2, 2004

Mr. Patrick Jacobsen, Manager
Nottingham Golf Club
957 Edgewood Boulevard
Green Bay, WI 54303-3498

Re: Purchase Order No. 47061

Dear Mr. Jacobsen

The design specifications for your new clubhouse reveal that you have spared no expense to provide members with spacious, multipurpose rooms complete with exquisite Williamsburg furnishings. Clearly, a sprinkler system designed to protect this valuable investment is one of your top priorities.

Currently your specifications include a traditional wet sprinkler system that carries water in the pipes to be used in case of fire. Over the years our experience has been that pipes often freeze when exposed to subfreezing temperatures over extended periods, a common condition in Wisconsin. The expansion that results from freezing water in the pipes causes the pipes to break, which results in extensive damage to the structure and its furnishings.

For this reason, we believe that a dry sprinkler system is preferable in our cold climate, especially for structures with exquisite furnishings such as yours. In the dry system, pressurized air in the pipes releases a valve that pumps water into the pipes *only* when a fire is detected. Although the dry system carries additional installation costs, you save money in the long run by preventing the unnecessary costs of structural repair, replacement of expensive furnishings, and the inconvenience caused by a burst water pipe. Please take a look at the enclosed brochure that illustrates the operation of the dry sprinkler system.

Mr. Jacobson, we will gladly consult with your architect to redesign the blueprints to include the dry system or a wet system with a heat source in the attic to warm the pipes during subfreezing temperatures. Just call us at 617-555-1900 with your instructions.

Sincerely

Anya Maxey

Anya Maxey
Owner

Enclosure

Format Pointers

- Uses reference line to direct reader to source documents.
- Includes enclosure notation to alert reader that other information is enclosed.

Denying Credit

Objective  7

Prepare message denying credit.

Legal & Ethical Constraints

Critical Thinking

What motivation does a business have for maintaining goodwill when writing a credit refusal?

Critical Thinking

Why discuss reasons for a credit refusal?

Legal & Ethical Constraints

Once you have evaluated a request for credit and have decided "No" is the better answer, your primary writing problem is to refuse credit so tactfully that you keep the business relationship on a cash basis. When requests for credit are accompanied with an order, your credit refusals may serve as acknowledgment letters. Of course, every business message is directly or indirectly a sales message. Prospective customers will be disappointed when they cannot buy on a credit basis. However, if you keep them sold on your goods and services, they may prefer to buy from you on a cash basis instead of seeking credit privileges elsewhere.

When the credit investigation shows that applicants are poor credit risks, too many credit writers no longer regard them as possible customers. They write to them in a cold, matter-of-fact manner. They do not consider that such applicants may still be interested in doing business on a cash basis and may qualify for credit later.

In credit refusals, as in other types of refusals, the major portion of the message should be an explanation for the refusal. You cannot expect your receiver to agree that your "No" answer is the right answer unless you give the reasons behind it. Naturally, those who send you credit information will expect you to keep it confidential. If you give the reasons without using the names of those from whom you obtained your information, you are not violating confidence. You are passing along the truth as a justification for your business decision.

Both writers and readers benefit from the explanation of the reasons behind the refusal. For writers, the explanation helps to establish fair-mindedness; it shows that the decision was not arbitrary. For receivers, the explanation not only presents the truth to which they are entitled, it also has guidance value. From it they learn to adjust habits and, as a result, qualify for credit purchases later.

Because of the legal implications involved in refusing credit, a legal counsel should review your credit refusal letters to ensure that they comply with laws related to fair credit practices. For example, the Equal Credit Opportunity Act (ECOA) requires that the credit applicant be notified of the credit decision within 30 calendar days following application. Applicants who are denied credit must be informed of the reasons for the refusal. If the decision was based on information obtained from a consumer reporting agency (as opposed to financial statements or other information provided by the applicant), the credit denial must include the name, address, and telephone number of the agency. It must also remind applicants that the Fair Credit Reporting Act provides them the right to know the nature of the information in their credit file. In addition, credit denials must include a standard statement that the ECOA prohibits creditors from discriminating against credit applicants on the basis of a number of protected characteristics (race, color, religion, national origin, sex, marital status, age). Additional information related to this legislation is included in the accompanying Strategic Forces feature "The Fair Credit Reporting Act."

The Fair Credit Reporting Act

If you have ever applied for a charge account, a personal loan, insurance, or a job, someone is probably keeping a file on you. Your credit report contains information on how you pay your bills, and whether you have been sued, arrested, or have filed for bankruptcy in the past seven years. Also included in your report are your Social Security number, date of birth, current and previous addresses, telephone numbers, and employment information. The companies that gather and sell this information are called credit reporting agencies, of which the most common type is the credit bureau. The three main credit bureaus, Equifax, Experian (formerly TRW), and Trans Union, sell information to employers, insurers, and other businesses in the form of consumer, or credit, reports. Anyone with a "legitimate business need" can gain access to your credit history, including lenders, landlords, insurance companies, prospective employers to whom you have given consent, and state child support enforcement agencies.

In 1970, Congress passed the Fair Credit Reporting Act (FCRA) to give consumers specific rights in dealing with credit reporting agencies. The act was significantly overhauled in 1996, and various amendments have been enacted since then. The Fair Credit Reporting Act (FCRA) gives consumers specific protections when they apply for and are denied credit:

- When credit or employment is denied based on information in a credit report, the credit grantor must tell the consumer the name and address of the credit bureau used to secure the information.

- The credit bureau must supply the consumer with a free copy of his or her credit report if the consumer asks for it within 30 days of being denied credit. (Credit bureaus voluntarily extend this time to within 60 days of applying for credit.)

- If the consumer believes that information on the credit report is inaccurate, the credit bureau must investigate the item within a "reasonable time," generally defined as 30 days, and remove the item if it is inaccurate or cannot be verified as accurate.

- Consumers may request that the credit bureau not distribute their names and contact information for unsolicited credit and insurance offers.

- Complaints against credit reporting agencies may be filed with the Federal Trade Commission, Washington, DC.

Responsible consumers should check their credit reports periodically, since information in them could affect their ability to get jobs, mortgages, loans, credit cards, or insurance. A *Consumer Reports* study reported that more than 50 percent of credit reports checked contained errors. An individual may request a copy of his or her credit report any time by contacting the credit reporting agency, who may not charge more than $9 for the report.[4]

Application

Visit the following Internet sites to obtain further information about the Fair Credit Reporting Act, credit bureaus, and abuses in credit reporting:

http://what-credit-report-scores-mean.com/

http://www.privacyrights.org/fs/fs6-crdt.htm

After reviewing the information, enumerate other specific consumer safeguards provided by the laws regarding credit reporting and some precautionary measures consumers can take to protect themselves against abuse.

Critical Thinking

Why is a poorly written refusal worse than an unsatisfactory spoken one?

To avoid litigation, some companies choose to omit the explanation from the credit denial letter and invite the applicant to call or come in to discuss the reasons. Alternately, they may suggest that the receiver obtain further information from the credit reporting agency whose name, address, and telephone number are provided.

Assume that a retailer of electronic devices has placed an initial order and requested credit privileges. After examining financial statements that were enclosed, the wholesaler decides the request should be denied. Review the letter in Figure 7-10 to identify techniques used to refuse credit while preserving relations with this customer—who may very well have good credit in the near future.

Critical Thinking

What is a good counterproposal in a credit refusal message?

The credit refusal in Figure 7-10 provides an explanation for the refusal and offers a 1 percent discount for goods purchased on a cash basis. No information about a credit reporting agency is necessary because the applicant provided all the information on which the decision was based. It makes no apology for action taken that would only cause the applicant to speculate that the decision was arbitrary.

Including resale is helpful in a credit refusal letter because it

- might cause credit applicants to prefer your brand and perhaps be willing to buy it on a cash basis.
- suggests that the writer is trying to be helpful.
- makes the writing easier—negative thoughts are easier to de-emphasize when cushioned with resale material and when you seem confident of future cash purchases.
- can confirm the credit applicant's judgment. (Suggesting the applicant made a good choice of merchandise is an indirect compliment.)

Delivering Constructive Criticism

Objective 8

Prepare messages that provide constructive criticism.

A person who has had a bad experience as a result of another person's conduct may be reluctant to write or speak about that experience. However, because one person took the time to communicate, many could benefit. Although not always easy or pleasant, communicating about negatives can be thought of as a civic responsibility. For example, a person who returns from a long stay at a major hotel might, upon returning home, write a letter or e-mail to the management commending certain employees. If the stay had not been pleasant and weaknesses in hotel operation had been detected, a tactful message pointing out the negatives would probably be appreciated. Future guests could benefit from the effort of that one person.

Before communicating about the problem, an individual should recognize the following risks: being stereotyped as a complainer, being associated with negative thoughts and perceived in negative terms, and

Critical Thinking

What can be gained from delivering a message that points out another person's mistakes? What are the risks?

Figure 7-10

Good Example of a Credit Denial

Implies receipt of order and uses resale to confirm applicant's good choice. Leads to explanation by implying approval of applicant's practice.

Leads to a discussion of the basis for the refusal and continues with the explanation.

De-emphasizes the refusal by using positive language recommending a counterproposal.

Looks confidently to the future and reminds the applicant of the commendable practice discussed earlier.

Encourages subsequent application and thus implies continued business. Reminds the merchant of the counterproposal.

Closes with sales promotion. Uses "timely" to remind the applicant of the commendable business practice and to develop unity.

LONESTAR ELECTRONICS

1800 Tally Ho Street ★ Reno, NV 89510-1800 ★ Telephone: (702) 555-3200 Fax: (702) 555-1039

May 16, 2004

Ms. Lila Ulsh
Purchasing Agent
Union Office Supply
1600 Main Street
Conroe, TX 77301-1600

Dear Ms. Ulsh:

The items listed in your order of May 6 have been selling very rapidly in recent weeks. Supplying customers' demands for the latest in electronic technology is sound business practice.

Another sound practice is careful control of indebtedness, according to specialists in accounting and finance. Their formula for control is to maintain at least a 2-to-1 ratio of current assets to current liabilities. Experience has taught us that, for the benefit of all concerned, credit should be available only to purchasers who meet that ratio. Because your ratio is approximately 1¼ to 1, you are encouraged to make cash purchases and take advantage of a 1 percent discount.

By continuing to supply your customers with timely merchandise, you should be able to improve the ratio. Then, we would welcome an opportunity to review your credit application. Use the enclosed envelope to send us your check for $1,487.53 to cover your current order, and your order will be shipped promptly.

Other timely items (such as the most recent in video games) are shown in the enclosed folder.

Sincerely,

Nancy Strasbaugh

Nancy Strasbaugh
Credit Manager

Enclosure

Legal and Ethical Constraints

Assures compliance with laws related to fair credit practices by including the reason for the denial.

appearing to challenge management's decisions concerning hotel operations. Yet such risks may be worth taking because of the benefits:

- The communicator gets a feeling of having exercised a responsibility.
- Management learns of changes that need to be made.
- The hotel staff about whom the message is written modifies techniques and is thus more successful.
- Other guests will have more enjoyable stays in the hotel.

In the decision to communicate about negatives, the primary consideration is intent. If the intent is to hurt or to get even, the message should not be sent. Including false information would be *unethical* and *illegal*. To avoid litigation charges and to respond ethically, include only specific facts you can verify and avoid evaluative words that present opinions about the person's character or ability. For example, instead of presenting facts, the message in Figure 7-11 judges the auditor sent to perform an audit at a client's office. In the sender's mind, the first sentence may be fair and accurate, but the reader may perceive "deplorable" as overly harsh. The phrase may convey the tone of a habitual fault-finder. Without details, the charges made in the second sentence lack force. If "deplorable" strikes the receiver as an exaggeration, the whole message loses impact. Overall, the message is short, general, and negative. By comparison, the

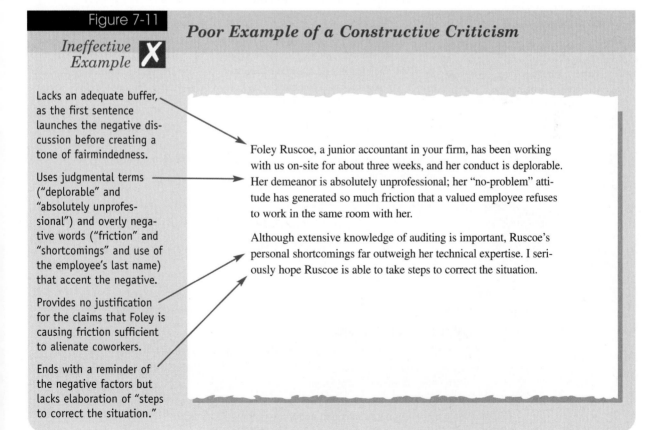

Figure 7-11

Ineffective Example ✗

Poor Example of a Constructive Criticism

Lacks an adequate buffer, as the first sentence launches the negative discussion before creating a tone of fairmindedness.

Uses judgmental terms ("deplorable" and "absolutely unprofessional") and overly negative words ("friction" and "shortcomings" and use of the employee's last name) that accent the negative.

Provides no justification for the claims that Foley is causing friction sufficient to alienate coworkers.

Ends with a reminder of the negative factors but lacks elaboration of "steps to correct the situation."

Foley Ruscoe, a junior accountant in your firm, has been working with us on-site for about three weeks, and her conduct is deplorable. Her demeanor is absolutely unprofessional; her "no-problem" attitude has generated so much friction that a valued employee refuses to work in the same room with her.

Although extensive knowledge of auditing is important, Ruscoe's personal shortcomings far outweigh her technical expertise. I seriously hope Ruscoe is able to take steps to correct the situation.

revision in Figure 7-12 has positive intent, is factual, uses positive language, and leaves judgment to the recipient.

Figure 7-12

Good Example of a Constructive Criticism

FSC
2500 Lincoln Green Road / Austin, TX 78710-2500 / Phone: 512.555.9000 / Fax: 512.555.6573
FREEMAN STEEL CORPORATION

February 17, 2004

Mr. Preston Larsen
N. R. Larsen & Co.
8640 Hazel Park Drive
Austin, TX 78710-8640

Dear Preston:

Introduces a discussion of the audit work underway.

Foley Ruscoe, a junior accountant in your firm, has been working with us on-site for about three weeks. She is a very proficient auditor and did an excellent job of straightening out a technical tangle in our electronic accounting system last week.

Tries to convey fair-mindedness and establish credibility by acknowledging good points in a letter that discusses bad points.

Her demeanor, while friendly and open, has caused some of our employees to complain that she does not take her work seriously. She jokes with other members of the audit team, which disrupts the attention of our employees. Two or three of our managers also commented on Foley's dress—more appropriate for a round of tennis than a business office.

Presents a statement of fact without labeling it in negative terms. Judgment is left to the reader.

Foley is obviously quite good at her job; I know from conversations with her that she is sincere and has sound judgment. Please convey my concerns to Foley confidentially so that the rest of her time in our office will go more smoothly for Foley and for us.

Includes verifiable statements. If such conduct is deplorable and unprofessional, the recipient will be aware of it without the sender's use of such terms.

Sincerely,

Kerinda Nowicki

Kerinda Nowicki
Controller

Ends on a pleasant note that seeks to add credibility to the preceding negatives.

Legal and Ethical Constraints

- Is written with the positive intent to help—not to hurt someone or to get even.
- Avoids potential litigation charges by including specific, verifiable facts and avoiding evaluative, judgmental statements.
- Uses "confidential" as a safeguard; the information is intended for professional use only, not designed to hurt and not to be thought of as gossip.

Communicating Negative Organizational News

Objective **9**

Prepare messages communicating negative organizational news.

Being able to initiate messages that convey bad news is as important as responding "No" to messages from customers/clients and others outside the company. Employees are seeking, and expecting, *honest* answers from management about situations adversely affecting the company and thus its employees—slumping profits, massive layoffs as a result of downsizing, a variety of major changes in the organization, negative publicity that affects the overall health of the business and retirement plans, to name a few.

Managers who can communicate negative information in a sensitive, honest, and timely way can calm employees' fears and doubts and build positive employee relations. Effective managers recognize that employee morale, like customer goodwill, is fragile—easily damaged and difficult to repair. If handled well, these bad-news messages related to the organization can be opportunities to treat employees with respect thus building unity and trust.

Strong internal communication is a key to involving employees in corporate strategies and building an important sense of community. The best companies use a variety of communication tools that promote an open exchange of honest, candid communication and welcome input from employees. Newsletters, e-mail updates, town hall or focus meetings, videoconferencing, phone calls, and discussion boards drive home relevant messages and allow employees to pose questions to management.

Honest, candid communication delivered on a regular, timely basis is more effective than occasional dire pronouncements made when disaster hits. This commitment to open internal communications builds a strong sense of community that prepares employees for bad news when it must be delivered.

© CINDY CHARLES/PHOTOEDIT

SPOTLIGHT COMMUNICATOR

Candid Communication Best in Any Situation

Following the Columbia disaster, the public face of NASA was a controlled, patient, and slightly bookish 50-year-old engineer, Ron Dittemore, NASA's space shuttle program manager. Those who know Dittemore described him as the perfect man to head the space shuttle program. They say he is open, painstakingly thorough, and unsurpassed in terms of overall, shuttle-related technical knowledge.

From his first press conference hours after Columbia was lost, Dittemore impressed many observers with thoughtful explanations, expansive answers to reporters' questions, and a willingness to share his off-the-cuff personal feelings about NASA's mission and his grief over the loss of friends. Though their questions were often pointed and antagonistic, most reporters and officials agree that Dittemore's answers were careful and well considered as well as candid and straightforward. "Human spaceflight is a passion," Dittemore said, a few hours after Columbia disintegrated over Texas. "It's an emotional event. And we work together, we work together as family members . . . It's a professional dependency.

And so, when we have an event like today where we lose seven family members, it is devastating to us."[5]

A firm believer in not passing the buck, Dittemore consistently took responsibility for decisions made throughout the shuttle program: "This is a team effort. When we succeed, we succeed as a team. When they go badly, we are together as a team, but I'm accountable to lead the team."[6] According to Aaron Cohen, a retired director of the center, Dittemore demonstrated the ability to express his knowledge so others could understand it: "If he didn't know, he said he didn't know. And if he made a mistake, he'd tell you he made a mistake and not be ashamed to do so. He has no hidden agenda. He wants people to know how it is."[7]

Two months following the Columbia disaster, Dittemore announced his intention to resign as manager of the space shuttle program. Though pre-Columbia discussions with NASA officials targeted a departure following the Columbia mission, the tragedy influenced Dittemore to stay on to

oversee the shuttle recovery effort and assist in a leadership transition. His replacement, William Parsons, says of Dittemore: "Ron showed us a strong character when we had our tragedy. I hope I don't have to deal with a situation like that, but I think I learned a lot from Ron and how he approached the event."[8] No matter what Ron Dittemore undertakes in his professional career, he will likely be best remembered by Americans and citizens of the world for his openness in handling the Columbia disaster.

Applying What You Have Learned

1. How did Dittemore's communication style prepare him for handling his responsibilities during the space shuttle Columbia disaster?

2. What is the relationship between accountability and communication?

Ron Dittemore, former NASA Space Shuttle Program Manager.

http://www.nasa.gov

Refer to ShowCASE, Part 3, at the end of the chapter to learn how organizations improve their crisis communication strategies through tragedies.

This quality two-way communication involves employees in corporate strategies; employees who are aware of company goals and potential problems feel connected and accountable. Informed employees are also better prepared for bad news than employees who only receive dire pronouncements of bad news. You will recall the discussion in Chapter 3 of the strong internal communications in place at Hallmark Cards to communicate openly, directly, and honestly about the company's long-term vision and financial goals. The sample employee newsletter, *Noon News*, on page 109 illustrates the valuable information provided to build a sense of community among employees.

Assuming this long-term commitment to keep employees informed, the following suggestions provide guidance in breaking bad news to employees:[9]

Critical Thinking

How does the phrase "knowledge is power" fit in situations when bad news is shared with employees?

- *Convey the bad news as soon as possible.* Timeliness will minimize damage caused by rumors and will give employees the concern and respect they deserve.
- *Give employees a complete, rational explanation of the problem.* Be candid about what is happening, why, and its effect on the employees. Provide enough detail to establish your credibility and provide context so employees can understand the situation. Stressing positive aspects will provide needed balance and avoid sugarcoating or minimizing the severity of the news to the point that the message is misunderstood.
- *Show empathy and respond to the employees' feelings.* Allow employees adequate time to react to the bad news. Listen attentively for understanding and then address the concerns, issues, and potential problems presented.
- *Follow up.* Let employees know what will happen next—what is expected of them and what the company will do and when. Plan to repeat your explanations and assurances that you are available to respond to concerns in several communications that extend over a given time.

Consider the company president who e-mailed employees about a relocation of the company's manufacturing facility in Figure 7-13. The president should not be surprised to learn that employees are resisting the relocation; some perceive the company to be an enemy uprooting families from their homes simply for financial gain. The president's revision, Figure 7-14, anticipates the employees' natural resistance to this stunning announcement and crafts a sensitive message using the following strategies: (a) uses a neutral subject line that introduces the topic without revealing the bad news, (b) includes a rational explanation focusing on benefits employees can gain from the move rather than a blunt statement that a decision had been made for the benefit of the company, (c) provides the bad news, (d) points out the silver lining associated with the move, and (e) follows the bad news with information and an offer of support.

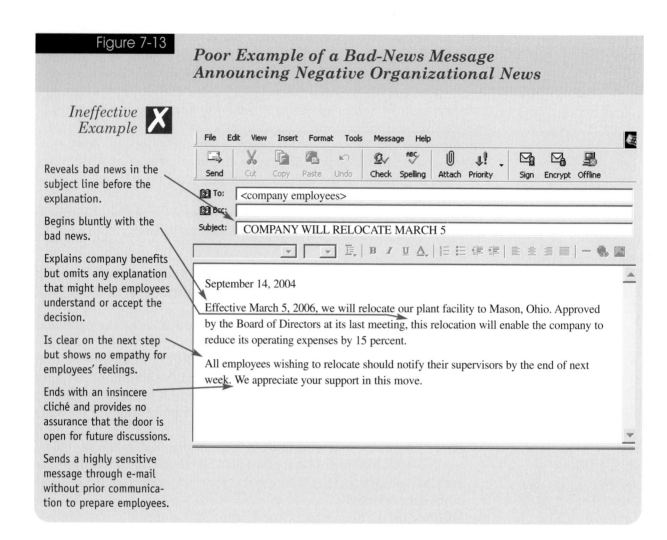

Figure 7-13

Poor Example of a Bad-News Message Announcing Negative Organizational News

Ineffective Example ✗

Reveals bad news in the subject line before the explanation.

Begins bluntly with the bad news.

Explains company benefits but omits any explanation that might help employees understand or accept the decision.

Is clear on the next step but shows no empathy for employees' feelings.

Ends with an insincere cliché and provides no assurance that the door is open for future discussions.

Sends a highly sensitive message through e-mail without prior communication to prepare employees.

File   Edit   View   Insert   Format   Tools   Message   Help

Send   Cut   Copy   Paste   Undo   Check   Spelling   Attach   Priority   Sign   Encrypt   Offline

To: <company employees>
Bcc:
Subject: COMPANY WILL RELOCATE MARCH 5

September 14, 2004

Effective March 5, 2006, we will relocate our plant facility to Mason, Ohio. Approved by the Board of Directors at its last meeting, this relocation will enable the company to reduce its operating expenses by 15 percent.

All employees wishing to relocate should notify their supervisors by the end of next week. We appreciate your support in this move.

A printed memo is a more effective channel for communicating this sensitive and official information than the efficient, yet informal, e-mail message. The revision indicates that the company's internal communications (newsletters and intranet) have been used to prepare the employees for this negative announcement. Thus, the official memo is no surprise; nor is the company's commitment to listen to the employees' concerns and to provide up-to-date information as it develops.

Before developing a bad news message, study the overall suggestions in the "General Writing Guidelines" placed before the activities in Chapter 5 and the specific suggestions in this chapter's "Check Your Communication" checklist. Compare your work with this checklist again after you have prepared a rough draft, and make any revisions.

Figure 7-14

Good Example of a Bad-News Message Announcing Negative Organizational News

Inductive Outline for Bad-News Memorandum

1. Begin with a neutral idea that leads to the reasons for the bad news.
2. Present the facts, analysis, and reasons for the bad news.
3. Present the bad news, using positive tone and de-emphasis techniques.
4. Include a counterproposal or silver lining idea to shift focus away from the bad news.
5. Close with an idea that shifts the emphasis away from the bad news.

Uses a subject line to introduce the topic but does not reveal the bad news.

Uses a buffer to introduce a topic familiar to employees through previous communication and lead into reasons.

Provides a rational explanation including benefits the company and employees will gain from the relocation.

Presents the bad news while reminding receiver of the benefits.

Shows empathy by assuring that no one's job is in jeopardy.

Follows up assuring continued exchange of timely information through discussions and web pages.

Ends with a positive appeal for unity.

Legal and Ethical Constraints Issue

Selects a memo rather than an e-mail as the appropriate channel for conveying a sensitive message.

INTEROFFICE MEMORANDUM

TO: All Employees
FROM: Wesley Moskal, President   WM
DATE: September 14, 2004
SUBJECT: PROPOSED PLAN FOR INCREASING MANUFACTURING CAPACITY

Growth presents its challenges. As we have projected, increased demand for our product will soon exceed the capabilities of our present production facilities as you know from information we've shared in recent newsletters and on the intranet. For some time we have been studying whether to expand our current manufacturing facility or relocate to another site.

High property taxes and transportation cost increases every year are compelling reasons to consider alternative sites. Likewise, attracting new talent into this high-cost metro area has become more difficult each year. In fact, both of our newly hired unit supervisors are commuting over one hour just to obtain affordable housing.

While relocating could provide a long-term economic benefit to the company, moving out of New York City could enhance the quality of life for us all. In a suburban city, we could enjoy day-to-day living in a relaxed, small-town environment with all the benefits of a large city only a short drive away. These factors have convinced us that moving the manufacturing facility to Mason, Ohio, a thriving suburb located approximately ten miles north of Cincinnati, would benefit the company and our employees.

Be assured you may resume your duties at the same structure should you choose to relocate. Your supervisor will explain the logistics of the relocation at your unit's next meeting. In the meantime, visit the Mason link on the company intranet to read preliminary information about the move and more about what Ohio can offer us and our families. You'll also want to visit this link periodically for relocation updates and to check the FAQ page we're compiling daily to respond to your concerns as they arise. Now let us all work together for a smooth transition to many challenging opportunities awaiting us in Mason.

Summary

1. **Explain the steps in the inductive outline and the importance of selecting an appropriate communication channel for bad news.** When the reader can be expected to be *displeased* by the message, the reasons for the refusal are presented before the main idea. The inductive approach is appropriate for letters denying an adjustment, refusing an order for merchandise, refusing credit, sending constructive criticism, or negative organizational messages.

   The steps in the inductive outline include (1) introducing the topic with a neutral idea that sets the stage for the explanation; (2) presenting a concise, logical explanation for the refusal; (3) implying or stating the refusal using positive language; (4) offering a counterproposal or silver lining statement that shifts focus toward the positive; and (5) closing with a positive, courteous ending that shifts the focus away from the bad news. While bad-news messages are typically expressed using paper documents or face-to-face means, electronic channels may be appropriate under certain circumstances.

2. **Identify exceptions to using the inductive approach to communicate bad news.** The deductive approach can be used to communicate bad news when (a) the letter is the second response to a repeated request; (b) a very small, insignificant matter is involved; (c) a request is obviously ridiculous, immoral, unethical, illegal, or dangerous; (d) a writer's intent is to "shake" the receiver; or (e) a writer-reader relationship is so close and long-standing that satisfactory human relations can be taken for granted.

3. **Discuss strategies for developing the five components of a bad-news message.** Follow these guidelines when developing the five components of a bad news message.

   Introductory Paragraph. The first sentence of a bad news letter should (a) buffer the bad news that will follow, (b) identify the subject of the message without stating the obvious, and (c) serve as a transition into the explanation. Avoid empty acknowledgments of the obvious, tipping off the bad news too early, and starting too positively so as to build false hopes. Effective beginning paragraphs might include a compliment, a point of agreement, good news, resale, a review of the circumstances related to the message, or an expression of gratitude.

   Facts, Analysis, and Reasons. This important section includes a concise, logical discussion of the reasons for the refusal that a receiver can understand and thus be prepared to accept the refusal statement as valid. The reasons section should (a) provide a smooth transition from the opening paragraph to the explanation, (b) present one or more reasons that are logical to the reader, (c) show reader benefit and/or consideration, and (d) avoid using "company policy" as the reason.

   Bad-News Statement. When writing the bad-news sentence, position the bad news strategically by (a) using the inductive approach to sandwich the bad news between a logical explanation and a positive closing, (b) avoiding the placement of the refusal statement in a paragraph by itself where it would be highlighted, and (c) placing the negative message in the dependent clause of a complex sentence to de-emphasize the negative. Avoid overly negative words and statements that automatically set up barriers to your message. Instead, use positive techniques such as stating what you can do rather than what you cannot do or including a positive fact in the same sentence with the negative idea. Use the subjunctive mood or imply the bad news if you believe the reader will understand your refusal clearly. If you must state the bad news directly, avoid using a simple sentence for the refusal unless your intention is to emphasize the "No."

   Counterproposal or Silver Lining Statement. Follow the bad news with a tangible or intangible counterproposal representing another outcome or course of action or with a silver lining statement that points to some positive aspect of the situation. This technique provides the shift away from the negative and provides a logical progression into the empathetic message of the closing paragraph.

   Closing Paragraph. The closing paragraph should demonstrate empathy and should not include statements that may cause the reader to question the fairness of your decision. Do not mention the refusal in the final paragraph. Instead, end with an idea that brings a positive, unifying quality to the message; e.g., referring to a pleasant idea mentioned earlier in the message or using resale, sales promotion, or a counterproposal.

4. **Prepare messages refusing requests.** A message refusing a request begins with a neutral idea and presents the reasons before the refusal. The close may offer a counterproposal—an alternative to the action requested.

5. **Prepare messages denying claims.** A message denying a claim begins with a neutral or factual sentence that leads to the reason for the refusal. In the opening sentence you might include resale to reaffirm the reader's confidence in the merchandise or services. Next, present the explanation for the refusal and then the refusal in a positive, nonemphatic manner. Close with a positive thought such as sales promotion that indicates you expect to do business with the customer again.

6. **Prepare messages handling problems with customers' orders.** A message refusing an order implies receipt of the order and uses resale to reaffirm the customer's

Content

- Be sure the principal idea (the unpleasant idea or the refusal) is sufficiently clear.
- Use sufficient supporting details, and present them in a logical sequence.
- Verify accuracy of facts or figures.
- Structure the message to meet ethical and legal requirements.

Organization

- Structure the first sentence to introduce the general subject
  - without stating the bad news.
  - without leading a receiver to expect good news.
  - without making such an obvious statement as "I am replying to your letter" or "Your letter has been received."
- Precede the main idea (bad news) with meaningful discussion.
- Follow up the bad news with a counterproposal or silver lining statement that moves discussion into a positive mood.
- Use a closing sentence that is positive (an alternative, resale, or sales promotion).

Style

- Write clearly and concisely (e.g., words are easily understood).

- Use techniques of subordination to keep the bad news from emerging with unnecessary vividness. For example, bad news may
  - appear in a dependent clause.
  - be stated in passive voice.
  - be revealed through indirect statement.
  - be revealed through the use of subjunctive mood.
- Use first person sparingly or not at all.
- Make ideas cohere by avoiding abrupt changes in thought.
- Keep sentences and paragraphs relatively short, and vary length and structure.
- Use original expression (sentences are not copied directly from the definition of the problem or from sample documents in the text); omit clichés.

Mechanics

- Assure that keyboarding, spelling, grammar, and punctuation are perfect.

Format

- Use a correct document format.
- Assure the document is appropriately positioned.
- Include standard document parts in appropriate position.
- Include special parts if necessary (subject line, enclosure, copy, etc.).

---

confidence in the merchandise or service. Continue with reasons for your procedures or actions and benefits to the customer. Close with information needed for the customer to reorder or anticipate later delivery.

7. **Prepare messages denying credit.** Credit refusal letters must comply with laws related to fair credit practices and should be reviewed carefully by legal counsel. Begin the letter by implying receipt of an order and using resale that could convince the applicant to buy your merchandise on a cash basis when he or she learns later that credit has been denied. You must provide an explanation for the refusal (in writing or verbally) and may encourage the customer to apply for credit later or offer a discount on cash purchases. Your legal counsel may advise that you omit the explanation and invite the applicant to call or come in to discuss the reasons or to obtain more information from the credit reporting

agency whose name, address, and telephone number you provide in the letter.

8. **Prepare messages providing constructive criticism.** The motive for delivering constructive criticism should be to help—not to get even. The message includes verifiable facts and omits evaluative words, allowing the recipient to make logical judgments based on facts.

9. **Prepare messages communicating negative organizational news.** Negative information about an organization should be communicated to employees and outside parties in a sensitive, honest, and timely manner. These messages include negative decisions related to declining financial position and major changes in the organization and its policies. Because of the importance of maintaining goodwill, use the inductive approach for organizational messages that convey bad news.

Discussion Boards Accommodate Online Brainstorming

One of the best uses of a company intranet is its ability to draw people together to share information. When Diane Watkins, State Farm senior marketing specialist, posted her ten best sales tips on the company's intranet discussion board, what happened next was a sales manager's dream come true. Over 40 agents nationwide added their own tips, and hundreds read the postings.* Online brainstorming through discussion boards, also known as electronic bulletin boards, is one of the most important success stories of the digital economy.

 InfoTrac College Edition. Access http://www.infotrac.thomsonlearning.com to read more about how discussion boards promote learning from others.

O'Leary, M. (2002, January). SupportPath.com: Bulletin board epitome; this site's support groups offer a valuable online communication service. *Information Today, 14–17.*

Compile a list of the unique advantages offered by discussion board communication.

 Text Support Web Site. Visit http://lehman.swlearning.com to learn more about discussion board communications. Refer to Chapter 7's Electronic Café that links you to an article on how to make sure your discussion board communications are effective.

 WebTutor Advantage. Your instructor will give you directions about how to access the discussion board in your WebTutor and post your thoughts on the following: Discussion board communication fills a niche not addressed by other forms of communication because . . .

 Professional Power Pak. Access your PPP CD for tips on making the most of your discussion board participation.

* Intranet use—smart, fast, efficient. (2002, January). *Work & Family, 7–8.*

Chapter Review

1. Explain the appropriate channel and outline for a message that conveys bad news. (Obj. 1)

2. Discuss two reactions the reader might have toward a message if the refusal precedes the explanation. (Obj. 1)

3. How can writers reduce the risk that recipients will become impatient while reading explanations that precede bad news? (Obj. 1)

4. List conditions under which a writer would be justified in stating bad news in the first sentence. (Obj. 2)

5. What three functions does the first paragraph of a bad-news message serve? Does "I am responding to your letter of the 25th" accomplish all of these functions? Explain. (Obj. 3)

6. Discuss how a counterproposal and implication can be used to de-emphasize the bad-news statement and assist a communicator in achieving the human relations goal of business communication. (Obj. 3)

7. What objectives should the final paragraph accomplish? Should the closing sentence apologize for action taken? Explain. (Obj. 3)

8. Should a communicator strive to achieve unity by referring to the statement of refusal in the last paragraph? Explain. (Obj. 3)

9. In which part of a refusal message would resale and sales promotional material be most appropriate? Explain. (Objs. 3–4)

10. List three reasons businesses might refuse to send merchandise customers have ordered. (Obj. 6)

11. Are form letters recommended when handling problems related to orders? Explain. (Obj. 6)

12. What advice would you give regarding use of template documents available with word processing software? (Objs. 1–7)

13. Discuss the legal implications involved in writing credit refusals. (Obj. 7)

14. What elements make criticism "constructive"? (Obj. 8)

15. Why is the effective handling of negative information of such importance to a company? (Obj. 9)

Digging Deeper

1. *Saying "no" is not difficult; the challenge is to do so while protecting goodwill.* Explain the rationale and significance of this statement.

2. Frequent channels for delivering business messages include written, electronic, and face-to-face means. What criteria would you use in selecting the appropriate channel for delivering bad news?

To check your understanding of the chapter, take the practice quizzes at **http://lehman.swlearning.com** or your WebTutor course.

Activities

1. **Appropriateness of the Inductive Outline (Objs. 1, 2)**

   In pairs, describe either a personal or business-related situation you faced in which you had to share bad news with someone. How did you structure your message? What channel did you use for sharing the news? Was your strategy effective?

2. **Effective Opening and Closing Paragraphs (Objs. 1–9)**

   Study each of the good examples in the chapter and compile a list of the approaches used to open and to close the document in a positive way.

3. **De-emphasizing Negative Ideas (Objs. 3, 4)**

   Prepare a list of techniques for de-emphasizing a refusal. You may wish to refer to the techniques discussed in Chapter 3 ("Project a Positive, Tactful Tone"). Provide an example of your own for each technique.

4. **Determining Appropriate Sequence of Ideas: Deductive or Inductive (Objs. 1, 2)**

   Identify whether each of the following messages should be written deductively or inductively based on the reader's likely reaction to the message.

   a. A message to the manufacturer of a national tread-mill company explaining dissatisfaction with the unit and requesting a refund. A television advertisement shows an exerciser running on the unit, but the customer cannot run on the unit without being pushed off the front.

   b. A message from a sales manager to a customer explaining inability to meet a promised deadline for delivery of goods.

   c. A message from a customer service manager saying no, once again, to a customer's third request for a refund that was previously denied.

   d. A message from a company president to reject a contract proposal offered by an international business partner whose cultural style is direct and forthright.

   e. A message from the manufacturer of a national-brand treadmill refusing to extend an adjustment to a customer who cannot run on the unit.

   f. A message to an investment client who is questioning the accuracy of his statement because he doesn't understand the differences between front-load or back-load mutual funds.

   g. A message refusing a customer's request to reduce his monthly payment for Internet services. He contends busy signals prevented him from connecting most of the time.

   h. A message from an automobile dealer informing a customer that the delivery of a custom-order vehicle will be delayed two months.

   i. A message from an appliance manufacturer authorizing the replacement of an under-the-counter ice machine that is still under warranty.

   j. A message from a human resources manager to refuse an employee's request that the manager "fudge" to a lender about his reported income to help him qualify for a home loan.

   k. A message from a financial planner apologizing for her failure to place an order to buy mutual funds for a customer.

   l. A message from the chief financial officer of a local business agreeing to serve on a fund-raising committee for a community service organization.

   m. A message extending appreciation for the outstanding work of a consulting firm that spearheaded your successful effort to obtain ISO 9000 certification.

   n. A message acknowledging shipment of an order and extending credit to a first-time customer.

5. **Choosing an Effective Channel. (Obj. 1)**

   For each of the situations in Activity 4, decide which communication channel would be most appropriate. Explain your reasoning.

6. **Writing Inductive Openings (Objs. 1–9)**

   Revise the following openings so that they are inductive.

   a. Because your three-in-one printer did not show any defects in workmanship until three months after the warranty expired, we cannot honor your claim.

   b. We received many applications for this position, but an internal candidate was selected.

   c. Dampier Enterprises cannot participate in the Magnolia Charity Benefit this year.

   d. This letter is in response to your complaint of April 9.

   e. Company policy does not allow me to approve the proposed transaction.

   f. We cannot grant you a refund. However, if you will agree to pay the shipping costs, we will send replacements for your defective spinning reels.

7. **Revising for Positive Tone (Obj. 3)**

   Revise the following refusal sentences to ensure positive tone.

   a. We cannot accept an application sent after May 9.

   b. Employees cannot smoke in the main office.

   c. I am sorry, but we cannot be responsible for the service charges on your car; the damage occurred at the dealership, not our factory.

   d. Your request for transfer to Kyoto, Japan, has been denied.

   e. We cannot accept this poorly organized report.

8. **Document for Analysis: Denying an Employee's Request (Obj. 4)**

   Analyze the following e-mail. Pinpoint its strengths and weaknesses and then revise the e-mail as directed by your instructor.

   Visit the Interactive Study Center at **http://lehman. swlearning.com** for a downloadable version of this activity.

   > Your desire to participate in this fund-raising activity is admirable, but we must refuse to support your relay team. Ashland Industries does not have any specific rules in place to handle this particular situation, but as the president it is my responsibility to safeguard expenditures of this type. Six-hundred dollars is a lot of money. Perhaps you should consider raising the money yourself.
   >
   > If you have questions about this decision, please contact your data control manager for a copy of our corporate policy on charitable contributions.

9. **Document for Analysis: Denying a Request (Obj. 4)**

   Analyze the following letter. Pinpoint its strengths and weaknesses and then revise the letter as directed by your instructor.

   Visit the Interactive Study Center at **http://lehman. swlearning.com** for a downloadable version of this activity.

   > Dear Kyle:
   >
   > I am pleased and honored to have been asked to serve as treasurer of the United Way campaign for the coming year.
   >
   > However, I regret to inform you that I cannot accept this position. Don't take this personally as it is my personal policy to refuse all nominations. The demands of my accounting practice keep me on the road an enormous amount of time, and you must understand that sleep is a luxury during the notorious "busy season" for accountants.
   >
   > Once again, I appreciate the confidence you have placed in me but am sorry that my plate is much too full to accept this outstanding service opportunity. Please contact me in the future if I can help in any way.

10. **Document for Analysis: Denying a Claim (Obj. 5)**

    Analyze the following letter. Pinpoint its strengths and weaknesses and then revise the letter as directed by your instructor.

    Visit the Interactive Study Center at **http://lehman. swlearning.com** for a downloadable version of this activity.

    > I am sorry you were dissatisfied with the sports celebrity we subbed for your dedication ceremony. Although you obviously feel your claim has merit, refusing to pay us is just not going to work for us.
    >
    > Ms. Vonetta Flowers' injury and hospitalization was out of our control—just not our fault. We felt sure you would be overjoyed we came through with someone at the last minute. Our contract states specifically that we would provide you a substitute; we did our part and we expect you to do your part and pay us for our services.
    >
    > We appreciate your business and hope that you will consider us the next time you need a sports celebrity for a function.

Applications

Read   Think   Write   Speak   Collaborate

1. **Communication Success Stories (Objs. 1–9)**

   Conduct an electronic search to locate an article that deals with successful negative communication in a company or organization. Prepare an abstract of the article that includes the following parts: (1) article citation, (2) name of organization/company, (3) brief description of communication technique/situation, and (4) outcome(s) of the successful communication. As an alternative to locating an article, write about a successful communication situation in the organization/company for which you work.

   Required: Present your abstract in a memo. Refer to Appendix B for examples for formatting citations. Be prepared to give a short presentation in class.

2. **Making Criticism Pay Off (Obj. 9)**

   Visit the text support site at **http://lehman. swlearning.com** and read the enrichment content,

   "Tips for Conducting an Effective Employee Performance Review." Then locate and read the following article available from InfoTrac (**http://www.infotrac.thomsonlearning. com**) or another database from your campus library:

   Pollock, T. (2003, January). Make your criticism pay off. *Electric Light & Power*, 91(1), 31.

   Required: Recall an experience where you received or gave constructive criticism in an academic or work situation. What was your perception of the sender's motive? What outcome(s) was achieved by the confrontation? Using the advice from your text and the readings, summarize the techniques that you believe kept the criticism on target. What advice would you give for delivering the criticism that would have led to more positive results? Be prepared to present your ideas in a brief presentation to the class.

Read   Think   Write   Speak   Collaborate

3. **Bad-News Speeches (Objs. 1–3, 9)**

   Refer to a recent political or business event in which bad news was shared. Prepare a written critique that includes (1) your assessment of the effectiveness of the message and the manner in which it was delivered, (2) an analysis of the results, and (3) a summary of what you learned from your analysis. Be prepared to share with the class in a brief presentation.

4. **Employee Bad News: Discontinue Downloading Audio Files (Obj. 9)**

   Opened during the late 1990s in southern California, Aspire Consulting has allowed its office employees the freedom of personal expression. At the extreme, some

   employees bring their pets to work, roller-blade to meetings, and play guitars to relieve stress. However, most employees simply enjoy playing music on their personal computers. As the director of computer security, it has come to your attention that the music industry has begun a campaign to prosecute and seek substantial fines against companies that allow employees to download copyrighted music files over the Web.

   Required: Write a memo to your employees instructing them to immediately delete and discontinue downloading music files. Identify the legal methods currently available that will enable them to continue listening to music and, therefore, preserve the current corporate culture.

Read   Think   Write   Speak   Collaborate

5. **Client Bad News: Going Paperless (Objs. 1–3)**

   Woodlands Mortgage Company sends its customers a printed monthly statement that reports the activity and balances of their mortgage and escrow accounts. The monthly statement has been an important element of a customer-service philosophy that has enabled the company to double in size over the past six years. Beginning next month, the company will discontinue sending printed statements to customers who pay their account using the company's online electronic payment service. Instead, customers will receive a monthly e-mail statement that includes the same account information and

   links to the online system where transaction history, tax information, and special promotions are available 24/7. However, a printed copy of the year-end tax information required for tax return preparation will be mailed.

   Required: Prepare the message that will appear in the bottom section of the last printed statement informing customers of the change in the monthly statement.

6. **Request Refusal: One Size Doesn't Fit All (Obj. 4)**

   Belmont Financing Corporation provides its regional managers with a car for travel among the retail locations within their regions. The corporate office purchases these cars from a single dealer and has purchased the same model and color for the past nine years. In your position as corporate controller, you have received a request from one manager who wants authorization to purchase a different model and color. The manager maintains that the car does not fit his personality and does not comfortably fit his 6'6" frame. After consulting with the legal department, you have decided to refuse his request to choose a color other than the "corporate color" but will allow him to select a larger car so long as it has a 5-star crash rating and portrays a professional, yet modest image.

Required: Send an e-mail to the manager, Josh Hundley, communicating your decision and requiring him to obtain your approval of the model selected.

7. Request Refusal: Parent Company Refuses to Continue Sponsoring Elementary School (Obj. 4)

Velson Mfg. Co., a family-owned business, has been the corporate sponsor for Lincoln Elementary School for the past ten years. The owner and the public relations director believe that supporting the community's education system has been a favorable public relations tool. Recently, Velson was merged into Wilson Industries. When approached by the school board president to renew financial commitment to the school, the president of Wilson refused. The president is not opposed to contributing to the community; however, top management at Wilson sees little, if any, merit in sponsoring an elementary school. Therefore, no financial resources are devoted to projects of this kind.

Required: As the public relations director, write the letter to the school board refusing to sponsor the school. Address it to Patty Leslie, School Board President, Lincoln Public Schools, P.O. Drawer 343, Lincoln, TX 78948-0343.

8. Request Refusal: Rejecting an Employee's Suggestion (Obj. 4)

Daniel Pelling, a driver for Atwood Corp., sent the following e-mail to the firm's suggestion box:

> Our manager informed us that you were looking for inexpensive ways of rewarding people who receive the employee-of-the month award. I believe you should give that person the week off with pay. You're going to pay the person anyway and the rest of us will work just a little harder to cover for that person.

Required: As the chief executive officer, write an e-mail message to Daniel Pelling rejecting his idea. Although you applaud his willingness to work a little harder, you are not sure that all employees would share his commitment. In addition, your human resources director pointed out that many employees work in unique jobs where vacation time must be planned in advance to keep the business operating efficiently.

9. Adjustment Refusal: Extended Warranty Claims Must Be Preauthorized (Obj. 5)

In your new position as manager of customer service department at Precision Warranty, you are reviewing form letters sent to customers in response to a number of standard claim issues. You are disturbed by the following form letter sent to customers who have submitted claims without preauthorization and feel sure this poor communication may be contributing to customer dissatisfaction and the increasing numbers of customers cashing out of their extended warranties. You begin to consider improvements in the letter that will help the customer understand the importance and simplicity of the preauthorization process. You're just asking the auto repair department to call your 800 number to verify that the repairs are covered under the warranty contract and to record your authorization number on the customer's copy of the auto repair invoice, which the customer will send directly to Precision Warranty.

> May 5, 2004
>
> KARYN ASH
> 90 FINCH COVE
> BATON ROUGE, LA 70821
>
> Re: Contract # 793810
> Date of claim: 2/8/04
>
> Dear Sir/Madam:
>
> We have reviewed your invoice for reimbursement of the above claim. Based upon this review, we are denying the claim due to the following reason(s):
>
> THE TERMS OF YOUR CONTRACT STATE THAT PRIOR AUTHORIZATION FROM THE ADMINISTRATOR IS REQUIRED FOR ANY REPAIR. THIS PROCEDURE WAS NOT FOLLOWED.
>
> Please review your service contract on procedures for filing a claim.
>
> Customer Service Department

Required: As the customer service manager, revise the form letter used to deny claims submitted without preauthorization. Your goal is to help the customer understand the policy and maintain confidence in your extended warranty.

10. Adjustment Refusal: Internet Connection Disrupts Business (Obj. 5)

Janice Bishop is a freelance photographer who operates from her home in Hillsboro, Oregon. Janice regularly uses e-mail to conduct her business, posting photograph samples on her web site and corresponding with customers via e-mail. A technical problem with her Internet service provider (ISP), PacLink, caused her web site to be down for two days. When service was restored, Janice learned that she missed the opportunity to sell $3,000 of photographs to a national magazine.

As an account representative of PacLink, you received a letter from Janice demanding payment for $3,000 in damages. PacLink's personal service contract includes a provision stating the company is not liable for any damages resulting from a loss in service. In contrast, the business service contract does provide for damages if service is not restored within eight hours. Janice chose to set up a personal account because of the significantly higher cost of business service accounts.

Required: Write the refusal to Janice Bishop, 89 Hawthorne Avenue, Crossville, TN 38555-3989.

11. **Adjustment Refusal: Monitoring Company Refuses Individual Payments (Obj. 5)**

Delta Monitoring Company provides home and business security system monitoring for customers throughout Kentucky. To minimize its administrative costs, Delta deals only with licensed security dealers. The dealers collect monitoring fees directly from their clients and forward the fees to Delta.

Avery Anderson, a client of Best Security Systems (BSS), called requesting that she be allowed to pay her monitoring fees directly to Delta. She states that BSS collects $30 a month, over twice the $14 monitoring rate charged by Delta. Although Ms. Anderson recognizes BSS deserves a reasonable fee for collecting the fee and arranging the monitoring service, she believes that $16 per month is exorbitant. Because security dealers use codes to lock the home controllers they install, Ms. Anderson is unable to switch security dealers without paying $500 to pay for a new home controller.

Required: Write the refusal to Avery Anderson, 2301 Webster Street, Lexington, KY 40523.

12. **Adjustment Refusal: Customer Seeks Adjustment of Bowling Fee (Obj. 5)**

Last month you opened Tiger Lanes, a modern bowling alley and entertainment center. Following the industry trend, you adopted a fee structure that charges by the minute rather than by the game. Rates vary from $.20 to $.50 per minute, based on the day of the week and the time of day. Charging customers by the minute has proven to be the most effective method to optimize lane usage and minimize wait time. Signs showing the fee structure are posted throughout the facility, and a minute counter constantly displays on the scoring monitor.

Despite your efforts to communicate this information, several customers have incurred relatively large bills because they kept the lane while taking frequent breaks and enjoying snacks from your deli. One customer, John

Sullivan, has written you a letter asking for a partial refund of the $180 bill his family incurred last Saturday night. His family of six used two lanes for three hours, bowling four games each. Mr. Sullivan remembers bowling for $1 per game when he was young and believes $48, or $2 a game per person, would be a fair price today.

Required: Write the refusal to John Sullivan, 8950 Rackley Way, Apartment #151, Pomona, CA 91766-0151.

13. **Telephone Response: Order Problem Tests Customer Loyalty (Obj. 5)**

As an account manager of Patriot, a manufacturer of limited-edition furniture, you recently shipped six highback, distressed-wood chairs to Nina Hughes, an interior designer who is one of your premier accounts. Because these chairs were a special order, Nina's customer had waited for over a year for delivery. You received a voice mail message from Nina explaining that the chairs will not stay together. The customer has tried gluing them, but the supports still come apart. You reported the problem to product development, who uncovered a flaw in the design of this chair—the supports are too short for the chair. Because you want to answer Nina's question as quickly as possible, you prepare to telephone her with an explanation and a promise to rush delivery of replacement chairs produced with the modified design, along with a $300 credit for the inconvenience this error has caused.

Required: Develop a voice script explaining how you intend to deliver this negative news with your long-standing customer (you're replacing the chairs but the remanufacture will require approximately three months for delivery).

14. **Order Refusal: Camera Accessories Needed to Ensure Customer Satisfaction (Obj. 6)**

HGA Electronics has received an order request from a new retailer for 100 units of three models of its digital video cameras. As the regional sales representative, you notice that the retailer has not ordered any of the normal accessories that would enable customers to utilize and enjoy their cameras fully.

Required: Research the Internet sites of companies that offer digital video cameras to identify the accessories that a retailer should stock to support the sales of today's digital video cameras. Write a letter to Joanne Gayle, buyer, suggesting that she add these specific accessories (at $15,000, her cost) to the order. Send the letter to Venice Electronic City, 530 Lakeland Mall, Annapolis, MD 21402.

15. **Order Refusal: Receiver's and Speakers' Capabilities Don't Match (Obj. 6)**

You have received a large order of a custom sound system from First National Bank. The bank plans to offer the system as a gift to customers purchasing a $25,000, five-year certificate of deposit. You have a problem with the order. The frequency response of the receiver is 20 to 20,000 Hz, but the frequency response for the speakers is only 35 to 18,000 Hz. Thus, the stereo receiver has the capacity to produce sound with deep, rich bass and high treble, but the speakers will not be capable of projecting these sounds. Suggest to the bank that they consider a system having components with matching frequency responses. The price for this new system will be slightly more than the system the bank ordered.

Required: Write the letter explaining the need to alter the component choices. Use an electronics catalog (printed or online) to specify the model numbers for the receiver and the speakers you are recommending; cite the frequency response of each model. Provide your telephone number and e-mail address so that the bank can call for additional information and authorize the order. Address the letter to Stephen Rogers, Vice President of Marketing, First National Bank, 54 Cloverleaf Mall, Harrisburg, PA 17105-0054.

16. Credit Refusal: Intern Must Manage Balances (Obj. 7)

Heritage Financial Services aggressively issues credit cards to college students. By maintaining low credit limits, the company is able to limit the nonpayment losses typically attributed to first-time credit cardholders. Angela Pearson, a current cardholder who has exhibited a good payment record, has requested her credit limit be raised from $500 to $3,000, noting she needs the higher limit to support the travel expenses inherent in her internship position with a national public relations firm.

Required: As a manager in the credit department, you can justify increasing the limit to only $1,000. Prepare a letter informing Angela of your decision and suggesting that she take advantage of the company's web site to monitor her balance and schedule bi-monthly payments directly from her checking account.

17. Credit Refusal: Loan Denied for Poor Credit Customer (Obj. 7)

Having decided to build an addition to their home, Larry and Alice Sherman made an application for a $35,000 loan from a personal finance company. A report from a consumer credit agency revealed a consistent record of slow payment. On more than one occasion, they paid only after forceful attempts at collection.

Required: As manager of the local branch of the finance company, write a refusal letter. Provide the name, address, and telephone number of the consumer reporting agency and invite the Shermans to come in to discuss the refusal. Write to Larry and Alice Sherman, P.O. Box 432, Baxter, WI 54321-5590.

18. Constructive Criticism: Golf Instruction Not Up to Par (Obj. 8)

As an avid golfer, you are constantly looking for anything that will enable you to improve your game. Until recently, you have consistently achieved positive results from the numerous training aids and golf lessons you have purchased. In a desperate attempt to take your game to the next level, you paid $1,000 to attend PineRidge Golf Academy, an exclusive golf school. During the first day, participants attend classes conducted by various instructors. On the second day, participants play one round of 18 holes accompanied by the instructor of their choice.

Because you were particularly impressed with the knowledge and teaching style of Stan Campbell, the putting instructor, you selected him to accompany you during your round. To your dismay, Stan did not exhibit the same qualities during the round that motivated you to select him. He rarely made comments or suggestions, even when you hit poor shots. In fact, you know he did not watch several of your shots. On numerous occasions he received and made calls on his cell phone, causing him to pay little or no attention to your shots. Although you were very pleased with the instruction received during the first day of the school, you are very disappointed with the quality of the second day. The chance to have a teaching golf professional accompany you on a round was the primary reason you were attracted to PineRidge.

Required: Prepare a letter to Thom Franks, Director, PineRidge Golf Academy, 34 Kinsey Drive, Kaukauna, WI 54130-9752. Your intent is to alert the director of Stan's shortcomings so that steps can be taken to help him modify his actions.

19. Employee Bad News: Employees to Pay for Fitness Center (Obj. 9)

For several years GTW Corporation has provided its members and their families with free memberships to the Fitness Club, a local health facility. The facility has recently undergone a significant expansion, including an indoor pool, climbing wall, and racquetball courts, and has notified its members of a rate increase effective next month. GTW's board of directors has rejected management's request to pay the incremental fees. Thus, management must inform employees that they must pay a portion of their membership fees. Specifically, each employee will be required to pay $10 per month and an additional $5 for each family member.

Required: As the director of human resources for GTW, write a memo announcing the rate increase. Your memo should request that employees complete a form authorizing an automatic withdrawal from their paychecks.

20. Employee Bad News: Pets No Longer Allowed in Office (Obj. 9)

When Andrea Fuller worked late at night or on the weekends, she brought her German Shepherd to the office to provide her with an added sense of security. The practice quickly gained popularity and soon spread to include other types of pets. Some employees have now begun bringing their pets during normal office hours. Not all of your employees are happy about this situation, and you have noticed that productivity appears to be declining. Therefore, you adopt a policy to ban the practice of bringing pets to the office.

Required: As managing partner of Synergy Consulting Group, write a memo to your employees informing them of the new no-pet policy.

Read   Think   Write   Speak   Collaborate

21. Critique of Bad-News Messages Produced by Real Companies (Objs. 1–9)

Locate an example of both a well-written and a poorly written bad-news message. Analyze the strengths and weaknesses of each document.

Required: Prepare a visual of each and present your critique to the class.

22. Request Refusal: Must Be Said in Person (Obj. 4)

Gulf South Communications Corporation has purchased a significant number of season tickets to the Riverside Community Theatre since its inaugural season in 1979. Gulf South distributes the tickets to special customers, vendors, and employees to foster goodwill and promote the company. Because of the financial crisis in the telecommunications industry, Gulf South's management has regrettably been forced to eliminate all noncritical expenditures. As a supervisor in the human resources department, you have been asked by management to inform Steve Cafferty, the business manager of the Theatre, that Gulf South will not purchase season tickets this year. Because the loss of your long-time support will be a hard blow to the Theatre, you decide to break the news to Steve over lunch at his favorite restaurant.

Required: Develop a voice script of the conversation you'd have with Steve conveying the company's disappointing decision. Your instructor may ask you to role play your conversation with another student in the class.

Read   Think   Write   Speak   Collaborate

23. Electronic Message Boards: The Good and the Bad (Objs. 1–9)

The Electronic Café for this chapter explores the powerful use of discussion boards to gather and share information on a topic and provides tips for effective participation in an online discussion. Despite the benefits of online brainstorming, storm waves are being generated as companies and individuals become victims of negative messages posted on the Internet. The widespread electronic distribution of these unflattering and possibly slanderous comments, often posted anonymously, is a major concern to many. Learn more about the negative effects of being "zapped in cyberspace" presented in the following articles, and examine the pros and cons of anonymity presented in the Internet Case for this chapter.

Zhivago, K. (2002). Loose cannons. CEOs, marketers, and message boards. *Adweek Magazine's Technology Marketing, 22*(3), 29.

Elvin, J. (2002). Grading the graders creates uproar. *Insight on the News, 18*(24), 35.

Required: Prepare a presentation that (a) summarizes the advantages and disadvantages of online discussions and (b) provides a checklist for writing an effective reply to an online posting calling for constructive criticism of a company or individual.

24. Evaluating Online Discussions (Objs. 1–9)

Visit the electronic bulletin board that allows students at your college/university to post faculty evaluations and select three to five postings for a professor(s) of your choice.

Required: Using the evaluation checklist developed in Application 23, critique the effectiveness of the postings, placing them in rank order of effectiveness. Make a brief team presentation to the class about your analysis that includes a visual illustrating an example of a poorly written and well-written posting. Be sure to omit all identification.

Communication Lessons Learned from Crisis Situations

In the years following the loss of Challenger, NASA scientists and engineers scrutinized the space shuttle program, seeking to reduce the chances of future tragedies. At the same time, the agency undertook to revise its crisis communications strategy that had been criticized as evasive. Learning from mistakes, however, can be difficult as there is often a tendency within an embattled company to want to get back to business as usual rather than seek to change its very culture.

- Visit the NASA web site at **http://www.nasa.gov** to learn about the ONE NASA initiative that emphasizes a unified strategic plan, a strong commitment to teamwork, tools and capabilities for greater collaboration, and more efficient systems within the Agency.
- Locate the following article that describes efforts of NASA and other organizations to learn from crisis situations and make positive changes as a result:

Creamer, M. (2003, February 17). Learning from past errors is vital to current crisis PR. *PR Week*, 9.

Write a short report on the evolutionary nature of a crisis communication plan. Use examples from your readings to illustrate your points.

Part 4 of the NASA ShowCASE focuses on media-friendly strategies for crisis communication and the role of supportive messages in coping with tragedy.

http://www.nasa.gov

Visit the text support site at **http://lehman.swlearning.com** to complete Part 4 of the NASA ShowCASE.

Anonymity in Cyberspace

Do you have a right to anonymity in cyberspace? Should you have this right? Two current views prevail about the right of anonymity. One view sees anonymity as limiting the free flow of information; by having a wealth of information available, people can communicate, shop, and conduct business with ease. Access to information allows you to find a friend's e-mail address that you had forgotten or to track down an old friend in another city. The opposing view sees the right to anonymity as a protection of individual privacy; without anonymity, unidentified parties can track where you go in cyberspace, how often you go there, and with whom you communicate. At the present time, you are typically required to reveal your identity when engaging in a wide range of activities. Every time you use a credit card, e-mail a friend, or subscribe to an online magazine, an identifiable record of each transaction is created and linked to you. But must this always be the case? Are there situations where transactions may be conducted anonymously, yet securely? Several methods currently exist for surfers to protect their anonymity in cyberspace:[10]

- ***Anonymous remailers:*** A completely anonymous remailer, or chain remailer, sends mail through remailing locations. Each location takes the header information off the mail and sends it to the next location. When the mail gets to its final destination, the recipient has no idea where the mail originated. What makes the system truly anonymous is that the remailing locations that the message goes through typically keep no records of the mail that comes in or goes out. This procedure makes the mail impossible to track.

- ***Pseudo-anonymous remailers:*** These single remailers work similarly to the chain remailer. The mail is sent to a remailing location, the header information is stripped at this site, and the mail is forwarded to its final destination. As with the chain remailer, the recipient has no idea where the mail originated. What makes the single remailer pseudo-anonymous is the fact that single remailers typically keep records of the mail that comes into and goes out of their systems. This procedure makes the mail traceable.

- *Pseudonymity:* This process consists of sending mail through cyberspace under a false name. Like the single remailer, the recipient will not immediately know who the mail came from, but the mail is completely traceable.

- *Anonymizer web site:* By visiting **http://www.anonymizer. com**, you can learn how to stop any specified web site from gathering information on you. When you use the anonymizer software to access a particular web site, the anonymizer goes to that web site for you, grabs the information, and sends you the information from the site. As far as the web site knows, they have been contacted only by the anonymizer web site. This secures your transactions and keeps "nosy" web sites from gathering information on you.

In spite of consumer interest in protecting anonymity, the federal government opposes total anonymity due to legitimate interests that are at stake. If total anonymity existed, the government would be unable to track down people who use cyberspace to violate the laws of libel, defamation, and copyrights.

Visit the text support site at **http://lehman. swlearning.com** to link to web resources related to this topic. As directed by your instructor, respond to one or more of the following:

1. Linking from the Internet sites listed for this case, locate an additional article on the issue of online anonymity. Print out the article and prepare a two-page abstract that includes the following sections: (1) reference citation, (2) overview, (3) major point, and (4) application.

2. Prepare a chart that summarizes the advantages and the disadvantages of online anonymity.

3. **GMAT** Take a position on the anonymity issue, either to support the right to anonymity or to defend the need for identification. In writing, present a defense of your position, giving reasons and/or evidence.

Sundance Catalog: Ethics and Environmental Responsibility

Sundance Village offers an art and nature community that preserves the natural beauty of the environment while fostering artistic pursuits (such as the Sundance Film Festival) and recreational activities (such as skiing, snowboarding, and hiking). The resort had its start in 1969 when Robert Redford purchased thousands of acres in the North Fork of Utah's Provo Canyon, home to Mount Timpanogos, a mountain surrounded by approximately 82,000 acres of wild lands. The following year the General Store was established; and soon thereafter guests began requesting special items they had seen at the store while visiting Sundance Village. To meet the increased demand, Sundance Catalog was launched in 1989 with the mailing of the first edition of its catalog.

The Sundance Resort works hand-in-hand with the North Fork Preservation Alliance (NFPA) to improve its environmental programs. NFPA, a not-for-profit organization, was established for the purpose of preserving and protecting the open spaces and wild lands of Provo's North Fork Canyon and to educate the public regarding conservation ethics and the human impact on fragile mountain ecosystems. The missions of both organizations, to respect the surrounding environment and employ sustainable practices, have resulted in Sundance's developing programs in recycling, energy efficiency, waste reduction, mountain mitigation, and other green initiatives.

In this video case, you will download a white paper from the Business for Social Responsibility (BSR) web site. The BSR is "a global organization that helps member companies achieve commercial success in ways that respect ethical values, people, communities and the environment. BSR provides information, tools, and advisory services to make corporate social responsibility an integral part of business operations and strategies . . . BSR member companies have nearly $2 trillion in combined annual revenues and employ more than six million workers around the world."*

View the video segment about Sundance Catalog on WebTutor or your Professional Power Pak CD.

Discussion Questions

1. What are the four principles that Sundance stands for?

2. In light of these principles, what are some of the ethical issues an organization has to be aware of when it has a well-known spokesperson, such as Sundance's Robert Redford?

3. In the catalog business, what is profitability based on, and how can ethics have an impact on that profitability factor?

Activities

1. Watch **http://www.nfpa-utah.org/** to learn more about NFPA.

2. Locate the Business for Social Responsibility (BSR) white paper entitled "Environment" at **http://www. bsr.org/BSRResources/WhitePaperDetail.cfm? DocumentID=252**. Note the links to the main headers that appear at the beginning of the paper. Read the "Introduction," link to "Implementation Steps," and become familiar with the ten areas typically addressed by companies that integrate environmental responsibility into business operations.

3. Evaluate Sundance's environmental initiatives using the ten areas identified in the BSR white paper.

Possible resources in addition to the Sundance Catalog video include the following:

a. Press Release: **http://www.sundanceresort.com/ environment/enviro_current.html**

b. Ski areas in Utah: **http://www.skiareacitizens. com/cgi-bin/report.cgi?region=ut**

c. Sundance Report Card: **http://www. skiareacitizens.com/cgi-bin/report. cgi?region=ut&area=9**

4. Choose *three* of the ten initiatives explained in the white paper and discuss actions Sundance has taken in each of the selected areas: environmental policy, environmental audit, employee involvement, toxics reduction, energy efficiency, waste minimization and recycling, green procurement, green design, measuring progress, and community involvement.

*BSR report on women's health needs in global supply chains underscores importance of business involvement and partnerships. (2002, November 6). Retrieved February 17, 2003, from **http://www.bsr.org/Meta/about/ PressReleasesDetail.cfm?DocumentID=48360**

Delivering Persuasive Messages

© SUSAN VAN ETTEN

Objectives *When you have completed Chapter 8, you will be able to:*

1 Develop effective outlines and appeals for messages that persuade.

2 Write effective sales messages.

3 Write effective persuasive requests (claim, favor, and information requests, and persuasion within an organization).

FEDEX RELIES ON THE PERSUASIVE POWER OF BRAND RECOGNITION

COURTESY OF FEDEX

What's in a name? Brand is one of the most important factors in positioning a company in the marketplace. It tells a company's story and provides consistent recognition exposure to customers and potential customers. Everything from a company's advertising, to the CEO's speech, to news releases should be part of the branding. Nevertheless, many companies don't synchronize their communications effectively around the concept of brand recognition.

FedEx is one company that recognizes the persuasive power of branding. In 2000, Federal Express unleashed the power of its global brand, bringing several of its subsidiaries under a single sales and marketing umbrella, renaming the company as FedEx Corporation. And in response to the demand for home delivery the company introduced FedEx Home Delivery, a new residential delivery service that operates as a separate business but relies in part on FedEx Ground's network. Although each of the subsidiaries continues to operate independently, the company provides customers with a single point of contact for support functions such as customer service, electronic commerce, and billing.[1]

In speaking of the extensive branding effort, Frederick W. Smith, chairman, president, and CEO of FedEx Corp., says, "We believe this change has major strategic implications for the company and for our customers. Specifically, our customers have told us that more and more they are attempting to manage supply and distribution on a strategic basis and that they need a broad portfolio of services, but that they want a single point of contact, single invoices, and a single point to track packages."[2] The new branding effort is apparently paying off, with FedEx earnings exceeding expectations—in spite of the September 11 attack, an anthrax scare, and a soft economy.[3]

Familiar uniforms and trucks, vans, and tractor-trailers bearing the FedEx name and logo help to visually promote the corporate brand. Collectively, the FedEx companies deliver millions of shipments every business day. With operations now under one recognized name, the corporation can effectively compete under the powerful FedEx brand worldwide.[4]

http://www.fedex.com

See ShowCASE, Part 2, on page 310 for Spotlight Communicator Rodger Marticke, executive vice-president of FedEx Ground.

Persuasion Strategies

Objective 1

Develop effective outlines and appeals for messages that persuade.

The FedEx feature illustrates persuasion at work. ***Persuasion*** is the ability to influence others to accept your point of view. It is not an attempt to trap someone into taking action favorable to the communicator. Instead, it is an honest, organized presentation of information on which a person may choose to act. In all occupations and professions, rich rewards await those who can use well-informed and well-prepared presentations to persuade others to accept their ideas or buy their products, services, or ideas.

How do you learn to persuade others through spoken and written communication? Have you ever made a persuasive request, written a cover letter, completed an application for a job, or written an essay for college entry or a scholarship? If so, you already have experience with this type of communication. While the persuasive concepts discussed in this chapter are directed primarily at written communication, they can also be applied in many spoken communication situations.

For persuasion to be effective, you must understand your product, service, or idea; know your audience; anticipate the arguments that may come from the audience; and have a rational and logical response to those arguments. Remember, persuasion need not be a hard sell; it can simply be a way of getting a client or your supervisor to say, "Yes." Although many of the examples and discussions in this chapter concentrate on selling *products and services*, similar principles apply to selling an *idea, your organization*, and *your own abilities*.

Critical Thinking

What is the difference between motivation and manipulation?

Before preparing an effective persuasive message, you must know as much as possible about your product, as well as the receivers' needs, doubts, and questions. Gateway went to extremes to develop empathy by scheduling surfing clinics to essentially "scare" staffers into understanding first-time customers' fears about getting started with computers. One enthusiastic employee shares with technophobic customers, "Hey, I went surfing—and I barely know how to swim. The important thing is to try."[5]

© HANK FOTOS/INDEX STOCK INAGERY

Plan Before You Write

Success in *writing* is directly related to success in preliminary *thinking*. If the right questions have been asked and answered, the composing will be easier and the message will be more persuasive. Specifically, you need information about (1) your product, service, or idea, (2) your audience, and (3) the desired action.

Know the Product, Service, or Idea

You cannot be satisfied with knowing the product, service, or idea in a general way; you need details. Get your information by (1) reading all available literature, (2) using the product and watching others use it, (3) comparing the product, service, or idea with others, (4) conducting tests and experiments, and (5) soliciting reports from users.

Before you write, you need concrete answers to such questions as these:

Critical Thinking

Consider a product you currently use. What is the major difference that makes it distinct from competing brands?

- What will the product, service, or idea do for the receiver(s)?
- What are its superior features (e.g., design and workmanship or receiver benefit)?
- How is the product or service different from its competition? How is the proposed idea superior to other viable alternatives?
- What is the cost to the receiver?

Similar questions must be answered about other viable alternatives or competing products. Of particular importance is the question, "What is the major difference?" People are inclined to choose an item (or alternative) that has some distinct advantage. For example, some people may choose a particular model of car because of its style and available options; still others may choose the model because of its safety record.

Know the Receiver

Who are the people to whom the persuasive message is directed? What are their wants and needs? Is a persuasive message to be written and addressed to an individual or to a group? If it is addressed to a group, what characteristics do the members have in common? What are their common goals, their occupational levels, their educational status? To what extent have their needs and wants been satisfied?

Critical Thinking

How can you determine receiver needs?

Recall the discussion of Maslow's need hierarchy in Chapter 2. Some people may respond favorably to appeals to physiological, security, and safety needs (to save time and money, to be comfortable, to be healthy, or to avoid danger). People with such needs would be impressed with a discussion of such benefits as convenience, durability, efficiency, or serviceability. Others may respond favorably to appeals to their social, ego, and self-actualizing needs (to be loved, entertained, remembered, popular, praised, appreciated, or respected). Consider the varying appeals used in a memo to employees and to supervisors seeking support of telecommuting. The memo to employees would appeal to the need for greater flexibility and reduced stress. Appeals directed at supervisors would focus on increased productivity and morale, reduced costs (office space), and compliance with the Clean Air Act (federal law requiring companies to find ways to get employees off the road to reduce air pollution and traffic congestion).

Identify the Desired Action

What do you want the receiver to do? Complete an order form and enclose a personal check? Receive a demonstration copy/model for trial examination? Return a card requesting a representative to call? E-mail for more information? Approve a request to allow you to telecommute two days a week? Accept a significant change in service, style, and procedures? Whatever the desired action, you need to have a clear definition of it before beginning to compose your message.

Apply Sound Writing Principles

The principles of unity, coherence, and emphasis are just as important in persuasive messages as in other messages. In addition, some other principles seem to be especially helpful in preparing persuasive messages:

- *Keep paragraphs short.* The spaces between paragraphs show the dividing place between ideas, improve appearance, and provide convenient resting places for the eyes. Hold the first and last paragraph to three or fewer lines; a one-line paragraph (even a very short line) is acceptable. You can even use paragraphs less than one sentence long! Put four or five words on the first line and complete the sentence in a new paragraph. Be careful to include key attention-getting words that either introduce the product, service, or idea or lead to its introduction.
- *Use concrete nouns and active verbs.* Concrete nouns and active verbs help receivers see the product, service, or idea and its benefits more vividly than do abstract nouns and passive verbs.
- *Use specific language.* General words seem to imply subjectivity unless they are well supported with specifics. Specific language is space consuming (saying that something is "great" is less space consuming than telling what makes it so); therefore, persuasive messages are usually longer than other messages. Still, persuasive messages need to be concise; they should say what needs to be said without wasting words.
- *Let receivers have the spotlight.* If receivers are made the subject of some of the sentences, if they can visualize themselves with the product in their hands, if they can get the feel of using it for enjoyment or to solve problems, the chances of creating a desire are increased.
- *Stress a central selling point or appeal.* A thorough analysis will ordinarily reveal some feature that is different from the features of

Critical Thinking

Brainstorm the possible central selling points for a particular automobile of your choice. With what type of audience would each selling point be most appropriate?

competing products or some benefit not provided by other viable alternatives. This point of difference can be developed into a theme that is woven throughout the entire message. Or, instead of using a point of difference as a central selling point, a writer may choose to stress one of the major satisfactions derived from using the item or doing as asked (approving a claim or responding favorably to a request). A central selling point (*theme*) should be introduced early and reinforced throughout the remainder of the message.

Critical Thinking

Does the AIDA strategy apply to persuasion through television advertisements? Explain.

• **Use an inductive outline.** Well over eighty years ago, Sherwin Cody summarized the persuasive process into four basic steps called AIDA.[6] The steps have been varied somewhat and have had different labels, but the fundamentals remain relatively unchanged. The AIDA steps for selling are

A Get the receiver's *attention.*

I Introduce the product, service, or idea and arouse *interest* in it.

D Create *desire* by presenting convincing evidence of the value of the product, service, or idea.

A Encourage *action.*

A persuasive message organized following these steps is inductive. The main idea, which is the request for action, appears in the *last* paragraph after presenting the details—convincing reasons for the receiver to comply with the request.

Each step is essential, but the steps do not necessarily require equal amounts of space. Good persuasive messages do not require separate sentences and paragraphs for each phase of the outline—getting attention; introducing the product, service, or idea; giving evidence; and stimulating action. The message *could* gain the receiver's attention and interest in the same sentence, and creating desire *could* require many paragraphs. Blend the steps in the four-step outline to prepare effective and persuasive (1) sales messages; (2) claims, favors, and information requests; and (3) requests within organizations.

Sales Messages

Objective 2

Write effective sales messages.

The four-point persuasive outline is appropriate for an **unsolicited sales message**, a letter, memo, or e-mail message written to someone who has not requested it. A **solicited sales message** has been requested by a potential buyer or supporter; that is, the message is prepared to answer this interested person's questions. With the use of persuasive e-mail on the rise, potential customers can also indicate willingness to receive electronic communication about products and services. Visit the text support site at http://lehman.swlearning.com to learn more about permission (opt-in) e-mail communication.

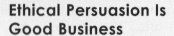

Ethical Persuasion Is Good Business

Businesses have learned that unethical behavior, such as overstating the capabilities of a product or service, is not beneficial in the long run. Developing effective persuasion skills will be important throughout your profession as you apply for a job, seek promotion or advancement, or seek to persuade your employer to adopt your ideas. Use the effective persuasion techniques you are learning to present your argument ethically—not to exploit the receiver. Ethical persuasion should include the following elements:[7]

- **Clear definition.** Persuaders should not present products and their characteristics without clear explanation. Although the Federal Trade Commission and Food and Drug Administration may legally allow some "puffery," unsubstantiated claims may confuse or mislead.

- **Scientific evidence.** Claims of superior performance or quality of a product imply that objective data exist to support the statements. Whenever possible, the persuader should provide the source and nature of the evidence. Failure to do so may lead to lawsuits, loss of credibility, and harm to both consumers and the company.

- **Context for comparison.** Better, faster, cleaner, easier, and similar terms imply a comparison.

Better than what? Better than it once was? Better than the competition? Or better than using nothing at all?

- **Audience sensitivity.** The multicultural and mixed-gender nature of most mass media audiences makes some messages objectionable. The persuader should consider those who might find the message offensive.

With these responsibilities in mind, the following two rules of thumb will assist you in presenting facts honestly, truthfully, and objectively:

- **Use concrete evidence and objective language to create an accurate representation of your product, service, or idea (and the competition if mentioned).** Be certain you can substantiate all claims made. Overzealous sales representatives or imaginative writers can use language to create less-than-accurate perceptions in the minds of receivers. However, legal guidelines related to truth in advertising provide clear guidance for avoiding misrepresentation. If you exaggerate or mislead in a letter delivered by the U.S. Postal Service, you can be charged with the federal offense of mail fraud and incur significant fines or even imprisonment.

- **Do not deliberately omit, distort, or hide important information that does not support your argument so that the receiver completely misses it.**

Consider the truthfulness of a president disclosing the financial benefits of a plant closing but omitting the fact that 3,000 employees were laid off in a town where the plant is the primary employer. The investor may realize the impact of the omission and lose faith in the manager's credibility.

Application

Consider a message, such as a letter or television advertisement, that promotes a product or service you have used or experienced (e.g., a new fast-food restaurant). How accurate was the message's representation of the product or service? Did the message embellish or exaggerate quality? Do you feel that you were misled in any way? Did your perception of the company change as a result of your experience? Write a memo to your instructor or be prepared to discuss your first-hand experience in class.

Ongoing consumer research by Apple Computer, Inc. allows the company to respond to the needs of the "net generation." "For this generation, the computer is like a hot rod," says Allen Olivo, Apple's senior director for worldwide marketing, who says kids are constantly comparing features and styling with their friends' systems.[8]

"Yes, I'm a PC guy that switched to Mac."

© SUSAN VAN ETTEN

Critical Thinking

Why are unsolicited sales letters often referred to as "junk mail"? What can the writer do to dispel this attitude?

Someone who has invited a persuasive message has given some attention to the product, service, or idea already; an attention-getting sentence is hardly essential. However, such a sentence is essential when the receiver is not known to have expressed an interest previously. The very first sentence, then, is deliberately designed to make a receiver put aside other thoughts and concentrate on the rest of the message.

Gaining Attention

Various techniques have been successful in convincing receivers to consider an unsolicited sales message. Some commonly used attention-getting devices include

- *A personal experience:* When a doctor gives you instructions, how often have you thought, "I wish you had time to explain" or "I wish I knew more about medical matters."
- *A solution to a problem (outstanding feature/benefit):* Imagine creating a customized multimedia presentation that . . .
- *A startling announcement:* More teens die as a result of suicide each month than die in auto accidents in the same time period.
- *A what-if opening:* What if I told you there is a savings plan that will enable you to retire three years earlier?
- *A question:* Why should you invest in a company that has lost money for six straight years?
- *A story:* Here's a typical day in the life of a manager who uses Wilson Enterprise's Pager.

... what works today may not work later. Pop-up ads that spring up uninvited over Internet sites are still getting results for many advertisers; but the majority of people find them "very annoying."[9] How much longer will this technique work as a growing number of Internet users install pop-up blockers?

© AP/WORLD WIDE PHOTOS

Critical Thinking

Visit a quotation site on the Internet and locate a quote that might be used to promote a product or service of your choice.

- *A proverb or quote from a famous person:* P. T. Barnum supposedly said, "There's a sucker born every minute." At Northland Candy Factory, we make the saying come true.
- *A split sentence:* Picture . . . your audience's enthusiastic response to dramatic video footage to support your major points.
- *An analogy:* With Wentman's innersole inserts, you'll be walking in the clouds.

Other attention-getters include a gift, an offer or a bargain, or a comment on an enclosed product sample. Regardless of the technique used, the attention-getter should achieve several important objectives:

- *Introduce a relationship between the receiver and the product, service, or idea.* Remaining sentences grow naturally from this beginning sentence. If receivers do not see the relationship between the first sentence and the sales appeal, they may react negatively to the whole message—they may think they have been tricked into reading. For example, consider the following poor attention-getter: *Would you like to be the chief executive officer of one of America's largest companies? As CEO of Barkley Enterprises, you can launch new products, invest in third-world countries, or arrange billion-dollar buyouts. Barkley Enterprises is one of several companies at your command in the new computer software game developed by Creative Diversions Software.*

Critical Thinking

How can your opening sentence backfire and not achieve the desired result?

The beginning sentence is emphatic because it is a short question. However, it suggests the message will be about obtaining a top management position, which it is not. All three sentences combined suggest high-pressure techniques. The computer software game has relevant virtues; one of them could have been emphasized by placing it in the first sentence.

- *Focus on a central selling feature.* Almost every product, service, or idea will in some respects be superior to its competition. If it is not, such factors as favorable price, fast delivery, or superior service may be used as the primary appeal. This primary appeal (central selling point) must be emphasized, and one of the most effective ways to emphasize a point is by position in the message. An outstanding feature mentioned in the middle of a message may go unnoticed, but it will stand out if mentioned in the first sentence. Note how the following opening sentences introduce the central selling feature and lead naturally into the sentences that follow:

> A complete collection of Salvador Dali prints—only at the PosterShop!
>
> You can select complete sets of prints by Doré and Monet, as well as Dali, at the PosterShop, the only fine arts poster dealer with this comprehensive selection of works of art by the "masters." PosterShop will also frame these prints professionally so you can display them in your home as proudly as you would the originals.

- *Use an original approach.* To get the reader's attention and interest, you must offer something new and fresh. Thus, choose an anecdote likely unfamiliar to your receiver or use a peculiar combination of words to describe how a product, service, or idea can solve a receiver's problem. The following personal story grabs the receiver's attention and leads into a presentation of the new features available with a new release of *WordPerfect*.[10]

> I step into my favorite restaurant, and the waiters all dive for cover. Only the restaurant owner has the guts to take my order—as if she really needs to ask. "I'll have the usual," I say. "Give me . . . the *All You Can Eat Buffet*." For the next two hours, I stuff myself. I indulge at the salad bar and I gorge at the taco bar. As much as I consume, though, I haven't tried everything—I just don't have room.
>
> In many ways, WordPerfect is like that gigantic buffet. The new WP is packed with powerful, useful features. . . .

Critical Thinking

In a group, use one of the techniques presented to write a creative attention-getter for a product, service, or idea of your choice.

Introducing the Product, Service, or Idea

A persuasive message is certainly off to a good start if the first sentences cause the receiver to think, "Here's a solution to one of my problems," "Here's something I need," or "Here's something I want." You may lead the receiver to such a thought by introducing the product, service, or idea in the very first sentence. If you do, you have succeeded in both getting attention and arousing interest in one sentence. An effective introduction of the product, service, or idea is cohesive and action centered, and continues to stress a central selling point.

- *Be cohesive.* If the attention-getter does not introduce the product, service, or idea, it should lead naturally to the introduction. Note the abrupt change in thought and the unrelatedness of the attention-getter to the second paragraph in the following example:

> Employees appreciate a company that provides a safe work environment.
>
> The Adcock Human Resources Association has been conducting a survey for the last six months. Their primary aim is to improve the safety of office work environments.

The last words of the first sentence, "safe work environment," are related to "safety of office work environments"—the last words of the last sentence. No word or phrase in the first sentence connects the words of the second sentence, which creates an abrupt, confusing change in thought. In the following revision, the second sentence is tied to the first by the word "that's." "Safety" in the second sentence refers to "protection" in the third. The LogicTech low-radiation monitor is introduced as a means of providing a safe work environment. Additionally, notice that the attention-getter leads smoothly to the discussion of the survey results.

> Employees appreciate a company that provides a safe work environment.
>
> That's one thing the Adcock Human Resources Association learned from its six-month survey of the safety of the office work environment. For added protection from radiation emissions, more companies are purchasing LogicTech's low-radiation computer monitors. . . .

Critical Thinking

Refer to Figures 8-2 and 8-3 on pages 305 and 306. Is the receiver or product or idea the subject of most of the sentences? What benefits will the receiver gain from purchasing digital music? From attending the LASIK seminar?

- *Be action oriented.* To introduce a product, service, or idea in an interesting way, you must place the product, service, or idea in your receivers' hands and talk about their using it or benefiting from accepting your idea. They will get a clearer picture when reading about something happening than when reading a product description. Also, the picture becomes all the more vivid when the receiver is the hero of the story—the person taking the action. In a sense, you do not sell products, services, or ideas—you sell the pleasure people derive from their use. Logically, then, you have to focus more on that use than about the product, service, or idea. If you put receivers to work using your product, service, or idea to solve problems, they will be the subject of most of your sentences.

Some product description is necessary and natural. In the following example, the writer focuses on the product and creates an uninteresting, still picture: *The ClassicForm treadmill is powered by a two horsepower motor. The patented electronic control system features a digital display screen with variable speed and pause controls.* In the revision, a person is the subject of many of the sentences and is enjoying the benefits of the treadmill.

> As you step on the ClassicForm treadmill to begin your workout, you will immediately enjoy the smooth, even movement. No more jarring starts and stops of other treadmills. That's because our unique electronic control center puts *you* in total control of your workout. All you have to do is press the ON button to start accelerating to your desired speed, which you can easily monitor on the clear digital display. Getting tired? Just press COAST to reduce the speed. Need to stop for a moment? Press the PAUSE button to bring your treadmill to a gradual stop. The strength of the two-horsepower motor will provide you this smooth, even movement for years to come.

Critical Thinking

Where should the central selling point be mentioned in a persuasive message?

- **Stress a central selling point.** If the attention-getter does not introduce a distinctive feature, it should lead to it. You can stress important points by position in the message and by space allocated to the point. As soon as receivers visualize the product, service, or idea, they need to have attention called to its outstanding features; the features are therefore emphasized because they are mentioned first. If you want to devote much space to the outstanding features, introduce them early. Note how the attention-getter introduces the distinctive selling feature (ease of operation) and how the following sentences keep the receivers' eyes focused on that feature:

> If you know how to write a check and record it in your checkbook, then you can operate Easy Accounting. It's that *easy to use*. Just click the check icon to display a blank check. Use the number keys to enter the amount of the check and Easy Accounting fills in the word version of the amount. Doesn't that sound easy?
>
> Now click on the category box and *conveniently* view a complete listing of your accounts. Move the arrow to the account of your choice and click. The account is written on the check and posted to your records *automatically*.

By stressing one point, you do not limit the message to that point. For example, while *ease of operation* is being stressed, other features are mentioned. A good film presents a star who is seen throughout most of the film; a good term paper presents a central idea that is supported throughout; a school yearbook develops a theme—a sales message should stress a central selling point.

Providing Convincing Evidence

After you have made an interesting introduction to your product, service, or idea, present enough supporting evidence to satisfy your receivers' needs. Keep one or two main features uppermost in the receivers' minds, and include evidence that supports these features. For example, using appearance as an outstanding selling feature of compact cars while presenting abundant evidence to show economy of operation would be inconsistent.

Present and Interpret Factual Evidence

Few people will believe general statements without having supporting factual evidence. Saying a certain machine or method is efficient is not enough. You must say *how you know* it is efficient and present some data to illustrate *how* efficient. Saying a piece of furniture is durable is not enough. Durability exists in varying degrees. You must present information that shows what makes it durable and also define *how* durable. Durability can be established, for example, by presenting information about the manufacturing process, the quality of the raw materials, or the skill of the workers:

> KCC Publishing's Garnet Classics will last your child a lifetime—pages bound in durable gold-embossed hardback, treated with special protectants to retard paper aging, and machine-sewn (not glued) for long-lasting quality. The 100-percent cotton fiber paper can withstand repeated turning of pages. The joy of reading can last for years as your children explore the world of classic literature with KCC's Garnet Classics.

Critical Thinking

How can the writer establish credibility in the mind of the reader?

Presenting research evidence (hard facts and figures) to support your statements is another way to increase your chances of convincing receivers to buy. Presenting results of a research study takes space but makes the message much more convincing than general remarks about superior durability and appearance.

Evidence presented must not only *be* authentic; it must *sound* authentic, too. Talking about pages treated with special protectants to retard aging and machine-sewn construction suggests the writer is well informed, which increases receiver confidence. Facts and figures are even more impressive if the receiver can get some kind of internal verification of their accuracy. For example, the following paragraph presents figures and gives their source:

> We insulated 30 houses in Buffalo last year. Before installing the insulation, we asked each homeowner to tell us the total fuel bill for the four coldest months—November, December, January, and February. The average cost was $408, or $102 a month. After installation, we discovered the fuel bill for the same four-month period was $296, or $74 a month—a saving of $28 a month, or 25 percent.

Critical Thinking

Think of examples of concepts in your career field that might need interpretation.

Naturally, your receivers will be less familiar with the product, service, or idea and its uses than you will be. Not only do you have an obligation to give information, you should interpret it if necessary and point out how the information will benefit the receiver. Be prepared to interpret technical concepts in your field to a potential customer/client (e.g., finance majors might interpret tax-deferred annuities in terms of the needs of a specific target audience). Alternately, you could interpret a feature of a product. Notice how the following examples interpret the capability of the new oven in terms of receiver benefit and clearly interpret *why* infrared technology is superior to traditional keyboards. The interpretation makes the evidence understandable and thus convincing.

Cold Statement without Interpretation	Specific, Interpreted Fact
The revolutionary Speedcook Technology cooks oven-quality food faster than a conventional oven without sacrificing the taste.	New Speedcook technology harnesses light to cook the top and bottom of the food simultaneously, quickly searing in the natural juices and flavors. Speedcook broils, browns, roasts, and even grills food, with no preheating, delivering you oven-quality food cooked in one-fourth the time required in a conventional oven.
Infrared technology is the industry leader in wireless keyboarding.	Infrared technology uses infrared light to transmit information between the keyboard and the computer in the same way your remote control communicates with your television. Like your television remote, an infrared wireless keyboard requires that you have a somewhat clear line of sight between the keyboard and computer and keep the keyboard only a couple of feet away from the PC for optimal transmission.

The previous example about the wireless keyboard also uses a valuable interpretative technique—the comparison. You can often make a point more convincing by comparing something unfamiliar with something familiar. Most people are familiar with the television remote, so they can now visualize how the wireless keyboard will work. Comparison can also be used to interpret prices. Advertisers frequently compare the cost of sponsoring a child in a third-world country to the price of a fast-food lunch. An insurance representative might write this sentence: *The annual premium for this 20-year, limited-payment policy is $219, or 60 cents a day—about the cost of a cup of coffee.*

Do not go overboard and inundate your receivers with an abundance of facts or technical data that will bore, frustrate, or alienate. Never make your receivers feel ignorant by trying to impress them with facts and figures they may not understand.

Legal & Ethical Constraints

Be Objective

Use language people will believe. Specific, concrete language makes your message sound authentic. Unsupported superlatives, exaggerations, flowery statements, unsupported claims, incomplete comparisons, and remarks suggesting certainty all make your message sound like high-pressure sales talk. Just one such sentence can destroy confidence in the whole message. Examine the following statements to see whether they give convincing evidence. Would they make a receiver want to buy? Or do they merely remind the receiver of someone's desire to sell? *This antibiotic is the best on the market today. It represents the very latest in biochemical research.*

Identifying the best-selling antibiotic requires gathering information about all antibiotics marketed and then choosing the one with superior characteristics. You know the writer is likely to have a bias in favor of the particular drug being sold. However, you do not know whether the writer (or speaker) actually spent time researching other antibiotics or whether the communicator would know how to evaluate this information. You certainly do not know whether the communicator knows enough about biochemical research to say truthfully what the very latest is.

Legal & Ethical
Constraints

Similarly, avoid preposterous statements *(Gardeners are turning handsprings in their excitement over our new weed killer!)* or subjective statements *(Stretch those tired limbs out on one of our luscious water beds. It's like floating on a gentle dream cloud on a warm, sunny afternoon. Ah, what soothing relaxation!).* Even though some people may be persuaded by such writing, many will see it as an attempt to trick them. Note the incomplete comparison in the following example: *SunBlock provides you better protection from the sun's dangerous ultraviolet rays.* Is SunBlock being compared with *all* other sunscreens, *most* other sunscreens, *one* unnamed brand, or others? Unless an additional sentence identifies the other elements in the comparison, you do not know. Too often, the writer of such a sentence hopes the receiver will assume the comparison is with *all* others. Written with that intent, the incomplete comparison is *unethical.* Likewise, statements of certainty are often inaccurate or misleading.

Include Testimonials, Guarantees, and Enclosures

One way to convince prospective customers that they will like the product, service, or idea is to give them concrete evidence that other people like it. Tell what others have said (with permission, of course) about the usefulness of your product, service, or idea. Guarantees and free trials convey both negative and positive connotations. By revealing willingness to refund money or exchange an unsatisfactory unit if necessary, a writer confesses a negative: the purchase could be regretted or refused. However, the positive connotations are stronger than the negatives: the seller has a definite plan for ensuring that buyers get value for money spent. In addition, the seller exhibits willingness for the buyer to check a product, service, or idea personally and compare it with others. The seller also implies confidence that a free trial will result in a purchase and that the product will meet standards set in the guarantee. If terms of a guarantee are long or complex, they can be included in an enclosure.

Ordinarily, a message should persuade the receiver to read an enclosure, attachment, or file link that includes more detailed information. Thus, refer to the added material late in the message after the major portion of the evidence has been given. An enclosure or link is best referred to in a sentence that is not a cliché ("Enclosed you will find," or "We have enclosed a brochure") and says something else:

The enclosed annual report will help you understand the types of information provided to small- and medium-sized companies by Lincoln Business Data, Inc.

Click <u>here</u> to view the huge assortment of clearance-priced items and other end-of-season specials.

Critical Thinking

What does the buyer hope to pay for a product? What does the seller hope to charge? What is the ethical dilemma in justifying an appropriate price?

Subordinate the Price

Logically, price should be introduced late in the message—after most of the advantages have been discussed. Use the following techniques to overcome people's natural resistance to price:

- *Introduce price only after creating a desire for the product, service, or idea and its virtues.* Let receivers see the relationship of features and benefits to the price.
- *Use figures to illustrate that the price is reasonable or that the receiver can save money.* (Purigard saves the average pool owner about $10 in chemicals each month; thus, the $150 unit pays for itself in 15 months.)
- *State price in terms of small units.* (Twelve dollars a month seems like less than $144 a year.)
- *Invite comparison of like products, services, or ideas with similar features.*
- *Consider mentioning price in a complex or compound sentence that relates or summarizes the virtues of the product, service, or idea.* (For a $48 yearly subscription fee, Medisearch brings you a monthly digest of recent medical research that is written in nontechnical language.)

Critical Thinking

How can sentence position affect the reader's acceptance of the price?

Motivating Action

Critical Thinking

How can the writer overcome readers' potential objections so that they will take the desired action?

For proper clarity and emphasis, the last paragraph should be relatively short. Yet it must accomplish three important tasks: specify the specific action wanted and present it as easy to take, encourage quick action, and ask confidently.

- *Make the action clear and simple to complete.* Define the desired action in specific terms that are easy to complete. For example, you might ask the receiver to complete an order blank and return it with a check, place a telephone call, or order online. General instructions such as "Let us hear from you," "Take action on the matter," and "Make a response" are ineffective. Make action simple to encourage receivers to act immediately. Instead of asking receivers to fill in their names and addresses on order forms or return cards and envelopes, do that work for them. Otherwise, they may see the task as difficult or time consuming and decide to procrastinate.

- *Restate the reward for taking action (central selling point).* The central selling point should be introduced early in the message, interwoven throughout the evidence section, and included in the last paragraph as an emphatic, final reminder of the reason for taking action.

Critical Thinking

Why is procrastination such a common reaction to a persuasive appeal? What are some ways to reduce the likelihood of reader procrastination?

- *Provide an incentive for quick action.* If the receiver waits to take action on your proposal, the persuasive evidence will be harder to remember, and the receiver will be less likely to act. Therefore, you prefer for the receiver to act quickly. Reference to the central selling point (assuming it has been well received) helps to stimulate action. Commonly used appeals for getting quick action are to encourage customers to buy while prices are in effect, while supplies last, when a rebate is being offered, when it is a particular holiday, or when they will receive benefits.
- *Ask confidently for action.* If you have a good product, service, or idea and have presented evidence effectively, you have a right to feel confident. Demonstrate your confidence when requesting action: "To save time in cleaning, complete and return. . . ." Avoid statements suggesting lack of confidence, such as "If you want to save time in cleaning, complete and return. . . ," "If you agree. . . ," and "I *hope* you will. . . ."

Observe how the following closing paragraph accomplishes the three important tasks: refers to the central selling point, makes a specific action easy, and provides an incentive for quick action.

> From a Touch-Tone telephone, simply dial 1-800-555-8341. Then input the five-digit number printed in the top right corner of the attached card. Your name and address will be entered automatically into our system, an expedient way to get your productivity software to you within five working days along with a bill for payment. When you order by August 12, you will also receive a free subscription to *Time Resource Magazine*. TMC's new productivity software is as easy to use as it is to order!

Changing Technology

Figures 8-1 and 8-2 illustrate poor and good *unsolicited sales messages* for a product. Figure 8-3 presents an unsolicited sales message promoting a service. The same principles apply in writing a *solicited sales letter*, with one exception: Because the solicited sales letter is a response to a request for information, an attention-getter is not essential. Typically, sales messages are longer than messages that present routine information or convey good news. Specific details (essential in getting action) require space. While the rules that apply to effective persuasive letters and memos generally apply to e-mail messages, some particular guidelines are offered in the the Strategic Forces feature on "E-Mail as a New Wave of Persuasive Communication."

E-Mail as a New Wave of Persuasive Communication

More and more organizations are using e-mail as a means to persuade existing and potential customers to buy their products. Since e-mail marketing is a new field, rules have not been written in stone. However, marketers are learning how to use e-mail effectively with various audiences. To gain desired attention from customers, messages must be carefully timed to arrive when they will gain the most attention. Over-messaging can be annoying, while under-messaging may cause the company to miss potential sales opportunities. The subject line is of utmost importance, as it must catch the attention of the reader and create a desire to learn more. Other aspects of effective persuasive appeal are illustrated in the accompanying message from Palm:[11]

- Personalizes the message by using the recipient's name in the copy.

- Uses a graphical design to add visual appeal.

- Uses targeted e-mail as a two-step process; does not attempt to generate a sale directly from the message.

- Entices recipient to learn more about an offer; provides links to sites of possible interest.

- Allows for easy sharing of information with others.

- Keeps the message as short as possible, while adequately explaining the offer.

- Includes means to be removed from the list, ensuring that only interested parties continue to receive e-mailings.

E-commerce marketers such as Ticketmaster, eBags, and Victoria's Secret are using e-mail communications to acquire new customers, increase sales, notify customers of promotions and services, and, most importantly, develop and nurture an ongoing dialogue and relationship with their customers. Many marketers provide an incentive such as premiums or award points to reward their target audience for reading the content of the e-mail.

Persuasive e-mail communications have become an integral part of their overall marketing strategy.

Application

Print out a copy of an ineffective marketing e-mail message you have received. Why was the selected message ineffective? What was your reaction to it? What is your current attitude toward the company?

© AP TOPIC GALLERY

Figure 8-1

Poor Example of a Sales Message Promoting a Product

Ineffective Example X

Uses deductive approach inappropriately by placing the request to buy before gaining receiver's attention or providing convincing evidence.

Uses writer-centered, exaggerated language that diminishes receiver interest and confidence in the writer's objectivity.

Erodes reader confidence through arrogant attitude and presentation of technical information without explanation.

Lacks central selling point that reflects accurate knowledge of the receiver's needs. Provides no unity for the numerous details presented.

Places unnecessary emphasis on price by placing at the paragraph's beginning. Discusses features without showing receiver benefit.

States desired action with no mention of benefit; uses demanding tone and choppy sentence structure.

Dear Jessica:

Buy a $299 PearJam handheld music player from PearMusic, and we will let you download songs from our web site for 99 cents each.

Our 300,000 songs are great!!!! And we are adding songs all the time. Our web site can be navigated easily and is chock full of music we like. The quality is good and the music is better. We give you access to a wide variety of artists, and we also give you free 30-second previews of each song.

Our techies are using the new CPM format to release the songs, and you will love what it does for you! Our songs are legal and high quality because we negotiated with the big guys at the record companies, and we made the deals.

At 99 cents each and no subscription fees, you will spend about the same amount per song as with a traditional CD format, but we let you buy only the songs you want to hear. And you can mix songs from various artists to make your favorite playlists, all playable on our PearJam handheld music players and our comPear computers. Browse our collection by genre, artist, album, composer, or song title. Use our 30-second free previews to be certain the song is what you want.

You can use the enclosed authorization number to save $50 on the rather expensive PearJam. You have to go to our web site, comPear.com/PearMusic to use it. You can do it whenever you feel like it.

Figure 8-2

Good Example of a Sales Message Promoting a Product

Inductive Outline for Sales Messages

1. Gain the receiver's attention.

2. Introduce the product, service, or idea and arouse interest in it.

3. Present convincing evidence of the merits of the item being promoted and overcome any resistance.

4. Encourage the receiver to take the desired action (buy the product or service or accept the idea).

 **PearMusic** **Music downloads the right way** (a division of comPear Computers)
6223 North Frontgate Road ♪ Fort Wayne, IN 46485 ♪ 219-555-4877

May 20, 2004

Ms. Jessica Lawrence
500 Louisville Street
Oxford, MS 38655

Dear Ms. Lawrence

Do you want to access the music you love and arrange the songs how YOU want to? want CD-quality songs that are easy to download? want those songs to be portable? and want the peace of mind knowing that all your downloads are sanctioned by the record company and the original recording artist? Then you want PearMusic from comPear.com.

With comPear's new online digital music store PearMusic, you can find songs from Tom Petty, Richard Marx, Harry Connick, Jr., and every other Tom, Dick, and Harry in the music world for 99 cents per song with no subscription fees. With PearMusic, you also can

♪ Load the songs onto your PearJam handheld music player and up to three comPear computers.

♪ Mix songs from various artists to make your favorite playlists.

♪ Burn a single playlist up to ten times without changes.

♪ Get a free 30-second preview for every song.

♪ Listen to CD-quality music on your computer and your PearJam.

♪ Browse the PearMusic store by genre, artist, album, composer, or song title.

♪ Access cover art for CDs and watch exclusive full-length music videos.

Visit www.comPear.com/PearMusic today and check out the collection that is growing daily. Use the enclosed authorization number to save $50 on your purchase of a PearJam (regular price $299) so that you can take your PearMusic wherever you go. Just key the authorization number into the "special offer" box on the checkout screen. The $50 savings offer expires July 31, so get your PearJam today and start making your own music choices with PearMusic.

Sincerely

Adria D. Wayne

Adria D. Wayne
Sales Manager

Enclosure

Gains attention by introducing experiences that are familiar to the receiver. Presents customized music as the central selling point.

Presents the "online digital music store" as a solution to the problem and reinforces the central selling point.

Uses an easy-to-read bulleted list to present evidence that reflects understanding of the flexibility the receiver desires in digital music.

Keeps the focus on the receiver by use of second person, active-voice sentences.

States specific action with reward. Makes action easy and provides incentive for quick response.

Figure 8-3

Good Example of a Sales Message Promoting a Service

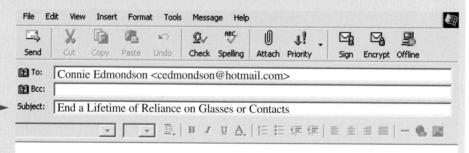

Sends a customized e-mail message to patients who are considered potential candidates for the procedure.

Gains attention by introducing familiar annoying experiences; presents freedom from corrective lenses as the central selling point.

Introduces the surgery as a potential solution to the reader's vision problem. Reduces resistance by indicating no pain is involved.

Builds interest by explaining the process and providing easy access to detailed information.

Creates a desire to learn more through the discussion of the seminar and the free surgery.

States the specific action to be taken and associates that action with the central selling point— excellent vision.

To: Connie Edmondson <cedmondson@hotmail.com>

Bcc:

Subject: End a Lifetime of Reliance on Glasses or Contacts

Connie,

Do you ever imagine being able to see the alarm clock when you wake each morning? No more hassle of daily contact maintenance? Perhaps you may have imagined playing your favorite sport with complete peripheral vision—no fogging or slipping glasses. Millions of people across the world have chosen LASIK, a laser vision correction procedure, as an alternative to glasses and contact lenses. They now are enjoying the freedom that you may have only imagined.

The Genesis Optical Center is eager to inform patients who are potential candidates for laser vision correction of the benefits of this remarkable new procedure. Take a moment to visit our web site at http://www.genesis/optical.com to see skilled surgeons use an excimer laser to correct the shape of the cornea with absolutely no pain to the patient. Many of your questions will be answered by reading about the vision improvements you can realistically expect, testimonials of our many satisfied patients, and the experience of our five resident surgeons.

You are also invited to attend a special laser seminar held at our clinic on February 18 at 7 p.m. that will feature a live laser vision correction procedure followed by a question/ answer period led by our laser correction experts. You'll have an opportunity to enter your name in a drawing for a free laser vision correction procedure to be presented at the close of the seminar.

Would you like to join the millions of people who have chosen LASIK vision correction and end a lifetime of reliance on glasses and contacts in a blink of an eye? Get started today by calling our clinic to register for the laser seminar or to schedule a personal consultation to determine whether you are a candidate for this life-changing procedure. Learn for yourself whether LASIK vision correction could do for you what it has done for so many.

Cordially,

Brian Johnson, Office Manager <bjohnson@genesis.com>

Legal and Ethical Considerations

Abides by the requirements for advertising under the Federal Trade Commission Act including guidance provided specifically for promotions related to LASIK (**http://www.ftc.gov**).

Persuasive Requests

Objective **3**

Write effective persuasive requests (claim, favor, and information requests, and persuasion within an organization).

The preceding discussion of sales messages assumed the product, service, or cause was sufficiently worthy to reward the receiver for taking action. The discussion of persuasive requests assumes requests are reasonable—that compliance is justified when the request is for an adjustment and that compliance will (in some way) be rewarded when the request is for a favor.

Common types of persuasive requests are claim messages and messages that request special favors and information. Although their purpose is to get favorable action, the messages invite action only after attempting to create a desire to take action and providing a logical argument to overcome any resistance anticipated from the receiver.

Making a Claim

Critical Thinking

What is the difference between a persuasive claim and the routine claim message discussed in Chapter 6? How can the writer decide which writing approach to use?

Claim messages are often routine because the basis for the claim is a guarantee or some other assurance that an adjustment will be made without need of persuasion. However, when an immediate remedy is doubtful, persuasion is necessary. In a typical large business, the claim message is passed on to the claims adjuster for response.

Often, any reasonable claim will be adjusted to the customer's satisfaction. Therefore, venting strong displeasure in the claim message is of little value. It can alienate the claims adjuster—the one person from whom cooperation is sought. Remember, adjusters may have had little or nothing to do with the manufacture and sale of the product or direct delivery of the service. They did not create the need for the claim.

Companies should welcome claims. First, research indicates two important facts: (1) complainers are more likely to continue to do business with a company than those who do not complain, and (2) businesses that know how to resolve claims effectively will retain 95 percent of the complainers as repeat customers.[12] Second, only a small percentage of claims are from unethical individuals; the great bulk is from people who believe they have a legitimate complaint. Thus, the way an adjuster handles the claim determines, to a large extent, the goodwill of the company.

For the adjuster, granting a claim is much easier than refusing it. Because saying "No" is one of the most difficult writing tasks, the sender of a persuasive claim message has an advantage over the adjuster.

Like sales messages, persuasive claims should use an inductive sequence. Unlike routine claim messages, persuasive claims do not begin by asking for an adjustment. Two major changes would improve the poor example in Figure 8-4: (1) writing inductively (to reduce the chance of a negative reaction in the first sentence), and (2) stressing an appeal throughout the message (to emphasize an incentive for taking favorable action). In a persuasive claim, an appeal serves the same purpose that a central selling feature does in a sales message. Both serve as a theme; both remind the receiver of a benefit that accrues from doing as asked. Note the application of these techniques in the revision in Figure 8-5.

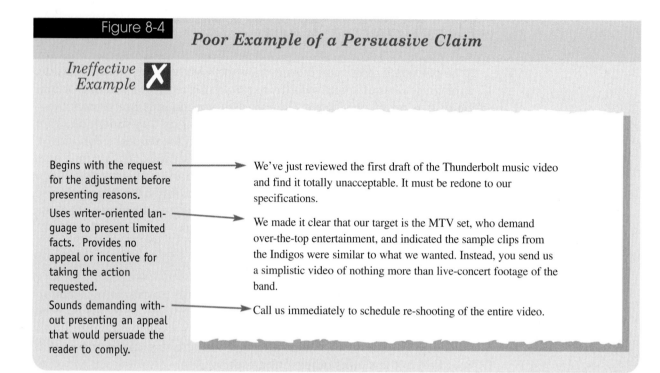

Figure 8-4 | *Poor Example of a Persuasive Claim*

Ineffective Example ✗

Begins with the request for the adjustment before presenting reasons. →

We've just reviewed the first draft of the Thunderbolt music video and find it totally unacceptable. It must be redone to our specifications.

Uses writer-oriented language to present limited facts. Provides no appeal or incentive for taking the action requested. →

We made it clear that our target is the MTV set, who demand over-the-top entertainment, and indicated the sample clips from the Indigos were similar to what we wanted. Instead, you send us a simplistic video of nothing more than live-concert footage of the band.

Sounds demanding without presenting an appeal that would persuade the reader to comply. →

Call us immediately to schedule re-shooting of the entire video.

Legal & Ethical Constraints

Knowledge of effective claim writing should never be used as a means of taking advantage of someone. Hiding an unjustifiable claim under a cloak of untrue statements is difficult and strictly unethical. Adjusters are fair-minded people who will give the benefit of the doubt, but they will not satisfy an unhappy customer simply to avoid a problem.

Asking a Favor

Occasionally, everyone has to ask someone else for a special favor—action for which there is little reward, time, or inclination. For example, suppose a professional association wants to host its annual fund-raiser dinner at an exclusive country club. The program chair of the association must write the club's general manager requesting permission to use the club. Will a deductive message be successful?

Critical Thinking

How might the receiver react to a persuasive message written in the deductive style?

When a deductive approach is used in a persuasive situation, chances of getting cooperation are minimal. For example, what might be a probable reaction to the following beginning sentence? *Please send me, without charge, your $450 interactive CD-ROM on office safety.*

If the first sentence gets a negative reaction, a decision to refuse may be made instantly. Having thought "No," the receiver may not read the rest of the message or may hold stubbornly to that decision in spite of a well-written persuasive argument that follows the opening sentence. Note that the letter in Figure 8-6 asks the favor before presenting any benefit for doing so.

Figure 8-5

Good Example of a Persuasive Claim

Inductive Outline for Persuasive Claims

1. Gain attention by appealing to a mutual need.

2. Present reasoning (details and evidence) that leads to the request in context of the central appeal presented in the first paragraph.

3. Present the request in context of the central appeal.

VideoSolutions
A leader in entertainment video production

3109 Overlook Terrace / Beverly Hills, CA 90213-8120 / (213) 555-3120 Fax (213) 555-3129

May 20, 2004

Mr. Chris Ragan
Creative Director
Harrelson Producers
3674 Elmhurst Avenue
Los Angeles, CA 90052-3674

Dear Chris

Seeks attention by giving a sincere compliment that reveals the subject of the message.

When Thunderbolt negotiated with your firm to produce our first music video, we were impressed with the clips of other Harrelson videos and your proven performance record. Especially intriguing to us was your video of the Indigos, with its subtle use of symbolism in the graphic images along with creative shots of the musicians.

Continues the central appeal—commitment to creative production—while providing needed details.

In our meeting with your creative team, we focused on the methods used in the Indigos video and specifically asked for graphic symbolism juxtaposed with shots of the band. After viewing the first draft of our video, we find the level of artistic expression disappointing. This video closely resembles a concert tape, focusing primarily on live-concert footage of the band and will have little appeal with our customers, the MTV set, who demand innovative and exciting new approaches in entertainment.

Presents reasoning that leads to the request for reshooting the video and a subtle reminder of the central appeal.

Connects a specific request with the firm's commitment to develop creative productions.

With Harrelson's reputation for creative productions, we are confident the video can be revised to meet our expectations. The band will do its part to assist in reshooting footage and will meet with the creative director at a mutually convenient time to discuss the kind of graphic imagery appropriate for interpreting our music and its message. Please call me at 555-3920 to schedule this meeting.

Sincerely

Cole Gallant

Cole Gallant
General Manager

Legal and Ethical Considerations

Sends a letter rather than an e-mail to emphasize the importance of these differences regarding a contractual agreement.

SPOTLIGHT COMMUNICATOR

FedEx Home Delivery Responds to Needs of Online Shoppers

Meeting ever-changing consumer needs is the key to staying competitive, a fact clearly recognized at FedEx. As a part of an ambitious strategic initiative in 2000, FedEx Corporation launched FedEx Home Delivery, a new home delivery service designed for online shoppers. Online purchases are projected to account for $184 billion by 2004, up from only $38 billion in 2000; and the company strives to be the preeminent delivery system for the growing number of shipments sold by retailers via the Internet. Initially serving 38 major U.S. cities, the service now covers the entire country and has brought FedEx thousands of new customers.[13]

Rodger Marticke, executive vice-president of FedEx Ground, describes

COURTESY OF FEDEX

FedEx Home Delivery as a necessary consequence of a much larger goal—to integrate the company to fit every client's shipping needs. "The residential business wasn't really a target market segment for us before. But now we're really going out there soliciting the business." The home delivery system collects consumers' specific delivery information from the shipper. FedEx transmits that information to one of its local delivery facilities, where it is printed and becomes part of a driver's delivery manifest. An automated vehicle routing system uses the customer information to determine which packages should go on which vehicles as well as the delivery routes drivers should take and their sequence of stops. Marticke explains that FedEx also uses a geographical information system to generate computerized maps and turn-by-turn directions for each driver, assuring that drivers cover the fewest miles in the shortest time.[14]

FedEx Home Delivery strives to set itself apart from competitors by offering a money-back guarantee, a

first in the home delivery market, along with a menu of service options, including Saturday evening and by appointment deliveries. The FedEx Home Delivery logo, illustrated here, features a dog named "Spot.com," and is designed to further solidify the brand recognition that is so important to customer loyalty.[15] Marticke and the staff at FedEx Home Delivery are banking on the persuasive power of Spot.com to clinch the growing online buyers market.

Applying What You Have Learned

1. How is FedEx Home Delivery meeting the needs of today's consumers?
2. Compare the use of the Spotcom logo with other successful product "personalities" that you recall.

Rodger Marticke, Executive Vice President, FedEx Ground

http://www.fedex.com

Refer to ShowCASE, Part 3, at the end of the chapter, to explore how FedEx uses the AIDA formula to persuade its web customers to use its services.

Figure 8-6

Poor Example of a Persuasive Request (asking a favor)

Ineffective Example **X**

Begins with an announcement that is already known.

Asks the favor before presenting a reason for accepting.

Sounds somewhat doubtful; is wordy and overuses the first person pronoun "I."

> The specials and promotions in your store are only announced in English. However, it's clear to me that many of your customers are Latino. Have you considered repeating these announcements in Spanish?
>
> Likely I'm not telling you anything you've not already considered, but I wanted to bring it to your attention.

The letter illustrated in Figure 8-7 uses an inductive approach. Note the extent to which it applies principles discussed earlier. As this letter shows, if the preceding paragraphs adequately emphasize a receiver's reward for complying, the final paragraph need not shout loudly for action.

Requesting Information

Requests for information are common in business. Information for research reports frequently is obtained by questionnaire, and the validity and reliability of results are strongly influenced by the percentage of return. If a message inviting respondents to complete a questionnaire is written carelessly, responses may be insufficient.

The most serious weaknesses of the e-mail in Figure 8-8 on page 313 are asking too quickly for action and providing no incentive for action. Sometimes the reward for taking action is small and indirect, but the message needs to make these benefits evident. Note the reward in the revision of the e-mail in Figure 8-9 on page 314 (it appeals to Maslow's higher order of needs as discussed in Chapter 2).

Persuading within an Organization

The majority of memos are of a routine nature and essential for the day-to-day operation of the business, for example, giving instructions for performing work assignments, scheduling meetings, providing progress reports on projects, and so on. In many organizations, such matters are

Critical Thinking

Why are routine requests shorter than persuasive requests?

Figure 8-7

Good Example of a Persuasive Request (asking a favor)

Inductive Outline for Persuasive Requests

1. Gain the receiver's attention.
2. Introduce the request and emphasize benefits the receiver can gain from complying with the request.
3. Address any major resistance to the request.
4. Request specific action.

Audrey Banzhaf-Wade
456 Bee Cave Drive   Austin, TX 39876-0456   (512)555-3819

February 18, 2003

Ms. Kathyrn Connors
General Manager
Fresh Foods
8976 Northeast Ninth Street
Austin, TX 39876-8976

Dear Ms. Connors:

Begins with a sincere compliment that sets the stage for the request that follows.

As a regular customer of Fresh Foods grocery store, I have enjoyed and bene-fited from your store's practice of announcing price specials and promotions over your public address system. These announcements have saved me money and alerted me to specials I might have missed had the announcement not drawn my attention to them.

Explains the rationale for the request with discussion of benefits to the store and its customers.

These announcements are currently made only in English. While I have no trou-ble understanding the English messages, many of your customers who live in the Latino community near your store have limited knowledge of spoken English and, therefore, do not benefit from these informative store announcements.

Connects the specific action to the rewards for taking action.

By providing both English and Spanish announcements for price specials and promotions, you could ensure that all your customers understand and can benefit from these announcements. Because these customers are now aware of your specials, they will be more likely to make additional purchases as well. It is a win for Fresh Foods and for the many customers patronizing your grocery store.

Sincerely,

Audrey Banzhaf-Wade

Audrey Banzhaf-Wade

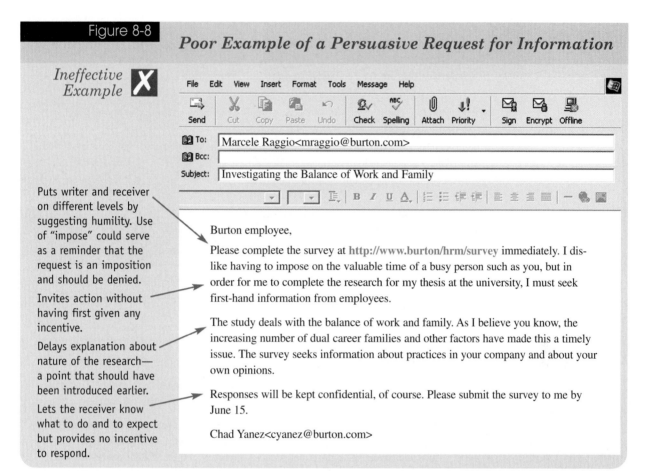

Figure 8-8

Poor Example of a Persuasive Request for Information

Ineffective Example ✗

Puts writer and receiver on different levels by suggesting humility. Use of "impose" could serve as a reminder that the request is an imposition and should be denied.

Invites action without having first given any incentive.

Delays explanation about nature of the research—a point that should have been introduced earlier.

Lets the receiver know what to do and to expect but provides no incentive to respond.

File   Edit   View   Insert   Format   Tools   Message   Help

Send   Cut   Copy   Paste   Undo   Check   Spelling   Attach   Priority   Sign   Encrypt   Offline

To: Marcele Raggio<mraggio@burton.com>
Bcc:
Subject: Investigating the Balance of Work and Family

Burton employee,

Please complete the survey at http://www.burton/hrm/survey immediately. I dislike having to impose on the valuable time of a busy person such as you, but in order for me to complete the research for my thesis at the university, I must seek first-hand information from employees.

The study deals with the balance of work and family. As I believe you know, the increasing number of dual career families and other factors have made this a timely issue. The survey seeks information about practices in your company and about your own opinions.

Responses will be kept confidential, of course. Please submit the survey to me by June 15.

Chad Yanez<cyanez@burton.com>

handled through the use of e-mail rather than paper memos. These routine memos and e-mail messages, as well as messages conveying good news, are written deductively. However, some circumstances require that a supervisor write a persuasive message that motivates employees to accept a change in their jobs that might have a negative effect on the employees or generate employee resistance in some form (e.g., being transferred to another position or office, automating a process that has been performed manually, changing computer software programs, etc.).

For example, Steak and Ale restaurant faced the challenge of communicating to its employees a significant change in service and style, accompanied by new uniforms. Rather than coercing or demanding that employees accept the change, a letter from Bob Mandes, president of Steak and Ale, emphasized reasons the changes were being made (benefits to guests, the company, and the employees) and the employee's important role in implementing the changes. Using a lighthearted, entertaining approach, the letter and accompanying magazine provide (a) a visual model of the fresh, crisp, and professional look the company expected with the uniform change; and (b) helpful information on ways to achieve this look. Note the "You" orientation in the "style flashes" interwoven throughout the magazine excerpt that follows:

Figure 8-9

Good Example of a Persuasive Request for Information

Inductive Outline for Persuasive Request for Information

1. Gain receiver's attention.

2. Introduce the request and emphasize benefits the receiver can gain from complying with the request.

3. Address any major resistance to the request such as assuring that the information will remain confidential.

4. Request specific action by a specified date.

File   Edit   View   Insert   Format   Tools   Message   Help

Send | Cut   Copy   Paste   Undo | Check   Spelling | Attach   Priority | Sign   Encrypt   Offline

To: Marcele Raggio<mraggio@burton.com>

Bcc:

Subject: Investigating the Balance of Work and Family

Seeks attention by establishing the message as work related and alludes to a way to find needed answers.

Introduces the survey and reward for taking action. Employees with an interest in the issue would see sharing of results as a positive.

Makes the request for action in a complex sentence that includes the reward for complying and mentions a deadline. Presents needed assurance that the effort will consume little time.

Expresses gratitude and adds unity by using words that tie in with the first paragraph's reference to quality of work life at Burton.

Burton employee:

Balancing work and family lives is an important issue for most employees. Your help is needed to learn more about how Burton employees handle this concern.

By participating in this doctoral study, you and other Burton employees have an opportunity to share ways you've learned to balance your work and family lives and give your opinions on this timely issue. A summary of the questionnaire results will be given to the Burton Human Resources Department, who will use this information as a starting point for initiating desired changes that will support your efforts to balance the demands of your work and family.

To ensure that the information represents the views of all employees, please visit **http://www.burton/hrm/survey** to complete the survey by **June 15**. Only 15 minutes or so of your time is needed to complete the survey, and your responses will be reported only as part of the group results.

I sincerely appreciate your help with this research project and in making Burton a better place to work. If you wish to receive a summary of this information, simply provide your e-mail address at the end of the survey.

Thanks,

Chad Yanez<cyanez@burton.com>

Legal and Ethical Consideration

Informs participant as to how individual responses will be treated.

Out of control hair is the biggest turnoff to Guests in restaurants—they don't want it wandering into their food. So pull your hair back and pull in a better tip.

If you wear a lot of jewelry, Guests may think you don't need as large a tip.

Your smile is the most important part of your appearance and it's the first signal to Guests that their Steak and Ale experience will be a memorable one. Your smile tells Guests, "I'm happy you're here!" But hey, don't take our word for it. Check out the recent study by Boston College which found that smiling suggests an awareness of the needs of others. Maybe that's the reason behind the phrase "winning smile."[16]

The detailed language leaves no doubt in an employee's mind as to what management considers clean, crisp, and professional. However, by continually emphasizing the benefits employees gain from the change, management garners support for the high standards being imposed.

Similarly, employees must often make persuasive requests of their supervisors. For example, they may recommend a change in procedure, acquisition of equipment or software, or attendance at a training program to improve their ability to complete a job function. They may justify a promotion or job reclassification or recommendation. Persuasive memos and e-mail messages are longer than most routine messages because of the extra space needed for developing an appeal and providing convincing evidence.

When preparing to write the memo in Figure 8-10, the store manager recalled a past attempt to computerize perpetual inventory that failed miserably. At that time, most employees could be easily categorized as computer illiterate; they required extensive training and were resistant to any effort to computerize. The company finally abandoned the computerization effort when the computer system could not be upgraded to handle higher inventory levels.

Anticipating the managing partner's resistance, the store manager decided to write the memo inductively. Thus, the subject line does not reveal how the manager proposes to improve the efficiency of maintaining inventory counts. To increase his chances of gaining approval, the store manager stresses the features designed to avoid known pitfalls (computer literacy of employees and obsolescence of computer systems) but does not mention the past failure.

Kate La Barge, the writer of the persuasive e-mail in Figure 8-11, may have been one more burnout statistic had it not been for her initiative and, most important, her excellent writing skills. Kate is a manager for a large national firm who enjoys her career and thrives on the challenge of performing at her peak while rearing her two children. However, last year she began showing signs of burnout. Managing her career and finding time to care for the children without feeling exhausted most of the time had become increasingly difficult. While skimming a business publication one day, she noticed an article about telecommuting—a plan that enables employees to work from home on certain days with the assistance of a computer with a modem and facsimile machine. Intrigued,

Changing
Technology

Figure 8-10

Good Example of a Persuasive Memo

Inductive Outline for Persuasive Memos

1. Gain the receiver's attention.
2. Build interest in the idea by presenting objective evidence, including benefits the company and the recepient can gain.
3. Address any major resistance to the idea.
4. Request specific action to be taken.

Gives the purpose of the memo without revealing the specific request.

Links a company strength that leads logically to the problem; does not reveal the actual request.

Builds interest by providing specific benefits of the computerized system.

Reduces resistance by discussing changes to alleviate prior problems with computerized system; does not refer directly to past failures.

Expands discussion of advantages of the proposed system.

Refers to attachment after presenting evidence. Alludes to benefits and closes with a specific action to be taken.

TO: Tracey Ellis, Managing Partner
FROM: Aparna Nadisen, Store Manager
DATE: September 20, 2004
SUBJECT: Proposal to Improve the Efficiency of Maintaining Inventory Counts

One of our competitive advantages is the wide variety of materials we offer crafts enthusiasts in our city. However, our manual system has become inadequate for maintaining this large inventory.

A computerized perpetual inventory would eliminate the need to close the store two days in each major season to count stock and update our records. This system would also provide management with timely and accurate information about inventory levels.

Our employees have been using computers for other applications (word processing and general ledger) for over a year; therefore, I would anticipate little resistance to this type of change in daily operations. In fact, several inventory clerks have suggested getting perpetual inventory on the computer already. Their prior computer training would likely reduce the cost of implementing this computerized system significantly.

Unlike older computer equipment, today's hardware is designed to be flexible. No longer must new computers be purchased to take advantage of new technologies. For example, more powerful microprocessors can be inserted directly into this system. Thus, as our business grows and technology changes, we would be able to upgrade this system to meet our changing demands.

Take a look at the attached brochure describing the exact specifications and the cost of a perpetual inventory system. After you have considered this change, please call so we can discuss this critical enhancement to our efficient delivery of products to our customers.

Attachment

Kate discovered that telecommuting offers numerous advantages for both employees and companies, and she concluded this work plan was a perfect solution for her.

Of course, she needed to obtain permission from her supervisor to begin telecommuting, so she developed a plan. First, Kate made a list of her job duties that could be performed at home and those that must be completed at the office. Then, she made a list of the benefits of telecommuting, emphasizing in particular how the company would benefit. She anticipated possible objections to her plan and developed responses for those protests. Finally, she drafted a proposal in the form of an e-mail message to her supervisor, including the information she had organized.

Because compliance with the Clean Air Act was the subject of a staff meeting, Kate opens her request (Figure 8-11) with a straightforward statement about the problem and her telecommuting proposal. She presents a thorough analysis of duties that could be efficiently completed away from the office, thus reducing her commuting time. This analysis provides convincing evidence that telecommuting is a feasible recommendation. The specific changes she suggests in scheduling required meetings and the progress report on equipping a home office aid her in counteracting any resistance to her proposal. Her call to discuss the proposal at the next meeting is clear and specific and reminds the supervisor of the benefits of the proposal. After some minor negotiating, Kate was allowed to begin telecommuting on a temporary basis while management evaluated its efficiency. Now she is a permanent telecommuter and plans to maintain this schedule until her children are older. She is more productive because of reduced stress and fewer interruptions, and the company is benefiting from this increased productivity.

Before writing a persuasive message, study carefully the overall suggestions in the "General Writing Guidelines" that appear just before the activities in Chapter 5. Then, study the specific suggestions in the following "Check Your Communication" checklist. Compare your work with this checklist again after you have written a rough draft; then make necessary revisions.

Summary

1. **Develop effective outlines and appeals for messages that persuade.** The purpose of a persuasive message is to influence others to take a particular action or to accept your point of view. Effective persuasion involves understanding the product, service, or idea you are promoting; knowing your audience; presenting convincing evidence; and having a rational response to anticipated resistance to your arguments.

   Effective persuasive communications build on a central selling point interwoven throughout the message.

   The receivers, rather than the product, serve as the subject of many of the sentences. Therefore, receivers can envision themselves using the product, contracting for the service, or complying with a request. Persuasive messages are written inductively.

2. **Write effective sales messages.** A sales message is written inductively following the four-point AIDA steps for selling:

Figure 8-11 | Good Example of a Persuasive E-Mail Message

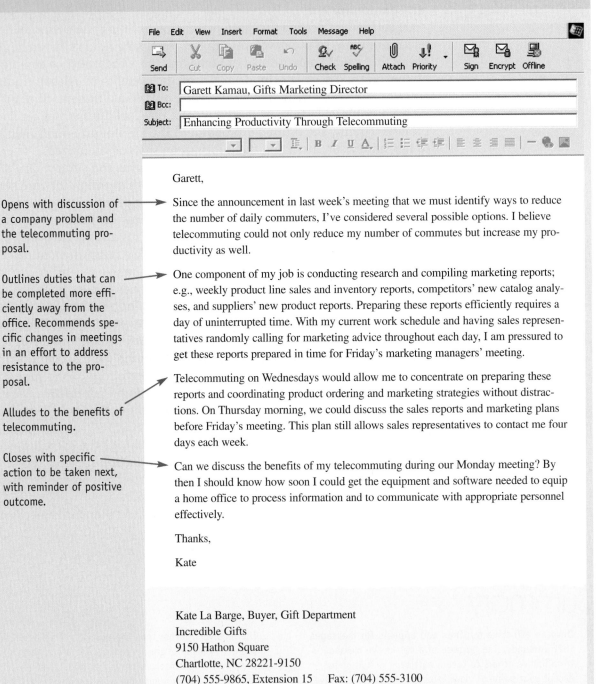

File   Edit   View   Insert   Format   Tools   Message   Help

Send | Cut | Copy | Paste | Undo | Check | Spelling | Attach | Priority | Sign | Encrypt | Offline

To: Garett Kamau, Gifts Marketing Director

Bcc:

Subject: Enhancing Productivity Through Telecommuting

Garett,

Opens with discussion of a company problem and the telecommuting proposal. → Since the announcement in last week's meeting that we must identify ways to reduce the number of daily commuters, I've considered several possible options. I believe telecommuting could not only reduce my number of commutes but increase my productivity as well.

Outlines duties that can be completed more efficiently away from the office. Recommends specific changes in meetings in an effort to address resistance to the proposal. → One component of my job is conducting research and compiling marketing reports; e.g., weekly product line sales and inventory reports, competitors' new catalog analyses, and suppliers' new product reports. Preparing these reports efficiently requires a day of uninterrupted time. With my current work schedule and having sales representatives randomly calling for marketing advice throughout each day, I am pressured to get these reports prepared in time for Friday's marketing managers' meeting.

Alludes to the benefits of telecommuting. → Telecommuting on Wednesdays would allow me to concentrate on preparing these reports and coordinating product ordering and marketing strategies without distractions. On Thursday morning, we could discuss the sales reports and marketing plans before Friday's meeting. This plan still allows sales representatives to contact me four days each week.

Closes with specific action to be taken next, with reminder of positive outcome. → Can we discuss the benefits of my telecommuting during our Monday meeting? By then I should know how soon I could get the equipment and software needed to equip a home office to process information and to communicate with appropriate personnel effectively.

Thanks,

Kate

Kate La Barge, Buyer, Gift Department
Incredible Gifts
9150 Hathon Square
Chartlotte, NC 28221-9150
(704) 555-9865, Extension 15   Fax: (704) 555-3100

SALES MESSAGES

Content

- Convince the reader that the product or service is worthy of consideration.
- Include sufficient evidence of usefulness to the purchaser.
- Reveal price (in the message or an enclosure).
- Make the central selling point apparent.
- Identify the specific action that is desired.
- Structure message to meet ethical and legal requirements.

Organization

- Use inductive sequence of ideas.
- Assure that the first sentence is a good attention-getter.
- Introduce the central selling point in the first two or three sentences, and reinforce it through the rest of the message.
- Introduce price only after receiver benefits have been presented.
- Associate price (what the receiver gives) directly with reward (what the receiver gets).
- Introduce a final paragraph that includes (a) the specific action desired, (b) the receiver's reward for taking the action, and (c) an inducement for taking action quickly. Present the action as easy to take.

Style

- Use objective language.
- Assure that active verbs and concrete nouns predominate.
- Keep sentences relatively short but varied in length and structure.
- Place significant words in emphatic positions.
- Make ideas cohere by avoiding abrupt changes in thought.
- Frequently call the central selling point to the receiver's attention through synonyms or direct repetition.
- Use original expression (sentences that are not copied directly from the definition of the problem or from sample documents in the text.) Omit clichés.
- Achieve unity by including in the final paragraph a key word or idea (central selling point) that was introduced in the first paragraph.

Mechanics

- Assure that keyboarding, spelling, and punctuation are perfect.

Format

- Use a correct document format.
- Assure the document is appropriately positioned.
- Include standard document parts in appropriate position.
- Include special parts if necessary (subject line, enclosure, copy, etc.).

PERSUASIVE REQUESTS

Content

- Convince the receiver that the idea is valid, that the proposal has merit.
- Point out the way(s) in which the receiver will benefit.
- Incorporate primary appeal (central selling feature).
- Identify specific action desired.

Organization

- Use inductive sequence of ideas.
- Use a first sentence that gets attention and reveals the subject of the message.
- Introduce a major appeal in the first two or three sentences and reinforce it throughout the rest of the message.
- Point out receiver benefits.
- Associate desired action with the receiver's reward for taking action.
- Include a final paragraph that makes reference to the specific action desired and the primary appeal. Emphasize the ease of taking action, and (if appropriate) include a stimulus for quick action.

Style

- Use language that is objective and positive.
- Assure that active verbs and concrete nouns predominate.
- Keep sentences relatively short, but vary them in length and structure.
- Place significant words in emphatic positions.
- Make ideas cohere by assuring that changes in thought are not abrupt.
- Call primary appeal to the receiver's attention frequently through synonyms or repetition of a word.

- Use original expression (sentences that are not copied directly from the definition of the problem or from sample documents in the text). Omit clichés.
- Achieve unity by including in the final paragraph a key word or idea (the primary appeal) that was used in the first paragraph.

Mechanics

- Assure that keyboarding, spelling, grammar, and punctuation are perfect.

Format

- Use a correct document format.
- Assure the document is appropriately positioned.
- Include standard document parts in appropriate position.
- Include special parts if necessary (subject line, enclosure, copy, etc.).

- *Gain attention.* Use an original approach that addresses one primary receiver's benefit (the central selling point) in the first paragraph.
- *Introduce the product, service, or idea.* Provide a logical transition to move the receiver from the attention-getter to information about the product, service, or idea. Hold the receiver's attention by using action-oriented sentences to stress the central selling point.
- *Provide convincing evidence.* Provide specific facts and interpretations that clarify the nature and quality of a feature, nonexaggerated evidence people will believe, and research and testimonials that provide independent support. De-emphasize the price by presenting convincing evidence first but not in the final paragraph, showing how money can be saved, stating price in small units, illustrating that the price is reasonable, and placing the price in a sentence that summarizes the benefits.
- *Motivate action.* State confidently the specific action to be taken and the benefits for complying. Present the action as easy to take, and provide a stimulus for acting quickly.

3. **Write effective persuasive requests (claim, favor, and information requests, and persuasion within an organization).** A persuasive request is written inductively, is organized around a primary appeal, and is longer than a typical routine message because you must provide convincing evidence of receiver benefit.

- *Persuasive claim*—When an adjuster must be convinced that a claim is justified, gain the receiver's attention, develop a central appeal that emphasizes an incentive for making the adjustment, and end with the request for an adjustment you consider fair.
- *Request for a favor or information*—Gain the receiver's attention, build interest by emphasizing the reward for taking action, and encourage the receiver to grant the favor or send the information.
- *Persuasion within an organization*—When persuading employees or supervisors to take specific actions, gain the receiver's attention, introduce and build interest and support for the proposed idea, address any major resistance, and encourage the receiver to take a specific action.

Chapter Review

1. Summarize the types of information you should gather as you plan a persuasive message. (Obj. 1)
2. List the writing principles that are important in writing an effective persuasive message. (Obj. 1)
3. What are the legal and ethical implications of persuasive messages? (Obj. 1)
4. Define "central selling feature." Where should it appear in a persuasive message? (Obj. 1)
5. List the four steps in the persuasive pattern. (Obj. 1)
6. What are the characteristics of a good attention-getter? List five techniques for getting receivers' attention. (Objs. 1, 2)

Interactivity Is Web's Third Wave

First it was cool to have a web site. Then it became expected that you would. Now you're lagging behind if your site doesn't offer interactivity. Interactivity makes the site visitor an active participant and can include discussion areas, password-protected zones, online price calculators, searchable databases, product directories with user reviews and comparison prices, and shopping baskets with secure checkouts. With an interactive site, every page can be tailored to particular customers. You can detect whether they have been to your site before, recall what they did, and suggest related things. The following electronic activities will allow you to explore aspects of web interactivity:

 InfoTrac College Edition. Access http://www. infotrac.thomsonlearning.com to read more about how companies are using interactive web sites to enhance their customer communication. Search for the following article that is available in full text:

Butcher, T. (2002, June 13). Keep cool over interactivity. *Computer Weekly*, p. 26.

Make a list of software products that can assist a company in extending the interactivity of its site. If your instructor specifies, further investigate each of the products to find out about features and price.

 Text Support Web Site. Visit http://lehman. swlearning.com to learn more about interactive web page design. Refer to Chapter 8's Electronic Café

activity that provides a link to an online article that describes various features of online interactivity. Select a favorite web site or visit one specified by your instructor. Analyze the selected site for the various features described in the online article.

 WebTutor Advantage. Your instructor will give you instructions about accessing the Quiz Bowl and Image Gallery. Complete the Quiz Bowl activities your instructor designates. Visit the Image Gallery to view images and complete an activity explained by your instructor.

 Professional Power Pak. Access your PPP CD for information on advanced features of web page design, including interactivity and animation.

---

7. Why are sales messages normally longer than routine messages? What guidelines apply as to the recommended lengths for paragraphs? (Obj. 2)

8. What types of words and phrases are effective in persuasive messages? (Objs. 1–3)

9. In addition to the general guidelines for sales messages, what specific guidelines apply to sales-oriented e-mail messages? (Objs. 1, 2)

10. Summarize the effective techniques for convincing the receiver that your product, service, or idea has value. (Obj. 2)

11. How should price be handled in a sales message? (Obj. 2)

12. Describe the characteristics of an effective action ending to a persuasive message. (Objs. 1–3)

13. What is the principal difference between a persuasive claim and a routine claim? (Obj. 3)

14. What is meant by an "appeal" in a persuasive message? (Obj. 3)

15. Should a persuasive memo to a supervisor address any known or anticipated resistance to a proposed idea? Explain. (Obj. 3)

Digging Deeper

1. Where does one cross the line between being persuasive and being coercive or overbearing?

2. How might a persuasive approach need to be modified when dealing with persons of other cultures?

To check your understanding of the chapter, take the practice quizzes at **http://lehman.swlearning.com** or your WebTutor course.

Activities

1. Critique of Sales Letters and Persuasive Requests Produced by Real Companies (Obj. 1)

Select an unsolicited sales message you (or a friend) have received. List (a) the principles it applies and (b) the principles it violates. Rewrite the message retaining its strengths and correcting its weaknesses.

2. Effective Opening Paragraphs (Objs. 1–3)

Analyze the effectiveness of each sentence as the opening for a persuasive message.

a. Don't you want to make the world a better place? Instead of worrying about the starving in Africa, let's take care of our own—donate canned food to the local Homeless Haven in time for the holidays!

b. John F. Kennedy said, "Ask not what your country can do for you; ask what you can do for your country." One of the best ways to support American capitalism is to let Carville Consultants make your business better.

c. You haven't lived until you've owned a Multi-Sound Compact Disc Storage Chest!

d. For an investment of $550, you can own the best high-pressure washer on the market from Sims, Inc.

e. The enclosed folder shows our latest prices on lead glass windows.

f. This new policy I am proposing will revolutionize our sales figures within three months. (request)

g. I am requesting to be promoted to regional sales manager because I have a proven track record of turning around sales revenues within two months. (request)

h. The merchandise you sent Maxwell Corporation on September 3 is defective, and we refuse to pay for it. (claim)

3. Convincing Evidence (Objs. 1–3)

Analyze the effectiveness of the convincing evidence included in the following sentences in a persuasive request.

a. Reorganizing the loan department will help us serve our clients better and cut costs.

b. I know you are extremely busy, but we would really like to have you come speak to us on effective investing.

c. Southside Recycling has four regional offices in each county in Texas, with headquarters in Dallas. Our professional staff consists of 15 members at each location.

d. You wonder if you can get quality education at our school and still save money? Dollar for dollar, tuition and fees at Carlton State give you the best education value for your money.

e. The infrared transfer available on your handheld personal assistant is a must-have in today's information explosion. Just beam it up and you're on your way.

4. Document for Analysis: Sales Message (Objs. 1, 2)

Analyze the following letter promoting bookings of a historic schooner. Pinpoint its strengths and weaknesses, and then revise the letter if directed by your instructor.

Visit the Interactive Study Center at **http://lehman. swlearning.com** for a downloadable version of this activity.

> January 3rd, 2004
> Clark S. Palotta
> 1366 Campus View Road
> Lake City, FL 32055-9019
>
> Dear Sir,
>
> I thank you for your inquiry regarding our schooner, The Mary Ann. Please find the enclosed information, which I hope you will find interesting.
>
> The Mary Ann is a 103 year-old gaffed rugged wooden schooner currently able to accommodate 32 passengers. Early next season we will be increasing our capacity to 49 passengers. The Mary Ann is 89 feet long and weighs approximately 60 gross tons.
>
> Our rates for the 2003 season were $300 per hour for a minimum of three hours. There will be a price increase next year but it will be minimal.
>
> Although the 2003 season is over, we are currently taking reservations for next season, which will commence during April 2004. Please consider advance booking with us if you are at all interested in that special day as each year we have to turn away so many people who request a particular time and day. We do offer discounts to customers who are able to make reservations and pay in full before March 31st, 2004.
>
> Should you have any questions or like to view our unique, historic sailing vessel then please do not hesitate to contact me.
>
> Yours sincerely,
>
> Carlos Pardue
> Office Manager

5. **Document for Analysis: Persuasive Claim (Objs. 1, 3)**

Analyze the following e-mail persuading a sports agent to reimburse a hospital for an acceptable substitute speaker. Pinpoint its strengths and weaknesses, and then revise the message if directed by your instructor.

Visit the Interactive Study Center at **http://lehman. swlearning.com** for a downloadable version of this activity.

> Please send a refund of $3,000, one half of the speaker's fee, for the unacceptable substitute you provided for the grand opening of the Brookridge Healthplex.
>
> We thought you clearly understood that John Dampier was our choice for the keynote speaker for this long-awaited grand opening. Not only is John an Olympic gold medalist and respected spokesperson for physical fitness, he is a native of nearby Kosciosko. Your substitute speaker, Sharron Mabry, saved us from total embarrassment, but she failed to meet the criteria we had established for this speaker. As you know, she is not an Olympian nor a native of our state. In fact, very few people at the event had a clue who she was. Many voiced complaints that John Dampier was not present as we had promoted.
>
> Considering the months of hard work we devoted to planning this event, we are sure you can understand our extreme disappointment with the community's response to this substitute speaker and will willingly agree to reimburse us one half the speaker's fee. Please call me at your convenience to discuss this issue further.

6. **Document for Analysis: Persuasive Request (Objs. 1, 3)**

Analyze the following memo written to encourage employees to attend a meeting to gain additional information about financial planning. The company hopes to increase enrollment of employees in its 403(b) plan that allows them to invest 15 percent of their gross wages in tax-deferred annuities. Presently only 22 percent of the company's employees have taken advantage of this plan. Pinpoint the strengths and weaknesses of the human resource director's memo, and then revise it if directed by your instructor.

Visit the Interactive Study Center at **http://lehman. swlearning.com** for a downloadable version of this activity.

> Despite our efforts, very few of you have taken advantage of the tax benefits afforded by the 403(b) plan. Contributing to a tax-deferred annuity enables you to shelter a portion of your income from current income taxes. The earnings in your annuity also grow tax free and you don't pay income taxes on these funds until you withdraw them at retirement.
>
> Contributing into a 403(b) plan is easy. Because the funds can be deducted automatically from your checking account, anyone can afford it.
>
> You've got one more chance to learn about this plan. An information session will be held next Wednesday in the conference room beginning at 1 p.m. All your questions will be answered by a representative of our human resources division.
>
> See you there.

Applications

| Read | Think | Write | Speak | Collaborate |

1. **Communication Success Stories (Objs. 1–3)**

Conduct an electronic search to locate an article that deals with the successful use of persuasive communication in a company or organization. Prepare an abstract of the article that includes the following parts: (1) article citation, (2) name of organization/company, (3) brief description of communication technique/situation, (4) and outcome(s) of the successful communication. As an alternative to locating an article, write about a successful communication situation in the organization/company for which you work.

Required: Submit your abstract to your instructor as an e-mail attachment. Be prepared to give a short presentation in class.

2. **Persuasive Message: Multimedia Presentations: Necessary or Pointless? (Objs. 1, 3)**

It happened again today. Your team had worked for weeks preparing its response to a request for proposal. Your plan to subcontract the investor services of the potential client was far superior to your competitors', but your presentation failed miserably. Although well done, your flip charts and overhead transparencies made your team look incompetent when your competitor appeared with a dazzling multimedia presentation. If the company is to win sizable contracts, you are convinced your employees must learn new tactics for developing and delivering presentations. You need projection equipment and intensive training in creating dynamic multimedia presentations. You are just as sure that the managing partner will be a hard sell because of her resistance to technology. To win a pitch for the move to electronic presentations, you must have cold, hard facts about the benefits of electronic presentations and be able to address any disadvantages associated with electronic presentations. Begin your research by locating the following articles:

Simons, T. (2000, February). Multimedia or bust? *Presentations*, 14(2), 40–48. Retrieved May 27, 2003, from Business Source Premier database.

Ganzel, R. (2000, February). Power pointless. *Presentations*, 14(2), 53–57. Retrieved May 27, 2003, from Business Source Premier database.

Required: Write a memo to Kim Macias, managing partner, persuading her to approve your proposal for investing in presentation design training, software, and projection equipment needed to enhance the company's presentation style. Prepare a short electronic presentation of your ideas. Be prepared to deliver your presentation to the class.

3. Designing Permission Marketing Communication (Obj. 2)

Permission (opt-in) marketing is a popular method used by advertisers to build an ongoing, personalized dialogue with customers who want to receive e-mail offers and updates. Visit the text support site at **http://lehman. swlearning.com** to learn more about how to design permission marketing communication effectively.

Required: Locate an additional article on the subject of permission marketing. Prepare a one-page abstract of the article that includes a bibliographic citation, an overview, important points, and application sections.

Read   Think   Write   Speak   Collaborate

4. Sales Message: Promoting a Product of Your Choice (Objs. 1, 2)

Select a product that you own, assume that you are its distributor, and write a sales letter addressed to customers who are your age. Regardless of whether you select an item as expensive as an SUV or as inexpensive as an MP3 player, choose a product on which you are sold. You have pride in it; you have benefited greatly from its use; you are well informed about it; and you could heartily recommend it to others. You may assume an accompanying picture, brochure, or web site is mentioned in the letter.

Required: Write a sales letter providing an address for a fictitious customer.

5. Desktop Publishing: Creating Effective Visual Elements (Objs. 1, 2)

Referring to the letter you wrote in Application 4, create effective visual elements to enhance your sales appeal.

Required: Use desktop publishing capabilities available to you to design a creative, attention-getting layout, including a letterhead, for the letter you prepared in Application 4. Provide a fictitious name and address for your company. Develop an effective flyer, or brochure to accompany your letter.

6. Persuasive Claim: Your Dilemma (Objs. 1, 3)

Identify a situation in which you believe an adjustment is warranted but you doubt the company will comply without persuasion. Perhaps a retailer has already refused to make an adjustment, but you believe the manufacturer should be informed of your dissatisfaction.

Required: Write the claim letter to the appropriate recipient.

7. Persuasive Message: Investigating Expanded E-Commerce Capability (Objs. 1, 3)

Your company's Internet site has remained relatively static for several years. Although customers can access a wealth of information about your company and its products, they cannot order products without calling your toll-free number. You have read extensively about the changing trends in consumer behavior that indicate that consumers increasingly favor companies that provide e-commerce capability. You are convinced that the recent loss of market share can be attributed to the loss of these Internet customers. Unfortunately, personnel in your information technology group do not seem to have the time or expertise to develop an e-commerce system. Through your involvement in a local community organization, you have developed a friendship with an Internet consultant who you believe should be contracted to develop the system.

Required: Write a persuasive memo to the president requesting his authority to prepare a request-for-proposal for development of an e-commerce system. Attach a copy of an article or a printout from a web site that outlines the value of e-commerce and provides specific examples of companies that have increased sales or market share via e-commerce.

8. Persuasive Request: Securing Volunteer Services for Service Organization (Objs. 1, 3)

You are responsible for finding a suitable person to perform a special activity for a service organization to which you belong. Using your own interests and creativity, specify the exact nature of this activity. For example, you might ask a financial planner to discuss mutual funds at a monthly meeting; an accountant to prepare tax returns for senior citizens; or a computer programmer to assist in automating membership records. Assume that the individual must be convinced to respond favorably because of circumstances that you specify (e.g., too busy, not a member of your organization, no previous experience in such civic activities, etc.).

Required: Write a letter or e-mail to the person of your choice inviting him/her to assist in the activity you specified. Include any details needed to make arrangements for his/her participation in this activity.

Read   Think   **Write**   Speak   Collaborate

9. Sales Message: Promoting Insurance for Legal Services (Objs. 1, 3)

You are an agent for a national insurance company that has begun offering a prepaid legal insurance plan. In exchange for a membership fee or premium, policyholders receive basic legal services at no cost and reduced rates for other legal services. Legal services are provided by a local attorney contracted through the insurance company. To promote this new coverage, you decide to send an e-mail message to clients who have homeowners coverage with you and have subscribed to receive your regular e-mail newsletters and electronic updates.

Required: In preparation for writing this message, use the Internet to expand your knowledge of prepaid legal insurance plans and the text support site at **http://lehman.swlearning.com** to learn more about the design of effective permission marketing communication. Write an e-mail message to your current clients persuading them to come by your office for an annual insurance checkup, including a short presentation on the benefits of prepaid legal insurance plans.

10. Sales Message: Mixing Your Own Music on a Custom CD (Objs. 1, 3)

The sale of music on the Internet has become very popular. From a list containing over 200,000 titles from nearly 2,000 artists, Songfly.com enables its customers to build custom-designed CDs containing titles from various artists. The company pays artists a royalty based on the number of times their songs are selected.

Required: Access Songfly.com or a similar site identified by searching "online music" in your favorite search engine. Identify a popular artist whose music is not currently available on the site. Write a letter persuading this artist to make a sample of his or her music available on the site for a royalty. Provide a fictitious address.

11. Sales Message: Setting Up an E-business Center for Business Travelers (Objs. 1, 2)

Many national motels/hotels have equipped their rooms to enable business travelers to connect their notebook and handheld computers to the Internet. Access to the Internet, however, is limited for business travelers who do not carry notebook computers. As an owner of a computer consulting firm, you have developed a niche installing e-business sites in hotels. Adapting a typical motel room, you install a network of computers, printers, scanners, fax machines, and Internet access that customers use for an hourly fee. The hotel simply provides the room and receives 10 percent of the revenues. Existing installations currently generate an average monthly revenue of $10,000.

Required: Write a letter persuading a local hotel to contract with you to install an e-business center in one of its rooms.

12. Sales Message: What's Cooking at Viking Range? (Objs. 1, 2)

As a new dealer of Viking Range Corporation, a manufacturer of commercial-type appliances for the home, you are preparing an e-mail sales promotion to customers who have recently purchased a Viking range or grill. Your e-mail will encourage these customers to attend one of the cooking classes held at the Viking Culinary Arts Center. Visit the Viking Range web site at **http://www.viking-range.com** and click "Instruction" to obtain information about class locations, calendar and description of classes offered, instructors, and retail stores for purchasing the special cooking equipment demonstrated.

Required: Write an e-mail message promoting the Culinary Arts Center to your new customers. Send the message to your instructor.

13. Persuasive Claim: Look Who's Talking (Objs. 1, 3)

You recently paid $250 to Keller & Jenkins for adding a provision in your will to establish a scholarship endowment at your alma mater. While eating lunch in a crowded restaurant, Sallie Wimberly, a clerk at Keller & Jenkins, stopped by your table to commend you on your planned generosity. Although no harm was intended, you were placed in the uncomfortable position of explaining the clerk's comments to your lunch guests. Keller & Jenkins provides its clients with a bill of rights that clearly states that client information will be kept strictly confidential.

Required: Write a letter to H. Daniel Keller, the lawyer who performed the legal work for you. Inform him of the situation and seek a full refund for the legal services.

14. Persuasive Claim: Golf Instruction Not Up to Par (Obj. 1, 3)

Refer to Application 18 in Chapter 7 on page 280 for this case.

Required: Write a letter persuading the director to reimburse you for half the cost of the tuition. You feel this amount is justified as the instruction provided during the first day of school was adequate. Address the letter to Will Mahan, Director, PineRidge Golf Academy, 34 Kinsey Drive, Kaukauna, WI 54130-9752.

15. Persuasive Claim: Equipment Malfunction Justifies an Exchange (Objs. 1, 3)

Six months ago you bought a digital camcorder from a computer retailer in your town. After a week of use, it no longer saves pictures to the memory stick. Because it had a two-year warranty, you returned it to the retailer for repair. One week later you took it home, and again you cannot take a photograph. After six months of continually returning the camcorder for repair, you feel you deserve a new camcorder. The local retailer will not give you a new unit, so you decide to write to the manufacturer.

Required: Write a persuasive letter explaining that you feel justified in asking for a new camcorder because yours has been in the repair shop more than it has been available for use. Address the letter to ScanScope, 580 West Lakes Blvd., Milwaukee, WI 53202-0580. (You may adapt this case to an actual problem you have experienced for which you would have written a persuasive claim.)

16. Persuasive Request: Challenge Courses Build Team Leadership (Objs. 1, 3)

The size of your accounting firm is about to double as it plans to absorb a large number of accountants from another firm that is being dissolved. Having previous experience with a merger, you recognize the inherent problems with merging two former competitors into a single, cohesive team. To help with this transition, you believe the staff would benefit from a ropes challenge course conducted at the local Boy Scout camp. The ropes course challenges groups to perform a variety of activities that develop teamwork, communication, and imaginative thinking. For example, blindfolded and unable to speak, group members must place themselves in order by birthdate. After each activity, groups are "debriefed" to identify how well they worked as a team to overcome each obstacle. To learn more about the organizational benefits of challenge courses, locate the following article available in full text from InfoTrac College or perhaps from another database available through your campus library:

Steinfield, C. (1997, April). Challenge courses can build strong teams. *Training & Development,* 51(4), 12–13.

Required: Write a memo persuading Sean Hargett, the managing partner, to organize a firm outing centered around the challenge course.

17. Persuasive Request: Kick Your Way to Good Health and More (Objs. 1, 3)

Several months ago a friend invited you to attend his test to attain a black belt in Tae Kwon Do (TKD). You were inspired to join his dojang and have been overwhelmed by the change this martial art has made in your life. Not only are you more physically fit, but your renewed confidence has had a positive impact on your job performance. You believe many of your coworkers could benefit from the same experience as many of them are overweight, exercising sporadically if at all, and increasingly have a poor attitude toward their jobs and the company.

Required: Write an e-mail to your manager, Karen Hunter, encouraging her to provide an incentive for employees to enroll in an introductory TKD session. The message should request that the company pay the nominal fee and encourage the manager to demonstrate her support by being the first person to register. (Alternately, you may choose to encourage participation in a similar fitness program that you advocate strongly.)

18. Persuasive Request: Technology Can Aid Local Pharmacy (Objs. 1, 3)

For many years your family has filled its prescriptions at a locally owned pharmacy. The pharmacist is a family friend, provides excellent service, and sells at competitive prices. However, the pharmacy has yet to adopt any technology to simplify the process of ordering refills. From your experiences as a customer with other types of businesses, you know that an automated telephone system could be installed that allows customers to order refills, day or night, by entering their prescription number and customer identification information using a touch-tone telephone.

Required: Write a letter to Mitchell Garrand, Garrand Pharmacy, 180 Center Grove Street, Grand Junction, MI 49056-3307, persuading him to install a telephone system to accept refill orders on prescription drugs.

19. Persuasive Request: Web Site Redesign Needed to Satisfy Repeat Customers (Objs. 1, 3)

As a small business owner, you regularly purchase office supplies using the web site of a national office supply company. Each time you place an order, you are required to search through the company's extensive online catalog to identify the items you need. You believe this time-consuming task could be more efficient if the web site allowed a repeat customer to enter an account number to obtain a list of the customer's most recent purchases that could be modified for the current order.

Required: Write a letter to the customer relations department of a national office supply company persuading the company to modify its web site.

20. Persuasive Request: Additional Information Needed to Evaluate Investments (Objs. 1, 3)

Many corporations enable investors to make monthly stock purchases using automatic drafts on the investors' checking accounts. While taking advantage of this investment opportunity, you notice that the monthly transaction advice from Harris Industries contains only some of the information you desire (shown below). In addition to information regarding the current month's purchase, the advice reports the total shares purchased to date. However, the advice does not report the total amount invested to date. Without this data you cannot compute the weighted-average price of shares purchased.

Dividend Reinvestment   **Transaction Advice**

Keller Corporation
Account # 4000-7650-64128

Frances R. Vanlandingham
912 Tanglewood Drive
Southaven, MS 38671-0912

Transaction Type:	Automatic Draft
Transaction Date:	07/20/04
Balance Forward:	129.784
Shares Purchased:	14.473
New Balance:	144.257
Funds Submitted:	$200.00
Transaction Fee:	$1.00
Funds Invested:	$199.00
Purchase Price:	$13.75

Important! Retain this advice for tax purposes.

Required: Assuming you have selected the "Customer Feedback" button on the company's web site, compose a message to Harris Industries persuading the company to modify its transaction advice to report the total amount invested to date and the weighted-average price per share.

21. Persuasive Request: Reduced Wait Time Enhances Park Experience (Objs. 1, 3)

Individuals who frequent amusement parks are all-too familiar with long waiting lines. During a recent visit to Disney World in Orlando, you experienced how Disney's FASTPASS^{sm} system and single-rider lines significantly reduced the time park guests spend waiting in lines. FASTPASS^{sm} allows a guest to obtain a reserved time for selected high-traffic attractions. Individuals waiting in the single-rider lines occupy empty seats that result when group sizes do not match the ride's seating capacity. For example, when a family of five boards a six-passenger car, an individual in the single-rider line is seated in the sixth seat.

Required: Research FASTPASS^{sm} on Disney's web site (**http://www.disney.com**). Write a letter to an amusement park in your area encouraging it to develop similar systems to reduce rider wait time and thus enhance the guest's entertainment experience.

22. Persuasive Request: Persuading Employees to Complete Community Service (Objs. 1, 3)

Your corporation strongly believes that it should give back to the community. Thus, each of the corporation's manufacturing plants is directed to select one community organization to sponsor. The corporation encourages, but does not require, its employees to donate one day each quarter in service to the organization and authorizes a $5,000 donation per year. Corporate policy requires that the sponsored organization be rotated every three years. By the slimmest margin, the employees at your plant recently voted to sponsor the local high school.

The athletic director at the high school has requested that your employees provide leadership in creating a field for the girls' softball team. The first work day would entail purchasing and installing pipe for a sprinkler system.

Required: Write an e-mail to the employees persuading them to participate in the work day, scheduled for the last Friday of this month. Lunch and refreshments will be served. Employees who do not participate in the work day must report to the plant to assist in regular maintenance of the production equipment.

Read   Think   Write   **Speak**   Collaborate

---

23. Sales Message: Practicing Sales Pitches (Objs. 1, 2)

Form groups of two and select a tangible item from a collection provided by your instructor or one of your own choice (your PDA, purple stapler, nifty white-out pen, cool backpack, or favorite tee-shirt or accessory, etc.).

Required:

1. Designate one member of the team as the buyer and one the seller. The seller will present a compelling sales pitch for the item to the buyer focusing on an appropriate central appeal and convincing evidence. Following the sales pitch, the buyer will give friendly feedback for making the pitch more convincing. Reverse roles except the buyer will sell himself/herself as a potential employee of the company that makes the item. Again, share friendly feedback for improving the presentation and discuss differences you encountered in selling a product versus promoting yourself. Be prepared to share your experiences with the class.

2. Use the experience gained from the previous activity to deliver a one- to two-minute sales pitch on a pet project or idea you genuinely support. Choose at least three points that prove your case.

24. Persuasive Request: Calling for Continued Support (Objs. 1, 3)

As a business professional, you may be asked to serve on the board of directors of a philanthropic organization. Assume you are on the board of directors of the Pearson Foundation, an organization dedicated to providing scholarships to first-generation college students in your state. The Foundation has recently seen its endowment funds shrink as a result of a bear market. As a result, the Foundation will be unable to fund the typical number of scholarships unless additional donations are received. You have been asked to assist in developing a plan to solicit the necessary funds.

Required: Write a voice script to be read by volunteers encouraging past donors to increase their annual contributions by 10 percent. In small groups, practice delivering your message as a conversation.

25. Persuasive Request: Volunteer Must Complete Commitment (Objs. 1, 3)

HomeBuilders, a not-for-profit organization that builds low-mortgage houses for needy families, recently initiated its annual fund-raising drive. Allison Ivey, the manager of Ivey Electronic Service, was among numerous business executives who volunteered to solicit pledges from 50 area businesses. These volunteers agreed to submit pledges weekly and to complete the drive by May 15. With the deadline only two weeks away, Allison has turned in only five pledge cards. Most of the other volunteers have completed at least 80 percent of their solicitations.

Required: Write a voice script of a telephone call to Allison persuading her to call on the remaining 45 businesses and to submit the pledges by the deadline.

Read Think Write Speak Collaborate

26. Persuasive Request: Company Logo: It's Time for a Change (Objs. 1, 3)

Company logos are often the centerpiece of advertising campaigns and are a crucial tool for developing consumer recognition. Do you, for example, recognize the logos of Nike, McDonalds, and Intel? Companies sometimes change their logos in an effort to project a new image or simply to give the logos a contemporary look.

Required: In small groups, identify a company whose logo you believe needs to be updated and draft a proposed change. Assuming you are an investor in that company, write a letter to its customer relations department persuading the company to change the company logo. Attach a draft of your proposed change. Be prepared to present your recommendation to the class in a brief report.

27. Tackling Your Own Persuasion Challenge (Objs. 1, 3)

In small groups, identify a situation in your work, educational experience, or school and community organizations that requires persuasion. How are you uniquely qualified for a scholarship, award, internship, admission into graduate school or honorary organization, or election to an officer position in a student or community organization? Could a fund-raising event for a student organization or class project benefit from the development of a sales letter and flyer? What changes could enhance services or operations on your campus (e.g., increase number of concerts offered each semester, expand campus shuttle routes to locations off campus, extend hours of operation for computer labs, etc.)? How could a change in a procedure improve the quality and efficiency of your work? How could a particular software

product, training program, or piece of equipment improve your ability to complete a job function? Why should you be promoted or your present job reclassified to a level of higher responsibility?

Required: Send your instructor an e-mail message describing the exact nature of your persuasive situation and asking approval for this topic. After receiving your instructor's approval, write the persuasive message to the appropriate person, convincing him or her to accept your idea or take the action you have recommended. Obtain the facts and figures necessary to present your argument, identify the benefits the receiver will derive from complying, anticipate the arguments that may come from the receiver, and have a rational and logical response to those arguments. Indicate the exact action you wish to be taken. Create visual aids to support your request and be prepared to make a brief presentation to the class.

28. Persuasive Request: Turning Away Customers—Not Again (Objs. 1, 3)

Gordon's Deli is filled to capacity during the lunch hour because of its convenient location in the center of the downtown business district and its reputation for delicious specialty foods. As a summer employee, daily you watch small groups of office workers stand impatiently checking their watches as they wait for a table; other groups leave as soon as they see the long lines. While waiting for a table, numerous customers have told you they prefer your wide selection of healthy food choices over the other fast-food restaurants in the area. Often they cannot leave the office for lunch because of pressing deadlines and are forced to skip lunch or eat snacks from a vending machine. No space is available for expanding the dining room to shorten the waiting line.

FedEx Uses AIDA Approach on the Web

The AIDA formula for inductive persuasion is a staple element in many advertising and promotional efforts. The four-step formula can also be applied to the design of web communications. Visit the FedEx web site at **http://www. fedex.com** to determine how FedEx Corp. has incorporated the four fundamental steps into its web message in order to attract and retain customers. Write a short report that presents your analysis.

Part 4 continues exploration of the persuasive power of electronic communication for FedEx and other organizations

http://www.fedex.com

Visit the text support site at **http://lehman.swlearning.com** to complete Part 4 of the FedEx ShowCASE.

However, you believe customers who are eating on the run would react favorably to what you are calling a FaxFood Line: Customers would fax their orders, with delivery to their office guaranteed within a half hour. You realize that not all your menu items can be delivered effectively, and you cannot afford to deliver small orders. Other resistance includes the logistics of receiving and confirming orders, especially for those ordering as a group from the same office but wanting individual totals.

Required:

1. Working in a team, write a memo to persuade the manager to introduce the FaxFood Line. Mention you are attaching a draft of a fax promoting the new service to downtown office workers and the order forms needed to expedite your plan.

2. Write a fax with a creative message including graphics to promote this new service to downtown office workers. (Provide your own name for the service if you wish.)

3. Design an order form for the FaxFood Line and the confirmation form you will send after the order is received. Use your own creativity to generate a list of menu items or select them from the menu of your favorite deli.

Internet Case

How to Get Off the Lists

The solicitation phone call interrupts dinner once again. The mailbox and the e-mail inbox are stuffed with the usual array of junk mail. What can consumers do about these unwelcomed contacts? Nine out of ten households have received at least one telemarketing call, according to the American Teleservices Association, an industry trade group. By some estimates, telemarketers make 18 million calls a day, or 12,500 a minute. Additionally, consumer mailboxes are crowded with catalogs, sweepstakes offers, and credit card solicitations. The U.S. Postal Service reports that the average household gets ten pieces of unsolicited third-class mail each week. All that is necessary to get on solicitation lists is to get a credit card, open a checking account, or complete a survey. But there are ways to get off the lists:[17]

- **Opt out.** The first step in preventing unwanted calls and mail is to "opt out" of sales lists through the National Do Not Call Registry launched by the Federal Trade Commission in July 2003 and industry associations such as the Direct Marketing Association (DMA), which also operates a free nationwide name-removal service for both phone and mail. Once your request takes effect, it should drastically reduce the number of calls from publishers, credit card companies, telecommunications and utilities corporations, and major non-profit groups. To reduce phone calls, sign up for the national-do-not-call list by calling a toll-free number or registering online at **(http://www.donotcall. gov/)**. Registrations must be renewed every five years. Register for the DMA's Telephone Preference Service (at **http://www.dmaconsumers.org/consumerassistance. html**) or send your full name, address, and phone number with area code to: Telephone Preference Service, c/o Direct Marketing Association, P.O. Box 9014, Farmingdale, New York 11735-9014. Removing your name from a spam e-mail list is more difficult; offers to remove your name from unwanted e-mail sender lists are generally untrue and often result in your name getting added to yet another list.

- **Maintain privacy.** In 1998, two thirds of American adults made purchases by mail or over the phone, according to the DMA. Though you might enjoy ordering from home, remember that companies with whom you do business will keep you on their sales lists unless you tell them not to. Once you are pegged as a buyer, an organization will sell your name to other companies and the calls and mail will just keep coming. To reduce your exposure, never enter contests or complete surveys with your name and address or from your private e-mail account, and use care when posting to newsgroups. Tell every company with which you do business not to sell your name. Set up a separate e-mail account just for ordering purposes.

- **Be persistent.** Laws do not prevent a company from sending you mail, unless it is pornographic, sexually offensive, or involves fraud. In that case, contact your postmaster to launch an investigation. If you continue to receive other unwanted mail, write directly to the companies to tell them to stop. With first-class mail, you can print that request right on the envelope, along with "refused" or "return to sender." But since the post office won't return third-class mail, the more common rate for solicitations, you will have to use your own stamps. Include the mailing label in your request so the company can find you on its sales list. Complain to your senator or representative about the need for laws to regulate unwelcomed solicitations.

- **Know the law.** Even after removing your name from sales lists, you may still get calls from telemarketers who simply dial random numbers. The Telephone Consumer Protection Act (TCPA) of 1991 restricts residential telemarketing calls to between 8 a.m. and 9 p.m. and requires that telemarketers keep a do-not-call list. You can also place your name on the "Do Not Call" national registry, which will enable you to be deleted from phone calling lists of most organizations for five years. Telemarketers who disregard the registry can be fined. To file a telemarketing complaint or request information about the TCPA, write to Federal Communications Commission, Consumer Complaints, Washington, DC 20554 or file online at **http://www.ftc. gov.** Report repeat offenders to your state attorney general, who may take legal action against them.[18]

- **Follow through.** Keep a log near the phone to document calls. Write down the telemarketer's name, company, and time of call. If you haven't done business with them before, telemarketers are required to state their company's address or phone number during the solicitation, but most do not—a violation worth up to $500. After asking to be put on a company's do-not-call list, request a copy of its do-not-call policy. Failure to send the policy is an additional violation of up to $500. Check your log to see whether the same organization calls twice within 12 months after you've asked to be put on their no-call list. If so, that's another $500 violation, which can be tripled if the company is found to be willfully disregarding the law.

- **Protect yourself.** Legally speaking, salespeople are not allowed to lie. Under the Federal Trade Commission's Telemarketing Sales Rule, callers must disclose the company's identity, the purpose of the call, the product or service offered and any requirements for obtaining it. If a telemarketer won't do those things, hang up. To determine whether a telemarketer or mail offer is fraudulent, contact the NFIC at 800-876-7060 or visit them at **http://www.fraud. org.** You can also check with your local consumer protection agency or Better Business Bureau.[19]

Visit the text support site at **http://lehman.swlearn-ing. com** to link to web resources related to this topic. As directed by your instructor, complete one or more of the following:

1. Prepare a presentation that describes current legal provisions that address the problem of unsolicited telephone calls, mailings, and e-mail. Make recommendations for enforcement of existing laws and/or the passage of further legal requirements.

2. Discuss the challenges faced by telemarketers. Prepare a list of suggestions for phone solicitors to aid them in completing more successful contacts.

3. **GMAT** Prepare a short paper in which you argue for the right of sellers to offer products and services via telephone or mail.

Ironbound Supply: The Power of Information Technology

Ironbound Supply, Newark, New Jersey, supplies the pipes that are used to move heat and chemicals through commercial buildings. Owner Howard Kent is responsible for building the business and implementing technology to streamline various systems.

In an effort to keep growing his business, Kent started a new business selling actuated valves primarily on the Internet. As its web site (**http://www.ironbound.com/**) says, "Ironbound Valve Actuation Company is dedicated to providing quality products at competitive prices to solve industry's problems today." Ironbound is the region's leading valve automation center. Their systems range in size from $1/2$ inch to 24 inches, and they also carry a comprehensive parts inventory and a full line of valve accessories.

In this video case, you will see how the seemingly unsophisticated business of industrial pipe valves and fittings with its bulky, and sometimes greasy and dusty, inventory is using technology in a variety of ways to improve its operations.

View the video segment about Ironbound Supply and related activities on WebTutor or your Professional Power Pak CD.

Discussion Questions

1. In what ways has technology been used to change the way Ironbound's products, which have not changed in over 30 years, are made and sold?

2. What are some ways that the technologies of the fax machine and the computerized inventory system and customer database can work together to increase sales?

3. Consider the statement from the video, "The right technology at the right time improves sales and service and lightens the load for employees." What issues has Ironbound addressed in relation to this quotation and its use of the Internet to sell selected products?

Activities

The largest company on the planet—based on sales revenues—according to the *2002 Fortune Global 500* is Wal-Mart Stores (**http://www.fortune.com/fortune/global 500**) with nearly $220 billion in revenues and $6.7 billion in profits. Wal-Mart Stores had a fiscal 2002 end-of-year worldwide store count of 4,414, which includes Discount Stores, Supercenters, Sam's Clubs, and Neighborhood Markets in the U.S., Argentina, Brazil, Canada, China, Germany, South Korea, Mexico, Puerto Rico, and the United Kingdom.[20]

Wal-Mart has long been known as a company that invests heavily in information technology to develop systems that allow everyone throughout the organization to have quick and reliable access to important information. In fact, many attribute Wal-Mart's phenomenal growth and success in large part to its expert use of technology.

Locate the following article available in full text from InfoTrac College or perhaps from another database available through your campus library:

Wal-Mart harnesses power of information technology. (2001, July 22). *Chain Drug Review*, 84.

Respond to the following questions in a short report or presentation to the class.

1. What four forms of technology discussed in this article does Wal-Mart use?

2. What kinds of information does Retail Link provide? Who gets access to the data?

3. How has Wal-Mart tried to help those who are less technologically savvy to use information in Retail Link?

4. What similarities can you identify between how Ironbound Supply uses technology and what you've learned in this article about Wal-Mart's use of technology?

Communication Through Reports and Business Presentations

iv

9 Understanding the Report Process and Research Methods

© JIM CALLAWAY/BLOOMBERG NEWS/LANDOV

Objectives *When you have completed Chapter 9, you will be able to:*

1 Identify the characteristics of a report and the various classifications of business reports.

2 Identify the four steps in the problem-solving process.

3 Select appropriate secondary and primary methods for solving a problem.

4 Locate both printed and electronic sources of information.

5 Explain the purpose of sampling and describe four sampling techniques.

6 Explain the process for documenting referenced information.

7 Apply effective techniques for collecting survey data.

8 Explain techniques for the logical analysis and interpretation of data.

RESEARCH AND DEVELOPMENT STRATEGIES OFFER NEW BEST SELLERS FOR PROCTER & GAMBLE

Procter & Gamble is a long-standing American success story. With nearly $40 billion in annual sales, it currently offers more than 300 brands in 140 countries. Virtually every kitchen and bathroom cabinet in the United States contains at least one P & G product, long-standing brands such as Ivory, Clearasil, Old Spice, Head & Shoulders, and Pepto-Bismol, and more recently—Dryel and Febreze.

Over its 160+ year history, Procter & Gamble traditionally aimed to double its sales every decade and largely succeeded by simply improving versions of the same classic products. Tide, for example, has gone through more than 60 product upgrades since its launch. But repeating the same formula works for only so long, and a growth slowdown during the 1980s emphasized the need to respond quickly to emerging trends and create demand for novel products. P & G's current strategy, however, is based on recognition that balance is needed in allocating resources for the maintenance of current brands and the research and development of new products.

Over the years, Procter & Gamble had a long-standing reputation of doing things right but doing them slowly. Aggressive corporate remake initiatives in the 1990s focused on the rapid introduction of various new offerings: Fit, an antibacterial fruit and vegetable cleanser; Thermacare, a portable heat wrap; Swiffer, a dry mop; Febreze, a spray-on odor eliminator; and of course, Dryel, the home dry-cleaning product. According to Alan G. Lafley, P & G's CEO, the transformation was costly to the company. In the company's effort to convince consumers they needed kinds of products they had never even heard of, promotion of some of its core products suffered, as did profits. "In hindsight, it's clear we changed too much too soon," says Lafley.[1] Now, the company is committed to doing things right, though perhaps not quite as quickly.

Following Lafley's appointment as CEO in mid-2000, P & G conducted extensive research of their current sales and spending to determine which efforts should be continued and which should be targeted for disposal. Factors considered in the analysis included global consumer markets, the reduction of trade barriers, and demographic and technological changes. Some well-established brands such as Coast and Prell were sold because they were deemed as not fitting into the global vision of the company. Presently, attention is focused on various products that reflect intensive scientific research efforts: Febreze Allergen Reducer—created to appeal to the 75 million U.S. allergy sufferers,[2] and Olay Regenerist, an amino peptide complex that signals a new approach to anti-aging skin care.[3]

Effective marketing research will enable P & G to continue the success of its well-known lines and the development of new product categories. As a manager, you will be faced with the challenge of maximizing results for your organization, division, or department. Conducting successful research will provide you with the information needed to propose and implement effective solutions.

http://www.pg.com

See ShowCASE, Part 2, on page 351 for Spotlight Communicator Alan Lafley, Procter & Gamble's CEO.

The Characteristics of Reports

"Hello, Kristen. This is Abe in customer service. The boss wants to know how things are going with the 400-case Stanphill order. Are we going to make the 4 p.m. shipping deadline?"

"Oh hi, Abe. We are going to make the deadline, with time to spare. We have about 250 cases on the loading dock, 100 on the box line, and 50 going through the labeling process. They'll all be ready for the loader at two o'clock."

This brief exchange illustrates a simple reporting task. A question has been posed; the answer given (along with supporting information) satisfies the reporting requirement. Although Kristen may never have studied report preparation, she did an excellent job; so Abe, in turn, can report to his supervisor. Kristen's spoken report is a simple illustration of four main characteristics of reports:

- *Reports typically travel upward in an organization because they usually are requested by a higher authority.* In most cases, people would not generate reports unless requested to do so.
- *Reports are logically organized.* In Kristen's case, she answered Abe's question first and then supported the answer with evidence to justify it. Through your study of message organization, you learned the difference between deductive and inductive organization. Kristen's report was deductively organized. If Kristen had given the supporting evidence first and followed that with the answer that she would meet the deadline, the organization of her reply would have been inductive and would still have been logical.
- *Reports are objective.* Because reports contribute to decision making and problem solving, they should be as objective as possible; when nonobjective (subjective) material is included, the report writer should make that known.
- *Reports are generally prepared for a limited audience.* This characteristic is particularly true of reports traveling within an organization and means that reports, like letters, memos, and e-mails can be prepared with the receivers' needs in mind.

Critical Thinking

How can receivers' needs be addressed in an organization's annual financial report?

Types of Reports

Based on the four characteristics, a workable definition of a **report** is an orderly, objective message used to convey information from one organizational area to another or from one organization to another to assist in decision making or problem solving. Reports have been classified in numerous ways by management and by report-preparation authorities. The form, direction, functional use, and content of the report are used as bases for classification. However, a single report might fit several classifications. The following brief review of classification illustrates the scope of reporting and establishes a basis for studying reports.

- *Formal or informal reports.* The formal/informal classification is particularly helpful because it applies to all reports. A **formal report** is carefully structured; it is logically organized and objective, contains much detail, and is written in a style that tends to eliminate such elements as personal pronouns. An **informal report** is usually a short message written in natural or personal language. The internal memo generally can be described as an informal report. All reports can be placed on a continuum of formality, as shown in Figure 9-1. The distinction among the degrees of formality of various reports is explained more fully in Chapter 11.
- *Short or long reports.* Reports can be classified generally as short or long. A one-page memo is obviously short, and a report of twenty pages is obviously long. What about in-between lengths? One important distinction generally holds true: as it becomes longer, a report takes on more characteristics of formal reports. Thus, the classifications of formal/informal and short/long are closely related.
- *Informational or analytical reports.* An **informational report** carries objective information from one area of an organization to another. An **analytical report** presents suggested solutions to problems. Company annual reports, monthly financial statements, reports of sales volume, and reports of employee or personnel absenteeism and turnover are informational reports. Reports of scientific research, real estate appraisal reports, and feasibility reports by consulting firms are analytical reports.
- *Vertical or lateral reports.* The vertical/lateral classification refers to the directions reports travel. Although most reports travel upward in organizations, many travel downward. Both represent vertical reports and are often referred to as **upward-directed** and **downward-directed** reports. The main function of vertical reports is to contribute to management *control*, as shown in Figure 9-2. Lateral reports, on the other hand, assist in *coordination* in the organization. A report traveling

Critical Thinking

Why do organizations need information generated from both informational and analytical reports?

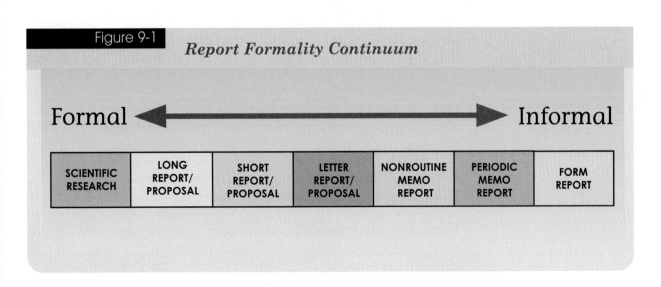

Figure 9-1

Report Formality Continuum

Formal ⟷ Informal

SCIENTIFIC RESEARCH	LONG REPORT/ PROPOSAL	SHORT REPORT/ PROPOSAL	LETTER REPORT/ PROPOSAL	NONROUTINE MEMO REPORT	PERIODIC MEMO REPORT	FORM REPORT

Figure 9-2

The General Upward Flow of Reports

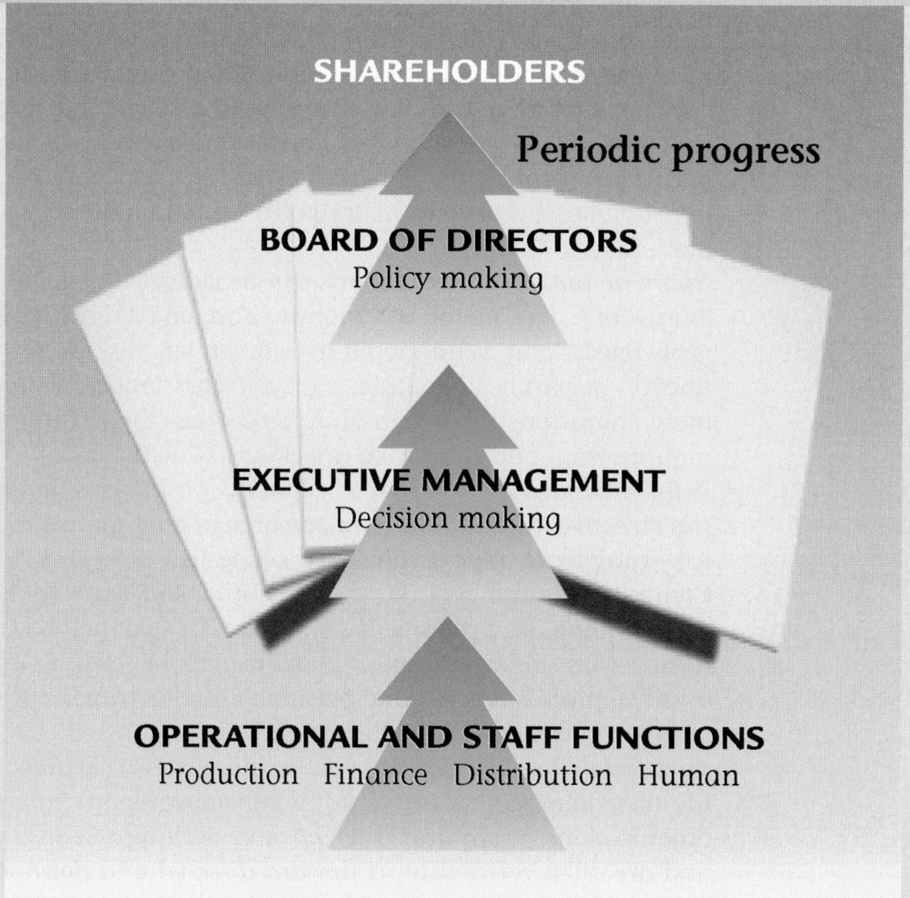

SHAREHOLDERS

Periodic progress

BOARD OF DIRECTORS
Policy making

EXECUTIVE MANAGEMENT
Decision making

OPERATIONAL AND STAFF FUNCTIONS
Production   Finance   Distribution   Human

between units on the same organizational level, as between the production department and the finance department, is lateral.

- *Internal or external reports.* An **internal report**, such as a production and a sales report, travels within an organization. An **external report**, such as a company's annual report to stockholders, is prepared for distribution outside an organization.
- *Periodic reports.* **Periodic reports** are issued on regularly scheduled dates. They are generally directed upward and serve management control purposes. Daily, weekly, monthly, quarterly, semiannual, and annual time periods are typical for periodic reports. Preprinted forms and computer-generated data contribute to uniformity of periodic reports.
- *Functional reports.* A **functional report** serves a specified purpose within a company. The functional classification includes accounting reports, marketing reports, financial reports, personnel reports, and a variety of other reports that take their functional designation from their ultimate use. For example, a justification of the need for additional personnel

or for new equipment is described as a *justification report* in the functional classification.

Proposals

Critical Thinking

What types of proposals do you think you might develop in your career field?

A **proposal** is a written description of how one organization can meet the needs of another; for example, provide products or services or solve problems. Businesses issue "calls for bids" that present the specifications for major purchases of goods and certain services. Most governmental agencies issue "requests for proposals," or RFPs. Potential suppliers prepare proposal reports telling how they can meet that need. Those preparing the proposal create a convincing document that will lead to their obtaining a contract.

In our information-intensive society, proposal preparation is a major activity for many firms. In fact, some companies hire consultants or designate employees to specialize in proposal writing. Chapter 11 presents proposal preparation in considerable detail.

As you review these report classifications, you will very likely decide—correctly—that almost all reports could be included in these categories. A report may be formal or informal, short or long, informational or analytical, vertically or laterally directed, internal or external, periodic or nonperiodic, functionally labeled, a proposal, or some other combination of these classifications. These report categories are in common use and provide necessary terminology for the study and production of reports.

Basis for Reports: The Problem-Solving Process

Objective **2**

Identify the four steps in the problem-solving process.

The upward flow of reports provides management with data that someone may use to make a decision. The purpose is to use the data to solve a problem. Some problems are recurring and call for a steady flow of information; other problems may be unique and call for information on a one-time basis. A problem is the basis for a report. The following steps are used for finding a solution:

1. Recognize and define the problem.
2. Select a method of solution.
3. Collect and organize the data.
4. Arrive at an answer.

Only after all four steps have been completed is a report written for presentation. Reports represent an attempt to communicate how a problem was solved. These problem-solving steps are completed *before* the report is written in final form.

Recognizing and Defining the Problem

Problem-solving research cannot begin until the researchers define the problem. Frequently, those requesting a report will attempt to provide a suitable definition. Nevertheless, researchers should attempt to state the problem clearly and precisely to ensure they are on the right track.

Using Problem Statements, Statements of Purpose, and Hypotheses

The **problem statement**, or statement of the problem, is the particular problem that is to be solved by the research. The **statement of purpose** is the goal of the study and includes the aims or objectives the researcher hopes to accomplish. Research studies often have both a problem statement and a statement of purpose. For example, a real estate appraiser accepts a client's request to appraise a building to determine its market value. The problem is to arrive at a fair market value for the property. The purpose of the appraisal, however, might be to establish a value for a mortgage loan, to determine the feasibility of adding to the structure, or to assess the financial possibility of demolishing the structure and erecting something else. Thus, the purpose may have much to do with determining what elements to consider in arriving at an answer. In other words, unless you know why something is wanted, you might have difficulty knowing what is wanted. Once you arrive at the answers to the *what* and *why* questions, you will be on your way to solving the problem.

Critical Thinking

Of what value is a research study in which the hypotheses are disproved?

A **hypothesis** is a statement to be proved or disproved through research. For example, a study of skilled manufacturing employees under varying conditions might be made to determine whether production would increase if each employee were part of a team, as opposed to being a single unit in a production line. For this problem, the hypothesis could be formulated in this way:

> **Hypothesis:** Productivity will increase when skilled manufacturing employees function as members of production teams rather than as single units in a production line.

Because the hypothesis tends to be stated in a way that favors one possibility or is prejudiced toward a particular answer, many researchers prefer to state hypotheses in the null form. The **null hypothesis** states that no relationship or difference will be found in the factors being studied, which tends to remove the element of prejudice toward an answer. The null hypothesis for the previous example could be written as follows:

Critical Thinking

Write a statement of purpose for this study of teams.

> **Null hypothesis:** No significant difference will be found in productivity between workers organized as teams and workers as individual production line units.

Using the problem/purpose approach and/or the hypothesis approach is a choice of the researcher. In many ways, the purpose of a study is determined by the intended use of its results.

Limiting the Scope of the Problem

Critical Thinking

How does the scope of a report serve a similar purpose as a scope on a rifle?

A major shortcoming that often occurs in research planning is the failure to establish or to recognize desirable limits. The *scope* of the report helps to establish boundaries in which the report will be researched and prepared. Assume, for instance, that you want to study salaries of office support staff. Imagine the enormity of such a task. Millions of people are employed in office support jobs. Perhaps a thousand or so different types of jobs fall into this classification. To reduce such a problem to reasonable proportions, use the *what, why, when, where,* and *who* questions to limit the problem. Here are the limits you might derive as the human resources manager at a metropolitan bank:

What:	A study of salaries of office support staff.
Why:	To determine whether salaries in our firm are competitive and consistent.
When:	Current.
Where:	Our metropolitan area.
Who:	Office support staff employees in banks.

Now you can phrase the problem this way:

Statement of Purpose:	The purpose of this study is to survey salaries of office support staff in local banks to determine whether our salaries are competitive and consistent.

Note that this process of reducing the problem to a workable size has also established some firm limits to the research. You have limited the problem to current salaries, to the local area, and to a particular type of business. Note, too, how important the *why* was in helping establish the limits. Limiting the problem is "zeroing in on the problem."

Critical Thinking

Why would a reader want to know about limitations and delimitations placed on a project?

In some reports, it is desirable to differentiate between the boundaries that were placed on the project outside the control of the researcher(s) and those that were chosen by the researcher(s). Boundaries imposed outside the control of the researchers are called *limitations*; they may include the assignment of the topic, allotted budget, and time for completion of the report. These boundaries affect what and how the topic can be researched. Boundaries chosen by the researcher(s) to make the project more manageable are called *delimitations*; they may include the sources and methods chosen for both primary and secondary research.

Defining Terms Clearly

Vague terms contribute greatly to faulty communication. Words often have more than one meaning; thus a definition of the specific terms in the current study would be necessary. Additionally, technical or special-use words may occur in the report that are not widely used or understood. These terms would also require a definition for the reader's understanding of the information presented. In the previously used example concerning the study of office support staff salaries, a comparison of one bank's salaries with those paid by others would be meaningful only if the information gathered from other banks relates to identical jobs. A job description defining the duties performed by an administrative assistant, for example, would help ensure that all firms would be talking about the same job tasks regardless of the job title. In addition, the term *salary* requires definition. Is it hourly, weekly, monthly, or yearly? Are benefits included?

Documenting Procedures

The procedures or steps a writer takes in preparing a report are often recorded as a part of the written report. This **procedures** section, or **methodology**, adds credibility to the research process and also enables subsequent researchers to repeat, or replicate, the study in another setting or at a later time if desired. Reports that study the same factors in different time frames are called **longitudinal studies**.

The procedures section of a report records the major steps taken in the research, and possibly the reasons for their inclusion. It may, for instance, tell the types of printed and electronic sources that were consulted and the groups of people interviewed and how they were selected. Steps in the procedures section are typically listed in chronological order, so that the reader has an overall understanding of when the research steps took place and the timetable that existed for the project.

Selecting a Method of Solution

Objective 3

After defining the problem, the researcher will plan how to arrive at a solution. You may use secondary and/or primary research methods to collect necessary information.

Select appropriate secondary and primary methods for solving a problem.

Secondary Research

Secondary research provides information that has already been created by others. Researchers save time and effort by not duplicating research that has already been undertaken. They can access this information easily through the aid of electronic databases, bibliographic indexes, and catalogs. Suppose that a marketing manager has been authorized to investigate the feasibility of implementing a strategic information system. The manager knows other companies are using this technology. By engaging in library research, the manager can determine the boundaries of knowledge before proceeding into the unknown.

Critical Thinking

Describe the proper balance between secondary research and primary research.

Certain truths have been established within the confines of a field of knowledge. These truths are treated as principles and reported in textbooks and other publications. However, because knowledge is constantly expanding, the researcher knows that new information is available. The job, then, is to become familiar with the library, canvass the literature of the field, and attempt to redefine the boundaries of knowledge. The researcher can then explore the unknown. Through redefinition of boundaries, secondary research accomplishes the following objectives:

- establishes a point of departure for further research
- avoids needless duplication of costly research efforts
- reveals areas of needed research
- makes a real contribution to a body of knowledge.

Secondary research can be gathered by means of traditional printed sources or by using electronic tools.

Objective 4

Locate both printed and electronic sources of information.

Printed Sources. Major categories of published sources are books, periodicals, and government documents. Books are typically cataloged in libraries by call number, with most larger libraries using the Library of Congress classification system. The card catalog in most libraries has been replaced by an "online catalog," which allows the user to locate desired books by author, title, subject, or key word. A wide assortment of reference books is typically available for use within the library; these include dictionaries, encyclopedias, yearbooks, and almanacs. Some of these volumes contain general information on a wide array of topics, while others are designed for a specific field of study.

Periodicals, referred to as *serials* by librarians, include various types of publications that are released on a regular, periodic basis. Thus, newspapers, magazines, and journals are all types of periodicals. Newspapers, which are usually published daily, are a good initial source for investigation, since they give condensed coverage of timely topics. Magazines may be published weekly, monthly, bimonthly, or in some other interval. They are typically written for a general readership, providing expanded coverage in an easy-to-read format. Journals, on the other hand, are written for more specialized audiences, and are more research oriented. Journal articles share the results of research studies and provide interpretive data that support their findings. They also provide bibliographies or citation lists that can be very useful for locating related materials. Articles on specific topics can be located using both published and online indexes. A noninclusive list of these sources is shown in Figure 9-3.

Electronic Sources. The availability of computer-assisted data searches has simplified the time-consuming task of searching through indexes, card catalogs, and other sources. Weekly and monthly updates keep electronic databases current, and they are easy to use. Databases such as Lexis-Nexis Academic Universe have full-text retrieval capability, meaning you can retrieve the entire article so that you can review it and print a copy. A

Changing Technology

Figure 9-3

Useful Reference Sources

Printed Indexes

Business Periodicals Index
Education Index
The New York Times Index
Readers' Guide to Periodical Literature
Social Science and Humanities Index
The Wall Street Journal Index

Electronic Databases

ABI/INFORM
Academic Search Elite
Business Source Premier
Business Dateline
DIALOG Information Services
ERIC
First Search
Lexis-Nexis Academic Universe
FSI Online
Periodical Abstracts
ProQuest
Westlaw

Biography

Who's Who in America
Similar directories for specific geographic areas, industries, and professions

General Facts and Statistics

Statistical Abstract of the United States
Bureau of the Census publications
Dictionaries (general and discipline specific)
Encyclopedia (*Americana* or *Britannica*)
Fortune Directories of U.S. Corporations
World Atlas
Lexis-Nexis Statistics
Almanacs

Report Style and Format

American Psychological Association. (2001). *Publication manual of the American Psychological Association*, (5th ed.). Washington, DC: Author.

Gibaldi, J. (2003). *MLA handbook for writers of research papers*, (6th ed.). New York: Modern Language Association.

research process that may have taken several hours can be completed in a matter of minutes. Note the list of electronic databases for business users listed in Figure 9-3.

The Internet and its subset, the World Wide Web, have made thousands of reference sources available in a matter of minutes. However, the vastness of this resource can be overwhelming to the novice researcher. Cautions related to the use of the Internet are discussed in the accompanying Strategic Forces feature, "Internet Sources Vary: Caution Advised." The following tips will help to make your Internet search more productive:

Critical Thinking

How have computer-assisted data searches revolutionized the research process?

- *Choose your search engine or database appropriately.* A *search engine* is a cataloged database of web sites that allows you to search on specific topics. Several popular search engines exist, including Google, Yahoo!, AltaVista, HotBot, and Excite. Megasearch engines, such as Google, which indexes more than three billion web pages, search through a number of other engines to produce "hits."[4] (A *hit* is a located web site that contains the word or words specified in the search.) You want to obtain a sufficient number of hits, but not thousands. Although the variety of these larger engines is greater, they pose more difficulty in narrowing a search. Start with a small search engine and then move to a larger one if necessary.

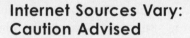

Internet Sources Vary: Caution Advised

The Internet has been likened to a wild, untamed frontier, open to all who desire to exercise their right to free speech. In its decision to declare the Communications Decency Act unconstitutional, the Supreme Court said, "The interest in encouraging freedom of expression in a democratic society outweighs any theoretical but unproven benefit of censorship."[5] Because of the uncensored status of the Internet, the serious researcher has several reasons for exercising caution in using information found there.

- **Internet resources are not always accurate.** Because the Internet is not centrally patrolled or edited, postings come from a wide variety of sources. Some of these sources are reliable and credible; some are not.

- **Certain uses of Internet sources may be illegal.** Some material available on the Internet is copyright protected and therefore not available for some uses by those who download the files. For instance, photograph files that are copyrighted may be viewed by Internet users but not incorporated into documents

that have commercial use, unless permission is granted by the copyright holder. Such permission often involves a royalty fee.

- **Internet resources are not always complete.** Selected text of articles and documents are often available via the Internet, while full text may be available only in published form. Additionally, Internet resources are not always updated to reflect current information.

- **Electronic periodicals are not always subjected to a rigorous review process.** Because most traditional magazines and journal articles are reviewed by an editorial board or peer reviewers, they are considered to be of more value than an article prepared by one or a few individuals that is not critiqued by other experts before its publication. Articles available over the Internet may not have benefited from such a review process.

Because of these limitations, the Internet should not be seen as a substitute for traditional library research, but rather as a complementary search tool. To help you evaluate the credibility and value of web material, apply the following criteria:[6]

- Who wrote this, and who would believe it?

- Is the source educational, commercial, gossip, or solid research?

- What are the credentials of the writer or producer?

- When was it originally published or produced?

- How accurate, current, and organized is the information?

- Why was it done, and where might I get more accurate information?

Application

Select a business topic, if one is not assigned to you by your instructor, and search for resources related to that topic using the Internet. Locate at least one article you feel is a reliable source of valuable information for use in a business report on the assigned topic. Locate at least one article you feel would not be a good choice for use as a reference in a business report. Compose a brief explanation of the reasons for your selections; attach printouts of the selected articles and submit the assignment to your instructor.

Critical Thinking

To what databases does your campus library subscribe?

Electronic databases provide access to articles from newspapers, magazines, journals, and other types of publications. The database provider may charge to access articles either as a subscription fee or a document delivery fee. These types of databases are not accessible by a search engine and are often described as the **hidden internet**. Many libraries provide access to these databases. Some databases are suited for topic searches of general interest; others are geared toward specialized fields. A topic search will produce a listing of references and abstracts for articles, or even full text of some. Databases available through your library might include Business Source Premier, Academic Search Elite, Lexis-Nexis Academic Universe, ABI Inform First Search, Periodical Abstracts, and others.

Critical Thinking

Boolean searches with "and" look for both keywords you include. "Or" searches look for either term.

- *Structure searches from broad to specific.* Use words for your topic that are descriptive and do not have multiple meanings. Once sites have been located for your general topic, you can use **Boolean logic** to narrow the selection. Boolean operands (and, or, not) serve to limit the identified sites. The following example shows how these delimiters can assist you in locating precisely what you want:
  - Using the key phrase "workplace productivity" will produce all sites that have either of the key words in the title or descriptors.
  - Placing "and" between the key words will produce only those hits that have both words.
  - Keying "workplace productivity not United States" will eliminate hits that refer to the United States.
- *Use quotation marks when literal topics are desired.* Putting quotation marks around your topic words can drastically affect the number of hits. The quotation marks cause the search engine to look for the designated words as a phrase, thus producing only those sites that have the phrase present. Without the quotation marks, the search engine will treat the words individually and produce many more hits, most of which may not be useful. For instance, if you are looking for sites related to international communication, placing quotation marks around the desired phrase would eliminate the sites that deal with international topics that are not communication oriented.
- *Look for web pages that have collections of links to other related topics.* Clicking on these hyperlinks will allow you to maximize your time investment in the data-gathering phase of your research.
- *Be adaptable to the various access format requirements.* Each search engine and database has its own particular format and instructions for use. Some require keyboard input and do not respond to your mouse. The method for specifying and narrowing your search will vary.

Primary Research

After reviewing the secondary data, you may need to collect primary data to solve your problem. **Primary research** relies on firsthand data, for example, responses from pertinent individuals or observations of people or phenomena related to your study. Recognized methods to obtain original information are observational studies, experimental research, and normative surveys.

Observational studies are those in which the researcher observes and statistically analyzes certain phenomena in order to assist in establishing new principles or discoveries. For example, market analysts observe buying habits of certain income groups to determine the most desirable markets. An information systems manager tabulates the number of input-operator errors made to assess the effectiveness of a computer training program. Executives analyze the frequency of ethical misconduct to determine the effectiveness of a comprehensive ethics program. Developing an objective system for quantifying observations is necessary to collect valid data. For example, to gain insight on the effect of a comprehensive ethics program, a researcher might record the number of incidents of ethical misconduct reported or the number of calls made to an ethics help-line to seek advice about proper conduct. Observational studies typically involve no contact with the human subjects under study.

Critical Thinking

What are some challenges faced in experimental research?

Experimental research typically involves the study of two samples that have exactly the same components before a variable is added to one of the samples. Any differences observed are due to the variable. Like scientists, businesses use experimental research to solve various problems. As a simple example, assume that a company has a large number of machinists doing the same routine job. Management decides to research the effects of work groups on productivity (hypothesis discussed earlier in this chapter). The study involves the machinists in two plants with similar previous productivity rates. The machinists in one plant are organized into work groups; each machinist in the other plant continues to work as a single person in the production line. During the period of the study, the difference in the two study groups is noted. Because the workgroup organization is assumed to be the only variable, any difference is attributed to its influence. Experimental research can require informed consent from participants that are subjected to experimental methods.

Normative survey research is undertaken to determine the status of something at a specific time. Survey instruments such as questionnaires, opinion surveys, checklists, and interviews are used to obtain information from participants. Election opinion polls represent one type of normative survey research. The term normative is used to qualify surveys because surveys reveal "norms" or "standards" existing at the time of the survey. A poll taken two months before an election might have little similarity to one taken the week before the election.

Critical Thinking

Why is the U.S. census conducted in ten-year intervals rather than longer or shorter ones?

Surveys can help verify the accuracy of existing norms. The U.S. Census is conducted every decade to establish an actual population figure, and each person is supposedly counted. In effect, the census tests the accuracy of prediction techniques used to estimate population during the years between censuses. A survey of what employees consider a fair benefits package would be effective only for the date of the survey. People retire, move, and change their minds often; these human traits make survey research of human opinion somewhat tentative. Yet surveys remain a valuable tool for gathering information on which to base policy making and decision making.

A feedback study of Federal Express's web site led to improved customer satisfaction and a phenomenal increase in the use of the site's package tracking function. At customers' request, FedEx moved the package-tracking window to conveniently appear on the home page (as shown) and developed an online application that allows customers to order supplies.[7]

Objective 5

Explain the purpose of sampling and describe four sampling techniques.

Researchers normally cannot survey everyone, particularly if the population is large and the research budget is limited. **Sampling** is a survey technique that eliminates the need for questioning 100 percent of the population. Sampling is based on the principle that a sufficiently large number drawn at random from a population will be representative of the total population; that is, the sample will possess the same characteristics in the same proportions as the total population. For example, a company collecting market research data before introducing a new low-fat food product would survey only a few people. The data are considered *representative* if the sample of people surveyed has the same percentage of ages, genders, purchasing power, and so on as the anticipated target market. A number of sampling methods are available that you will study in research and statistics courses. Some common methods include the following:

- **Simple random sampling** produces a random sample using a random number generator program. This is the easiest sampling technique. To determine the career plans of a college student body, a researcher could generate a list of random numbers, using software capabilities, and then select the students to be included in the survey. Because the entire student body is included in the computer system, each student would have an equal opportunity to be selected.

- **Stratified random sampling** involves dividing the population into subgroups so that each subgroup is proportionately represented in the sample. In surveying the student body using this method, you might divide the population into student classifications: for example, seniors, juniors, sophomores, and freshmen. Suppose the total student body of 10,000 is composed of 30 percent freshmen, 27 percent sophomores, 23 percent juniors, and 20 percent seniors. If you want to survey 1,000 students, you would randomly select students from each classification until you have

300 freshmen, 270 sophomores, 230 juniors, and 200 seniors. Stratified samples are useful for comparing responses between subgroups.

- **Systematic random sampling** is useful when the researcher has access to a listing of elements or persons within the population to be studied. For instance, a membership list of all members of an organization could give rise to a systematic random sample. The process involves selecting every nth listing for inclusion in the study. For instance, if the total membership of an organization is 1,000, and a sample of 100 is desired, the value of n would be 10. Thus, every tenth name would be selected for inclusion in the study. In this way, the sample will be drawn from throughout the entire membership list.

- **Convenient sampling** is merely a sample selected by the convenience of the researcher, with no assurance that it is representative of the population under study. Convenient sampling is not scientific and therefore not recommended for research gathering; it is, nevertheless, frequently used because it is easy and yields quick results. A professor, for example, might want to identify students' opinion on the adequacy of academic advising available in her university. For convenience, she might choose to survey students in her own classes. The opinions obtained would be questionable as to whether they accurately reflected the opinions of the entire student population, since no procedure was followed to select a random sample. Businesses, too, make frequent use of convenient sampling by conducting "straw polls" of employees, consumers, or other specific groups.

Critical Thinking

Why are public opinion polls often inaccurate?

As a researcher, you must be cautious about drawing conclusions from a sample and generalizing them to a population that might not be represented by the sample. For example, early-morning shoppers may differ from afternoon or evening shoppers; young ones may differ from old ones; men shoppers may differ from women shoppers. A good researcher defines the population as distinctly as possible and uses a sampling technique to ensure that the sample is representative.

Whether a survey involves personal interviewing or the distribution of items such as checklists or questionnaires, some principles of procedure and preplanning are common to both methods. These principles assure the researcher that the data gathered will be both valid and reliable.

Critical Thinking

What steps can you take to ensure that your data are valid and reliable?

- **Validity** refers to the degree to which the data measure what you intend to measure. It generally results from careful planning of the questionnaire or interview questions or items. Cautious wording, preliminary testing of items to detect misunderstandings, and some statistical techniques are helpful in determining whether the responses to the items are valid. A *pilot test* of the instrument is often conducted prior to the full-scale survey. Through this means, a smaller number of participants can test the instrument, which can then be revised prior to wide-scale administration.

- **Reliability** refers to the level of consistency or stability over time or over independent samples; that is, reliable data are reasonably accurate or

A major factor affecting the value of a survey is the way in which it is conducted. The results are only as valid and reliable as the methods the researchers use to select and question a representative sample of the population.

© CHUCK SAVAGE/STOCK MARKET

repeatable. Reliability results from asking a large enough sample of people so that the researcher is reasonably confident the results would be the same even if more people were asked to respond or if a different sample were chosen from the same population. For example, if you were to ask ten people to react to a questionnaire item, the results might vary considerably. If you were to add 90 more people to the sample, the results might tend to reach a point of stability, where more responses would not change the results. Reliability would then be reasonably established.

Responses to surveys conducted by mail often represent only a small percentage of the total mailings. In some cases, a return of 3 to 5 percent is considered adequate and is planned for by researchers. In other cases, depending on the population, the sample, and the information requested, a return of considerably more than half the mailings might be a planned result. Selecting an appropriate data collection method and developing a sound survey instrument are crucial elements of an effective research study.

Collecting and Organizing the Data

Objective 6

Explain the process for documenting referenced information.

Collecting the right data and assuring that they are recorded appropriately is paramount to the success of a business report. Various techniques can assist in this process when collecting both secondary and primary research.

Collecting Secondary Data

When beginning to collect secondary data, beware of collecting too much information—one of the major deterrents to good report writing. Although

SPOTLIGHT COMMUNICATOR

Changing Market Requires Clear Vision, New Strategies

Alan Lafley, Procter & Gamble's CEO, has the daunting task of assuring the continued financial success of a corporate empire into a new millennium. For much of its history, Procter & Gamble was highly innovative, pioneering nearly all the techniques now taken for granted in the consumer goods industry. It created teams of market researchers to find out what products the world wanted, set up laboratories to invent them, and marketed them with new techniques such as advertising during soap operas on radio and television. For as long as the world stayed much the same, the company's proven methods worked, delivering reliable profit growth year after year. Steady success, however, led to entrenched management styles and formal systems and procedures that were policed by headquarters. New products had to undergo years of scrutiny to make sure they could not fail. Individuality was frowned upon as employees learned the P & G way of doing things and operated as robot "Proctoids," as they became known to outsiders.

As the world business environment changed, P & G leadership became convinced that their product development and marketing practices had to be revamped. Extensive restructuring efforts in the 1990s resulted in a revamping of a corporate culture marked by secrecy and strict discipline. The loosening of the formal dress code was indicative of the relaxing of corporate methods. The practice of rewriting memos 20 times was discontinued, as were many of the review committees that stifled initiative and delayed product introduction. But the new culture that was intended to provide more cross communication of information and faster product development also resulted in staff reduction and sagging financial performance.[8]

Through Lafley's efforts, Procter & Gamble appears to have struck a healthy balance between tradition and innovation. Record revenue gains and a doubling in cash flow from operations indicate that Lafley has successfully built on dynamic company initiatives begun in the 1990s while winning support from employees and investors. Described as personable and energetic, Lafley has a reputation for doing a good job and motivating employees. In perhaps his biggest symbolic move, Lafley gutted the 11th floor of P & G corporate headquarters in Cincinnati, the untouched bastion of the company's top executives since the building was constructed 50 years ago. Gone are the offices of 11 division presidents, who have moved out to be closer to their teams. In their

place is a training center that draws employees from around the world.

Observers see Lafley not only as an effective motivator but as a strategic thinker who isn't afraid to make tough decisions, such as selling weak businesses. Lafley knows that new business conditions require new ideas. In commenting on effective change Lafley says, "The consumer is boss. Our scientists understand that innovation is in the consumer's eyes."[9] Gone are the good old predictable days of P & G. "The rate of change and the magnitude of change is accelerating. There is no way I can go back. That is a losing strategy."[10] New opportunities await as Procter and Gamble continues to explore its market potential and plan new product launches.

Applying What You Have Learned

1. How has the process of research and development changed at Procter & Gamble over its history?
2. Why is innovation important to the process of research?
3. Describe Lafley's management style of "gentle toughness."

Alan G. Lafley, Chief Executive Officer, Procter & Gamble

http://www.pg.com

Refer to ShowCASE, Part 3, at the end of the chapter to learn about P & G's use of technology to achieve research and development goals.

you want to be thorough, you do not want to collect and record such a large amount of information that you will hardly know where to begin your analysis.

The availability of computer-assisted data searches has simplified the time-consuming task of searching through indexes, card catalogs, and other sources. For example, suppose you select an online database such as Business Source Premier or an Internet search engine such as Google to research the role of instant messaging in the workplace. By inputting the key term *instant messaging*, you receive the screen output in Figure 9-4 (an Internet search engine) and Figure 9-5 (an online database). The screen output contains information that will facilitate your research.

First, you can quickly evaluate the relevance of each reference by reading the title and the brief summary that may be provided and then clicking on the hyperlink (underlined title) of each reference that appears to have merit. The full text of the selected articles, which can then be saved to disk or printed out, will be displayed. Retrieved articles can be read and analyzed for useful information. Be sure to obtain a full bibliographic citation for each reference you obtain. This procedure can eliminate the need to revisit the library or the online database.

After you have located the relevant sources, you can begin taking notes using various methods. Because your aim is to *learn*, not to accumulate, the following technique for taking notes is effective:

Critical Thinking

How does the statement, "Become an expert before becoming an author" apply to summarizing secondary research?

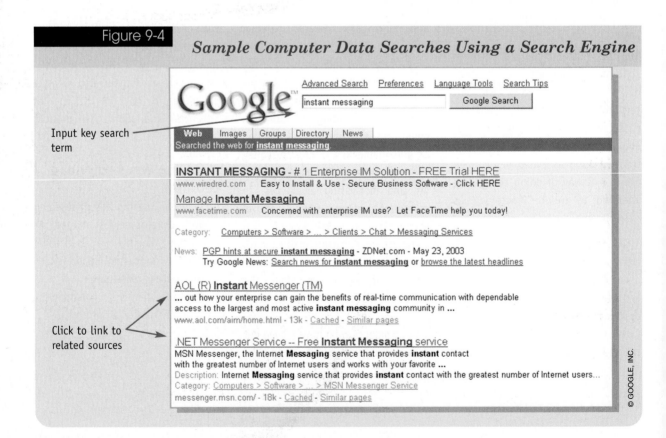

Figure 9-4

Sample Computer Data Searches Using a Search Engine

Figure 9-5

A Sample Computer Data Search Using an Online Database

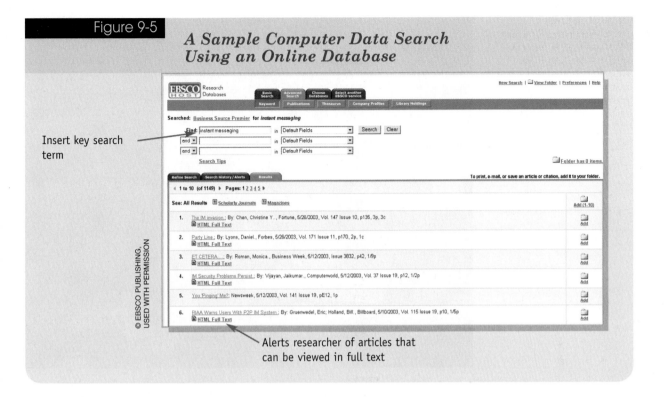

Insert key search term

Alerts researcher of articles that can be viewed in full text

1. Read an article rapidly.
2. Put the article aside.
3. List main and supporting points *from memory*.
4. Review the article to see whether all significant points have been included.

Rapid reading forces concentration. Taking notes from memory reinforces learning and reduces the temptation to rely heavily on the words of others. If you really learn the subject matter of one source, you will (as research progresses) see the relationship between it and other sources.

Traditionally, researchers have read the article and immediately written notes on cards. Currently, researchers often prefer highlighting important points on a photocopy or printout of the article; then from the highlighted material, they write note cards or compose notes at the keyboard. In addition, some researchers use portable computers to facilitate library research. Rather than spending time and money photocopying large volumes of information, researchers compose notes at the keyboard in the library and then return the reference material to the shelf.

Critical Thinking

When is an exact quote beneficial?

You can use two kinds of note-taking: direct quotation or paraphrase. The **direct quotation method** involves citing the exact words from a source. This method is useful when you believe the exact words have a special effect or you want to give the impact of an expert. The **paraphrase method** involves summarizing information in your own words without changing the author's intended meaning. Put direct quotations in quotation marks as a reminder that the material is quoted, and indicate the page numbers of

Charges of plagiarism can diminish your professional reputation and result in costly lawsuits. In 2002, Harry Potter author J. K. Rowling won a court battle against Nancy Stouffer, a U.S. writer who claimed Rowling lifted ideas from her book, *The Legend of Rah and the Muggles*.[11]

© AP/WIDE WORLD PHOTOS

Legal & Ethical Constraints

cited information. This information may save you time relocating the reference.

Plagiarism is the presentation of someone else's ideas or words as your own. To safeguard your reputation against plagiarism charges, be certain to give credit where credit is due. Specifically, provide a citation for each (1) direct quotation and (2) passage from someone else's work that you stated in your own words rather than using the original words (the words are your own, but the idea is not). After identifying the text that must be credited to someone else, develop complete, accurate citations and a reference page according to some recognized referencing method.

Documenting Referenced Material

A crucial part of ethical honest research writing is documenting or referencing sources fairly and accurately. Although time consuming and tedious, meticulous attention to documentation marks you as a respected, highly professional researcher. The *Publication Manual of the American Psychological Association* points out the importance of documentation with a forceful quote by K. F. Bruner: An inaccurate or incomplete reference "will stand in print as an annoyance to future investigators and a monument to the writer's carelessness."[12]

An important first step is to pledge that you will not, for any reason, present someone else's ideas as your own. Then, develop a systematic checklist for avoiding plagiarism. Carelessly forgetting to enclose someone else's words within quotation marks or failing to paraphrase another's words can cause others to question your ethical conduct. When you feel that the tedious work required to document sources fairly and accurately is not worth the time invested, remind yourself of the following reasons for documentation:

- *Citations give credit where it is due—to the one who created the material.* People who document demonstrate high standards of ethical conduct and responsibility in scholarship. Those exhibiting this professional behavior will gain the well-deserved trust and respect of peers and superiors.
- *Documentation protects writers against plagiarism charges.* Plagiarism occurs when someone steals material from another and claims it as his or her own writing. Besides embarrassment, the plagiarist may be assessed fines, penalties, or professional sanctions.
- *Documentation supports your statements.* If recognized authorities have said the same thing, your work takes on credibility; you put yourself in good company.
- *Documentation can aid future researchers pursuing similar material.* Documentation must be complete and accurate so that the researcher can locate the source.

Many style guides are available to advise writers how to organize, document, and produce reports and manuscripts. Figure 9-3 includes two of the most popular authoritative style manuals. The *Publication Manual of the American Psychological Association* has become the most-used guide in the social and "soft" sciences and in many scholarly journals. The *MLA Handbook for Writers of Research Papers* is another authoritative source used in the humanities. These style guides and their format requirements are discussed further in Appendix B.

Follow these general suggestions for preparing accurate documentation:

Critical Thinking

What are the legal and ethical consequences of failing to document the sources for quoted and paraphrased material?

- *Decide which authoritative reference manual to follow for preparing in-text parenthetical citations or footnotes (endnotes) and the bibliography (references).* Some companies and most journals require writers to prepare reports or manuscripts following a particular reference manual. Once you are certain you have selected the appropriate style manual, follow it precisely as you prepare the documentation and produce the report.
- *Be consistent.* If you are carefully following a format, you shouldn't have a problem with consistency. For example, one style manual may require an author's initials in place of first name in a bibliography; another manual requires the full name. The placement of commas and periods and other information varies among reference manuals. Consult the manual, apply the rules methodically, and proofread carefully to ensure accuracy and consistency. If you cannot locate a format for an unusual source in the reference manual you are using, use other entries as a guide for presenting information consistently.
- *Follow the rule that it is better to include more than enough than too little.* When you are in doubt about whether certain information is necessary, include it.

Citations. Two major types of citations are used to document a report: source notes and explanatory notes. Depending on the authoritative style manual used, these notes may be positioned in parentheses within the report, at the bottom of the page, or at the end of the report.

- **Source notes** acknowledge the contributions of others. These citations might refer readers to sources of quotations, paraphrased portions of someone else's words or ideas, and quantitative data used in the report. Source notes must include complete and accurate information so that the reader can locate the original source if desired.
- **Explanatory notes** are used for several purposes: (1) to comment on a source or to provide information that does not fit easily in the text, (2) to support a statistical table, or (3) to refer the reader to another section of the report. The following sample footnote describes the mathematics involved in preparing a table:

> *The weighted opinion was derived by assigning responses from high to low as 5, 4, 3, 2, 1; totaling all respondents; and dividing by the number of respondents.

In this case, the asterisk (*) was used rather than a number to identify the explanatory footnote both in the text and in the citation. This method is often used when only one or two footnotes are included in the report. If two footnotes appear on the same page, two asterisks (**) or numbers or letters are used to distinguish the second from the first. An explanatory note that supports a visual or a source note that provides the reference from which data were taken appears immediately below the visual.

Critical Thinking

Why do numerous referencing methods exist?

Referencing Methods. Various reference methods are available for the format and content of source notes: in-text parenthetical citations, footnotes, and endnotes. Note the major differences among the methods in the following discussion.

- ***In-text parenthetical citations.*** The *APA Manual, MLA Handbook,* and other documentation references eliminate the need for separate footnotes or endnotes. Instead, an in-text citation, which contains abbreviated information within parentheses, directs the reader to a list of sources at the end of a report. The list of sources at the end contains all publication information on every source cited. This list is arranged alphabetically by the author's last name or, if no author is provided, by the first word of the article title.

  The in-text citations contain minimal information needed to locate the source in the complete list. In-text citations prepared using APA include the author's last name and the date of publication; the page number is included if referencing a direct quotation. An MLA citation includes the author's last name and the page number but not the date of publication.
- ***Footnote citation method.*** Placing citations at the bottom of the page on which they are cited is the footnote citation method. It is often referred to as the *traditional method* because of its historic use. The reader can conveniently refer to the source if the documentation is

Changing Technology

positioned at the bottom of the page. A list of footnotes can also be collected at the end of the document in the order they appeared. This numbered listing is appropriately referred to as an *endnotes page*. Footnotes and endnotes are easily created with word processing software and automatically updated each time the report is revised. Footnotes and endnotes are not used in APA and MLA referencing, as these styles permit the use of in-text citations only.

- *References (or Works Cited).* This document is an alphabetized list of the sources used in preparing a report. Each entry contains publication information necessary for locating the source. In addition, the bibliographic entries give evidence of the nature of sources the author consulted. *Bibliography* (literally "description of books") is sometimes used to refer to this list. A researcher often uses sources that provide information but do not result in citations. To acknowledge that you may have consulted these works and to provide the reader with a comprehensive reading list, you might include them in the list of sources. The APA and MLA styles use different terms to distinguish between these types of lists, as shown in Appendix B. See Appendix B for additional information on APA and MLA formats.

Collecting Data Through Surveys

Objective *7*

Apply effective techniques for collecting survey data.

The method of distribution and the makeup of the questionnaire are critical factors in successful survey research.

Selecting a Data Collection Method. Selecting an appropriate data collection method is crucial to effective research. Researchers must consider various factors when selecting an appropriate method for collecting data:

- **Questionnaire surveys** by mail are inexpensive and not limited geographically. Respondents may remain anonymous, which might result in honest answers, and a mailed survey removes difference-in-status barriers. For example, a corporation president may respond readily to a mailed questionnaire whereas the researcher might never succeed in getting a response by telephone or by personal interview. At the same time, mail survey instruments must be concise or they will be discarded. Most people who respond have strong feelings about the topic, so this group of respondents might not be representative of the intended population. The researcher must prepare a persuasive transmittal message that indicates how the respondent can benefit by answering. That persuasion often takes the form of a thank-you gift for participating.
- **Telephone surveys** are inexpensive as a rule, but calls are often seen as disruptive or as a sales ploy. For these reasons, only a small percentage of total calls will provide usable information.
- **E-mail polling** has become popular with researchers and participants and typically yields quick results. Another advantage is that response results can be electronically updated as responses are received. A disadvantage is that research participants are limited to those with computer access

Critical Thinking

Why might e-mail polling lead to a biased response?

who use e-mail. The Electronic Café at the end of Chapter 9 will allow you to explore the use of electronic research methods in greater depth.

- **Personal interviews** allow the interviewer to obtain in-depth answers and perhaps explore otherwise sensitive topics. But interviews are expensive in terms of time and money spent traveling, and more so if interviewers are paid; additionally, many people simply don't want their opinions identified.
- **Participant observation** is frequently used in consumer research with the observer simply noting how people seem to make selections. A problem, of course, is that observation is limited to what can be seen or otherwise sensed and does not give clues about the reasons for behavior.

Critical Thinking

What are the major advantages of electronic, mail, or telephone surveys? Do personal interviews offer additional advantages or disadvantages? Explain.

Developing an Effective Survey Instrument. No matter which survey technique or combination of techniques is used, the way in which the survey instrument is designed and written has much to do with response validity and reliability, response rate, and quality of information received.

The construction of the survey instrument—usually a questionnaire or interview guide—is critical to obtaining reliable and valid data. Before formulating items for a questionnaire or opinion survey, a researcher should visualize the ways responses will be assembled and included in a final report. Here are some suggestions for developing effective questionnaires:

- *Provide brief, easy-to-follow directions.* Explain the purpose of the study in the cover letter or in a brief statement at the top of the questionnaire so that the respondents understand your intent. Avoid "skip-and-jump" instructions; confusion results from instructions such as these:

Ineffective Example

> If you answered Yes to item 4, skip directly to item 7; if you answered No, explain your reason in items 5 and 6.

- *Arrange the items in a logical sequence.* If possible, the sequence should proceed from easy to difficult items. Easy, nonthreatening items involve respondents and encourage them to finish. You might group related items such as demographic data or those that use the same response options (multiple choice, rating scales, open-ended questions).
- *Create an appealing, easy-to-comprehend design using word processing or desktop publishing software.* Use print enhancements such as typefaces, bold, underline, and italics to emphasize important ideas. Use graphic lines and boxes to partition text so that the reader can identify and move through sections of a questionnaire quickly.
- *Use short items that ask for a single answer to one idea.* Include only the questions needed to meet the objectives of your study, since long questionnaire length affects the return rate negatively.
- *Design questions that are easy to answer and to tabulate.* Remember that participants may not take the time to answer numerous open-ended questions that require essay-style answers. When open-ended questions are included, provide enough space for respondents to answer adequately.

- *Strive to write clear questions that all respondents will interpret in the same way.* Avoid words with imprecise meanings (e.g., several, usually) and specialized terms and difficult words that respondents might not understand. Be sure you have used accurate translations for each concept presented if other cultures are involved. Provide examples for items that might be difficult to understand.
- *Ask for factual information whenever possible.* Opinions may be needed in certain studies, but opinions may change from day to day. As a general rule, the smaller the sample, the less reliable are any conclusions based on opinions.
- *Ask for information that can be recalled readily.* Asking for information going back in time may not result in sound data.
- *Provide all possible answer choices on multiple-choice items.* Add an "undecided" or "other" category so that respondents are not forced to choose a nonapplicable response.
- *Decide on an optimal number of choices to place on a ranking scale.* Ranking scales, also called Likert scales, allow participants to indicate their opinion on a numbered continuum. When deciding the numbers to place on the scale, consider the tendency of some groups to choose the noncommittal midpoint in a scale with an odd number of response choices (for instance, choosing 3, on a scale from 1–5).
- *Avoid questions that may be threatening or awkward to the respondent.* For sensitive issues, such as age and income, allow respondents to select among ranges if possible. Assure that ranges do not overlap, and provide for all possible selections.
- *Consider the advisability of prompting a forced answer.* A forced answer question can be used to determine which single factor is most critical to a respondent, as shown in the following examples:

Critical Thinking

What does convergence toward the middle on questionnaire items reveal about human nature?

> Of all the problems listed, which is the *single* most critical problem for you personally?
>
> Should city taxes be levied to fund a city recreational complex?
> ❑ Yes
> ❑ No
> ❑ Undecided

When using forced choice items, avoid "leading questions" that cause people to answer in a way that is not their true opinion or situation. The following item is an example of such a question:

Ineffective Example **X**

> Have you stopped humiliating employees who question your management decisions?
> ❑ Yes
> ❑ No
> ❑ Undecided

- *Include a postage-paid envelope with a mailed questionnaire.* A higher response rate results when this courtesy is provided. Include your return information at the bottom of the questionnaire in the event the envelope is misplaced.

Various types of items can be used in questionnaire design, depending on your purpose and the characteristics of your participants. Figure 9-6 illustrates principles of effective questionnaire design.

A final step in questionnaire design is to test the instrument by asking others to complete and/or critique the questionnaire. For survey research of major importance, researchers typically conduct a **pilot test**, sending out the questionnaire to a small group of the population involved. This process allows them to correct problems in clarity and design, and typically leads to better response and quality of answers. A pilot study may uncover factors affecting your results, which you can address in the final research design and before conducting the actual survey.

Researchers must select from among the several formats available the one best suited to the situation. Criteria for selecting one alternative over the others might include the following: Which format leaves the least chance for misinterpretation? Which format provides information in the way it can best be used? Can it be tabulated easily? Can it be cross-referenced to other items in the survey instrument?

Avoiding Data Gathering Errors

If acceptable data gathering techniques have been used, data will measure what they are intended to measure (have validity) and will measure it accurately (have reliability). Some common errors at the data gathering stage seriously hamper later interpretation:

- Using samples that are too small.
- Using samples that are not representative.
- Using poorly constructed data gathering instruments.
- Using information from biased sources.
- Failing to gather enough information to cover all important aspects of a problem.
- Gathering too much information (and then attempting to use all of it even though some may be irrelevant).

Hopefully, the carefully designed research process will yield useful data for analysis.

Critical Thinking

A pilot study helps to validate a research instrument.

Objective 8

Explain techniques for the logical analysis and interpretation of data.

Arriving at an Answer

Even the most intelligent person cannot be expected to draw sound conclusions from faulty information. Sound conclusions can be drawn only when information has been properly organized, collected, and interpreted.

Figure 9-6

Example of an Effective Questionnaire

Uses a variety of items to elicit different types of responses.

Uses clear, concise language to minimize confusion.

Provides clear instructions for answering each item.

Provides additional lines to allow for individual opinions.

Provides an even number of rating choices to eliminate "fence" responses.

Asks for easily recalled information.

Provides nonoverlapping categories of response and an open-ended final category.

Format Pointers

- Provides adequate space for answering open-ended item.

- Keeps length as short as possible while meeting the objectives of the survey.

- Includes instructions for submitting the completed questionnaire.

1. Rank the following job factors in order of their importance to you. Two blank lines are provided for you to add and rank other factors that are important to you.

		1	2	3	4	5	6	7
a.	Acceptance by others	○	○	○	○	○	○	○
b.	Interest in job	○	○	○	○	○	○	○
c.	Economic security	○	○	○	○	○	○	○
d.	Health and retirement benefits	○	○	○	○	○	○	○
e.	[_____]	○	○	○	○	○	○	○
f.	[_____]	○	○	○	○	○	○	○

2. Which of the following is the single job satisfaction factor that you feel needs more attention in our company? (Please check only one.)

○ Acceptance by others
○ Interest in job
○ Economic security
○ Health and retirement benefits
○ Opportunity for advancement
○ Other (specify) [_____▼]

3. To what degree has your job satisfaction changed since you first were employed in your current position?

It is more negative		It is about the same			It is more positive
1	2	3	4	5	6
○	○	○	○	○	○

4. How would you rate your overall job satisfaction?

Very negative		Moderate			Very positive
1	2	3	4	5	6
○	○	○	○	○	○

5. Indicate your age group:

○ 20–29
○ 30–39
○ 40–49
○ 50–59
○ 60–69
○ 70 years and over

6. Indicate your time with the company:

○ Less than one year
○ 1–3 years
○ 4–6 years
○ 10–12 years
○ Over 12 years

7. Please provide any additional comments you have about job satisfaction as related to your position with this company.

[_____]

Thanks for your participation. Click to submit your questionnaire.

[Submit]

Analyzing the Data

Having decided on a method, researchers must outline a step-by-step approach to the solution of a problem. The human mind is susceptible to digressions. Although these digressions may be short lived, they distract from the job at hand; if given free rein, they can lead you to demolish the real object of the study.

Therefore, *keep on the right track.* Plan the study and follow the plan. Question every step for its contribution to the objective. Keep a record of actions. In a formal research study, the researcher is expected to make a complete report. Another qualified person should be able to make the same study, use the same steps, and arrive at the same conclusion. Thus, a report serves as a guide.

Suppose you have conducted a survey and collected several hundred replies to a 20- or 30-item questionnaire in addition to many notes from printed and electronic sources. What do you do next? Notes must be carefully considered for relevance and organized for relationships among ideas. Appropriate statistical analysis must be applied to interpret what has been found through the survey. **Tabulation** techniques should be used to reduce quantitative data such as numerous answers to questionnaire items. For instance, you may want to tabulate the number of males and females participating in the study, along with the appropriate percentages for each gender.

For many kinds of studies, ***measures of central tendency*** may help in describing distributions of quantitative data. The **range** assists the researcher in understanding the distribution of the scores. The ***mean***, ***median***, and ***mode*** are descriptions of the average value of the distribution. For information about how to compute the measure of central tendency, visit the text support site at http://lehman.swlearning.com.

Critical Thinking

What other statistical techniques are you aware of that could be useful in data analysis? Explain.

Other statistical techniques may be used. For example, ***correlation analysis*** might be used to determine whether a relationship existed between how respondents answered one item and how they answered another. Were males, for example, more likely to have chosen a certain answer to another item on the survey than were females?

The report process is one of reducing the information collected to a size that can be handled conveniently in a written message, as shown in Figure 9-7. Visualize the report process as taking place in a huge funnel. At the top of the funnel, pour in all the original information. Then, through a process of compression within the funnel, take these steps:

1. Evaluate the information for its usefulness.
2. Reduce the useful information through organization of notes and data analysis.
3. Combine like information into understandable form through the use of tables, charts, graphs, and summaries. (See Chapter 10.)
4. Report in written form what remains. (See Chapter 11.)

Figure 9-7 — The Report Process

RESEARCH

Secondary Research
- Review of printed and online sources
- Company records

Primary Research
- Surveys
- Observations
- Experiments

CONDENSATION

Compiling using notes, cards, or inputting into to a computer file
- Direct quotations
- Paraphrased citations

COMBINATION
- Charts
- Tables
- Graphs
- Summaries

ASSIMILATION

Analysis
- Findings
- Conclusions
- Recommendations

WRITING
- Finished Report

Interpreting the Data

Legal & Ethical Constraints

Your ethical principles affect the validity of your interpretations. Through all steps in the research process, you must attempt to maintain the integrity of the research. Strive to remain objective, design and conduct an unbiased study, and resist any pressure to slant research to support a particular viewpoint (e.g., ignoring, altering, or falsifying data). Some common errors that seriously hinder the interpretation of data include the following:

- *Trying, consciously or unconsciously, to make results conform to a prediction or desire.* Seeing predictions come true may be pleasing, but objectivity is much more important. Facts should determine conclusions.

- *Hoping for spectacular results.* An attempt to astonish supervisors by preparing a report with revolutionary conclusions can have a negative effect on accuracy.

- *Attempting to compare when commonality is absent.* Results obtained from one study may not always apply to other situations.

Critical Thinking

The women's basketball team has won every game since you began attending the college. Is this record a coincidence or your influence? How does this example reveal the difference between correlation and causation?

Similarly, research with a certain population may not be consistent when the same research is conducted with another population.

- *Assuming a cause-effect relationship when one does not exist.* A company president may have been in office one year, and sales may have doubled. However, sales might have doubled in spite of the president rather than because of the president.

- *Failing to consider important factors.* For example, learning that McDonald's was considering closing its restaurants in Kassel, Germany, a manager of an industrial supply company recommended that his firm reconsider its plans to expand its operation into Germany. The manager failed to recognize that the adverse impact of a new tax on disposable containers, not an unfavorable German economy or government, was the reason McDonald's was considering closing its restaurants.[13] Other diversity issues that affect research are explored in the accompanying Strategic Forces feature "International Marketing Research".

- *Basing a conclusion on lack of evidence.* "We have had no complaints about our present policy" does not mean that the policy is appropriate. Conversely, lack of evidence that a proposed project will succeed does not necessarily mean that it will fail.

- *Assuming constancy of human behavior.* A survey indicating 60 percent of the public favors one political party over the other in March does not mean the same will be true in November. Because some people paid their bills late last year does not mean a company should refuse to sell to them next year since reasons for slow payment may have been removed.

Critical Thinking

Do you agree with the statement that statistics can be used to prove just about anything? Why?

The research process has been revolutionized by web access to millions of sources. Knowing how to cut through the many irrelevant sources to find useful information is a valuable skill. Your PPP CD offers suggestions and strategies to help you effectively evaluate web resources.

© PHOTODISC/GETTY IMAGES

International Marketing Research

Cautious interpretation should be given to the results of research conducted within particular cultural settings as to their appropriateness for other groups. For instance, concluding that a certain product would sell well in Canada or Mexico because it sold well in the United States is risky.

Disney executives presumed company policies successful in the United States would be equally as successful at their French theme park, EuroDisney. This *faulty logic* caused immediate problems. Employees resisted Disney's disregard for national customs—the unpopular dress code prohibiting facial hair and limiting makeup and jewelry. Visitors to the park were unhappy with the no-alcohol-in-the-park policy, as the French generally include wine with most meals.[14]

Coldwater Creek, a U.S. firm that began selling in Japan recently, found through research that Japanese favor clothing in brighter colors than the dark palette popular in the United States. They also found it necessary to add petite sizes to Japanese catalogs. Coca-Cola and McDonald's products sold successfully across international boundaries until they managed to offend the entire Muslim world by putting the Saudi Arabian flag on their packaging. The flag's design includes a passage from the *Koran*, and Muslims feel very strongly that their Holy Writ should never be wadded up and tossed as garbage. Hence the first rule of international marketing: Never assume what works in one country will work in another.

While information about related populations may serve as a basis for study, effort should be made to conduct research within the particular group that will be affected by the business decision. A good source for secondary research on international markets is the Columbus, Ohio-based Trade Point, USA, a nonprofit online and print information service that was set up in cooperation with the United Nations in 1994. However, second-hand information can take you only so far. In many cases, it will be necessary to go to the target country yourself or to hire an outside firm with solid experience in that country to do grassroots primary research in the country. Some products will be unsuitable or unattractive to certain nations because of differences in culture, lifestyle, or preferences.

Experts recommend thorough country-by-country testing before a product launch to help identify problems inherent in cross-cultural marketing. Testing provides insights into potential market sizes and responses and uncovers the extent to which language and consumer preference will be problematic. While such market research is expensive, it is justified when considering the essential information that will result.[15]

Application

Conduct an online search to discover an example of a company whose product(s) experienced a negative reception in another country's consumer market. What issues were involved in the poor sales performance? How could the problem have been avoided?

If you avoid common data collection errors, you are more likely to collect valid and reliable data and reach sound conclusions. However, if you interpret valid and reliable data incorrectly, your conclusions will still *not* be sound.

Keep in mind the differences in meaning of some research terms as you analyze your material and attempt to seek meaning from it.

- *Finding:* A specific, measurable fact from a research study

- *Conclusion:* Summation of major facts and evidence derived from findings
- *Recommendation:* A suggested action based on your research

Consider the following examples of conclusions and recommendations generated by analyzing research findings:

Example 1

Finding: Nearly 75 percent of responding recruiters indicated they were more likely to hire a candidate who was involved in extracurricular activities.

Conclusion: Active involvement in extracurricular activities is an important job-selection criterion.

Recommendation: Students should be involved in several extracurricular activities prior to seeking a job.

Example 2

Finding: Only 16 percent of the consumers interviewed knew that Hanson's Toy Company sells educational computer software.

Conclusion: Few consumers are knowledgeable of our line of educational software.

Recommendation: An advertising campaign focusing on educational software should be launched.

Visit the text support site at http://lehman.swlearning.com for additional information about interpreting data and arriving at conclusions and recommendations.

Summary

1. **Identify the characteristics of a report and the various classifications of business reports.** The basis of a report is a problem that must be solved through data collection and analysis. Reports are usually requested by a higher authority, are logically organized and highly objective, and are prepared for a limited audience. Reports can be classified as formal/informal, short/long, informational/analytical, vertical/lateral, internal/external, or a proposal.

2. **Identify the four steps in the problem-solving process.** The four steps in the problem-solving process must be followed to arrive at a sound conclusion: (a) Recognize and define the problem; (b) select an appropriate secondary and/or primary method for solving the problem; (c) collect and organize data, using appropriate methods; and (d) interpret the data to arrive at an answer.

3. **Select appropriate secondary and primary methods for solving a problem.** Research methods in report preparation involve locating information from appropriate secondary sources to identify research that has already been done on the topic and then collecting primary data needed to solve the problem.

4. **Locate both printed and electronic sources of information.** Location of secondary sources of information involves appropriate use of printed indexes and application of electronic search techniques that can lead the researcher to books, periodicals, and other documents needed for topic exploration.

5. **Explain the purpose of sampling and describe four sampling techniques.** Selecting a sample that is representative of the entire population affects the validity and reliability of the data reported. Simple random sampling, stratified random sampling, and systematic random

Problem Formation

- Decide what type of report is required.
- Formulate the problem statement.
- Determine the boundaries for the research.
- Define specialized terms used in the report.

Research Methodology

- Select appropriate methods of solution, including relevant secondary and primary resources.
- Gather appropriate published and electronic sources.
- Plan appropriate primary research, using observational, experimental, or normative techniques.

Data Collection and Organization

- Document all quoted and paraphrased information using an appropriate referencing method.
- Develop effective data collection instruments; pilot test and refine prior to conducting research.
- Avoid data collection errors that can minimize your research effort.

Data Interpretation

- Analyze data accurately and ethically.
- Interpret data to reach logical conclusions.
- Make recommendations that are well supported by the data presented.
- Avoid overgeneralizing the results of research conducted in one setting to another group or setting.

---

sampling are recognized techniques used to produce a representative sample for study. Convenient sampling, while often used, does not assure representativeness of data.

6. **Explain the process for documenting referenced information.** Notetaking methods, such as preparing note cards or highlighting on paper copies or printouts, can assist in organizing large amounts of information. To avoid plagiarism, both direct quotes and paraphrases must be referenced, using an acceptable method.

7. **Apply techniques for collecting survey data.** Methods for collecting survey data include mailed questionnaires, telephone surveys, e-mail polling, personal interviews, interviews, and participant observation. Developing an

effective survey instrument is critical to obtaining valid and reliable data. Effective questionnaires are clear, ask for information the respondent can recall and is willing to answer, and are easy to complete and tabulate. A pilot test involving a small subset of the population provides feedback for improving the survey instrument and fine-tuning the data collection process.

8. **Explain techniques for the logical analysis and interpretation of data.** Arriving at an answer in the research process involves proper analysis using appropriate statistical techniques. To maintain the integrity of the research, the interpretation of data should be objective and unbiased. Carefully presented findings give way to sound conclusions that lead to logical recommendations.

Chapter Review

1. What characteristics do all reports have in common? (Obj. 1)

2. In a bank, the internal auditing division performs semiannual audits of each branch. Then the audit reports are sent to the bank's chief executive officer and chief financial officer and to the manager of the audited branch. The purpose of the audits is to determine whether policies and practices are properly followed. Into what report classifications might the audit report fall? Explain. (Obj. 1)

3. How do the four steps in problem solving apply when a student realizes that he or she does not have enough money to pay the upcoming tuition bill? (Obj. 2)

4. How might a null hypothesis be stated for a research study attempting to determine whether television or magazine advertising has greater influence on athletic shoe sales? (Obj. 2)

5. How does library research make a contribution to all studies? (Obj. 3)

// electronic café //

E-Research—An Expanding Internet Application

The Internet has accelerated the pace of business and has also given us e-research—research conducted online or using online databases. Surveys, panels, and focus groups have all moved to the Web, where they function as super-fast decision-making support for various activities. And unlike television, radio, or billboards, the Internet comes with not only the means to send and receive large volumes of information but also to describe its audience. The following electronic activities will allow you to explore the e-research process in more depth:

 InfoTrac College Edition: Access http://www.infotrac-thomsonlearning.com to read more about taking polls on the Web. Search for the following article that is available in full text:

Let's go to the survey: Poll taking on the Net. (2001, June). *The Information Advisor*, 13(6), 1.

 Text Support Web Site: Visit http://lehman.swlearning.com to learn more about how e-mail surveys work. Refer to Chapter 9's Electronic Café activity that links you to the site of an online marketing company and descriptions of its various resources. Be prepared to discuss in class the techniques of e-mail surveys, web panels, and online focus groups; or follow your instructor's directions about how to use this information.

 WebTutor Advantage: Your instructor will give you directions about how to respond to a quiz provided in WebTutor.

 Professional Power Pak. Access your PPP CD for information related to effective e-research strategies.

---

6. How are observational and experimental research different? (Obj. 3)

7. What techniques can help make the Internet search process more efficient? (Obj. 4)

8. Describe a situation in which a stratified random sample might be desirable. (Obj. 5)

9. Distinguish between reliability and validity. How are both important to quality research? (Obj. 5)

10. What purpose do quotes and paraphrases serve in the findings of a report? (Obj. 6)

11. Why should a research study document information taken from other sources? (Obj. 6)

12. What questions might you ask of someone who wants assistance in planning a questionnaire survey to determine automobile-owner satisfaction with certain after-the-sale services provided by dealers? (Obj. 7)

13. What factors should be considered in developing a Likert scale for a survey questionnaire? (Obj. 7)

14. Gathering so much information that the researcher is "snowed under" by the amount is often a barrier to good reporting. How might researchers protect themselves against this possibility? (Obj. 8)

15. How does the assumption that human beings behave in consistent ways over time present a danger in data interpretation? (Obj. 8)

Digging Deeper

1. How has the process of research changed in recent years? How have the changes been both beneficial and detrimental?

2. What communication skills should an effective researcher possess?

To check your understanding of the chapter, take the practice quizzes at **http://lehman.swlearning.com** or your WebTutor course.

Activities

1. **Classifying Business Reports (Obj. 1)**

   Working in teams of three or four, classify each of the following reports in one or more of the ways described in this chapter.

   a. Your company's two-year study of traditional classroom training versus distance-learning instruction is to be written for publication in an industrial training journal.

   b. You have surveyed company personnel on their perceptions of the need for a company-sponsored fitness center. You are preparing a report for the president that conveys the results.

   c. You have completed your department's weekly time sheets to send to payroll.

   d. As department head, you have sent a report to the vice president for finance requesting additional funding for equipment acquisition.

   e. You have prepared an article on software updates for publication in your employee newsletter that is made available online and in printed form to all employees.

   f. As director of end-user computing, you have prepared a report for circulation to all departments. The report summarizes hardware, software, and training offerings available through your department.

2. **Writing a Hypothesis (Obj. 2)**

   Write a positive hypothesis and then restate it as a null hypothesis for each of the following research topics. Hypotheses for topic (a) are given as an example.

   a. A study to determine functional business areas from which chief executive officers advanced in their organizations. Functional areas are legal, financial, accounting, marketing, production, and other.

      Positive Hypothesis: Chief executives advanced primarily through the legal area.

      Null Hypothesis: No relationship exists between chief executives' advancement and their functional field backgrounds.

   b. A study to determine whether a person's career success is related to mentoring experiences.

   c. A study to determine the relationship between college students' gender and their final grades in the business communication course.

3. **Limiting the Scope of the Problem (Obj. 2)**

   What factors might limit or influence your findings in any of the studies in Activity 2? Could you apply the findings of Activity 2 studies to a broader population than those included in the studies? Why or why not?

4. **Selecting a Research Method (Obj. 3)**

   What research methods would you use for each of the research problems identified in Activity 2?

5. **Outlining a Search Strategy (Obj. 4)**

   Outline a secondary search strategy for one of the topics in Activity 2. What printed indexes would you use? What electronic search techniques would you use?

6. **Using Sampling Techniques (Obj. 5)**

   If you were to conduct a survey of residents' attitudes toward recycling in a town of 35,000 people, describe how you might construct a sampling procedure to avoid having to survey the entire population.

7. **Collecting and Documenting Secondary Data (Objs. 4, 6)**

   Select one of the research problems in Activity 2. Locate four related articles using both printed and electronic sources. Prepare a References (APA) or Works Cited (MLA) page that includes the located sources. (See Appendix B.)

8. **Developing Questionnaire Items (Obj. 7)**

   In teams of three or four, develop a customer satisfaction questionnaire for a fast-food restaurant of your choice.

9. **Computing Measures of Central Tendency and Preparing a Table (Obj. 8)**

   Refer to the text support site at **http://lehman. swlearning.com** for information about measures of central tendency. The following figures represent the value of stock options in thousands of dollars issued to executive management of 25 local high-tech firms.

   Visit the Interactive Study Center at **http://lehman. swlearning.com** for a downloadable version of this activity.

   a. Compute the range, mean, median, and mode of the following distribution.

50	91	164	217	425
60	130	170	260	596
65	139	170	283	600
70	143	170	350	650
78	159	204	390	690

   b. Tally the scores in Exercise 9a in seven classes beginning with 0–99, 100–199, and so on to 700–799. When you have tallied the scores, compute the mean, median, and modal class.

   c. Prepare a table for the data and indicate the appropriate percentages for each class. Write a sentence to introduce the table in a report.

Applications

Read | Think | Write | Speak | Collaborate

1. **Identifying Challenges Posed by Human Subjects (Obj. 3)**

   Using an online database, locate and read an article related to challenges associated with experimental research. What legal and ethical challenges do researchers face when conducting experimental research with human subjects? How can they be managed?

2. **Performing an Electronic Search (Obj. 4)**

   This application will allow you to perform an electronic search of a business research topic selected by you or assigned by your instructor.

   Instructions:

   a. Select a business topic for investigation; for example, challenge education, computer viruses, diversity training, electronic privacy, electronic meeting management, or translation software.

   b. Access the Internet, using Netscape, Internet Explorer, or some other browser.

   c. Look up your topic, using two of the following search engines/databases:
      Google (**http://google.com**)
      Yahoo! (**http://www.yahoo.com**)
      AltaVista (**http://www.altavista.com**)
      Go.com (**http://infoseek.go.com**)
      Search.com (**http://www.search.com**)

   d. Print out appropriate pages from the sites you identify.

   e. Using your campus library database selection, select one or more online databases to research your topic. Refer to the list of available electronic databases in Figure 9-3.

   f. Locate one or more appropriate articles on your topic and save them to disk.

   Send your instructor an e-mail message explaining how you located the articles. How did the information you gathered using the search engine approach differ from the information gained from the database search? Attach a copy of one of the articles to your e-mail message.

Read | **Think** | Write | Speak | Collaborate

3. **Gathering Research Information (Objs. 2-4)**

   Visit the text support site at **http://lehman.swlearning. com** and read the enrichment content "Interpreting Research Data." To learn more about the research process and using various types of printed and electronic resources, complete the TILT tutorial at **http://tilt.lib. utsystem.edu**. Submit your scores for each module to your instructor according to the directions provided in TILT. Then develop a list of possible sources of information for a topic of your choice or one assigned by your instructor. For each item on your list, indicate the type of information that the source will likely yield (background facts, latest figures, theoretical base, expert opinions, etc.).

4. **Designing a Research Study (Objs. 1–5)**

   Prepare a one-page description of your plan to solve the problem for each of the following research studies. Use the following headings for the problem assigned: (1) Statement of the Problem, (2) Research Method and Sources of Information, (3) Nature of Data to Be Gathered and Analyzed, (4) Hypothesis or Hypotheses to Be Proved or Disproved (if feasible).

   Visit the Interactive Study Center at **http://lehman. swlearning.com** for a downloadable version of this activity.

   a. Investigate a problem occurring on your campus (declining enrollment in some major(s), increasing tuition, delayed financial aid payments, high cost of textbooks, or closed classes) or in a job or student organization position you hold.

   b. Rainbow Pool and Spas initiated a web site to provide answers to frequently asked questions and product-update information. Customer response has been outstanding, freeing up the company's toll-free telephone lines for calls about more technical, nonrecurring problems—a primary goal of the service. As marketing manager, you are considering the possibility of allowing customers to order pools and spas via the web site.

   c. Karen's Frozen Foods, Inc., is considering adding frozen breakfast pizza to its product line in an effort to overcome the flat profit line it has experienced for several years. The marketing staff intends to target the product to teenagers and working couples whose busy schedules require foods that can be heated quickly. Because all production facilities are currently operating at full capacity, introducing the frozen pizza will require adding production capacity.

   d. As administrator of Greater Lewisville Health Services, a family health clinic, you have mailed an informative brochure to each patient that describes the need to receive the influenza vaccine. Although the flu season is approaching, very few patients have come in to receive their injections.

e. For the first time, Greenwood Consulting Group held an all-company retreat that included customer service training, team building sessions, and numerous social activities. Eight months following the conference, neither customer service nor employee morale seems to have had any noticeable improvement, and the time is near when you must decide whether to schedule the retreat for the coming year.

Read	Think	**Write**	Speak	Collaborate

5. **Real-World Case: Analyzing the Use of "E-Research" (Objs. 1–8)**

Meal times may be less likely to be interrupted by telemarketing calls as e-research continues to catch on. Companies such as InfoPoll offer downloadable software and other services for developing and executing online surveys. Offered at an average of $1,000 per project, these polls are delivered via e-mail or on popup web windows and offer a significant savings over traditional phone and paper surveys that can cost upwards of $25,000. Despite the advantages, many market researchers feel that web audiences don't give the random representation of the general population.

a. One organization that offers e-research services is InfoPoll. Visit their web site at **http://www.infopoll.com** and review the services offered.

b. Read the suggestions offered under "How to Write a Good Survey."

c. Prepare a short written report or presentation that describes how to plan, conduct, and interpret results of an e-poll.

Read	Think	Write	**Speak**	Collaborate

6. **Overcoming Problems in Data Collection and Interpretation (Objs. 7–8)**

Locate an article using either printed or electronic sources that addresses a problem that has occurred for some organization when it failed to realize that research findings that were true for one country or culture were not accurate for another. Make a brief presentation to the class about your findings.

Read	Think	Write	Speak	**Collaborate**

7. **Developing a Survey Instrument (Obj. 7)**

In teams of three, design a survey instrument for one of the research studies you analyzed in Application 4.

Research & Development at Procter & Gamble Changes with the Times

In early years, Procter & Gamble conducted concept testing by inviting consumers to come in and participate in focus groups, a time consuming and expensive process. Now, according to Chief Information Officer Stephen David, all that is done via the Web at a twentieth of the cost and time that was previously required.[16]

- Visit the Procter & Gamble web site at **http://www.pg.com**. What information does the company provide concerning its research and development activity?

- Locate the following article that describes ways that information technology is being used to accomplish the Organization 2005 initiative:

Sandoval, G. (2002, June 13). The tech success that Ivory built. *News.com*. Retrieved May 14, 2003, from **http://news.com. com/1200-1120-975484.html**

Write a short report that summarizes Procter and Gamble's current goal for its R & D division. Include discussion of how today's goal and strategies differ from that of early years.

Part 4 of the Procter & Gamble Show-CASE focuses on online Latino research at P & G and the CEO's philosophy about change.

http://www.pg.com

Visit the text support site at **http://lehman.swlearning.com** to complete Part 4 of the Procter & Gamble ShowCASE.

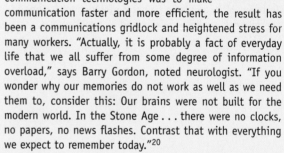

Internet Case

Coping with Information Overload

The greatest challenge of our times is to reduce information, not to increase it. Until about 50 years ago, more information was always a good thing. Now we can't see our way through the "data smog." An ever-growing universe of information translates to masses of data through which people must search to find what is useful and meaningful to them.[17] Consider the following statistics:

- The average businessperson in the United States, Canada, and the United Kingdom sends or receives 190 messages a day.[18]

- Managers report that e-mail demands an average of two hours a day.

- A typical manager reads about a million words a week.

- Senior managers report spending an average of three-quarter hours per day accessing information on the Internet.[19]

While the original intent of advanced communication technologies was to make communication faster and more efficient, the result has been a communications gridlock and heightened stress for many workers. "Actually, it is probably a fact of everyday life that we all suffer from some degree of information overload," says Barry Gordon, noted neurologist. "If you wonder why our memories do not work as well as we need them to, consider this: Our brains were not built for the modern world. In the Stone Age . . . there were no clocks, no papers, no news flashes. Contrast that with everything we expect to remember today."[20]

Some companies are going so far in battling information overload as hiring people whose job it is to filter and sort through the communications gridlock. These "information architects" are the translators and traffic controllers who help to bridge the communication gaps in the organization and deliver usable information in a concise way. The information architect reorganizes information for more effective communication, gives structure and order to pertinent information, and maps out the best way for the organization's people to access it.[21]

Whether for improved job performance, a better product, or increased productivity, more and more organizations are recognizing that good information means good business. And good information must somehow be made available in spite of increasing information overload.

Visit the text support site at **http://lehman.swlearning.com** to link to web resources related to this topic. As directed by your instructor, complete one or more of the following:

1. In teams of four, visit the listed sites and prepare a presentation on Information Overload (IO). The pres-entation should include the following elements: (1) seriousness of the problem, (2) suggestions for reducing IO in e-mail usage, (3) suggestions for reducing IO in Internet usage, and (4) suggestions for reducing stress that results from IO.

2. **GMAT** "The information age has brought about a reduction in the quality of life." Choose to either support or defend the statement; write a one- to two-page paper that explains your position and gives supporting evidence and/or examples.

3. Select a personal example from your academic or work life in which you have experienced information overload (IO). Prepare a written analysis that (1) describes the situation, (2) identifies the reasons for the IO that occurred, and (3) outlines strategies for reducing your IO.

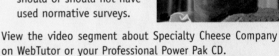

Video Case

Specialty Cheese Company: Old Business Transformed by Market Research

In 1839 Specialty Cheese Company (SCC) had its beginnings as one of over 4,000 cheese factories in Wisconsin. Today fewer than 150 cheese factories exist in the state. SCC now owns and operates three of the oldest and smallest cheese plants in the United States, where over sixty small family farmers supply them with their milk every day. Their sixty employees, led by ten Wisconsin licensed cheesemakers, make over 35 varieties of cheese representing dozens of ethnic traditions, including Hispanic and Mideastern cheeses. In this video case, you will be introduced to Vicki and Paul Scharfman, both with Harvard MBAs, and learn how they rebuilt this 160+-year-old business—Wisconsin's oldest continuously running cheese factory—by using market research.

Discussion Questions

1. Did Vicki and Paul Scharfman use *observational studies* in their market research? If yes, describe; if no, explain whether you think they should or should not have used observational studies.

2. Did Vicki and Paul Scharfman use *experimental research* in their market research? If yes, describe; if no, explain whether you think they should or should not have used experimental studies.

3. Did Vicki and Paul Scharfman use *normative surveys* in their market research? If yes, describe; if no, explain

whether you think they should or should not have used normative surveys.

View the video segment about Specialty Cheese Company on WebTutor or your Professional Power Pak CD.

Activities

Assume your college's student newspaper has a special feature in every issue entitled "For Business Students Only." For this feature, you have been asked to write a review of a web site that will be published in the next issue. The title of your review is "A Research Resource for Business Students: **http://www.ceoexpress.com**." The outline of your review will follow the judging criteria used by the members of The International Academy of Digital Arts and Sciences when they select the winners of the Webby Awards—awards in 30 categories that recognize the best of the Web in both quality and in quantity.

1. Become familiar with each of the judging criteria available at **http://www.webbyawards.com/main/webby_awards/criteria.html**. Criteria include (a) content, (b) structure and navigation, (c) visual design, (d) functionality, (e) interactivity, and (f) overall experience.

2. Access the web site at **http://www.ceoexpress.com**. Write your review and e-mail it to your instructor.

Managing Data and Using Graphics

Objectives *When you have completed Chapter 10, you will be able to:*

1 Communicate quantitative information effectively.

2 Apply principles of effectiveness and ethical responsibilities in the construction of graphic aids.

3 Select an appropriate type of graphic for specific data interpretation and design meaningful graphics.

4 Integrate graphics within documents.

YAHOO! CREATING VISUAL APPEAL FOR VIRTUAL VISITORS

In the decade since the Web became public, entrepreneurs and venture capitalists have turned this communication network into a bustling marketplace of goods and services. With the explosion of web sites, search engines such as Yahoo! help consumers in navigating the wild jungle. CEO Terry Semel says Yahoo! used to boast of running the greatest Internet "funnel," a place to gather briefly before passing on to other things on the Web. Now, rather than passing surfers along, Yahoo! increasingly tries to keep them so it can build a big audience for its advertisers.[1]

Sounds simple, but it's a tall order for Yahoo! to juggle the dual identity as web portal and service provider. After clinging for a few years to its directory role with a plain-text look, Yahoo! recently expanded the use of photos and graphics in its ads and animated commercials for big advertisers such as Pepsi. Shopping pages provide links to sports, music, and movie channels. The web-mail interface was improved, giving it a softer look with optional colors and better tools for organizing messages. The web search feature that made Yahoo! famous had its type downsized to make room for all the splashy new features.[2]

Unlike network television, where everyone sees the same broadcast, Internet capabilities allow Yahoo! to offer personalization to the user's visual experience. You can customize your home pages so that as soon as you log on, you see links to breaking news stories on topics you have selected, a glimpse of your stock portfolio, and a menu of your favorite destinations. What you see is what you want to see. Yahoo! realizes that vast information is useless unless you can manage it. If information is organized in easy-to-navigate visual clusters, you greatly speed the process of discovering what you want to know about a given topic.

In much the same way that Yahoo! successfully exploits the capabilities of Internet appeal, you can use creative and engaging graphics to interpret complex numerical data or highlight important ideas in your business reports and presentations. Your success in these activities depends largely on how successful you are at organizing and interpreting your data and at getting and keeping your audience's interest.

http://www.yahoo.com

See ShowCASE, Part 2, on page 381 for Spotlight Communicator Farzad Nazem, senior vice president of engineering and site operations, and chief technical officer at Yahoo!.

Communicating Quantitative Information

Objective 1

Communicate quantitative information effectively.

Before you can interpret quantitative data, the elements must be classified, summarized, and condensed into a manageable size. This condensed information is meaningful and can be used to answer your research questions. For example, assume that you have been given 400 completed questionnaires from a study of employee needs for financial planning. This large accumulation of data is overwhelming until you tabulate the responses for each questionnaire item by manually inputting or compiling responses received through an online survey or optically scanning the responses into a computer. Then, you can apply appropriate statistical analysis techniques to the tabulated data.

The computer generates a report of the total responses for each possible answer to each item. For example, the tabulation of responses from each employee about his or her most important need in financial planning might appear like this:

Retirement Annuities	128
Traditional and Roth IRA	104
Mutual Funds	80
Internet Stock Trading	52
Effective Charitable Giving	36
	400

The breakdown reduces 400 responses to a manageable set of information. The tabulation shows only five items, each with a specific number of responses from the total of 400 questionnaires. Because people tend to make comparisons during analysis, the totals are helpful. People generally want to know proportions or ratios, and these are best presented as percentage parts of the total. Thus, the numbers converted to percentages are as follows:

Personal Development Need	Number	Percentage	
Retirement Annuities	128	32	} Combine two categories to simplify data (58%)
Traditional and Roth IRA	104	26	
Mutual Funds	80	20	
Internet Stock Trading	52	13	
Effective Charitable Giving	36	9	
	400	100	

Now analyzing the data becomes relatively easy. Of the survey participants, 13 percent selected Internet stock trading, and only 9 percent selected effective charitable giving. Other observations, depending on how exactly you intend to interpret percentages, could be that a fifth of the employees selected mutual funds. Combining data in two categories allows you to summarize that slightly more than one half of the employees selected retirement annuities and individual retirement accounts.

When tabulating research results of people's opinions, likes, preferences, and other subjective items, rounding off statistics to fractions helps paint a clear picture for readers. In actuality, if the same group of people were asked this question again a day or two later, a few probably would have changed their minds. For example, an employee who had not indicated a desire for retirement planning may have learned of the benefits of a Roth IRA during a civic club meeting. The next day, the employee might indicate a desire for training in IRAs and Retirement Annuities.

Fractions, ratios, and percentages are often examples of **common language**. In effect, common language reduces difficult figures to the "common denominators" of language and ideas. Although "104 of 400 prefer traditional and Roth IRAs" is somewhat easy to understand, "26 percent prefer . . ." is even easier, and "approximately one out of four indicate a preference for traditional and Roth IRAs" is even more understandable.

Common language also involves the use of indicators other than actual count or quantity. The Dow Jones Industrial Averages provide a measure of stock market performance and are certainly easier to understand than the complete New York Stock Exchange figures. "Freight car loadings" are weight measurements used in railroad terminology rather than "pounds carried," and oil is counted in barrels rather than in the quart or gallon sizes purchased by consumers. Because of inflation, dollars are not very accurate items to use as comparisons from one year to another in certain areas; for example, automobile manufacturers use "automobile units" to represent production changes in the industry. The important thing for the report writer to remember is that reports are communication media, and everything possible should be done to make sure communication occurs.

Critical Thinking

What are the most understandable terms for presenting your score of 112 points out of a possible 150 on an exam?

Critical Thinking

How could you describe the storage capacity of a ZIP disk or a CD-ROM so that a computer novice could understand? What are other examples of common language?

Using Graphics

Objective *2*

Apply principles of effectiveness and ethical responsibilities in the construction of graphic aids.

Imagine trying to put in composition style all the information available in a financial statement. Several hundred pages might be necessary to explain all material that could otherwise be contained in three or four pages of balance sheets and income statements. Even then, the reader would no doubt be thoroughly confused! To protect readers from being overwhelmed or simply bored with data, report writers must design a visually appealing graphic that is appropriate for the data being presented. Data reported in a table, graph, or picture will make your written analysis clearer to the reader.

The term **graphics** is used in this chapter to refer to all types of illustrations used in written and spoken reports. The most commonly used graphics are tables, bar charts, line charts, pie charts, pictograms, maps, flow charts, diagrams, and photographs.

MTV has effectively harnessed the power of visual appeal to its target market of 18–to–34 year olds. A 25-person graphics and production department stays busy churning out visual images and sound for their animated programming.

© REUTERS NEWMEDIA, INC./CORBIS

Effective and Ethical Use of Graphics

Critical Thinking

"A picture is worth a thousand words." Discuss this adage from a business perspective.

Graphics go hand in hand with the written discussion for three purposes: to clarify, to simplify, or to reinforce data. As you proceed through the remainder of this chapter, ask yourself if the discussion would be effective if the accompanying graphic figures were not included. Use the following questions to help you determine whether using a graphic presentation is appropriate and effective in a written or spoken report:

- Is a graphic needed to clarify, reinforce, or emphasize a particular idea? Or can the material be covered adequately in words rather than in visual ways? To maintain a reasonable balance between words and graphics, save graphics for data that are difficult to communicate in words alone.
- Does the graphic presentation contribute to the overall understanding of the idea under discussion? Will the written or spoken text add meaning to the graphic display?
- Is the graphic easily understood? Does the graphic emphasize the key idea and spur the reader to think intelligently about this information? Follow these important design principles:
    - Avoid *chartjunk*. This term, coined by design expert Edward Tufte, describes decorative distractions that bury relevant data.[3] Extreme use of color, complicated symbols and art techniques, and unusual combinations of typefaces reduce the impact of the material presented.

Changing Technology

- Develop a consistent design for graphics. Arbitrary changes in the design of graphics (e.g., use of colors, typefaces, three-dimensional or flat designs) within a written or spoken report can be confusing as the reader expects consistency in elements within a single report.
- Write meaningful titles that reinforce the point you are making. For example, a reader can interpret data faster when graphics use a talking title; that is, a title that interprets the data. Consider the usefulness of the following graphic titles for a junior doctor browsing through a complex table in the middle of the night:[4]

Descriptive Title: White-Cell Counts During April
Talking Title: White-Cell Count Has Fallen Throughout April

Obviously the talking title saves the doctor time in reaching the writer's interpretation but also ensures the accuracy of the doctor's interpretation and proper diagnosis and/or treatment. Similarly, poor business decisions may be averted if graphic titles reveal the key information. You will learn more about the appropriate use of descriptive and talking headings as you study the preparation of informational and analytical reports in Chapter 11.
- Is the graphic honest? Visually presented data can be distorted easily, leading the reader to form incorrect opinions about the data. The Strategic Forces feature "Ethical Implications in Creating Graphs" provides directions for preparing ethical graphics.
- Can a graphic used in an spoken presentation be seen by the entire audience? Flip charts, white boards, overhead transparencies, and electronic presentations are the visual means most often used to accompany spoken reports. You will learn more about designing graphics for a visual presentation in Chapter 12.

Visit the text support site at http://lehman.swlearning.com to learn about other design techniques that enhance the professional appearance of graphics.

Legal & Ethical Constraints

Critical Thinking
When would an informational hand-out to each audience member be appropriate during a presentation?

Types of Graphic Aids

Objective **3**

Select an appropriate type of graphic for specific data interpretation, and design meaningful graphics.

The greatest advantage of computer graphics is their value to the individual decision maker who formerly had to battle through a maze of computer-printed output. With powerful software programs available on personal computers, managers can perform the data management functions discussed in this chapter to produce highly professional graphics. The information can be reproduced in a variety of ways for integrating into reports and for supporting highly effective presentations.

Selecting the graphic type that will depict data in the most effective manner is the first decision you must make. After identifying the primary idea you want your receiver to understand, you can choose to use a table, a bar chart, line chart, pie chart, flow chart, organization chart,

Ethical Implications in Creating Graphs

Creators of visuals can mislead their audience just as surely as can creators of text. In fact, visuals can sometimes have more impact than their accompanying text, for three reasons:

- Visuals have an emotional impact that words often lack.

- Skimmers of items will see visuals even when they don't read text.

- Readers remember visuals longer.

Ethical considerations become an issue in visual communication because graphic designers mislead their audiences either through lack of expertise or deliberate ambiguity. Today's professionally oriented communicators will need to defend themselves from unethical uses of visual aids and determine what choices are ethical in the design of their own visuals.

Visual distortion can occur in a number of ways. For instance, distortion can occur in bar charts when the value scale starts at some point other than "0," as illustrated in the accompanying chart. The left bar chart seems to indicate a much greater improvement in test scores over the covered time period than actually occurred. This distortion could lead a student, parent, taxpayer, or employee to form a false impression about the schools' performance.

Another type of distortion can occur in bar charts when increments on the Y-axis that are visually equal are used to represent varying values. For instance, if intervals are set at 100, then each additional increment must also represent an increase of 100. When graphic placement or eye appeal would be jeopardized by including all intervals, a break line can be used to show that intervals have been omitted, as shown in Figure 10-4. This technique makes accurate reader interpretation more likely.

Other visual distortions, such as the misuse of relative-size symbols in pictograms, as illustrated in Figure 10-8, can also confuse or mislead a reader. The researcher has a responsibility to report data as clearly and accurately as possible and should be able to answer the following questions favorably:[5]

- Does the visual actually do what it seems to promise to do? Does the design cause false expectations?

- Is it truthful? Does it avoid implying lies?

- Does it avoid exploiting or cheating its audience?

- Does it avoid causing pain and suffering to members of the audience?

- Where appropriate, does it clarify text? Does the story told match the data?

- Does it avoid depriving viewers of a full understanding? Does it hide or distort information?

Application

Construct a bar chart for data you select with intervals of unequal value on the Y-axis; then construct the same chart using intervals of equal value. Describe the difference in interpretation that the reader might have in viewing the two visuals.

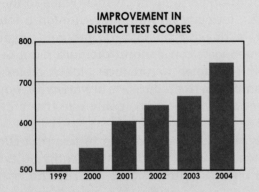

IMPROVEMENT IN DISTRICT TEST SCORES

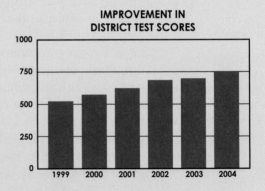

IMPROVEMENT IN DISTRICT TEST SCORES

SPOTLIGHT COMMUNICATOR
Less Can Be More in Graphic Appeal

If you are one of the 80 million visitors a month to Yahoo!, you'll see the results of a five-month overhaul achieved in 2003. The "new Yahoo!" features enhanced visuals, better personalization tools, and event programming while still affording users a clear entry to Internet searching. The success of this new strategy is due in large part to Yahoo!'s Farzad "Zod" Nazem, senior VP for engineering and site operations and chief technical officer. As web sites get ultragraphic, Nazem works with Yahoo! designers and engineers to keep his site efficient for users, while constantly expanding available services and content.

"What people care about is how fast their pages turn," says Nazem. "It doesn't make sense to make pages complex and use a lot of graphics. If you make a site look really fancy, it looks great the first time. The second time, it's amusing. And the third time, it's just plain annoying."[6] Nazem never forgets that there is a user on the other end whose main concern is being able to surf easily from point to point.

Nazem joined Yahoo! a month before it went public to head the engineering operations and provide supervision for a young staff of seven—which has since grown to several hundred. Nazem's technological savvy has been crucial to Yahoo!'s success, as it has transformed itself from a mere launching pad to the Internet to a prominent advertising service provider. The Iranian immigrant is the person whose care and maintenance of Yahoo!'s simple format has assured the site's success as daily visits have soared to 6.5 million unique visitors a month.[7] A primary goal for Nazem is to provide engaging

© YAHOO! INC.

content while avoiding the cyber "slo-mo" that can result from information overload and visual excess.

Applying What You Have Learned

1. Nazem has been described by an industry peer as possessing skills as both an engineer and a business person. How is this important to his successful approach to graphic design for Yahoo!?

2. Compare the repeat visit phenomenon that Nazem describes to the experience of viewing a television re-run. How can the same communication be perceived differently by the viewer when it is experienced again?

Farzad Nazem, Yahoo! Senior Vice-President for Engineering and Site Operations and Chief Technical Officer

http://www.yahoo.com

Refer to ShowCASE, Part 3, at the end of the chapter to learn how visual elements make Yahoo! a best-known URL.

Changing Technology

photographs, models, and so on. Use Figure 10-1 to help you choose the graphic type that matches the objective you hope to achieve.

A variety of graphics commonly used in reports is illustrated in Figures 10-2 through 10-15. These figures illustrate acceptable variations in graphic design: placement of the caption (figure number and title), inclusion or exclusion of grid lines, proper labeling of the axes, proper referencing of the source of data, and others. When designing graphics, adhere to the requirements in your company policy manual or the style manual you are instructed to follow. Then be certain that you design all graphics consistently throughout a report. When preparing a graphic for use as a visual aid (transparency or on-screen

Figure 10-1

Choosing the Appropriate Graphic to Fit Your Objective

Graphic Type		Objective	Graphic Type		Objective
Table	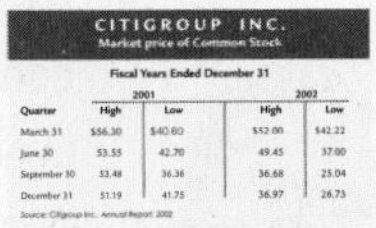	To show exact figures	Gantt chart	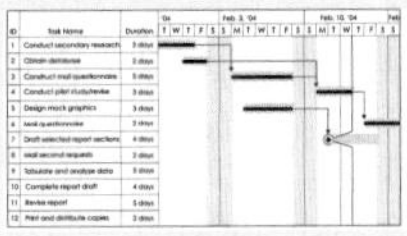	To track progress toward completing a project
Bar chart	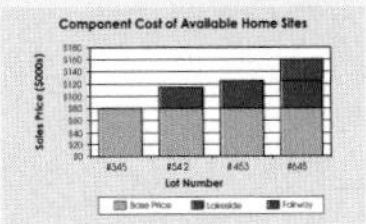	To compare one quantity with another	Map	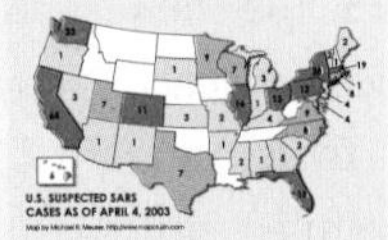	To show geographic relationships
Line chart	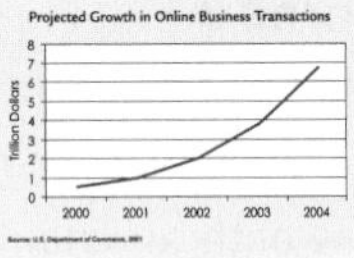	To illustrate changes in quantities over time	Flow chart	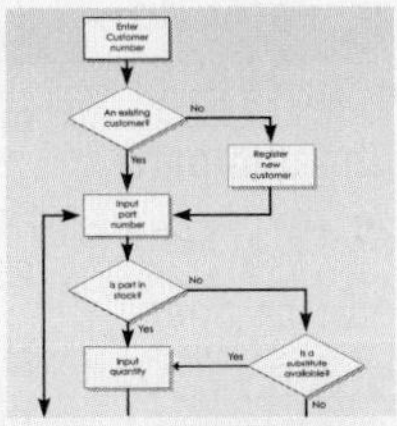	To illustrate a process or procedure
Pie chart	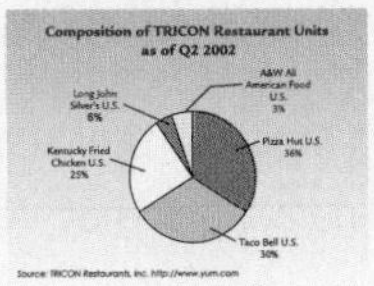	To show how the parts of a whole are distributed	Photograph		To provide a realistic view of a specific item or place

display) in a spoken presentation, you may wish to remove the figure number and include the title only.

Tables

A *table* presents data in columns and rows, which aid in clarifying large quantities of data in a small space. Proper labeling techniques make the content clear. Guidelines for preparing an effective table follow and are illustrated in Figure 10-2:

- *Number tables and all other graphics consecutively throughout the report.* This practice enables you to refer to "Figure 1" rather than to "the following table" or "the figure on the following page." Incidentally, the term *figure* can be used to identify all tables, graphs, pictures, and charts. Note that all illustrations in this chapter are identified as figures.
- *Give each table a title that is complete enough to clarify what is included without forcing the reader to review the table.* Table titles may be quite long as they may contain sources of data, numbers included in the table, and the subject, as shown in the accompanying illustration. Titles may be written in either all capitals or upper- and lowercase letters. Titles that extend beyond one line should be arranged on the page so that

Critical Thinking

Why should a multiple-line title resemble an inverted pyramid?

Figure 10-2

Effective Table Layout, Identifying Information, Labels, and Source

CITIGROUP INC.
Market Price of Common Stock

Fiscal Years Ended December 31

Quarter	2001		2002	
	High	Low	High	Low
March 31	$56.30	$40.60	$52.00	$42.22
June 30	53.55	42.70	49.45	37.00
September 30	53.48	36.36	36.68	25.04
December 31	51.19	41.75	36.97	26.73

Source: Citigroup Inc., Annual Report, 2002

lines do not extend into the margins. The second line should be generally shorter than the first and centered under it as shown below:

Incorrect: Base Salaries of Chief Executives of the 200 Largest Financial Institutions in the United States

Correct: Base Salaries of Chief Executives of the 200 Largest Financial Institutions in the United States

- *Label columns of data clearly enough to identify the items.* Usually, column headings are short and easily arranged. If, however, they happen to be lengthy, use some ingenuity in planning the arrangement.
- *Indent the second line of a label for the rows (horizontal items) two or three spaces.* Labels that are subdivisions of more comprehensive labels should be indented, as should summary labels such as *total*.
- *Place a superscript beside an entry that requires additional explanation and include the explanatory note beneath the visual.*
- *Document the source of the data presented in a visual by adding a source note beneath the visual.* If more than one source was used to prepare a visual, use superscripts beside the various information references and provide the sources beneath the figure.

Bar Charts

Critical Thinking

How effective is a three-dimensional bar chart? Why?

A **bar chart** is an effective graphic for comparing quantities. The bar chart is often referred to as a *column chart* when the bars are presented vertically. The length of the bars, horizontal or vertical, indicates quantity, as shown in Figures 10-3 and 10-4. The quantitative axis should always begin at

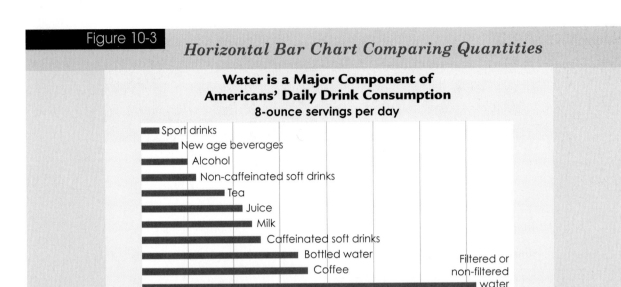

Figure 10-3 | *Horizontal Bar Chart Comparing Quantities*

**Water is a Major Component of
Americans' Daily Drink Consumption**
8-ounce servings per day

- Sport drinks
- New age beverages
- Alcohol
- Non-caffeinated soft drinks
- Tea
- Juice
- Milk
- Caffeinated soft drinks
- Bottled water
- Coffee
- Filtered or non-filtered water

0.0 0.5 1.0 1.5 2.0 2.5 3.0 3.5 4.0

Source: International Bottled Water Association, 2002

zero and be divided into equal increments. The width of the bars should be equal, or the wider bar will imply that it represents a larger number than the narrower bar. Here are further suggestions:

Critical Thinking

Should specific quantities and grids be included in bar charts? Provide an example to justify your answer.

- *Use shadings (or cross-hatchings) or variations in color to distinguish among the bars.* Shadings must be used when printing in black and white since colors could be indistinguishable from one another.
- *Consider the audience's use of the data to determine the need for labeling specifics.* Printing the specific dollar or quantity amount at the top of each bar assists in understanding the graph. Readers tend to skim the text and rely on the graphics for details. Omit actual amounts if a visual estimate is adequate for understanding the relationships presented in the chart. Excluding nonessential information such as specific amounts, grids, and explanatory notes actually increases the readability of the chart by reducing the clutter.
- *Include enough information in the scale labels and bar labels to be understandable but not so complicated that readers will skip over the graph.* The horizontal bar chart in Figure 10-3 shows average per capita consumption of carbonated soft drinks. Amounts appear in the horizontal (x-axis) scale labels; drinks, in the vertical (y-axis) labels.
- *Break the bars to indicate omission of part of each bar if some quantities are so large that the chart would become unwieldy.* A broken-bar chart is illustrated in Figure 10-4.

Critical Thinking

How does a grouped bar chart differ from a simple bar chart?

Grouped Bar Chart. A **grouped bar chart**, also called a *clustered bar chart*, is useful for comparing more than one quantity (set of data) at each point along the x-axis (vertical or column chart) or y-axis (horizontal chart). Figure 10-5 shows changes in the popularity of four cellular phone options

Figure 10-4

Vertical Bar (Column) Chart Indicating Omission of Part of the Bar

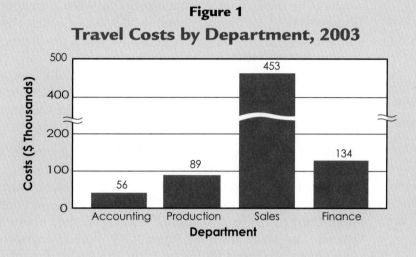

Figure 1

Travel Costs by Department, 2003

during two quarters of 2003. The bars indicate increased sales of each option during Quarter 4 with the greatest volume in voice mail. Because the chart was printed using a color printer, each quantity appears in a specific color to facilitate comparison.

Figure 10-5

Grouped Bar Chart Comparing More Than One Quantity Over Time

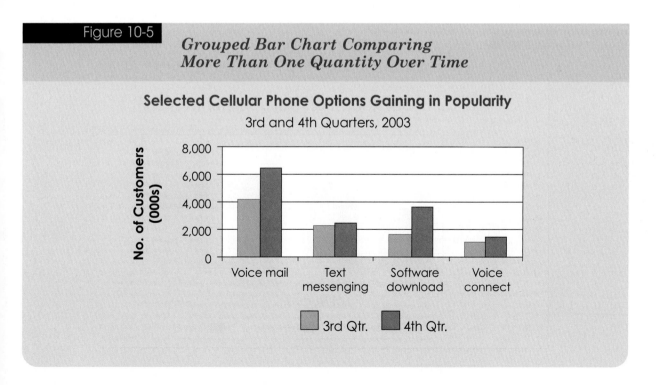

Selected Cellular Phone Options Gaining in Popularity

3rd and 4th Quarters, 2003

Segmented Bar Chart. The **segmented bar chart**, also called a *subdivided, stacked bar chart,* or *100 percent stacked bar,* is shown in Figure 10-6. When you want to show how different facts (components) contribute to a total figure, the segmented chart is desirable. This graphic is also useful when components for more than one time period are being compared. Figure 10-6 shows the basis for the cost of four available home sites. The segments show the relative price of lots that are adjacent to the development's lake or golf course. Actual percentages are omitted to reduce excessive clutter when you believe the reader can assess the proportions visually. Specific values can be displayed if needed for proper decision making. Because this graph was printed using a color printer, colors distinguish the components, with a legend included to identify each of the three types of home sites.

Stock Charts. A **stock chart** tracks the market price of a stock over a period of time. The traditional stock chart shows the high, low, and closing price for each trading day. Variations of the stock chart allow investors to evaluate other data such as the opening price and daily volume. The stock chart can be used to display two or more data points for a single time period. The stock chart in Figure 10-7 enables investors to assess the growth and the range of change (high and low) in the price/earnings ratio for Abercrombie & Fitch.

Critical Thinking

Clip a pictogram from USA Today and share with groups in class. Discuss the effectiveness of the symbols used and the ethical presentation of the data.

Pictograms

A pictogram uses pictures to illustrate numerical relationships. A pictogram can convey a more literal, visual message to the reader than can a bar

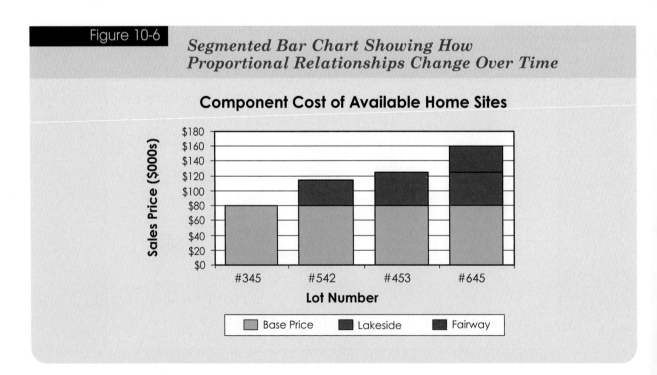

Figure 10-6

Segmented Bar Chart Showing How Proportional Relationships Change Over Time

Component Cost of Available Home Sites

Figure 10-7

Stock Chart (High-Low) for Analyzing Stock Performance

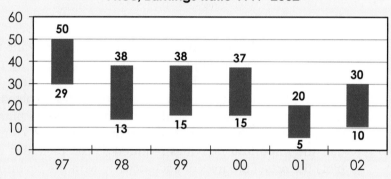

Recession Erodes Investor Confidence in Abercrombie & Fitch Co.

Price/Earnings Ratio 1997–2002

Source: E*Trade Financial, April 5, 2003

chart. For example, the pictogram in Figure 10-8 uses visual images of trees instead of bars to depict lumber production in the United States. However, pictograms can be more dramatic than meaningful if they are not planned properly. For example, doubling the height and width of a picture increases the total area four times. Therefore, all symbols must be the same size so

Figure 10-8

Relative-Size Symbols (left) Distorting Data; Same-Size Symbols (right) Depicting Relationships Accurately

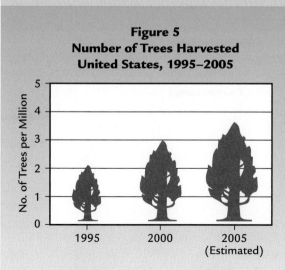

Figure 5
Number of Trees Harvested
United States, 1995–2005

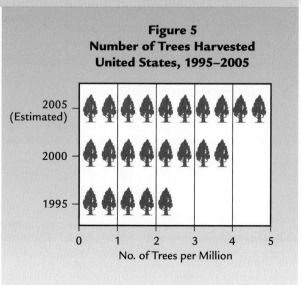

Figure 5
Number of Trees Harvested
United States, 1995–2005

Critical Thinking

What icon would you choose to illustrate growing tuition costs in a pictogram representation? to illustrate number of households with Internet access?

that true relationships are not distorted. Note that the relative sizes of the trees in the pictogram on the left in Figure 10-8 are misleading and make the actual amounts and relationships hard to understand. In the pictogram on the right, using the same-size trees makes both amounts and relationships instantly clear. Refer to the Strategic Forces feature on page 380 for additional discussion of the ethical implications of graphical presentation.

Gantt Charts

A *Gantt chart*, named for Henry L. Gantt, is a specific type of bar chart that is useful for tracking progress toward completing a series of events over time. The Gantt chart in Figure 10-9, prepared using Microsoft® Project, plots the output on the y-axis (activities involved in planning and implementing a research study) and the time (days planned to complete the activity) on the x-axis. This version of the Gantt chart not only schedules the important activities required to complete this research but also plots the *actual* progress of each activity with the *planned* progress.

The Gantt chart clearly indicates that this research study is running behind schedule on the drafting of selected report sections, but questionnaires have been mailed ahead of schedule. To interpret this chart, notice that the shaded bars indicate the duration of the activity (the number of days allotted to complete). For example, the pilot study (Activity 4) was

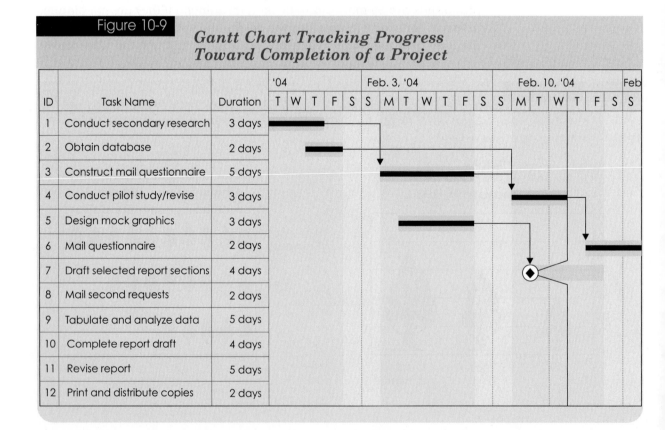

Figure 10-9

Gantt Chart Tracking Progress Toward Completion of a Project

ID	Task Name	Duration
1	Conduct secondary research	3 days
2	Obtain database	2 days
3	Construct mail questionnaire	5 days
4	Conduct pilot study/revise	3 days
5	Design mock graphics	3 days
6	Mail questionnaire	2 days
7	Draft selected report sections	4 days
8	Mail second requests	2 days
9	Tabulate and analyze data	5 days
10	Complete report draft	4 days
11	Revise report	5 days
12	Print and distribute copies	2 days

Critical Thinking

Describe a work activity in your career field that could be depicted in a Gantt chart.

planned to be completed within three days from February 11 to 13. The solid line within the task bar indicates actual progress (the percentage of the task completed). The pilot study was completed on schedule. The arrows feeding into the task bars indicate predecessor activities, work that must be done before another activity is begun. For example, the questionnaire (Activity 6) cannot be mailed until Activities 1–4 have been completed, but Activity 5 can be completed at any time prior to Activity 10. Finally, the dotted line marks the current date as February 12, and a series of lines points the reader's attention to a diamond within the Activity 7 task bar that highlights the one incomplete activity, the preparation of portions of the report.

Line Charts

A *line chart* depicts changes in quantitative data over time and illustrates trends. The line chart shown in Figure 10-10 shows the projected growth in online business transactions. The steep slope of the line clearly shows how the dollars generated from online transactions are expected to nearly double annually. The three lines plotted in Figure 10-11 allow for easy comparison of Exxon's safety record by its employees, contractors' employees, and employees in the petroleum industry.

When constructing line charts, keep these general guidelines in mind:

- *Use the vertical axis for amount and the horizontal axis for time.*

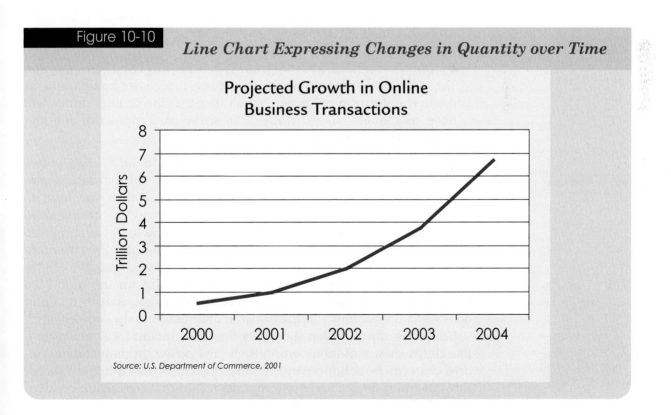

Figure 10-10

Line Chart Expressing Changes in Quantity over Time

Projected Growth in Online Business Transactions

Source: U.S. Department of Commerce, 2001

Figure 10-11

Line Chart Plotting Three Lines

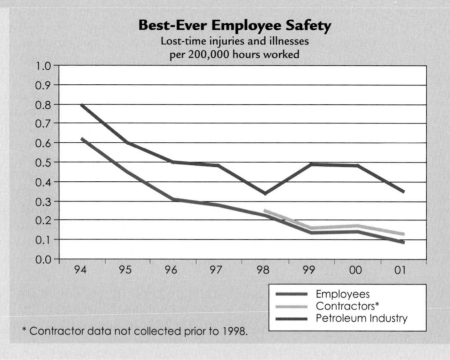

Best-Ever Employee Safety
Lost-time injuries and illnesses
per 200,000 hours worked

Legend:
— Employees
— Contractors*
— Petroleum Industry

* Contractor data not collected prior to 1998.

- *Begin the vertical axis at zero.* If the height of the chart becomes unwieldy, break it the same way the vertical scale was broken in Figure 10-4.
- *Divide the vertical and horizontal scales into equal increments.* The vertical or amount increments, however, need not be the same as the horizontal or time increments so that the line or lines drawn will have reasonable slopes. (Unrealistic scales might produce startling slopes that could mislead readers.)

An **area chart**, also called a *cumulative line chart* or a *surface chart*, is similar to a segmented bar chart because it shows how different factors contribute to a total. An area chart is especially useful when you want to illustrate changes in components over time. For example, the area chart in Figure 10-12 illustrates changes in the actions of visitors to a company's web site. A company decision maker can easily recognize the growth in the number of hits and orders placed. The cumulative total of the number of hits, registrations, and orders is illustrated by the top line on the chart. The amount of each component can be estimated by visual assessment. Color adds visual appeal and aids the reader in distinguishing the components.

Unlike bar charts, which show only the total amount for a time period, line charts show variations within each time period. In presentations, an area chart can be enhanced by introducing an animated graphic object or separate transparency for each component. During the presentation, each

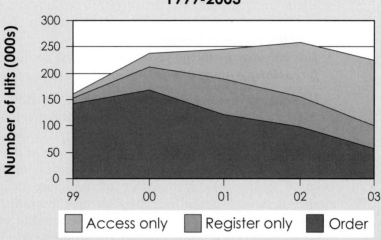

Figure 10-12

Area Chart Showing How Proportional Relationships Change over Time

Internet Site Visits Yielding More Orders
1999-2003

object could be displayed in progression or a transparency laid over the previous one for a cumulative effect. In the example shown in Figure 10-12, for instance, the first animated object or transparency may show only number of times a site was visited; the second, number of times a viewer registered at a site; and the third, the number of times an order was placed—the completed chart.

Critical Thinking

Can the information in a pie chart also be represented in a bar chart? Can the information in a bar chart also be represented in a pie chart? Explain.

Pie Charts

A *pie chart*, like segmented charts and area charts, shows how the parts of a whole are distributed. As the name indicates, the whole is represented as a pie, with the parts becoming slices of the pie. Pie charts are effective for showing percentages (parts of a whole), but they are ineffective in showing quantitative totals or comparisons. Bars are used for those purposes. The pie chart in Figure 10-13 shows the composition of TRICON's total restaurant units by providing percentages for its five restaurants (Kentucky Fried Chicken, Pizza Hut, Taco Bell, Long John Silver's U.S., and A&W All American Food U.S.).

Here are some generally used guidelines for constructing pie charts:

• *Position the largest slice or the slice to be emphasized at the twelve o'clock position.* Working clockwise, place the other slices in descending order of size or some other logical order of presentation.

- *Label each slice and include information about the quantitative size (percentage, dollars, acres, square feet, etc.) of each slice.* If you are unable to attractively place the appropriate labeling information beside each slice, use a legend to identify the color or pattern for each slice. Note the labeling in Figure 10-13.
- *Draw attention to one or more slices for desired emphasis.* Special effects include exploding the slice(s) to be emphasized, (that is, removing it from immediate contact with the pie) or displaying or printing only the slice(s) to be emphasized.
- *Use color or patterns (cross-hatchings) to aid the reader in differentiating among the slices and to add appeal.*

Use your own judgment in constructing a pie chart. Your software may limit your ability to follow rules explicitly. Likewise, the nature of the data or the presentation selected may require slight deviations to increase the clarity of the graphic. For example, if you intend to explode the largest slice, placing it in the twelve o'clock position may not be desirable because the slice is likely to intrude into the space occupied by a title positioned at the top of the page. If your style manual or company policy requires that titles be positioned above the graphic, starting with a slice other than the largest is acceptable. For dramatic effect, many periodicals and reports vary from these general rules. Other deviations are discussed in the Strategic Forces feature on page 395, "Presentation Software and Graphic Design Principles."

Changing Technology

Critical Thinking

Can you think of other situations that might warrant slight deviation from the rules presented in this chapter?

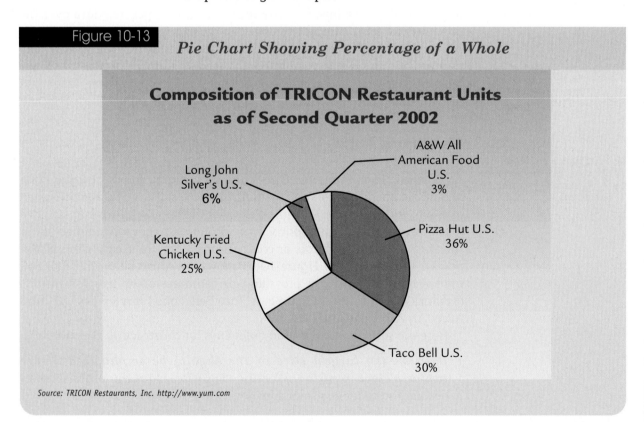

| Figure 10-13 | *Pie Chart Showing Percentage of a Whole* |

Composition of TRICON Restaurant Units as of Second Quarter 2002

A&W All American Food U.S. 3%

Long John Silver's U.S. 6%

Kentucky Fried Chicken U.S. 25%

Pizza Hut U.S. 36%

Taco Bell U.S. 30%

Source: TRICON Restaurants, Inc. http://www.yum.com

Maps

A *map* shows geographic relationships. A map is especially useful when a reader may not be familiar with the geography discussed in a report. The map shown in Figure 10-14 effectively presents the number of suspected cases of an infectious disease by state. The map gives the information visually and thus eliminates the difficulty of explaining the information in words. In addition to being less confusing, a map is more concise and interesting than a written message would be.

Flow Charts

Critical Thinking

Sketch a flow chart outlining the procedure that shipping dock employees should follow when shipping packages. Decisions may include priority of package, destination (in-state, out-of-state), and weight of package.

A *flow chart* is a step-by-step diagram of a procedure or a graphic depiction of a system or organization. A variety of problems can be resolved by using flow charts to support written analyses. For example, most companies have procedures manuals to instruct employees in certain work tasks. Including a flow chart with the written instructions minimizes the chance of errors.

A flow chart traces a unit of work as it flows from beginning to completion. Symbols with connecting lines are used to trace a step-by-step sequence of the work. A key to a flow chart's symbols may be included if the reader may not readily understand standard symbols. For example, the flow chart in Figure 10-15 illustrates the procedures for processing a

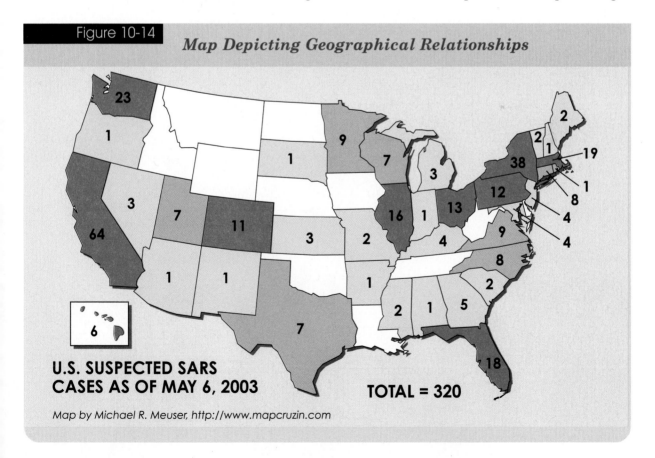

Figure 10-14

Map Depicting Geographical Relationships

U.S. SUSPECTED SARS CASES AS OF MAY 6, 2003

TOTAL = 320

Map by Michael R. Meuser, http://www.mapcruzin.com

Figure 10-15

Flow Chart Simplifying Understanding of Work Tasks

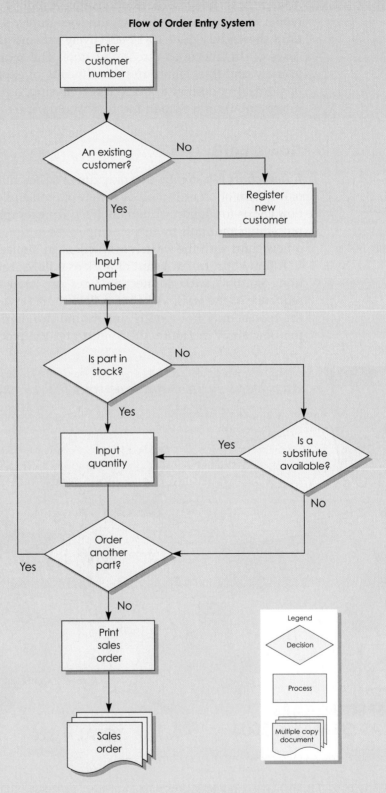

Flow of Order Entry System

Presentation Software and Graphic Design Principles

In the early days of software development, some businesspeople made the mistake of assuming that because technical capabilities existed for creating a variety of graphic materials, everyone could perform the job of designer. This was not, and still is not, the case. Fortunately, the latest generation of presentation software packages do try to guide the user away from the worst errors of taste and judgment. For instance, PowerPoint® offers wizards that lead the user through the process of preparing a presentation that follows one of a series of style templates.[8] Other vendors have inserted relevant rules into their products, such as incorporating graphic design principles in presentation applications.

In spite of ongoing improvements in presentation software applications, developers of products still often do not reflect good rules for formation of graphic aids in the default settings. For instance, many programs automatically arrange pie slices in random-size order; if the pie contains many small slices, the program may intersperse the small slices with the larger slices to increase readability and enhance appearance. Some programs also do not start pie charts at the twelve o'clock position. Software applications often include an unnecessary series legend indicator for charts, even when only one value is represented.

With a little work on your part, you can usually achieve accurate graphic depictions when using presentation and graphics applications. Many times you can select options, optional settings, or some similar command and instruct the program to arrange the graphic according to the appropriate rules. For example, the pie chart customized to follow design rules (shown at right, below) is much more effective than the default pie chart created in Microsoft Excel® (shown at the left). Three simple format changes simplified the design and made it easier to interpret: (a) beginning the largest slice at the twelve o'clock position and positioning the remaining slices in descending order of size, (b) positioning the labels and percentages beside the slide to enhance readability, and (c) adding a second line to the title for added description. Thus, to ensure clarity and appeal, a competent software user never assumes the software application will produce the desired arrangement automatically.

Application

1. Select two different presentation or graphics software products (PowerPoint®, Corel® Presentations®, Freelance®, Harvard Graphics®, etc.). Using the following data and the default settings of the application, construct a simple bar chart and a simple pie chart in both of the selected products.

   Operating Budget for Administrative Support Department, XYZ Company: salaries & benefits, 62%; training & development, 11%; supplies & materials, 12%; and operating chargeback, 15%.

2. Print out your results. What differences did you find in the output of each product? How did the outcomes deviate from the rules in this chapter? How did they comply with the rules?

Projected Expenses by Department

- Production
- Marketing
- Human Resources
- Finance
- Accounting

Chart built with default values

Projected Expenses by Department Fiscal Year 2004

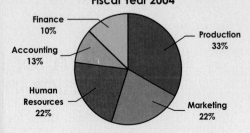

Finance 10%
Accounting 13%
Human Resources 22%
Production 33%
Marketing 22%

Chart enhanced for optimal appeal and readability

telephone order. If this information had been presented only in a series of written steps, the customer service manager would have to rely not only on the input operator's reading ability but also on his or her willingness to read and study the written procedures.

Organization charts, discussed in Chapter 1, are widely used to provide a picture of the authority structure and relationships within an organization. They provide employees with an idea of what their organization looks like in terms of the flow of authority and responsibility. When businesses change (because of new employees or reorganization of units and responsibilities), organization charts must be revised. Revisions are simple if the organization chart is prepared using graphics software and can be revised easily when changes must be made.

Critical Thinking

Locate an organization chart of a company with a flat organizational structure. Compare it with the tall structure shown in Figure 1-3.

Other Graphics

Critical Thinking

What legal precautions should be taken when scanning photographs and other artistic items for use in a business report?

Other graphics, such as floor plans, photographs, cartoons, blueprints, and lists of various kinds, may be included in reports. The availability of graphics and sophisticated drawing software facilitate inclusion of these more complex visuals in reports and spoken presentations. Because managers can prepare these visuals themselves less expensively and more quickly than having them prepared by professional designers, these sophisticated graphics are being used increasingly for internal reports. Photographs are used frequently in annual reports to help the general audience understand a complex concept and to make the document more appealing to read. Frequently, you must include some material in a report that would make the narrative discussion unwieldy. In this case, the material might be placed in an appendix and only referred to in the report.

Including Graphics in Text

Objective 4

Integrate graphics within documents.

Text and graphics are partners in the communication process. If graphics appear in the text before readers have been informed, they will begin to study the graphics and draw their own inferences and conclusions. For this reason, always give a text introduction to a graphic immediately preceding the positioning of the graphic. A graphic that follows an introduction and brief explanation will supplement what has been said in the report. Additional interpretation and analysis that may be needed should follow the graphic.

Pattern for Incorporating Graphics in Text

The pattern, then, for incorporating graphics in text is (1) introduce, (2) show, and (3) interpret and analyze.

Note how the language in the following sentences introduces graphic or tabular material:

Poor:	Figure 1 shows preferences for shopping locations.	*This sentence is poor because it tells the reader nothing more than would the title of the figure.*
Acceptable:	About two thirds of the consumers preferred to shop in suburban areas rather than in the city. (See Figure 1.)	*This sentence is acceptable because it does the job of interpreting the data, but it puts the figure reference in parentheses rather than integrating it into the sentence.*
Improved:	As shown in Figure 1, about two thirds of the consumers preferred to shop in suburban areas rather than in the city.	*Although improved over the previous examples, this sentence puts reference to the figure at the beginning, thus detracting from the interpretation of the data.*
Best:	About two thirds of the consumers preferred to shop in suburban areas rather than in the city, as shown in Figure 1.	*This sentence is best for introducing figures because it talks about the graphic and also includes introductory phrasing, but only after stressing the main point.*

Positioning of Graphics in Text

Critical Thinking

Assume a graphic was introduced on page 8 of a report, but the graphic will not fit on the page. Where should the graphic be positioned? What should be done with the blank space at the bottom of page 8?

Ideally, a graphic should be integrated within the text material immediately after its introduction. A graphic that will not fit on the page where it is introduced should appear at the top of the following page. The previous page is filled with text that would have ideally followed the graphic. In this chapter, figures are placed as closely as possible to their introductions in accordance with these suggestions. However, in some cases, several figures may be introduced on one page, making perfect placement difficult and sometimes impossible.

When interpreting and analyzing the graphic, avoid a mere restatement of what the graphic obviously shows. Instead, emphasize the main point you are making. This analysis may include summary statements about the data, compare information in the figure to information obtained from other sources, or extend the shown data into reasonably supported speculative outcomes. Contrast the boring style of the following discussion of data presented in a graphic with the improved revision:

Obvious Restatement of Data:	Among the respondents, 35 percent are pleased with their rate of return from online investing, 12 percent are not pleased with their rate of return from online investing, 31 percent are not investing online but plan to begin, 8 percent only invest using a broker, and 15 percent do not trade stocks.
Emphasis on Main Point:	Over one third of the respondents are pleased with their rate of return on online investing.

Absorption and retention of information are unquestionably enhanced by the use of graphics.

Strive to transition naturally from the discussion of the graphic into the next point you wish to make.

Throughout the discussion of tables and graphics, the term *graphics* has been used to include all illustrations. Although your report may include tables, graphs, maps, and even photographs, you will find organizing easier and writing about the illustrations more effective if you label each item as a "Figure" followed by a number; then number the items consecutively. Some report writers prefer to label tables consecutively as "Table 1," etc., and graphs and charts consecutively in another sequence as "Graph 1," etc. When this dual numbering system is used, readers of the report may become confused if they come upon a sentence saying, "Evidence presented in Tables 3 and 4 and Graph 2 supports. . . ." Both writers and readers appreciate the single numbering system, which makes the sentence read, "Evidence presented in Figures 3, 4, and 5 supports. . . ."

Summary

1. **Communicate quantitative information effectively.** Graphics complement text by clarifying complex figures and helping readers visualize major points. Tabulating data and analyzing data using measures of central tendency aid in summarizing or classifying large volumes of data into manageable information you can interpret. You can then communicate this meaningful data using common language—fractions, ratios, and percentages—that the reader can easily understand.

2. **Apply principles of effectiveness and ethical responsibilities in the construction of graphic aids.** A graphic aid should clarify, reinforce, or emphasize a particular idea and should contribute to the overall

understanding of the idea under discussion. It should be uncluttered and easily understood and depict information honestly. Graphic aids used in spoken presentations should be large enough to be seen by the entire audience.

3. **Select an appropriate type of graphic for specific data interpretation and design meaningful graphics.** The type of graphic presentation should be chosen based on the ability to communicate the information most effectively. Tables present data in systematic rows and columns. Bar charts (simple, grouped, and stacked) compare quantities for a specific period. Line charts depict changes in quantities over time and illustrate trends. Pie charts, pictograms, and segmented and area charts show the proportion of components to a whole. Gantt charts track progress toward completing a series of events over time. Maps help readers visualize geographical relationships. Flow charts visually depict step-by-step procedures for completing a task; organization charts show the organizational structure of a company. Floor plans, photographs, cartoons, blueprints, and lists also enhance reports.

4. **Integrate graphics within documents.** A graphic should always be introduced by text before it is presented. The graphic will then reinforce your conclusions and discourage readers from drawing their own conclusions before encountering your ideas. An effective introduction for a graphic tells something meaningful about what is depicted in the graphic and refers the reader to a specific figure number. The graphic should be placed immediately after the introduction if possible or positioned at the top of the next page after filling the previous page with text that ideally would have followed the graphic. Analysis or interpretation follows the graphic, avoiding a mere repetition of what the graphic clearly shows.

Chapter Review

1. In what ways does managing data help protect researchers and readers from being overwhelmed by information? (Obj. 1)

2. What is meant by common language? Provide several examples. (Obj. 1)

3. What basic rules are used to determine whether a graphic should be used to present certain information? (Obj. 2)

4. What is meant by the term *chartjunk*? Provide suggestions for eliminating chartjunk. (Obj. 2)

5. What are some examples of distortions in graphics that can mislead the reader about the data presented? (Obj. 2)

6. What are potential pitfalls of using presentation software to create graphics? What advice do you suggest for producing an effective graphic using presentation software? (Obj. 2)

7. Discuss the major principles involved in preparing effective tables. (Obj. 3)

8. Why should increments on the vertical axis of a graphic be equal? Is variation in the sizes of horizontal increments acceptable? (Obj. 3)

9. What purpose does a Gantt chart serve? (Obj. 3)

10. Under what conditions can data be represented in either a pie chart or a bar chart? When is that not possible? (Obj. 3)

11. When would a pictogram be preferred to a bar chart? Why? (Obj. 3)

12. Give several examples of how flow charts can be used to present information. (Obj. 3)

13. Where should a graphic be placed in relation to the text that describes it? (Obj. 4)

14. Should every graphic be introduced before it appears in a report? Is interpreting a self-explanatory graphic necessary? Explain. (Obj. 4)

15. Discuss the appropriate way to introduce and to interpret a graphic in a report. (Obj. 4)

Digging Deeper

1. "A picture is worth a thousand words." Discuss the significance of this statement in regard to business information.

2. How much is "too much" when considering the use of graphics in a business document?

To check your understanding of the chapter, take the practice quizzes at **http://lehman.swlearning.com** or your WebTutor course.

Digital Collaboration Overcomes Geographical Barriers

Digital collaboration is defined as the use of technology to enhance and extend the abilities of individuals and organizations to collaborate, independent of their geographical location. While collaboration has traditionally occurred in the same physical place, digital collaboration involves the creation of a "virtual place" that participants share. Various software applications are available that enable the technology for collaboration, but the success of the process depends on the willingness of people to work together. Effective digital collaboration integrates people, processes, and technology.

 InfoTrac College Edition. Access http://www.infotrac.thomsomlearning.com to read about different technologies that enable digital conferencing. Search for the following article that is available in full text:

Grigonia, R. (2001, November). Conferencing technology in the spotlight: The electronic conferencing industry got some unexpected "help": First a recession, then the fear factor, and now the hassle factor. Will it last? *Communications Convergence*, 9(11), 58(9).

Make a list of the various types of electronic conferencing that are mentioned in the article, along with advantages and limitations of each.

 Text Support Web Site. Visit http://lehman.swlearning.com to learn more about how the events of September 11, 2001, gave the world of digital collaboration an unplanned assignment. Refer to Chapter 10's Electronic Café activity that guides you in a search of information about the expanded uses of digital collaboration for education and business activity. Be prepared to discuss this information or use it as directed by your instructor.

 WebTutor Advantage. Your instructor will give you instructions about how to join an electronic meeting involving collaboration on a graphics document posted to the whiteboard.

 Professional Power Pak. Access your PPP CD for information on how to download and use Microsoft NetMeeting.

Activities

1. **Selecting Appropriate Graphics (Obj. 3)**

   Select the most effective graphic means of presenting the following data. Justify your decision.

   a. Data showing the growth in the number of students using PDAs during the past three years.

   b. Data showing the distribution of contributions to the company's education matching gifts program by functional unit.

   c. Data showing the availability of apartments by type (studio, number of bedrooms) in a designated area.

   d. The growth in subscriptions of a magazine over the past four years by state.

   e. Data showing the functional areas of a company from the CEO to the vice presidents to the line supervisors.

   f. Predicted senior citizen population by state for the year 2007.

   g. Instructions to human resources managers for conducting team interviews.

   h. Figures comparing the percentage of warranty claims of a company's three product lines for the past four quarters.

   i. Data showing the total number of calls to a company's ethics hotline over the past two years. The data should show changes in the classifications of reported issues (e.g., financial fraud, employment discrimination, etc.).

   j. Data showing the number of people utilizing the portfolio option of a financial investment firm's web site. The data should depict the number of portfolios opened by investors in five age categories during each of the past four quarters.

k. Data showing percentage of organizational projects that are delayed, on time, or ahead of schedule.

l. Figures showing the number of MBA or graduate business employees hired by Addy Industries during the past five years.

m. Company capital investments in each of five countries during the last fiscal year.

n. Graphic tracking the progress of a product development team that is working on a new refrigeration product for a 2007 launch date.

2. **Evaluating Graphics (Objs. 2–4)**

Evaluate each of the following graphics for its ethical presentation of the data and the effectiveness of its design. Be prepared to discuss your critique in class. Your instructor may ask you complete Application 7 that involves revising the graphics.

a. Dollar sales (in thousands of dollars) over a six-year period. The graphic will be included in the company's annual report.

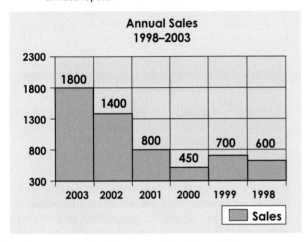

b. Number of employment offers for 2003.

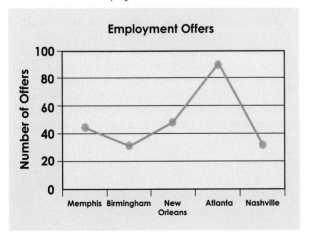

c. Breakdown of the calls made to a software developer's customer service hotline for March 2003.

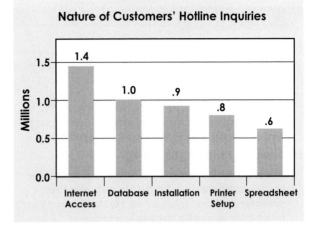

3. **Improving Introductions to Graphics (Obj. 4)**

Improve the following statements taken from reports:

a. As can be seen in Table 3, the correlation between interest rates and credit card sales was .68.

b. Professional salaries in the Southeast have increased about 12 percent while the national average has increased 3 percent. (See Figure 1).

c. Take a look at Figure 3, where a steady decline in the price of writeable CD-ROMs during the year is shown.

d. The data reveal (Figure 4) that only 7 out of 10 customers are satisfied with our service department.

e. Figure 1 summarizes data related to college students' investment patterns. Of the college students surveyed, 45 percent believe their companies' pension plan will adequately fund their retirement, 25 percent plan to begin investing for retirement after their children complete college, 15 percent plan to begin investing in their 30's, 10 percent plan to begin investing in their 20's, and 5 percent have already begun their retirement investment plans.

Applications

Read   Think   Write   Speak   Collaborate

1. Recognizing Common Language (Obj. 1)

Using an online database, select an article from a business journal that presents the findings of a research study. Find examples of how percentages and common language are used in the reporting of the data. Describe how effective or ineffective the author(s) was/were in assuring that the data were understood by the intended audience.

2. Drawing a Bar Chart (Objs. 2–4)

Using appropriate presentation software, prepare a bar chart showing the sales for the top carbonated soft drinks for the latest fiscal period. Locate the most current information by visiting the web site of one of the leading drink manufacturers (e.g., Coca-Cola, Pepsico). Write a talking title that clearly identifies the data depicted in the chart. Write a sentence to introduce the graphic and emphasize the most important idea(s) in the graphic.

3. Drawing a High-Low Stock Chart (Objs. 2–4)

Prepare a high-low stock chart for a company of your choice or one designated by your instructor. Show the high and low stock price for the last five years. Include a source note below the graphic. Obtain the data from either a printed or an online copy of the company's annual report. Write a talking title that interprets the data depicted in the chart and a sentence to introduce the graphic and emphasize the most important idea(s) in the graphic.

Hint: If creating this graph in Excel, select the stock chart type and open high low closing chart subtype. Enter the appropriate data in Columns A, B, and E in the spreadsheet, leaving Columns C and D blank.

Sample DataSheet

Column A (Date)	Column B (Opening Price)	Column C (High)	Column D (Low)	Column E (Closing Price)
2003	42.25			35.50

Read   Think   Write   Speak   Collaborate

4. Selecting and Drawing an Appropriate Graphic (Objs. 2–4)

Create the graphic that would most effectively aid a human resources manager in identifying potential areas for training and development. Write a descriptive or a talking title that interprets the data depicted in the chart and a sentence to introduce the graphic and emphasize its most important idea(s).

Interest in Computer Training by Department January 2004

Dept.	Security	Instant Messaging	Video-conferencing	Video Production
Acct./ Finance	87	69	78	83
Marketing	25	71	64	95
Production	35	56	45	22

5. Adding Creative Enhancements (Objs. 2–4)

Visit the text support site at **http://lehman.swlearning. com** and read the enrichment content for Chapter 10, "Giving Graphics a Contemporary Look."

Required: As directed in the reading. analyze the creative techniques used in graphics appearing in various sources: annual reports, corporate web sites, and news publications (printed and online), and television broadcasts.

Prepare a brief list of the techniques you identified and discuss the benefits and drawbacks of each technique as it relates to effective graphic design. What recommendations would you give to information designers as a result of your analysis? Select one graphic that violates the principles presented in the text enrichment content; revise incorporating your suggestions for improvement. Be prepared to give a short report to the class that includes a summary of the creative techniques you compiled and an analysis of the ineffective graphic. Use a transparency or slide of the graphic to support your report. Alternatively, your instructor may require you to apply one or more of the creative techniques presented in the enrichment content to an application at the end of the chapter.

6. Preparing a Table (Objs. 2–4)

Prepare a table to show the *total* revenue Nashville Sports Connection earned from membership fees for a fiscal period. Fees were collected by type of membership: single, $25; double, $40; family (3+ members), $50; corporate, $22.50; senior, $20. Nashville Sports Connection has 1,439 single memberships, 642 double, 543 family, 3,465 corporate, and 786 senior memberships.

7. Revising Graphics (Objs. 2–4)

Download the three graphics shown in Activity 2 from the text web site. Revise each of the graphics, incorporating your suggestions for improvement. Write a descriptive or talking title and a sentence to introduce each graphic and emphasize the most important idea(s) in each graphic.

Visit the Interactive Study Center at **http://lehman. swlearning.com** for a downloadable version of this activity.

8. Drawing a Segmented Chart (Objs. 2–4)

The director of the Nashville Sports Connection wishes to compare the usage rate of various activities offered to its members over the past four quarters. Using the data provided in the following table, prepare a segmented chart that will make comparison of these usage rates easier to understand.

Activity	1st Q	2nd Q	3rd Q	4th Q
Aerobics classes	2,451	2,315	2,248	2,258
Aerobics machines (treadmills, steppers)	6,245	6,458	6,835	6,994
Strength machines	4,212	4,259	4,205	4,213
Free weights	945	845	758	789
Swimming pool	894	974	1,048	1,245

Write a descriptive or a talking title that interprets the data depicted in the chart. Write a sentence to introduce the graphic and emphasize the most important idea(s) in the graphic.

9. Drawing a Line Chart (Objs. 2–4)

The information technology group of First National Bank has prepared estimates on the number of its customers expected to actively use its Internet banking site. Prepare a line chart showing the actual number of customers for 2000–2002 with the estimates for 2003–2006:

2000	645		2004	7,500
2001	1,247		2005	9,000
2002	2,456		2006	10,000
2003	5,000			

To distinguish projected data from actual data, create a dashed line or add an explanatory note below the graph (e.g, Projected Data for ___). Write a descriptive or a talking title that clearly identifies the data depicted in the chart. Write a sentence to introduce the graphic and emphasize its most important idea(s).

10. Drawing an Area Chart (Objs. 2–4)

Prepare an area chart showing how the Wal-Mart Stores' retail divisions contributed to the total number of stores over a ten-year period. Use the data presented in the following table or obtain current data from Wal-Mart's latest annual report or web page. Include a source note below the chart.

Write a descriptive or talking title that clearly identifies the data depicted in the chart. Write a sentence to introduce the graphic and emphasize its most important idea(s).

11. Drawing a Pie Chart (Objs. 2–4)

Prepare a pie chart showing the percentage of revenue Video Connection generated from rentals in the following categories during the second quarter of the current year: VHS (55%), DVD (35%), PlayStation (4%); Xbox (3%), and GameCube (2%). Write a descriptive or talking title that interprets the data depicted in the chart. Write a sentence to introduce the graphic and emphasize its most important idea(s).

Pie Chart Data

Division	1993	1994	1995	1996	1997	1998	1999	2000	2001	2002
Wal-Mart	1,848	1,950	1,985	1,995	1,960	1,921	1,869	1,801	1,736	1,647
Supercenter	34	72	147	239	344	441	564	721	888	1,066
SAM's Club	256	417	426	433	436	443	451	463	475	500
International	10	24	226	276	314	601	715	1,004	1,071	1,170

12. Drawing a Map (Objs. 2–4)

Haley Manufacturing Company is initiating a distance education program for delivering instruction on new production methods to its 15 manufacturing plants. Use computer software such as a spreadsheet with a map option to prepare a map showing (a) Haley's home office in Kansas City, the live site where the instruction will originate, and (b) the locations of the 15 remote sites:

Los Angeles, Seattle, Houston, New Orleans, Little Rock, Denver, Chicago, Orlando, Philadelphia, Boston, Atlanta, Indianapolis, Cincinnati, Albuquerque, and Green Bay. Write a descriptive or talking title that interprets the data depicted in the map. Write a sentence to introduce the graphic and emphasize its most important idea(s).

Read   Think   Write   **Speak**   Collaborate

13. Mastering Graphic Design: Tufte Style (Obj. 2)

Locate the following information related to Edward Tufte's principles of information design from **http://www.infotrac.thomsonlearning.com**:

Martin, M. H. (1997). The man who makes sense of numbers: Yale professor dazzles business people by making rational the data that rule their work lives. *Fortune*, 136(8), 273–275.

Rosen, S. (2000). The more words, the merrier. *Communication World*, 17(4), 64.

Conduct an online search to locate other articles that discuss and apply Tufte's concepts or obtain a copy of one of Tufte's three books on information design: (a) *Visual Explanations: Images and Quantities, Evidence and Narrative*, (b) *Envisioning Information*, and (c) *The Visual Display of Quantitative Information*.

Prepare a presentation explaining Tufte's principles of information design for printed and web pages. Include at least one of Tufte's classic examples that illustrates the importance of data design in proper decision making. Compile a list of basic principles for presenting data clearly and attractively following Tufte's theory.

14. Evaluating Graphics in Annual Reports (Objs. 2–4)

Obtain a copy of a corporate annual report and follow these steps to critique a graphic in the report:

a. Identify *one* graphic that violates one or more of the principles presented in this chapter. For example, the graphic may be an inappropriate type to present the data meaningfully, may be drawn incorrectly, may distort the true meaning of the data, have too much clutter, contain typographical or labeling errors, or contain other ineffective design elements.

b. Revise the graphic, incorporating your suggestions. Send your instructor an e-mail message outlining the major weaknesses in the graphic and your suggestions for improving it. Attach the computer file containing your revised graphic.

c. Be prepared to present a report to the class. To support your report, prepare a slide or transparency of the poor and revised graphic and a list of the weaknesses if your graphic contained several errors.

Read   Think   Write   Speak   **Collaborate**

15. Drawing a Gantt Chart (Objs. 2–4)

 In teams assigned by your instructor, prepare a Gantt chart to schedule the activities involved in completing a team project assigned by your instructor. The chart should include timelines that compare the actual progress with the planned progress. Your instructor will designate the software that should be used for preparing the Gantt chart or you may download a trial version of Microsoft Project® from the Internet. Refer to *Building High-Performance Teams* (your team handbook) and your instructor's guidelines for identifying the activities and time requirements for the project.

16. Evaluating Graphics in Annual Reports (Objs. 2–4)

In teams of three, obtain a copy of a corporate annual report for a U.S. based firm and one for a non-U.S. based firm. Prepare a one-page memo to your instructor that evaluates the use of graphics in each report, the graphics' effectiveness in clarifying or reinforcing major points, and any noted differences between the graphics presentation of each report. Share your analysis in a short report to the class.

Visual Elements Make Yahoo! a Best-Known URL

While search engines such as Yahoo!, Excite, GeoCities, Netscape's NetCenter, and Microsoft Network have been referred to as web portals, the developers of each of these sites want to do more than provide a ramp to other resources. Greater user time in the search engine ensures greater exposure to the site's advertisers.

- Visit the Yahoo! web site at **http://www.yahoo.com** and the Excite web site at **http://www.excite.com**.
- What visual similarities and differences do you note in the sites?

Write a short report on the part visual elements have played in making Yahoo! one of the best-known URLs in existence.

Part 4 of the Yahoo! ShowCASE focuses on how Yahoo! uses visual design strategies to showcase its advertisers.

http://www.yahoo.com

Visit the text support site at **http://lehman.swlearning.com** to complete Part 4 of the Yahoo! ShowCASE.

Internet Case

Lying Statistics

Three kinds of lies are possible, according to Benjamin Disraeli, a British prime minister in the nineteenth century—lies, damned lies, and statistics. A related notion exists that "you can prove anything with statistics." Such statements bolster the distrust that many people have for statistical analysis. On the other hand, many nonmathematicians hold quantitative data in awe, believing that numbers are, or at least should be, unquestionably correct. Consequently, it comes as a shock that various research studies can produce very different, often contradictory results. To solve this paradox, many naive observers conclude that statistics must not really provide reliable indicators of reality after all, and if statistics aren't "right," they must be "wrong." It is easy to see how even intelligent, well-educated people can become cynical if they don't understand the concepts of statistical reasoning and analysis.

Consider, for instance, the frequent reporting of a "scientific discovery" in the fields of health and nutrition. The United States has become a nation of nervous people, ready to give up eating pleasures at the drop of a medical report. Today's "bad-for-you" food was probably once good for you, and vice versa. Twenty years ago, many consumers were turned away from consuming real butter to oily margarine, only recently to learn that the synthetically solidified oils of margarine, trans-fatty acids, are worse for our arteries than any fat found in nature. In the year following the publication of this latest finding, margarine sales dropped 8.2 percent and butter sales rose 1.4 percent.

Distrust also arises concerning studies that link exercise to health. Numerous studies have established statistically that people who exercise live longer. But the conclusion that exercise is good for you may put the cart before the horse. Are people healthy because they exercise? Or do they exercise because they are healthy? Correlation, once again, does not establish causation.

How do such incorrect and partial research findings become published and consequently disseminated through the media? Some of the responsibility should probably be cast upon researchers who may overstate the significance or the generalizability of their findings. The media should also shoulder some blame, as preliminary findings of small or limited studies are often reported as foregone conclusions. Consumers should also assume some responsibility in the interpretation of reported research. Questions such as the following should be asked when considering the value of reported findings.

- Is the study sample representative of the population involved?
- Were the statistical procedures used appropriate to the data?
- Has the research involved a sample of significant size and a sufficient time period of study?
- Were adequate controls applied to assure that outcomes are actually the result of the studied variable?
- Has the margin for error been taken into account in interpreting the results?
- Has any claim of causation been carefully examined using appropriate approaches?

The statement that "you can prove anything with statistics" is true only if statistics are used incorrectly. Understanding the basics of statistics is becoming increasingly important. With the prevalence of computers, vast amounts of data are available on every subject; and statistical packages allow analysis of these data with the press of a button, regardless of whether the analysis makes sense. Our professional and business lives thrive on numbers and our ability to interpret them correctly.

Visit the text support site at **http://lehman.swlearning. com** to link to web resources related to this topic. As directed by your instructor, complete one or more of the following:

1. Compile a list of behaviors or practices that can lead to the reporting of "lying statistics." For each item on your list, indicate whether the behavior or practice is likely an intentional or unintentional attempt to distort.

2. **GMAT** Write a one- to two-page analysis of the researcher's ethical responsibilities in reporting statistical results of a study versus the consumer's responsibilities in reading and interpreting the results.

3. Prepare a short spoken report in which you describe some of the issues that arise when reporting international economic statistics.

Video Case

Renegade Animation: Animated Graphics Technology

Located in downtown Burbank, California, Renegade Animation was founded in 1992 by Ashley Quinn and Darrell Van Citters. In its first year, Renegade did $1.2 million in sales. And even though it is slightly larger in sales today, there are only four full-time employees along with 35 freelance artists. Renegade Animation does everything from low-budget public service announcements to 90-second spots that have aired on the Super Bowl.

Renegade's impressive production list (found at **http://www.renegadeanimation.com/projects.html**) includes a variety of animation projects, such as computer games and animation consulting, design, and development projects. If you enjoy animation and are using a fast Internet connection, you may want to view several of the QuickTime clips of Renegade's work at **http://www. renegadeanimation. com/movies.html**, such as "Trix Yogurt Magic Wand" and "Cheetos Stunt Double."

View the video segment about Renegade Animation and related activities on WebTutor or your Professional Power Pak CD.

Discussion Questions

1. What might be one reason that Ashley Quinn and Darrell Van Citters chose the name *Renegade Animation* for their new company, when one definition of the word "renegade" is "an individual who rejects . . . conventional behavior"?

2. What part, if any, of Ken McDonald's explanation of the animation process was new information to you? If you already knew how the animation process works before viewing this video, when and from whom did you gain your knowledge?

3. Why do you think companies such as Kraft General Foods, Midas, and Vlasic Pickles are willing to pay $120,000 to $180,000 for a 30-second animated commercial?

Activities

Locate the following article available in full text from InfoTrac College or perhaps from another database available through your campus library:

Watson, M. (2002, August 21). Memphis, Tenn.-area companies put animation technology to use in business, *Knight Ridder/Tribune Business News*. ITEM 02233083.

1. Write a brief summary of the article that discusses primary applications of 3-D animation and the benefits gained from this technology.

2. The Internet provides a platform for many types of animated graphics options. One option—touted on its web site as serving over 100 million image views per day on web sites worldwide*—is provided by Internet Pictures Corporation (iPIX):

    a. See for yourself what this animated graphics technology can do by going on a virtual tour of the White House at **http://www.whitehouse.gov/ history/whtour/360index.html**

    b. Learn how the technology works by visiting **http://www.ipix.com/products/im/publishing/ index.shtml**. Look under the heading on the right side of the window that reads "Information Quick Links" and select the hyperlink "View an Introduction." (Be forewarned the link also includes a sales pitch.)

    c. View several samples of various types of animated graphics technology at the following links:

    http://www.kmgi.com/

    http://www.editflorida.com/

    http://www.virtual3dinc.com/anima.html#

    http://www.andylackow.com/animate_filmstrips. html

3. Write a conclusion to the following introduction and submit it to your instructor: "After reviewing various types of animated graphics technologies in this video case, I believe the impact these technologies have on the communication process is . . . ."

*Solving mission-critical imaging needs with high-quality, reliable, market-proven technology. (2003) International Pictures Corporation. Retrieved August 6, 2003, from **http://www.ipix.com/company/overview.shtml**

11 Organizing and Preparing Reports and Proposals

Objectives *When you have completed Chapter 11, you will be able to:*

1. Identify the parts of a formal report and the contribution each part makes to the report's overall effectiveness.

2. Organize report findings.

3. Prepare effective formal reports using an acceptable format and writing style.

4. Prepare effective short reports in letter, memorandum, and e-mail formats.

5. Prepare effective proposals for a variety of purposes.

AFLAC INCORPORATED: CAPITALIZING ON THE COMMUNICATION POWER OF THE ANNUAL REPORT

Of all the documents corporations publish, none receives as much attention as the annual report. Offering a valuable glimpse into the workings and financial performance of companies, these annual scorecards guide investors' decisions. Furthermore, annual reports serve as an ideal public relations mechanism to influence various stakeholders, including employees and the general public. Managers of many companies are seizing the apparent opportunity to articulate their company's corporate personality and philosophy effectively.

One company that is successfully capitalizing on the communication power of its annual report is AFLAC Incorporated. A Fortune 500 company, AFLAC insures more than 40 million people worldwide and is the leading underwriter of supplemental insurance. AFLAC's annual reports have been honorably recognized every year since the inception of *Chief Executive* magazines's rating system of the best annual reports. AFLAC's reports have consistently been assigned "World-Class" status by scoring at least 100 of a potential 135 points on the evaluation system. Commenting on the outstanding recognition, AFLAC's CEO Dan Amos said: "We are extremely pleased to see AFLAC's annual report at the top of the list of the best annual reports. Our shareholders are our most valuable customers, and we believe that effective communication with our customers is crucial to the success of our business."[1]

The annual report rating is based on a 135-point copyrighted evaluation system that factors in elements ranging from extensive CEO involvement to more financial disclosure than is required by the Securities and Exchange Commission. According to Sid Cato, contributing editor and judge for *Chief Executive's* annual report listing, AFLAC's exemplary reports include multiple-year financial data, biographical information on company officers, and fully captioned graphs, all of which helped place it as one of the best.[2]

Careful design and organization of AFLAC's annual report has led to positive public recognition and likely improved its competitive edge. Similarly, you will want the reports you are called on to produce to be effective for their desired purpose. Each part must be carefully crafted and reviewed to make sure it is as perfect as possible and contains all necessary support and documentation. Finally, your skills in combining all the various parts into a clear, concise whole will assure that your report receives a "number one" rating.

http://www.aflac.com

See ShowCASE Part 2, page 443, for Spotlight Communicator Sid Cato, contributing editor for Chief Executive *and author of the Official Annual Report web site.*

Parts of a Formal Report

Objective 1

Identify the parts of a formal report and the contribution each part makes to the report's overall effectiveness.

The differences between a formal report and an informal report lie in the format and possibly in the writing style. The type of report you prepare depends on the subject matter, the purpose of the report, and the readers' needs. At the short, informal end of the report continuum described in Chapter 9, a report could look exactly like a brief memorandum. At the long, formal extreme of the continuum, the report might include most or all of the parts shown in Figure 11-1.

A business report rarely contains all of the parts shown but may include any combination of them. The preliminary parts and addenda are mechanical items that support the body of a report. The body contains

Figure 11-1

Parts of a Formal Report: Preliminary Parts, Report Text, and Addenda

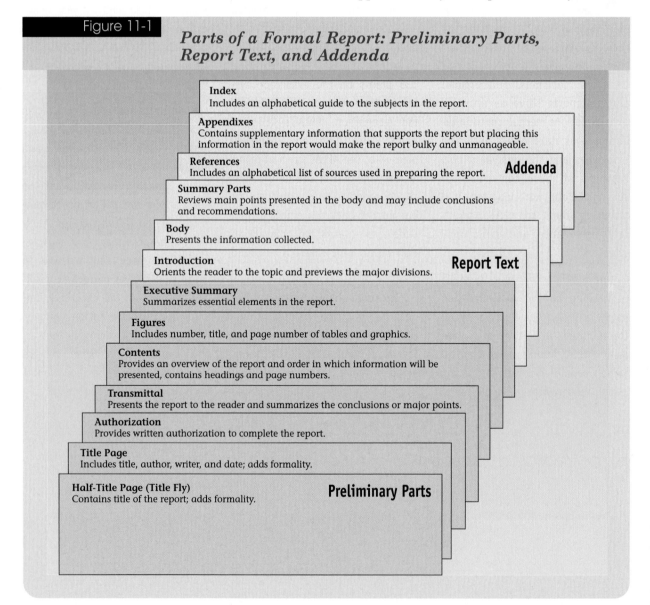

Index
Includes an alphabetical guide to the subjects in the report.

Appendixes
Contains supplementary information that supports the report but placing this information in the report would make the report bulky and unmanageable.

References
Includes an alphabetical list of sources used in preparing the report.

Addenda

Summary Parts
Reviews main points presented in the body and may include conclusions and recommendations.

Body
Presents the information collected.

Introduction
Orients the reader to the topic and previews the major divisions.

Report Text

Executive Summary
Summarizes essential elements in the report.

Figures
Includes number, title, and page number of tables and graphics.

Contents
Provides an overview of the report and order in which information will be presented, contains headings and page numbers.

Transmittal
Presents the report to the reader and summarizes the conclusions or major points.

Authorization
Provides written authorization to complete the report.

Title Page
Includes title, author, writer, and date; adds formality.

Half-Title Page (Title Fly)
Contains title of the report; adds formality.

Preliminary Parts

the report of the research and covers the four steps in the research process. The organization of the body of a report leads to the construction of the contents page.

Because individuals usually write to affect or influence others favorably, they often add parts as the number of pages increases. When a report exceeds one or two pages, you might add a cover or title page. When the body of a report exceeds four or five pages, you might even add a finishing touch by placing the report in a plastic cover or ring binder, or binding in a professional manner. Reports frequently take on the characteristics of the formal end of the continuum simply by reason of length. First, note how the preliminary parts and addenda items shown in Figure 11-2 increase in number as the report increases in length. Second, notice the order in which report parts appear in a complete report.

Memo and letter reports are seldom longer than a page or two, but they can be expanded into several pages. As depicted, long reports may include some special pages that do not appear in short reports. The format you select—long or short, formal or informal—may help determine the supporting preliminary and addenda items to include.

To understand how each part of a formal report contributes to reader comprehension and ease of access to the information in the report, study the following explanations of each part shown in Figure 11-1. The three basic sections—preliminary parts, report text, and addenda—are combined to prepare a complete formal report.

Critical Thinking

What factors determine the parts of a report that are desirable to include?

Preliminary Parts

Critical Thinking

How would you respond to the statement that preliminary pages are mere window dressing?

Preliminary parts are included to add formality to a report, emphasize report content, and aid the reader in locating information in the report quickly and in understanding the report more easily. These parts include the half-title page, title page, authorization, transmittal, contents, figures, and executive summary. Preliminary pages are numbered with small Roman numerals (i, ii, iii, and so on).

Half-Title Page

Often called a **title fly**, the **half-title page** is a single page containing only the report title. This page simply adds formality and enhances the appearance of a report. In less formal reports, including letter and memorandum reports, the half-title page is omitted.

Title Page

The **title page** includes the title, author, date, and frequently the name of the person or organization that requested the report. A title page is often added when the writer opts to use a formal report format rather than a memorandum or a letter arrangement.

Figure 11-2

The Number of Assisting Parts Increases as the Length of a Report Increases

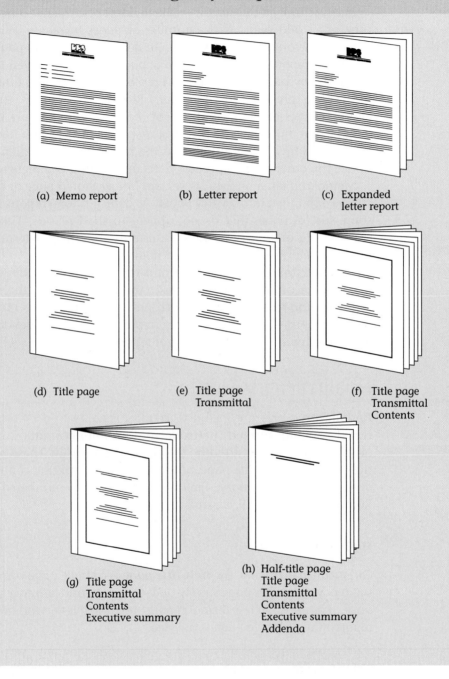

(a) Memo report

(b) Letter report

(c) Expanded letter report

(d) Title page

(e) Title page
Transmittal

(f) Title page
Transmittal
Contents

(g) Title page
Transmittal
Contents
Executive summary

(h) Half-title page
Title page
Transmittal
Contents
Executive summary
Addenda

The selected title should be descriptive and comprehensive; its words should reflect the content of the report. Avoid short, vague titles or excessively long titles. Instead, use concise wording to identify the topic adequately. For example, a title such as "Marketing Survey: Noncarbonated

Beverages" leaves the reader confused when the title could have been "Noncarbonated Beverage Preferences of College Students in Boston." To give some clues for writing a descriptive title, think of the "Five Ws": *Who, What, When, Where,* and *Why.* Avoid such phrases as "A Study of . . .," "A Critical Analysis of . . . ," or "A Review of . . . ."

Follow company procedures or a style manual to place the title attractively on the page. If the title is longer than one line, arrange it in the inverted pyramid format; that is, make each succeeding line shorter than the line preceding it. Arrange the title consistently on the half-title page, title page, and the first page of a report. The inverted pyramid format also should be used in titles of graphics. Note the arrangement of the following title of a graphic:

Incorrect:	AVERAGE PER CAPITA INCOME IN 2003 FOR TEN STATES
Incorrect:	AVERAGE PER CAPITA INCOME IN 2003 FOR TEN STATES
Correct:	AVERAGE PER CAPITA INCOME IN 2003 FOR TEN STATES

Authorization

Critical Thinking

Write an effective title for a report to select a mobile phone carrier and rate plan for a pharmaceutical sales force.

An **authorization** is a letter or memorandum authorizing the researcher to conduct a specific research project. The authorization is included as a formal part of the report and follows the title page. If no written authorization is provided, authorization information may be included in the letter of transmittal or the introduction. This information might include a clear description of the problem, limitations restricting the research, resources available, and deadlines.

Transmittal

As a report becomes more formal, the writer may attach a **letter** or **memorandum of transmittal**. The transmittal serves two purposes: (1) to present the report to the one who requested it, and (2) to provide the conclusion from an analytical study or highlights from an informational report. If the writer has prepared a report for a person or a department inside the company, the writer uses the memorandum format for the transmittal. A consultant preparing a report for another company or client arranges the transmittal in a letter format.

The transmittal letter or memorandum is the writer's opportunity to speak directly to the reader in an informal tone. Thus, the writer may include first- and second-person pronouns in the transmittal. If the report includes an executive summary or a detailed introduction, the transmittal is short. Use the deductive approach and follow these suggested steps:

1. Let the first sentence present the report and remind the reader that he or she requested it.
2. Explain the subject of the report in the first paragraph.
3. Present brief conclusions and, if called for, the recommendations.
4. Close cordially. The closing paragraph may also express appreciation for the cooperation given by the company.

Contents

Critical Thinking

How does the contents page contribute to the coherence of a formal report?

The **contents** provides the reader with an analytical overview of the report and the order in which information is presented. Thus, this preliminary part aids the reader in understanding the report and in locating a specific section of it. The list includes the name and location (beginning page number) of every report part except those that precede the contents page. Include the list of figures and the transmittal, executive summary, report headings, references, appendixes, and index. Placing spaced periods (leaders) between the report part and the page numbers helps lead the reader's eyes to the appropriate page number.

Changing Technology

Word processing software simplifies the time-consuming, tedious task of preparing many of the preliminary and addenda report parts, including the contents. Because the software can generate these parts automatically, report writers can make last-minute changes to a report and still have time to update preliminary and addenda parts.

Figures

To aid the reader in locating a specific graphic in a report with many graphics, the writer might include a list of figures separate from the contents. The list should include a reference to each figure that appears in the report, identified by both figure number and name, along with the page number on which the figure occurs. The contents and the figures can be combined on one page if both lists are brief. Word processing software can be used to generate the list of figures automatically.

Executive Summary

Critical Thinking

How can the executive summary serve a useful purpose without being redundant?

The executive summary (also called the *abstract*, *overview*, or *précis*) summarizes the essential elements in an entire report. This overview simplifies the reader's understanding of a long report. The executive summary is positioned before the first page of the report.

Typically, an executive summary is included when the writer believes it will assist the reader in understanding a long, complex report. Because of the increased volume of information that managers must review, managers tend to require an executive summary regardless of the length and complexity of a report. The executive summary presents the report in miniature: the introduction, body, and summary as well as conclusions and recommendations, if they are included in the report. Thus, an executive summary should (1) introduce briefly the report and preview the major divisions, (2) summarize the major sections of the report, and (3) summarize the report summary and any conclusions and recommendations. Pay special attention to topic sentences and to concluding sentences in paragraphs or within sections of reports. This technique helps you write concise executive summaries based on major ideas and reduces the use of supporting details and background information.

Critical Thinking

An executive summary, or abstract, is said to serve the immediate reader as well as "distant readers." Explain.

To assist them in staying up-to-date professionally, many busy executives require assistants to prepare executive summaries of articles they do not have time to read and conferences and meetings they cannot attend. Many practitioner journals now include an executive summary of each article. Reading the executive summary provides the gist of the article and alerts the executive to pertinent articles that should be read in detail. According to public relations consultant Cynthia Pharr, the executive summary is probably the most important part of a report being presented to top management. She advises that summaries be prepared with the needs of specific executive readers in mind. For instance, a technically oriented executive may require more detail; a strategist, more analysis. An executive summary should "boil down" a report to its barest essentials, yet without brevity so severe that the overview is meaningless. Essentially, an executive summary should enable top executives to glean enough information and understanding to feel confident making a decision.

Report Text

The report itself contains the introduction, body, summary, and any conclusions and recommendations. Report pages are numbered with Arabic numerals (1, 2, 3, and so on).

Introduction

The introduction orients the reader to the problem. It may include the following items:

- what the topic is.
- why it is being reported on.
- the scope and limitations of the research.
- where the information came from.
- an explanation of special terminology.
- a preview of the major sections of the report to provide coherence and transitions:
  - how the topic is divided into parts.
  - the order in which the parts will be presented.

Body

The **body**, often called the heart of the report, presents the information collected and relates it to the problem. To increase readability and coherence, this section contains numerous headings to denote the various divisions within a report. Refer to "Organization of Formal Reports" in this chapter for an in-depth discussion of preparing the body.

Summary, Conclusions, and Recommendations

An informational report ends with a brief *summary* that serves an important function: It adds unity to a report by reviewing the main points presented in the body. A summary includes only material that is discussed in a report. Introducing a new idea in the summary may make the reader wonder why the point was not developed earlier. It may suggest that the study was not completed adequately or that the writer did not plan the report adequately before beginning to write. Finally, a summary, which is expected to be fairly short, does not provide enough space for developing a new idea.

An *analytical report*, designed to solve a specific problem or answer research questions, will end with an "analysis," which may include a summary of the major research findings, particularly if the report is lengthy. Reviewing the major findings prepares the reader for the conclusions, which are inferences the writer draws from the findings. If required by the person/organization authorizing the report, recommendations follow the conclusions. *Recommendations* present the writer's opinion on a possible course of action based on the conclusions. Review the examples of findings, conclusions, and recommendations presented in Chapter 9 if necessary.

For a long report, the writer may place the summary, the conclusions, and the recommendations in three separate sections or in a section referred to as "The Analysis." For shorter reports, all three sections are often combined.

Critical Thinking

What is the difference between an informational and an analytical report? What applications do the two types have in business settings?

Addenda

The *addenda* to a report may include all materials used in the research but not appropriate to be included in the report itself. The three basic addenda parts are the references, appendixes, and index. Addenda parts continue with the same page numbering system used in the body of the report.

Critical Thinking

What addenda parts might be added to a report making a recommendation for a health care plan for company personnel?

References

The *references* (also called *works cited* or *bibliography*) section is an alphabetical listing of the sources used in preparing the report. Because the writer may be influenced by any information consulted, some reference manuals require all sources consulted to be included in the reference list. When the reference list includes sources not cited in the report, it is referred to as a *bibliography* or a *list of works consulted*. If a report includes endnotes rather than in-text parenthetical citations (author and date within the text), the endnotes precede the references. Using word processing software to create footnotes and endnotes alleviates much of the monotony and repetition of preparing accurate documentation. Refer to "Documenting Referenced Material" in Chapter 9, Appendix B, or a style manual for specific guidelines for preparing citations.

Appendix

An **appendix** contains supplementary information that supports the report but is not appropriate for inclusion in the report itself. This information may include questionnaires and accompanying transmittal letters, summary tabulations, verbatim comments from respondents, complex mathematical computations and formulas, legal documents, and a variety of items the writer presents to support the body of the report and the quality of the research. Placing supplementary material in an appendix helps prevent the body from becoming excessively long.

If the report contains more than one appendix, label each with a capital letter and a title. For example, the four appendixes (or appendices) in a report could be identified as follows:

Appendix A:	Cover Letter Accompanying End-User Questionnaire
Appendix B:	End-User Questionnaire
Appendix C:	Means of 20 Technology Competencies
Appendix D:	Number and Percentage of Ratings Given to 20 Technology Competencies

Each item included in the appendix must be mentioned in the report. References within the report to the four appendixes mentioned in the previous example follow:

A copy of the cover message (Appendix A) and the end-user questionnaire (Appendix B) were distributed by e-mail to 1,156 firms on February 15, 2004.

Means were computed, and the total means were ranked to establish an order of importance for the 20 technology competencies as shown in Table 10. The means are shown in Appendix C, and the frequency distribution from which these means were computed is provided in Appendix D.

Index

The **index** is an alphabetical guide to the subject matter in a report. The subject and each page number on which the subject appears are listed. Word processing software can generate the index automatically. Each time a new draft is prepared, a new index with revised terms and correct page numbers can be generated quickly and easily.

Organization of Formal Reports

Objective 2

Organize report findings.

The authors of certain types of publications known as tabloids typically have no valid documentation to support their claims, so they make up their own support. Hopefully, absolutely no one believes them. The purpose of such publications is to entertain, not to inform. The writer of a bona fide report must, however, do a much more convincing and thorough job of reporting.

Writing Convincing and Effective Reports

As discussed in Chapter 9, reports often require you to conduct research to find quotes, statistics, or ideas from others to back up the ideas presented. This support from outside sources serves to bolster the research as well as your credibility. Doing research and taking notes, however, are only parts of the process of putting together a well-documented, acceptable report. Careful organization and formatting assure that the reader will be able to understand and comprehend the information presented. While many companies have their own style manuals that give examples of acceptable formats for reports, this section presents some general organization guidelines.

Critical Thinking

Complete the following analogy: Outline is to report as _____ is to _____.

Outlining and Sequencing

The content outline serves as a framework on which to build the report. In the development of the outline, the writer identifies the major and minor points that are to be covered in the report and organizes them into a logical sequence. Outlining of a formal report is an essential prerequisite to writing the report. The outline is a planning document and is thus subject to modification as the writer develops the report.

Critical Thinking

Why is an outline considered to be a "penciled" document?

Development of an outline requires that the writer think about the information to be presented and how it can best be organized for the clear understanding of the reader. Assume, for instance, that you must select a PDA (personal digital assistant) from among three comparable brands from three vendors—Palm, Handspring, and Sony. You must choose the PDA that will best serve the portable computing needs of a small office and present your reasons and recommendations in a *justification report*.

You gather all information available from suppliers of the three PDAs; you operate each PDA personally; and you compare the three against a variety of criteria. Your final selection is the Palm. Why did you select it? What criteria served as decision guides? When you write the report, you will have to tell the reader—the one who will pay for the equipment—how the selection was made in such a way that the reader is "sold" on your conclusion.

Significant business scandals and failures led in 2002 to tightened reporting requirements by the Securities and Exchange Commission (SEC). Current SEC guidelines require that companies' annual reports include comprehensive and detailed financial information, as well as thorough analysis.

© DENNIS BRACK/BLOOMBERG NEWS/LANDOV

If you organize your report so that you tell the reader everything about the Palm, the Handspring, and the Sony each in a separate section, the reader may have trouble making comparisons. Your content outline might look like this:

> I.   Introduction
>   A. The Problem
>   B. The Method Used
> II. Palm
> III. Handspring
> IV. Sony
> V.   Conclusion

Note that this outline devotes three Roman-numeral sections to the findings, one to the introduction that presents the problem and the method, and one to the conclusion. This division is appropriate because the most space must be devoted to the findings. However, the reader may have difficulty comparing the expansion capacity of the PDAs because the information is in three different places. Would discussing the expansion capacity of all three in the same section of the report be better? Would prices be compared more easily if they were all in the same section? Most reports should be divided into sections that reflect the criteria used rather than into sections devoted to the alternatives compared.

If you selected your computer based on cost, service/warranties, and expandability, these criteria (rather than the computers themselves) might serve as divisions of the findings. Then your content outline would appear this way:

> I. Introduction
>   A. The Problem
>   B. The Methods Used
> II. Product Comparison
>   A. Handspring Is Least Expensive
>   B. Service/Warranties Favor Palm
>   C. Expandability Is Best on Palm
>   D. Availability of Applications Is Equal
> III. Conclusion: Palm Is the Best Buy

The outline now has three major sections, with the product comparison consisting of four subsections. When the report is prepared in this way, the features of each PDA (the evaluation criteria) are compared in the same section, and the reader is led logically to the conclusion.

Critical Thinking

What relation does a report outline have to the final report document?

Note the headings used in Sections II and III. These are called **talking headings** because they talk about the content of the section and even give a conclusion about the section. Adding page numbers after each outline item will convert the outline into a contents page. Interestingly, the headings justify the selection of the Palm. As a result, a knowledgeable reader who has confidence in the researcher might be satisfied by reading only the content headings.

In addition to organizing findings by criteria, report writers can use other organizational plans. The comparison of three PDAs was an analytical process. When a report is informational and not analytical, you should use the most logical organization. Treat your material as a "whole" unit. A report on sales might be divided by geographic sales region, by product groups sold, by price range, or by time periods. A report on the development of a product might use chronological order. By visualizing the whole report first, you can then divide it into its major components and perhaps divide the major components into their parts.

A final caution: Beware of overdividing the sections. Too many divisions might make the report appear disorganized and choppy. On the other hand, too few divisions might cloud understanding for the reader.

When developing content outlines, some report writers believe that readers expect the beginning of the body to be an introduction, so they begin the outline with the first heading related to findings. In our example, then, Section I would be "Product Comparison." Additionally, when they reach the contents page, readers may eliminate the Roman numeral or other outline symbols.

The research process consists of inductively arranged steps as shown in Figure 11-3: (1) Problem, (2) Method, (3) Findings, and (4) Conclusion. Note how the four steps of research have been developed through headings in the Roman-numeral outline and to a contents page for a report, as shown in Figure 11-3. When the report is organized in the same order, its users must read through the body to learn about the conclusions—generally the most important part of the report to users. To make the reader's job easier, report writers may organize the report deductively, with the conclusions at the beginning. This sequence is usually achieved by placing a synopsis or summary at the beginning:

> **REPORT TITLE IN DEDUCTIVE SEQUENCE REVEALS THE CONCLUSION**
>
> I. Conclusion Reported in the Synopsis
> II. Body of the Report
>   A. Problem
>   B. Method
>   C. Findings
> III. Conclusion

This arrangement permits the reader to get the primary message early and then to look for support in the body of the report. The deductive arrangement contributes to the repetitious nature of reports, but it also facilitates understanding.

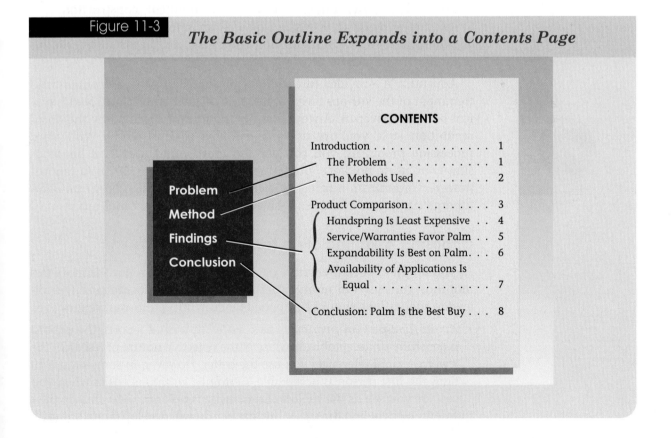

Figure 11-3

The Basic Outline Expands into a Contents Page

CONTENTS

Introduction	1
The Problem	1
The Methods Used	2
Product Comparison	3
Handspring Is Least Expensive	4
Service/Warranties Favor Palm	5
Expandability Is Best on Palm	6
Availability of Applications Is Equal	7
Conclusion: Palm Is the Best Buy	8

Problem
Method
Findings
Conclusion

Using Headings Effectively

Critical Thinking

What formatting techniques can be used to differentiate levels of headings?

Headings are signposts informing readers about what text is ahead. Headings take their positions from their relative importance in a complete outline. For example, in a Roman numeral outline, "I" is a first-level heading, "A" is a second-level heading, and "1" is a third-level heading:

```
I.   First-Level Heading
     A. Second-Level Heading
     B. Second-Level Heading
          1. Third-Level Heading
          2. Third-Level Heading
II.  First-Level Heading
```

Two important points about the use of headings also relate to outlines:

- *Because second-level headings are subdivisions of first-level headings, you should have at least two subdivisions (A and B).* Otherwise, the first-level heading cannot be divided—something divides into at least two parts or it is not divisible. Thus, in an outline, you must have a "B" subsection if you have an "A" subsection following a Roman numeral, or you should have no subsections. The same logic applies to the use of third-level headings following second-level headings.

Critical Thinking

Make the following headings from a sales analysis parallel: Sales in Northeast Are Flat; Sales Increase Dramatically in Southwest; Increasing Sales in West; Midwest Experienced No Change in Sales.

- *All headings of the same level must be treated consistently.* Consistent elements include the physical position on the page, appearance (type style, underline), and grammatical construction. For instance, if Point A is worded as a noun phrase, Point B should be worded in the same manner. Or if Point I is a complete sentence, Points II and III should also be worded as sentences.

Appendix A provides further information about the placement and treatment of the various levels of headings. The method illustrated is typical but not universal. Always identify the format specified by the documentation style you are using and follow it consistently. With word processing programs, you can develop fourth- and fifth-level headings simply by using boldface, underline, and varying fonts. In short reports, however, organization rarely goes beyond third-level headings; thoughtful organization can limit excessive heading levels in formal reports.

Changing Technology

Choosing a Writing Style for Formal Reports

As you might expect, the writing style of long, formal reports is more formal than that used in many other routine business documents. The following suggestions should be applied when writing a formal report:

- *Avoid first-person pronouns as a rule.* In formal reports, the use of *I* is generally unacceptable. Because of the objective nature of research, the fewer personal references you use the better. However, in some organizations the first person is acceptable. Certainly, writing is easier when you can use yourself as the subject of sentences. People who can change their writing by avoiding the use of the first person will develop a genuine skill.

The federal government has taken strides to improve the readability of reports it creates. Its web site, Writing User-Friendly Documents, provides numerous suggestions for using plain language. Visit this useful site at **http://www.blm.gov/nhp/NPR/pe_toc.html.**

Plain Language

WRITING USER-FRIENDLY DOCUMENTS

TABLE OF CONTENTS

- *Use active voice.* "Authorization was received from the IRS" might not be as effective as "The IRS granted authorization." Subjects that can be visualized are advantageous, but you should also attempt to use the things most important to the report as subjects. If "authorization" were more important than "IRS," the writer should stay with the first version.
- *Use tense consistently.* Because you are writing about past actions, much of your report writing is in the past tense. However, when you call the reader's attention to the content of a graphic, remember that the graphic *shows* in the present tense. If you mention where the study *will take* the reader, use a future-tense verb.
- *Avoid placing two headings consecutively without any intervening text.* For example, always write something following a first-level heading and before the initial second-level heading.

Critical Thinking

Compose a transition sentence that could be used to move from a discussion of Company A phone plan to Company B phone plan as the better choice for company personnel.

- *Use transition sentences to link sections of a report.* Because you are writing a report in parts, show the connection between those parts by using transition sentences. "Although several advantages accrue from its use, the incentive plan also presents problems" may be a sentence written at the end of a section stressing advantages and before a section stressing problems.
- *Use a variety of coherence techniques.* Just as transition sentences bind portions of a report together, certain coherence techniques bind sentences together: repeating a word, using a pronoun, or using a conjunction. If such devices are used, each sentence seems to be joined smoothly to the next. These words and phrases keep you from making abrupt changes in thought.

Time Connectors	**Contrast Connectors**
finally	although
further	despite
furthermore	however
initially	in contrast
meanwhile	nevertheless
next	on the other hand
since	on the contrary
then	yet
thereafter	
while	
at the same time	
Similarity Connectors	**Cause-and-Effect Connectors**
for instance	but
for example	conversely
likewise	because
in the same way	consequently
just as	hence
similarly	therefore
thus	

Additional ideas about transitional wording are covered in Chapter 4, "Link Ideas to Achieve Coherence" and "Apply Visual Enhancements." Other ways to improve transition include the following:

- *Use tabulations and enumerations.* When you have a series of items, bullet them or give each a number and list them consecutively. This list of writing suggestions is easier to understand because it contains bulleted items.
- *Define terms carefully.* When terms are not widely understood or have specific meanings in the study, define them. Definitions should be written in the term-family-differentiation sequence: "A dictionary (*term*) is a reference book (*family*) that contains a list of all words in a language (*point of difference*)." "A sophomore is a college student in the second year." Refer to Chapter 9 for additional information on defining terms in a research study.

- **Check for variety.** In your first-draft stage, most of your attention should be directed toward presenting the right ideas and support. When reviewing the rough draft, you may discover certain portions with a monotonous sameness in sentence length or construction. Changes and improvements in writing style at this stage are easy and well worth the effort.

Enhancing Credibility

Legal & Ethical Constraints

Readers are more likely to accept your research as valid and reliable if you have designed the research effectively and collected, interpreted, and presented the data in an objective, unbiased manner. The following writing suggestions will enhance your credibility as a researcher:

- **Avoid emotional terms.** "The increase was fantastic" doesn't convince anyone. However, "The increase was 88 percent—more than double that of the previous year" does convince.
- **Identify assumptions.** Assumptions are things or conditions taken for granted. However, when you make an assumption, state that clearly. Statements such as "Assuming all other factors remain the same, . . ." inform the reader of an important assumption.
- **Label opinions.** Facts are preferred over opinion, but sometimes the opinion of a recognized professional is the closest thing to fact. "In the opinion of legal counsel, . . ." lends conviction to the statement that follows and lends credence to the integrity of the writer.
- **Use documentation.** Citations and references (works cited) are evidence of the writer's scholarship and honesty. These methods acknowledge the use of secondary material in the research.

Critical Thinking

How can the report writer "dignify" an included opinion?

Effective writing requires concentration and the removal of distractions. A writing procedure that works well for one person may not work for another. However, some general guidelines for creating an environment conducive to effective writing are available on the text web site at http:// lehman.swlearning.com.

A writing environment that works well for one person may not work for another.

Diversity Challenges

Cultural variances, as well as legal and business requirements in some countries, may dictate the content and style of reports, as discussed in the Strategic Forces feature, "Disclosure in Annual Financial Reports of International Firms."

Analyzing a Formal Report

Objective **3**

Prepare effective formal reports using an acceptable format and writing style.

A complete, long report following APA format is illustrated in Figure 11-4. The notations next to the text will help you understand how effective presentation and writing principles are applied. APA style requires that reports be double-spaced and that the first line of each paragraph be indented a half inch; however, a company's report-writing style manual may override this style and stipulate single-spacing without paragraph indents. The sample report in Figure 11-4 is single-spaced, and paragraphs are not indented to save space and give a more professional appearance. The report may be considered formal and contains the following parts:

Title Page

Transmittal

Contents

Executive Summary

Figures

Report Text (Introduction, Body, Summary, Conclusions, and Recommendations)

References

Appendix

This sample should not be considered the only way to prepare reports, but it is an acceptable model. The "Check Your Communication" section at the end of the chapter provides a comprehensive checklist for use in preparing effective reports.

Short Reports

Objective **4**

Prepare effective short reports in letter, memorandum, and e-mail formats.

Short reports incorporate many of the same organizational strategies as do long reports. However, most **short reports** include only the minimum supporting materials to achieve effective communication. Short reports focus on the body—problem, method, findings, and conclusion. In addition, short reports might incorporate any of the following features:

• personal writing style using first or second person.
• contractions when they contribute to a natural style.
• graphics to reinforce the written text.
• headings and subheadings to partition portions of the body and to reflect organization.
• memorandum, e-mail, and letter formats when appropriate.

Disclosure in Annual Financial Reports of International Firms

The annual financial report is the basic tool used by investors to compare the performance of various companies. While U.S. firms must comply with Security and Exchange Commission (SEC) requirements for disclosure, the extent to which information is reported by companies based abroad varies. For the most part, companies in English-speaking countries do a good job with disclosure. Annual reports of American and British firms provide much more than just a balance sheet and a profit-and-loss statement; they typically provide a comprehensive set of notes giving additional information—for instance, on how a firm's pension liabilities are calculated or whether assets have been sold and leased back. Heightened requirements for disclosure in the United States, enacted in 2002 in light of widely publicized corporate scandals, represent solid progress in enhancing the user's understanding of the choices and judgments that underlie a set of financial statements. On the other hand, some information published in the annual report must be limited in detail to prevent competitors and possible takeover bidders from gaining useful but damaging knowledge of the organization.[3]

In some countries such as Germany, any information beyond the basic annual report is often nonexistent, in published form or otherwise. National requirements vary, as do the voluntary responses of individual companies within a given country. More and more international firms, however, are reporting their financial results according to the International Accounting Standards (IAS)—a body of rules developed in the 1970s, and currently under revision by an international committee of accountants, financial executives, and equity analysts. The IAS is a step in the right direction for improving disclosure, and its new requirements will go into effect for listed companies in 2005.[4] In the United States, the SEC requires that international firms that wish to list their shares on an American exchange must comply with the United States' Generally Accepted Accounting Principles (GAAP).

Currently, in the United States and some other countries, the annual financial report of a firm is recognized as communicating much more than just the accounting summary for the organization's performance. Management realizes that this single communication document is scrutinized by three groups of vital partners: the customers, the owners, and the employees. In addition to projecting profitability, many U.S. firms see the annual report as a vehicle for illuminating prevailing management philosophy, projecting corporate charisma, and humanizing themselves to their publics.

Application

Using the Internet or a published source, obtain the annual financial report for a company based abroad. Write a short report that analyzes your responses to the following questions:

- Did the report contain the company's mission statement?

- Was the company's code of ethics, or credo, included?

- Was information provided about the company directors, officers, and/or executives?

- Were the major shareholders reported?

- What currency was used in the financial reporting (dollars, yen, pounds, etc.)?

- Was evidence provided of company concern for the environment or charities?

- How extensive and sophisticated were the report's graphics and photos?

Figure 11-4   *Long, Formal Report*

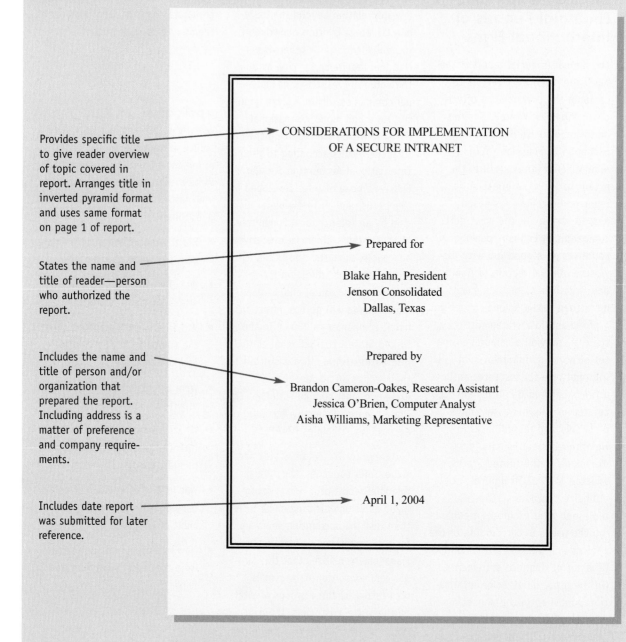

Provides specific title to give reader overview of topic covered in report. Arranges title in inverted pyramid format and uses same format on page 1 of report.

States the name and title of reader—person who authorized the report.

Includes the name and title of person and/or organization that prepared the report. Including address is a matter of preference and company requirements.

Includes date report was submitted for later reference.

CONSIDERATIONS FOR IMPLEMENTATION
OF A SECURE INTRANET

Prepared for

Blake Hahn, President
Jenson Consolidated
Dallas, Texas

Prepared by

Brandon Cameron-Oakes, Research Assistant
Jessica O'Brien, Computer Analyst
Aisha Williams, Marketing Representative

April 1, 2004

Format Pointers
- Omits page number but counts the page.
- Uses all capital letters and boldface, large font size to emphasize title.
- Uses different font for remaining items to add interest and to distinguish them from titles.
- Uses double border to add professional flair.

Figure 11-4 *continued*

JENSONCONSOLIDATED

2600 Conover Street
Dallas, TX 75260-2600
(214) 555-3900 Fax: (214) 555-9815

TO:　　　Blake Hahn, President

FROM:　　Brandon Cameron-Oakes, Research Assistant *BCO*
　　　　　Jessica O'Brien, Computer Analyst *JO*
　　　　　Aisha Williams, Marketing Representative *AW*

DATE:　　April 1, 2004

SUBJECT:　Report on Implementation of a Secure Intranet

Presents the report and reminds reader that he authorized it. Uses informal, natural tone that involves reader. →

Here is the report on the implementation of a secure intranet that you authorized on February 24. Current business literature was examined, and a survey was conducted of 20 business people from various organizations in Texas who have implemented an intranet.

Discusses methods used (secondary and primary) to solve the problem and summarizes major conclusions. →

The report discusses the various benefits of intranets that account for their phenomenal growth in popularity. Limitations are also addressed, with attention given to methods for overcoming security risks. The intranet experiences of several surveyed organizations are summarized as examples of successful implementations. A recommendation is made for Jenson to proceed with the implementation of a secure intranet, while following several suggested guidelines.

Expresses willingness to discuss the results. →

Thank you for allowing us the opportunity to participate in this worthwhile study. We are confident that this report will aid you in making appropriate decisions about the implementation of a secure intranet, and we will be happy to discuss the findings with you.

asl

Attachment

ii

Format Pointers

- Uses an acceptable memorandum format for a report submitted to an organization insider.
- Adds enclosure notation to indicate report is included.
- Centers page numbers in small Roman numerals at bottom of page; may omit number but count as a page.

Figure 11-4   *continued*

Omits the word "table" or "list," an obvious fact.

Presents each heading exactly as it appears in the report; thus, the page is prepared after the report is completed.

Omits outline numbering system (I, II, A, B) but reflects the outline to indicate the importance of the headings (main heads placed at the left margin; minor ones indented).

Includes the page number on which each major and minor section begins.

1½"

Contents
DS

Figures

iii

Format Pointers

- Combines contents and figures on the same page to save space.
- Adds leaders (spaced periods) to guide the eyes from the heading to the page number.
- Allows word processing software to generate the contents so it can be updated quickly with each draft of the report.

Figure 11-4   *continued*

Uses "Executive Summary," a term commonly used in business, rather than "Abstract," the term APA recommends.

Provides background and explains problems leading to need for the study. Presents purpose of study and identifies person authorizing it.

Describes methods used to solve the problem.

Synthesizes major findings focusing on specific findings needed to support conclusions. Highlights the conclusions and recommendations based on analysis of the findings.

Executive Summary_{DS}

1½"

Jenson Consolidated, a small but growing industrial supplies business, had operated in Dallas, Texas for ten years. Blake Hahn, President, had considered the implementation of an intranet to facilitate internal communications. He had concerns, however, about the various security risks that would be posed by such a move. Hahn authorized a cross-functional team to study the possibility of implementing an intranet while providing an acceptable level of security.

Research was conducted in two ways: (1) current business literature was examined, and (2) 20 business people whose organizations had intranets were surveyed about their intranet experiences.

The report addressed the following topics: (1) background and popularity of intranets, (2) benefits and limitations of intranets, (3) intranet security measures, and (4) organizational uses of intranets. The study concluded that intranets have become extremely popular because of the various benefits they offer. The potential limitations can be addressed adequately by proper planning and implementation of recommended security measures. Jenson should proceed with plans to implement a secure intranet.

iv

Figure 11-4   *continued*

CONSIDERATIONS FOR IMPLEMENTATION OF A SECURE INTRANET

DS

Uses centered heading to denote a major division.

$1^{1}/_{2}''$ **Introduction**

Jenson Consolidated has increased its staff size from 5 to 57 over the last ten years and is considering the implementation of an intranet to enhance corporate communication. In light of growing threats of hacking and virus attack, the company must have reasonable assurance that the intranet can be made secure in order to proceed with the implementation.

Gives specific purpose and scope of study in separate sections to form a basis for information that follows.

Purpose of the Study

The purpose of this report is to examine the possibility of implementing an intranet while providing an acceptable level of security. Answers to the following questions are provided:

1. How does an intranet work?
2. What are some advantages and disadvantages of intranets?
3. How can an intranet be made secure?
4. How are organizations using their intranets?

Scope of the Study

Uses side heading to move reader from one minor division of introduction to another.

The project was limited by the topic assignment, the five-week time period allowed for its completion, and the absence of a research budget. The team delimited the project by gathering research only through the Steen Library on the campus of Stephen F. Austin State University and through interviews with 20 conveniently selected business people in Texas whose organizations have intranets.

Definitions

Provides definitions needed by the reader to understand the report.

The following terms are defined to assist the reader:

Uses paragraph heading to denote the third-level division of the outline.

Intranet. A network of computers, based on Internet-style technology, that is completely within an organization. Intranets are different from local area networks and wide area networks used in many organizations that are based on network platforms and use network software to communicate with one another (Pagan & Fuller, 1997).

1

Format Pointers
- Sinks first page to 1½ inches for added eye appeal.
- Centers title in all capital letters; overrides APA format (upper- and lowercase) as directed in company style manual. Uses larger, boldface font for emphasis.
- Formats center, side, and paragraph headings in boldface font. Note capitalization style for each level.
- Centers Arabic numeral one inch from bottom of page, or omits but counts it.

Figure 11-4 | *continued*

2

Encryption. A technique for rendering information unintelligible to anyone other than the intended recipient that uses an algorithm (mathematical formula) and a key (string of bits or characters) (National Computer Security Center, 1985).

Methods and Procedures

Secondary research was conducted through traditional and electronic searches of periodicals, books, and government documents. Interviews were conducted during March, 2004, with 20 conveniently selected business managers from throughout Texas. The sample represented a cross section of business types (See Appendix A for a list of participants). Interviewees were asked a set of questions dealing with the application of a secure intranet in the respective organizations. (See Appendix B for survey questionnaire.)

Findings

Intranets have grown in popularity with the commercial use of the Internet. Various advantages have been found by participating companies, as well as a few disadvantages. While security has typically been the largest challenge to organizations using intranets, recommended measures can reduce information risks.

Background on Intranets

The Internet is a network of computer networks, interlinked at various points around the world, which can communicate with each other. A local area network (LAN) is a group of computers located in a relatively limited area and connected by communication links that allow them to interact with each other. The Internet and LANs were both designed to permit computer users to communicate and share information. The newest phenomenon is integrating Internet technologies with LANs to create what is known as an intranet.

An intranet is a group of web sites that are internal and function as a network using Internet protocols (Bartlett, 1998). While intranets use the enabling technologies of the Internet, they are intended to provide information for internal communication and decision making (Perry, 1998). The two most important functions of intranets are the mass publishing of information and the widespread sharing of data, and these functions mirror the two biggest information responsibilities of most corporations (Pagan & Fuller, 1997). Intranets are being used throughout corporations for electronic publishing, electronic mail, employee conferencing, electronic forms completion, database searches, groupware projects, and technical support and help desk assistance (Reynolds, 2002).

The number of companies implementing intranets grew phenomenally in the first four years of their existence, as shown in Figure 1:

Provides methods and procedures and sources of information used to add credibility. Refers reader to Appendix for additional information.

Uses centered heading to move reader from introduction to first major division.

Includes lead-in paragraph that previews information to be presented and provides intervening text to separate major and minor headings.

Uses in-text citations to indicate ideas paraphrased from secondary sources.

Format Pointers

- Numbers page 2 and remaining pages with an Arabic numeral at the top right margin one inch from top of page.
- Singe-spaces final copy of report for efficiency; APA style requires double-spacing.

Figure 11-4 *continued*

Places Figure 1 following its textual reference as closely as possible. Provides title specific enough to assist readers who skim the report.

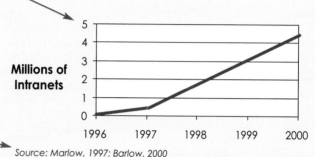

3

Figure 1
Growth in Number of Intranets
Over 4-Year Period

Millions of Intranets

Source: Marlow, 1997; Barlow, 2000

Includes source note for correct documentation.

Summarizes major points in the figure and provides expanded information.

By 2003, it was estimated that 90 percent of U.S. enterprises had an intranet in some stage of evolution (Intranet Road Map, 2003). Intranets are a fundamental element in creating an online community within an organization that improves productivity and morale, reduces turnover, and heightens company competitiveness (Holtz, 2003).

Uses side heading to divide the major section into minor divisions.

Benefits and Limitations of Intranets

Various benefits and limitations have been experienced by the 90 percent of U.S. enterprises that now have an intranet (Intranet Road Map, 2003).

Uses paragraph heading to denote the third-level division of the outline.

Benefits. Intranets have been popularized by the numerous benefits they offer of communicating within an organization.

Uses bullets to emphasize benefits; would use numbers if sequence were important.

- **Reduction in cost.** As with most computer system decisions, a major factor is cost. Internet-type technology is less costly for the same number of users than traditional groupware, especially as the number of users grows (Pagan & Fuller, 1997).
- **Ease of use.** Because intranet technology is based upon the user-friendly atmosphere of the World Wide Web, users are able to become proficient quite easily (Pagan & Fuller, 1997).
- **Freedom of choice.** Web technology is based on open standards and therefore does not lock companies into limited, costly choices. Web technology is available for all leading operating systems and hardware platforms (Pagan & Fuller, 1997).

Format Pointers

- Ensures the page does not end or begin with a single line of a paragraph (applies to all pages in a report).
- Labels a line chart as a figure and numbers consecutively with one numbering system. Formats the two-line title in inverted pyramid format.

Figure 11-4   *continued*

4

Uses in-text citations to reflect paraphrased or quoted items. Page number is provided for direct quotations.

Uses paragraph heading to denote the third-level division of the outline.

Uses bullets to emphasize the limitations; would use numbers if sequence were important.

- **Increased productivity.** While it is difficult to measure how much productivity has increased where intranets are in use, the consensus of users is that it is significant (Vowler, 1999).
- **Reduction in information access costs.** All relevant information is readily available on everyone's desktop. Time is saved in looking for materials, and money is saved in copying and distribution (Reynolds, 2002).
- **Improved communications.** Intranet collaboration "increases communication and the capture and sharing of knowledge within the company" (Murray, 2002, p. 21).

Limitations. Limitations have also been noted in the use of intranets.

- **Bandwidth.** A major limiting factor in intranet usage is bandwidth, the capacity of an organization's network to transmit data. An intranet breaks data into small packets for transmission, and data cannot be seen until all of the packets reach their destination and are reassembled for display. That means that materials containing large groups of video and audio files take longer to transmit (Curtin & Canterucci, 1997).
- **Network use patterns.** Heavy intranet use at certain times of the day or days of the week can mean extended delays in user access time. Each time a user links to a page, he or she has to wait for the network to deliver it. Slow access time can mean long waits and discouragement in accessing needed information (Curtin & Canterucci, 1997).
- **Security risks.** Risks to organizational information include viruses, unauthorized access to data by hackers and disgruntled employees, and inadvertent display of sensitive information. Various measures can be implemented to protect intranet data (Greengard, 1998).
- **Maintenance requirements.** Content changes and the ripple effect associated with them require on-going attention. Management and maintenance of the web site can tax the availability and skills of existing technical personnel and require expenditures for hiring outside consultants (McCluskey-Moore, 2000).

Uses transition statement and side heading to summarize previous section and move the reader to the next subpoint within a major section.

Thoughtful implementation and proper controls can help overcome limitations concerning usage and security.

Security Measures

While intranets are inherently vulnerable to intrusion, various practices can reduce the security risks associated with their use.

Figure 11-4   *continued*

5

Uses paragraph heading to denote the third-level division of the outline.

Encrypt sensitive pages. Encryption is essential when employees are allowed to view sensitive information on an intranet, such as 401(k) statements or salary records. Various encryption programs are available (Greengard, 1998).

Assure user identity. A traditional and widely used means of user authentication is with the implementation of a PIN or password system. Newer techniques include digital signatures, which can be used to further authenticate a user's identity. When using a digital signature, a document is encrypted using an assigned password that is required by both the sender and the receiver. Without the password, the message is garbled. When personal data is changed via the intranet, the person originating the transaction should confirm it by sending a letter or e-mail to the individual who will verify its accuracy and send a confirmation reply (Greengard, 1998).

Summarizes major points in the diagram and refers reader to figure.

Use firewalls. A firewall is typically located between a company's Internet server and its intranet in an attempt to prevent unauthorized access. Figure 2 illustrates the function of a firewall in controlling access to information within an intranet:

Places Figure 2 immediately following its textual reference.

Figure 2
Function of a Firewall in
Restricting User Access

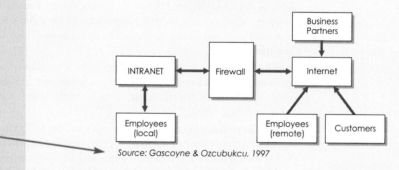

Includes source note for correct documentation.

Source: Gascoyne & Ozcubukcu, 1997

Discusses significance of information presented in the figure.

As illustrated, employees accessing the intranet from computers physically located within the organization can directly access the intranet, while those in other locations who desire to access the organization's intranet would have to clear the firewall barrier. The FBI's National Computer Crime Squad recommends the use of firewalls for organizations and individuals as a measure to guard against computer crime (Pagan & Fuller, 1997).

Format Pointer

• Centers figure number and title on separate lines separated by a double space. Uses inverted pyramid format for a two-line title.

Figure 11-4 *continued*

6

Manage intranet data. Management must know what is on the intranet and regulate unofficial applications and information that can crash networks and lead to liability threats. In establishing access controls, it is essential to consider what data different employees need, and establish controls to limit access to appropriate information. Workers must be educated as to how to use the system correctly. All the protection in the world will not help if employees do not follow standard guidelines and procedures (Greengard, 1998).

Summarizes major findings of the survey described in the Introduction section.

How Organizations Are Using Intranets

Intranets have gained wide acceptance as a means for disseminating information to internal constituents. Interviews with representatives of 20 organizations revealed that intranets are beneficial for a number of purposes, as indicated in the following selected summaries.

According to James Holloway, assistant manager at Wal-Mart, Nacogdoches, Texas, Wal-Mart uses its intranet, the "Wal-Mart Pipeline" to disseminate information for training, videos, promotions, present and past calendars, policies, history of the business, stock profit, and scholarships. Holloway cited increased access to information as a major advantage and security risks as a major disadvantage. Wal-Mart's security controls include limiting access via passwords and requiring levels of access.

British Petroleum/Amoco uses its intranet, "Connect," to distribute software applications, conduct training, report problems to centralized help desks, and provide communication among its worldwide staff of employees. An advantage noted by Al O'Neill, staff geologist, is the reduction in the use of paper and e-mail traffic and increased access to Internet search engines. A disadvantage can occur because of the massive expanse of information located via the intranet; employees can tend to spend too much time exploring the intranet instead of working. A small percentage of workers who are afraid of the technology miss out on vital information. BP/Amoco relies on a firewall to keep unauthorized parties out, and uses levels of passwords to control internal access.

Craig Perry, an investment officer with GE Capital, reported that his organization uses its intranet to share desired and achieved goals for the company and to provide stock information, earnings, and revenues. Announcements of promotions and changes in organizational structure are posted; and new product information and annual reports can be accessed as well as company forms. Links are provided to the web sites of other companies. Improved efficiency and productivity have resulted

Figure 11-4   *continued*

7

from the implementation of the company intranet. A noted disadvantage is the vulnerability to incorrect information. If false or incomplete information is posted to the intranet, the result is widespread. GE uses an FOB system that requires each employee to carry a watch face that has a six-digit number that changes every 30 seconds. To access the intranet, the correct six-digit number must be entered.

Dave Tedder, director of information systems at Nacogdoches Memorial Hospital, reported that their intranet allows for information to be shared among departments without unnecessary duplication. A library of medicine can also be accessed as needed. A major advantage has been the improved patient care, which has resulted from a better flow of timely information. The major disadvantage is the increased maintenance, upkeep, and knowledge requirements that are associated with their intranet. A firewall protects the hospital's intranet from intrusion, and passwords are required.

Interviewees were asked to provide advice for an organization contemplating the implementation of an intranet. The results are summarized below; those receiving the greatest number of responses are listed first:

Uses bullets to emphasize the advice provided by the interviews; would use numbers if the sequence were important.

- Provide adequate security, including a quality firewall.
- Conduct a thorough needs analysis before beginning design.
- Avoid taking shortcuts or cutting corners.
- Gather thorough information through interviews, product comparison, etc.
- Train employees adequately on the use of the intranet.
- Calculate the ongoing maintenance costs accurately.
- Hire qualified people to design, install, and maintain the intranet.
- Involve users in the design process.
- Strive for simplicity.
- Limit access appropriately.
- Provide other means for information dissemination in case of system failure or user reluctance.

The consensus of interviewed managers is that intranets offer obvious organizational advantages but must be carefully designed and managed to assure effective, secure operation. Lampron (2003) offers two additional suggestions for assuring a successful intranet:

Figure 11-4   *continued*

8

Work with the marketing communications department to develop the look and feel of the intranet itself. It should be consistent with the company's web site and other external marketing materials. To help ensure the success of your new intranet, remember to start with a simple application that affects a large proportion of your workforce (p. 69).

Properly designed and implemented, an intranet offers numerous benefits and minimal limitations.

Analysis

Consideration of primary and secondary research about intranets has led to the following analysis.

Summary

Most companies have implemented the use of an organizational intranet. Intranets have grown in popularity due to their use of familiar Internet protocols and their ability to facilitate the organization's ability to create, process, and disseminate intracompany information.

Intranets provide benefits including reduced cost for multiple users, ease of use, freedom of choice of operating platforms, and increased productivity. Limitations of intranets include transmission delays due to limited bandwidth and heavy intranet usage patterns and the various security risks that are posed.

Solutions for reducing security risks are available. Encrypting sensitive information helps assure delivery of information to only the desired parties. User authentication measures, such as passwords and digital signatures, help assure the legitimate user's identity. The use of firewalls helps to prevent unauthorized access from parties outside the organization. Appropriate management of an intranet includes understanding the data that are contained and the various needs for access, educating employees as to proper system use, and requiring that employees follow standard guidelines for usage.

The survey of 20 organizations revealed common usages of intranets, including the dissemination of various types of information related to training, policies, and financial position. Reduction in paper and increased communication were cited as primary advantages, and these achievements lead to improved efficiency and greater productivity. Recommended advice for intranet implementation

Callouts (left margin):

Includes a transition statement that summarizes the discussion of the findings and signals the analysis that will follow.

Combines "Summary, Conclusions, and Recommendations" in an appropriate heading for a report designed to solve a problem.

Includes a logical lead-in to a subsection to avoid stacked headings.

Uses side heading to denote the summary as a minor division.

Figure 11-4   *continued*

9

included the use of adequate security, a thorough needs analysis prior to design, and adequate expenditure to assure a quality system.

Uses side heading and lead-in sentence to transition the reader to the conclusion section.

Conclusions

Based on the research presented, the following conclusions were drawn:

Includes broad generalizations drawn from the findings and does not repeat specific findings. Uses bullets to add emphasis and clarity.

- Intranets are popular because they offer various advantages for improving productivity and effectiveness.
- While intranets have certain limitations and risks, appropriate planning and implementation can help to overcome them.
- Businesses are using their intranets in a variety of ways that increase efficiency and productivity.

Uses side heading and lead-in sentence to transition the reader to the recommendations section.

Recommendations

Jenson Consolidated should proceed with the implementation of a secure intranet according to the following guidelines:

Includes logical actions that follow from the research. Uses bullets to add emphasis and clarity.

- Conduct an extensive needs analysis to determine what features and capabilities are needed in the intranet.
- Contract with a qualified consultant to design an intranet and train company personnel on its use.
- Consider available security measures and implement those that are deemed appropriate for the company's needs.
- Assure ongoing evaluation and maintenance of the intranet, by providing training for selected current personnel or hiring additional personnel with intranet maintenance experience.

Provides logical closure to convince reader that report is thorough and complete.

Jenson can minimize the information security risks through a successful intranet implementation. Any potential risk is convincingly justified by improvements in communication, productivity, and competitiveness.

Figure 11-4   *continued*

10

Uses "References" as the title to indicate list contains only sources cited in report.

Presents alphabetical listing of sources cited in the report formatted in APA style.

Includes timely, valid sources from a variety of periodicals (scholarly journals and magazines, books), and electronic media (Internet and online databases).

References

Barlow, J. (2000, May 7). Intranet replaces office grapevine. *Houston Chronicle*, Business, p. 1.

Bartlett, J. E. (1998). Using an Intranet in business education. *In Integrating the intranet into the business curriculum. 1998: NBEA Yearbook, No 36*, pp. 139–147. Reston, VA: National Business Education Association.

Curtin, C., & Canterucci, J. (1997, February). Getting off to a good start on intranets, *Training & Development*, 42–46.

Greengard, S. (1998, September). Ten ways to protect intranet data. *Workforce*, 78–82.

Holtz, S. (2003). *The intranet advantage.* San Francisco: International Association of Business Communicators.

Intranet Road Map. (2003). Growth of intranet development. Retrieved June 10, 2003, from *http://www.intranetroadmap.com/growth.cfm*

Lampron, F. (2003, January). Intranet development requires teamwork: Before rollout, make sure tech support can handle employee self-service glitches. *HR Magazine*, 48(1), 67(3). Retrieved June 10, 2003, from GeneralBusinessFile database.

Marlow, E. (1997). *Web visions: An inside look at successful business strategies on the Net.* New York: Van Nostrand Reinhold.

McCluskey-Moore, N. (2000). Untangling Web content management. *Intranet Journal.* Retrieved September 29, 2003, from *http://www.intranetjournal.com/articles/200004/im_04_18_00a.html*

Murray, W. E. (2002, October 10). Empowering staff through the intranet. *New Media Age*, 21. Retrieved June 10, 2003, from InfoTrac database.

National Computer Security Center. (1985). Personal computer security considerations. (Report No. NCSC-WA-002-85). Fort Meade, MD: NCSC.

Pagan, K., & Fuller, S. (1997). *Intranet firewalls.* Triangle Park, NC: Ventana.

Perry. W. G. (1998). What is an intranet and how is it going to change systems analysis and design? *Journal of Computer Information Systems, 39*(1), 55–59.

Reynolds, P. (2002, October 21). Intranets help agencies organize info. *National Underwriter Life & Health-Financial Services Edition, 106*(42), 14–15.

Vowler, J. (1999, January 28). Does investment in intranets pay off? *Computer Weekly,* 44.

Format Pointers
- Continues page numbering used in the report.
- Centers "References" and uses larger, boldface font used for similar headings in the report (title, contents, executive summary, and appendix).
- Single-spaces references to be consistent with single spacing in the report. Double-spaces between references for differentiation.
- Uses paragraph indentions for each entry; alternately, APA allows for beginning each item at the left margin and indenting subsequent lines. Italicizes titles of books and periodicals and volume numbers.

Figure 11-4 *continued*

11

Appendix A

Interview Participants

(n = 20)

Increases credibility of research by including list of interviewees referenced on page 2.

Name	Title	Organization	Location
Ackerman, Sallie	Office Manager	AA Emergency Ambulance	Houston, TX
Adams, Lee	PC Specialist	Berrydirect	Nacogdoches, TX
Archer, Chet	Computer Programmer	Computer Task Group	Dallas, TX
Blair, Bob	VP-Contracts & Marketing	Diamond Offshore Drilling	Houston, TX
Boland, Chris	Software Consultant	Wang International	Houston, TX
Czubik, Greg	District Service Manager	General Motors Corp	Houston, TX
Ferris, Mary	Lending Officer	Bank of Texas	Dallas, TX
Harrison, Rick	Controller	Citizen's 1st Bank	Rusk, TX
Holloway, James	Assistant Manager	Wal-Mart	Nacogdoches, TX
Huerta, Dan	Technical Service Manager	Brookshire Brothers Warehouser	Lufkin, TX
Montes, Kevin	Senior LAN Administrator	B.J. Services	Tyler, TX
Morris, Ken	Technical Learning Manager	Shell Oil Company	Houston, TX
Nguyen, Duc	Computer Network Specialist	Moore North American	Nacogdoches, TX
O'Neill, Al	Staff Geologist	British Petroleum/ Amoco	Houston, TX
Perry, Craig	Investment Officer	GE Capital	Dallas, TX

Format Pointers

- Continues page numbering used in the report.
- Centers "Appendix A" and uses larger, boldface font used for similar headings in the report (title, contents, executive summary, and references).

12

Appendix B

Interview Questionnaire

Increases credibility by including interview questionnaire referenced on page 2.

1. What is the history of your organization's intranet?
2. What are the primary purposes of your intranet?
3. What are some advantages and disadvantages of having a company intranet?
4. How is information in your company's intranet secured? Do you feel that these measures are adequate?
5. What advice would you give to a company contemplating the creation of an intranet?
6. What other comments about secure intranets would you like to add?

SPOTLIGHT COMMUNICATOR

Promoting Annual Reports that Make the Grade

As contributing editor and the judge for *Chief Executive* magazine's annual report listing, Sid Cato is recognized by many as the world's foremost authority on annual reports. The annual listing, which has appeared in the magazine's November issue for over 20 years, is based on evaluations of reports submitted from around the world, according to a 135-point copyrighted evaluation system.

In speaking of the annual report, Cato says, "This is the No. 1 document a company can produce. It's the key corporate communiqué. It indicates how the company feels about itself."[5] Important factors that Cato looks for include clear financial disclosures, biographical data on corporate officers and board members, a brief and forward-looking letter from the company's chairman, and design continuity that suggests the company's accountants work well with its communication people. The use of understandable language and four-color artwork and photos are also valued. These design

factors helped propel AFLAC to the top of the numeric scoring. Cato says, "If a company doesn't know enough to produce an annual report that says 'Open me, read me,' you should toss it in the wastebasket."[6]

In addition to his annual report rating, Cato authors a monthly newsletter on annual reports and provides report critiques at the request of companies with an offer of tips for improvement. While encouraging companies to develop a clear theme and to use their reports to document their competitive advantages, Cato recognizes that the companies often fear revealing so much that they erode their competitive edge. Instead of attempting to satisfy so many different audiences with one annual report, some companies are spending time and energy breaking information into component parts. Digital media like the Internet and CD-ROMs have the facility to present large amounts of information in different ways.

COURTESY SID CATO/CATO COMMUNICATIONS

Cato feels that the worst thing that can happen in an annual report is for management not to explain the numbers. His caution: If you see something in the financial data that raises questions, such as an operating loss, and it's not explained anywhere in the report, that should raise suspicion.

Applying What You Have Learned

1. How does an annual report reveal what a company feels about itself?
2. What additional communication options are possible when annual reports are delivered over the Internet or by CD-ROM instead of in traditional paper form?

Sid Cato, Contributing Editor, Chief Executive *and Author of the Official Annual Report Web Site*

http://www.aflac.com
http://sidcato.com

Refer to ShowCASE, Part 3 at the end of the chapter to learn about the effective use of a theme in annual reports.

Memorandum and Letter Reports

Critical Thinking

Besides the difference in length, how do short reports differ from long, formal reports?

Short reports are often written in memorandum, e-mail, or letter format. The memorandum report is directed to an organizational insider, as are most e-mail reports. The letter report is directed to a reader outside the organization. Short reports to internal and external readers are illustrated in Figures 11-5 and 11-6. The commentary in the left column will help you understand how effective writing principles are applied.

The memo report in Figure 11-5 communicates the activity of a company's child care services during one quarter of the fiscal period. This periodic report is formatted as a memorandum because it is prepared for personnel within the company and is a brief, informal report. An outside consultant presents an audit of a company's software policy in the letter report in Figure 11-6.

The report in Figure 11-7 is written deductively. Implementation of a conservative business dress policy is described in an expanded letter report written by a consultant to a client (external audience). The consultant briefly describes the procedures used to analyze the problem, presents the findings in a logical sequence, and provides specific recommendations.

Form Reports

Critical Thinking

What form reports are you familiar with?

Form reports meet the demand for numerous, repetitive reports. College registration forms, applications for credit, airline tickets, and bank checks are examples of simple form reports. Form reports have the following benefits:

- When designed properly, form reports increase clerical accuracy by providing designated places for specific items.
- Forms save time by telling the preparer where to put each item and by preprinting common elements to eliminate the need for any narrative writing.
- In addition to their advantages of accuracy and time saving, forms make tabulation of data relatively simple. The value of the form is uniformity.

Most form reports, such as a bank teller's cash sheet, are informational. At the end of the teller's work period, cash is counted and totals entered in designated blanks. Cash reports from all tellers are then totaled to arrive at period totals and perhaps to be verified by computer records.

In addition to their informational purpose, form reports assist in analytical work. A residential appraisal report assists real estate appraisers in analyzing real property. With this information, the appraiser is able to determine the market value of a specific piece of property.

Many form reports are computer generated. For example, an automated hospital admission process expedites the repetitive patient reports that must be created. The admission clerk inputs the patient information using the carefully designed input screen beginning with the patient's

Changing Technology

Figure 11-5

Short, Periodic Report in Memorandum Format

Includes headings to serve the formal report functions of transmittal and title page.

Includes a horizontal line to add interest and to separate the transmittal from the body of the memo.

Uses deductive approach to present this periodic report requested by management on a quarterly basis.

Uses headings to highlight standard information; allows for easy update when preparing a subsequent report.

Includes primary data collected from a survey completed by parents.

Attaches material to the memorandum. The attachment would be an appendix item in a formal report.

THE PLAY STATION *(Child Care and Learning Center)*

1560 Kingsbury Lane / Arlington, VA 22922 / (703)555-6412 FAX (703)555-0919

TO: Melanie R. Adams, Director, Human Resources
FROM: Corey Camerino, Coordinator, Child Care Services *CC*
DATE: July 14, 2004
SUBJECT: Quarterly Report on In-House Child Care Center, Second Quarter, 2004

The in-house child care center experienced a successful second quarter. Data related to enrollment and current staffing follow:

Enrollment: 92 children, up from 84 at end of first quarter.
Staff: Ten full-time staff members, including six attendants, three teachers, and one registered nurse.

Registration for the upcoming school year is presently underway and is exceeding projected figures. Current staff size will necessitate an enrollment cap of 98. Further increases in enrollment will be possible only if additional personnel are hired.

The payroll deduction method of payment, instituted on January 1, has assured that operations remain profitable. It has also eliminated the time and expense of billing. Parents seem satisfied with the arrangement as well.

Full license renewal is expected in August as we have met and/or exceeded all state and county requirements for facilities, staff, and programs.

Favorable results were obtained from the employee satisfaction poll, which was administered to parents participating in the child care program. Ninety-one percent indicated that they were very satisfied or extremely satisfied with our in-house child care program. The most frequently mentioned suggestion for improvement was the extension of hours until 7 p.m. This change would allow employees time to run necessary errands after work, before picking up their children. We might consider this addition of services on a per hour rate basis. A copy of the survey instrument is provided for your review.

Call me should you wish to discuss the extended service hours idea or any other aspects of this report.

Attachment

Format Pointer

- Uses a memorandum format for a brief periodic report prepared for personnel within a company.

Figure 11-6   *Audit Report in Letter Format, Page 1*

GSI Technology Consulting Group

290 RBC Parkway, West • Los Angeles, CA 90046-9439
(213)555-9087 • Fax (213)555-3872
www.gsi.com

April 3, 2004

Ms. Kerry Tang, CEO
Pacific Systems Design Centre
P. O. Box 17963
Long Beach, CA 90810-1796

Dear Ms. Tang:

The personal computer software audit for Spectrum Analysis has been completed according to the procedures recommended by Software Publishers Association. These procedures and our findings are summarized below.

PROCEDURES

Specific procedures involved

- Reviewing the software policy of the organization and its implementation and control.
- Reviewing the organization's inventory of software resources, including a list of all personal computers by location and serial number. Using SPAudit, we obtained a list of all the software on the hard disk of each computer.
- Matching purchase documentation with the software inventory record we had established. This procedure included reviewing software purchase records, such as invoices, purchase orders, check registers, canceled checks, manuals, disks, license agreements, and registration cards.

FINDINGS

In the area of software policy and controls, we found that the organization owns a total of 432 copies of 11 applications from seven vendors. No record of registration with the publisher was available for 81 of the programs owned. In addition, we identified 47 copies of software programs for which no corresponding purchase records existed. These copies appear to be illegal.

Of the 113 personal computers, we found 14 machines with software that had been brought from home by employees.

Letterhead and letter address function as a title page and transmittal.

Introduces the overall topic and leads into procedures and findings.

Uses side heading to denote the beginning of the body.

Uses bulleted list to add emphasis to important information.

Format Pointer

- Uses letter format for a short report prepared by an outside consultant.

Figure 11-6

Audit Report in Letter Format, Page 2

Ms. Kerry Tang, CEO
Page 2
April 3, 2004

Summarizes major point in table and refers the reader to it. Does not number this single figure. Formats data in four-column table to facilitate reading and uses a clear title and column headings.

A summary of the software license violations identified follows:

Identified Software License Violations

Software	Total Copies Found	Legal Copies	Copies in Violation
Corel WordPerfect	56	52	4
Microsoft Office	110	100	10
Windows XP	115	75	40

We have deleted all copies in excess of the number of legal copies, and you are now in full compliance with applicable software licenses. We have also ordered legal software to replace the necessary software that was deleted.

Uses side heading to denote the beginning of the recommendation section.

CONCLUSIONS AND RECOMMENDATIONS

While some departments had little or no illegal software, others had significant violations. Therefore, the following recommendations are made:

Uses enumerations to emphasize the recommendations.

1. Institute a one-hour training program on the legal use of software and require it for all employees. Repeat it weekly over the next few months to permit all employees to attend. Additionally, require all new employees to participate in the program within two weeks of their start date.

2. Implement stricter software inventory controls, including semi-annual spot audits.

Thank you for the opportunity to serve your organization in this manner. Should you wish to discuss any aspects of this report, please call me.

Sincerely,

Kyle A. Cruse

Kyle A. Cruse
Software Consultant

slr

Format Pointer

• Includes reference initials of typist who is not the letter's author.

Figure 11-7   *Short Report in Expanded Letter Format, Page 1*

SPL STRATEGIC SOLUTIONS   *Management Consulting and Corporate Training*

761 Westgate Avenue   Atlanta, GA 30319-8718   (404)555-1768   Fax (404)555-6221

April 3, 2004

Ms. Jill A. Rowland
President, MetroBank
1660 Fremont Street
Marietta, GA 30360-1660

Dear Ms. Rowland:

RECOMMENDATIONS FOR IMPLEMENTING A RETURN TO
CONSERVATIVE BUSINESS DRESS POLICY

Thank you for allowing us to assist you in determining whether to implement a return to conservative business dress policy for MetroBank employees. This trend is gaining wide support throughout the business community and deserves careful consideration by your organization.

Procedures

In preparing this report, a variety of resources were consulted, including paper and online resources. Additionally, interviews were conducted with 20 businesspersons from a variety of organizations in Texas that have returned to business dress policies. Their perceptions, along with published research on the advantages and disadvantages of the strategy, led to the recommendations in this report.

Published resources, as well as firsthand interviews, generally support the implementation of a return to a business dress policy.

Findings

Research revealed useful information concerning the development and current status of business attire.

Trend from Casual Back to Conservative Business Attire

The casual dress movement gained rapid momentum in the 1990s, spurred by the casual dot-com heyday. In 1992, only 24 percent of businesses

Annotations (left margin):

Letterhead, letter address, and subject line function as a title page and transmittal.

Uses deductive approach to present this informational report to the president.

Provides research methods and sources to add credibility to the report.

Uses centered heading to denote a major division of the body and a transition sentence that leads the reader to subpoint denoted by its own heading.

Format Pointer
• Uses Subject line to introduce topic of letter report.

Figure 11-7 *continued*

Includes second page heading to denote continuation; appears on plain matching paper.

Ms. Jill A. Rowland
Page 2
April 3, 2004

surveyed by the Society for Human Resource Management allowed casual attire at the office, and nearly 75 percent of those permitted it on just one day of the week. By 1999, 95 percent of employers surveyed by the same group had a dress-casual policy, and more than 40 percent of those businesses permitted it every work day (White, 2001).

Advocates pushing a decade ago to loosen dress codes claimed that more casual, comfortable wear at the office would mean happier employees who would work harder and produce more than they would cinched up in buttoned-down collars, ties, and suits. While casually clad employees did enjoy new-found freedom and comfort, much research and anecdotal evidence has indicated "that relaxed dress leads to relaxed manners, relaxed morals, and relaxed productivity" (Hudson, 2002, p. 6). A 1999 study by the employment law firm Jackson Lewis found that casual clothes could lead to increased on-the-job flirting, harassment, tardiness, and absenteeism (White, 2001). Furthermore, problems with dress-down policies frequently resulted from the lack of clear standards as to what constituted business casual (Jones, 2003).

Uses side heading to denote a minor section.

Implementation of Conservative Business Dress in Other Organizations

Uses a transition sentence to move the reader smoothly to this minor section.

Following the lax dress policies of the past 15 years, more companies are tightening their dress policies by bringing back business professional attire. Some attribute the shift to a slowing economy in which the laid-back look was linked to an overall lack of professionalism and business acumen (White, 2001). The Bush administration is also credited for the shift back to formal. Within days of his inauguration in 2001, President George W. Bush announced a new formal dress code that reinstated the business suit as appropriate office attire and banned jeans and T-shirts from White House business meetings. The reason, he said, was to restore dignity and sobriety to the office of the presidency (Brody, 2003). In the same year, various firms reversed their business-casual dress policies, including Bear Stearns, Deutsche Bank, and Lehman Brothers.

Figure 11-7   *continued*

Ms. Jill A. Rowland
Page 3
April 3, 2004

A 2002 survey commissioned by the Men's Apparel Alliance showed that 19 percent of over 200 companies with more than $500 million in annual revenues were returning to formal business attire (Egodigwe & Alleyne, 2003). A 2003 survey by Kurt Salmon Associates revealed that only 24 percent of all businesses currently offered casual days—down from 87 percent in 2000 during the height of the trend (Brody, 2003).

Although most employees understand terms such as "business dress" and "business professional," others may need more graphic definitions, such as "traditional suits and ties" (Brody, 2003, p. 7). In reversing its business casual policy, Lehman brothers detailed its requirements in a memo to employees. "Business dress for men is a suit and tie, and for women, a suit with either a skirt or slacks, a dress, or other equivalent attire" (Egodigwe & Alleyne, 2003, p. 59). Many find the new requirements much more straightforward than the vagary of business casual. A paralegal of a law firm reversing its business casual dress code expressed relief at the elimination of confusion: "Now I don't have to guess what I should and shouldn't wear to work" (Egodigwe & Alleyne, 2003, p. 59).

Advantages of Conservative Business Dress

Various positive outcomes have been attributed to the implementation of business dress policies:

- **Improved attitudes.** People tend to behave in ways that complement their clothing. They are more likely to act like professionals if they are wearing a suit and tie (Brody, 2003).

- **Increased productivity.** Improvements in the overall quality of work, professional commitment, and company loyalty have been reported when business dress was enforced (Hudson, 2002).

- **Enhanced image.** The clothing people wear can affect their careers, as well as the organization's image (Best Business Attire, 2003).

[Margin annotations:]

Provides APA citations for direct quotes and paraphrased information.

Uses side heading and transition sentence to move reader smoothly to this minor section.

Uses bullets to highlight advantages and disadvantages of business dress.

Figure 11-7

continued

Ms. Jill A. Rowland
Page 4
April 3, 2004

- **Greater versatility.** The tried-and-true business uniform means that employees can go anywhere and meet anyone, knowing they are properly attired (Hudson, 2002).

- **Increased respect for women and minorities.** John T. Molloy, the original dress-for-success author, asserts that business attire enhances the authority of women, minorities, and short men, placing everyone on a more even playing field (Malloy, 1999).

Disadvantages have been associated with a shift to a more formal business dress policy:

- **Additional wardrobe expenditures.** Many workers will have to purchase new wardrobe selections to comply with the business dress standard (Clifford, 2002).

- **Resistance to change.** The business casual movement remains strong, and a shift back to more formal attire will be resisted by many (White, 2001).

Implementation of Conservative Business Dress Policy

Establishing an official dress code is the first step in making the shift from casual to business dress. The code establishes a clear set of rules for all employees as to what is acceptable. Guidelines should be simple but specific, in writing, and well distributed; they should not conflict with Title VII of the Civil Rights Act, which protects employees' cultural and religious rights (Brody, 2003).

Because a dressier code can involve wardrobe updating, employees may need assistance in understanding fashion trends and making smart purchases. Various clothing manufacturers, retailers, and business consultants provide information and training in wardrobe selection:

Figure 11-7   *continued*

Uses three-column table to make information easy to access. Table immediately follows its introduction; is not numbered because it is the only figure.

Ms. Jill A. Rowland
Page 5
April 3, 2004

Sources of Information About Conservative Business Dress

Brooks Bros.	Holds seminars and fashion shows; offers special clothing discounts through Corporate Image Program	http://www.brooksbrothers.com
Neiman Marcus	Offers instructional video on business dress	http://www.neimanmarcus.com
Dayton Hudson Corp.	Conducts fashion seminars	http://www.targetcorp.com
Men's Wearhouse	Offers free instructional video on dress for success	http://www.menswearhouse.com
Executive Communications Group	Offers web site with attire tips for men and women	http://www.ecglink.com

Summary

The following guidelines are offered to assure a successful implementation of a return to a conservative business dress policy:

Uses bulleted list to summarize points for emphasis.

- Access information from organizational sources described in this report and consider consultant options.
- Appoint an employee committee to investigate the particulars of an appropriate business dress policy for MetroBank and to make a recommendation to management as to implementation guidelines.
- Consider phasing in the more formal policy, allowing time for employees to adjust their wardrobes for full implementation.
- Evaluate the success of the program from the perspectives of management, employees, and customers; make any indicated changes.

Figure 11-7   *continued*

Ms. Jill A. Rowland
Page 6
April 3, 2004

Closes with a courteous offer to provide additional service.

Thank you for the opportunity to provide this information concerning a return to a conservative dress policy. Please let us know how we can assist you further with this project or with other related endeavors.

Sincerely,

Patricia Sykes

Patricia Sykes, Consultant

ksm

Includes enclosure notation to alert reader of the enclosed reading list.

Enclosure: Reading list

Reading List

Best business attire. (2003). Executive Communications Group. Retrieved June 13, 2003, from *http://ecglink.com*

Brody, M. (2003, March 1). Dress codes: 'Business conservative' is making a comeback. *HR Briefing*, 7.

Clifford, L. (2002, March 18). Suitable stocks. *Fortune*, 145(6), 150.

Egodigwe, L., & Alleyne, S. (2003, March). Here come the suits. *Black Enterprise*, 33(8), 59.

Hudson, R. (2002, April 15). 'Business causal' on the wane. *St. Louis Post Dispatch*. Retrieved June 13, 2003, from *http://seattlepi.nwsource.com*

Jones, C. (2003, June 8). Experts discuss ways to dress in business attire for summer. *Las Vegas Review*. Retrieved June 13, 2003, from InfoTrac database.

McPherson, W. (1997). "Dressing down" in the business communication curriculum. *Business Communication Quarterly*, 60(1), 134–146.

Molloy, J. T. (1999, December 9). Executives find as dress gets sloppier, attitudes slip. *The Houston Chronicle*, p. 2.

White, R. D. (2001, August 26). Clashing dress styles. *Careerbuilder.* Retrieved June 13, 2003, from *http://www.latimes.com*

social security number. If the patient has been admitted previously, the patient's name, address, and telephone number are displayed automatically for the clerk to verify. When the clerk inputs the patient's date of birth, the computer calculates the patient's age, eliminating the need to ask a potentially sensitive question and assuring accuracy when patients cannot remember their ages. All data are stored in a computer file and retrieved as needed to generate numerous reports required during a patient's stay: admissions summary sheet, admissions report, pharmacy profile, and even the addressograph used to stamp each page of the patient's record and the identification arm band.

Using the computer to prepare each report in the previous example leads to higher efficiency levels and minimizes errors because recurring data are entered only once. Preparing error-free form reports is a critical public relations tool because even minor clerical errors may cause patients or customers to question the organization's ability to deliver quality service.

Proposals

Objective 5

Prepare effective proposals for a variety of purposes.

Managers prepare **internal proposals** to justify or recommend purchases or changes in the company; for instance, installing a new computer system, introducing telecommuting or other flexible work schedules, or reorganizing the company into work groups. An **external proposal** is a written description of how one organization can meet the needs of another, for example, provide products or services, as defined in Chapter 9. Written to generate business, external proposals are a critical part of the successful operation of many companies.

Proposals may be solicited or unsolicited. **Solicited proposals** are invited and initiated when a potential customer or client submits exact specifications or needs in a bid request or a request for proposal, commonly referred to as an **RFP**. Governmental agencies such as the Department of Defense solicit proposals and place orders and contracts based on the most desirable proposal. The bid request or RFP describes a problem to be solved and invites respondents to describe their proposed solutions.

An **unsolicited proposal** is prepared by an individual or firm who sees a problem to be solved and submits a proposal. For example, a business consultant is a regular customer of a family-owned retail store. On numerous occasions she has attempted to purchase an item that was out of stock. Recognizing that stock shortages decrease sales and profits, she prepares a proposal to assist the business in designing a computerized perpetual inventory with an automatic reordering system. For the business to accept the proposal, the consultant must convince the business that the resulting increase in sales and profits will more than offset the cost of the computer system and the consulting fee.

Critical Thinking

Give examples of situations in your career field for which a proposal may need to be prepared.

Structure

Critical Thinking

When would price be the only deciding factor for distinguishing between competing proposals?

A proposal includes (1) details about the manner in which the problem would be solved and (2) the price to be charged or costs to be incurred. Often the proposal is a lengthy report designed to "sell" the prospective buyer on the ability of the bidder to perform. However, a simple price quotation also constitutes a proposal in response to a request for a price quotation.

The format of a proposal depends on the length of the proposal and the intended audience:

Format	Proposal Length and Intended Audience
Memo or e-mail report	Short; remains within the organization
Letter report	Short; travels outside the organization
Formal report	Long; remains within the organization or travels outside the organization

Most work resulting from proposals is covered by a working agreement or contract to avoid discrepancies in the intents of the parties. In some cases, for example, users of outside consultants insist that each consultant be covered by a sizable general personal liability insurance policy that also insures the company. Many large firms and governmental organizations use highly structured procedures to assure understanding of contract terms.

The following general parts, or variations of them, may appear as headings in a proposal: (1) Problem or Purpose, (2) Scope, (3) Methods or Procedures, (4) Materials and Equipment, (5) Qualifications, (6) Follow-up and/or Evaluation, (7) Budget or Costs, (8) Summary, and (9) Addenda. In addition to these parts, a proposal may include preliminary report parts, such as the title page, transmittal message, and contents as well as addenda parts, such as references, appendix, and index.

Problem and/or Purpose

Critical Thinking

How can the writer make the proposal more successful in the competitive process?

Problem and purpose are often used as interchangeable terms in reports. Here is the introductory purpose statement, called "Project Description," in a proposal by a firm to contribute to an educational project:

Project Description: Logan Community College has invited business and industry to participate in the creation of *Business Communication*, a television course and video training package. These materials will provide effective training in business communication skills to enhance the performance of individuals in business and contribute to organizational skills and profitability. In our rapidly evolving information society, skill in communication is integral to success.

Note how the heading "Project Description" has been used in place of "Purpose." In the following opening statement, "Problem" is used as the heading:

> **Problem:** The Board of Directors of Oak Brook Village Association has requested a proposal for total management and operation of its 1,620-unit permanent residential planned development. This proposal demonstrates the advantages of using Central Management Corporation in that role.

The purpose of the proposal may be listed as a separate heading (in addition to "Problem") when the proposal intends to include objectives of a measurable nature. When you list objectives such as "To reduce overall expenses for maintenance by 10 percent," attempt to list measurable and attainable objectives and list only enough to accomplish the purpose of selling your proposal. Many proposals are rejected simply because writers promise more than they can actually deliver.

Scope

[Info to Remember]

When determining the scope of your proposal, you can place limits on what you propose to do or on what the material or equipment you sell can accomplish. The term *scope* need not necessarily be the only heading for this section. "Areas Served," "Limitations to the Study," and "Where (*specify topic*) Can Be Used" are examples of headings that describe the scope of a proposal. Here is a "Scope" section from a consulting firm's proposal to conduct a salary survey:

> **What the Study Will Cover:** To assist Sun Valley Technologies in formulating its salary and benefits program for executives, Patterson Consulting will include an analysis of compensation (salary and benefits) for no fewer than 20 of Sun Valley's competitors in the same geographic region. In addition to salaries, insurance, incentives, deferred compensation, medical, and retirement plans will be included. Additionally, Patterson Consulting will make recommendations for Sun Valley's program.

Another statement of scope might be as follows:

> **Scope:** Leading figures in business and industry will work with respected academicians and skilled production staff to produce fifteen 30-minute interactive video training courses that may be used in courses for college credit or as modules dealing with discrete topics for corporate executives.

Methods and/or Procedures

The method(s) used to solve the problem or to conduct the business of the proposal should be spelled out in detail. In this section, simply think through all the steps necessary to meet the terms of the proposal and write them in sequence. When feasible, you should include a time schedule to indicate when the project will be completed.

Materials and Equipment

For large proposals, such as construction or research and development, indicate the nature and quantities of materials and equipment to be used. In some cases, several departments will contribute to this section. When materials and equipment constitute a major portion of the total cost, include prices. Much litigation arises when clients are charged for "cost overruns." When contracts are made on the basis of "cost plus XX percent," the major costs of materials, equipment, and labor/personnel must be thoroughly described and documented.

Qualifications

Critical Thinking

How can you establish your credibility without being perceived as boastful?

Assuming your proposal is acceptable in terms of services to be performed or products to be supplied, your proposal must convince the potential buyer that you have the expertise to deliver what you have described and that you are a credible individual or company. Therefore, devote a section to presenting the specific qualifications and special expertise of the personnel involved in the proposal. You may include past records of the bidder and the recommendations of its past customers, and the proposed cost. Note how the brief biography of the principal member in the following excerpt from a proposal contributes to the credibility of the proposer:

> **Principals:** Engagement Principal: Charles A. McKee, M.B.A., M.A.I., Partner in Property Appraisers, Inc., consulting appraiser since 1974. Fellow of the American Institute of Appraisers, B.A., M.B.A., Harvard University. Phi Kappa Phi and Beta Gamma Sigma honorary societies. Lecturer and speaker at many realty and appraisal conferences and at the University of Michigan.

In another related section, the proposal might mention other work performed:

> **Major Clients of Past Five Years:** City of Tulsa, Oklahoma; Dade County, Florida; City of San Francisco, California; City of Seattle, Washington; Harbor General Corporation, Long Beach, California; Gulf and Houston, Incorporated, Houston, Texas. Personal references are available on request.

Follow-Up and/or Evaluation

Although your entire proposal is devoted to convincing the reader of its merit, clients are frequently concerned about what will happen when the proposed work or service is completed. Will you return to make certain your work is satisfactory? Can you adjust your method of research as times change?

If you propose to conduct a study, do not promise more than you can deliver. Not all funded research proves to be successful. If you propose to prepare a study in your firm's area of expertise, you may be more confident. A public accounting firm's proposal to audit a company's records need not be modest. The accountant follows certain audit functions that are prescribed by the profession. However, a proposal that involves providing psychological services probably warrants a thoughtful follow-up program to evaluate the service.

Budget or Costs

The budget or cost of the program should be detailed when materials, equipment, outside help, consultants, salaries, and travel are to be included. A simple proposal for service by one person might consist of a statement such as "15 hours at $200/hour, totaling $3,000, plus mileage and expenses estimated at $550." Present the budget or costs section after the main body of the proposal.

Summary

You might conclude the proposal with a summary. This summary may also be used as the initial section of the proposal if deductive sequence is desired.

Addenda

Critical Thinking

What other types of items might appear in a proposal addendum?

When supporting material is necessary to the proposal but would make it too bulky or detract from it, include the material as addenda items. A bibliography and an appendix are examples of addenda items. References used should appear in the bibliography or as footnotes. Maps, questionnaires, letters of recommendation, and similar materials are suitable appendix items.

A short, informal proposal that includes several of the parts previously discussed is shown in Figure 11-8. This proposal consists of three major divisions: "The Problem," "Proposed Course of Instruction," and "Cost." The "Proposed Course of Instruction" section is divided into five minor divisions to facilitate understanding. Wanting to increase the chances of securing the contract, the writer made sure the proposal was highly professional and had the impact needed to get the reader's attention. In other words, the writer wanted the proposal to "look" as good as it "sounds." To add to the overall effectiveness of the proposal, the writer incorporated appealing, but not distracting, page design features. Printing the proposal with a laser printer using proportional fonts of varying sizes and styles resulted in a professional appearance and an appealing document. The reader's positive impression of the high standards exhibited in this targeted proposal is likely to influence his or her confidence in the writer's ability to present the proposed seminar.

Figure 11-8

Short Proposal, Page 1

PROPOSAL FOR STAFF DEVELOPMENT SEMINAR: CONSERVATIVE BUSINESS DRESS POLICY IMPLEMENTATION

for MetroBank

by Patricia Sykes, Communications Consultant

May 14, 2004

Purpose

Describes the problem and presents the proposed plan as a solution to the problem.

After careful study, the management of MetroBank has decided to implement a conservative business dress policy for its employees. The proposed training course is designed to help participants understand the purposes of the policy and assure appropriate response to the new dress policy.

Uses headings to aid the reader in understanding the organization of the proposal. Boldface font adds emphasis.

Proposed Course of Instruction

The training course will be delivered by Janine Raymond, a dynamic associate with more than ten years of business experience in professional settings. Because clothing is a reflection of one's personality and personal tastes, the program will actively involve participants and facilitate personal application of the new policy.

Divides the "Proposed Course of Instruction" into five minor divisions for easier comprehension. Describes the course content, instructional method, and design in detail.

Teaching/Learning Methods

This activity-oriented training program will involve response to videos, role playing, and case discussion. The trainer will act as a facilitator to assist each participant in assessing wardrobe choices and planning outfit selections that comply with the new dress policy.

Program Content

The following topics constitute the content core of the program:

Uses bullets to highlight course components.

- history and background of conservative business dress policies
- advantages and disadvantages of conservative business dress
- organizational goals in implementing conservative business dress

Format Pointer

- Incorporates page design features to enhance appeal and readability (e.g., print attributes, headings, bulleted lists, laser print on high-quality paper).

Figure 11-8

Short Proposal, page 2

Includes heading to → Staff Development Proposal   Page 2
identify second page.
Adds horizontal line to
increase professional   • what "conservative business dress" means
appearance.   • consequences of proper and improper conservative business dress
                           • wardrobe planning for conservative business dress
                           • modeling, fashions courtesy of the Men's Wearhouse and Fashion Corner

                           Learning Materials

                           The following materials will be provided to facilitate learning:

                           • Dress for Success video: Men's Wearhouse
                           • consultant-developed workbook for each participant

                           Length of Course

                           As requested by management, this course will consist of three two-hour ses-
                           sions held on a selected day of the week for three consecutive weeks.

                           Number of Participants

                           The seminar will serve all MetroBank employees, which is reportedly 67.
                           Upward adjustments can be made and reflected in the materials fee.

                           Cost

                           All teaching-learning materials will be provided by the consulting firm and
                           include workbooks, videos, and video camera and recorder. Exact cost figures
                           are as follows:

Itemizes costs so reader →   Workbooks and other materials for 67 participants $ 335.00
understands exactly how   Equipment lease fees   100.00
the figure was calculated.   Professional fees (6 hours' instruction @ $250/hour)   1,500.00
Disclosing detailed break-   Travel/meals   75.00
down gives the reader   ──────────
confidence that the cost   Total $2,010.00
is accurate.

Preparation

Writers have much flexibility in preparing proposals. When they find a particular pattern that seems to be successful, they no doubt will adopt it as their basic plan. The ultimate test of a proposal is its effectiveness in achieving its purpose. The writer's task is to assemble the parts of a proposal in a way that persuades the reader to accept it.

To put the proposal together expeditiously, determine the parts to include, select one part that will be easy to prepare, prepare that part, and then go on to another. When you have completed the parts, you can arrange them in whatever order you like, incorporate the transitional items necessary to create coherence, and then put the proposal in finished form. As with most report writing, first prepare the pieces of information that you will assemble later as the "whole" report. Trying to write a report by beginning on line one, page one, and proceeding to the end may prove to be frustrating and time consuming. Keep in mind that you should allow adequate time after completing the research and writing for proofreading and editing. Figures should be checked carefully for accuracy, since underreporting costs can lead to a financial loss if the proposal is accepted, and overreported costs may lead to refusal of the proposal. If you fail to allow sufficient time for proposal completion, you may miss the required deadline for proposal submission.

If you become part of a collaborative writing team producing a proposal of major size, you probably will be responsible for writing only a small portion of the total proposal. For example, a proposal team of 16 executives, managers, and engineers might be required to prepare an 87-page proposal presenting a supplier's plan to supply parts to a military aircraft manufacturer. After the group brainstorms and plans the proposal, a project director delegates responsibility for the research and origination of particular sections of the proposal. Finally, one person compiles all the sections, creates many of the preliminary and addenda parts, and produces and distributes the final product.

The accompanying Strategic Forces feature, "Collaborative Skills for Team Writing," provides additional information about writing in teams.

Critical Thinking

What message does Aesop's Fable about the tortoise and the hare have for the writer of a report or proposal?

Team Environment

Collaborative Skills for Team Writing

Many problems faced by organizations cannot be solved by an individual because no one person has all the experience, resources, or information needed to accomplish the task. Team writing produces a corporate document representing multiple points of view. Group support systems (GSSs) are interactive computer-based environments that support coordinated team efforts. Numerous GSS products have been developed, and the style of the team-editing process dictates which GSS application will be most appropriate:

- **Sequential editing.** Collaborators divide the task so that the output of one stage is passed to the next writer for individual work. Software editors that support this process are called markup tools.

- **Parallel editing.** Collaborators divide the task so that each writer works on a different part of the document at the same time. Then the document is reassembled in an integration stage.

- **Reciprocal editing.** Collaborators work together to create a common document, mutually adjusting their activities in real time to take into account each other's changes.

Early attempts at collaborative writing typically used an unstructured process that often proved to be dysfunctional and frustrating to participants. Successful collaborative writing projects typically involve a multistage process:

1. **Open discussion.** Collaborators develop the objectives and general scope of the document using brain-storming or parallel-discussion software.

2. **Generation of document outline.** Collaborators develop main sections and subsections that will provide the structure for the document.

3. **Discussion of content within outline.** Collaborators interactively generate and discuss document content in each section using parallel discussions.

4. **Composing by subteams.** Subteams may consist of a few people (or sometimes only one person) who take the content entries from a section and organize, edit, and complete the section as a first draft.

5. **Online feedback and discussion.** The team reviews each section and makes suggestions in the form of annotations or comments. The section editors accept, reject, or merge suggestions to improve their own sections.

6. **Verbal walkthrough.** Using a collaborative writing tool, the team does a verbal walkthrough of the document.

Stages 1 through 3 are sequential and are undertaken only once. Stages 4 through 6 are circular in nature, and in some cases multiple loops are carried out before the document is finalized. As synchronous group time may be limited and valuable, it is used to add and refine document content. Formatting can be accomplished later by team members or an outside editor.

Disputes can arise when collaborative team members have incorrect or incomplete information or different philosophical approaches to an issue. In such cases, the disputing team members can be assigned to work together as a subteam, negotiating their differences without an audience. When the subteam returns to the group with compromised text, the group readily accepts it, knowing that multiple points of view went into its composition.[7]

Application

In teams of four, research a GSS product. Prepare a five-minute oral report about the product that includes the following: (1) description of the product, (2) applications for which it is suited, (3) requirements and specifications for use, and (4) limitations of the product.

Formal Reports

The following checklist provides a concise, useful guide as you prepare a report.

Transmittal Letter or Memorandum

(Use a letter-style transmittal in reports going outside the organization. For internal reports, use a memorandum transmittal.)

The transmittal letter or memo should:

- Transmit a warm greeting to the reader.
- Open with a "Here is the report you requested" tone.
- Establish the subject in the first sentence.
- Follow the opening with a brief summary of the study. Expand the discussion if a separate summary is not included in the report.
- Acknowledge the assistance of those who helped with the study.
- Close the message with a thank-you and a forward look.

Title Page

The title page should:

- Include the title of the report, succinctly worded.
- Provide full identification of the authority for the report (the person or organization for whom the report was prepared).
- Provide full identification of the preparer(s) of the report.
- Provide the date of the completion of the report.
- Assure an attractive layout.

Contents Page

For a contents page:

- Use *Contents* as the title.
- Use indention to indicate the heading degrees used in the report.
- List numerous figures separately as a preliminary item called *Figures*. (Otherwise, figures should not be listed because they are not separate sections of the outline but only supporting data within a section.)

Executive Summary

In an executive summary or abstract:

- Use a descriptive title, such as Executive Summary, Synopsis, or Abstract.
- Condense the major sections of the report.
- Use effective, generalized statements that avoid detail available in the report itself. Simply tell the reader what was done, how it was done, and what conclusions were reached.

Report Text

In writing style, observe the following guidelines:

- Avoid the personal *I* and *we* pronouns. Minimize the use of *the writer, the investigator*, and *the author*.
- Use active construction to give emphasis to the *doer* of the action; use passive voice to give emphasis to the *results* of the action.
- Use proper tense. Tell naturally about things in the order in which they happened, are happening, or will happen. Write as though the reader were reading the report at the same time it is written.
- Avoid ambiguous pronoun references. (If a sentence begins with *This is*, make sure the preceding sentence uses the specific word for which *This* stands. If the specific word is not used, insert it immediately after *This*.)
- Avoid expletive beginnings. Sentences that begin with *There is, There are*, and *It is* present the verb before presenting the subject. Compared with sentences that use the normal subject-verb-complement sequence, expletive sentences are longer and less interesting.
- Use bulleted or enumerated lists for three or more items if listing will make reading easier. For example, a list of three words such as *Growth, Adaptability*, and *Cost* need not be bulleted; but a list of three long phrases, clauses, or sentences would probably warrant bulleting or enumeration.
- Incorporate transition sentences to ensure coherence.

In physical layout, observe the following guidelines:

- Use headings to assist the reader by making them descriptive of the contents of the section. Talking headings are preferred.
- Maintain consistency in the mechanical placement of headings of equal degree.

- Use parallel construction in headings of equal degree in the same section of the report.
- Incorporate the statement of the problem or purpose and method of research as minor parts of the introduction unless the research method is the unique element in the study.
- Use the picture-frame layout for all pages, with appropriate margins that allow for bindings.
- Number all pages appropriately.

In using graphics or tabular data, observe the following guidelines:

- Number consecutively figures (tables, graphics, and other illustrations) used in the report.
- Give each graph or table a descriptive title.
- Refer to the graph or table within the text discussion that precedes its appearance.
- Place the graph or table as close to the textual reference as possible and limit the text discussion to analysis. (It should not merely repeat what can be seen in the graph or table.)
- Use effective layout, appropriate captions and legends, and realistic vertical and horizontal scales that help the table or graph stand clearly by itself.

In reporting the analysis, observe the following guidelines:

- Question each statement for its contribution to the solution of the problem. Is each statement either descriptive or evaluative?
- Reduce large, unwieldy numbers to understandable ones through a common language, such as units of production, percentages, or ratios.
- Use objective reporting style rather than persuasive language; avoid emotional terms. Identify assumptions and opinions. Avoid unwarranted judgments and inferences.

In drawing conclusions:

- State the conclusions carefully and clearly, and be sure they grow out of the findings.

- Repeat the major supporting findings for each conclusion if necessary.
- Make sure any recommendations grow naturally from the stated conclusions.

Citations

If citations are used:

- Include a citation (in-text reference, footnote, or endnote) for material quoted or paraphrased from another source.
- Adhere to an acceptable, authoritative style or company policy.
- Present consistent citations, including adequate information for readers to locate the source in the reference list.

References

If a reference list is provided:

- Include an entry for every reference cited in the text.
- Adhere to an acceptable, authoritative style or company policy.
- Include more information than might be necessary in cases of doubt about what to include in an entry.
- Include separate sections (e.g., books, articles, and nonprint sources) if the references (works cited) section is lengthy and your referencing style allows it.

Appendix

If an appendix is provided:

- Include cover messages for survey instruments, maps, explanations of formulas used, and other items that provide information but are not important enough to be in the body of a report.
- Subdivide categories of information beginning with Appendix A, Appendix B, and so on.
- Identify each item with a title.

Summary

1. **Identify the parts of a formal report and the contribution each part makes to the report's overall effectiveness.** As reports increase in length from one page to several pages, they also grow in formality with the addition of introductory and addenda items. As a result, reports at the formal end of the continuum tend to be repetitious. These report parts and their purposes are summarized as follows:

Preliminary Parts

Half-Title Page (Title Fly)—contains title of report; adds formality.

Title Page—includes title, author, writer, and date; adds formality.

Authorization—provides written authorization to complete the report.

Transmittal—presents the report to the reader and summarizes the conclusions or major points.

Contents—provides an overview of the report and the order in which information will be presented; contains report headings and beginning page numbers.

Figures—includes number, title, and page number of tables and graphics.

Executive Summary—summarizes essential elements in a report.

Report Text

Introduction—orients the reader to the topic and previews the major divisions.

Body—presents the information collected.

Summary—reviews main points presented in the body.

Conclusions—draws inferences based on the findings.

Recommendations—presents possible actions based on the conclusions.

Addenda

References—includes an alphabetical list of sources used in preparing the report.

Appendixes—contains supplementary information that supports the report but placing this information in the report would make the report bulky and unmanageable.

Index—includes an alphabetical guide to the subjects in the report.

2. **Organize report findings.** Organizing the content of a report involves seeing the report problem in its entirety and then breaking it into its parts. After the research or field work has been completed, the writer may begin with any of the report parts and then complete the rough draft by putting the parts in logical order. Short reports, that don't require the many supporting preliminary and addenda parts, usually are written in memorandum, e-mail, or letter format. Although reports grow in formality as they increase in length, writers determine whether to prepare a report in formal style and format before they begin writing. As they organize and make tentative outlines, writers determine the format and style best able to communicate the intended message.

3. **Prepare effective formal reports using an acceptable format and writing style.** In preparing effective long reports, outlining assists the writer with logical sequencing. Appropriate headings lead the reader from one division to another. The writing style should present the findings and data interpretation clearly and fairly, convincing the reader to accept the writer's point of view, but in an unemotional manner. Opinions should be clearly identified as such. The writer should lay the first draft aside long enough to get a fresh perspective, then revise the report with a genuine commitment to making all possible improvements.

4. **Prepare effective short reports in letter, memorandum, and e-mail formats.** Short reports are typically written in a personal writing style and in memorandum, e-mail, or letter format. Form reports provide accuracy, save time, and simplify tabulation of data when a need exists for numerous, repetitive reports.

5. **Prepare effective proposals for a variety of purposes.** Proposals can be written for both internal and external audiences. Proposals call for thorough organization and require writing methods that will be not only informative but convincing. Because they have discrete parts that can be prepared in any order and then assembled into whole reports, they are conducive to preparation by teams.

Chapter Review

1. List each of the parts of a formal report and briefly discuss the purpose of each one. (Obj. 1)

2. How does a report writer determine which preliminary or addenda parts to include in a report? (Obj. 1)

3. Briefly discuss the primary principles involved in writing an executive summary. What is the significance of other names given to this preliminary report part? (Obj. 1)

Extranets—Intranets' Cyberspace Cousins

Extranets can be thought of as cyberspace cousins to intranets. Whereas intranets allow only internal colleagues to communicate with each other, extranets typically include on their guest lists selected business partners, suppliers, and customers. This selective sharing is in addition to the company's public web site, which is accessible to everyone.

Extranets are becoming an increasingly important means of delivering services and communicating efficiently. The following electronic activities will allow you to learn more about the role of extranets in companies' external communications:

 InfoTrac College Edition. Access http://www.infotrac.thomsonlearning.com to read about how Showtime Networks Inc. is using its extranet to act as a virtual office for business affiliates:

Hogan, M. (2002, July 8). Showtime launches affiliate extranet. *Multichannel News*, 23(27), 28.

Write a brief summary of the advantages the extranet provides for both Showtime and its affiliates.

 Text Support Web Site. Visit http://lehman.swlearning.com to learn more about extranets. Refer to Chapter 11's Electronic Café activity that provides links to an online site that provides

information on how extranets work and how companies are using them to improve customer service, increase revenues, and save time and resources.

 WebTutor Advantage. Your instructor will assign you to a project group. Go to your WebTutor site and locate your group information; respond to the initial message your instructor has posted for your group.

 Professional Power Pak. Access your PPP CD to learn more about how to use an extranet as a channel for external communication effectively.

---

4. What purposes are served by the findings, conclusions, and recommendations sections? How are they related, yet distinctive? (Obj. 1)

5. Give two or three examples of emotional terms that should be avoided in a formal report. (Obj. 2)

6. Why is impersonal, third person style frequently used in formal reports? How is it achieved? (Obj. 2)

7. Explain the relationship between the content outline of a report and the placement of headings within the body of a report. (Obj. 2)

8. How would a writer decide the best organization for a formal report and what parts to include? (Obj. 3)

9. In addition to length, what are the differences between long and short reports? (Objs. 3, 4)

10. How are memorandum, letter, and e-mail reports similar? In what ways are they different? (Obj. 4)

11. How do form reports increase the accuracy of information? (Obj. 4)

12. What is the primary purpose of a proposal, and what can the writer do to assure that the purpose is achieved? (Obj. 5)

13. What is meant by RFP? Why is it important to the preparation of a proposal? (Obj. 5)

14. Discuss the typical parts of a proposal. (Obj. 5)

15. How does team preparation of a proposal differ from preparation by an individual? How can technology assist in team writing? (Obj. 5)

Digging Deeper

1. How do diversity considerations impact the choices made in report style and and format?

2. Considering general trends in society toward more informality in many situations, how might the style of reports be impacted?

To check your understanding of the chapter, take the practice quizzes at **http://lehman.swlearning.com** or your WebTutor course.

Activities

1. **Outlining an Analytical Report (Obj. 2)**

   In small groups, develop an outline for a report that would explain the criteria for choosing a college major.

2. **Critiquing a Report Outline (Obj. 2)**

   Analyze the table of contents at the right. What suggestions do you have for improving it?

   Visit the Interactive Study Center at **http://lehman.swlearning.com** for a downloadable version of this activity.

3. **Identifying a Writing Environment that Works (Obj. 2)**

   Visit the text support site at **http://lehman.swlearning.com** and read the "Guidelines for Creating an Effective Environment for Writing." Add three or more additional suggestions to those given.

Applications

Read	Think	Write	Speak	Collaborate

1. **Researching the Importance of Readability in Reports (Objs. 1–3)**

   Locate and read the following article on the importance of readable writing in reports:

   Goldbort, R. (2001, April). Readable writing by scientists and researchers. *Journal of Environmental Health, 63*(8), 40–41.

   Prepare a detailed outline of the article, including major and minor points related to readability.

2. **Gathering Background Information for a Report (Objs. 2, 4)**

   Using databases available through your campus library, locate and read three articles on firewalls as a means of securing a company's intranet. Mark the main points of each article and prepare a bibliographic citation for each.

Read	Think	Write	Speak	Collaborate

3. **Developing a Report Outline (Objs. 1, 2)**

   Select one of the report topics listed in Application 13. Develop an outline for the described report. Identify possible sources for locating the necessary information.

4. **Summarizing a Professional Meeting (Objs. 2, 4)**

   Attend a professional meeting of a campus or community organization. Take notes on the program presented, the issues discussed, and so on. Submit a short report to your instructor summarizing the events of the meeting, and include a section that describes the benefits that might be derived from membership in that organization.

Informational Reports

5. Evaluating a Career Field (Objs. 2, 4)

Select a career field in which you have some interest. Study government handbooks, yearbooks, and online materials that project the outlook of that career. Submit an e-mail report to your instructor that includes the following sections: (1) the career you have chosen, with reasons; (2) the relative demand for that career over the next five to ten years; and (3) the pay scale and other benefits that are typical of that career.

6. Auditing a Computer Lab (Objs. 2, 4)

Visit the computer lab on your campus. Through observation and interviews, prepare an audit report of the lab's offerings. Include the following items in your report: (1) the types of equipment available (e.g., PCs, Macs, mainframe terminals), (2) the quantity of each type, and (3) the operating systems and applications software available (product, version). Attach a table that summarizes your analysis. Submit the letter report to your instructor.

7. Evaluating the Performance of a Stock Portfolio (Objs. 2, 4)

Create a stock portfolio of ten stocks on a financial web site (e.g., **http://www.stockmaster.com**, **http://moneycentral.msn.com/content/P58723.asp**). Assume that you will purchase 100 shares of each of the ten stocks at the prices listed at the market close on a particular day. The stock portfolio will record the changes in each of the ten stocks for each trading day. Print this report for a one-week period—five trading days.

Required: Submit a memorandum report to your instructor on the purchase date reporting your ten stocks according to the following format:

Name of Stock   Price per Share   Total Cost (× 100)

At the end of the five-day period, submit another memorandum to your instructor detailing how your investments fared during the week. Record the Dow Jones Industrial Average for both your purchase date and the end of the five-day period. Compare your total performance—percentage gain or loss—with that of the Dow Jones average.

8. Promoting International Understanding (Objs. 2, 4)

Research the cultural differences between business executives in the United States and China; write a memorandum report communicating this information to U.S. managers working in China. Write another memo to Jeanne Pitman, director of international assignments, persuading her to develop other ways to promote international understanding in the company. You may vary this case by selecting a country of your choice.

9. Communicating Concern for Employees (Objs. 2, 4)

Review research related to cell phone safety and identify ways to solve businesses' problems resulting from accidents among workers. Write a short informational report. To make the case more meaningful, address the issue in an employee group or environment with which you are familiar.

10. Communicating during a Crisis (Objs. 2, 4)

Review research and write an informational report related to crisis communication and the sharing of information with employees about a financial, ethical, health, or environmental crisis. Your instructor may vary this assignment so that your report will be directed to stockholders, the public, or another specified group.

Analytical Reports

11. Comparing the Merits of Franchising Versus Starting an Independent Business (Objs. 2, 4)

You and a silent partner plan to open a business establishment in your city. You are unsure whether to obtain a franchise for such an establishment or to start your own independent restaurant. Select a franchise opportunity of your choice and research it. Include in your findings the initial investment cost, start-up expenses, franchise requirements and fees, and success and failure rate. Compare the franchise opportunity to the option of an independent business.

Required: Prepare a report for your intended silent partner that compares the options of franchising versus independent ownership. Make a recommendation as to the more desirable action to take.

12. Assessing the Feasibility of Constructing a Recreational Complex (Objs. 2, 4)

Oakdale University has established a committee to study the feasibility of constructing a recreational center for students, faculty, and staff. To help determine the interest of faculty and staff, the committee has administered a questionnaire. The findings will be combined with other aspects of the feasibility study in a presentation to the president. The committee believes the 668-person sample is representative of the faculty and staff. The results of the survey follow:

1. On average, how often do you exercise each week?
   136   0–1 day
   274   2–3 days
   197   4–5 days
   61   6–7 days

2. During a week, in which of the following activities do you participate? Check all that apply.
   171   Aerobic exercise
   157   Jogging
   147   Weightlifting
   299   Walking
   67   Tennis
   42   Other

3. If you had access, in which of the following activities would you participate? Check all that apply.
   196   Racquetball
   361   Swimming
   72   Basketball
   126   Running or walking on an indoor track
   165   Weight machines

4. If a recreation center were constructed for employees, what is the maximum amount you would be willing to pay per month to provide use of the center to your immediate family members?
   125   $0–$10
   69    $11–$20
   156   $21–$30
   261   $31–$40
   57    $41–$50

Required: As a member of the committee, prepare a short report for the president, Michelle Karratassos. You asked respondents to estimate the amounts they would be willing to pay a month for their families to use the center as $0 to $10, $11 to $20, and so on. If you were to do mathematical computations, you would probably use midpoints such as $5, $15.50, $25.50, and so on as values for each class. In this case, however, write in generalities simply using percentages. Measures of central tendency are not necessary.

13. Preparing an Analytical Report (Objs. 2, 4)

In teams of three or four, prepare a short report on *one* of the following cases. Make any assumptions and collect any background information needed to make an informed decision. Reviewing this list may help you identify a business-related problem you have encountered that you would like to investigate; evaluate possible alternative solutions, and make a recommendation.

a. Recommend one of three laptop computers for use by the company's sales representatives to update accounts, process orders, prepare sales proposals, and so forth. The computer must have a modem for connecting to the central office for transmission of daily reports.

b. Recommend how you would invest $2 billion of excess cash that your company will not need until the plant expands in two more years.

c. Recommend a printer for a company installing a personal computer-based information system. The company will use the printer for both internal and external correspondence; some correspondence requires graphics.

d. As director of human resources, recommend the type of network configuration that would best serve the needs of the department's 26 employees. Your computers are presently not networked, and only three can access the company mainframe. Investigate the advantages and disadvantages of the star, ring, and bus topologies. Make a recommendation to upper management.

e. Your insurance agency employs 200 people at four locations. A high volume of e-mail with accompanying attachments is sent among the four offices. Determine the most effective virus protection software for your firm.

f. Your government agency has always purchased the automobiles used by its social workers. The cars are typically driven approximately 30,000 miles a year and are sold for about 20 percent of their purchase value at the end of three years. Consider the cost effectiveness of the current policy and a car dealer's offer to lease the cars. Recommend whether the agency should purchase or lease the automobiles.

g. One of your sales representatives has provided literature that cites health problems related to the use of cellular telephones. Study the issue and make a recommendation to the company as to how to respond to this issue.

h. A family-owned business with a growing Web presence is considering a DSL cable connection to replace its current telephone modem. Evaluate the costs, benefits, and any disadvantages related to this change.

i. You have noticed a substantial increase in the number of employees who spend their lunch hour exercising at one of several health clubs in your community. Furthermore, your insurance agent has reported that health claims of your company are increasing at less than the national average. Attributing this positive fact to your employees' commitment to physical fitness, you are considering either installing exercise equipment in underused areas of your plant or subsidizing membership dues. You are also thinking about extending the lunch hour to make exercising more convenient. Weigh the alternatives and make a recommendation.

j. As vice president of production, investigate whether introducing background music would improve productivity in a manufacturing environment.

14. Considering Adoption of Linux Operating System (Objs. 2, 3)

Your company, Support, Inc., is considering the possibility of adopting Linux as your network operating system. You have been asked by the owner and president of your organization to research the possibility of converting from Windows NT to Linux. You have surveyed 66 companies that are using the Linux operating system and have obtained the following results:

1. What operating system were you using prior to Linux? (Check one)
   - 48 Windows/Windows NT
   - 12 Unix
   - 6 Other

2. In general, how would you rate the quality of Linux as compared to your previous operating system? (Check one)
   - 4 Linux's quality is very inferior to that of the previous operating system.
   - 7 Linux's quality is somewhat inferior to that of the previous operating system.
   - 19 Linux's quality is about the same as that of the previous operating system.
   - 25 Linux's quality is somewhat better than that of the previous operating system.
   - 11 Linux's quality is much better than that of the previous operating system.

3. What, if anything, do you like about Linux? (Check all that apply)
   - 40 Better reliability, fewer crashes
   - 34 Ease of use
   - 51 Greater power
   - 9 Other
   - 7 Nothing

4. What, if any, complaints do you have about Linux? (Check all that apply)
   - 6 Inadequate documentation
   - 7 Glitch(es) in the program
   - 27 Inadequate availability of applications that run on it
   - 17 Inferior applications that run on it
   - 6 Lack of technical support
   - 5 Other problems
   - 16 No problems

5. Where have you used Linux? (Check one)
   - 22 Only on a network system
   - 17 Only on a desktop system
   - 27 On both a network and a desktop system

6. How did you obtain your Linux operating system? (Check one)
   - 34 Free company download
   - 21 Free add-on with other software purchase
   - 10 Other

7. What is your advice to a company considering converting to the Linux operating system? (Circle one)

(9)	(4)	(15)	(19)	(9)	(10)
1	2	3	4	5	6

Definitely would not recommend					Definitely would recommend

Required: As director of information systems, write a report with findings, conclusions, and recommendations. Prepare any preliminary and addenda parts you believe will enable the reader to understand the report.

15. Studying the Merits of Mentoring (Objs. 2, 3)

Your company, Ultron Oil, is considering implementing a formal mentoring program as a means for developing managerial talent. Your supervisor, the division director, has commissioned you to prepare a report on the effectiveness of mentoring. As a part of the study, you have surveyed 70 managers representing a variety of businesses; 44 were male, and 26 were female. They ranged in age from 22 to 69, with the median age being 45. Their responses follow:

1. In your career development, have you ever had a mentor?
   - 66 Yes. Answer all items.
   - 4 No. Skip to Item 6.

2. Which of the following describes your mentoring relationship(s)?
   - 6 Formal; my mentor(s) was/were appointed or assigned to me.
   - 38 Informal; the relationship(s) just evolved.
   - 22 One or more was formal, and one or more was informal.

3. How long did the typical mentoring relationship last?
   - 10 Less than one year
   - 12 One to two years
   - 16 Three to five years
   - 14 More than five years
   - 14 Varying lengths of time (answers varied from one month to life)

4. Did you perceive that you benefited from the mentoring relationship?
   - 63 Yes
   - 3 No

5. Did you perceive that your mentor benefited from the relationship?
   60 Yes
   6 No
6. Have you ever been a mentor to another person?
   54 Yes
   16 No
7. Does your company have a mentoring program in place?
   32 Yes
   38 No

Required: Prepare the report for the division director. Present your findings, draw conclusions, and make recommendations. Prepare any preliminary and addenda parts you believe will enable the reader to understand the report.

16. **Assessing Attitudes Toward Software Piracy (Objs. 2, 3)**

    You are conducting a study of college seniors concerning their awareness of and attitudes toward software piracy. You have surveyed 100 students as a part of your project. The first category of questions dealt with their knowledge of software piracy. The correct answer to each of these questions is "true." Their responses are as follows:

1. Purchased software is covered by copyright law and generally allows for only a backup copy to be made by the purchaser.
   84 True
   16 False
2. Making copies of copyrighted software for distribution to others (software piracy) is a federal crime.
   94 True
   6 False
3. Making a copy of a software program owned by my company for use at home, unless expressly allowed, is a violation of copyright law.
   82 True
   18 False
4. Software piracy is punishable by both fine and imprisonment.
   92 True
   8 False

The second category of questions dealt with specific situations. To each, students were instructed to give their *honest* responses. Their responses are as follows:

1. Your employer has purchased *Visual Communicator* for use on your computer at work. You have a computer at home and would like to have a copy of the program for you and your family's personal use. You would
   38 Make a copy of the disk for use at home and buy a manual from Walden Books.
   50 Make a copy of the disk and photocopy the manual for home use.
   12 Wait until you could afford to purchase a copy yourself.
2. You visit a local computer software store and see *Visual Communicator* with a price of $149. You would
   100 Buy it now or if money is short, come back later to buy
   0 Shoplift the software
3. You obtain a copy of *Visual Communicator*. A friend asks you for a copy of it. You would
   58 Give your friend a copy of the program.
   22 Trade your friend a copy of *Visual Communicator* for a copy of *Adobe PhotoShop*.
   6 Sell your friend a copy for $25.
   14 Tell your friend that he/she must purchase a copy.

Required: Present your findings, conclusions, and recommendations in a formal report to your college administrators. Prepare any preliminary and addenda parts you believe will enable the reader to understand the report.

17. **Solving a Business Problem (Objs. 2, 3)**

    Select one of the following problems to solve. Provide the necessary assumptions and background data. Then write a formal report of your analysis, conclusions, and recommendations. Include preliminary and ending parts you believe appropriate. You may need to design a questionnaire and administer it to an appropriate sample. Reviewing this list may help you identify a business-related problem you have encountered during your employment or cooperative education and intern experiences. If you choose to solve your own problem, provide the necessary assumptions and background data.

    a. Choose from the five research studies presented in Chapter 9, Application 4.

    b. You have read articles about the advantages of having Global Positioning Satellite (GPS) trackers in automobiles to help stranded motorists. Propose how GPS trackers could be used to monitor the movement of remote employees and investigate the implications of this action.

c. Your human resources department is considering the implementation of a full criminal background check in the selection of employees. Study the advisability of this practice.

d. Your department handles highly sensitive information and, as a result, requires extremely reliable user identification. You are considering ocular scanning or perhaps some other type of biometric identification. Investigate the advantages and disadvantages of such a system and recommend whether your organization should pursue it.

e. A committee of employees has recommended that the company establish a recycling center where employees can deposit recyclable items when entering the parking lot. The president has asked you to think the idea through and present a report of the cost, public relations implications, employee relations, and logistics of operating the recycling center.

f. You have received reports that several of your major competitors have installed electronic auditing procedures to monitor employees' computer usage. The president wants your immediate attention on this issue. Investigate the implications of using technology to monitor employees' computer activities. Will employees consider this procedure an invasion of privacy? Anticipate all possible problems and present strategies for dealing with them.

g. Although no employees have made formal complaints of sexual harassment in the workplace, information from the grapevine has convinced you that the company needs a formal policy concerning sexual harassment. To develop this company policy, research the legalities related to this issue and gather information (strategies) from other companies with sexual harassment policies.

h. The upcoming downsizing of your company will result in the displacement of approximately 10 percent of your middle- and upper-level managers. Investigate strategies for supporting these managers in their search for new employment. Many of these managers have worked for your company 15 to 20 years; therefore, they are quite apprehensive about the job search process.

i. Investigate the possibility of hiring senior citizens to fill selected positions in your company.

j. A client has $10,000 to invest for her children's college education. Their ages are 12, 9, and 4. Investigate alternatives and prepare a proposal for her consideration.

Proposals

18. Bidding for a Convention Site (Obj. 5)

The National Insurance Appraisers Association is planning an upcoming convention. This association of 500 members conducts a three-day conference during late October that includes at least one general session and as many as five breakout groups of 50–75 participants. The chair of this group's convention site committee has invited your city (instructor will assign) to submit a proposal bidding for the convention's 2006 national convention.

Required: As the executive director of the Economic Development Council, write a proposal including specific information to convince the group that your city (choose a location) can provide the needed meeting facilities, hotel accommodations, economical transportation from major U.S. cities, and a variety of social and recreational activities for members and guests. Obtain the necessary information via the Internet.

19. Applying for a Franchise to Open a Paint Ball Range (Obj. 5)

Interested in opening a paint ball range, Vicente Cruz wrote Combat Fantasy, Inc., a popular franchiser of paint ball ranges, to solicit franchise information. In answer to his request, Vicente received an extremely receptive letter requesting standard information designed to help Combat Fantasy determine the economic viability of the proposed location. After analyzing this preliminary information, Combat Fantasy will decide whether to accept Vicente's franchise application.

Combat Fantasy has requested preliminary information regarding the economic and social environment of the proposed site. Specifically, Vicente must provide valid, objective data concerning the population of the service area, the economic status of the population, the impact of the climate on the operation of an outdoor business, the nature and extent of competing entertainment businesses, the local tourist industry, and any other information that would support the economic success of the proposed franchise.

Required: As Vicente Cruz, prepare a letter report to the franchiser. Address it to Combat Fantasy, 9700 Gulfside Drive, Pensacola, FL 32501-9700.

20. Proposing Additional Employee Benefit to Management (Obj. 5)

As human resources manager at Innovative Solutions, you are preparing a proposal to be submitted to company management that would institute a tuition reimbursement program for employees who return to college.

Required: Write a proposal that includes the following information: (1) an explanation of how the tuition reimbursement program described in your proposal would increase overall morale and productivity of employees, (2) complete explanation of how the reimbursement program would work, and (3) a budget for anticipated costs.

21. Analyzing an Organization's Report (Objs. 1, 2)

Obtain a copy of a report prepared by an organization and analyze it in the following ways:

a. Purpose

b. Intended audience

c. Degree of formality

d. Use of graphic support

e. Parts included (see Figure 11-1)

f. Referencing method

Make a brief presentation to your class about your findings.

22. Responding to Problem of Computer Virus Hoaxes (Objs. 2, 4)

Prepare an oral report on computer virus hoaxes and appropriate response to them. Include the following parts in your report outline: (1) Why are virus hoaxes problematic for individuals and organizations? (2) What are some common virus hoaxes? (3) How can virus hoaxes be "checked out"? Prepare appropriate visuals for your presentation. End your report with a recommendation as to how to best respond to virus hoaxes. Submit your report outline and a copy of your visuals to your instructor after delivering your presentation.

23. Writing as a Team (Objs. 1-4)

Your instructor has provided detailed instructions for completing a long or short report or proposal in teams. *Building High-Performance Teams* (your team handbook) contains instructions, sample formats, and guidelines for electronically communicating with your instructor in the following ways:

a. Send your instructor a weekly progress report via e-mail. The report should contain the following information about each meeting held during the week: date, place, and duration of meeting; members present; report of work accomplished since the last meeting; brief description of work accomplished during the current meeting; and work allocated to be completed before the next meeting. (See *Building High-Performance Teams* for format.)

b. About midway in your report preparation, or when you are instructed, send your instructor an e-mail message containing your evaluation of each member of the group. Assign a percentage indicating the contribution each member has made to the group thus far. Ideally each member should contribute his or her fair share of 100 percent. However, assume that a group consisted of four members; one person contributed more than his or her equal share, and one person contributed less. You might assign these two members 30 percent and 20 percent respectively and rank the other two members 25 percent each. Note the total percentages awarded must equal 100 percent. Write a brief statement justifying the rating you assigned each member; provide specific, verifiable evidence. (A form for completing this evaluation is included in *Building High-Performance Teams*.)

c. After your report is completed, complete the team member evaluation provided in your team handbook. E-mail a debriefing memo to your instructor that describes your perceptions about your team's performance. (See *Building High-Performance Teams* for details of this assignment).

AFLAC/Sid Cato: Analyzing Report Theme

Sid Cato recommends the use of a unifying theme in the preparation of an annual report, a discernible point of view that is well-conceived and woven throughout, more than simply stated on the cover. Visit the following sites to identify the theme used in the award-winning AFLAC report and the strategy for developing the theme throughout the report.

- Visit the AFLAC web site at **http://www.aflac.com**
- Visit Sid Cato's web site at **http://www.sidcato.com**

Form a small group and prepare a memo report directed to your instructor that addresses the following issues: (1) identification of the AFLAC annual report theme, (2) examples of how the theme was developed in the report, (3) reasons Cato deemed the development to be successful, and (4) advice for companies concerning the use of themes in their annual reports.

Part 4 of the ShowCASE focuses on how AFLAC achieves world class status with its annual reports and the need to provide adequate explanation in annual reports.

http://www.aflac.com
http://sidcato.com

Visit the text support site at **http://lehman.swlearning.com** to complete Part 4 of the ShowCASE.

Internet Case

Cybertheft: It's a Big Deal

One of the World Wide Web's most attractive features, easy access to a universe of information and data, is also one of its greatest vulnerabilities. Computer users can easily access, download, copy, cut, paste, and publish any of the text, pictures, video, sound, program code, and other data forms available on the Internet. An inherent conflict of interest prevails because of the consumer's appetite for data and the creator's right to remuneration for original work.

Copyrights provide an economic incentive for the development of creative works in literature, computer applications, and the performing arts. For instance, songwriters in the United States are paid royalties by radio stations for broadcasting their copyrighted musical works. Because of copyrights, it is illegal to make and sell an authorized audio duplicate of a commercial CD or a video or DVD copy of a movie. The law assures that creators receive remuneration from sales for their investment of time, talent, and energy. The information superhighway, however, crosses borders where U.S. copyright laws do not apply. With proper equipment and the aid of file sharing web sites, cyberfans can make high-quality digital copies of downloaded music and movies, effectively bypassing copyright requirements.

Passage of the Patriot Act gave the FBI easier access to information about cyberspace theft by allowing examination of Internet databases without search warrants. Internet service providers have been compelled to turn over the names of subscribers traced by the music industry to their IP addresses. The Recording Industry Association has also targeted college campuses in its aggressive campaign to curtail unauthorized music downloading. In 2003, for example, four students agreed to fines of $12,000–$17,500 each and promised to stop illegally downloading music on their campus computer servers as part of an out-of-court settlement. Some universities are also denying Internet access to students who download films and music illegally.[8]

Web pages are another type of creative expression falling victim to cybertheft. Dealernet, an organization that helps car dealers sell vehicles over the Internet, was shocked to discover that a Southern California company had downloaded Dealernet web pages and reproduced them on its own web site. The competing site deleted the pages when Dealernet threatened legal action.

Cybertheft deprives musicians, artists, and other creative parties from the income that would otherwise result from the sale and licensing of their artistic works. The World Intellectual Property Organization, sponsored by the United Nations, is working to assure copyright protection worldwide. Representatives of the United States and 160 other countries who are members of the group have signed treaties that extend copyrights to the Internet and strengthen copyright laws in many of the world's nations. On the home front, various representatives of the computer industry have joined entertainment groups such as the Recording Industry Association of America and the Motion Picture Association of America to form the Creative Incentive Coalition; a major activity of the group is to lobby Congress for legislation and treaties that would provide better copyright protection.[9]

Every business entity has a responsibility to avoid situations of copyright infringement and to assure that its employees do so as well. Companies are legally responsible for violations if the copyright owner can prove that they knew or should have known about the infringement.

Texaco, for instance, agreed to a $1 million settlement in 1995 after a federal appellate court ruled that it was liable for copyright violations.[10] While it is rare for employees to be taken to court for copyright violation, it does occur and carries heavy penalties. Such liability makes it advisable for organizations to develop policies against copyright violation and to provide training to employees about the risks and responsibilities.

Visit the text support site at **http://lehman.swlearning. com** to link to web resources related to this topic. As directed by your instructor, complete one or more of the following:

1. Visit the listed sites to determine current international copyright issues or cases. Provide a one-page written summary to your instructor that describes the issue and the country(ies) involved.

2. Write a short, informative report describing how a company's web site can violate the copyrights of others and giving advice to organizational web page developers for avoiding possible copyright infringement.

3. **GMAT** "The nature of cyberspace defies copyright enforcement." In a one- to two-page report, justify or refute this statement, giving reasons and/or examples.

Video Case

Mir, Fox, & Rodriguez, PC: Celebrating Diversity

Mir, Fox, & Rodriguez, PC (MFRPC), the eighth largest professional accounting firm in Houston and the largest locally owned firm, was established in January 1988 by Gasper Mir, Carolyne Fox, and Roland Rodriguez. The founding group represented more than 40 years of collective experience at KPMG, an international accounting firm. MFRPC, located in the Galleria area of Houston and easily accessible to any part of the city, now includes 50 professional and support personnel engaged in providing assurance and tax services.

Since its founding, MFRPC has been committed to growing its practice and expanding the number of career opportunities for minorities and women in public accounting. Statements used to describe the emphasis on diversity at MFRPC include "a corporate family celebrating diversity" and "ethnically diverse bilingual workforce." The MFRPC

core values include honesty and integrity, client focus, and respect for each other.

View the video segment about Mir, Fox, & Rodriguez, PC and related activities on WebTutor or your Professional Power Pak CD.

Discussion Questions

1. What evidences of MFRPC's core value of "respect for each other" did you see in the video segment?

2. What relationships exist among MFRPC's three core values: (a) honesty and integrity, (b) client focus, and (c) respect for each other?

3. What examples of "a corporate family celebrating diversity" did you see in the video segment?

Activities

Locate the following articles available in full text from InfoTrac College or perhaps from another database available through your campus library:

DiversityInc Magazine announces top 50 companies for diversity; rigorous methodology positions annual study as corporate benchmark for best practices. (2003, April 15). *PR Newswire*. Retrieved June 17, 2003, from InfoTrac College database.

Hickman, J. (2002, July 8). America's 50 best companies for minorities. *Fortune, 146*(1), 110+. Retrieved June 17, 2003, from InfoTrac College database.

1. Summarize the similarities and differences between the two approaches to ranking companies.

2. Identify at least five companies that appear on both the *Fortune* 50 list and the *DiversityInc* 50 list.

3. Note that Fannie Mae appears at the #1 or #2 spot of both lists. Go to the recruitment document "Our Mission Your Mission" at **http://www.fanniemae. com/global/pdf/careers/recruitment.pdf** and print page 15 ("Committing to Diversity"). Highlight what you believe is the most innovative diversity initiative at Fannie Mae and submit to your instructor the highlighted printout along with your responses to the previous questions.

12

Designing and Delivering Business Presentations

© JEFF GREENBERG/PHOTOEDIT, INC.

Objectives *When you have completed Chapter 12, you will be able to:*

1   Plan a business presentation that accomplishes the speaker's goals and meets the audience's needs.

2   Organize and develop the three parts of an effective presentation.

3   Select, design, and use presentation visuals effectively.

4   Deliver speeches with increasing confidence.

5   Discuss strategies for presenting in alternate delivery situations such as culturally diverse audiences, team, and distance presentations.

SUN MICROSYSTEMS: TECHNOLOGY ADVANCEMENTS REVOLUTIONIZE BUSINESS PRESENTATIONS

While Sun Microsystems was originally involved with the manufacture of computer workstations, it is now most associated with Java, one of the hottest Internet-based programming languages. Because of the capabilities of Java, Internet sites can now effectively offer splashy graphics, animation, and real-time data updates.

One of Java's most noticeable abilities is the delivery of small programs, called applets, over the Web. Java applets have wide applicability because they are system independent. The same Java applet can be used by Windows, Mac, or Unix computers. This flexibility has attracted many developers to use Java to enhance their web sites and wireless communication capabilities. In Japan, Java-enabled cell phones allow users to access calendars, expense reports, e-mail, and more. In Brazil, Java offers doctors instant access to the medical records of 12 million people, assuring accurate information wherever residents need care. And U.S. carmakers hope to beam ads to drivers via onboard Java-equipped GPA navigation systems.[1]

Before the Web was regarded as a viable business tool, presentations were created with smaller audiences in mind. Presentation choices came in the form of slides, handouts, or an automated slide show that could be stored to a floppy disk. Now, however, you can upload your presentation to a web site and let viewers watch at their leisure. Special considerations in using this capability include keeping graphics small, since the larger the image, the longer it will take to appear. Using universally available fonts such as Times Roman and Arial will help assure that your audience is able to view what you intended. No matter how nice your presentation looks on your own PC, you will want to visit the site and view the show, ideally on different computers and using different browsers.[2]

Whether designing visual presentations for the Web or developing face-to-face presentations for delivery to your staff or customers, you will want to relate your ideas clearly and effectively—skills that you develop through your own critical thinking and for which no amount of innovative technology can substitute. This chapter provides guidelines for refining your presentation skills. You will learn how to plan and organize your presentation, develop dynamic presentation media, refine your delivery, and adapt your presentation for an intercultural audience or alternate delivery methods, such as team and distance presentations.

http://www.java.sun.com

See ShowCASE, Part 2, on page 492 for Spotlight Communicator Scott McNealy, president, Sun Microsystems.

Planning an Effective Business Presentation

Objective 1

Plan a business presentation that accomplishes the speaker's goals and meets the audience's needs.

Critical Thinking

Which is the most critical component of a presentation: content, quality of visual support, or delivery?

A business presentation is an important means of obtaining and exchanging information for decision making and policy development. Because several people receive the message at the same time, and the audience is able to provide immediate feedback for clarification, presentations can significantly reduce message distortion and misunderstanding.

Many of the presentations you give will be formal, with sufficient time allowed for planning and developing elaborate visual support. You may present information and recommendations to external audiences such as customers and clients whom you've never met or to an internal audience made up of coworkers and managers you know well. You can also expect to present some less formal presentations, often referred to as *oral briefings*. An oral briefing might entail a short update on a current project requested during a meeting without advance notice or a brief explanation in the hallway when your supervisor walks past. Sales representatives give oral briefings daily as they present short, informal pitches for new products and services.

Regardless of the formality of the presentation, the time given to prepare, the nature of the audience (friends or strangers), or the media used (live, distant, web or CD or DVD delivery on demand) your success depends on your ability to think on your feet and speak confidently as you address the concerns of the audience. Understanding the purpose you hope to achieve through your presentation and conceptualizing your audience will enable you to organize the content in a way the audience can understand *and* accept.

Now mobile presentations are easier than ever. Software available for most PDAs converts and stores presentation files in a compressed format. All you need to do is connect your PDA to a projector, turn on the application, and begin presenting.

© ROYALTY-FREE/CORBIS

Identify Your Purpose

Determining what you want to accomplish during a presentation is an important fundamental principle of planning an effective presentation. Some speech coaches recommend completing the following vital sentence to lay the foundation for a successful presentation, "At the end of my presentation, the audience will _____." In his book, *Do's and Taboo's of Public Speaking*, Axtell provides two excellent mechanisms for condensing your presentation into a brief, achievable purpose that will direct you in identifying the major points to be covered and the content to support those points:[3]

- Ask yourself, "What is my message?" Then, develop a phrase, a single thought, or a conclusion you want the audience to take with them from the presentation. This elementary statement likely may be the final sentence in your presentation—the basic message you want the audience to remember.
- Imagine your audience is leaving the room and someone has asked these people to summarize the message they had just heard in as few words as possible. Ideally, you would want to hear the people describe your central purpose.

Know Your Audience

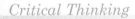

Critical Thinking

How is preparation of written messages and presentations similar in terms of empathy for the audience?

A common mistake for many presenters is to presume they know the audience without even attempting to find out about them. If you expect to get results, you must commit the time to know your audience and focus your presentation on it—from planning your speech to practicing its delivery.

As a general rule, audiences *do* want to be in tune with a speaker. Yet, people listen to speeches about things of interest to them. "What's in it for me?" is the question most listeners ask. A research scientist should not deliver a speech to a lay audience in highly technical terms. A speech about acid rain to a farm group should address the farmers' problems, for example, and not focus on scientific causes of acid rain. Additionally, different strategies are needed for audiences who think and make decisions differently. For instance, different strategies are needed for making a successful presentation to sell software to a group of lawyers than to a group of doctors. Lawyers typically think quickly and are argumentative and decisive while doctors are often cautious, skeptical, and don't make quick decisions.[4]

To deliver a presentation that focuses on the wants and expectations of an audience, you must determine who they are, what motivates them, how they think, and how they make decisions. Helpful information you can obtain about most audiences includes ages, genders, occupations, educational levels, attitudes, values, broad and specific interests, and needs, if any. Your analysis of these factors enables you to direct your speech specifically to your audience. In addition to these factors, you should also consider certain things about the occasion and location. Patriotic speeches to a group

Diversity Challenges

of military veterans will differ from speeches to a group of new recruits, just as Fourth of July speeches will differ from Memorial Day speeches. Seek answers to the following questions when you discuss your speaking engagement with someone representing the group or audience:

Critical Thinking

What other questions would you seek to answer when planning for a speaking engagement?

1. *Who* is the audience and *who* requested the presentation? General characteristics of the audience should be considered, as well as the extent of their knowledge and experience with the topic, attitude toward the topic (receptive or not eager to listen), anticipated response to the use of electronic presentation technology, and required or volunteer attendance.
2. *Why* is this topic important to the audience? What will the audience do with the information presented?
3. *What* environmental factors affect the presentation?
   - How many will be in the audience?
   - Will I be the only speaker? If not, where does my presentation fit in the program? What time of day?
   - How much time will I be permitted? Minimum? Maximum?
   - What are the seating arrangements? How far will the audience be from the speaker? Will a microphone or other equipment be available?

Answers to these questions reveal whether the speaking environment will be intimate or remote, whether the audience is likely to be receptive and alert or nonreceptive and tired, and whether you will need to develop additional motivational or persuasive techniques.

To illustrate the planning stage of a presentation, assume that you are a promotional representative for Project COPE (Challenging Outdoor Personal Experiences), a personal development program. Through a weekend of mentally and physically challenging events, participants develop self-confidence, trust, communication, and teamwork. Participants build these valuable managerial skills as they attempt to do things they have never done before and work together to develop creative ways to overcome various obstacles. The "trust fall" (falling backwards to be caught by a team member) and climbing a 30-foot tower and leaning out to catch a bar being held by team members are examples of these demanding events. Several of the senior executives of a large multinational company are sold on your program as a means to develop a trust-based corporate culture, and you have been invited to speak during the company's annual two-day management retreat. You are scheduled to speak at 10 a.m. and will have 30 minutes to present your message to 300 managers of various ages, genders, and cultures. Your analysis of the purpose and your audience follows:

Purpose: To guide participants in the use of COPE techniques in order to facilitate their development of self-confidence, trust, communication, and teamwork.

Audience: Intended purpose will be well received by managers desiring to improve the corporate culture in the organization and in their units. Audience should be alert for this early morning presentation; retreat environment should minimize mental distractions. Managers will likely welcome a captivating electronic presentation with realistic images of the described activities.

Organizing the Content

Objective *2*

Organize and develop the three parts of an effective presentation.

With an understanding of the purpose of your business presentation—why you are giving it, what you hope to achieve—and a conception of the size, interest, and background of the audience, you are prepared to outline your presentation and identify appropriate content. First introduced by Dale Carnegie, a famous speaker and speech trainer, and still recommended by speech experts today, the simple but effective presentation format includes an introduction, a body, and a close:

Introduction:	Tell the audience what you are going to tell them.
Body:	Tell them.
Close:	Tell them what you have told them.

Critical Thinking

What purpose does each main part of a presentation serve? How can the speaker avoid redundancy in the delivery of the three parts?

This design may sound repetitive; on the contrary, it works quite well. The audience processes information verbally and cannot slow the speaker down when information is complex; nor can they reread a confusing section. Thus, the repetition aids the listener in processing the information that supports the speaker's purpose.

Introduction

What you say at the beginning sets the stage for your entire presentation and initiates your rapport with the audience. However, inexperienced speakers often settle for unoriginal and overused introductions, such as "My name is . . ., and my topic . . ." or "It is a pleasure . . .," or negative statements, such as apologies for lack of preparation, boring delivery, or late arrival, that reduce the audience's desire to listen. An effective introduction accomplishes the following goals:

Critical Thinking

How would you gain attention for a presentation on your firm's entry into the Latin American market?

- *Captures attention and involves the audience.* Choose an attention-getter that is relevant to the subject and appropriate for the situation. Attention-getting techniques may include:
  - a shocking statement or startling statistic.
  - a quotation by an expert or well-known person.
  - a rhetorical or open-ended question that generates discussion from the audience.
  - an appropriate joke or humor.
  - a demonstration or dramatic presentation aid.
  - a related story or anecdote.
  - a personal reference, compliment to the audience, or a reference to the occasion of the presentation.

To involve the audience directly, ask for a show of hands in response to a direct question, allow the audience time to think about the answer to a rhetorical question, or explain why the information is important and how it will benefit the listeners. For example,

A speech on highway safety might begin with a startling statistic:

> "Just last year 15 young people from our community were killed in the prime of their lives by automobile crashes that could have been avoided."

A drug awareness speech to young people might begin with a true story:

> "I live in a quiet, middle-class, comfortable neighborhood. That is, until just a few months ago—when four young people from three different families were killed in an automobile accident following a party at which drugs were used."

A report presenting a site-selection recommendation could introduce the subject and set the stage for the findings (inductive sequence) or the recommendation (deductive sequence):

> **Inductive:** "When we were granted the approval to open a new distribution facility in Madison, South Carolina, we assigned a team to select the best possible suburban location."
>
> **Deductive:** "I want to inform you about why and how we selected Madison, South Carolina, as the location for the distribution facility.

Critical Thinking

How can the speaker effectively guide the audience from one major section of the presentation to another?

- **Establishes rapport.** Initiate rapport with the listeners; convince them that you are concerned that they benefit from the presentation and that you are qualified to speak on the topic. You might share a personal story that relates to the topic but reveals something about yourself, or discuss your background or a specific experience with the topic being discussed.
- **Presents the purpose statement and previews the points that will be developed.** To maintain the interest you have captured, present your purpose statement directly so that the audience is certain to hear it. Use original statements and avoid clichés such as "My topic today is . . ." or "I'd like to talk with you about . . ." Next, preview the major points you will discuss in the order you will discuss them. For example, you might say,

> "First, I'll discuss . . ., then . . ., and finally. . . ."
>
> "The acquisition and construction cost of all three sites were comparable. The decision to locate the new distribution facility in Madison, South Carolina, is based on three criteria: (1) quality of living, (2) transportation accessibility, and (3) availability of an adequate work force."

Revealing the presentation plan will help the audience understand how the parts of the body are tied together to support the purpose statement, thus increasing the coherence of the presentation. For a long, complex presentation, you might display a presentation visual that lists the points in the order they will be covered. As you begin each major point, display a slide that contains that point and perhaps a related image. These divider slides partition your presentation as headings do a written report and thus move the listener more easily from one major point to the next.

Body

Critical Thinking

Consider an effective presentation you have heard. What factors made it successful?

In a typical presentation of 20 to 30 minutes, limit your presentation to only a few major points (three to five) because of time constraints and your audience's ability to concentrate and absorb. Making every statement in a presentation into a major point—something to be remembered—is impossible, unless the presentation lasts only two or three minutes.

Once you have selected your major points, locate your supporting material. You may use several techniques to ensure the audience understands your point and to reinforce it.

- *Provide support in a form that is easy to understand.* Two techniques will assist you in accomplishing this goal:
  1. *Use simple vocabulary and short sentences that the listener can understand easily and that sound conversational and interesting.* Spoken communication is more difficult to process than written communication; therefore, complex, varied vocabulary and long sentences often included in written documents are not effective in a presentation.
  2. *Avoid jargon or technical terms that the listeners may not understand.* Instead, use plain English that the audience can easily comprehend. Make your speech more interesting and memorable by using word pictures to make your points. Hughes, a speech consultant, provides this example: If your message is a warning of difficulties ahead, you could say: "We're climbing a hill that's getting steeper, and there are rocks and potholes in the road."[5] Drawing analogies between new ideas and familiar ones is another technique for generating understanding. For example, comparing the power supply of a computer to the horsepower of an automobile engine, disks or CD-Roms to a briefcase, and a hard drive to a filing cabinet would help a computer novice comprehend complex concepts easily.
- *Provide relevant statistics.* Provide statistics or other quantitative measures available to lend authority and believability to your points. In your presentation about COPE, you could (1) locate evidence to support your thesis that trust environments can be created, and (2) obtain statistics from companies that have participated in COPE (e.g., reduced turnover and absenteeism, improved internal communication, stronger relationships with customers/clients, and other measures of increased effectiveness).

A word of warning: Do not overwhelm your audience with excessive statistics. Instead, use broad terms or word pictures that the listener can remember. Instead of "68.2 percent" say "over two thirds"; instead of "112 percent rise in production" say "our output more than doubled." Hearing that a CD-ROM holds "over 400 times as much as a 3½-inch floppy disk" is less confusing and more memorable than hearing the exact number of megabytes for each medium. Choose novel, interesting metaphors and word pictures such as "McDonald's has sold enough burgers to feed lunch to every person in the world" rather than trite images such as the number of football fields that could be covered with the burgers sold or how many times the burgers would reach around the world.[6]

- *Use quotes from prominent people.* Comments made by other authorities are helpful in establishing credibility. In the case of COPE, comments from top management of leading companies represent a credible source of quotations.

- *Use jokes and humor appropriately.* A joke or humor can create a special bond between you and the audience, ease your approach to sensitive subjects, disarm a nonreceptive audience, make your message easier to understand and remember, and make your audience more willing to listen. Plan your joke carefully so that you can (1) get the point across as quickly as possible, (2) deliver it in a conversational manner with interesting inflections and effective body movements, and (3) deliver the punch line effectively. If you cannot tell a joke well, use humor instead—amusing things that happened to you or someone you know, one-liners, or humorous quotations that relate to your presentation. Refrain from any humor that may reflect negatively on race, color, religion, gender, age, culture, or other personal areas of sensitivity.

For the COPE presentation, you could incorporate a few amusing incidents that actually occurred during a COPE session. Each incident should be relevant to your speech and appropriate to your audience. You believe these humorous accounts will make the audience more receptive to the idea of a weekend of intense activities.

- *Use interesting anecdotes.* Audiences like anecdotes or interesting stories that tie into the presentation. Like jokes, be sure you can get straight to the point of the story. You might include stories about leading companies that have participated in COPE and can relate their firsthand experiences.

- *Use presentation visuals.* Presentation visuals, such as handouts, whiteboards, flip charts, transparencies, electronic presentations, and demonstrations enhance the effectiveness of the presentation. Develop presentation visuals that will enable your audience to see, hear, and even experience your presentation.

Although stories, statistics, quotations, and the like may seem trivial, they are critical to effective speaking. They retain listener interest, provide proof and evidence supporting major points, and often provide the humor and enlightenment that turn an otherwise dreary topic into a

Diversity Challenges

Critical Thinking

Why do audiences generally respond positively to the use of statistics, human interest stories, quotes, and humor? How can these techniques produce negative results?

stimulating message. They are among the professional speaker's most important inventory items. You can begin accumulating these items from personal reading and by accessing quotations from prominent people, information about your topic, and techniques for speaking effectively from commercial media and the Internet. Start a file for materials you come across that seem worth remembering.

Close

The close provides unity to your presentation by "telling the audience what you have already told them." The conclusion should be "your best line, your most dramatic point, your most profound thought, your most memorable bit of information, or your best anecdote."[7] Because listeners tend to remember what they hear last, use these final words strategically. Develop a close that supports and refocuses the audience's attention on your purpose statement.

- *Commit the time and energy needed to develop a creative, memorable conclusion.* An audience is not impressed with endings such as "That's all I have" or "That's it." Because an audience tends to remember what they hear last, you must use these final words strategically to accomplish your speaking goal. Techniques that can be used effectively include summarizing the main points that have been made in the presentation and using anecdotes, humor, and illustrations that can also be used in the introduction. When closing an analytical presentation, you would state your conclusion and support it with the highlights from your supporting evidence: "In summary, we selected the Madison, South Carolina, location because it had. . . ." In a persuasive presentation, the close is often an urgent plea for the members of the audience to take some action or to look on the subject from a new point of view.
- *Tie the close to the introduction to strengthen the unity of the presentation.* For example, you might answer the rhetorical question you asked in the opening, refer to and build on an anecdote included in the introduction, and so on. A unifying close to a drug awareness presentation might be "So, my friends, make your community drug free so you and your friends can grow up to enjoy the benefits of health, education, family, and freedom."
- *Use transition words that clearly indicate you are moving from the body to the close.* Attempt to develop original words rather than rely on standard statements such as "In closing," or "In conclusion."
- *Practice your close until you can deliver it without stumbling.* Use your voice and gestures to communicate this important idea clearly, emphatically, and sincerely rather than swallow your words or fade out at the end as inexperienced speakers often do.
- *Smile and stand back to accept the audience's applause.* A solid close does not require a "thank you"; the audience should respond spontaneously with applause to thank you for a worthwhile presentation.[8]

At this point of development, a working outline of your presentation about COPE might take this form:

COPE (Challenging Outdoor Personal Experiences):
Skills for Creating Trust Environments in Today's Dynamic Workplace

I. Introduction
   A. Attention-getter that involves the audience and establishes credibility
   B. Purpose statement
   C. Preview of three major points
II. Body
   A. Self-confidence
   B. Communication skills
   C. Team-building skills
III. Close: Restatement of primary benefits to be derived or statement that refocuses the audience's attention to the purpose in a memorable way

Visit the text support site at http://lehman.swlearning.com to download a Presentation Planning Guide. This planning guide will simplify your preparation for future presentations as you follow a systematic process of selecting a topic, analyzing your audience and speaking environment, and organizing a logical, concise presentation.

Designing Compelling Presentation Visuals

Speakers who use presentation visuals are considered better prepared and more persuasive and interesting, and achieve their goals more often than speakers who do not use visuals. Presentation visuals support and clarify a speaker's ideas and help the audience visualize the message. A speaker using presentation visuals hits the listener (receiver) with double impact—through the eyes and the ears—and achieves the results quoted in an ancient Chinese proverb: "Tell me, I'll forget. Show me, I may remember. But involve me and I'll understand." Research studies have confirmed this common-sense idea that using visual support will enhance a presentation. The effective use of presentation visuals provides several advantages:[9]

- clarifies and emphasizes important points.
- increases retention from 14 percent to 38 percent.
- reduces the time required to present a concept.
- results in a speaker's achieving goals 34 percent more often than when presentation visuals are not used.
- increases group consensus by 21 percent when presentation visuals are used in a meeting.

Types of Presentation Visuals

A speaker must select the appropriate medium or combination of media to accomplish the purpose and to meet the needs of a specific audience. The most common presentation visuals are illustrated in Figure 12-1. Visit the text support site at http://lehman.swlearning.com for additional explanation about each type.

Figure 12-1

Selecting an Appropriate Presentation Visual

Visual	Advantages	Limitations
 Handouts	• Provide detailed information that audience can examine closely • Extend a presentation by providing resources for later use • Reduce the need for note taking and aid in audience retention	• Can divert audience's attention from the speaker • Can be expensive
 Boards and flip charts	• Facilitate interaction • Are easy to use • Are inexpensive if traditional units are used	• Require turning speaker's back to audience • Are cumbersome to transport, can be messy, and not professional looking. • Are not reusable, provide no hard copy, and must be developed on-site if traditional units are used
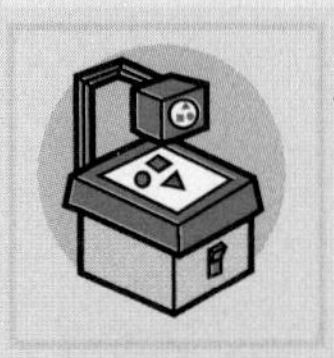 Overhead transparencies	• Are simple to prepare and use • Allow versatile use; prepare beforehand or while speaking • Are inexpensive and readily available	• Are not easily updated and are awkward to use • Must have special acetate sheets and markers unless using a document camera • Pose potential for equipment failure
 Electronic presentations	• Meet audience expectations of visual standards • Enhance professionalism and credibility of the speaker • Provide special effects to enhance retention, appeal, flexibility, and reuse	• Can lead to poor delivery if misused • Can be expensive, require highly developed skills, and are time-consuming • Pose technology failure and transportability challenges
 35 mm. slides	• Are highly professional • Depict real people and places	• Require darkened room • Creates a formal environment not conducive to group interaction • Lacks flexibility in presentation sequence
 Models or physical objects	• Are useful to demonstrate an idea	• Can compete with the speaker for attention

Design of Presentation Visuals

Changing Technology

Computer technology has raised the standards for presentation visuals; however, inexperienced designers often use the power of the technology to make visuals overly complex and difficult to understand. Your goal is to create an appealing, easy-to-read design that supports your main points. Additionally, your presentation visuals should possess the same degree of professionalism as your delivery and personal appearance. You can create dynamic and useful presentation visuals including slides, handouts, and notes pages by composing effective slide content and applying basic design rules related to space usage, typography, and color.

Effective Slide Content

Well-organized, crisp slide content enhances the audience's ability to grasp the speaker's meaning and find immediate value in the information. Follow these simple rules for writing concise, meaningful slide content. Study the samples slides in Figures 12-2 and 12-3:

- *Limit the number of visual aids used in a single presentation.* Too many visuals can overwhelm, bore, and tire the audience. While the

---

Figure 12-2

Concise, Targeted Bulleted List:
Poor (left) and Good (right) Examples

Humor

- Important element in any presentation
- Easy connection with audience
- Gets attention
- Alleviates boredom
- Reduction of mental tension
- Discourages conflect
- Enhances comprehension
- Shouldn't embarrass people
  - Ethnic jokes are inappropriate
  - Profane language is definitely not recommended

Value of Humor in a Presentation

- Establishes a connection with the audience
- Increases audience's willingness to listen
- Makes message more understandable and more memorable
- Alleviates negativity associated with sensitive subjects

- Uses a descriptive title that captures the single idea—the value humor adds to a presentation.
- Omits bulleted items that don't reflect the value of using humor (common element of the list). The first item can be used as a verbal transition for the list; the final two items, moved to new slide presenting tips for using humor.
- Corrects misspelled word to maintain credibility ("conflict").
- Uses parallel structure for remaining bulleted items (all singular action verbs).

audience values being able to "see" your points, they also welcome the variety provided by listening and the break from concentrating on visuals, especially if they are being displayed in a darkened room. Take a thorough look at the entire presentation and prepare visuals needed to direct the reader's attention to major points and to clarify or illustrate complex information.

Critical Thinking

How does the advice "more is not necessarily better" apply to the design of presentation visuals?

- ***Include only one major idea on each visual with a descriptive title highlighting the idea.*** The title should reflect the exact content of the slide in a way that will engage the audience's attention. Note the improvement in Figure 12-2 when the revised title prepares the audience for a list of benefits gained from incorporating humor into a business presentation. A subsequent slide could discuss specific guidelines for using humor effectively.

- ***Compose concise, to-the-point statements that you want the audience to remember.*** Avoid the tendency of many speakers to clean up their notes and put everything they intend to say on the slide as illustrated in the first item in the poor slide in Figure 12-2 ("important element in any presentation"). The clarity of precise language will enable an audience to focus briefly on key points while directing primary attention to the speaker's explanations. Good slides will facilitate an extemporaneous delivery rather than a speaker's monotonous reading of scripted slides. Short text lines also are easier for the eye to follow and open up the slide with appealing white space.

- ***Develop powerful bulleted lists.*** Begin by making the items in a bulleted list parallel. If one item is presented in a different way grammatically, it appears out of place and weakens the emphasis given to each item in the list; it also may distract the audience's attention from the message. Second, be certain each item in a bulleted list appears together for a similar purpose. Does each major point relate to the key concept presented in the slide title? Does each subpoint relate to its major point, and so on? Lastly, limit the number of items in a bulleted list to increase audience retention and facilitate a smooth flow of ideas; in your draft, look for overlap and repetition that will allow you to collapse content into a short list that an audience can remember more easily. Note the application of each of these principles for powerful bulleted lists in the slides in Figure 12-2.

- ***Use powerful visual communication for quick and effective conveyance of information.*** Images and shapes are more visually appealing and memorable than words, and enable audiences to grasp information more easily. What's more, today's audiences expect media-rich, dynamic visuals, not a speaker's dense notes simply cleaned up, put onscreen, and used as a crutch during a boring and unbearable delivery. In Figure 12-3, for example, to reinforce the dire need for improved business presentations, the speaker rejects the standard design of bulleted lists and random clip art and instead creates a strong conceptual image of an ineffective presentation complete with boring speaker and inattentive audience. Note the power of this visual design as you compare the slides in Figure 12-3.

SPOTLIGHT COMMUNICATOR
Don't Lose the Forest in the Trees

According to Peter Drucker, management guru of the twentieth century, "We are prone both in academia and management to mistake the surface gloss of brilliance for the essence of performance."[10] While this visionary statement was made prior to the exploding technology revolution, it offers a sober precaution for the use of current technology applications.

The very success of electronic presentations has inspired a backlash of sorts. Some companies have declared electronic presentations as too formal for internal communications; others have offered guidelines to limit the number of slides used in a presentation, or even dictated what colors could or could not be used. Scott McNealy, Sun Microsystem's president, went so far in 1997 as to ban the use of PowerPoint by his 25,000 employees. McNealy's reason-ing for prohibiting slide usage was that Sun employees were spending too much time preparing slides, pre-sumably at the expense of other kinds of preparation. While the ban was reportedly not enforced, it pro-vided wide exposure to the problem with overuse and abuse of slide pre-sentations.[11]

A major argument against elec-tronic presentations is that they divert attention of both the audi-ence and speaker from the presen-ter's message to what is essentially a series of pictures. The slide show, once peripheral to a presentation (visual *aid*), becomes the center focus. A good presentation will have the presenter as its major focus; visuals should be used sparingly and only to reinforce the speaker's credibility. Another important point is that presenters should choose visuals only after they have a firm

© REUTERS NEWMEDIA, INC./CORBIS

idea of what they want to say.

McNealy may not be as vocally opposed to slide usage now that Sun offers its own presentation soft-ware product, Impress, as a compo-nent of its Star Office free software download. But his philosophy that presentation software should be a medium and not the message has remained the same.[12]

Applying What You Have Learned

1. What are some other ways that the use of presentation slides can weaken the overall presentation?
2. Develop a list of suggestions for the appropriate use of an elec-tronic slide presentation.

Scott McNealy, President, Sun Microsystems

http://www.java.sun.com

Refer to ShowCASE, Part 3, at the end of the chapter to learn how Sun Microsystems distributes presentations to virtual audiences.

Legal & Ethical Constraints

- **Reflect legal and ethical responsibility in the design of presenta-tion visuals.** Like the graphics you developed in Chapter 10, presen-tation visuals should be uncluttered, easily understood, and depict information honestly. You will learn that copyright compliance is imperative as you explore the perils of copyright violations covered in the the Strategic Forces feature "Copyright Violations: A Presenter's Peril" on page 501.

Figure 12-3

Engaging Conceptual Slide Design: Poor (left) and Good (right) Examples

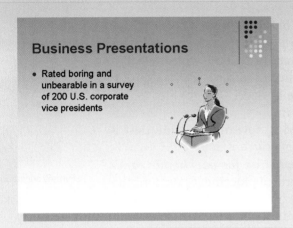

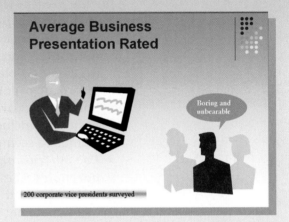

- Uses a descriptive title that captures the central idea of the contempt in which a typical business presentation is held.
- Selects images that imply the intended message—the ineffectiveness of today's business presentations; enlarges the images for appeal and balance on the slide.
- Pares the text to emphasize the central idea and eliminates the bullet as a bulleted list must have at least two items.
- Moves the source note to a less prominent position on the slide to add credibility to the research data while keeping the focus on the central idea.

- *Proofread the visual carefully following the same systematic procedures used for printed letters and reports and electronic communication.* Misspellings in handouts or displays are embarrassing and diminish your credibility. When preparing visuals customized for a prospective client/customer, double-check to be certain that names of people, companies, and products are spelled correctly.

Space Design and Typography

Follow these guidelines related to the use of space on the visual and the presentation of the text:

- *Limit the amount of text on the slide.* To avoid clutter and keep the audience's attention on important ideas, generally, do not fill more than 75 percent of the slide with text. Limit headings to four words and follow the 7 × 7 rule as a general rule that limits text to 7 lines per slide and 7 words per line.
- *Use graphic devices to direct the audience's attention and to separate items.* Options include borders, boxes, shadows, lines, and bullets. Unless sequence is important, use bullets as they add less clutter

Critical Thinking
The 7 × 7 rule keeps slides concise.

and are easier than numbers to follow. Note the enhancements shown in Figure 12-1.

Landscape orientation

- *Select a page layout orientation appropriate for the presentation visual you are creating:*
  - *Use landscape orientation for computer presentations and 35-millimeter slides.* This horizontal placement provides a wide view that (a) creates a pleasing, soothing feeling similar to looking over the horizon, (b) provides longer lines for text and images, and (c) ensures that no text is included so low on the slide that it cannot be seen properly.

Portrait orientation

  - *Use portrait orientation for overhead transparencies.* This vertical placement positions the text to be read across the shortest side of the page, which makes additional lines available for text on an overhead transparency.

- *Use left alignment of text as a general rule.* **Left alignment** that begins flush at the left margin and ends at various points along the line creates an informal, personal appearance and easily leads the viewer's eyes consistently back to the same position for reading each item. Left alignment also provides consistent spacing between each word, unlike justified alignment that adds extra spacing to create an even right margin. Centered alignment is appropriate for positioning a few words on the slide and creating a formal look; right alignment is used to format numerical data.

- *Follow these capitalization and punctuation rules for easy reading:*
  - *Use capital letters sparingly as they are difficult to read from a distance.* Capitalize the first letter of important words in slide titles (initial caps) and the first letter of the first word and proper nouns in a bulleted list (sentence case).
  - *Omit punctuation at the end of bulleted lists.* Avoid punctuation elsewhere on the slide because punctuation is too small to be read from a distance. Consider inserting special characters when punctuation such as an exclamation point is needed.
  - *Avoid abbreviations and hyphenations that may cause confusion.*

Follow these guidelines concerning fonts to help assure that your textual message supports the tone of your presentation.

- *Limit the number of fonts within a single presentation to no more than three to prevent a cluttered, confusing look.* Create special effects by using various fonts in the same family; by applying an attribute such as boldface, italics, shadow, outline; or by using color.
- *Choose interesting fonts that convey the mood of your presentation and are a fresh change from the fonts most commonly used.* For example, for a less formal presentation, consider informal fonts such as **Comic Sans MS** and Tahoma over Arial and Times New Roman.

- *Choose sturdy fonts that can be easily read from a distance.* Avoid delicate fonts with narrow strokes that wash out especially when displayed in color. Italic, decorative, and condensed fonts are also difficult to read. Choose an especially strong font for the title to draw the audience's attention naturally to this idea first and a less prominent but readable font for the text.
- *Create a hierarchy of importance among the standard slide elements by varying the font face and font size.*
    - *Use a sturdy sans serif font for the slide title and a serif font for the bulleted text to distinguish the slide from the other text.*
    - *Vary font sizes.* Vary sizes as shown in the following table to ensure that the text can be easily read by the people in the back row and to draw the audience's attention first to the title, then the bulleted list, and then other text (e.g., source notes, callouts). For point of reference, one **point**, the measurement scale used for text, equals 1/72 of an inch. A one-inch letter measured from the top of the highest part of the letter to the lowest part of the letter is 72 points.

Critical Thinking

Identify several additional fonts that would be recommended for slide use.

Slide Element	Recommended Font Type	Recommended Font Size	Examples
Slide title	**Sans Serif** A font with short cross-strokes, known as **serifs**, that has a simple, blocky look appropriate for displaying text as in the headlines of newspaper or the title of a slide.	24 to 36 points	Arial Univers
Bulleted list	**Serif** A font with short cross-strokes that project from the top and bottom of the main stroke of a letter—the type that typically is read as the main print in books and newspapers.	18 to 24 points	Times New Roman CG Times
Other text	**Serif**	No smaller than 14 points	See serif examples.

Effective Use of Color

Color is the most exciting part of presentation design. The colors you choose and the way you combine them determine the overall effectiveness of your presentation and add a personal touch to your work. Your strategic choice of color will aid you in (a) conveying the formality of the presentation, (b) creating a desired tone, (c) associating your presentation with your company, a product, or the subject of the presentation, and (d) emphasizing important components of your slide.

Critical Thinking

Give examples of other colors associated with certain themes or ideas.

- *Formality.* Conservative colors (blue) add formality; brighter colors (yellow) lend a less formal and perhaps trendy look.
- *Effect.* Generally, warm colors such as reds, oranges, and yellows stimulate your audience; cool colors such as blues and greens create a more relaxed and receptive environment.
- *Association.* Audiences naturally associate colors with certain ideas: green for money or go; yellow for caution; red for stop, danger, or financial loss; and blue for calm. Because of a natural association of red with financial loss, red would be inappropriate in a table of numbers or a graph depicting growth or a healthy financial situation. Colors also can be used to create an association with a company or a product (e.g., red and white and Coca-Cola or blue and white and Pepsi).
- *Differentiation.* Color helps the audience distinguish between different elements such as the slide title appearing a color brighter than the bulleted list. Other ways color can be used to distinguish information include
  - highlighting specific text or emphasizing key elements in a graph.
  - connecting a set of numbers in a table that are to be considered as a group.
  - color coding related components in a line drawing or an organizational chart.
  - printing pages on different colors of paper to help the audience find a particular sheet in handouts. The speaker can simply say, "On the yellow sheet . . ."

    Red and green should be avoided when differentiating important points as almost 10 percent of the population is color impaired and cannot distinguish between red and green. The red and green bars in a graph would be seen as one large area.

Diversity
Challenges

To avoid an overwhelming, distracting design, limit colors to no more than three colors on a slide and follow these steps for selecting an effective color scheme for presentation visuals:

1. *Determine the medium you will use for displaying the visual.* The color scheme needed for optimal readability varies depending on your use of an electronic presentation, overhead transparencies, or a web page.

Output Medium	Background/Foreground
Overhead transparencies shown in a well-lit room	Light background Dark text
Electronic presentations and 35-millimeter slides presented in a darkened room	Medium to dark background Light text
Web page	Light background Dark text

2. *Choose the background color first, as this area displays the largest amount of color.* Consider the preliminary issues of formality and mood discussed previously.
3. *Choose foreground colors—one for the slide title and a second color for the text.* Both colors must contrast highly with the background color selected so that the text can be read easily. Black text against a white background, the color scheme used traditionally in overhead transparencies, has the greatest contrast. A blue background with yellow text contrasts well, but a yellow background with white text would be difficult to read because of low contrast.

Black text on a white background provides high contrast and is easy to read.

White text on a light blue background provides low contrast and is difficult to read.

Yellow text on a dark blue background provides high contrast and is easy to read.

Critical Thinking

What colors do you consider to be complementary?

After you have chosen the background and foreground colors, evaluate the readability of the font(s) you have chosen. Colored text tends to wash out when projected; therefore, be certain that the fonts are sturdy enough and large enough to be read easily using the color scheme you selected.

4. *Choose the accent colors that complement the color scheme.* Accent colors are used in small doses to draw attention to key elements: bullet markers; bars in graphs, backgrounds (fills) of boxes, geometric shapes, lines, selected text; or drawings that are color coded for emphasis.

Project your presentation ahead of time in the room where you are to present so you can adjust the color scheme. This process is essential because colors display differently on a computer monitor than they do on projection devices. You can also check the readability of the text and double-check for typographical errors at the same time.

The slides in Figure 12-4 provide an opportunity to review these design guidelines. First, study carefully the poor example (left) and identify design principles that you believe have been violated. Note changes needed in the following major areas: (a) content, (b) choice of template and graphics, (c) space usage and layout, (d) typography, and (e) color scheme. Then, compare your suggestions with the revised slide and the explanation of the principles violated provided in the accompanying commentary.

Figure 12-4

Effective Slide Design: Poor (left)
and Good (right) Examples

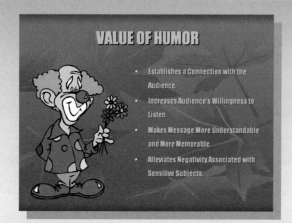
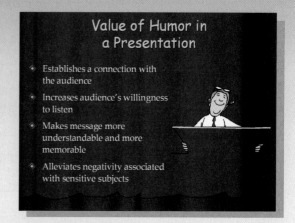

Template and Graphics

- Substitutes "curtain call" template for unrelated "maple leaves" template.
- Substitutes clip art of clown with relevant image of a happy presenter.
- Chooses effective color scheme:
  - Uses a cool color that is more relaxing than the warm color orange and fits the informal, relaxed mood of the topic.
  - Uses background color and foreground colors (slide title and bulleted list) that have high contrast with the background for easy readability. Placing the brighter color in the slide title pulls the audience's eyes first to this important description of the slide's major idea, then to the list.
  - Chooses accent colors that complement the background and foreground colors (i.e., yellow and orange in bullets and clip art).

Space Use and Layout

- Provides appropriate white space (no more than 75 percent coverage) and follows the 7 × 7 rule by dividing content into two slides (value of humor and guidelines).
- Moves clip art to the lower right quadrant, the optimal position for impact. Balances size of clip art with text
- Formats slide title in inverted pyramid format—each succeeding line is shorter than the line preceding it.

Typography

- Selects fonts to create an informal tone and to differentiate slide title from bulleted lists:
  Slide title: Sans serif font, Comic Sans MS, 40 points
  Bulleted list: Serif font, Palatino Linotype, 28 points
- Uses initial caps in the slide title and capitalizes only the first word in the bulleted list.
- Omits periods at the end of the bulleted items.

Design Tips for Audience Handouts

Audience handouts should add value for individual audience members; otherwise, the information can better be conveyed in a projected format for group benefit. An effective handout can help audience members remember your message, serve as a reference for later consideration or action, and encourage involvement when space is provided for notetaking. Follow these guidelines for preparing a well-designed, highly professional handout:

Critical Thinking

How would you decide whether to present certain information in an electronic slide or in a handout?

- *Keep the handout simple.* Summarize major points, but do not provide the audience with your entire presentation. Omit any information that does not directly support your purpose.
- *Limit the amount of text you include on the page.* Even though you can include much more information on a printed page than on other visuals, generally, at least 50 percent of your handout should be white space. Arrange the information in an uncluttered, easy-to-read format with wide margins. Short sentences and bulleted lists are easy to scan.
- *Use graphics when possible.* Graphics such as clip art, a chart, or diagram, create visual appeal and may bring an audience's attention to an item more effectively than a verbal explanation.
- *Make sure the handout conveys a positive impression of your company.* The handout should look good to the audience through the quality of the paper, printing, and copying. For professional appearance and future advertisement, include contact information and your company logo in a strategic location as shown in Figure 12-5.
- *Choose an appealing format that supports the purpose of your presentation.* After completing the presentation visuals, you can generate professional handouts easily in several formats. Varying numbers of miniature slides can be printed to a page (e.g., 2, 3, 6) by selecting from the software's print options as shown in Figure 12-5 (left). Slides can be imported into a word processing program to produce highly professional handouts as shown in Figure 12-5 (right). This detailed, professional format is especially useful if the audience will make decisions related to the presentation, summarize ideas for coworkers or supervisors, or use the information at a future date. Binding can be added to generate an attractive take-home packet. The notes page format shown in Figure 12-5 can also be used to generate detailed handouts (one slide per page) but may be cost prohibitive depending on the page count and the number of copies to be distributed.

Changing Technology

Design Tips for Notes Pages

Useful notes for reference during the presentation can be prepared on small index cards or on pages generated by electronic presentation software. Follow these guidelines:

Figure 12-5

Professional Handout Formats

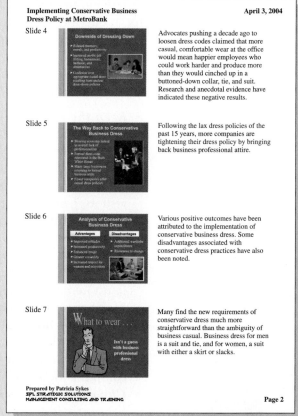

- *Include brief phrases that you can scan easily and will trigger the next point you are to discuss.* To ensure accuracy and high impact, write out completely sections you must deliver without stumbling: segments of the introduction, a quotation, exact statistics or figures, the punch line of a joke, and closing statements.
- *Prepare legible notes that are neat and large enough to read easily.* Use a 14-point font if the room will be darkened or 10–12 point in a well-lit room.
- *Make generous use of bulleted lists and other formats that are easily read.* Use boldface and all capitals for emphasis only. Keying text in boldface, underline, or all capitals will make the notes difficult to read.
- *Keep notes clean and uncluttered.* Highlight important points with a colored marker, but avoid drawing arrows during a rehearsal to indicate a change in order of material; these changes will be confusing during the pressure of a presentation.

Copyright Violations: A Presenter's Peril

When preparing presentations, you will likely want to use copyrighted materials to support your ideas. Your informed use of copyrighted materials may save you embarrassment and your company the cost of an expensive lawsuit.

Under the Copyright Act of 1976, copyright is automatic when an original work is first "fixed" in a tangible medium of expression (including electronic files, Internet postings, and e-mail) regardless of whether a notice of copyright appears with the material. Copyright owners have five exclusive rights that protect their ability to obtain commercial benefit from the work and control what is done with the work by others: (1) the right to reproduce the copyrighted work; (2) the right to distribute copies of a copyrighted work to the public; (3) the right to prepare derivative works, or creations based on the original; (4) the right to perform the copyrighted work publicly; and (5) the right to display copyrighted work publicly. Statutory damages for infringing on copyright can be as much as $100,000 in cases of willful violation, and commercial copyright violation of more than 100 copies and a value of more than $2,500 is a felony in the United States.[13]

Presenters are more likely than ever to be tempted to commit copyright infringements as a result of scanning and duplicating technologies and the wealth of high quality, downloadable graphics, sound, and video. At the same time, copyright owners and watchdog organizations are becoming more aggressive, using new tactics and technologies to enforce their rights. Recent court cases, such as the highly publicized Napster trial regarding music copyrights, indicate a shift in the legal tides in favor of copyright owners.[14]

To avoid copyright abuse when preparing presentation materials:

1. **Commit to learning the basics of copyright law.** Don't gamble that you won't get caught or that you will be safe if you plead ignorance.

2. **Assume that any pre-existing work is copyrighted and requires permission from the copyright owner to use or copy.** Plan ahead so you will have plenty of time to secure permissions and negotiate a fair price with the copyright owner.

3. **Note the precautions that relate to fair use.** The "fair use" defense is generally applicable in education, research, and scholarly uses, and rarely applies in for-profit settings.[15]

4. **Acquire your own library of multimedia content by purchasing royalty-free multimedia content from reputable companies.** Royalty-free multimedia content provides unlimited use for a one-time fee, because all copyrights have been cleared for the purchased content. However, be wary of advertisers that sell "royalty-free" content but fail to clear the copyrights.

5. **Stay abreast of changes in the copyright law.** Owners and information users will continue to devise ways to make the copyright law work in an electronic environment.

Application

1. Test your knowledge of copyright law by taking the quiz at **http://literacy.kent.edu/Oasis/Workshops/copytoc.html**.

2. Locate the following web site that describes the ten common myths related to copyright. **http://www.templetons.com/brad/copymyths.html**.

   • Write a short report that explains the discussed myths related to copyright law.

   • Prepare a handout that effectively conveys this information for office staff.

Refining Your Delivery

Changing Technology

After you have organized your message, you must identify the appropriate delivery method, develop your vocal qualities, and practice your delivery.

Delivery Method

Four presentation methods can be used: memorized, scripted, impromptu, and extemporaneous. Impromptu and extemporaneous styles are generally more useful for business presentations.

Memorized presentations are written out ahead of time, memorized, and recited verbatim. Memorization has the greatest limitations of the speech styles. Speakers are almost totally unable to react to feedback, and the speaker who forgets a point and develops a mental block may lose the entire speech. Memorized speeches tend to sound monotonous, restrict natural body gestures and motions, and lack conviction. For short religious or fraternal rites, however, the memorized presentation is often impressive.

Scripted, also known as written-and-read, delivery involves the speaker's writing out the entire speech and reading it to the audience. For complex material and technical conference presentations, scripted presentations ensure content coverage. Additionally, this style protects speakers against being misquoted (when accuracy is absolutely critical) and also fits into exact time constraints, as in television or radio presentations. Speeches are sometimes read when time does not permit advance preparation, or several different presentations are given in one day (e.g., the speaking demands of the President of the United States and other top-level executives). Scripted presentations limit speaker-audience rapport, particularly when speakers keep their eyes and heads buried in their manuscripts. Electronic devices make it possible to project manuscripts on transparent screens on each side of the speaker. The speaker may read the rolling manuscript but appear to be speaking extemporaneously.

Impromptu delivery is frightening to many people because the speaker is called on without prior notice. Experienced speakers can easily analyze the request, organize supporting points from memory, and present a simple, logical response. In many cases, businesspeople can anticipate a request and be prepared to discuss a particular idea when requested (e.g., status report on an area of control at a team meeting). Because professionals are expected to present ideas and data spontaneously on demand, businesspeople must develop the ability to deliver impromptu presentations.

Extemporaneous presentations are planned, prepared, and rehearsed but not written in detail. Brief notes prompt the speaker on the next point, but the exact words are chosen spontaneously as the speaker interacts with the audience and identifies this audience's specific needs. Extemporaneous presentations allow natural body gestures, sound conversational, and can be delivered with conviction because the speaker is speaking "with" the listeners and not "to" them. The audience appreciates a warm, genuine communicator and will forgive an occasional stumble or groping for a word that occurs with an extemporaneous presentation. Learning to construct useful notes will aid you in becoming an accomplished extemporaneous speaker; guidelines are provided in the "Design Tips for Notes Pages" section on page 499.

Vocal Qualities

The sound of your voice is a powerful instrument used to deliver your message and to project your professional image. To maximize your vocal strengths, focus on three important qualities of speech—phonation, articulation, and pronunciation.

Phonation involves both the production and the variation of the speaker's vocal tone. You project your voice and convey feelings—even thoughts—by varying your vocal tones. Important factors of phonation are pitch, volume, and rate. These factors permit us to recognize other people's voices over the telephone. Changes in phonation occur with changes in emotional moods.

Critical Thinking

How do the "voice of experience" and the "voice of authority" sound? Name at least two individuals who you believe exhibit these vocal qualities.

Pitch is the highness or lowness of the voice. Pleasant voices have medium or low pitch; however, a varied pitch pattern is desirable. The pitch of the voice rises and falls to reflect emotions; for example, fear and anger are reflected in a higher pitch; sadness, in a lower pitch. Lower pitches for both men and women are perceived as sounding more authoritative; higher pitches indicate less confidence and suggest pleading or whining. Techniques to be discussed later in this section can help you lower the pitch of your voice.

Volume refers to the loudness of tones. Generally, good voices are easily heard by everyone in the audience but are not too loud. Use variety to hold the audience's attention, to emphasize words or ideas, or to create a desired atmosphere (energetic, excited tone versus quiet, serious one).

Rate is the speed at which words are spoken. Never speak so quickly that the audience cannot understand your message or so slowly that they are distracted or irritated. Vary the rate with the demands of the situation. For example, speak at a slower rate when presenting a complex concept or emphasizing an important idea. Pause to add emphasis to a key point or to transition to another major section of the presentation. Speak at a faster rate when presenting less important information or when reviewing.

An inherent problem related to speaking rate is verbal fillers—also called *nonwords*. Verbal fillers, such as *uhhh, ahhh, ummm, errr* are irritating to the audience and destroy your effectiveness. Many speakers fill space with their own verbal fillers; these include *you know, I mean, basically, like I said, okay, as a matter of fact.* Because of the conversational style of impromptu and extemporaneous presentations, a speaker will naturally grope for a word or the next idea from time to time. Become aware of verbal fillers you frequently use by critiquing a tape or video recording and then focus on replacing them with a three- to five-second pause. This brief gap between thoughts gives you an opportunity to think about what you want to say next and time for your audience to absorb your idea. Presenting an idea (sound bite) and then pausing briefly is an effective way to influence your audience positively. The listener will not notice the slight delay, and the absence of meaningless words will make you appear more confident and polished. Also avoid annoying speech habits, such as clearing your throat or constantly uttering a soft cough, that shift the audience's attention from the speech to the speaker.

The following activities will help you achieve good vocal qualities: medium to low pitch and audible, steady pace, with variations to reflect mood:

- *Breathe properly and relax.* Nervousness affects normal breathing patterns and is reflected in vocal tone and pitch. The better prepared you are, the better your phonation will be. Although relaxing may seem difficult to practice before a speech, a few deep breaths, just as swimmers take before diving, can help.
- *Listen to yourself.* A recording of your voice reveals much about pitch, intensity, and duration. Most people are amazed to find their voices are not quite what they had expected. "I never dreamed I sounded that bad" is a common reaction. Nasal twangs usually result from a failure to speak from the diaphragm, which involves taking in and letting out air through the larynx, where the vocal cords operate. High pitch may occur from the same cause, or it may be a product of speaking too fast.
- *Develop flexibility.* The good speaking voice is somewhat musical, with words and sounds similar to notes in a musical scale. Read each of the following sentences aloud and emphasize the underscored word in each. Even though the sentences are identical, emphasizing different words changes the meaning.

I am happy you are here.	Maybe I'm the only happy one.
I *am* happy you are here.	I really am.
I am *happy* you are here.	Happy best describes my feeling.
I am happy *you* are here.	Yes, you especially.
I am happy you *are* here.	You may not be happy, but I am.
I am happy you are *here.*	Here and not somewhere else.

Articulation involves smooth, fluent, and pleasant speech. It results from the way in which a speaker produces and joins sounds. Faulty articulation is often caused by not carefully forming individual sounds. Common examples include

- dropping word endings—saying *workin'* for *working*.
- running words together—saying *Snoo* for *What's new*, *kinda* for *kind of*, *gonna* for *going to*.
- imprecise enunciation—saying *Dis* for *this*, *wid* for *with*, *dem* for *them*, *pin* for *pen*, or *pitcher* for *picture*.

Critical Thinking

Poorly articulated expressions can diminish your acceptance as a credible speaker. What words do you use incorrectly or enunciate poorly?

Critical Thinking

Of what region is your accent typical? Is your accent stronger at certain times? If so, why? Does your accent give you an advantage or disadvantage in a professional environment?

Diversity
Challenges

Critical Thinking

What does a dictionary show as the preferred pronunciation of status, often, economics, and envelope?

These examples should not be confused with *dialect*, which people informally call an *accent*. A **dialect** is a variation in pronunciation, usually of vowels, from one part of the country to another. Actually, everyone speaks a dialect; and speech experts can often identify, even pinpoint, the section of the country from where a speaker comes. In the United States, common dialects are New England, New York, Southern, Texan, Mid-Western, and so forth. Within each of these, minor dialects may arise regionally or from immigrant influence. The simple fact is that when people interact, they influence each other even down to speech sounds. Many prominent speakers have developed a rather universal dialect, known as General American Standard Speech pattern, that seems to be effective no matter who the audience is. This model for professional language is the most widely used of all regional dialects in the United States, is used by major broadcasters, and is easily understood by those learning English as a second language because they likely listened to this speech pattern as they learned the language.[16] The Internet case at the end of the chapter provides you with the opportunity to further explore the impact of accents on your potential for advancement.

You can improve the clarity of your voice, reduce strain and voice distortion, and increase your expressiveness by following these guidelines:

- *Stand up straight with your shoulders back and breathe from your diaphragm rather than your nose and mouth.* If you are breathing correctly, you can then use your mouth and teeth to form sounds precisely. For example, vowels are always sounded with the mouth open and the tongue clear of the palate. Consonants are responsible primarily for the distinctness of speech and are formed by an interference with or stoppage of outgoing breath.
- *Focus on completing the endings of all words, not running words together, and enunciating words correctly.* To identify recurring enunciation errors, listen to a recording and seek feedback from others.
- *Obtain formal training to improve your speech.* Pursue a self-study program by purchasing tapes that help you reduce your dialect and move more closely to the General American Standard Dialect. You can also enroll in a course to improve your speech patterns or arrange for private lessons from a voice coach.

Pronunciation involves using principles of phonetics to create accurate sounds, rhythm, stress, and intonation. People may articulate perfectly but still mispronounce words. A dictionary provides the best source to review pronunciation. Two pronunciations are often given for a word, the first one being the desired pronunciation and the second an acceptable variation. For example, to adopt a pronunciation commonly used in England such as *shedule* for *schedule* or *a-gane* for *again* could be considered affected speech. In other cases, the dictionary allows some leeway. The first choice for pronouncing *data* is to pronounce the first *a* long, as in *date*; but common usage is fast making pronunciation of the short *a* sound, as in *cat*, acceptable. Likewise, the preferred pronunciation of *often* is with a silent *t*. Good speakers use proper pronunciation and refer to the dictionary frequently in both pronunciation and vocabulary development.

When your voice qualities combine to make your messages pleasingly receptive, your primary concerns revolve around developing an effective delivery style.

Delivery Style

Critical Thinking

What are the causes and symptoms of public speaking anxiety?

Speaking effectively is both an art and a skill. Careful planning and practice are essential for building speaking skills.

Before the Presentation

Follow these guidelines when preparing for your presentation:

- *Prepare thoroughly.* You can expect a degree of nervousness as you anticipate speaking before a group. This natural tension is constructive because it increases your concentration and your energy and enhances your performance. Being well prepared is the surest way to control speech anxiety. Develop an outline for your presentation that supports your purpose and addresses the needs of your audience. Additionally, John Davis, a successful speech coach, warned: "Never, never, never give a speech on a subject you don't believe in. You'll fail. On the other hand, if you prepare properly, know your material, and *believe* in it . . . your audience will not only hear but *feel* your message."[17]

Changing Technology

- *Prepare effective presentation support tools.* Follow the guidelines presented in the prior section to select and design presentation support tools appropriate for your audience and useful in delivering the presentation: visuals, handouts, and notes pages. Additionally, develop a contingency plan in the real event of technical difficulties with computer equipment. Prepared presenters have backup overheads and hard copies of their presentations and may have a backup computer pre-loaded and ready. Arrive early so you can troubleshoot unexpected technological glitches. Despite your degree of planning, however, technical problems may occur during your presentation. Remain calm and correct them as quickly and professionally as you can. Take heart in the fact that Bill Gates' computer crashed when he introduced a new version of Windows!

- *Practice, but do not rehearse.* Your goal is to become familiar with the key phrases on your note cards so that you can deliver the presentation naturally as if you are talking with the audience—not reciting the presentation or acting out a role. Avoid overpracticing that may make your presentation sound mechanical and limit your ability to respond to the audience.

- *Practice the entire presentation.* This practice will allow you to identify (1) flaws in organization or unity, (2) long, complex sentences

Present or perish! Are poor speaking skills jeopardizing your career success? To improve your presentation skills, begin by taking *every* opportunity to practice your speaking skills in public.

or impersonal expressions inappropriate in a presentation, and (3) "verbal potholes." Verbal potholes include word combinations that could cause you to stumble, a word you have trouble pronouncing ("irrelevant" or "statistics"), or a word you perceive accentuates your dialect ("get" may sound like "git" regardless of the intention of a Southern speaker).

- *Spend additional time practicing the introduction and conclusion.* You will want to deliver these important parts with finesse while making a confident connection with the audience. A good closing serves to leave the audience in a good mood and may help overcome some possible mistakes made during the speech. Depending on the techniques used, consider memorizing significant brief statements to ensure their accuracy and impact (e.g., direct quotation, exact statistic, etc.).

- *Practice displaying presentation visuals so that your delivery appears effortless and seamless.* Your goal is to make the technology virtually transparent, positioned in the background to support *you* as the primary focus of the presentation. First, be sure you know basic commands for advancing through your presentation without displaying distracting drop-down menus and the computer's untidy work areas (menu bars and icons). Develop skill in returning to a specific slide in the event of a computer glitch or a spontaneous question from the audience.

- *Seek feedback on your performance that will enable you to polish your delivery and improve organization.* Critique your own performance by practicing in front of a mirror and evaluating a videotape of your presentation. If possible, present to a small audience for feedback and to minimize anxiety when presenting to the real audience.

- *Request a lectern to hold your notes and to steady a shaky hand, at least until you gain some confidence and experience.* Keep in mind, though, that weaning yourself from the lectern will eliminate a physical barrier between you and the audience. Without the lectern, you will speak more naturally. If you are using a microphone, ask for a cordless or portable microphone so that you can move freely.

Changing Technology

- *Insist on a proper, impressive introduction if the audience knows little about you.* An effective introduction will establish your credibility as the speaker on the subject to be discussed and will make the audience eager to hear you speak. You may prepare your own introduction as professional speakers do, or you can provide concise, targeted information that answers these three questions: (1) Why is the subject relevant? (2) Who is the speaker? and (3) What credentials qualify the speaker to talk about the subject? Attempt to talk with the person introducing you to verify any information, especially the pronunciation of your name, and to review the format of the presentation (time limit, question-and-answer period, etc.). Be certain to thank the person who made the introduction. "Thank you, Mr. President" or "Thank you for your kind introduction, Ms. Garcia" are adequate. Then, follow with your own introduction to your presentation.
- *Dress appropriately to create a strong professional image and to bolster your self-confidence.* An audience's initial impression of your personal appearance, your clothing and grooming, affects their ability to accept you as a credible speaker. Because first impressions are difficult to overcome, take ample time to groom yourself immaculately and to select clothing that is appropriate for the speaking occasion and consistent with the audience's expectations.
- *Arrive early to become familiar with the setup of the room and to check the equipment.* Check the location of your chair, the lectern, the projection screen, and light switches. Check the microphone and ensure that all equipment is in the appropriate place and working properly. Project your electronic presentation so you can adjust the color scheme to ensure maximum readability. Finally, identify the technician who will be responsible for resolving any technical problems that may occur during the presentation.

During the Presentation

Critical Thinking

What can you do as a speaker to build rapport with the audience? How do you know when you have succeeded?

The following are things you can do during your presentation to increase your effectiveness as a speaker:

- *Communicate confidence, warmth, and enthusiasm for the presentation and the time spent with the audience.* "Your listeners won't care how much you know until they know how much you care," is pertinent advice.[18] Follow these guidelines:
  - *Exhibit a confident appearance with alert posture.* Stand tall with your shoulders back and your stomach tucked in. Stand in the "ready position"—no slouching or hunching over the lectern or leaning back on your feet. Keep weight forward with knees slightly flexed so you are ready to move easily rather than rooted rigidly in one spot, hiding behind the lectern.
  - *Smile genuinely throughout the presentation.* Pause as you take your place behind the lectern and smile before you speak the

first word. Smile as you finish your presentation and wait for the applause.

- *Maintain steady eye contact with the audience in random places throughout the room.* Stay with one person approximately three to five seconds—long enough to finish a complete thought or sentence to convince the listener you are communicating individually with him or her. If the audience is large, select a few friendly faces and concentrate on speaking to them rather than a sea of nondescript faces.

Critical Thinking

Considering a speaker's mannerisms, what are some nonverbal actions that could have different interpretations among cultures?

- *Refine gestures to portray a relaxed, approachable appearance.* Vary hand motions to emphasize important points; otherwise, let hands fall naturally to your side. Practice using only one hand to make points unless you specifically need two hands, such as when drawing a figure or showing dimensions or location. Eliminate any nervous gestures that can distract the audience (e.g., clenching hands in front or behind body, steepling hands in praying position, placing hands in pocket, jingling keys or change, or playing with ring or pencil).

- *Move from behind the lectern and toward the audience to reduce the barrier created between you and the audience.* You may stand to one side and casually present a relaxed pose beside the lectern. However, avoid methodically walking from place to place without a purpose.

- *Exercise strong vocal qualities.* Review the guidelines provided for using your voice to project confidence and credibility.

- *Watch your audience.* They will tell you how you are doing and whether you should shorten your speech. Be attentive to negative feedback in the form of talking, coughing, moving chairs, and other signs of discomfort.

- *Use your visuals effectively.* Many speakers will go to a great deal of effort to prepare good presentation visuals—and then not use them effectively. Inexperienced speakers often ignore the visual altogether or fall into the habit of simply nodding their heads toward the visual. Neither of these techniques is adequate for involving the audience with the visual. In fact, if the material is complex, the speaker is likely to lose the audience completely.
    - *Step to one side of the visual so the audience can see it.* Use a pointer if necessary. Direct your remarks to the audience, so that you can maintain eye contact and resist the temptation to look over your shoulder to read the information from the screen behind you.
    - *Paraphrase the visual rather than reading it line for line.* To increase the quality of your delivery, develop a workable method of recording what you plan to say about each graphic. Detailed guidelines for preparing useful notes are included on pages 499–500.

- *Handle questions from the audience during the presentation.* Questions often disrupt carefully laid plans. At the same time, questions provide feedback, clarify points, and ensure understanding. Often people ask questions that will be answered later in the presentation. In these cases, you should say, "I believe the next slide will clarify that point. If not, we will come back to it." If the question can be answered quickly, the speaker should do so while indicating that it will also be covered later.

Attempt to anticipate and prepare for questions that might be raised. You may generate presentation visuals pertaining to certain anticipated questions and display them only if the question is posed. An audience will appreciate your thorough and complete explanation and your willingness and ability to adjust your presentation to their needs—much more professional than stumbling through an explanation or delaying the answer until the information is available. Speakers giving electronic presentations have ready access to enormous amounts of information stored in other software programs or in other presentation files that can be instantly displayed for audience discussion. Hyperlinks created within a presentation file will move a speaker instantaneously to a specific slide within the presentation, a different presentation, or even a spreadsheet file. The hyperlink can be used to play a music file embedded in a presentation, to start a CD in the computer's CD drive, or to connect to an Internet site.

Changing Technology

- *Keep within the time limit.* If your presentation is part of a busy program, be prepared to complete the presentation within the allotted time. In many organizations, speakers have one or more rehearsals before delivering reports to a group such as a board of directors. These rehearsals, or dry runs, are made before other executives, and are critiqued, timed, revised, and rehearsed again. Presentation software makes rehearsing your timing as simple as clicking a button and advancing through the slides as you practice. By evaluating the total presentation time and the time spent on each slide, you can modify the presentation and rehearse again until the presentation fits the time slot.

After the Presentation

How you handle the time following a presentation is as important as preparing for the presentation itself:

Critical Thinking

How will you prepare for the question-and-answer period?

- *Be prepared for a question-and-answer period.* Encourage the audience to ask questions, recognizing an opportunity to ensure that your presentation meets audience needs. Restate the question, if necessary, to ensure that everyone heard the question and ask the questioner if your answer was adequate. Be courteous even to hostile questioners so you will maintain the respect of your audience. Stay in control of the time by announcing that you have time for one or two more questions and then invite individual questions when the presentation is over.
- *Distribute handouts.* Distribute the handout when it is needed rather than at the beginning of the presentation. Otherwise, the audience may read the handout while you are explaining background information needed to understand the idea presented in the handout. If you expect the audience to take notes directly on the handout (see Figure 12-5) or if the audience will need to refer to the handout immediately, distribute the

handout at the beginning of the presentation or before it begins. To keep control of the audience's attention, be sure listeners know when they should be looking at the handout or listening to you. If the handout is intended as resource material only, post the handout to a web page or place it on a table at the back of the room and on a table at the front for those who come by to talk with you after the presentation.

Adapting to Alternate Delivery Situations

Objective 5

Discuss strategies for presenting in alternate delivery situations such as culturally diverse audiences, team, and distance presentations.

Diversity Challenges

As you've learned, the ability to present a dynamic presentation that focuses on the audience's needs and expectations is the fundamental principle in presenting effectively. Along with the solid foundation you've set for spoken communication, you'll also need to be prepared to adapt your presentation style to ever-present changes in the business environment. You will need to be prepared to respond to the special needs of a culturally diverse audience, a frequent scenario for many business people. Delivering team presentations and presenting in distance formats are other common situations you'll need to master.

Culturally Diverse Audiences

When speaking to a culturally diverse audience, you will want to be as natural as possible, while adjusting your message for important cultural variations. Using empathy, you can effectively focus on the listener as an individual rather than a stereotype of a specific culture. Be open and willing to learn, and you will reap the benefits of communicating effectively with people who possess a variety of strengths and creative abilities. Additionally, follow these suggestions for presenting to people from outside your own culture:

- *Speak simply.* Use simple English and short sentences. Avoid acronyms and expressions that may be confusing to nonnative English speakers, namely, slang, jargon, figurative expressions, and sports analogies. The Strategic Force feature, "Did I Make Myself Clear???" provides more information about avoiding confusion in terminology.
- *Avoid words that trigger negative emotional responses such as anger, fear, or suspicion.* Such "red flag" words vary among cultures; thus, try to anticipate audience reaction and choose your words carefully.
- *Enunciate each word precisely and speak somewhat more slowly.* Clear, articulate speech is especially important when the audience is not familiar with various dialects. Avoid the temptation to speak in a loud voice, a habit considered rude in any culture and especially annoying to the Japanese who perceive the normal tone of North Americans as too loud.

- *Be extremely cautious in the use of humor and jokes.* Cultures that prefer more formality may find your humor and jokes inappropriate or think you are not serious about your purpose. Asians, for instance, do not appreciate jokes about family members and the elderly.
- *Learn the culture's preferences for a direct or indirect presentation.* While North Americans tend to prefer directness, with the main idea presented first, many cultures, such as the Japanese, Latin American, and Arabic cultures, consider this straightforward approach tactless and rude. The Strategic Forces feature, "Basic Values Influence Communication Styles," in Chapter 6 explores this practice in greater detail.
- *Adapt to subtle differences in nonverbal communication.* Direct eye contact expected by most North Americans is not typical of Asian listeners who keep their eyes lowered and avoid eye contact to show respect. Arab audiences may stare into your eyes in an attempt to "see into the window of the soul." Cultures also vary on personal space and degree of physical contact (slap on the back or arm around the other as signs of friendship).
- *Adapt your presentation style and dress to fit the degree of formality of the culture.* Some cultures prefer a higher degree of formality than the casual style of North Americans. To accommodate, dress conservatively, strive to connect with the audience in a formal, reserved manner, and use highly professional visuals rather than jotting ideas on a flip chart.
- *Seek feedback to determine whether the audience is understanding your message.* Observe listeners carefully for signs of misunderstanding, restating ideas as necessary. Consider allowing time for questions after short segments of your presentation. Avoid asking "Is that clear?" or "Do you understand?" as these statements might elicit a "Yes" answer if the person perceives saying "No" to be a sign of incompetence.

Critical Thinking

How can you become more comfortable when speaking to culturally diverse audiences?

Potential frustrations can also occur when presentations or meetings bring together people of cultures who are not time conscious and who believe that personal relationships are the basis of business dealings (e.g., Asian, Latin American) with North Americans who see "time as money." When communicating with cultures that are not time driven, be patient with what you may consider time-consuming formalities and courtesies and lengthy decision-making styles when you would rather get right down to business or move to the next point. Recognize that the presentation may not begin on time or stay on a precise time schedule. Be prepared to allow additional time at the beginning of the presentation to establish rapport and credibility with the audience, and perhaps provide brief discussion periods during the presentation devoted to building relationships.

Be patient and attentive during long periods of silence; in many cultures people are inclined to stay silent unless they have something significant to say or if they are considering (not necessarily rejecting) an idea. In fact, some Japanese have asked how North Americans can think and

Proper introductions require presenting business cards in cultures such as the Chinese and Japanese with respect. Because these cultures consider the business card an extension of the self, damage to the card is damage to the individual.

© MARK RICHARDS/PHOTOEDIT, INC.

talk at the same time. Understanding patterns of silence can help you feel more comfortable during these seemingly endless moments and less compelled to fill the gaps with unnecessary words or to make concessions before the other side has a chance to reply.

Other significant points of difference between cultures are the varying rules of business etiquette. Should you use the traditional American handshake or some other symbol of greeting? Is using the person's given name acceptable? What formal titles should be used with a surname? Can you introduce yourself, or must you have someone else who knows the other person introduce you? Are business cards critical, and what rules should you follow when presenting a business card? A business card printed in two languages can be an efficient and effective tool.

Gift-giving can be another confusing issue. When you believe a gift should be presented to a speaker, investigate the appropriateness of gift giving, types of gifts considered appropriate or absolutely inappropriate, and colors of wrapping to be avoided in the speaker's culture. Liquor, for example, is an inappropriate gift in Arab countries.

Gaining competence in matters of etiquette will enable you to make a positive initial impression and concentrate on the presentation rather than agonizing over an awkward, embarrassing slip in protocol. Your audience will appreciate your willingness to learn and value their customs. Being sensitive to cultural issues and persistent in learning specific differences in customs and practices can minimize confusion and unnecessary embarrassment.

Team Presentations

Team Environment

Because much of the work in business today is done in teams, many presentations are planned and delivered by a team of presenters. Team presentations give an organization an opportunity to showcase its brightest

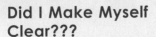

Did I Make Myself Clear???

Even though English is the generally recognized international business language, presenting in English is not without its problems. Non-native speakers may be fairly fluent in English, but they may have difficulty with common expressions such as these:

Acronyms: FYI, ASAP, CPU, HMO, IPO, NYSE, FASB

Slang: Referring to a dollar as a *buck*, using *cool* and *bad* to indicate approval, *rad* for excellence, and *dis* for critical remarks.

Figurative expressions: Break a leg, hanging by a thread, went up in smoke, bent out of shape, fly off the handle, right on the money, hold the fort, hit the nail on the head, down the tubes, worn to a frazzle, hard road to travel, sharp as a tack, dead ringer, brainstorm.

Sports analogies: Batting a thousand, struck out, made it to first base, out of the ball park, drop back and punt, touch base, on target, right on line, up to par, kick off, shot down, springboard, caught off guard.

To ensure understanding, substitute dictionary terms:

Your analysis was *right on the money* [or *right on target*] (accurate).

Can you *pinch hit* (substitute) for the rep assigned to the Cox account?

The proposal *went over like a lead balloon* (was not well received).

I *blew it* (failed).

He was caught *redhanded* (committing the act).

The speaker was *dying on the vine* (doing a very poor job).

That doesn't *ring a bell* (I can't remember).

His actions were *out of line* (inappropriate).

Go for it (you have approval to . . .).

Mastering a large vocabulary in a second language is a daunting task, and Simplified English was developed to aid in communicating with diverse audiences. A joint project of the Association Europeene des Constructeurs deMateriel Aerospatial and the Aerospace Industries Association, the language has a core vocabulary of 1,500 words and a set of approximately 40 rules of style and grammar. With few exceptions, each word has only one meaning and can be used as only one part of speech. Necessary technical words can be added to the core vocabulary. Although developed initially for use in preparing documents for aircraft maintenance, Simplified English has generated

wide interest because of its potential for adaptation to other communication situations.[19]

Application

1. Visit the following web site for detailed information about the rules and vocabulary of Simple English: **http://www.userlab. com/SE.html**

2. Using Simple English, translate the following excerpt from a presentation on the use of digital images in a PowerPoint slideshow:

> Two methods will allow you to convert images into digital files that can be imported into a presentation: Use a graphics scanner to scan photographs taken with a regular camera or a digital camera to capture the photograph directly onto disk without developing the film. Using a digital camera saves time and money and eliminates the use of chemicals that are not environmentally friendly.

Submit your translation to your instructor, along with a short summary of your effort. Is your translation longer or shorter than the original? What is the reading level of the original? Of the revision? Did you encounter any problems?

talent while capitalizing on each person's unique presentation skills. E-mail, collaborative software, and other technologies make it easy to develop, edit, review, and deliver team presentations.

The potential payoff of many team presentations is quite high—perhaps a $200,000 contract or a million-dollar account. Yet, according to experts, team presentations fail primarily because presenters don't devote enough time and resources to develop and rehearse them.[20] Resist the sure-to-fail strategies of many presenters who decide to "wing it" or "blow off" team presentations. Instead, adapt the skills you already possess in planning and delivering an individual presentation to assure a successful team presentation. Follow these guidelines:

- *Select a winning team.* Begin by choosing a leader who is well liked and respected by the team, is knowledgeable of the project, is well organized, and will follow through. Likewise, the leader should be committed to leading the team in the development of a cohesive strategy for the presentation as well as the delegation of specific responsibilities to individual members. Frank Carillo, president of Executive Communications Group, warns team presenters that the problem with "divvying up" work into pieces is that the "pieces don't fit together well when they come back."[21]

    The core team members, along with management, should choose a balanced mix of members to complete the team. Use these questions to guide team selection: What are this member's complementary strengths and style; e.g., technical expertise, personality traits, and presentation skills? Can this member meet the expectations of the audience (e.g., a numbers person, technical person, person with existing relationship with the audience)? Is this member willing to support the team strategy and commit to the schedule?[22]

- *Agree on the purpose and schedule.* The team as a whole should plan the presentation using the same process used for an individual presentation. Agreeing on the purpose to be achieved and selecting content that focuses on a specific audience will prevent the panic and stress caused by an individual's submitting material that does not support the presentation. The quality of the presentation deteriorates when material must be hastily redone in the final days before the deadline or when unacceptable material is included because the presenter worked so hard on it. Mapping out a complete presentation strategy can also minimize bickering among team members because of uneven workloads or unfavorable work assignments.

    The team will also need to agree on a standard design for presentation visuals to ensure consistency in the visuals prepared by individual presenters. Assign a person to merge the various files, to edit for consistency in design elements and the use of jargon and specialized terminology, and to proofread carefully for grammatical accuracy.

    Developing a rehearsal schedule assures adequate time for preparation and practice. Many experts recommend five practice sessions to produce team presentations that are delivered with a unified look.

Planning time in the schedule to present before a review team is especially useful for obtaining feedback on team continuity and adjustments needed to balance major discrepancies in the delivery styles of individual presenters.

- *Plan seamless transitions between segments and presenters.* A great deal of your rehearsal time for a team presentation should be spent planning and rehearsing appropriate verbal and physical transitions between team members. The transitions summarize each part of the presentation and make the whole presentation cohesive. This continuity makes your team look polished and conveys the tone that each member really cares about the team. Follow these suggestions for ensuring seamless presentations:
  - *Decide who will open and conclude the presentation.* The team member who knows the audience and has established rapport is a logical choice for these two critical sections of a presentation. If no one knows the audience, select the member with the strongest presentation skills and personality traits for connecting well with strangers. This person will introduce all team members and give a brief description of the roles they will play in the presentation.

Critical Thinking

What behaviors demonstrate to the
audience that the presenters are
functioning as an effective team?

  - *Build natural bridges between segments of the presentation and presenters.* A lead presenter must build a bridge from the points that have been made that will launch the following presenter smoothly into what he or she will discuss. If a lead presenter forgets to make the connection to the next section clear, the next person must summarize what's been said and then preview his or her section. These transitions may seem repetitive to a team that has been working with the material for a long time; however, audiences require clear guideposts through longer team presentations. Also, courtesies such as maintaining eye contact, thanking the previous speaker, and clearing the presentation area for the next speaker communicates an important message that the presenters are in sync—they know each other and work well together.[23]
- *Deliver as a team.* You must present a unified look and communicate to the audience that you care about the team. Spend your time on the "sideline" paying close attention to team members as they are presenting and monitoring the audience for subtle hints of how the presentation is going. Be on guard to assist the presenter wherever needed—the presenter has not noticed that a wrong presentation visual is displayed, but the audience has; equipment malfunctions; and so on. To keep an audience engaged in a team presentation, Carillo, president of Executive Communications Group, recommends that team members not presenting should focus on the presenter at least two thirds of the time. "It may be the 27th time you've heard it, but for that audience it's the first time. Keep it fresh for the listeners."[24]
- *Field questions as a team.* Decide in advance who will field questions to avoid awkward stares and silence that erode the audience's confidence in your team. Normally, the person presenting a section is

Travel restrictions caused by terrorism and severe acute respiratory syndrome (SARS) have intensified the search for communication alternatives. Successful remote communication requires more than the right technology; the key is training people to communicate confidently and naturally with a non-face-to-face audience and establishing etiquette policies that alleviate negative experiences associated with video-conferencing.

the logical person to field questions about that section. You may refer questions to team members who are more knowledgeable, but avoid pleading looks for that person to rescue you. Rather, check visually to see if the person wants to respond and ask if he or she would like to add information. Tactfully contradict other presenters *only* when the presenter makes a mistake that will cause major problems later. While you should be ready to help presenters having difficulty, resist the urge to tack on your response to a presenter's answer when the question has already been answered adequately.

Distance Presentations

Changing Technology

Videoconferencing has been used for some time for large, high-exposure activities, such as quarterly executive staff presentations, company-wide addresses, new product launches, and crisis management. The technology's decreased cost, improved quality, and increased ease of use have opened videoconferencing to myriads of settings. In fact, any business that has people scattered at multiple sites or that interacts with vendors or clients—and that's everybody—may find videoconferencing worthwhile.

Substantial cost savings from reduced travel has been a compelling reason for companies to use videoconferencing. Additionally, terrorism and the threat of contagious disease have provided more reasons for companies to restrict business travel and look for alternative delivery methods. Videoconferencing also leads to important communication benefits that result from[25]

- improving employee productivity by calling impromptu videoconferences to clear up issues.

- involving more people in key decisions rather than limiting important discussions to those who are allowed to travel.
- involving the expertise critical to the mission, regardless of geographic boundaries.
- creating a consistent corporate culture rather than depending on memos to describe company policy.
- improving employees' quality of life by reducing travel time that often cuts into personal time (e.g., Saturday night layovers for a reasonable airfare).

Critical Thinking

Why has the Internet been referred to as a virtual presentation auditorium?

Internet conferencing or *webcasting* is the emerging new method of real-time conferencing that allows companies to conduct a presentation in real time over the Internet simultaneously with a conference telephone call. Because it runs on each participant's Internet browser (rather than the user's hard drive), a presentation can reach hundreds of locations at once. While listening to the call, participants can go to a designated web site and view slides or a PowerPoint presentation that is displayed in sync with the speaker's statements being heard on the telephone. Participants key comments and questions in chat boxes or press a keypad system to respond to an audience poll, thus giving valuable feedback without interrupting the speaker.

Major software products being used for live web presentations include Contigo Internet Conferencing System, Netpodium Interactive Broadcasting Suite, and Placeware Conference Center. Microsoft PowerPoint® in conjunction with Microsoft NetMeeting® can also be used for online presentations in real time.

Companies are delivering live web presentations on issues ranging from internal briefings on new developments and organizational and procedural changes to product strategy and training presentations. For example, Ernst & Young, who uses Netpodium to announce organizational changes, has found it to be an effective alternative for memos and e-mails that weren't always remembered or understood. People most affected by an organizational change are able to interact with leaders in the firm who are announcing the change. Also, the seamless, spontaneous approach to obtaining questions from the audience helps management understand what's on the employees' minds and thus focus their presentation to answer those questions. Businesses using the web presentation method report that more questions are typically asked than in other meeting formats, resulting in more effective communication.

Follow these guidelines for adapting your presentation skills to videoconferences and web presentations:

Critical Thinking

What challenges are faced by the audience in a distance presentation?

- *Determine whether a distance delivery method is appropriate for the presentation.* Is the presentation purpose suited to the technology? Can the costs in time, money, and human energy be justified? Are key people willing and able to participate? For example, a videoconference for a formal presentation such as an important speech by the CEO to a number of locations justifies the major expense and brings attention to the importance of the message. Distance delivery formats are inappropriate for presentations that cover highly sensitive or confidential issues, for persuasive or problem-solving meetings where no relationship has been established among the participants, and whenever participants are unfamiliar with and perhaps unsupportive of the technology.

Critical Thinking

What are some other ways to build rapport with a virtual audience?

- *Establish rapport with the participants prior to the distance presentation.* If possible, meet with or telephone participants beforehand to get to know them and gain insights about their attitudes. This rapport will enhance your ability to interpret subtle nonverbal cues and to cultivate the relationship further through the distance format. E-mailing or faxing participants a short questionnaire or posting presentation slides with a request for questions is an excellent way to establish a connection with participants and to ensure that the presentation is tailored to audience needs. Some enterprising distance presenters engage the participants in e-mail discussions before the presentation and then use this dialogue to develop positive interaction among the participants during the presentation.

- *Become proficient in delivering and participating through distance technology.* Begin by becoming familiar with the equipment and the surroundings. While technical support staff may be available to manage equipment and transmission tasks, your goal is to concentrate on the contribution you are to make and not your intimidation with the delivery method.

  - *Concentrate on projecting positive nonverbal messages.* Keep a natural, friendly expression; relax and smile. Avoid the tendency to stare into the lens of the camera. Instead of this glassy-eyed stare, look naturally at the entire audience as you would in a live presentation. Speak clearly with as much energy as you can. If a lag occurs between the video and audio transmission, adjust your timing to avoid interrupting other speakers. Use gestures to reinforce points, but avoid fast or excessive motion that will appear blurry. Avoid side conversations and coughing and throat clearing that could trigger voice-activated microphones. Pay close attention to other presenters to guard against easy distraction in a distance environment and to capture subtle nonverbal cues. When giving a web presentation, you will need to judge the vocal tone of the person asking a question because you won't see faces.

  - *Adjust camera settings to enhance communication.* Generally, adjust the camera so that all participants can be seen, but zoom in more closely on participants when you wish to clearly observe nonverbal language. Project a wide-angle shot of yourself during rapport-building comments at the presentation's beginning and zoom in to signal the start of the agenda or to emphasize an important point during the presentation. While some systems accommodate a split screen, others allow participants to view either you or your presentation visuals only. You will want to be conscientious in switching the camera between a view of you and your presentation visuals, depending on what is needed at the time.

Critical Thinking

How do television news broadcasts provide relief from the "talking head?"

- ***Develop high-quality graphics appropriate for the particular distance format.*** Even more than in a live presentation, you will need graphics to engage and maintain participants' attention. Graphics are a welcome variation to the "talking head"—you—displayed on the monitor for long periods. Some companies provide assistance from a webmaster or graphics support staff in preparing slide shows specifically for distance presentations. Also, e-conferencing companies will develop and post presentation slides and host live web presentations including managing e-mail messages and audience polling. Regardless of the support you receive, you should understand basic guidelines for preparing effective visuals for videoconferencing and web presentations.

  - ***Videoconferences.*** Readability of text will be a critical issue when displaying visuals during a videoconference because text becomes fuzzy when transmitted through compressed video. Thus, select large, sturdy fonts and choose a color scheme that provides high contrast between the background and the text. Stay with a tested color scheme such as dark blue background, yellow title text, and white bulleted list text to ensure readability. Projecting your visuals ahead of time so you can adjust the color scheme and other design elements (font face and size) is an especially good idea for video presentations.

  - ***Web presentations.*** In addition to considering overall appeal, clarity, and readability, web presentations must be designed for minimal load time and compatibility with various computers. For your first presentation, consider using a web template in your electronic presentations software and experiment with the appropriateness of other designs as you gain experience.

Stand-alone presentations designed specifically for web delivery require unique design strategies to compensate for the absence of a speaker.[26]

- Consider posting text-based explanations in the notes view area or adding vocal narration.
- Develop interactive slide formats that allow viewers to navigate to the most useful information in your presentation. For example, design an agenda slide that includes hyperlinks to the first slide in each section of the presentation.
- Select simple, high-quality graphics that convey ideas effectively.
- Plan animation that focuses audience attention on specific ideas on the slide.
- Consider adding video if bandwidth is not an issue.

Additional information related to developing web content is included in Chapter 5.

Before planning a business presentation and designing effective presentation visuals, study carefully the specific suggestions in the "Check Your Communication" checklist in this chapter. Practice your delivery at least once, and then compare your style with the points listed in the delivery section of the checklist. Make necessary improvements as you continue to polish your presentation skills.

Summary

1. **Plan a business presentation that accomplishes the speaker's goals and meets the audience's needs.** First, determine what you want to accomplish in your presentation. Second, know your audience so you can direct your presentation to the specific needs and interests of the audience. Identify the general characteristics (age, gender, experience, etc.), size, and receptiveness of the audience.

2. **Organize and develop the three parts of an effective presentation.** An effective presentation has an introduction, body, and close. The introduction should capture the audience's attention, involve the audience and the speaker, present the purpose statement, and preview major points. The body is limited to a few major points that are supported and clarified with relevant statistics, anecdotes, quotes from prominent people, appropriate humor, presentation visuals, and so forth. The close should be a memorable idea that supports and strengthens the purpose statement.

3. **Select, design, and use presentation visuals effectively.** Using visual aids reduces the time required to present a concept and increases retention for the audience. Available aids include handouts, models and physical objects, whiteboards, flip charts, overhead transparencies, electronic presentations, videotapes, and audiotapes. Each type provides specific advantages and should be selected carefully. Guidelines for preparing visual aids include limiting the number of visuals, presenting one major idea in a simple design large enough for the audience to read, selecting fonts and color schemes that convey appropriate tone and can be read easily, and proofreading to eliminate all errors. Permissions should be obtained for the use of copyrighted multimedia content. Effective visual aid use includes paraphrasing rather than reading the visual and stepping to one side so the audience can see the visual.

4. **Deliver speeches with increasing confidence.** Business speakers use the impromptu and extemporaneous speech methods more frequently than the memorized or scripted methods. Professional vocal qualities include a medium or low voice pitch, adequate volume, varied tone and rate, and the absence of distracting verbal fillers. Articulate speakers enunciate words precisely and refer to a dictionary to ensure proper pronunciation. Before your presentation, prepare thoroughly, develop any presentation visuals needed to support your presentation, prepare useful notes to aid your delivery, request a lectern to hold notes but not to hide behind, request a proper introduction, dress appropriately, and arrive early to check last-minute details. During the presentation, communicate confidence and enthusiasm for the audience, watch your audience for feedback, answer questions from the audience politely, and stay within your time limit. After the presentation answer questions from the audience and distribute handouts.

5. **Discuss strategies for presenting in alternate delivery situations such as culturally diverse audiences, team, and distance presentations.** When communicating with other cultures, use simple, clear speech. Consider differences in presentation approach, nonverbal communication, and social protocol that may require flexibility and adjustments to your presentation style. To deliver an effective team presentation, select an appropriate leader and team members with complementary strengths and styles. Plan the presentation as a team, and agree on a schedule to ensure a cohesive presentation focused on audience needs. Rehearse thoroughly to assure a coordinated, cohesive, and uniform team presentation. When delivering a distance presentation (videoconference or live web presentation), determine whether a distance delivery method is appropriate for the presentation, attempt to establish rapport with the participants prior to the distance presentation, become proficient in delivering and participating using distance technology, and develop high-quality graphics appropriate for the distance format being used.

Chapter Review

1. How does the purpose of a presentation affect the process of planning a presentation? What two techniques can you use to condense the purpose of a presentation into a brief statement? (Obj. 1)

2. What important facts should a speaker know about the audience when planning a presentation? (Obj. 1)

3. What is the basic three-part structure of an effective presentation? What are the purposes of each part? (Obj. 2)

4. How many major points should a speaker develop? Explain. (Obj. 2)

5. What does a speaker hope to accomplish in the close? What suggestions will help a speaker accomplish this goal? (Obj. 2)

6. How can presentation visuals be used to enhance a presentation? (Obj. 3)

Planning and Organizing a Presentation

- **Identify your purpose.** Be certain you understand exactly what you hope to accomplish so you can choose content that will support your purpose.
- **Analyze your audience.** Identify characteristics common to the audience and the speech setting (number in audience, seating arrangements, time of day).
- **Develop an effective opening.** The opening must capture attention, initiate rapport with the audience, present the purpose, and preview the main points.
- **Develop the body.** Select a few major points and locate support for each point: statistics, anecdotes, quotes, and appropriate humor. Use simple, non-technical language and sentences the listener can understand; avoid excessive statistics and use word pictures when possible; and use jokes or humor appropriately.
- **Develop an effective close.** The close calls for the audience to accept your idea or provides a conclusion with recommendations.

Selecting an Appropriate Presentation Visual

- Select a presentation visual appropriate for the audience and the topic.
- Use whiteboards and flip charts for small audiences in an informal setting and when no special equipment is available. Prepare flip charts in advance.
- Use overhead transparencies for small, informal audiences and when it is desirable to write audience comments that can be displayed.
- Use slides for presentations requiring photography; prepare them from visuals displayed on computer; arrange in a planned sequence and show in a darkened room.
- Use electronic presentations for large audiences and to enliven the topic and engage the audience with text, images, sound, and animation. Last-minute changes to visuals are possible.
- Use video- and audiotapes to illustrate major points in an engaging manner; use as a supplement to the presentation, not a replacement.

- Use models and physical objects to allow the audience to visualize and experience the idea being presented.

Designing and Using Presentation Visuals

- Limit the number of visual aids used in a single presentation to avoid overload.
- Clear all copyrights for multimedia content.
- Write descriptive titles and parallel bulleted lists.
- Create a standard design for each visual following these slide design principles:
  - Include only the major idea the audience is to remember.
  - Make the design concise, simple, and large enough to be read by the entire audience.
  - Choose fonts and a color scheme that convey the formality and tone of the presentation and can be read easily by the audience.
  - Design horizontal (landscape) visuals for electronic presentations and vertical (portrait) visuals for overhead transparencies.
  - Avoid graphics that distort facts.
  - Proofread the visual carefully to eliminate any errors.
- Use the presentation visuals effectively. Paraphrase rather than reading line for line and step to one side of the visual so the audience can see it.

Delivering a Presentation

Before the presentation

- Prepare thoroughly to minimize natural nervousness.
- Prepare easy-to-read note cards or pages to prompt your recall of the next point.
- Practice to identify any organizational flaw or verbal potholes; do not rehearse until your delivery is mechanical.
- Request a lectern to steady your hands but not to hide behind.
- Insist on a proper, impressive introduction.
- Dress appropriately to create a professional image.
- Arrive early to acquaint yourself with the room and check last-minute details.

During the Presentation

- Use clear, articulate speech and proper pronunciation.
- Use vocal variety and adjust volume and rate to emphasize ideas.
- Avoid irritating verbal fillers and other annoying speech habits.
- Maintain steady eye contact with audience members in random places.
- Smile genuinely and use gestures naturally to communicate confidence and warmth.
- Watch your audience for important feedback and adjust your presentation accordingly.
- Handle questions from the audience politely.
- Keep within the time limit.

After the Presentation

- Be prepared for a question-and-answer period.
- Distribute handouts.

Adapting to a Culturally Diverse Audience

- Use simple English and short sentences and avoid abbreviations, slang, jargon, figurative expressions, or "red flag" words.
- Enunciate precisely and speak slowly. Observe the audience carefully for signs of misunderstanding.
- Consider the appropriateness of jokes and humor.
- Use a straightforward, direct approach with the main idea presented first.
- Be aware of differences in nonverbal communication, preference for formality, gift-giving practices, and social protocol that may require flexibility and adjustments of presentation style.

Delivering a Team Presentation

- Select a leader who will lead the team in developing a cohesive presentation strategy and team members with complementary strengths and styles.
- Plan the presentation as a team and agree on a schedule to ensure a cohesive presentation focused on audience needs.
- Rehearse thoroughly until a team presentation is cohesive and uniform (e.g., plan seamless transitions between segments and presenters, support team presenters, and field questions).

Delivering a Distance Presentation

- Determine whether a distance delivery method (e.g., videoconference or web presentation) is appropriate for the presentation.
- Attempt to establish rapport with the participants prior to the distance presentation.
- Become proficient in delivering and participating using distance technology.
- Develop high-quality graphics appropriate for the distance format being used.

//electronic café //

Communicating Through Secure Electronic Documents

What happened to the concept of the paperless office? Firms have been interested in the idea of a paperless work environment since personal computers were introduced. Eliminating the space needed to store documents, reduced time spent handling and looking for information, and making better use of documents are all promising outcomes. However, studies show that offices continue to increase their paper output each year. Securely storing documents, conveniently locating information, and reliably retrieving desired information are ongoing challenges of paperless information management.

 InfoTrac College Edition. Access http://www. infotrac.thomsonlearning.com to read about how a large United Kingdom tour operation has streamlined its statement distribution process through online delivery:

AXS-One is First Choice for online statement delivery; First Choice Holidays Pic makes moves towards the paperless office with Web access system designed to replace 180,000 paper statements a year. (2003, January 29). M2 *Presswire*.

Research other software that competes with AXS-One's products for automating statement delivery. Write a brief analysis of how such products provide efficiency of time and resources.

 Text Support Web Site. Visit http://lehman. swlearning.com to locate and read an article that offers suggestions to firms that want to move toward a paperless environment.

 WebTutor Advantage. Your project team can exchange files and information securely through WebTutor. As instructed by your instructor, share information related to your assignment with other members of your team.

 Professional Power Pak. Access your PPP CD to learn more about how to keep your electronic information organized and accessible.

---

7. Discuss general guidelines for preparing an effective presentation visual. (Obj. 3)

8. Briefly explain the provisions of the Copyright Law of 1976 as it applies to multimedia content (graphics, sound, and video). What steps can presenters take to ensure they are complying with copyright law? (Obj. 3)

9. Provide suggestions for preparing professional audience handouts and useful notes pages. (Obj. 3)

10. Which delivery methods are used most often by business speakers? What are the advantages and limitations of each? (Obj. 4)

11. How can a speaker communicate to the audience that he/she is enthusiastic about the topic and committed to helping the audience benefit from the presentation? (Obj. 4)

12. What ethical responsibility does a speaker have when planning and delivering a presentation? (Objs. 1, 4)

13. What can a speaker do to ensure that a presentation is understood and not offensive to audience members of various cultures? (Obj. 5)

14. What strategies are recommended for delivering an effective team presentation? (Obj. 5)

15. What unique presentations skills are needed to adapt to videoconferencing and live web presentations? (Obj. 5)

Digging Deeper

1. What is the single, most important piece of advice you would give for making an effective business presentation?

2. With current advancements in technology, how has the business presenter's role been simplified? How has it become more difficult?

To check your understanding of the chapter, take the practice quizzes at **http://lehman.swlearning.com** or your WebTutor course.

Activities

1. **Preparing a Top Ten List for Effective Business Presentations (Objs. 1–5)**

   Generate a list of the top ten mistakes speakers make based on your experience as a speaker and listener. In small groups assigned by your instructor, discuss the points listed by each student and compile your ideas into a comprehensive top ten list that reflects the consensus of the group. Next, discuss strategies team members have used to avoid each of the mistakes you've listed. Be prepared to share your valuable advice with the class in an informal presentation.

2. **Focusing on an Effective Introduction and Close (Objs. 1, 2)**

   In a small group, develop a captivating introduction and memorable close for the COPE presentation discussed in this chapter or for a topic your instructor provides. Be prepared to discuss the techniques you used in the introduction to capture the audience's attention, to involve yourself with the audience, to present your purpose, and to preview the major points and the unity and closure achieved through the close.

3. **Presenting an Impromptu Presentation for Self-Critique (Objs. 1, 2, 4)**

   In groups of four assigned by your instructor, select four topics from the following list or questions provided by your instructor. A group leader may randomly assign a topic to each member or allow the members to select a topic. Following a brief preparation time, each member will give a one- to two-minute presentation to the group. After all presentations are given, the group will briefly discuss the strengths and weaknesses of each presentation and strive to provide each member with a few specific suggestions for improvement.

   a. Choose one of the following thought-provoking questions from *The Conversation Piece* by Nicholaus and Lowrie:[27]

      - What is one of the simple pleasures of life you truly enjoy?
      - What is something you forgot once that you will never forget again?
      - What thought or sentiment would you like to put in one million fortune cookies?
      - Almost everyone has something that he/she considers a sure thing. What is your "ace in the hole"?
      - Most people have a story or experience they love to share. What's your story?

   b. Why are communication skills a key ingredient in your career (specify a career)?

   c. What is the most critical component of a business presentation: content, visual support, or delivery?

   d. Why are effective intercultural communication skills important in an increasingly competitive global economy?

   e. How has downsizing affected the need for communication skills?

   f. Why is being a team player an important element of success in today's economy?

   g. What actions reflect the values of a team player who is focused on helping an organization succeed?

   h. How has rapidly changing technology revolutionized communication in business organizations?

   i. What would business be like if legality were a company's only ethical benchmark or criterion?

   j. Are business organizations less (or more) ethical today than they were a decade ago?

4. **Critiquing Presentation Visuals (Obj. 3)**

   Evaluate the effectiveness of each of the following slides. Identify the design guidelines that have been violated and offer suggestions for improvement. Classify your changes in these areas: (a) slide content, (b) choice of template and graphics, (c) space usage and layout, (d) typography and color choices. Be prepared to present your analysis to the class. Your instructor may ask you to download these slides from the web text site and revise them incorporating your suggestions.

   A downloadable version of this text is available at **http://lehman.swlearning.com**.

   a. Suggest enhancements to the bulleted list layout of each slide. Revise the title and the bulleted items to reflect the content in a descriptive, engaging manner. Select an appropriate template.

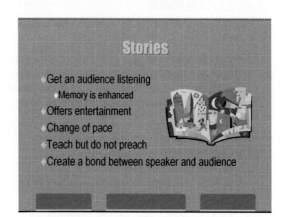

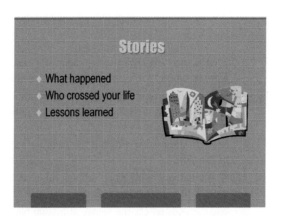

b. Suggest drawing tools and/or graphics to design three creative links to other slides that expand on each topic presented in the following slide. Revise the title and the bulleted items to reflect the content in a descriptive, engaging manner. Select an appropriate template.

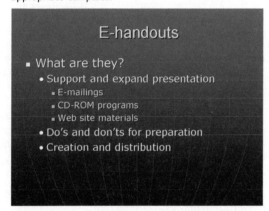

c. Redesign this mundane list of interview mistakes to create an appealing conceptual slide such as the one illustrated in the good example of Figure 12-3. Use powerful visual communication techniques and minimal text to create the appealing image of an interviewee committing these interview mistakes made during actual interviews. If you wish, substitute other interview mistakes based on your own experience or your own research of an online database or popular career web sites. (Creative teaser: Build on the analogy of interview mistakes and the "uncut" portions of a movie.)

Mistakes Made During Actual Interviews

- Graduated Moran University, 2002
- I was the first runner-up for Miss Fort Worth, 2002
- Objective: Employee
- Responsibilities included checking customers out

Applications

Read	Think	Write	Speak	Collaborate

1. Real-World Case: Analyzing an Executive Speech (Objs. 1–4)

Effective public speaking is especially important in today's fast-changing business environment. Locate the following article that is available from **http://www. infotrac. thomsonlearning.com** or possibly from your campus library:

Wilson, A. B. (1996, June/July). Ache for the impact: Four steps to powerful oratory. *Executive Speeches*, 6–7.

Answer the following questions:

- Describe the audience and the purpose the speaker intended to accomplish with this audience.
- What techniques were used to ensure an effective introduction, body, and close?
- Discuss three techniques you believe set this presentation apart from a typical presentation. Justify your choices.
- Discuss the elements of a presentation template that would fit the speaker's audience and topic. If your instructor directs, create one slide to illustrate a point made in the speech using your presentation template idea. Be prepared to present it to the class.

2. Selecting Appropriate Presentation Visuals (Obj. 3)

A speaker must select the appropriate medium or combination of media to accomplish the speech's purpose and to meet the needs of a specific audience. Visit the text support site at **http://lehman.swlearning.com** to learn about the most common types of presentation visuals and the design guidelines for presentation visuals.

Required: Develop a standard slide layout for a slide that (a) displays the advantages and disadvantages of each type of presentation visual and a slide that (b) provides tips for using each type of presentation visual effectively. For easier comparison, collapse the information into four categories: (a) electronic presentations, (b) boards and flipcharts, (c) still projection objects (overheads), and (d) hard copy visuals (handouts). Be prepared to present in a presentation to the class.

3. **Creating On-Demand Presentations: Delivering Crucial Information to Vast Numbers (Objs. 3, 5)**

Presentations incorporating video focus attention, convey information, increase retention and compel action *better* than static web pages or PowerPoint slides. Now, easy-to-use software allows users with no video training to produce professional presentations at a reasonable cost. The corporate communication applications for this rich communication medium are endless with powerful messages being delivered on-demand via a web site, e-mail, PowerPoint

show, or DVD or CD. Visit **http://www.seriousmagic.com** to view a demo of Visual Communicator (a software program for producing professional video presentations). Read users' success stories and view dramatic video samples from training presentations to video scrapbooks and birthday cards.

Required: Write a memo to your instructor summarizing the benefits of video presentations in enhancing business communications.

4. **Adapting Presentations for International Audiences (Obj. 5)**

Locate the following article that offers suggestions for developing business presentations for an international audience:

Agry, B. W. (2001, September). Presenting to an international audience. *Selling*, 8.

Required: Prepare a grid that compares the cultural groups mentioned in regard to differences in presentation preferences; research further as necessary to complete your informational comparison.

| Read | Think | Write | Speak | Collaborate |

5. **Evaluating a Speaker (Objs. 1–5)**

Evaluate the speaking skill of a well-known television newscaster, political figure, commentator, or a recognized speaker on your campus. What are the strengths? weaknesses? Use the "Check Your Communication" (positioned before the chapter summary) to direct your attention to the various components of effective speaking. Offer suggestions for improving the person's spoken communication skills. Pay special attention to vocal qualities, audience eye contact, audience rapport, and organization.

6. **Developing Vocal Power (Objs. 1–4)**

For this activity, you are to prepare a recording of your voice for analysis. For the recording, select an article from a newspaper or magazine or locate an actual speech using an online database and searching specifically for a speech (e.g., *Executive Speeches, Vital Speeches of the Day*). Listen to your recording and seek constructive feedback from friends or classmates, especially those from other regions or cultures who can help you identify speech problems affecting understandability and impression.

Required: Write a memo to your instructor that includes an honest critique of your voice and a description of the modifications you believe are needed to develop a voice that projects your professional image and truly means business. Use the following questions as a guide for your analysis.

- What words describe your overall perception of your voice?

- Do you use clear, articulate speech, and proper pronunciation that is easily understood and conveys a positive impression? List specific problem areas such as dropping word endings, adding, omitting, or substituting sounds, placing the accent on the incorrect syllable, or using incorrect pronunciation.

- Do you use vocal variety and adjust volume and rate to emphasize ideas, create meaning, and add energy and dynamics to your presentation? Do you speak loudly enough for everyone in the room to hear you easily?

- Do you include irritating fillers and other annoying speech habits?

- Is your regional dialect an asset or a liability to your career advancement? What deviations from General American Standard Speech Pattern can you detect?

7. **Critiquing Your Speaking Ability (Objs. 1–2, 4)**

Videotape your delivery of a presentation on one of the topics listed in Activity 3 or a topic of your choice. Review the videotape and complete the following activities. Be prepared to discuss with your instructor and to incorporate changes in your preparation for your next presentation.

- What was your overall impression of your performance after you completed the presentation?

- Use the "Check Your Communication" to direct your attention to the various components of effective speaking, and identify at least three strengths and three weaknesses that you noted as you viewed the videotape.

- Ask two other people in your class to view the videotape and critique your performance; they should provide at least two strengths and two suggestions for improvement.

- Finally, what is your overall impression of your performance after you analyzed the videotape and received feedback from class members? Does this impression differ from your impression before viewing the videotape? Explain.

8. **Critiquing an Electronic Slide Show (Objs. 1–5)**

   Download the following electronic presentation from the web site: *team presentation*. Assume this presentation will be given in an orientation seminar for new hires for the purpose of preparing them to deliver team presentations effectively. Critique the content and design of this presentation using the "Check Your Communication" checklist at the end of this chapter. Revise the slide show incorporating your changes. Be prepared to show your revised slide show to the class with justification for the changes you made. Viewing the sample presentation posted at the web site before you begin your critique would be beneficial. The file name is *team presentation*.

   A downloadable version of this file is available at **http://lehman.swlearning.com**.

Read   Think   Write   Speak   Collaborate

9. **Embracing a Presenter's Code of Conduct (Objs. 1–5)**

   Locate and read the following professional codes of ethics for professional communicators and a related article available from **http://www.infotrac.thomsonlearning.com** or possibly from your campus library:

   National Speakers Association: **http://www.nsaspeaker.org/about/code_of_ethics.shtml**

   International Association of Business Communicators (IABC): **http://www.iabc.com/members/joining/code.htm**

   Zielinski, D. (2002, August). The presenters pledge: Do presenter's need a code of conduct? *Presentations, 16*(8), 24+.

   Required: Consider the ethical challenges presenters face and the behavioral guideposts presented in these readings. Write your own presenter's pledge to ensure honesty and integrity in your professional presentations. Be prepared to explain to the class your rationale for the actions included.

10. **Supporting Major Points (Obj. 2)**

    Online databases and the Internet provide instant access to numerous sources of timely information to support your points. Access a database available to you and key in a subject of your choice (perhaps an issue that currently is receiving media coverage). Visit one of the following Internet sites or locate similar sites to locate a relevant quotation or anecdote to support your topic. Share with the class at least two possible sources including a quotation or anecdote to support your topic.

    http://www.cyber-nation.com/victory/quotations/authors/quotes_hammarskjold_dag.html

    http://www.quotationspage.com/

    http://quotes.s5.com/

11. **Organizing and Researching a Presentation Topic (Objs. 1–5)**

    Visit one of the following Internet sites that provide guidelines for organizing and delivering business presentations and using technology in presentations. Using these resources, develop an outline for a short (two- to three-minute) presentation on an aspect of presentation skill development. Send your instructor an e-mail message containing (a) the purpose statement, (b) audience analysis, (c) the outline, and (d) a list of the sources you intend to use. The outline should indicate the introduction, major points (body), and the summary. If required by your instructor, prepare two to three presentation visuals and deliver the presentation to the class or post the presentation to the course web site for other students to view. Bookmark these sites for your own professional development.

    http://www.presentations.com

    http://www.powerpointers.com

    http://www.presentersonline.com

12. **Critiquing a Slide Show Prepared to Support a Written Report (Objs. 1-3)**

    Visit the text support site at **http://lehman.swlearning.com** to explore the process of creating dynamic electronic presentations. Download the electronic presentation file, *business professional dress*, from the text web site; this slide show was developed to support a consultant's presentation of her study of the implementation of a professional business policy at MetroBank. Compare the slide show to the consultant's written report shown in Figure 11-7.

    Required: Write a memo to your instructor (a) analyzing the overall effectiveness of the slides in supporting the consultant's purpose and (b) summarizing the use of key

---

multimedia elements (e.g., template, clip art, photos, animation, and sound).

A downloadable version is available at **http://lehman. swlearning.com**.

13. **Preparing an Extemporaneous In-House Presentation (Objs. 1–4)**

Your instructor has provided specific instructions for presenting a proposal to management. Select a topic from the following list of suggested topics or use them as a springboard for other in-house presentations. Obtain your instructor's approval for your topic before beginning work.

a. Proposal for implementing a relaxed dress policy.

b. Proposal for opening an on-site childcare center or long-term care plan for parents of employees (or another employee benefit of your choice).

c. Proposal to a local business to increase sales to college students.

d. Proposal to the Board of Directors to forge a strategic alliance with another company. Choose two likely companies and present the concept and the benefits that could be derived for each company.

e. Proposal to management for creating a joint venture with another company to offer a business to business (B2B) exchange for online commerce and supply chain services. Choose two feasible companies that could take advantage of the benefits of supply chain management (e.g., HomebuildersXchange links suppliers, distributors, and trade contractors and builders to bring efficiencies to every participant in the construction process).

f. Proposal to extend your company's domestic retail market into an international market of your choice.

14. **Preparing an Extemporaneous Presentation on a Chosen Topic (Objs. 1, 2, 4)**

Your instructor has provided specific instructions for preparing a presentation of approximately five-to-ten minutes. Select a topic from the following list of suggested topics or use them as a springboard for other appropriate topics that will provide timely, relevant information to your class. Obtain your instructor's approval for your topic before beginning work.

a. What adjustments would be required for a presentation given to an audience from (supply a culture)? as a team presentation? as a videoconference? as a seated presentation? (choose one)

b. How can presentation slides weaken a presentation? What strategies can ensure the effective use of presentation support?

c. What effect has increased exposure to profanity in current society had on the workplace and professional settings? What are the legal implications of using unacceptable language in the workplace? What steps are companies taking to deal with this issue?

d. What are the major differences in the management styles of men and women?

e. What are major differences in the speaking styles of men and women? How do these differences affect speaking effectiveness?

f. What challenges has the aging population presented in the workplace? What can companies do to face these challenges?

g. What are common examples of computer abuse in today's companies and what can be done to combat it?

h. What are common uses of videoconferencing and live web presentations in today's companies? What benefits are being realized through the use of this technology?

i. How has the electronic revolution changed the way a person seeks a job?

j. What effect has technology had on presenters' and trainers' compliance with copyright law? What challenges must be addressed if the copyright law is to work in an electronic environment?

k. Discuss several business applications for multimedia. What benefits do they provide?

l. Does an employer have the right to read an employee's e-mail (or conduct other forms of electronic surveillance)? What laws govern this issue?

m. How can business professionals manage their time (or stress) more effectively?

n. What benefits are realized by working cooperatively in diverse work groups?

o. What are characteristics of effective and noneffective team members (choose one)?

p. What can corporate leaders do to increase employees' sensitivity toward diversity (cultures, genders, ages of coworkers, and potential markets)?

q. How can the use of a company intranet enhance a company's productivity?

r. Explain the use of the Internet, an intranet, and an extranet to improve a company's effectiveness.

s. Discuss a timely issue related to communication effectiveness in your field (may have been addressed recently in a business-related magazine or practitioner journal).

15. Developing a Presentation Plan (Objs. 1–5)

The foundation of an effective presentation is selecting an appropriate topic, one that is narrow in scope, fits the time slot, appeals to the speaker's interests and meets audience needs. Download the Presentation Planning Sheet from the text support site at **http://lehman.swlearning.com.**

a. In preparation for a ten-minute presentation, select a topic from this list or one approved by your instructor:

1. How to cope with an ethical dilemma in your profession

2. Internet-based learning

3. Lessons learned from corporate scandals

4. Salary inequities of average workers versus high-level executives

5. Digital music downloads and the law

6. Digital photography morphing and the law

7. Communication and the generation gap

8. Identity theft

9. Employment skills needed for the twenty-first century

10. Communication and career success

b. Complete the "Topic and Purpose" section of the Presentation Planning Sheet as you develop a purpose statement and preview statement (points to be covered in the presentation). In groups of two or three, critique each member's topic and preview statements; revise your own work, and submit the original and revised statements to your instructor. Be prepared to discuss your improvements in an informal presentation to the class.

16. Preparing a Team Presentation (Objs. 1–5)

Select one of the topics in Application 15 and develop it into a team presentation for delivery to the class. To ensure the quality and efficiency of the presentation, first outline a detailed action plan for the preparation and delivery of the team presentation following the guidelines for team presentations in your textbook. Complete the remaining sections of the Presentation Planning Sheet making your own assumptions about the audience and logistics or following those assigned by your instructor. To support your ideas, use at least two periodicals, a newspaper, a book, an electronic source, and a government publication. List the sources in a references page formatted in APA Style; use Appendix B as a format guide. Following the team presentation, prepare a debriefing memo to your instructor outlining the strengths of the team's work and planned improvements for future presentations.

17. Preparing an Oral Briefing (Objs. 1, 2, 4)

In small groups assigned by your instructor, give a one-to three-minute oral briefing regarding progress completed on an assigned team project. Alternately, each member may present a one- to two-minute presentation explaining a key concept or new development in his or her career field. A *brief* preparation time will be provided; however, the purpose of the activity is to prepare for impromptu spoken presentations. After all presentations are given, the group will briefly discuss the strengths and weaknesses of each presentation and provide each member with a few specific suggestions for improvement in delivering an impromptu presentation.

18. Preparing an Extemporaneous Report to Stockholders (Objs. 1–4)

As a part of a team of four, present a mock annual shareholders' meeting before the class. You should work from an annual report of a major company. One person should be the chief executive officer, one the chief operating officer, one the financial officer, and one the chief marketing officer. Each will speak for two to three minutes. The CEO should preside and introduce members appropriately before each speaks. Your report should include a review of the year's activities, plans for the next year, and information about the firm's role in the community. Design effective visuals and use them effectively in your presentation.

Sun Microsystems: Presenting to a Virtual Audience

Why limit a presentation to the number of people that can fit in a conference room? Companies can now expand their training program or sales pitch appeal to thousands or even millions. By distributing your presentation via the Web, you can extend it to a widely scattered audience.

- Visit the Java site at **http://java.sun.com**. Read about applets and how they are being used to enhance visual communication on the Web.
- Locate and read the following article:

Mucciolo, T. (2003, April). Meet me on the Web: Expert do's and don'ts for presenting via the Internet. *Presentations*, *17*(4), 42–45.

Prepare a short report that presents guidelines for effective web-delivered presentations.

http://www.java.sun.com

Visit the text support site at **http://lehman.swlearning.com** to complete Part 4 of the Sun Microsystems ShowCASE.

Internet Case

Now About that Accent . . .

Most individuals "pick up" the accent spoken in the region in which they live, and those who learn English as a second language typically retain some elements of pronunciation that are indicative of their first language. When you leave your native area, your accent may be a subject of interest, humor, or even ridicule.

Studies have indicated that salespersons with a standard accent or dialect are often perceived more favorably by customers than foreign-accented salespersons.[28] The U.S. media promotes the acceptance of "general American standard dialect," and the seeming lack of accent among public broadcasters is often the result of extensive retraining in vocal delivery. Corporations often also desire to enhance universal acceptance by cultivating "standard English" among their management. Corporate accent-reduction speech clients have included executives from Beech Aircraft, Mitsubishi Bank, NCR Corporation, Union Carbide, and Wells Fargo Bank.[29]

Not everyone, however, feels that accents are detrimental. A countering opinion is that an accent may at times serve as an asset to the speaker. It reflects personhood and adds dimension and interest to the individual. Furthermore,

the "best English" is often dictated by audience expectation and the circumstances in which a speaker functions. Regardless of the charm value of an accent, your audience must be able to understand you. The following guidelines are suggested when the speaker's dialect is different from that of the audience:

- Speak more slowly and distinctly than usual during the opening minutes of your presentations, to allow the audience to adjust to your speech patterns and style.
- Don't apologize for your accent. The audience will likely not find it offensive once they can understand your speech patterns.
- To avoid emphasizing the wrong syllables, ask someone fluent in the dialect of the audience to pronounce unfamiliar words, names, etc. Devise a kind of shorthand for marking the pronunciation and accented syllables in your notes.
- Try not to let your concern over dialect interfere with your interaction with the audience. Be enthusiastic and let your personality show through.

Visit the text support site at **http://lehman.swlearning.com** to link to web resources related to this topic. As directed by your instructor, complete one or more of the following:

1. Locate at least one additional web site on the subject of accents that you found interesting. What is the URL of the site? Summarize the important aspects of the information in outline form.

2. Analyze your own accent, responding to the following questions: Of what region is it typical? What distinguishes your accent from others? Is your accent stronger at certain times? If so, why? E-mail your instructor with your self-analysis.

3. How are accent and dialect different yet related? Prepare a chart that illustrates the relationship.

4. **GMAT** What are the advantages and disadvantages of a regional accent? How can accent work either to enhance or worsen a businessperson's communication? Write a one- to two-page summary of your position on the issue.

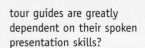

MeetingsAmerica: Public Speaking Confidence

Utah Business Magazine in 2002 chose MeetingsAmerica as the best Destination Management Company in Salt Lake City, Utah. MeetingsAmerica serves the needs of (a) inbound clients who hold conventions, meetings, or retreats in the Salt Lake City/Intermountain area, (b) local clients who hold conventions in other areas of the world, and (c) national clients who convene in cities around the world.

When it comes to event planning, MeetingsAmerica has arranged everything from quiet dinner receptions to near-Broadway-style productions. Descriptions of some events MeetingsAmerica has planned, such as Cirque D'Berserque and Night in Casablanca are available at **http://meetingsamerica.net/events.php**.

In addition to event planning, MeetingsAmerica offers tours of their Olympic City, Utah's five National Parks, and the Intermountain West. Samples of their popular tours can be seen at **http://meetingsamerica.net/tours.php**.

View the video segment about MeetingsAmerica and related activities on WebTutor or your Professional Power Pak CD.

Discussion Questions

1. Which characteristics identified by Kathleen Barnes as essential for her tour guides reinforce the fact that tour guides are greatly dependent on their spoken presentation skills?

2. Based on your experience listening to public speakers, give an example of what Kathleen referred to as her tour guides' presenting information "via their personality."

3. Many individuals fear public speaking. What connection do you see between the MeetingsAmerica tour guides' obvious lack of fear of public speaking with their enjoyment in "creating a memory for their customers"?

Activities

Locate the following articles available in full text from InfoTrac College or perhaps from another database available through your campus library:

Stage fright: Conquer your public speaking phobia. (2003, March 18). *Info-Tech Advisor Newsletter*. Retrieved June 16, 2003, from InfoTrac College database.

Eppley, M. (2003, March). Now that's scary: Conquer your fear of the speaker's podium. *Successful Meetings, 52*(3), 28.

Write a brief summary of the content of these articles that provide helpful insights on overcoming fear of public speaking. Include information about steps to be taken before, during, and after the presentation. Title your summary "Overcoming Fear of Public Speaking."

Communication for Employment

V

13 Preparing Résumés and Application Letters

COURTESY THE CONTAINER STORE

Objectives *When you have completed Chapter 13, you will be able to:*

1 Prepare for employment by considering relevant information about yourself as it relates to job requirements.

2 Identify career opportunities using traditional and electronic methods.

3 Prepare a persuasive résumé that reflects the most effective organizational pattern.

4 Adapt the résumé for alternate presentation and delivery options, including print (designed) formats, scannable versions, and electronic postings.

5 Utilize employment tools other than the résumé that can enhance employability.

6 Write an application message that effectively introduces an accompanying print (designed) or electronic résumé.

THE CONTAINER STORE: HIRING WELL RESULTS IN STABLE EMPLOYEE BASE

One great person is equal to three good people. That's a Foundation Principle and employment philosophy at The Container Store. The Dallas-based firm that specializes in storage and organization products for the home employs over 1,700 people in its 28 retail stores as well as in its large catalog and web site operations. Annual sales of $300 million suggest that the company is doing some things well.[1]

In addition to its continued financial success and steady expansion, The Container Store has consistently been named as number one or two in *Fortune* magazine's "100 Best Companies to Work for in America" list. The company believes that the first step in forging a great workforce is to hire only employees willing and able to use their creativity, enthusiasm, and intuition to devote themselves to customer service. All employees assist in the recruitment process and carry gold job interview invitations to give to friends, relatives, and even store customers who they feel would be great additions to the company. Once a great employee is found, ample training is a vital factor in turning that worker into someone who can reach his or her potential. The Container Store invests 241 hours of formal training in every first-year employee, while the retail industry average is a measly 7 hours. And high-quality employees are paid high-quality salaries, with The Container Store paying their workers 50 to 100 percent more than the retail average.[2]

Extensive training and enviable salaries are not the only ways that The Container Store empowers its people. Another Foundation Principle is to openly and fully communicate what is going on at the company with everyone who works there. Instead of tightly guarding financial information, The Container Store opens its ledger to all employees. The outcome is an annual turnover rate that is a fraction of the industry average, with the company losing just 8 percent of its full-time salespeople to voluntary turnover. In his book *Discovering the Soul of Service*, Texas A & M Professor Leonard Berry explains the reasons for The Container Store's success: "One of their keys to success is that they hire very well. It's such a generous place, such a high-trust place, that employees love it. They hire people with the same values as the leaders."[3]

The successful job search process involves matching the needs and values of the individual with those of the organization. A careful match results in a long-lasting, satisfying relationship that is mutually beneficial. This chapter presents the employment process you will need to follow to land your "ideal" job. From the careful self-analysis and identification of prospective employers to the preparation of a powerful résumé and application message, each step in the employment process is important to obtaining the right position with the right organization.

---

http://www.containerstore.com

See ShowCASE, Part 2, on page 578 for Spotlight Communicator KipTindell, president, CEO, and co-founder of The Container Store.

Preparing for the Job Search

Objective 1

Prepare for employment by considering relevant information about yourself as it relates to job requirements.

Managing your career begins with recognizing that securing a new job is less important than assessing the impact of that job on your life. Work isn't something that happens from 8 to 5, five days a week, with life happening after 5 p.m. Life and work are interconnected, and true satisfaction comes from being able to fully express yourself in what you do. This means merging who you are—your values, emotions, capabilities, and desires—with the activities you perform on the job.[4]

An ideal job provides satisfaction at all of Maslow's needs levels, from basic economic to self-actualizing needs. The right job for you will not be drudgery; the work itself will be satisfying. It will give you a sense of well-being, and you will sense its positive impact on others. Synchronizing your work with your core beliefs and talents leads to enthusiasm and fulfillment. If you're like most employees, you will work for 10,000 days of your life, not including time spent commuting and on other peripheral activities. Why spend all this time doing something unfulfilling when you could just as easily spend it doing what you enjoy?

Students often devote too little time and thought to career goals, or they unnecessarily postpone making career decisions. Are you willing to spend the necessary time gathering, recording, and analyzing information that will lead to a satisfying career? Are you ready to start compiling information that will guide you to the best career for you? Finding a job is a process, not an event; it's not too early to start work on that all-important process.

Just as finding the right career is important for you, finding the right employees is important for the employer. Before they can offer you a job, employers need information about you—in writing. Your *résumé* is a vital communication that provides a basis for judgment about your capabilities on the job. In preparing this essential document, your major concerns should be gathering essential information about yourself and the job using traditional and electronic resources, planning and organizing the résumé to showcase your key qualifications, and adapting the résumé for various types of delivery. You may also recognize the need to supplement your résumé with examples of your accomplishments and abilities. Finally, you'll prepare persuasive application message(s) appropriate for the option(s) you've used for delivering your résumé.

Critical Thinking

Have you set your career goals? What is your plan for reaching them?

Gathering Essential Information

The job search begins with research—collecting, compiling, and analyzing information—in order to assess your marketability. The career planning guides available at the text support site (http://lehman.swlearning.com) will help you identify key qualifications as they relate to an employer's needs, ensure that you have selected the right career, and compare your qualifications to the duties and responsibilities of the job you are seeking. The key accomplishments that surface from this thoughtful analysis will be the main ideas touted in a résumé or an interview. The research phase of the job search involves the steps shown in Figure 13-1 and summarized as follows:

1. *Gather relevant information for decision-making.* Complete (a) a self-assessment to identify your own qualifications related to the job, and (b) an analysis of the career field that interests you and a specific job in that field. Follow up with an interview of a career person in your field to provide additional information for your analysis.
2. *Prepare a company/job profile.* Compile the information you gathered into a format that allows you to compare your qualifications with the company and job requirements—to determine whether a match between you and the potential job is possible.
3. *Identify unique selling points and specific support.* Determine several key qualifications and accomplishments that enhance your marketability. These are the key selling points you'll target in your résumé and later in a job interview.

The company/job profile for an entry-level audit accountant in an international public accounting firm shown in Figure 13-2 shows a strong match between the job requirements and the applicant's basic qualifications and expectations for salary and advancement. This in-depth analysis also reveals some incompatibility in the work style and travel/ overtime requirements the applicant desires and weaknesses in several relevant job skills.

Critical Thinking

What reasons account for the fact that most entry-level employees are in the job market again within six months?

Identifying Potential Career Opportunities

Objective 2

Identify career opportunities using traditional and electronic methods.

Plan to begin your job search for prospective employers months beforehand. Waiting too long to begin and then hurrying through the job search process could affect your ability to land a satisfying job.

Before you begin, take the time to develop an organized strategy for your search efforts. You might download a template such as Microsoft's job search log (http://search.officeupdate.microsoft.com/Template Gallery) or invest in software such as Winway Résumé, Résumé Maker Deluxe, or ResuMail to simplify the task of tracking your contacts. You'll need a record of the name, address, and telephone number of each employer who has a job in which you have an interest. Later, record the date of each job call you make and receive (along with what you learned from the call), the date of each returned call, the name of the person who called, the date you sent a résumé, and so on. Maintaining this list alphabetically will enable you to find a name quickly and respond effectively to a returned telephone call.

Your search for potential career and job opportunities likely will involve traditional and electronic job search sources.

Figure 13-1

Process of Applying for a Job

Conduct research and analysis of self, career, and job
1. Gather essential information
2. Prepare a company/job profile
3. Identify key qualifications

Identify a job listing using traditional and electronic sources

Prepare targeted résumé and application message in required formats
Print, scannable, and electronic postings

Consider supplementing the résumé
- Portfolio (printed or electronic)
- Video recording

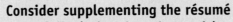

Interview with companies

Figure 13-2

Sample Company/Job Profile

Entry-Level Audit Staff—International Accounting Firm

Skill	Company/Job Requirements	My Qualifications and Needs
Education	Master's degree in accounting with 3.5 or higher GPA.	Will receive M.P.A. degree with 3.8 GPA.
Certification	CPA preferred; expected within three years.	Committed to earning CPA within two years.
General Knowledge	Broad understanding of all business (marketing, finance, management, information systems, etc.); history; world cultures; economic, political, and social systems; and ethical theories.	Curriculum provided courses in each area.
Intellectual Skills	Highly analytical; able to solve unstructured problems for unfamiliar settings (represent clients in various businesses); meticulous attention to detail.	Excelled in quantitative courses; performed well in preparing cases requiring creative solutions to problems without clear-cut answers.
Computer Skills	Proficiency in database, spreadsheet, word processing and Windows; knowledgeable of ERP systems and Internet.	Proficient in Windows, Microsoft Office; familiar with ACL and Internet.
Communication Skills	Secure and transfer information easily; present and defend views formally and/or informally in writing or orally.	Proficient in written communication; often reluctant to defend ideas; attempting to overcome speech anxiety.
Interpersonal Skills	Work efficiently in groups of diverse members; must withstand and resolve conflict with peers and clients.	Prefer working independently; have had poor experiences completing class team projects.
Management Skills	Organize and delegate tasks; motivate and develop others.	Part-time work and leadership roles provided opportunities to refine these skills.
Work Environment	Work primarily on location at the client's office with temporary work sites; share desk with staff when in the office.	Must feel in control of my own work space; need a desk organized for my sole use.
Work Style	Able to manage simultaneous audits and meet tight, coinciding deadlines; willing to revise work to meet high standards.	Prefer completing a project before moving to another; difficulty managing multiple projects; often take criticism personally.
Ethical Standards	Must abide by the AICPA Code of Professional Conduct.	High moral standards as result of family background; willing to abide by professional code.
Salary Range	$43,000–$45,000 annually.	$38,000–$42,000 annually.
Travel and Overtime	Approximately 25%; average 15 hours per month peaking between February 1 and April 1.	Prefer no more than 10% travel and limited overtime.
Career Path	Well-defined career path with frequent promotions every 3 years; eligible for partner after 10 years.	Well-defined career path with frequent changes in responsibilities.

Using Traditional Sources

Traditional means of locating a job include printed sources, networks, career services centers, employers' offices, employment agencies and contractors, help-wanted ads, and professional organizations.

Changing Technology

Critical Thinking

Make a list of network contacts who might assist you in your job search.

Printed Sources. Numerous printed sources are useful in identifying firms in need of employees. These include company newsletters, industry directories, and trade and professional publications. Many of these sources are also available on the Internet. Visit the text support site (http://lehman.swlearning.com) to review a list of useful resources available in print form.

Networks. The majority of job openings are never advertised. Therefore, developing a network of contacts may be the most valuable source of information about jobs. Your network may include current and past employers, guest speakers in your classes or at student organization meetings, business contacts you met while interning or participating in shadowing or over-the-shoulder experiences, and so on. Let these individuals know the type of job you are seeking and ask their advice for finding employment in today's competitive market.

Career Services Centers. Be certain to register with your college's career services center at least three semesters before you graduate. Typically, the center has a web site and a browsing room loaded with career information and job announcement bulletins. Career counseling is available including workshops on résumé writing, interviewing, etiquette, mock interviews, "mocktail" parties for learning to mingle in pre-interview social events, and more. Through the center, you can attend job fairs to meet prospective employers and schedule on-campus interviews and video interviews with company recruiters.

Critical Thinking

Visit your campus career services center. What services and materials are available? Register if your expected graduation date is within a year.

Most career services centers use electronic tracking systems just as companies are doing. Rather than submitting printed résumés, students input their résumés into a computer file following the specific requirements of the tracking system used by the college or university. A search of the database of résumés generates an interview roster of the top applicants for a campus recruiter's needs. Some centers assist students in preparing electronic portfolios to supplement the résumé, as discussed in a later section of this chapter.

Employers' Offices. Employers who have not advertised their employment needs may respond favorably to a telephoned or personal inquiry. The receptionist may be able to provide useful information, direct you to someone with whom you can talk, or set up an appointment.

Employment Agencies and Contractors. Telephone directories list city, county, state, and federal employment agencies that provide free or inexpensive services. Some agencies offer a recorded answering service; by dialing and listening, callers can get information about job opportunities and the procedure for using the agency's services. Fees charged by private agencies are paid by either the employee or the employer. This fee usually is based on the first month's salary and must be paid within a few months. Some agencies specialize in finding high-level executives or specialists for major firms. Employment contractors specialize in providing temporary employees. Instead of helping you find a permanent job, a contractor may be able to use your services on a temporary basis until you find a full-time job.

Classified Ads. Responses to advertised positions should be made as quickly as possible after the ad is circulated. If your résumé is received early and is impressive, you could get a favorable response before other applications are received. If an ad invites response to a box number without giving a name, be cautious. The employer could be legitimate but does not want present employees to know about the ad or does not want applicants to telephone or drop by the premises. However, you have a right to be suspicious of someone who wants to remain obscure while learning everything you reveal in your résumé.

Team Environment

Professional Organizations. Officers of professional organizations, through their contacts with members, can be good sources of information about job opportunities. Much job information is exchanged at meetings of professional associations. In response to help-wanted and position-wanted listings in journals or web sites of some professional organizations, interviews are sometimes arranged and conducted at hotels or schools in which the organization holds its annual meeting.

In addition to the professional growth that comes from membership in professional organizations, active participation is a good way to learn about job opportunities. Guest speakers share valuable information about the industry and career and often provide job information. In addition, employers are favorably impressed when membership and experiences gained are included on the résumé and discussed during an interview. They are even more impressed if the applicant is (or has been) an officer in the organization (implies leadership, community commitment, willingness to exert effort without tangible reward, social acceptance, or high level of aspiration). By joining and actively participating in professional, social, and honorary organizations for your major, you increase your opportunities to develop rapport with peers and professors and get an edge over less involved applicants.

Using Electronic Job Searches

Changing Technology

Increasing numbers of companies and applicants are harnessing the power of the Internet to assist job hunters in various stages of the job search process. Convenience, speed, accessibility, and a tight labor market are reasons for the popularity of electronic job searches among cost-conscious human resources managers. The cost of electronic recruiting is lower than traditional methods, and applicants can respond more quickly. Employment experts agree, however, that it is too early for applicants to

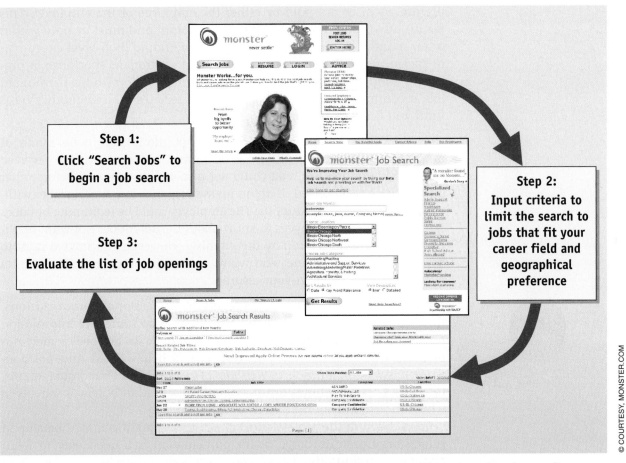

Step 1:
Click "Search Jobs" to begin a job search

Step 2:
Input criteria to limit the search to jobs that fit your career field and geographical preference

Step 3:
Evaluate the list of job openings

Easy-to-navigate, appealing web pages guide you in an electronic job search at Monster.com, one of the most popular web career sites.

© COURTESY, MONSTER.COM

rely solely on the Internet for locating a job. Instead job seekers should use the Internet to complement rather than replace the traditional methods previously discussed.

Numerous printed sources and excellent online assistance are available for learning to tap into the power of online job hunting. For a list of some of these resources, visit the text support site (http://lehman.swlearning. com). In this chapter, you'll explore the vast availability of useful career information and job postings on job banks and corporate home pages that match your qualifications. Later, you'll apply effective techniques for online job searching, including ways to protect your privacy while job hunting in cyberspace.

Critical Thinking

Some writers have criticized the use of electronic recruiting, stating that it impersonalizes the employment process. Do you agree or disagree?

Locating Career Guidance Information. According to one career consultant, "Most people in the old days could go into an organization [during a job interview] and not really know about it and hope for the best. Now, people can understand the organization before they even apply."[5] The Internet places at your fingertips a wealth of information that will prepare you for the job interview, that is, if you are wise enough to use the Internet as a research tool and not just a place to post your résumé in many job banks. Suggestions follow for effectively using the career guidance information you can locate on the Internet:

- *Visit career sites for information related to various phases of the job search.* You'll find a wide range of timely discussions at the career sites: planning a job search, finding a job you love, researching employers, working a career fair, crafting winning résumés and cover letters, negotiating a salary, and on and on. Visit the text support site (http://lehman.swlearning.com) to link conveniently to the top career sites and begin exploring career topics of interest to you.

Critical Thinking

How does online recruiting benefit the employer? the applicant?

- *Visit corporate web sites to learn about the company.* From the convenience of your desktop, you can locate information you'll need to target your résumé appropriately and to prepare for the job interview. Read mission statements or descriptions of services to see how the organization describes itself and review the annual report and strategic plan to learn about the financial condition and predicted growth rates. Search for sections touting new developments on "What's New" or "News" links and career opportunities and job postings. Evaluating the development and professional nature of the web site will give you an impression of the organization. Supplement this information with independent sources to confirm the company's financial health and other sensitive information as negative news will likely not be posted on the web site.

- *Identify specific skills companies are seeking.* Study the job descriptions provided on corporate home pages and job sites to identify the skills required for the job and the latest industry buzzwords. Use this information to target your résumé to a specific job listing and to generate keywords for an electronic résumé.

Critical Thinking

How has the employment process in your career field changed as a result of electronic technologies?

- *Network electronically with prospective employers.* It's easy to network online by attending electronic job fairs, chatting with career counselors, participating in news groups and listservs applicable to your field, and corresponding by e-mail with contacts in companies. The value of these electronic networking experiences is to learn about an industry and career, seek valued opinions, and uncover potential job opportunities. Applying the strategies for communicating in an online community you've already developed in this course, you can make a good impression, create rapport with employment contacts online, and polish your interviewing skills.

Identifying Job Listings. You can use the Internet to locate job opportunities in several ways:

- Look in the employment section of companies' corporate web pages to see if they are advertising job openings.
- Search the electronic databases of job openings of third-party services such as those listed at the text support site (http://lehman.swlearning.com).
- Access online job classifieds from daily and trade newspapers. CareerPath (http://www.careerpath.com) runs the classifieds of a number of major newspapers.

- Subscribe to a newsgroup through Usenet that gives you access to jobs by geographic location and specific job categories.
- Subscribe to services such as America Online that provide job-search sites and services by keying "Career."

Online and printed sources will help you learn to search particular databases. The following general suggestions will help you get started:

Critical Thinking

What words describe your skills?

- Input words and phrases that describe your skills rather than job titles because not every company uses the same job title.
- Use specific phrases such as "entry-level job" or "job in advertising" rather than "job search."
- Start with a wider job description term, such as "pharmaceutical sales jobs," then narrow down to the specific subject, geographic region, state, and so forth.
- Don't limit yourself to just one search engine. Try several and book-mark interesting sites.
- Don't get distracted as you go.

Searching for useful career sites among the hundreds available can be quite time-consuming. The five major career sites are AOL Workplace, Monster.com, CareerPath.com, Career Mosaic, and Headhunter.net, according to Media Metrix, a New York City-based firm that monitors site traffic.[6] Independent ratings of the effectiveness of job sites are also helpful in untangling the web of choices. Ratings are prepared by *WebWeek*, *Internet World*, and others including Richard Bolles, career expert and author of the long-time leading career guide *What Color Is Your Parachute?* His top ratings, "Parachute Picks: My Personal Rating System," and career advice from this expert are published at http://www.jobhuntersbible.com.

Planning a Targeted Résumé

Objective 3

Prepare a persuasive résumé that reflects the most effective organizational pattern.

In order to match your interests and qualifications with available jobs, you'll need an effective résumé. To win a job interview in today's tight market where job seekers outnumber positions, you need more than a general résumé that documents your education and work history. The powerful wording of a **targeted résumé** reflects the requirements of a specific job listing that you have identified through traditional and electronic job search methods.

An employer typically scans résumés quickly looking for reasons to reject the applicant, schedule an interview, or place in a stack for reread-ing. This initial scan and a second brief look for those who make the cut give little time to explain why you are the best person for the job.[7] To grab an employer's attention in this brief time, your writing must be powerful. You must selectively choose *what to say*, *how to say it*, and *how to arrange it* on the page so that it can be read quickly but thoroughly. A concise, informative, easy-to-read summary of your relevant qualifications will

Critical Thinking

What three decisions must you make when planning a résumé? Which requires the most time?

Athletes know that a split second or a fraction of an inch often determines who wins. Today's job market is almost that competitive. Even a minor error can mean the difference between employment and joblessness.

© PAUL A. SOUDERS/CORBIS

Legal & Ethical Constraints

demonstrate that you possess the straightforward communication skills demanded in today's information-intensive society.

The goal of the résumé is to get an interview, so ask yourself this question: "Does including this information increase my chances of getting an interview?" If the answer is "Yes," include the information; if the answer is "No," omit the information and use the space to develop your qualifications. When selecting information to be included, you must also be wary of the temptation to inflate your résumé to increase your chances of being hired. The Strategic Forces feature, "Inflated Résumés: High Price of Career Lies," later in this chapter discusses the consequences of inflating résumés.

Standard Parts of a Résumé

The standard parts of a winning résumé and an overview of the content of each section are shown in Figure 13-3. Study this overview carefully before reading the more in-depth explanation that follows and study the sample résumés provided in Figures 13-5 to 13-8 later in this chapter.

Identification

Changing Technology

Your objective is to provide information that will allow the interviewer to reach you. Include your name, current address, and telephone number. You may also include your e-mail address and Internet address to facilitate an interviewer's communication with you and to entice him/her to view your web page. Including these electronic addresses will bring attention to your ability to communicate electronically—important skills in a technological age.

Figure 13-3

Standard Sections of a Résumé

Identification

Provides name and where you can be reached.

Objective

Specifies the job sought.

Career Summary

Allows employer to grasp immediately why the applicant should be hired.

Qualifications

- **Education**—begins with most recent degree earned, institution, major, GPA if above 3.0, special abilities (computer or foreign language), and experiences that set you apart. Omits high school graduation.

- **Work Experience**—specifies job title and employer, describes related job duties and derived skills (interpersonal skills, time management, dependability). Ties derived skills to specific job duties to enhance credibility. Arranged with most relevant experience first.

- **Honors and Activities**—divides these experiences into short readable sections. Includes only those that enhance qualifications.

Personal Information

- Omits potentially discriminatory information.
- Portrays applicant as productive and well-rounded.

References

Provides names and contact information for three people who will support applicant's qualifications, or notes availability from other source.

RÉSUMÉ

- Identification
- Objective
- Career Summary
- Qualifications
- Personal Information
- References

To ensure that the interviewer can quickly locate the identification information, center it on the page or use graphic design elements to target attention to your name (e.g., change the font face and size, add graphic lines and borders, etc.). You may also include a permanent address (parent's or other relative's address) if you are interviewing when classes are not in session. If you are rarely at home during typical office hours (the time the interviewer is likely to call), provide a telephone number where messages can be left. Explain to those taking messages that prospective employers may be calling; thus, the accuracy of their messages and the impression they make while taking the message could affect your job search. Evaluate the personal message on your answering machine to be certain that it portrays you as a person serious about securing a job.

Job and/or Career Objective

Critical Thinking

What are the characteristics of a good job/career objective?

Following the "Identification" section, state your job/career objective—the job you want. Interviewers can see immediately whether the job you are seeking matches the one they have to offer. A good job/career objective must be specific enough to be meaningful yet general enough to apply to a variety of jobs. The following example illustrates a general objective that has been revised to describe a specific job.

General Objective	Specific Objective
A position that offers both a challenge and a good opportunity for growth.	Entry into management training program with advancement to commercial lending.
A responsible position with a progressive organization that provides opportunity for managerial development and growth commensurate with ability and attitudes.	Enter a challenging management position with special interest in mergers and acquisitions.

Some experts argue that a statement of your job or career objective may limit your job opportunities. Your objective should be obvious from your qualifications, they say. In general, however, making your objective clear at the beginning assures the interviewer that you have a definite career goal.

Career Summary

To survive the interviewer's 40-second scan, you must provide a compelling reason for a more thorough review of your résumé. Craft a persuasive introductory statement that quickly synthesizes your most transferable skills, accomplishments, and attributes and place it in a section labeled "Summary" or "Professional Profile."

In this synopsis of your key qualifications, communicate why you should be hired. Your answer should evolve naturally from the career objective and focus on your ability to meet the needs of the company you have identified from your extensive research. Combining the career objective with the career statement is an acceptable strategy as noted in the following examples.

Critical Thinking

What statement would capture your major qualifications and convince an employer to hire you?

Separate Objective and Career Summary

Objective	Obtain a challenging entry-level sales position for a high-growth consumer products company. Desire advancement into international sales management.
Career Summary	Honors graduate with a bachelor's degree in marketing with strong international emphasis including study abroad; three semesters' of related co-op experience with a large retail store; effective team worker and communicator.

Combined Objective with Career Summary

Professional Profile	Sales position, leading to sales management. International sales/ marketing manager with three years' experience in pharmaceutical sales, advertising, and contract negotiation with international suppliers. Strong technology, presentation, and interpersonal skills.

> **Linked Objective and Career Summary**
>
> **Profile**   Position as sales representative where demonstrated commission selling and hard work bring rewards.
>
> **Accomplishments:**
> - three years' straight-commission sales
> - average of $35,000–$55,000 a year in commissioned earnings
> - consistent success in development and growth of territories

A high-impact career summary, once considered optional, has become a standard section of résumés in today's fast-paced information age. No longer is it limited only to employees with varied or extensive qualifications that could be lost among the details. Develop your résumé that skillfully targets the requirements of a specific position; then compose a career summary sure to interest any interviewer who instantly sees an applicant with exactly the skills needed.

Qualifications

The "Qualifications" section varies depending on the information identified in the self-, career, and job analyses. This information is used to divide the qualifications into appropriate parts, choose appropriate labels for them, and arrange them in the best sequence. Usually, qualifications stem from your education and work experience (words that appear as headings in the résumé). Arrange these categories depending on which you perceive as more impressive to the employer, with the more impressive category appearing first. For example, education is usually the chief qualification of a recent college graduate; therefore, education appears first. However, a sales representative with related work experience might list experience first, particularly if the educational background is inadequate for the job sought.

Critical Thinking

*Is **your** education or your work experience the stronger factor?*

Education

Beginning with the most recent, list the degree, major, school, and graduation date. Include a blank line between schools so that the employer can see them at a glance. Using empathy for the interviewer's needs, determine the order for this information and follow that order consistently for each school attended. For example, the interviewer would probably want to know first whether you have the appropriate degree, then the institution, and so on. Recent or near college graduates should omit high school activities because that information is "old news." However, include high school activities if they provide a pertinent dimension to your qualifications. For example, having attended high school abroad is a definite advantage to an applicant seeking employment in an international firm. In addition, high school accomplishments may be relevant for freshmen or sophomores seeking cooperative education assignments, scholarships, or part-time jobs. Of course, this information will be replaced with college activities when the résumé is revised for subsequent jobs or other uses.

Inflated Résumés: High Price of Career Lies

Corporate downsizing and a slowed economy have created intense competition for fewer jobs, and desperate job seekers are increasingly more willing to lie or at least "enhance" their résumés. According to credentials specialist John Tonsick, as many as one third of job applicants will lie when the job market is tight or when they think it will help on something such as salary.[8] Many applicants feel lying is necessary to get past the initial screening and "get their feet in the door." Some rationalize their actions by saying, "Nobody is checking, so who will ever know?"; "Everyone does it"; or "I deserve it."

Common ways to lie on résumés include the following:

- **Fabricating or embellishing academic experience.**

Applicants claim they earned degrees from institutions they never attended or earned degrees they only partially completed. Applicants also fudge on their class ranks and grade-point averages and list fictitious honors and activities.

- **Fudging employment dates to hide gaps in employment.** Rather than lying, applicants should answer honestly: "Yes, I was laid off at Company X and spent six months looking for the right employer, so there is a gap in my employment dates for that year."

- **Overinflating job title and exaggerating job duties.** For example, a job seeker might report a job title as "supervisor" rather than "senior clerk." To further embellish the résumé, he or she might write "facilitated daily production of property/casualty documentation" when "typed and processed 200 insurance forms a day" would be more truthful and useful to the recruiter.

Companies cannot risk the safety of their people and resources to people they can't trust; therefore, they generally will not hire an applicant who submits false information and will terminate employment as soon as the deception is discovered. Deceptive employees who are retained face negative consequences for their unethical action. Loss of trust may prevent advancement in the company, and job performance will eventually suffer if an employee lacks the qualifications to perform the job. Bill Trau, a leading search firm executive, comments on the issue of fraudulent credentials: "It's surprising that people are still trying to fudge this stuff. We are going to find them out. Background checking has gotten much easier to do well."[9]

When selecting information to be included, honestly ask yourself, "Does this information present my qualifications honestly and ethically, or does it inflate my qualifications to increase my chances of getting the job?" If you have the slightest inclination that including a piece of information will inflate your qualifications, omit it. What you believe is a "career booster" could end your career.

Application

Review your résumé carefully. Is it truthful? Does it promote your accomplishments in a direct, simple, and accurate way? Is it clear where you were working when you gained the experience that you describe?

Murphy's Law No. 2

The _one_ little exaggeration on your résumé is the one they check!

HELLO... IS THIS THE WHITE HOUSE?

PERSONNEL

© WHEELER GROUP, INC. 1985

C86-4 The Drawing Board™ Box 660429 Dallas, Texas © Wheeler Group, Inc., 1985

Include overall and major grade-point averages if they are B or better—but be prepared to discuss any omissions during an interview. Some recruiters recommend that every candidate include grade-point average, since an omission may lead the reader to assume the worst. Honors and achievements that relate directly to education can be incorporated in this section or included in a separate section. Listing scholarships, appearance on academic lists, and initiation into honor societies will be simple, but highlight business-relevant skills you developed in active classroom experiences such as, client projects, team building, field experiences, etc. If honors and achievements are included in the "Education" section, be sure to include plenty of white space or use bullets to highlight these points (see Figures 13-5 and 13-8 later in this chapter).

Critical Thinking

What educational experiences do you have other than degrees earned?

The "Education" section could also include a list of special skills and abilities such as foreign language and computer competency. A list of courses typically required in your field is unnecessary and occupies valuable space. However, you should include any courses, workshops, or educational experiences that are not usual requirements. Examples include internships, cooperative education semesters, "shadowing," "over-the-shoulder" experiences, and study abroad.

Work Experience

The "Work Experience" section provides information about your employment history. For each job held, list the job title, company name, dates of employment, primary responsibilities, and key accomplishments. The jobs may be listed in reverse chronological order (beginning with the most recent) or in order of job relatedness. Begin with the job that most obviously relates to the job being sought if you have gaps in your work history, if the job you are seeking is very different from the job you currently hold, or if you are just entering the job market and have little, if any, related work experience.

Arrange the order and format of information about each job (dates, job title, company, description, and accomplishments) so that the most important information is emphasized—but format all job information consistently. If you have held numerous jobs in a short time, embed dates of employment within the text rather than surround them with white space. Give related job experience added emphasis by listing it first or surrounding it with white space.

Employers are interested in how you can contribute to their bottom line, so a winning strategy involves concentrating on accomplishments and achievements rather than rushing through a boring list of obvious duties. Begin with the job title and company name that provides basic information about your duties, then craft powerful descriptions of the quality of your performance, the pride you have in the skills you developed, and the pleasure of using them. These glittering bullet points will provide deeper insight into your capability, ambition, and personality and set you apart from other applicants who take the easy route of providing only a work history.

Return to the in-depth analysis you completed at the beginning of the job search process to recall insights as to how you can add immediate value to this company. Did your personal involvement play a key role in the success of a project? Did you uncover a wasteful, labor-intensive procedure that was resolved through your innovation? Did you bridge a gap in a communication breakdown? Consider the following questions to spur your recognition of marketable skills from your education, work, and community experiences.[10]

Critical Thinking

How can you most effectively summarize your work experience?

- How does my potential employer define success for the job I'm applying for? How do I measure up?
- What is my potential employer's bottom line (money, attendance, sales, etc.)? When have I shown that I know how to address that bottom line?
- What project am I proud of that demonstrates I have the skill for my job objective?
- What technical or management skills do I have that indicate the level at which I perform?
- What problem did I solve, how did I solve it, and what were the results?

Because interviewers spend such a short time reading résumés, the style must be direct and simple. Therefore, a résumé should use crisp phrases to help employers see the value of the applicant's education and experiences. To save space and to emphasize what you have accomplished, use these stylistic techniques:

1. Omit pronouns referring to yourself (*I, me, my*).
2. Use subject-understood sentences.
3. Begin sentences with action verbs as shown in the following examples:

Instead of	Use
I had responsibility for development of new territory.	*Developed* new territory.
My duties included designing computer systems and writing user documentation manuals.	*Designed* computer programs to monitor accounting systems including writing user documentation that enables users to operate these sophisticated systems efficiently.
I was the store manager and supervised employees.	*Managed* operations of store with sales volume of $1,000,000 and supervised eight employees.
My sales consistently exceeded sales quota.	*Earned* average of $35,000 a year in commissioned earnings. *Received* service award for exceeding sales quota two of three years employed.
I was a member of the Student Council, Society for the Advancement of Management, Phi Kappa Phi, and Chi Omega Social Sorority.	*Refined* interpersonal skills through involvement in student organizations such as the Student Council . . . .

Critical Thinking

Describe the value you gained from a previous job experience that can be transferred to a job you might seek after graduation.

Because employers are looking for people who will work, action verbs are especially appropriate. Note the subject-understood sentences in the right column of the previous example: action words used as first words provide emphasis. The following list contains action verbs that are useful in résumés:

accomplished	drafted	participated
achieved	expanded	planned
analyzed	increased	presented
assisted	initiated	proposed
compiled	maintained	recruited
counseled	managed	streamlined
developed	organized	wrote

To give the employer a vivid picture of you as a productive employee, you may find some of the following adjectives helpful as you describe your work experience:

adaptable/flexible	dependable	resourceful
analytical	efficient/productive	sensitive
conscientious	independent	sincere
consistent	objective	tactful
creative	reliable	team oriented

To avoid a tone of egotism, do not use too many adjectives or adverbs that seem overly strong. Plan to do some careful editing after writing your first draft.

Honors and Activities

Critical Thinking

The titles of sections may vary, depending on the items listed within the section. What section titles will you include on your résumé?

Make a trial list of any other information that qualifies you for the job. Divide the list into appropriate divisions and then select an appropriate label. Your heading might be "Honors and Activities." You might include a section for "Activities," "Leadership Activities," or "Memberships," depending on the items listed. You might also include a separate section on "Military Service," "Civic Activities," "Volunteer Work," or "Interests." If you have only a few items under each category, use a more general term and combine the lists. If your list is lengthy, divide it into more than one category; interviewers prefer "bite-size" pieces because they are easier to read and can be remembered more readily.

Resist the urge to include everything you have ever done; keep in mind that every item you add distracts from other information. Consider summarizing information that is relevant but does not merit several separate lines—for example, "Involved in art, drama, and choral groups." To decide whether to include certain information, ask these questions: How closely related is it to the job being sought? Does it provide job-related information that has not been presented elsewhere?

Personal Information

Because a résumé should contain primarily information that is relevant to an applicant's experience and qualifications, you must be selective when including personal information (not related to the job). The space could be used more effectively to include more about your qualifications or to add more white space. Personal information is commonly placed at the end of the résumé just above the "References" section because it is less important than qualifications (education, experience, and activities).

Legal & Ethical Constraints

Under the 1964 Civil Rights Act (and subsequent amendments) and the Americans with Disabilities Act (ADA), employers cannot make hiring decisions based on gender, age, marital status, religion, national origin, or disability. Employers prefer not to receive information that provides information about gender, age, and national origin because questions could be raised about whether the information was used in the hiring decision.

This topic is explored further in the Strategic Forces feature, "Diversity Issues Affecting Employability." Follow these guidelines related to personal information:

- *Do not include personal information that could lead to discriminatory hiring.* Exclude height, weight, and color of hair and eyes and a personal photograph on the résumé.
- *Reveal ethnic background (and other personal information) only if it is job related.* For example, certain businesses may be actively seeking employees in certain ethnic groups because the ethnic background is a legitimate part of the job description. For such a business, ethnic information is useful and appreciated.
- *Include personal information (other than the information covered by employment legislation) that will strengthen your résumé.* Select information that is related to the job you are seeking or portrays you as a well-rounded, happy individual off the job. Typically, include interests, hobbies, favorite sports, avocations, and willingness to relocate. You can also include these topics if you have not covered them elsewhere in the résumé: spoken and written communication skills, computer competency, foreign-language or computer skills, military service, community service, scholastic honors, job-related hobbies, and professional association memberships.
- *Consider whether personal information might be controversial.* For example, listing a sport that an interviewer might perceive to be overly time-consuming or dangerous would be questionable. An applicant seeking a position with a religious or political organization may benefit from revealing this affiliation.

Critical Thinking

What personal information will you include on your résumé?

Diversity Issues Affecting Employability

The objective of a responsible employer's recruitment policy and selection process should be to find the most suitable person to fill a particular job in terms of skills, experience, aptitude, and other qualifications. Employers may face claims of discrimination if they deny equality of opportunity by relying on selection criteria such as sex, race, ethnic origin, marital status, age, or disability. While gender discrimination in employment has been illegal in the United States for 40 years, it still persists in some instances, often subtly.

Recent research suggests that employers may be selecting or overlooking prospective job candidates for interviews based on their assumed race as suggested by names. Researchers submitted 5,000 bogus résumés in response to job ads, with half the résumés bearing stereotypical African-American names such as LaTonya and Tyrone and the other half sporting traditionally Anglo names such as Kristin and Brad. Of the candidates with Caucasian-sounding names, 10 percent were contacted, in contrast to only 6.7 percent of those with a presumed ethnic identity and identical résumés.[11] In the wake of the September 11 tragedy, frequent reports have surfaced of Muslims and Arabs shortening or changing their foreign-sounding names to English ones to gain more favorable employment opportunities.[12]

Women, too, continue to report dissimilar treatment in employment situations. Consider the following situations:

- **Marital status:** A man who includes marital status on the résumé may enhance his desirability as an applicant. For instance, indication of "married" may be associated with stability. A woman who indicates "married" may be viewed as unreliable or temporary because she may have children who could interfere with her job performance. She may also be seen as likely to leave the company if her husband is transferred or relocates. Indicating "single" is not necessarily a plus for a woman either. She may be viewed as seeking temporary work until she marries.

- **Physical appearance:** Given that qualifications among candidates are equal, physical attraction has been found to be positively correlated with job offers and with total lifetime earning potential.[13] However, physical attractiveness has been found in some cases to work against women. While unattractive men and women are rejected by potential employers about equally, a woman who is very attractive may be bypassed because a feeling still persists in some camps that a woman cannot be both beautiful and smart. Thus, a woman can be too attractive for employment.

Employers should be aware that illegal discrimination can have negative repercussions, not only from the courts but in terms of lower productivity resulting from the selection of less capable employees. Business people who have overcome discriminatory situations frequently say that networking with friends, former teachers, college alumni, and other acquaintances has helped them break the glass, or concrete, ceilings they encountered and land better jobs.[14]

Application

In small groups, brainstorm a list of other ways that discrimination may occur in employment. For each incidence of possible discrimination, propose an action that the applicant may take to minimize or eliminate it. Compose a class list that summarizes the small group discussions.

References

Providing potential employers a list of references (people who have agreed to supply information about you when requested) is an important component of your employment credentials. Listing names, addresses, telephone numbers, and e-mail addresses of people who can provide information about you adds credibility to the résumé. Employers, former employers, instructors, and former instructors are good possibilities. Friends, relatives, and neighbors are not (because of their perceived bias in your favor). Some career experts recommend including a peer to document your ability to work as a member of a team, an important job skill in today's team-oriented environment.[15]

Critical Thinking

Who could serve as a positive work reference for you?

References can be handled on the résumé in several ways. As the closing section of your résumé, you can provide a list of references, include a brief statement that references are available on request or from a career service center, or omit any statement regarding references assuming that references are not needed until after an interview. Research related to the employers' preferences for references supports omitting a list of references and using the remaining space for developing qualifications.[16] You might list references directly on the résumé if you have limited qualifications to include, if you know a company interviews applicants *after* references are contacted, or when you believe the names of your references will be recognizable in your career field. You may include a statement such as "For references . . ." or "For additional information . . ." and give the address of the career services center of your college or university, the job bank posting your credentials, or the URL of your electronic portfolio.

Critical Thinking

What are the advantages and disadvantages of including a list of references in your résumé?

Withholding references until they are requested prevents unnecessary or untimely requests going to your present employer. The interview gives an applicant a chance to assess the desirability of the job. Until then, the applicant may not want the present employer to receive inquiries (which may be interpreted as dissatisfaction with the present job). This action also conveys genuine courtesy to the references. Even the most enthusiastic references may become apathetic if required to provide recommendations to endless interviewers. For this same reason, be sure to communicate with references regularly if your job search continues longer than expected. A letter of thanks and an update on the job search will assure references that you appreciate their efforts. Suggestions for communicating with references are discussed in Chapter 14.

When preparing a separate list of references to be given after a successful interview, place the word *References* and your name in a visible position as shown in Figure 13-5. Balance the list (name, address, and telephone number) attractively on the page and use the same paper used for printing the résumé. When asked for references at the end of a successful interview, you can immediately provide the references page to the interviewer. If you need additional time to consider the interview, you can send the references page within a day or so by postal or electronic mail. Whether it is handed to the interviewer personally or mailed, the references page professionally complements your résumé. Furthermore, you have impressed the interviewer with your promptness in completing this task—a positive indicator that you will handle other duties similarly. Your résumé will need to meet high standards of content. All parts are important, but the most important portion is the one that covers your qualifications. If they seem compatible with job requirements, you have a good message to present. Confident that you have a good message, you are now ready to put it in writing—to construct a résumé that will impress an employer favorably.

Appropriate Organizational Plan

Critical Thinking

Five years after graduation, would education or experience likely appear first on your résumé? Why?

The general organization of all résumés is fairly standard: identification (name, address, telephone number, and e-mail address), job objective, qualifications, personal information, and references. The primary organizational challenge is in dividing the qualifications section into parts, choosing labels for them, and arranging them in the best sequence. When you review your self-, career, and job analyses data and company/job profile, you will recognize that your qualifications stem mainly from your education and your experience. Your task is to decide how to present these two categories of qualifications. Résumés usually are organized in one of three ways: reverse chronological order (most recent activity listed first), functional order (most important activity listed first), or a chrono-functional which combines the chronological and functional orders as the name implies. To determine which organizational plan to use, make trial outlines using each one.

Chronological Résumé

The **chronological résumé** is the traditional organizational format for résumés. Two headings normally appear in the portion that presents qualifications: "Education" and "Experience." Which one should appear first? Decide which one you think is more impressive to the employer, and put that one first. Within each section, the most recent information is presented first (reverse chronological order). Reverse chronological order is easier to use and is more common than functional order; however, it is not always more effective.

The chronological résumé is an especially effective format for applicants who have progressed up a clearly defined career ladder and want to move up another rung. Because the format emphasizes dates and job titles, the chronological résumé is less effective for applicants who have gaps in their work histories, are seeking jobs different from the job currently held, or are just entering the job market with little or no experience.[17]

If you choose the chronological format, look at the two headings from the employer's point of view, and reverse their positions if doing so is to your advantage. Under the "Experience" division, jobs are listed in reverse order. Assuming you have progressed typically, your latest job is likely to be more closely related to the job being sought than the first job held. Placing the latest or current job first will give it the emphasis it deserves. Include beginning and ending dates for each job.

Functional Résumé

Critical Thinking

How do functional résumés report experience and education?

In a **functional résumé**, points of primary interest to employers—transferable skills—appear in major headings. These headings highlight what an applicant can *do* for the employer—functions that can be performed well. Under each heading, an applicant could draw from educational and/or work-related experience to provide supporting evidence.

A functional résumé requires a complete analysis of self, career, and the job sought. Suppose, for example, that a person seeking a job as an assistant hospital administrator wants to emphasize qualifications by placing them in major headings. From the hospital's advertisement of the job and from accumulated job appraisal information, an applicant sees this job as both an administrative and a public relations job. The job requires skill in communicating and knowledge of accounting and finance. Thus, headings in the "Qualifications" section of the résumé could be (1) "Administration," (2) "Public Relations," (3) "Communication," and (4) "Budgeting." Under "Public Relations," for example, an applicant could reveal that a public relations course was taken at State University, from which a degree is to be conferred in June, and that a sales job at ABC Store provided abundant opportunity to apply principles learned. With other headings receiving similar treatment, the qualifications portion reveals the significant aspects of education and experience.

Order of importance is probably the best sequence for functional headings. If you have prepared an accurate self- and job analysis, the selected headings will highlight points of special interest to the employer. Glancing at headings only, an employer could see that you have the qualities needed for success on the job. By carefully selecting headings, you reveal knowledge of the requisites for success on that job.

Having done the thinking required for preparing a functional résumé, you are well prepared for a question that is commonly asked in interviews: "What can you do for us?" The answer is revealed in your major headings. They emphasize the functions you can perform and the special qualifications you have to offer.

If you consider yourself well qualified, a functional résumé is worth considering. If your education or experience is scant, a functional résumé may be best for you. Using "Education" and "Experience" as headings (as in a chronological résumé) works against your purpose if you have little to report under the headings; the format would emphasize the absence of education or experience.

Chrono-functional Résumé

The **chrono-functional résumé** combines features of chronological and functional résumés. This format can give quick assurance that educational and experience requirements are met and still use other headings that emphasize qualifications. For example, the "Qualifications" section could have headings such as these:

Education	List the degree, major, school, and graduation date.
Experience	Briefly list jobs held currently and previously.
Administration	Provide details drawn from education and/or experience.
Communication	Give examples of tasks, activities, or achievements that indicate communication skills.
Budgeting	Give examples drawn from education and/or experience.
Public Relations	Give examples of tasks, activities, or achievements that indicate public relations skills.

Critical Thinking

What do the headings in the chrono-functional résumé emphasize? What important question do they answer?

Functional headings vary for different jobs. In fact, two people applying for the same job would likely choose different headings or list similar headings in a distinctive sequence. Select headings that are appropriate for you and that the employer will see as directly related to the job.

When planning the résumé, take note of specific job requirements. They are good possibilities for functional headings. For example, for a job that requires bonding, "Top Security Clearance" gets deserved attention as a heading. Each of the following conditions, if it applies to the job sought, could be the basis for a heading: The work is in small groups; the work requires much overtime in certain seasons; travel is frequent; overseas assignments are a possibility; adaptability to rapid changes is desirable; ability to take criticism is essential; long and detailed reports are required; or lateral transfers can be expected. Choosing appropriate headings is a critical decision in résumé preparation.

Adapting Résumés for Alternate Presentation and Delivery Options

Objective 4

Adapt the résumé for alternate presentation and delivery options, including print (designed) formats, scannable versions, and electronic postings.

Format requirements for résumés have changed significantly in recent years. No longer is a paper résumé sent by mail the only way your résumé will be presented and delivered. Whether presented on paper or electronically, the arrangement of a résumé is just as important as the content. If the arrangement is unattractive, unappealing, or in poor taste, the message may never be read. Errors in keyboarding, spelling, and punctuation may be taken as evidence of a poor academic background, lack of respect for the employer, carelessness, or haste. Recognize that résumés serve as your introduction to employers, and indicate the quality and caliber of work you'll produce. Imperfect résumés are unacceptable. Put forth your best effort to this important task—one that could open the door to the job you really want.

Critical Thinking

Explain how poor mechanics in a résumé counteract superior content, organization, and style.

As in preparing other difficult documents, prepare a rough draft as quickly as you can and then revise as many times as needed to prepare an effective résumé that sells you. After you are confident with the résumé, ask at least two other people to check it for you. Carefully select people who are knowledgeable about résumé preparation and the job you are seeking and can suggest ways to present your qualifications more effectively. After you have incorporated those changes, ask a skillful proofreader to review the document.

To accommodate employers' preferences for the presentation and delivery of résumés, you'll need three versions of your résumé as shown in Figure 13-4. Enhanced résumé printed on paper, scannable résumé to be read by a computer, and an electronic résumé accessible through e-mail and web sites are versions you'll need to prepare.

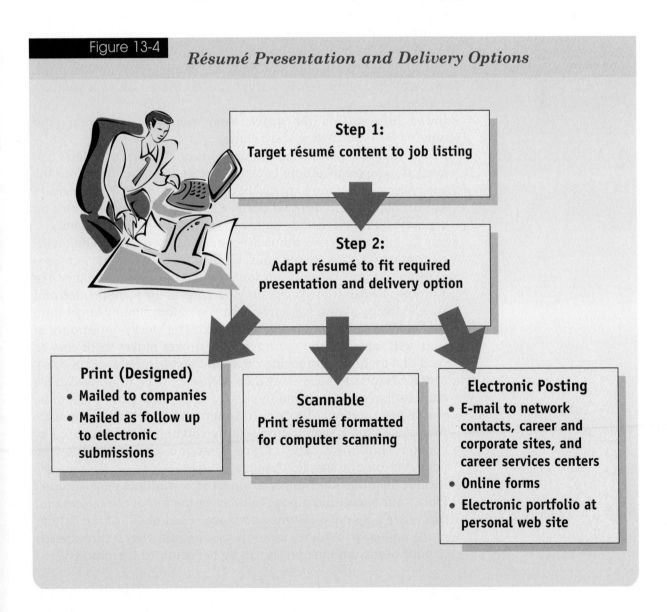

Figure 13-4

Résumé Presentation and Delivery Options

Step 1:
Target résumé content to job listing

Step 2:
Adapt résumé to fit required presentation and delivery option

Print (Designed)
- Mailed to companies
- Mailed as follow up to electronic submissions

Scannable
Print résumé formatted for computer scanning

Electronic Posting
- E-mail to network contacts, career and corporate sites, and career services centers
- Online forms
- Electronic portfolio at personal web site

Preparing a Print (Designed) Résumé

Your print (designed) résumé is considered your primary marketing document, and appearance is critical. To win out among hundreds of competing résumés, it must look professional and reflect current formatting and production standards while maintaining a distinctive conservative tone. Follow these guidelines for designing and producing a highly professional résumé with your own computer:

- *Develop an appealing résumé format that highlights your key qualifications and distinguishes your résumé from the many look-alikes created with résumé templates.* Use the power of your word processing software for style enhancements rather than settle for outdated template formats and the frustration of working with inflexible template layouts that are difficult to use when sequencing and reformatting are required for appropriate emphasis. Study the example résumés in this chapter and models from other sources for ideas for enhancing the style, readability, and overall impact of the document. Then create a custom design that maximizes the exposure of your key qualifications.

- *Format information for quick, easy reading.* To format your résumé so that it can be read at glance,

  - Use headings to partition major divisions and add graphic lines and borders to separate sections of text. These design techniques draw the interviewer's attention to pertinent information quickly and easily.

  - Use an outline format when possible to list activities and events on separate lines and include bullets to emphasize multiple points.

  - Use font sizes no smaller than 10 point. Interviewers shouldn't need a magnifying glass to read your résumé.

  - Use type styles and print attributes to emphasize key points. For example, to draw the reader's attention first to the identification and then to the headings, select a bold sans serif font slightly larger than the serif font used for the remaining text. The blocky appearance of sans serif fonts that do not have cross strokes makes them easy to read and useful for displaying important text (e.g., Arial or Univers). Serif fonts such as Times New Roman or New Century Schoolbook have cross strokes and are primarily used for large amounts of text to be read carefully. Capitalization, indention, and print enhancements (underline, italics, bold), are useful for adding emphasis. Word of caution: Limit the number of type styles and enhancements so the page is clean and simple to read.

  - Include identification on each page of a multiple-page résumé. Place your name and a page number at the top of the second and successive pages of a résumé and place "Continued" at the bottom of the first page. With each new page, the interviewer is reexposed to your name, and the pages can be reassembled if separated.

- *Create an appealing output to produce top professional quality:*
  - Check for consistency throughout the résumé. Consistency in spacing, end punctuation, capitalization, appearance of headings, and sequencing of details within sections will communicate your eye for detail and commitment to high standards.
  - Balance the résumé attractively on the page with approximately equal margins. Allow generous white space so the résumé looks uncluttered and easy to read.
- *Consider adding a statement of your creativity and originality.* Be certain, however, that your creativity will not be construed as gimmicky and consequently distract from the content of the résumé. For example, preparing a highly effective résumé layout including borders, lines, and graphics communicates creativity as well as proficiency in the use of technology. Demonstrating creativity is particularly useful for fields such as advertising, public relations, and graphic design and in those requiring computer competency.
  - Select paper of a standard size (8 ½" by 11") neutral colored (white, buff, or gray), high-quality (preferably 24-pound, 100-percent cotton fiber). Review Appendix A for additional discussion of paper quality. Because an application letter will accompany a résumé, use the large (No. 10) envelope. Consider using a mailing envelope large enough to accommodate the résumé without folding. The unfolded documents on the reader's desk may get favorable attention and will scan correctly if posted to an electronic database. (A detailed discussion of scannable résumés follows this section.)
  - Print with a laser printer that produces high-quality output. Position paper so the watermark is read across the sheet in the same direction as the printing.

Critical Thinking

What kinds of creative résumé features might be well received by a prospective employer in your career field?

Critical Thinking

What is the ideal length for a résumé for your career field?

Some employers insist that the "best" length for a résumé is one page, stating that long résumés are often ignored. However, general rules about length are more flexible. Most students and recent graduates can present all relevant résumé information on one page. However, as employees gain experience, they may need two or more pages to format an informative, easy-to-read résumé. A résumé forced on one page will likely have narrow margins and large blocks of run-on text (multiple lines with no space to break them). This dense format is unappealing and complicates the interviewer's task of skimming quickly for key information.

The rule about length is simple. Be certain your résumé contains only relevant information presented as concisely as possible. A one-page résumé that includes irrelevant information is too long. A two-page résumé that omits relevant information is too short.

The résumés illustrated in Figures 13-5, 13-7, and 13-8 demonstrate the organizational principles for the chronological, functional, and chronofunctional résumé. A references page is illustrated in Figure 13-6. Study the various layouts illustrated in these print (designed) résumés to find the layout that will highlight your key qualifications most effectively.

Figure 13-5

Chronological Résumé

Includes e-mail address for job search that reflects a professional image.

Russell B. Taylor
147 White Arches Cove
Aurora, IL 60505-0147
630-555-6543 (home) 630 555-7831 (cell)
rtaylor@netdoor.com

Reveals type of work sought and powerful summary statement explaining why the employer would want to hire Russell.

CAREER OBJECTIVE	Challenging position in the design and implementation of web, e-commerce, and supply chain applications.
CAREER SUMMARY	• Professional, core skills in Windows and Unix systems and software code; knowledge of Internet protocol and LAN administration. • Computer knowledge applied through cooperative education experience with a leading company and volunteer work. • Honors student pursuing B.B.A. in information systems. • Willingness to relocate.

Positions education as top qualification for this recent graduate. Includes high GPA (B or better) and conveys responsibility for financing his education.

EDUCATION	B.B.A., INFORMATION SYSTEMS, Barrett University. To be conferred June, 2004. Grade-point average: 3.6 (4.0 scale). Financed 80 percent of education with scholarships and part-time work.

Edges out the competition reflecting experience related to the job objective including work achievements.

RELATED EXPERIENCE	*Webmaster assistant*, Cooperative-Education Program, Pearson Industries, Wheaton, Illinois, three semesters, 2002–2003. • Performed system maintenance for HTML, CGI, and JavaScript applications. • Assisted design team in improving and developing new web applications, including initial design of a payroll application. • Received commendation for strong web design skills.

Emphasizes volunteer work that portrays service attitude and people-oriented experiences.

VOLUNTEER WORK	Volunteer Assistant, Lincoln School District Faculty Development Technology Program, Summer 2001. • Served as unpaid assistant. • Assisted teachers in upgrading technology skills.

Uses separate section to emphasize technology proficiency listed in the job requirements.

COMPUTER SKILLS	Microsoft Certified Professional (MCP), 2002 completion date. MCP + Site Building Certification pending. *Environments:* Windows and Unix, Novell networks *Languages:* HTML, CGI, Java, and C++ *Applications:* Microsoft Office Suite, Internet browsers

Lists academic recognitions and highlights business-relevant skills gained from involvement in student activities.

HONORS AND ACTIVITIES	Dean's List for seven semesters (3.6 GPA or higher) Gamma Beta Phi Honorary Society (upper 5% of senior class) Information Technology Association • Selected to design the organization's web page for competition. Site earned first place state and third place national recognition. • Networked with information systems professionals to enhance knowledge of the field.

Omits references section to use space for additional qualifications; references will be furnished when requested.

Format Pointers

• Places name at the top center where it can be easily seen when employers place it in a file drawer (top right is also acceptable). Uses a bold sans serif font to distinguish identification section and headings from the remaining text in serif font.

• Uses a two-column format for easy location of specific sections.

• Creates visual appeal through custom format rather than a commonly used template, short readable sections focusing on targeted qualifications, and streamlined bulleted lists.

Figure 13-6

References Page

Russell B. Taylor
147 White Arches Cove
Aurora, IL 60505-0147
630 555-6543 (home) 630 555-7831 (cell)
rtaylor@netdoor.com

References include two former employers and a professor. The list does not include friends, relatives, or clergy.

Mr. C. Thomas Hendrix
Web Site Manager
Pearson Industries
P.O. Box 47399
Wheaton, IL 60187-1894
708 555-9000
chendrix@pi.com

Dr. Victor Zikratov
Associate Professor
Information Systems Department
Barrett University
P.O. Box 5937
St. Charles, IL 60174-5937
708 555-4382
vzikratov@bu.edu

Each reference includes courtesy title, full name, company affiliation, address, telephone number (where the person can be reached during regular office hours), and e-mail address if available.

Ms. Marilyn L. Robertson
Information Technology Services Officer
Lincoln County School District
2150 North Hamilton Avenue
Naperville, IL 60540-4950
630 555-4385
marilyn_robertson@lincolncountysd.edu

Format Pointers

- The reference page is prepared at the same time as the résumé and can be provided immediately following a successful interview. Paper (color, texture, and size) and print type match the résumé.

- References are balanced attractively on the page.

Figure 13-7

Functional Résumé

Courtney Holzhauer
7310 Henley Street
Houston, TX 77001-7310
281 555-6743 (home) 281 555-1396 (cell)
cholzhauer@hotmail.com

Includes a clear objective and descriptive summary statement to grab interviewer's attention and provide incentive for reading the résumé more closely.

Uses headings to emphasize qualities as a solution to the employer's problem. Headings suggest that Courtney knows important requisites for success in sales.

Lists references because Courtney is confident she wants to work for this company and believes providing them will strengthen her résumé.

OBJECTIVE	Position in retail clothing sales with advancement to sales management.
CAREER SUMMARY	• Honors student majoring in marketing. • Related sales experience demonstrating superior inter-personal skills and commitment to customer satisfaction
SALES-ORIENTED	A strong interest in sales and fashion since childhood; began designing and making clothes for self and others at age 14. Have three years' part-time experience in fast foods. Currently, a senior majoring in marketing at West State College graduating in May 2004. Subscribe to *Retail Selling*.
PUBLIC RELATIONS SKILLS	Learned tactfulness when taking and filling orders in the fast-food business (Marketplace Bagel, part-time from August 2002 to May 2004). Commended by manager for diplomacy with customers and staff. Earned an "A" in Interpersonal Communication and will take Public Relations next semester. Gained experience coping with various personality types while volunteering as a counselor at Camp Seminole for three summers.
RECORDKEEPING SKILLS	Balanced receipts against records each day at Marketplace Bagel. Now taking two classes (accounting and computer applications) that emphasize keeping records electronically.
DEPENDABILITY	Report consistently and promptly when scheduled for work. In three years, have never been late for work. Attend classes regularly. Open and close store and make bank deposits.
LEARNING CAPACITY	Commended for learning work procedures quickly. Achieved Dean's List for the last two semesters. Earned 3.3 grade-point average (on a 4.0 scale) in major courses to date.
REFERENCES	Dr. Rick Trice, Advisor, Marketing Department, West State College, P.O. Box 4293, Temple, TX 76501-3293, (817) 555-2746. Ms. Marge Sherman, Camp Director, Camp Seminole, 1493 Dunlap Drive, Kingsville, TX 78363-1493, (512) 555-8934. Mr. Oscar Perez, Manager, Marketplace Bagel, 151 Woodlake Street, Corpus Christi, TX 78469-7310, (512) 555-6789.

Format Pointers

- Places name at the top center where it can be easily seen.
- Uses a bold sans serif font to distinguish identification section and headings from the remaining text in serif font.
- Creates visual appeal with a horizontal line, easy-to-read columnar format, and balanced page arrangement.

Figure 13-8

Chrono-functional Résumé

Marc R. Pollard
P. O. Box 739
Wilmington, DE 19735-7189
302 555-6753 (phone) 302 555-8312 (cell)
mpollard@aol.com ◆ http://www.mpollard.com

CAREER OBJECTIVE	Human resources director of a small progressive firm.
PROFILE	• Award-winning business graduate with more than ten years' supervisory experience. • Superior interpersonal skills, strong organizer with excellent planning and technical skills; proficiency in Microsoft Word and Access, Windows operating system, and web browsers. • Fluent in Spanish. • Online portfolio available for viewing at http://www.mpollard.com.
EXPERIENCE	**Assistant manager,** Freemont Inn, Smyrna, May 1990 – July 2000. • Began as desk clerk and promoted to desk manager after one year and assistant manager after three years. • Managed 6 to 10 desk clerks and bellhops during an eight-hour shift. • Recognized as Employee of the Month four times. **Director,** Fretz College, August 2000 to present (concurrent with education). • Supervised 72 upper-class male residents and enforced college regulations. • Provided individual and group counseling to residents having academic and personal problems. • Prepared work schedules and handled payroll for 5 resident assistants and 13 desk assistants. • Designed a computer-based work scheduling program adopted for use by all other residence hall directors.

Continued

Marginal notes (left column):

Summarizes key qualifications related to job requirements listed in the job posting. Uses this visible location to advertise the availability of an online portfolio where Marc has posted digital evidence of his skills.

Includes "Education" and "Experience," traditional headings in a chronological résumé but positions "Experience" first as the key qualifier.

Addresses requirements stated in the job posting that support Marc's ability to contribute to a potential employer. Adding "concurrent with education" emphasizes the initiative and discipline required to finance education and maintain academic honors.

Format Pointers

• Use a two-column format for easy location of specific sections.

• Creates visual appeal through custom format, two convenient columns with headings that emphasize relevant qualifications, and streamlined bulleted lists.

• Includes "Continued" at the bottom so the unstapled two-page résumé can be easily collated if separated.

Figure 13-8   *continued*

Marc R. Pollard   **Page 2**

EDUCATION	Bachelor of Science, Fretz College, Wilmington, Delaware. To be conferred May 1, 2004. **Major:** MANAGEMENT with a concentration in human resources. **Related courses:** International Management, International Communication, Spanish (three semesters), and technology courses.
	GPA: Major: 3.4; overall 3.5 (based on 4.0 scale).
	Honors: Phi Kappa Phi (top 10% of junior/senior class). Society of Human Resources Management (SHRM) National Championship HR team, 1st place winner, 2003.
COMMUNICATION SKILLS	Developed effective communication skills while counseling residents; learned the value of empathic listening and seeing ideas from the other person's perspective—skills relevant to quality employee training. Developed effective interpersonal skills through continuous interactions with hotel guests and supervision of 12 employees. Wrote memos, letters, business reports, and term papers and delivered presentations in business courses.
COMFORT WITH CRITICISM	Benefited from criticism of written materials and from critiques of presentations. Sensitive at first, came to recognize criticism as intent to help. Improved delivery skills after self-criticisms of taped presentations. Appreciate the need for tact in giving constructive criticism.
TECHNICAL PROFICIENCY	Elected to take three computer courses in addition to the two required for management majors. Most recently studied software programs (Microsoft Word and Access) are especially useful in producing effective reports. Applied basic computer skills and learned software programs specific to hotel management while working for Freemont Inn. Designed computer-based work scheduling program for residence hall management.
REFERENCES	Available through MonsterTRAK at http://www.monster.com.

Includes honors under "Education" because they are highly relevant to his job objective and were achieved as a part of his education. Divides section into short chunks that emphasize key points and increase readability.

Uses functional headings that represent factors in managerial success. Headings were identified through self- and career analysis (including an interview with a successful manager who had completed a management training program).

Notes that references can be accessed through Marc's registration with MonsterTRAK, a job bank for college students.

Format Pointers

- Places name and page number on page 2 for easy recognition of a multiple-page document.

- Removes hyperlink that is automatically added to e-mail addresses and URLs to increase appeal and to prevent blurring that would occur if the résumé is copied, faxed, or scanned.

Preparing a Scannable Résumé

Changing Technology

In addition to the traditional postal résumé read by a human, your résumé may be uploaded from a variety of sources into an electronic database where it will be read by a computer. Companies of all sizes are using **electronic applicant-tracking systems** to increase the efficiency of processing the volumes of résumés being submitted in a competitive market. Likely the career services center at your college uses an academic tracking system designed for processing résumés for campus recruiters.

Your efforts to adapt your traditional résumé will be more effective if you understand the demands of these tracking systems. The system processes incoming résumés in the following ways:

1. *Stores incoming résumés in an electronic database.* Résumés are uploaded from a variety of sources: Print résumés received by mail or fax, e-mail submissions, or postings to Internet job banks or corporate web sites. Because print résumés must first be scanned and converted into a digital format, they are often referred to as *scannable résumés*. However, any of these résumés is technically an *electronic résumé* because it will be read by the computer and not by a human.
2. *Compares the electronic résumés to a list of keywords and ranks applicants based on the number of keywords.* The keywords describe an ideal candidate and include mandatory and desired traits. The computer scans each résumé; the more matches of keywords included in a résumé, the higher the ranking on the computer's short list of candidates.
3. *Prepares letters of rejection and interview offers.* This automation is beneficial to job seekers who may receive no communication from companies processing applications manually.
4. *Stores the résumés, and accesses them for future openings.* The résumé remains in the system and is accessed whenever a new position is posted. A résumé is transferred into an employee tracking system when the applicant is hired to allow consideration for any job postings and internal promotions.

Critical Thinking

What are the advantages and disadvantages of an electronic tracking system?

Computerized résumé searches provide several distinct advantages to job seekers. Applicants are considered for every position in the company (not just reviewed by the recruiter whose desk on which the résumé happens to land); therefore, an applicant's résumé may be matched with a position he or she would not have applied for otherwise. The résumé remains in the system and is accessed whenever a new position is posted.[18]

When seeking a job with a company that scans résumés into an electronic database, you will need to submit a *scannable résumé*, one that can be read by a computer, and then follow up with a print (designed) résumé that will be read by a human if you are among the applicants selected to be interviewed. If you are unsure whether a company scans résumés, call and ask. If still in doubt, take the safe route and submit your résumé in both formats.

Formatting a Scannable Résumé

Critical Thinking

How will your print résumé need to be changed to comply with electronic format guidelines?

To ensure that the scanner can read your résumé accurately and clearly, you must prepare a plain résumé with no special formatting, often referred to as a "vanilla, no-frills" résumé.[19] Your objective is to use distinctive print that can still be read after it has been mushed and run together in the scanning process, and to resist the temptation to add graphic enhancements that cannot be read by a scanner. Follow these guidelines to prepare an electronic résumé that can be scanned accurately:

- *Use popular, nondecorative typefaces.* Typefaces such as Helvetica, Univers, Times New Roman, and New Century Schoolbook are clear and distinct and will not lose clarity in scanning.
- *Use 10- to 14-point font.* Computers cannot read small, tight print. With a larger font, your résumé may extend to two pages, but page length is not an issue because a computer is reading the résumé.
- *Do not include italics, underlining, open bullets, or graphic lines and boxes.* Use boldface or all capitals for emphasis. Italicized letters often touch and underlining may run into the text above; therefore, the scanned image may be garbled. Design elements, such as graphic lines, shading, and shadowing effects, confuse equipment designed to read text and not graphics. Use solid bullets (●); open bullets (○) may be read as o's.
- *Use ample white space.* Use at least one-inch margins. Leave plenty of white space between the sections of a résumé so that the computer recognizes the partitions.
- *Print on one side of white, standard-size paper with sharp laser print.* Send an original that is smudge-free; the scanner may pick up dirty specks on a photocopy. Colored and textured paper scans poorly.
- *Use a traditional résumé format.* Complex layouts that simulate catalogs or newspaper columns are confusing to the scanner.
- *Do not fold or staple your résumé.* If you must fold, do not fold on a line of text. Staples, when removed, make the pages stick together.

Making a Scannable Résumé Searchable

A few significant changes must be made in a print résumé to make it "computer-friendly." You have two concerns: (1) You want to be certain information is presented in a manner the computer can read, and (2) you want to maximize the number of "hits" your résumé receives in a computerized résumé search and thus enhance your ranking in the computer's short list of candidates. You may use more than one page if needed to present your qualifications. The more information you present the more likely you are to be selected from the database of applicants, and computers can read your résumé more quickly than humans can. Be sure to send a cover letter to reinforce your electronic résumé.

Follow these guidelines for modifying the content of your print résumé to make it searchable:

- *Position your name as the first readable item on the page.* Follow with your address, telephone number, fax number, and e-mail below your name on separate lines to avoid possible confusion by the systems.

Critical Thinking

Identify keywords from your print résumé that should appear in the electronic version.

- *Add powerful keywords in a separate section called "Keywords" or "Keyword Summary" that follows the identification.* To identify key words, highlight on a copy of your print (designed) résumé nouns you think the computer might use as keywords in the search. Ask yourself if these words describe your qualifications and continue looking for other words that label your qualifications. Make maximum use of industry jargon and standard, easily recognizable abbreviations (B.A., M.S.) in the keyword summary and the body of the résumé as these buzzwords will likely be matches with the computer's keywords.

Techniques for hammering out keywords offered by Kennedy and Morrow, leading consultants in the electronic job revolution, include asking yourself "What achievements would I discuss with my supervisor if I were meeting to discuss a raise?" Consider a job-related problem and describe the solution and every step required to solve the problem; consider the results. Consider actions, if done poorly, that would affect goals of the job and then state them positively. For example, a negative action is "an employee not getting to work on time"; stated positively, it becomes "efficiency minded and profit conscious."[20]

- *Format the keyword summary following these guidelines:* Capitalize the first letter of each word and separate each keyword with a period. Position the keywords describing your most important qualifications first and move to the least important ones. Order is important because some systems stop scanning after the first 80 keywords. The usual order is (a) job title, occupation, or career field, (b) education, and (c) essential skills for a specific position. Be certain to include keywords that describe interpersonal traits important to human resource managers. Examples of such keywords are *adaptable, flexible, sensitive, team player, willing to travel, ethical, industrious, innovative, open minded,* and *detail oriented.*

Critical Thinking

Make a list of industry jargon terms for your profession, along with their synonyms.

- *Support your keywords with specific facts in the body of the résumé.* Keep the keyword summary a reasonable length so that you have space to support your keywords. Use synonyms of your keywords in the body in the event the computer does not recognize the keyword (e.g., use M.B.A. in the keyword summary and Master of Business Administration in the body; use presentation graphics software in the keyword summary and a specific program in the body). One unfortunate applicant reported using "computer-assisted design" consistently throughout his résumé when the computer was searching for "CAD." Also, use a specific date of graduation in the education section. Some computer programs read two dates beside an institution to mean the applicant did not earn the degree (e.g., 2000–2004). If the degree is programmed as a requirement for the job (rather than a desirable qualification), this applicant would be excluded from the search.

The scannable résumé Jeanne Fulton prepared when seeking an entry-level audit position in a public accounting firm appears in Figure 13-9. Note how she presents qualifications that correspond to the company/job profile shown in Figure 13-2. The scannable résumé is formatted so that it can be scanned into an electronic database, and the content is searchable for an employer attempting to match applicants with an entry-level audit position.

Adapting to Varying Electronic Submission Requirements

Changing Technology

To this point you have focused on the preparation of paper documents: the print (designed) résumé that is read by humans and the scannable résumé that is submitted by mail or fax for computer scanning and processing. However, in the digital age of instant information, there are various other online methods for applying for a job and presenting your qualifications to prospective employers.

The easiest and most common method of putting your résumé online is through e-mailing a résumé to a job bank for posting or to a networking contact who asked you to send a résumé. Many job banks, corporate sites, and career services centers require you to respond to specific openings by completing an online form which may require you to paste your résumé into a designated section of the form. Frequently, you may input information directly on the web site or download the form to be submitted by e-mail, fax, or mail. You may also choose to post your résumé on your personal web page as a part of an electronic portfolio that showcases evidence of your qualifications.

Electronic submissions are quick and easy but present new challenges and many opportunities to jeopardize your employment chances and compromise your privacy. Just consider recent struggles you may have faced in dealing with viruses and unwelcomed e-mails, attempting to access nonworking links, and more. Before sending your résumé into cyberspace, follow these suggestions to ensure that your electronic submission is both professional and technically effective:

Legal & Ethical Constraints

- *Choose postings for your résumé with purpose.* Online resume postings are not confidential. Once your résumé is online, anyone can read it, including your current employer. You may also begin to receive junk mail and cold calls from companies who see your résumé online, and, even more seriously, you could become a victim of identify theft. To protect your privacy online, limit personal information disclosed in the résumé and post only to sites with password protection allowing you to approve the release of your résumé to specific employers. Dating your electronic résumé will also prevent embarrassment should your employer find an old version of your résumé, which could occur as result of exchange of résumés between career sites and delays in updating postings.

Figure 13-9

Scannable Résumé

Positions name as the first readable item. Entices employer to e-mail or visit her web site for additional qualifications; displays computer proficiency. →

Includes "Professional Profile" section that identifies job sought and reason to hire (same as a print résumé). →

Includes "Keyword Summary" section listing qualifications that match the job description. →

Supports keywords with specific facts; uses as many nouns as possible that might match those in the job description.

Uses synonyms of keywords in the body to ensure a match with the database (e.g., includes B.B.A. and M.P.A. and spells out degrees; includes general references to software applications and Internet browsers as well as names of specific software). →

JEANNE FULTON
89 Lincoln Street
San Antonio, TX 78285-9063
512 555–9823
jfulton@netdoor.com
www.netdoor/jfulton

Professional Profile

- First-year audit staff with an international accounting firm; interest in working in forensic accounting in an information systems environment.
- Technical proficiency in ERP systems, ACL, database, and spreadsheet.
- Realistic audit experience through cooperative education position with a regional CPA firm.
- Superior leadership abilities and team orientation developed through active involvement in student organizations; strong written and spoken communication skills.
- Fluency in Spanish.

Keywords

Entry-level audit position. Master's and bachelor's degrees in accounting. Sam Houston State University. 3.5 GPA. Beta Alpha Psi. Cooperative work experience. Inventory control. Spanish fluency. Traveled Mexico. Analytical ability. Computer proficiency. Communication skills. Team player. Ethical. Creative. Adaptable. Willing to relocate. Windows. Software applications. Word, Excel, Access, PowerPoint. ACL. ERP Systems. Internet. Netscape. Web design.

Education

M.P.A., Accounting, Systems Emphasis, Sam Houston State University, August 2004, GPA 3.8.
B.B.A., Accounting, Sam Houston State University, May 2003, GPA 3.6.
- President's Scholar 2000–2004
- Beta Alpha Psi (honorary accounting society)
- Mortar Board
- Lloyd Markham Academic Scholarship

Technical Skills

- Proficient in Windows, database and spreadsheet, ERP systems, ACL, Internet browsers (Netscape, Internet Explorer), and web design.
- Fluent Spanish; have traveled to Mexico.

Format Pointers

- Keeps résumé simple and readable by the computer: ample white space especially between sections; font style that does not allow letters to touch; font size within the font range of 10 to 14 points; solid bullets; and no italics, underlining, or graphic lines or borders.
- Mails the résumé with a cover letter and a print résumé unfolded and unstapled in a large envelope.

Figure 13-9   *continued*

Can extend beyond one page without concern because a computer will read résumé.

Jeanne Fulton   **Page 2**

Employment

Cooperative Education Program, Smith & Lewis, CPAs, San Antonio, Texas, June–December 2004

- Participated in the rollout of a client's supply chain management system.
- Upgraded the firm's web site to provide prospective clients with assistance in learning the benefits to be achieved by implementing supply chain management and customer relationship management systems.
- Developed time management skills, team building, and communication skills while completing independent projects with teams of accounting staff at various levels.
- Demonstrated ability to accept and respond to criticism, learn job tasks quickly, and perform duties with minimal supervision.

Projectionist/cashier/usher, DeVille Cinema, Marshall, Texas, March 2002–August 2003.

- Learned the technical skills needed to run and maintain projection equipment and selected to train other employees.
- Completed tasks under pressure with speed and accuracy and attention to positive customer service.

Leadership Activities

Phi Beta Lambda, national business organization, 2001–present

- Served as state president and local chapter treasurer.
- Managed the activities of state chapter, planned meetings/agenda for state board and conferences, and coordinated various conferences and leadership workshops.
- Refined communication skill by presenting speeches and workshops statewide and presiding over board meetings and the state conference.
- Used Microsoft Office Suite to prepare registration materials, informational mailings, and conference programs and manage organization's database.
- Received commendation from state executive board and others for strong organizational skills and excellent written and spoken communication.

Student Government Association, assistant director, University Services, Sam Houston University, 2003

- Organized and led a committee to identify ways to improve campus transportation. Resulted in the implementation of an on-campus shuttle service.
- Applied strong organizational and leadership skills and research and written and spoken communication skills.

Emphasizes willingness to provide a professional, more impressive document.

An attractive and fully formatted hard copy version of this document is available upon request.

Includes date of last revision to avoid confusion or embarrassment if the résumé is accessed after she has accepted a position.

Last revised 10/15/04

Format Pointers

- Alerts reader that a print résumé is available.

Online job searching can benefit both the applicant and the employer. It can, however, erode privacy for both parties. Those who post résumés or job vacancies should be fully aware of their potential audience.

Legal & Ethical Constraints

Protect your references' privacy by omitting their names when posting online. Withholding this information will prevent unwelcomed calls by recruiters needed to fill vacancies or other inappropriate contacts and threats to privacy. Although technology allows broadcast of your résumé to all available positions on a career site, read postings carefully and apply only to those that match your qualifications. This action improves the inefficiency of the job selection process for the company and the applicant and depicts fair, ethical behavior.

- ***Don't get in a hurry.*** The speed, convenience, and informality of filling in online boxes or composing an e-mail cover letter for an attached résumé can easily lead to sloppiness that is sure to reflect negatively on your abilities and speak volumes about your attitude. Make sure every aspect of your electronic submission is top-notch just as you would for a print résumé. Provide all information exactly as requested, write concise, clear statements relevant to the job sought, and proofread carefully for grammatical and spelling errors. Should you direct an employer to an electronic portfolio, devote necessary time to make it attractive, informative, and technically sound. Double-check your files to ensure that they can be opened and retain an appealing format. Finally, read the posting carefully so you understand how long your résumé will remain active, how to update it, and how to delete it from the site.

Changing Technology

- ***Include your résumé in the format requested by the employer or job bank.*** You may be instructed to send the résumé as an attachment to the message or include it in the body of an e-mail message, known as an **inline résumé**. The inline résumé is becoming the preferred choice as fear of computer viruses and daily e-mail overload prevent employers from opening attachments.

    Unless instructed to send your attachment in a specific format such as Word, save your résumé and cover letter in one file beginning with the cover letter as an ASCII or Rich Text Format file with line length limited to 65 characters and spacing. This plain text version, referred to as a **text résumé** removes formatting and lacks the appeal of your designed résumé; however, you can be confident that an employer can open the file and won't have to spend time "cleaning up" your résumé if it doesn't transmit correctly. For this reason, you'll also paste the text version of your résumé below your e-mail message when sending an inline résumé.

As an added safeguard regardless of the format you've chosen, send yourself and a couple of friends a copy of the résumé and see how it looks on different computers before sending it out to an employer. If you wish, follow up with a print résumé and cover letter on high quality paper.

- *Include a keyword summary after the identification section.* Just as you did in the scannable résumé, you'll want to grab the employer's attention by placing the keywords—a strong list of skills employers want—on the first screen (within the first 24 lines of text). Providing this relevant information will motivate the employer to keep scrolling down to see how the keywords are supported in the body rather than to click to the next résumé.

- *E-mail a cover letter to accompany an online résumé.* Some companies consider this cover e-mail message to be prescreening for a job interview. Send the message promptly and write a formal, grammatically correct message just as you would if you were sending an application letter in the mail.

Supplementing a Résumé

Objective 5

Utilize employment tools other than the résumé that can enhance employability.

Changing
Technology

Some candidates may feel their career accomplishments are not appropriately captured in a standard résumé. Two additional tools for communicating your qualifications and abilities are the portfolio and the employment video.

Professional Portfolios

The professional portfolio (also called the *electronic* or **e-portfolio** when presented in a digital format) can be used to illustrate past activities, projects, and accomplishments. It is a collection of artifacts that demonstrate your communication, people, and technical skills. Although portfolios were once thought of as only for writers, artists, or photographers, they are now seen as appropriate for other fields of work when the applicant wants to showcase abilities.

Many portfolios are now presented in digital format making the portfolio easier to organize and distribute to prospective employers via a web site, or burned on a CD-ROM or other media. With the availability of user-friendly software, college campuses are offering e-portfolio systems that aid students in reflecting on their experiences and producing e-portfolios. Just as students are currently not asked if they have an e-mail account, predictions are that soon they will also be expected to have "a web space that represents their learning and their assessment."[21]

A clear understanding of your audience's needs and your qualifications will allow you to develop a logical organizational structure for your portfolio. You may find the planning forms available at the text support site (http://lehman.swlearning.com) helpful for planning your showcase of accomplishments. Some possible items for inclusion are

Critical Thinking

What items would you include in your professional portfolio?

- sample speeches with digitized audio or video clips of the delivery.
- performance appraisals.
- awards.
- certificates of completion.
- reports, proposals, or computer samples from classes.
- brochures describing workshops attended.
- records or surveys showing client or customer satisfaction with service.
- attendance records.
- thank-you letters.

Critical Thinking

What types of information do you think Jeanne could include to showcase her education, work experience, and leadership activities? What work samples might she include?

After selecting the items for inclusion in your portfolio, you will need to select the appropriate software or binders you will use to showcase your accomplishments. Once you're organized, you can add items that demonstrate that you have the characteristics the employer is seeking. The portfolio should be continually maintained even after you are hired because it can demonstrate your eligibility for promotion, salary increase, advanced training, or even justify why you should not be laid off.[22]

For illustration purposes, take a look at Jeanne Fulton's electronic portfolio shown in Figure 13-10 that was created using a Microsoft web template and posted to her personal web page. Her name appears in a highly visible location along with her objective and career statement copied directly from her print résumé. To ensure online privacy and avoid discriminatory hiring, she omits all personal information (address, phone numbers, and photos) but provides a handy link to her e-mail. An employer can access two versions of her résumé: a text version for download into an electronic database and a print (designed) version that can be printed with one command for filing or closer reading. Finally, attractive links communicate the table of contents for the evidence she has selected. Note the labels reflect the key job qualifications that employers can immediately recognize from a targeted print résumé (education, experience, achievements). The links provide freedom to explore the information in any order desired. Subsequent screens are appealing, uncluttered pages that display the selective evidence she has chosen to include.

Critical Thinking

What additional items would you link to your electronic portfolio résumé?

Employment Videos

A video recording may be used to extend the impact of the printed résumé visually. A video can capture your stage presence and ability to speak effectively and add a human dimension to the written process. The most current technology enables applicants to embed video segments into ***multimedia***

Changing Technology

Figure 13-10

Electronic Portfolio Posted to an Applicant's Personal Web Site

Begins with name and professional profile just as on her résumé. Omits information that might encourage illegal discrimination, such as age or photo.

Jeanne Fulton

Includes link to an ASCII or Rich Text Format version of her résumé (no special formatting) that an employer can download into an electronic database.

Text Only Résumé
Download a text version of my résumé.

Complete Résumé
View or print a fully formatted copy of my résumé.

Includes link to a formatted résumé that can be read by scrolling down the screen and printed with one command.

Provides a link to e-mail to facilitate communication with a prospective employer.

Feedback
www.netdoor/jfulton

Includes links to additional information with titles that employers will recognize as sections typically found in a print résumé.

Includes date of latest revision to avoid confusion or embarrassment if résumé postings are not updated regularly.

Professional Profile

- First-year audit staff with an international accounting firm; interest in working in forensic accounting in an information systems environment.
- Technical proficiency in ERP systems, ACL, database, and spreadsheet.
- Realistic audit experience through cooperative education experience with a regional CPA firm.
- Superior leadership abilities and team orientation developed through active involvement in student organizations; strong written and spoken communication skills.
- Fluency in Spanish.

Additional information to support my qualifications

- Education
- Work Experience
- Leadership Activities
- Work Samples

Last updated 07/10/04

résumés created with presentation software such as PowerPoint® or Visual Communicator® and sent to prospective employers on a CD-ROM or DVD or posted on the applicant's personal web page. Accessing this information from a computer that is likely positioned on a recruiter's desk is much more convenient than having to move to a VCR to play a videotape.

Employment videos are more commonly used to obtain employment in career fields for which verbal delivery or visual performance is a key element. These fields include broadcasting and the visual and performing arts.

The following guidelines apply when preparing an employment video:

- Make sure the video makes a professional appearance and is complimentary to you. A "home movie" quality recording will be a liability instead of an asset to your application.
- Avoid long "talking head" segments. Include segments that reflect you in a variety of activities; shots that include samples of your work are also desirable.
- Remember that visual media (such as photographs and videos) encourage the potential employer to focus on your physical characteristics and attributes, which may lead to undesired stereotyping and discrimination.

Legal & Ethical Constraints

Be sure to advertise the availability of your portfolio and employment video to maximize its exposure. List your URL address in the identification section of your résumé. In your application letter, motivate the prospective employer to view your portfolio or video by describing the types of information included. Talk enthusiastically about the detailed supplementary information available during your a job interview and encourage the interviewer to view it when convenient. Note Jeanne Fulton's promotion of her e-portfolio when you read her application letter later in this chapter (Figure 13-11).

Critical Thinking

Would a video enhance employability in your career field? If so, what elements would you include in your video?

Composing Application Messages

Objective **6**

Write an application message that effectively introduces an accompanying print (designed) or electronic résumé.

When employers invite you to send a résumé regardless of whether the résumé is sent by mail or electronically, they expect you to include an **application** or **cover message**. A mailed paper résumé should be accompanied by an application letter. When a résumé is submitted electronically, the application "letter" can take the form of an e-mail message. As you have learned, a résumé summarizes information related to the job's requirements and the applicant's qualifications. An application message (1) seeks to arouse interest in the résumé, (2) introduces it, and (3) interprets it in terms of employer benefits. The application message is placed on top of (or above) the résumé so it can be read first.

Because it seeks to arouse interest and to point out employer benefits, the application message is persuasive and, thus, written inductively. It is designed to convince an employer that qualifications are adequate just as a sales message is designed to convince a buyer that a product will satisfy a need. Like sales messages, application messages are either solicited or unsolicited. Job advertisements *solicit* applications. Unsolicited application messages have greater need for attention-getters; otherwise, solicited and unsolicited application messages are based on the same principles.

Critical Thinking

What is the purpose of an application message?

SPOTLIGHT COMMUNICATOR

Open Employee Communication Fosters Superior Productivity

Imagine the two-minute warning sounding at a hotly contended game. Your team is driving down the field, determined to pull out a last-minute, come-from-behind victory. It's the ultimate team adventure, yet you have two players sitting on the bench that don't even know the score. What good are they? Kip Tindell, president, CEO, and co-founder of The Container Store, believes that company players must know the score at all times if they are to contribute to overall team success.

"We share just about everything with our employees . . . from daily sales to expansion plans," says Tindell. "We even distribute financial information, and yes, I know that occasionally information falls into the wrong hands. We decided . . . that communicating valuable information empowers our employees, strengthens their development,

enhances their contributions and reinforces their loyalty. The advantages far outweigh the disadvantage of the information settling in the wrong hands."[23]

Every day, the company "huddles" all employees to distribute sales results from the previous day. Sales goals for the day are also clearly communicated to everyone. Employees are trained in the company philosophy that selling is good for the customer—and the sales associate (profit sharing can significantly boost the typical $45,000 a year salary).[24] Additionally, periodic staff meetings of the company's top 200 employees are held in Dallas for up to a week, where staffers view the same PowerPoint presentation as the board of directors. Following that meeting, copious and meticulous notes are sent to every employee nationwide.[25]

COURTESY THE CONTAINER STORE

Tindell and other The Container Store managers actively practice the belief that information is power. According to Tindell, being well-informed generates a fierce sense of ownership by all employees in the company, and customers can sense the resulting energy. Low employee turnover results in significant savings for the company in terms of employment search costs.

Applying What You Have Learned

1. How is an environment of trust developed at The Container Store?
2. Describe the relationship between employee loyalty and financial performance.

Kip Tindell, President, CEO, and Co-Founder, The Container Store

http://www.containerstore.com

Refer to ShowCASE, Part 3, at the end of the chapter to learn about the company's creative employee incentives.

Refer to ShowCASE, Part 3, at the end of the chapter to learn about the company's creative employee incentives.

Critical Thinking

What does an application message have in common with a sales message?

Unsolicited application messages are the same basic message (perhaps with slight modifications) sent to many prospective employers. By sending unsolicited messages, you increase your chances of locating potential openings and may alert employers to needs they had not previously identified for someone of your abilities. However, sending unsolicited messages has some disadvantages. Because the employer's specific needs are not known, the opening paragraph will likely be more general (less targeted to a specific position) than the opening paragraph in solicited messages. The process could also be expensive.

Persuasive Organization

A persuasive message is designed to persuade the reader to take action, which in this case is to get the reader to read the résumé and invite you to an interview. Because an application message is a persuasive communication, organize it as you would a sales message:

Sales Message	Application Message
Gets attention	Gets attention
Introduces product	Introduces qualifications
Presents evidence	Presents evidence
Encourages action	Encourages action
(sells a product, service, or idea)	(results in an interview)

Critical Thinking

What central appeal could you develop to convince an employer to hire you? How might you introduce it in the attention-getting paragraph?

Like a well-written sales message, a well-written application message uses a central selling feature as a theme. The central selling feature is introduced in the first or second paragraph and stressed in paragraphs that follow. Two to four paragraphs are normally sufficient for supporting evidence. Consider order of importance as a basis for their sequence, with the most significant aspects of your preparation coming first.

Gain the Receiver's Attention

To gain attention, begin the message by identifying the job sought and describing how your qualifications fit the job requirements. This information will provide instant confirmation that you are a qualified applicant for a position open in that company. An employer required to read hundreds of application letters and résumés will appreciate this direct, concise approach.

If you are applying for a job that has been announced, you may indicate in the first paragraph how you learned of the position—for example, employee referral, customer referral, executive referral, newspaper advertising, or job fair. Your disclosure will not only confirm you are seeking a job the manager has open but will facilitate evaluation of the company's recruiting practices. Note the opening of the letter in Figure 13-11 on page 587 indicates the applicant learned of the position through a referral from a professor.

Critical Thinking

How does an unsolicited application message differ from one responding to an announced position? How are they similar?

An opening for an unsolicited message must be more persuasive: you must convince the interviewer to continue to read your qualifications even though a job may not exist. As in the opening of a solicited message, indicate the type of position sought and your qualifications but be more creative in gaining the receiver's attention. The following paragraph uses the applicant's knowledge of recent company developments and an intense interest in the company's future to gain the receiver's attention.

> During the past few years, TelCom has experienced phenomenal growth through various acquisitions, mergers, and market expansion. With this growth comes new opportunities, new customers, and the need for new team players to work in sales and marketing. While following the growth of TelCom, I have become determined to join this exciting team and am eager to show you that my educational background, leadership abilities, and internship experience qualify me for the job.

Provide Evidence of Qualifications

Critical Thinking

How can a job applicant assure that the application message is not just a "rehash" of the résumé?

For graduating students entering the world of full-time work for the first time, educational backgrounds usually are more impressive than work histories. They can benefit from interpreting their educational experiences as meaningful, job-related experiences. An applicant for acceptance into an auditor's trainee program should do more than merely report having taken auditing theory and practice:

> In my auditing theory and practice class, I could see specific application of principles encountered in my human relations and psychology classes. Questions about leadership and motivation seemed to recur throughout the course: What really motivates executives? Why are auditors feared at many levels? How can those fears be overcome? How can egos be salvaged? The importance of the human element was a central focus of many courses and my research report, "The Auditor as a Psychologist."

Because the preceding paragraph included questions discussed in a class, do not assume that your application message should do likewise. Or because this paragraph gives the title of a research project, do not assume the same technique is a must for your message. The techniques illustrated are commendable because they help to portray the educational experience as meaningful and related to the job sought. Recognizing that auditors must be tactful (a point on which the person reading the message will surely agree), the applicant included some details of a class. That technique is a basic in persuasion: Do not just say a product or idea is good; say what makes it good. Do not just say that a certain educational or work experience was beneficial; say what made it so.

By making paragraphs long enough to include interpretation of experiences on the present or previous job, you can give an employer some confidence that you are well prepared for your next job. For example, the following excerpt from an applicant whose only work experience was at a fast-food restaurant is short and general: *For three months last summer, I worked at Marketplace Bagel. While the assistant manager was on vacation, I supervised a crew of five on the evening shift. Evaluations of my work were superior.*

As the only reference to the Marketplace Bagel experience, the paragraph conveys one employer's apparent satisfaction with performance. Superior evaluations and some supervisory responsibility are evidence of that satisfaction, but added details and interpretation could make the message more convincing:

> In my summer job at Marketplace Bagel, I learned the value of listening carefully when taking orders, making change quickly and accurately, offering suggestions when customers seemed hesitant, and keeping a cheerful attitude. Supervising a crew of five while the assistant manager was on vacation, I appreciated the importance of fairness and diplomacy in working with other employees.

Apparently, the applicant's experience has been meaningful. It called attention to qualities that managers like to see in employees: willingness to listen, speed, accuracy, concern for clients or customers, a positive attitude, fairness, and tact. As a *learning* experience, the Marketplace Bagel job has taught or reinforced some principles that the employer will see can be transferred to the job being sought.

Critical Thinking

How can an applicant give the impression of confidence in the application message without appearing overly aggressive?

In this section, you can discuss qualifications you have developed by participating in student organizations, student government, athletics, or community organizations. Be specific in describing the skills you have gained that can be applied directly on the job—for example, organizational, leadership, spoken and written communication skills, and budgeting and financial management. You can also use your involvement in student activities as a vehicle for discussing important personal traits vital to the success of a business—interpersonal skills, motivation, imagination, responsibility, team orientation, and so forth.

> For the past year, I have served as state president of Phi Beta Lambda, a national business student organization. By coordinating various statewide meetings and leadership seminars, I have refined communication, organizational, and interpersonal skills.

Finally, end this section with an indirect reference to the résumé. If you refer to it in the first or second paragraph, readers may wonder whether they are expected to turn from the message at that point and look at the résumé. Avoid the obvious statement *"Enclosed please find my résumé"* or *"A résumé is enclosed."* Instead, refer indirectly to the résumé while restating your qualifications. The following sentence emphasizes that references confirm the statements the applicant has made about his/her qualifications:

> References listed on the enclosed résumé would be glad to comment on my accounting education and experience.

Encourage Action

Critical Thinking

How does a successful application message lead the reader to the desired action?

Now that you have presented your qualifications and referred to the enclosed résumé, the next move is to encourage the receiver to extend an invitation for an interview. The goal is to introduce the idea of action without apologizing for doing so and without being demanding or "pushy." If the final paragraph (action closing) of your message is preceded by paragraphs that are impressive, you need not press hard for a response. Just mentioning the idea of a future discussion is probably sufficient. If you have significant related experience and have developed this experience as a central selling feature, mentioning this experience in the action closing would add unity and stress your strongest qualification one last time. Forceful statements about *when* and *how* to respond are unnecessary and could arouse resentment. Do avoid some frequently made errors:

- *Setting a date.* "May I have an appointment with you on March 14?" The date you name could be inconvenient; or even if it is convenient for the employer, your forwardness in setting it could be resented.
- *Expressing doubt.* "If you agree," "I hope you will," and "Should you decide" use subjunctive words that indicate lack of confidence.
- *Sounding apologetic.* "May I take some of your time" or "I know how busy you are" may seem considerate, but an apology is inappropriate when discussing ways you can contribute to a company.
- *Sounding overconfident.* "I know you will want to set up an appointment." This statement is presumptuous and egotistical.
- *Giving permission to call.* "You may call me at 555-6543." By making the call sound like a privilege ("may call") you could alienate the reader. Implied meaning: You are very selective about the calls you take, but the employer does qualify.
- *Reporting capability of response.* "You can call me at 555-6543." When a number or address is given, employers are aware they are capable of using it ("can call").

The following sentences are possible closing sentences that refer to an invitation to interview. They are not intended as model sentences that should appear in your message. Because finding the right job is so important, you will be well rewarded for the time and thought invested in original wording.

- *"When a date and time can be arranged, I would like to talk with you."* The statement does not indicate who will do the arranging, and the meeting place and the subject of the conversation are understood.
- *"I would appreciate an opportunity to discuss the loan officer's job with you."* The indirect reference to action is not forceful. However, if the applicant has impressive qualifications, the reader will want an interview and will not need to be pushed.
- *"I would appreciate an appointment to discuss your employment needs and my information systems experience."* The statement asks

for the interview and re-emphasizes the applicant's strong related work experience.

General Writing Guidelines

Critical Thinking

Is an employer's busy schedule a valid argument for keeping an application message short?

Writing an excellent application message may be the most difficult message you ever attempt to write. It's natural to feel uncomfortable writing about yourself; however, your confidence will increase as you study the wealth of model documents available through your career services center as well as other sources and writing principles you've been introduced to in this chapter. Then, commit to the challenging task of writing a thoughtful, original message that impresses the interviewer. Instead of standard verbiage included in dozens of models, your self-marketing connects *your* experiences to your future at a specific company and reflects *your* personality and values. The following writing techniques will help in distinguishing your application message from the dozens of competing ones:

Critical Thinking

What other "filler statements" can you identify that add no real content to the application letter?

- ***Substitute fresh, original expressions that reflect contemporary language.*** Outdated expressions, overused, and obvious statements will give your message a dull, unimaginative tone and may be perceived as disrespectful. Overly casual language is also inappropriate. Obvious ideas such as "This is an application," "I read your ad," and "I am writing to apply for," are sufficiently understood without making direct statements. With the application message *and* résumé in hand, a reader learns nothing from "I am enclosing my résumé for your review." Observe caution in choosing overused words such as *applicant, application, opening, position, vacancy, interview.*

- ***Avoid overuse of "I" and writer-focused statements.*** Because the message is designed to sell your services, some use of "I" is natural and expected; but restrict the number of times "I" is used, especially as the first word in a paragraph. Focus on providing specific evidence that you can meet the company's needs. The employer is not interested in reading about your need to earn more income, to be closer to your work, to have more pleasant surroundings, or to gain greater advancement opportunities.

- ***Avoid unconvincing generalizations that may sound boastful.*** Self-confidence is commendable, but overconfidence (or worse still, just plain bragging) is objectionable. Overly strong adjectives, self-judgmental terms, and unsupported generalizations damage your credibility. Instead of labeling your performance as "superior" or "excellent," or describing yourself as "an efficient, technically skilled team player" give supporting facts that show the interviewer you can deliver on what you're selling.

- ***Tailor the message to the employer's need.*** To impress the interviewer that your message is not a generic one sent to everyone, provide requested information and communicate an understanding of the particular company, job requirements, and field.

- *Provide requested information.* Job listings often request certain information: "Must provide own transportation and be willing to travel. Give educational background, work experience, and salary expected." Discuss these points in your application message. Preferably, the question of salary is left until the interview, allowing you to focus your message on your contributions to the company—not what you want from the company (money). Discussion of salary isn't meaningful until after a mutually successful interview; however, if an ad requests a statement about it, the message should address it. You may give a minimum figure or range, indicate willingness to accept a figure that is customary for work of that type, or indicate a preference for discussing salary at the interview.

- *Communicate knowledge of the company, job requirements, and language of the field.* Your statements about a company's rapid expansion or competitive advantage show you really are interested in the company, read widely, do more than you are required to do, gather information before making decisions, and so on. However, phrase these statements carefully to avoid the perception of insincere flattery. For example, referring to the employer as "*the* leader in the field," "*the* best in the business," or "a great company" may appear as an attempt to get a favorable decision as a reward for making a complimentary statement. To reflect your understanding of the job requirements, use indirect statements that are informative and tactful. Direct statements such as "The requirements of this job are . . . " presents information the employer presumes you already know; "An auditor should be able to . . . " and "Sales personnel should avoid . . . " sound like a lecture and may be perceived as condescending. Discussing experiences related to a specific job requirement or your preference for work that requires this skill reveals your understanding without a direct statement. Including terminology commonly used by the profession allows you to communicate clearly in terms the reader understands; it also saves space and implies your background in the field.

- *Focus on strengths and portray a positive attitude.* Concentrate on the positive aspects of your education or experience that have prepared you for the particular job. Apologizing for a shortcoming or admitting failure only weakens your case and raises questions about your self-esteem. Do not discuss your current employer's shortcomings. Regardless of how negatively you perceive your present employer, that perception has little to do with your prospective employer's needs. Also, if you speak negatively of your present employer, you could be perceived as someone who would do the same to the next employer.

Finishing Touches

The importance of professional formatting and careful proofreading of a print document is generally understood. However, proofing and formatting a "real" résumé and letter appears more important to some applicants than producing quality e-mail submissions. Employers frequently voice concern with the sloppiness and unprofessional appearance and content of electronic submissions. To survive the skeptical eye of an interviewer scanning for ways to reject an applicant, allow yourself time to produce a professional-looking document regardless of the presentation or delivery option you've chosen. Get opinions from others and make revisions where necessary.

Regardless of your delivery option, address your application letter or e-mail message to the specific individual who is responsible for hiring for the position you are seeking rather than sending the document to the "Human Resources Department" or "To Whom It May Concern." If necessary, consult the company's annual report or web site, or call the company to locate this information. Verify the correct spelling, job title, and address, and send a personalized message to the appropriate individual. Keep the message short and easy to read. A one-page letter is sufficient for most applications but especially for students and graduates entering the job market. Apply visual enhancements learned previously to enhance the appeal and readability of the message and to draw attention to your strengths. Definitely keep the paragraphs short and consider listing your top four or five achievements or other important ideas in a bulleted list.

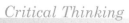

Critical Thinking

What color paper is best for an application letter in your career field?

Use paper that matches the résumé (color, weight, texture, and size). The watermark should be readable across the sheet in the same direction as the printing. Since you're using plain paper, include your street address and city, state, and ZIP Code above the date or formatted as a letterhead at the top of the page. Include "Enclosure" a double-space below the signature block to alert the employer that a résumé is enclosed. The proper letter format is shown in the example in Figure 13-11. If necessary, refer to Appendix A for more on professional letter layouts and pages 560–561 for formatting tips for print résumés that also relate to the accompanying letter.

When preparing an application message for e-mail submission, career experts recommend formatting it as a business letter with the complete address of the company exactly as presented in a letter sent by mail. To compete with the high volumes of junk mail, daily messages, and fear of computer viruses, you must provide a motive for an interviewer to open an unexpected message from an unknown person. Messages with missing or vague subject lines are annoying and may be ignored or deleted immediately. To bring attention to your message, include the name of the person referring you to the position directly in the subject line or mention your e-mail is a follow-up to a conversation (RE: Follow-up: Résumé for . . .). If the message is totally "cold," describe the specific value you can add to the company (Résumé for Forensics Accountant with Extensive ACL Skills). Stay away from tricks such as marking an e-mail "urgent" or adding "re" to pass your message off as a reply to an earlier message. Typically, you will want to send a complete letter and copy of your résumé by regular mail as a follow-up to the e-mail submission.

Legal & Ethical Constraints

Examples of Application Messages

Critical Thinking

How can you be sure that your application message is error free?

Jeanne Fulton wrote the letter in Figure 13-11 to accompany a chronological résumé she prepared after completing the company/job profile of an entry-level auditor shown in Figure 13-2. The time Jeanne devoted to analyzing the job, the company, and her qualifications was well spent. Notice how Jeanne discusses qualifications that correspond closely with the job requirements listed in the company/job profile: intellectual skills, technical skills, interpersonal skills, knowledge of work environment, ethical standards, and communication skills.

Before writing a résumé and application message, study carefully the overall suggestions in the "General Writing Guidelines" near the end of Chapter 6. Then study the specific suggestions in the "Check Your Communication" checklist on the following page. Compare your work with this checklist again after you have written a rough draft and make any necessary revisions.

Summary

1. **Prepare for employment by considering relevant information about yourself as it relates to job requirements.** A job candidate should complete systematic self-, career-, and job analyses. As in other important decisions, you must gather information to make wise career decisions, asking questions about yourself, about a possible career, and about a specific job in the chosen field. Interview people already working at the job. Recording and analyzing this information will assist you in selecting a satisfying career and preparing an effective résumé.

2. **Identify career opportunities using traditional and electronic methods.** The job candidate can widen employment opportunities by using traditional and electronic methods for the employment search. Names and addresses of possible employers may be obtained from networks, career services centers at schools, employers' offices, employment agencies and contractors, help-wanted ads, online databases and printed sources, and professional organizations. Information is available via the Internet about how to conduct a successful electronic job search. Company web sites can be accessed that provide information about the organizations and list job vacancies. The job seeker can also network with prospective employers through electronic job fairs, news groups, and chat sessions. General job listings are available by career field through a variety of online sources.

3. **Prepare a persuasive résumé that reflects the most effective organizational pattern.** The most effective résumé for a particular candidate could be a chronological,

functional, or chrono-functional résumé. A résumé typically includes identification, objective, career summary, qualifications, personal information, and references. To compete favorably for a job, use the full capability of computer technology to develop an appealing, easy-to-read design and print a high-quality copy. Chronological résumés have headings such as "Education" and "Experience" and list experiences in reverse chronological order; they are appropriate for applicants who have the apparent qualifications for the job. Functional résumés show applicant qualifications as headings; this format is especially effective for applicants who lack the appropriate education and experience. The chrono-functional résumé lists education and experience as headings and uses functional headings that emphasize qualifications.

4. **Adapt the résumé for alternate presentation and delivery options, including print (designed), scannable versions, and electronic postings.** Effective print (designed) résumés concisely highlight key qualifications and are formatted for quick, easy reading. Appropriate choices in arrangement, formatting, and paper quality add interest and visual appeal. Scannable résumés are designed so that the information can be scanned and processed by an applicant-tracking system. An effective keyword section that summarizes the applicant's qualifications helps assure that the résumé is identified during a search for matching requirements. Omission of special print effects aids in scanning accuracy. Electronic résumé posting varies considerably, with popular options including a job bank posting, a web site

Figure 13-11

Example of an Application Letter

Inductive Outline for an Application Letter

1. Gain the employer's attention by identifying the job sought and describing how qualifications fit the job requirements.
   Solicited: May indicate how applicant learned of position (ad or referral).
   Unsolicited: Must convince employer to read. Could begin by showing knowledge of recent company developments.
2. Provide convincing evidence of qualifications.
3. Refer to the résumé indirectly while restating qualifications. Mention the availability of a web site or portfolio for additional information (optional).
4. Encourage the employer to extend an invitation for an interview.

Addresses the letter to a specific person using correct name and job title.

Reveals how she learned of the position, identifies a specific job sought, and introduces her background.

Discusses how education relates to the job requirements.

Highlights skills related to the job requirements (ideas from the company/job profile where she identified the job requirements and her qualifications).

Introduces the résumé and a web site for additional information.

Encourages employer to take action without sounding pushy or apologetic.

Format Pointers

- Formats as a formal business letter since the message is accompanying a print résumé. An abbreviated e-mail message followed by an inline résumé in ASCII or RTF format would be appropriate for an electronic submission.

- Uses the same high-quality paper used for the résumé (neutral color, standard size); includes writer's address because letter is printed on plain paper.

Jeanne Fulton | *89 Lincoln Street* | *San Antonio, TX 78285-9063*

October 15, 2004

Mr. Colin Franklin, Partner
Foster & Daniel, CPAs
1000 Plaza Court
Austin, TX 78710-1000

Dear Mr. Franklin:

Dr. Lindsay, an accounting professor at Sam Houston State University, told me that Foster & Daniel has an auditing position available. A systems emphasis in my masters degree and my related work experience qualify me for this auditing position.

Because of my interest in fraud, I utilized my elective courses to enhance my skills in the area of forensic accounting. Courses in computer programming, networks, computer security, and criminology have given me the skills to extract data from today's enterprise resource planning software and search for frauds using ACL, IDEA, Excel, and Access. I especially enjoyed my elective courses in Internal Auditing and Information Technology Auditing. Unstructured, often ambiguous problems that require creative solutions are among my favorite assignments.

My experience at Smith & Lewis also gave me countless opportunities to interact with practicing auditors, often assisting them at client locations. These firsthand experiences have prepared me for working long, irregular hours; working effectively as a member of an audit team; and building trust and credibility with clients. My performance ratings were excellent with commendations for superior technical proficiency and strong written and spoken communication skills.

Please review the enclosed résumé for additional information about my accounting education and related work experience. Work samples and further detail are available in my electronic portfolio at jfulton@netdoor.com. Please call or write so we can discuss my joining the audit staff at Foster & Daniel.

Sincerely,

Jeanne Fulton

Jeanne Fulton

Enclosure

Résumés and Application Messages

Print (Designed) Résumé

Content

- Include relevant qualifications compatible with job requirements generated from analyses of self, career, and the job.
- Present qualifications truthfully and honestly.

Organization

- Choose organizational pattern that highlights key qualifications: chronological, functional, or chrono-functional.
- Arrange headings in appropriate sequence.
- Place significant ideas in emphatic position.
- List experiences consistently, either in time sequence or in order of importance.

Style

- Omit personal pronouns.
- Use action verbs.
- Use past tense for previous jobs; present tense for present job.
- Place significant words in emphatic positions.
- Use parallelism in listing multiple items.
- Use positive language.
- Use simple words (but some jargon of the field is acceptable).

Mechanics

- Assure there are *no* keying, grammar, spelling, or punctuation errors.
- Balance elements on the page.
- Use ample margins even if a second page is required.
- Include a page number on all pages except the first and "continued" at the bottom of the first page to indicate a multiple-page document.
- Position headings consistently throughout.
- Use an outline format or a bulleted list to emphasize multiple points.
- Use indention, underlining, capitalization, font changes, and graphic lines and borders to enhance overall impact.
- Laser print on high-quality (24-pound, 100-percent cotton-fiber content), neutral-colored paper.

SCANNABLE RÉSUMÉ

Content

- Follow general guidelines for résumé preparation.
- Position name as the first readable item on each page.
- Include "Objective" section to identify the job sought (same as a print résumé).
- Include "Keyword Summary" listing qualifications that match the job description.
- Support keywords with specific facts; use as many nouns as possible that might match those in the job description.
- Use synonyms of the keywords in the body to ensure a match with the database.

Mechanics

- Use nondecorative font with size range of 10 to 14 points.
- Omit design elements that could distort the text (italics, underline, open bullets, graphic lines and borders, two-column or other complex formats, and so on).
- Allow ample white space, especially between sections.
- Laser print on one side of white, standard-size paper.
- Mail unfolded and unstapled with an application letter.

ELECTRONIC RÉSUMÉS

Content

- Adapt general guidelines for résumé preparation to fit the particular requirements of the submission.
- Place "Keyword Summary" listing qualifications that match the job description on first screen (within first 24 lines of text).
- Support keywords with specific facts; use as many nouns as possible that might match those in the job description.
- Use synonyms of the keywords in the body to ensure a match with the database.
- Include link or reference to electronic portfolio.

Mechanics

- Save résumé in appropriate format for transmitting as an attachment, or paste into e-mail message.

PROFESSIONAL PORTFOLIO

Content

- Include items that showcase abilities and accomplishments.

Mechanics

- Choose an appropriate traditional or electronic format.
- Organize logically to assist in ease of use.
- For electronic formats, include links to print résumé, plain text version of résumé, e-mail address, and appropriate supplementary documents.

APPLICATION MESSAGE

Content

- Identify the message as an application for a certain job.
- Include valid ideas (statements are true).
- Emphasize significant qualifications and exclude nonessential ideas.
- Make reference to enclosed or attached résumé.
- End with action closing that is neither apologetic nor pushy.

Organization

- Begin by revealing the job sought in the attention-getter.
- Present paragraphs in most appropriate sequence (order of importance is possibly best).
- End with a reference to action employer is to take (call or write to extend an invitation for an interview).

Style

- Use simple language (no attempt to impress with a sophisticated vocabulary; some professional jargon is justified).
- Use relatively short sentences with sufficient variety.
- Place significant words and ideas in emphatic positions.

Mechanics

- Assure that there are *no* keying, grammar, spelling, or punctuation errors.
- Include writer's address above the date or format as a letterhead as letter is presented on plain paper that matches the résumé.
- Include equal side margins (approximately one inch).
- Balance on the page.
- Keep first and last paragraphs relatively short; hold others to six or seven lines.

---

entry, a link to a personal web page, an e-mail attachment, and an inline résumé within the body of an e-mail message. Formats for electronic résumés vary with the type of submission.

5. **Utilize employment tools other than the résumé that can enhance employability.** The résumé may be supplemented with other employment tools that include a professional portfolio and a video recording of the applicant. The portfolio, whose use is broadening to include many career fields, showcases projects, creative activities, and accolades. It may be prepared as a traditional notebook document or as an electronic resource saved to CD or DVD or linked to a personal web page. A video recording transmits a visual impression that may help convince the potential employer of your competence but may also lead to stereotyping and discrimination. Content for a portfolio or video should be carefully chosen to reflect skills necessary for effective job performance and should complement information in the résumé.

6. **Write an application message that effectively introduces an accompanying print (designed) or electronic résumé.** An application message, which may be in the form of a printed letter or e-mail communication, effectively introduces an accompanying résumé. The purposes of the application message are to introduce the applicant and the résumé, arouse interest in the information given on the résumé, and assist an employer in seeing ways in which the applicant's services would be desirable. As such, it is a persuasive message—beginning with an attention-getter, including a central appeal and convincing evidence, and closing with an indirect reference to the enclosed résumé and desired action (invitation to an interview). Use terminology that indicates your familiarity with the field and avoid using overused words and expressions. Encourage the reader to extend an interview without apologizing or being too demanding. Proofread your message and accompanying documents carefully to ensure your employment credentials are error free, an example of your best work.

Chapter Review

1. How is self-evaluation related to career choice? (Obj. 1)

2. Where can you obtain information about the responsibilities, compensation, and career potential of a certain job? (Obj. 1)

3. List five sources from which prospective employers' names and addresses may be obtained; include traditional and electronic sources. (Obj. 2)

4. How can a job applicant conduct a successful job search without leaving home? (Obj. 2)

5. What are the standard parts of a résumé? What are some optional parts? How does a job candidate decide which parts to include?(Obj. 3)

6. What are the possible consequences of inflating your qualifications on a résumé? (Obj. 3)

7. What are the advantages of using subject-understood sentences in résumés? Action verbs? Crisp phrases? Descriptive but not overly strong adjectives? Provide examples of each technique. (Obj. 3)

8. Under what conditions might you choose to include or not include references on a résumé? Is obtaining permission from references necessary? (Obj. 3)

9. Describe the three organizational patterns of résumés and explain under what circumstances each would be effective. (Obj. 3)

10. How does the format and content of a scannable résumé differ from a print résumé? (Obj. 4)

11. What safeguards should be taken when posting a résumé electronically? (Obj. 4).

12. What should a professional portfolio include? (Obj. 5)

13. Describe a job for which a video recording might be an effective résumé enhancement. What should the video include? (Obj. 5)

14. List techniques for effective persuasion that should be applied in application messages. Refer to Chapter 8 for ideas if necessary. (Obj. 6)

15. Describe an effective "action ending" for an application message. (Obj. 6)

Digging Deeper

1. Explain the rise in popularity of the "Career Summary" section on résumés. How else have résumés changed in recent years?

2. Is it possible for a candidate to "try too hard" when preparing a résumé? Explain your answer.

To check your understanding of the chapter, take the practice quizzes at **http://lehman.swlearning.com** or your WebTutor course.

Activities

1. **Preparing to Harness the Monster (Objs. 1–2, 4)**

   Browse the career sites available at the text support site at **http://lehman.swlearning.com**. Select the one that provides career guidance that you believe would be most useful in your job search. Register to receive the site's free online newsletter for timely job search information. You instructor may also require you to prepare a brief summary of the information in each newsletter that you found especially timely or relevant to your needs. Below the last summary, write a brief statement describing the effectiveness of the information provided and the presentation of these e-mail updates. Refer the discussion for e-mail marketing in Chapter 8 if necessary to review criteria important to effective campaigns. Be prepared to share in small groups or in class.

2. **Document for Analysis: Chronological Résumé (Objs. 1–4)**

   In your position as a career counselor, review the narrative of qualifications available at the text support site that you have received from Shane Austin, who is seeking

   a position as a senior loan officer in a major banking firm. In small groups, discuss the following questions and be prepared to present a short report to the class: (a) What information is relevant to Shane's career objective and thus should be included in his résumé? (b) Which of the three organizational plans for résumés would present Shane's qualifications most effectively? Explain. (c) What details could be included in a "Career Summary" section to strengthen Shane's résumé? (d) How should Shane communicate information about his references? Which of the references would you recommend he use? If directed by your instructor, prepare Shane's résumé incorporating your decisions. Provide fictitious information if needed.

   Visit the Interactive Study Center at **http://lehman.swlearning.com** for a downloadable version of this application.

3. **Document for Analysis: Application Letter (Obj. 6)**

   Analyze the following message. Pinpoint its strengths and weaknesses and then revise as directed by your instructor.

//electronic café //

Use of Time Speaks Volumes

Time is a language, and how we spend our 1,440 minutes a day speaks much about our interests, priorities, and commitment. In addition, how we use other people's time and attention communicates our attitudes about them. While we can't increase the total minutes in a day, we can do much to improve our use of the available time we have so that our goals are met.

 InfoTrac College Edition. Access http://www.infotrac.thomsonlearning.com to read more about the importance of time management to corporate communications. Search for the following article that is available in full text:

Jenson, B. (2001, April). It's about time. *Communication World, 18*(3), 16.

Make a list of the time management suggestions offered in the article. Star those that you most need to put into practice. Send an e-mail to your instructor, explaining your course of action for improving your time management.

 Text Support Site. Visit http://lehman.swlearning.com to learn more about becoming an effective time manager. Refer to Chapter 13's Electronic Café activity that provides a link to a web article that discusses how time management can improve your communication life. Be prepared to discuss in class the tips that are offered or follow your instructor's directions about how to use the information.

 WebTutor Advantage. Visit the Café feature in WebTutor for directions for accessing your class calendar to read important postings.

 Professional Power Pak. Access your PPP CD for time management tips that will help you be more efficient and effective.

April 5, 2004

Bailey Stores Incorporated
Roanoke VA 24022

Dear Sirs:

I am looking for an opportunity for advancement with a new employer. My background is in retail management and I fell well qualified for the Store Manager position in the Bailey's West location you advertised on your web site. I would like to be considered as an applicant for the position. The primary advantage I would have as a manager is my heavy educational background. Among the courses I have taken are consumer behavior, retailing, marketing, public relations, and advertising. I am sure you realize the many ways in which these courses can prepare one for a career in sales management.

In addition to my classes, my educational background includes work in the university bookstore, service on the school yearbook, and president of my fraternity. I will be receiving my degree on May 5, 2004. I will appreciate you studying the résumé which you will find inclosed. If you can use an energetic young man with my educational background as I hope, will you grant me an interview at your earliest convenience. So I can put my educational background to work for you. I will followup this letter with a phone call so we can talk more about the position.

Sincerely,

Visit the Interactive Study Center at **http://lehman.swlearning. com** for a downloadable version of this application.

4. **Locating Employment Opportunities (Objs. 1–4)**

    Jennifer Simms, a graduating senior in computer information systems, has sought your advice as to how to locate job opportunities in her field. Outline a course of action for her that includes traditional and electronic methods that may help her locate the right job.

Applications

Read | Think | Write | Speak | Collaborate

1. Surfing Cyberspace to Land a Job (Objs. 1, 2)

Visit one of the career sites using the links provided at the text support site at **http://lehman.swlearning.com** and note the types of career guidance information available. Print the page of a resource that you believe will be beneficial to you as you search for a job. Summarize the results of your exploration in a short report to your instructor. Your instructor may ask you to complete the activities in the Internet case related to Internet recruiting.

2. Spotting Common Résumé Blunders (Objs. 3, 4)

Visit one of the career sites and develop a list of the top ten résumé blunders. Be prepared to share your list with the class or in small groups. Choose a career site from the list available at the text support site (**http://lehman. swlearning.com**).

Read | **Think** | Write | Speak | Collaborate

3. Assessing Career Interests (Obj. 1)

Various career, or vocational, tests are available that can help you assess your areas of job interest. Visit the following site that discusses the value and use of such assessments and links you to some representative examples of career tests:

http://www.jobhuntersbible.com/counseling/ctests. shtml#interests

After considering the seven rules about taking career tests, take the Birkman Test. Write a one-page summary of what your test results revealed and how you will use the information in your career planning.

4. Getting Essential Information to Make a Wise Career Decision (Obj. 1)

Select a job listing for a job for which you wish to be interviewing (full- or part-time, internship or co-op position). Complete the planning forms available at the text support site to direct your reflection on your interests and abilities and understanding of your career and job sought. To validate your career and job analyses, interview a person currently working in your career field. Give honest, insightful answers to each question; add additional questions that you deem appropriate for a complete analysis in the planning form for each part of the analysis.

Visit the Interactive Study Center at **http://lehman. swlearning.com** for a downloadable version of this application.

5. Preparing a Company/Job Profile (Obj. 1)

Use information obtained from completing Application 4 to prepare a company/job profile for the company/job in which you expect to be interviewing. Using Figure 13-2 as a guide, complete these steps:

a. Review the completed profile and note the degree of compatibility between your qualifications and the company and job requirements.

b. Compile a list of strengths and weaknesses (lack of a match between your qualifications and job requirements) as they relate to the job requirements.

c. Consider carefully the deficiencies you must overcome before your qualifications fully match the job requirements. What are possible strategies for overcoming these deficiencies? Are any of these strategies feasible, or is overcoming these deficiencies out of your control?

d. Analyze the final comparison and decide whether interviewing for this job would be wise.

6. Critiquing a Sample Résumé (Objs. 3, 4)

Your instructor will distribute a sample résumé to the class. Critique the document's effectiveness using the guidelines and the examples provided in the chapter. Send an e-mail message to your instructor giving your overall impression of the résumé and specific suggestions for improving it. Printscreen to obtain a copy of your message and submit it to your instructor. Submit a copy of the résumé if you critiqued a student's résumé.

7. Critiquing a Peer's Résumé (Objs. 3, 4)

Exchange a rough draft of your résumé with another class member. Critique the document's effectiveness using the guidelines and the examples provided in the chapter. Send an e-mail message to the student giving your overall impression of the résumé and specific suggestions for improving it. Printscreen to obtain a copy of your message and submit it to your instructor with a copy of the student's résumé.

8. Applying for a Job of Your Choice: Print and Scannable Résumé with Accompanying Application Letter (Objs. 1, 3–4, 6)

Prepare print and scannable versions of your résumé and an application letter for a job of your choice using information compiled in Applications 4 and 5. Assume you are applying for an immediate part-time job, a full-time job for the summer, a cooperative education assignment or internship, or a full-time job immediately after you graduate. Look at the list of courses you plan to take and write as though you had taken them and satisfied the requirements for a degree. Follow the guidelines for preparing a print résumé, and then incorporate the valid comments of at least two others competent in proofreading and résumé design. Use the desktop publishing capability available to you to produce a highly effective, professional document.

9. Mastering Electronic Submissions (Obj. 6)

Assume one of your networking contacts asked you to e-mail your résumé for a potential opening in his firm. Prepare an abbreviated version of the application letter you prepared in Application 8. E-mail the application message with an inline résumé positioned below the letter. E-mail to your instructor using a subject line that stands out in an overloaded mailbox as an expected message from a known person.

10. Completing Electronic Postings (Obj. 4)

If you are within three semesters of graduation, register with your career services center and acquaint yourself with the services they provide. Follow instructions precisely for posting your résumé to your University's career services web site for submission to prospective employers. Alternately, your instructor may request that you post your résumé to a company's web site. Access the web site of a company of your choice and follow instructions carefully in order to prepare a résumé suitable for the company's use.

11. Designing an Electronic Portfolio (Obj. 5)

Sketch the information you would include on the first page of an electronic portfolio posted at your personal web site. Brainstorm about the types of information you might include in links to additional qualifications. Create your electronic résumé if your instructor directs you to do so. Consider using a template in a high-level word processing program. Post to your student home page in WebTutor or your personal web page. Send your instructor an e-mail message providing the URL address if posted to your personal web page.

12. Analyzing Résumé Critiques Made by Experts (Objs. 3–4)

Study the "before and after" versions of résumés, including recommendations from career experts, available at major career sites. Compile a list of suggestions that reinforce and/or supplement the information related to résumé construction presented in the chapter. Note any discrepancies in this information and your textbook or current knowledge. Share your suggestions in a short presentation to the class. Link to the career sites from the text support site at **http://lehman.swlearning.com.**

13. Launching a Newsletter to Boost Career Skills (Objs. 1–6)

A student organization that you're a member of is initiating an online monthly recruiting newsletter available to members at the organization's home page. The vision is to create a fresh, personalized approach to career information specifically related to the needs of the members of your group and the current competitive market. Each newsletter will include at least one article addressing specific job search skills, highlights of special recruiting events and previews of upcoming events, and an interview providing insights from an employer, returning co-op students, campus recruiters, etc. In small groups, generate an issue of the newsletter for an organization of your choice. Consider using a newsletter template from a high-level word processing program to assist you in generating the document. E-mail your newsletter to your instructor; distribute to the class through e-mail or an electronic posting to your WebTutor student home page or a personal web page.

Attracting Employees Through Creative Incentives

In receiving recognition as the best company to work for in America, The Container Store impressed *Fortune* magazine with its employee perks such as a paid sabbatical from work after ten years. Other companies that have made the list also offer creative incentives to attract employees in a tight labor market:

• MBNA, a credit card company, gives its newly married employees a week off and a limo on their wedding day.
• BMC software washes its employees' cars and changes the oil.
• The pharmaceutical company Pfizer's employees receive free drugs, including Viagra.
• In addition to monthly performance bonuses, employees at Continental Airlines can win a Ford Explorer for perfect attendance.

Locate the issue of *Fortune* that includes the latest "best company" award winners. Prepare a short report that summarizes incentives and rewards offered by award-winning companies in an effort to attract qualified employees. Conclude with the incentives you personally find most appealing.

Part 4 of the The Container Store ShowCASE focuses on how the company stays on top as an exemplary employer.

http://www.containerstore.com

Visit the text support site at **http://lehman. swlearning.com** to complete Part 4 of The Container Store ShowCASE.

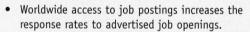

Internet Case

Employment Market Undergoes Cyber Revolution

The cyberspace employment market is here and advancing rapidly. What is being witnessed is nothing less than a transformation in the way people look for jobs and how organizations look for qualified employees. Those who do not engage in electronic employment searching may soon be left out entirely from the digital economy.

Until recently, employers and prospective employees carried on their mutual searching process in physical space. Now, information can be exchanged totally electronically. In a recent study of members of the Society of Human Resource Managers and the Recruitment Marketplace, 82 percent of respondents said they use online advertising to fill open positions. In fact, Internet recruiting is now second only to newspaper advertising in terms of volume of applicants generated and recruited.[26] Large and small companies alike are realizing the advantages offered by online recruiting:

• Worldwide access to job postings increases the response rates to advertised job openings.
• More and better information on applicants is available since a résumé document can provide links to publications, reference letters, and other informational items.
• The ability to quickly scan files, looking for keywords emphasizing experience, knowledge, and abilities, is replacing the tedious task of sorting through volumes of paper résumés, thus reducing the number of days necessary to fill a vacant position.
• A company can instantly ask an applicant to supply additional or missing information.
• The search process can be programmed to run the necessary security, criminal, or credit checks on the applicant automatically.

In sum, the process by which organizations gather necessary information from and about applicants can be made much more efficient through the application of an Internet-based recruiting process. Likewise, the communications garnered through such an automated procedure can be gathered much more quickly—at the speed of light rather than the speed of bureaucratic action and snail mail delivery.

Making use of the Internet allows companies to expand their geographic reach greatly. The paradox, however, of the increasing use of the Internet for corporate recruiting is the potential for both less and greater diversity in organizations. Although an applicant's gender, race, and even physical disabilities play no role in the decision-making process, current statistics on the Internet community reflect a built-in bias. While the demographics are beginning to change to be more reflective of society as a whole, the Internet is currently overwhelmingly male and white. In fact, it has been speculated that employers who would solely rely on the Internet for recruiting might well be in violation of Title VII of the Civil Rights Act. Employers should thus be aware of the potential for discrimination inherent in Internet-based recruiting. The EEOC currently requires that companies with more than 100 employees store all submitted résumés for one year and compile demographic data on applicants; EEOC officials can use the data to look for discriminatory hiring practices.[27]

Complete one or more of the following activities as directed by your instructor.

1. Locate the web page of an organization for whom you would like to work. Print the page. Does the web page provide information about job vacancies? Does it invite résumé postings? How effectively is the company using its web page for recruiting applicants? Report your findings to the class.

2. Locate the online résumé of a job applicant in your chosen field. Print it out. Is the résumé effectively designed? Are linked files used, and if so, do they enhance the candidate's appeal? What personal information is included? Does the information presented give rise to possible discrimination? Send an e-mail to your instructor reporting what you found.

3. **GMAT** Visit the following web site that presents information on recent Internet recruiting polls and statistics: **http://www.recruitersnetwork.com.**

Write a short informative paper that describes the current status of Internet recruiting. Give examples to substantiate trends and practices.

Video Case

Texas Jet: Gathering Essential Information

Texas Jet, operating out of Meacham International Airport, Fort Worth, Texas, provides all the ground-based services required by aircraft owners and operators and is one of more than 4,000 independent fixed-base operators (FBOs) in the United States.

For the fourth consecutive year, Texas Jet has been ranked as one of the ten best FBOs in the nation. Texas Jet was recognized for its line service, customer service, facilities, quick turn performance, and value for cost. Texas Jet's wide array of services ranges from gourmet catering to aircraft cleaning and washing. You can learn more about their wide variety of services at its web site.

View the video segment about Texas Jet and related activities on WebTutor or your Professional Power Pak CD.

Discussion Questions

1. In what ways might Texas Jet's ranking as one of the ten best FBOs in the United States be related to its hiring process?

2. Which steps in Texas Jet's hiring process for line service technicians relate to the fact that these employees will be dealing with airplanes that cost upwards of $30 to $40 million?

3. If you were a recruiter for Texas Jet seeking to hire employees who have a customer-service focus, what would you look for on their résumés to give you insight into their customer service skill level?

Activities

As you saw in the video segment and read in Chapter 13, employers must gather a great deal of information about prospective employees to help them make a hiring decision. Completing this exercise will help you locate information essential for launching a successful employment search.

You will be using O*NET, the U.S. Department of Labor's comprehensive database on job requirements and worker competencies for over 950 occupations. The O*NET Online welcome page (**http://online.onetcenter.org/online. onetcenter.org**) states that students can use O*NET to:

1. Find out which jobs fit with their interests, skills, and experience.

2. Explore growth career profiles using the latest available labor market data.

3. Research what it takes to get their dream jobs.

4. Maximize earning potential and job satisfaction.

5. Know what it takes to be successful in their fields and in related occupations.

The following activities will guide you through the completion of Items 1, 3, and 5 listed above. Once you see how easy it is to use the wealth of information available at this site, you may wish to gather further information on your own.

Activities

1. To provide an overview of this exercise, read the explanation of the O*NET® Skills Search feature at **http://online.onetcenter.org/help/online/skills**

2. Complete the Skills Search at **http://online. onetcenter.org/gen_skills_page**

3. Review the Skills Search Results, which provide three options: Summary, Details, and Custom. Select at least one, O*NET-SOC Title, that relates to a career you would like to pursue and print out the Summary Report.

4. At the Wages & Employment Link, select the state in which you would like to work.

   a. Read the Occupation Report for your career and view the "Related Career Video" (average viewing time is between two and three minutes).

   b. Be sure to check out several links of interest that appear along the left sidebar.

5. Print out your Occupation Report. Use the space provided after the headings that appear throughout the report (Tasks, Knowledge, Skills, Abilities, etc.) to comment briefly on the information in each section. Your comments should reflect that you've carefully read the information and responded appropriately based on your chosen occupation. Attach your Occupation Report to the Summary Report and submit to your instructor.

14

Interviewing for a Job and Preparing Employment Messages

© AP/WIDE WORLD PHOTOS

Objectives *When you have completed Chapter 14, you will be able to:*

1 Explain the nature of structured, unstructured, computer-assisted, group, and stress interviews.

2 Explain the steps in the interview process.

3 Prepare effective answers to questions often asked in job interviews and questions that will communicate initiative to an interviewer.

4 Recognize and bypass illegal interview questions.

5 Complete application forms accurately and write effective messages related to employment (follow-up, thank-you, job acceptance, job-refusal, resignation, and recommendation request).

6 Write positive and negative recommendations that are legally defensible.

GE ASSET MANAGEMENT: THE *I*'s HAVE IT: DO YOU?

Integrity, intellect, initiative, and intensity. Those are the qualities GE considers most important when seeking employees. As a wholly owned subsidiary of General Electric Company, GE Asset Management (GEAM) manages investments for GE employee pension and benefit plans and provides investment management services to institutional and retail investors. GEAM is a registered investment adviser, with offices in the U.S., Canada, Europe, and Japan. GEAM knows that its strong worldwide presence is made possible by the efforts of its hundreds of talented employees.[1]

GE employees around the globe share common traits that unite them as associates of a premier financial services company. The company describes its "4 *I*'s" platform as follows:

Integrity. Integrity is an uncompromising characteristic for all GE employees. It is an implicit factor in customer relationships and the cornerstone of all GE business activities. Integrity cannot be compromised and is the baseline by which everything else is measured.

Intellect. GE's continued success is the result of its employees' creativity. Teams of GE people push the frontiers, developing new products and services for customers. Focusing on highly specialized financial services segments, GE people develop a unique understanding of customer requirements as they apply their collective talents.

Initiative. GE never separates ideas and actions—viewing both as essential elements of the competitive equation. Developing the most advanced financial product or innovative service is meaningless if the company fails to move quickly to get products to the market and delivered to customers.

Intensity. GE's strategic objective—to maintain the leading market position in its niche business market—demands an intense focus on customer needs and market dynamics.

GE seeks qualified applicants who possess the 4 *I*'s and are willing to learn the skills necessary for company success. Some candidates are hired directly into leadership development programs that combine work experience with education and training. The Risk Management Leadership Program develops risk management leaders in a combination of rotation in various risk management positions and education in state-of-the-art risk management techniques. The Global Leadership Development Program grooms international leaders through a combination of global assignments and management training.[2]

At GE, "bringing good things to life" begins with offering opportunities to those who have a vision and the energy and confidence to pursue it. Success for GE, as for every company, begins with hiring well. The interview process provides the prospective employer with the opportunity to observe your talents and abilities, as well as your people skills. The interview is also your opportunity to form an impression of the company, its culture, and your future supervisors and coworkers.

http://www.ge.com

See ShowCASE, Part 2, on page 617 for Spotlight Communicator Marquette Wilson, Human Resources Manager, GE Asset Management.

Understanding Types of Employment Interviews

Objective 1

Explain the nature of structured, unstructured, computer-assisted, group, and stress interviews.

Critical Thinking

In what types of interviews have you participated?

Changing Technology

Most companies conduct various types of interviews before hiring a new employee. The number and type of interviews vary among companies. Typically, however, applicants begin with a screening interview, an in-depth interview, an on-site interview with multiple interviewers, and sometimes a stress interview. Depending on the goals of the interviewer, interviews may follow a structured or an unstructured approach.

Structured Interviews

In a **structured interview**, generally used in the screening process, the interviewer follows a predetermined agenda, including a checklist of items or a series of questions and statements designed to elicit the necessary information or interviewee reaction. Because each applicant answers the same questions, the interviewer has comparable data to evaluate. A particular type of structured interview is the behavior-based interview, in which applicants are asked to give specific examples of occasions in which they demonstrated particular behaviors or skills. The interviewer already knows what skills, knowledge, and qualities successful candidates must possess. The examples you provide will allow him or her to determine whether you possess them.[3]

Companies are finding computer-assisted interviews to be a reliable and effective way to conduct screening interviews. Applicants use a computer to provide answers to a list of carefully selected questions. A computer-generated report provides standard, reliable information about each applicant that enables an interviewer to decide whether to invite the applicant for a second interview. The report flags any contradictory responses (e.g., an applicant indicated he was terminated for absenteeism but later indicated that he thought his former employer would give him an outstanding recommendation), highlights any potential problem areas (e.g., an applicant responded that she would remain on the job less than a year), and generates a list of structured interview questions for the interviewer to ask (e.g., "Terrance, you said you feel your former employer would rate you average. Why don't you feel it would be higher?").

Research has shown that applicants prefer computer interviews to human interviews and that they respond more honestly to a computer, feeling less need to give polite, socially acceptable responses.[4] Because expert computer systems can overcome some of the inherent problems with traditional face-to-face interviews, the overall quality of the selection process improves. Typical interviewer errors include forgetting to ask important questions, talking too much, being reluctant to ask sensitive questions, forming unjustified negative first impressions, obtaining unreliable and illegal information that makes an applicant feel judged, and using interview data ineffectively. Regardless of whether the interview is face-to-face or computer assisted, you will need to provide objective, truthful evidence of your qualifications as they relate to specific job requirements.

Unstructured Interviews

Critical Thinking

Why have unstructured interviews decreased in popularity in recent years?

An **unstructured interview** is a freewheeling exchange and may shift from one subject to another, depending on the interests of the participants. Some experienced interviewers are able to make a structured interview seem unstructured. The goal of many unstructured interviews is to explore unknown areas to determine the applicant's ability to speak comfortably about a wide range of topics.

Stress Interviews

A **stress interview** is designed to place the interviewee in an anxiety-producing situation so an evaluation may be made of the interviewee's performance under stress. In all cases, interviewees should attempt to assess the nature of the interview quickly and adjust behavior accordingly. Understanding that interviewers sometimes deliberately create anxiety to assess your ability to perform under stress should help you handle such interviews more effectively. As the following discussion of different interviewer styles reveals, you, as an interviewee, can perform much better when you understand the interviewer's purpose.

Group Interviews

Team Environment

As organizations have increased emphasis on team approaches to management and problem solving, selecting employees who best fit their cultures and styles has become especially important. Involving key people in the organization in the candidate selection process has led to new interview styles. In a series interview, the candidate meets individually with a number of different interviewers. Each interviewer will likely ask questions from a differing perspective; for instance, a line manager may ask questions related to the applicant's knowledge of specific job tasks while the vice president of operations may ask questions related to the applicant's career goals. Some questions will likely be asked more than once in the process. A popular trend in organizations that desire a broad range of input in the hiring decision but want to avoid the drawn-out nature of series interviews is to conduct team interviews. The accompanying Strategic Forces feature, "The Team Interview: What to Expect When the Interviewer Turns Out to Be a Team," provides additional information about team interviews.

Virtual Interviews

Many companies, ranging from IBM, Microsoft, Nike, and Hallmark Cards, are now screening candidates through video interviews from

The Team Interview: What to Expect When the Interviewer Turns Out to Be a Team

Today, the hiring process is often a team effort. Once a hiring manager has identified a need, it is likely that Human Resources (HR) will pull together a team to fill it. A team of four to seven members is common, but teams can be larger, depending on the position to be filled. A team typically has an HR facilitator, employees who will work with the individual, the hiring manager, a peer of the hiring manager, subordinates of the position, and experts in the position's field. After the job description is developed, the team meets to discuss other attributes of the job, such as leadership and interpersonal skills. While HR screens the résumés using the job description and the desired attributes, the team develops questions to use in one or more of the team interviews. HR circulates the résumés that best match the job requirements to the hiring team, and the team reviews them individually and collaboratively to identify the candidates to be invited for a team interview.

Some or all of the hiring team may participate in the interview process. As the interview begins, the facilitator explains the interview process to the candidate; then the team spends several hours asking the questions that have been determined earlier. Each interviewer is likely to be armed with tailored questions designed to bring out information concerning specific competencies that have been identified as important for the job. The applicant is typically given the opportunity to ask questions, which can be directed to a particular member of the hiring team or to the team as a whole. Each member of the team takes notes for further discussion. After the interview, the hiring team discusses the candidate's performance and makes collective notes before moving to the next candidate. After all candidates have completed the interview process, the group discusses the results and determines to whom, if any, to offer the job or to ask back for an additional interview. Using the group selection process, the "right" person for the job usually emerges quickly.[5]

In some cases, a group of candidates may participate together in a team interview. The applicants may be brought in together and placed in teams to solve problems, while being observed directly or through two-way mirrors by company personnel. At the end of the day, each candidate participates in a traditional interview with one person, who may ask questions based on the observations made of the person during the day's activities. Serious contenders may be asked to return for a second-round interview.

In groups of three as assigned by your instructor, search the Internet to learn more about the team interview; then complete the application below.

Application

- In small groups, compare and contrast the team interview and the traditional interview with one interviewer.

- Outline advice for the applicant for (a) pre-interview preparation, (b) interview behaviors, and (c) the post-interview follow-up for both a traditional interview and a team interview.

Critical Thinking

Why is a face-to-face interview preferred for the final selection interview?

remote locations and saving money and time in the process. Virtual interviews conducted via videoconferencing technology is a more productive use of a recruiter's valuable time. Companies may replay the taped interviews to take another look at a candidate. Positions are filled quickly after interviewing applicants from around the world and achieved with a significant reduction in travel costs.[6] The general consensus is that the video interview is excellent for screening applicants, but a "live interview" is appropriate for the important final interview.

Various companies have direct hookups with the career services centers of colleges and universities to interview students. These virtual interviews allow students to meet large companies who typically would not visit colleges with small applicant pools and to interview with companies who could not travel because of financial constraints or other reasons. Students simply sit in front of a camera, dial in, and interview with multiple interviewers; in some cases, several applicants are interviewed simultaneously. Some photocopy stores are now equipped for video interviews. Companies and executive search firms use higher quality systems set up in specially equipped rooms for middle-level and senior management jobs.

As you would imagine, some candidates who would interview well in person may fail on camera. Because of the additional stress of functioning under the glare of a camera, videoconferencing is an excellent method to screen out candidates who cannot work under pressure. Likewise, a candidate who can't operate the controls would likely be eliminated from a highly technical position.

You should prepare for a virtual interview differently than you would for a traditional interview. First, suggest a preliminary telephone conversation with the interviewer to establish rapport. Arrive early and acquaint yourself with the equipment; know how to adjust the volume, brightness, and other camera functions so you can adjust the equipment for optimal performance after the interview begins. Second, concentrate on projecting strong nonverbal skills: speak clearly but do not slow down; be certain you are centered in the frame, sit straight; look up, not down; and use gestures to communicate energy and reinforce points while avoiding excessive motion that will appear blurry. Third, realize voices may be out of step with the pictures if there is a lag between the video and audio transmissions. You will need to adjust to the timing (e.g., slow down voice) to avoid interrupting the interviewer.[7]

Changing Technology

Preparing for an Interview

College students frequently schedule on-campus interviews with representatives from various business organizations. Following the on-campus interviews, successful candidates often are invited for further interviews on the company premises. The purpose of the second interview is to give executives and administrators other than the human resources interviewer an opportunity to appraise the candidate. Whether on campus or on company premises, interview methods and practices vary with the situation. Preliminary planning can pay rich dividends.

Pre-interview planning involves learning something about the company or organization, doing some studying about yourself, and making sure your appearance and mannerisms will not detract from the impression you hope to make.

Study the Company

Nothing can hurt a job candidate more than knowing little about the organization. No knowledge indicates insincerity, and the interviewer does not want to waste precious interview time providing the candidate with information that should have been gathered long before.

Companies that have publicly traded stock are required to publish annual reports that are available in school libraries or online. Other information can be obtained from the printed and electronic sources you consulted when preparing the company/job profile discussed in Chapter 13. Employees of the company or other students who have been interviewed may be of help to the interviewee. Some universities have prepared videotape interviews with various company recruiters and make the tapes available to students. Pertinent information about the company and the job sought needed for an interview includes the following:

Critical Thinking

Make a list of sources you would consult to gain information about a company with which you want to interview.

Company Information

Be sure to research the following on the companies with whom you interview:

- *Name.* Know, for example, that *Exxon* was a computer-generated name selected in the 1970s to identify the merged identity of an old, established oil company.
- *Status in the industry.* Know the company's share of the market, its Fortune 500 standing if any, its sales, and its number of employees.
- *Latest stock market quote.* Be familiar with current market deviations and trends.
- *Recent news and developments.* Read current business periodicals for special feature articles on the company, its new products, and its corporate leadership.
- *Scope of the company.* Is it local, national, or international?
- *Corporate officers.* Know the names of the chairperson, president, and chief executive officer.
- *Products and services.* Study the company's offerings, target markets, and innovative strategies.

Job Information

Be sure to know the following about the job you are seeking:

- *Job title.* Know the job titles of typical entry-level positions.
- *Job qualifications.* Understand the specific knowledge and skills desired.
- *Probable salary range.* Study salaries in comparable firms, as well as regional averages.
- *Career path of the job.* What opportunities for advancement are available?

Study Yourself

Critical Thinking

What three points could you use to persuade an interviewer you are right for the job? Refer to the company/job profile and the career planning guide you developed in Chapter 13.

When you know something about the company, you will also know something about the kinds of jobs or training programs the company has to offer. Next, review your answers to the company/job profile (Figure 13-2). This systematic comparison of your qualifications and job requirements helps you identify pertinent information (strengths or special abilities) to be included in your résumé. If you cannot see a relationship between you and the job or company, you may have difficulty demonstrating the interest or sincerity needed to sell yourself.

Plan Your Appearance

An employment interviewer once said that if the job applicant did not meet her *extremities* test, the interview might as well not take place. The applicant's personal appearance is critical; fingernails must be clean and neat, shoes shined, or at least clean, and the hair clean and well groomed. This interviewer felt that if the candidate did not take care of those items, the candidate could not really be serious about, or fit into, her organization. General guidelines include being clean and well groomed and avoiding heavy makeup and large, excessive jewelry. Select conservative clothes, and be certain clothing is clean, unwrinkled, and properly fitted. Additionally, avoid smoking, drinking, or wearing heavy cologne.

You can locate a wealth of information on appropriate interview dress from numerous electronic and printed sources (many are listed in Chapter 13). Additionally, talk with professors in your field, professors of professional protocol (business etiquette), personnel at your career services center, and graduates who have recently acquired jobs in your field. Research the company dress code—real or implied—ahead of time. If you *look* and *dress* like the people who already work at the company, the interviewer will be able to visualize you working there.

Plan Your Time and Materials

Critical Thinking

What other materials would you take to an interview?

One of the worst things you can do is be late for an interview. If something should happen to prevent your arriving on time, telephone an apology. Another mistake is to miss the interview entirely. Plan your time so that you will arrive early and can unwind and review mentally the things you plan to accomplish. Be sure to bring a professional portfolio that contains everything you will need during the interview. These items might include copies of your résumé, a list of references and/or recommendations, a professional-looking pen, paper for taking notes, highlights of what you know about the company, a list of questions you plan to ask, and previous correspondence with the company.

Practice

The job interview may be the most important face-to-face interaction you ever have. You will be selling yourself in competition with others. How you listen and how you talk are characteristics the interviewer will be able to measure. Your actions, your mannerisms, and your appearance will combine to give the total picture of how you are perceived. Added to the obvious things you have acquired from your education, experience, and activities, your interview performance can give a skilled interviewer an excellent picture of you. Practicing for an interview will help you learn to handle the nervousness that is natural when interviewing. Practice is what you want to do; do not memorize verbatim answers that will sound rehearsed and insincere. Instead, think carefully about how your accomplishments match the job requirements and practice communicating these ideas smoothly, confidently, and professionally.

The section "Presenting Your Qualifications" that appears later in this chapter will provide suggestions for preparing for standard interview questions and other interview issues. Once you are satisfied you have identified your key selling points, have a friend ask you interview questions you have developed and surprise you with others. Participate in mock interviews with a friend or someone in your career services center, alternating roles as interviewer and interviewee. Then follow each practice interview with a constructive critique of your performance.

Conducting a Successful Interview

The way you handle an interview will vary somewhat depending on your stage in the hiring process. Regardless of whether you are being screened by a campus recruiter or have progressed to an on-site visit, an interview will have three parts: the opening formalities, an information exchange, and the close.

The Opening Formalities

Critical Thinking

How can you "put your best foot forward" during the few minutes you have in a job interview?

Larry Hayes, president of Hayes Marketing Communication, emphasizes that skills missing during the interview are important because he assumes these same deficiencies will carry over during employment. "The good and the bad are obvious in the first five to ten seconds," says Hayes.[8] Clearly, since the impression created during the first few seconds of an interview often determines the outcome, you cannot afford to take time to warm up in an interview. You must come in the door selling yourself!

Common courtesies and confident body language can contribute to a favorable first impression in the early few seconds when you have not yet had an opportunity to talk about your qualifications:

Four minutes . . . that's about how long an interviewer will take to make a decision about you. Projecting a confident, mentally alert impression through your speech and appearance from the moment you walk into an interview is vital, as is your ability to provide quick, intelligent responses to questions. The Professional Power Pak CD that accompanies this text provides you with a host of tools to help you prepare for your first job and will also enable you to maintain that essential competitive edge as you advance through your career.

© TIM BROWN/STONE

Diversity Challenges

- *Use the interviewer's correct name and pronounce it correctly.* Even if the interviewer calls you by your first name, always use the interviewer's surname unless specifically invited to do otherwise.
- *Apply a firm handshake.* Usually, the interviewer will initiate the handshake, although you may do so. In either case, apply a firm handshake. You do not want to leave the impression that you are weak or timid. At the same time, you do not want to overdo the firm grip and leave an impression of being overbearing.
- *Wait for the interviewer to ask you to be seated.*
- *Maintain appropriate eye contact, and use your body language to convey confidence.* Sit erect and lean forward slightly to express interest. For a professional image, avoid slouching, chewing gum, and fidgeting.
- *Be conscious of nonverbal messages.* If the interviewer's eyes are glazing over, end your answer, but expand it if they are bright and the head is nodding vigorously. If the interviewer is from a different culture, be conscious of subtle differences in nonverbal communication that could affect the interviewer's perception of you. For example, a North American interviewer who sees eye contact as a sign of trust may perceive an Asian female who keeps her eyes lowered as a sign of respect to be uninterested or not listening.[9] Women should also be aware of typical "feminine behavior" during the interview. For instance, women nod more often than men when an interviewer speaks. Women are also likely to smile more and have a rising intonation at the end of sentences; such behaviors can convey a subservient attitude.[10]

Following the introductions, many interviewers will begin the conversation with nonbusiness talk to help you relax and to set the stage for the information exchange portion of the interview. Other interviewers may bypass these casual remarks and move directly into the interview.

The Information Exchange

Objective 3

Prepare effective answers to questions often asked in job interviews and questions that will communicate initiative to an interviewer.

Much of the information about you will appear on your résumé or application form and is already available to the interviewer. Thus, the interviewer most likely will seek to go beyond such facts as your education, work experience, and extracurricular activities. He or she will attempt to assess your attitudes toward work and the probability of your fitting successfully into the organization.

Presenting Your Qualifications

Your preparation pays off during the interview. Like a defense attorney ready to win a case, you are ready to present evidence that you should be hired. According to Kennedy & Morrow, leading career consultants, your case will have three major points: You must convince the interviewer that you (1) can do the job, (2) will do the job, and (3) will not stress out everyone else while doing the job.[11] That's an overwhelming task. Where do you begin? You learned during your study of persuasive writing that saying you're the best salesperson (supply other skills) is not convincing. To convince an interviewer to allow you to continue to the next interview or to extend you a job offer, you must provide specific, concrete evidence that your qualifications match the job description. Use the following guidelines to help you relate your skills and knowledge to the job.

Critical Thinking

What personal abilities and skills would you emphasize in a job interview?

- *List five or six key points that you want to emphasize.* Likely, you will want to present your education as a major asset. You should point out its relationship to the job for which you are being considered. Even more important, the fact that you have succeeded in academics indicates that you have the ability to learn. Because most companies expect you to learn something on the job, your ability to learn and thus quickly become productive may be your greatest asset. So your most important response to the interviewer's questions may be about your ability to learn. Even lack of work experience may be an asset: You have acquired no bad work habits that you will have to unlearn.

  Additionally, be sure to provide evidence of your interpersonal skills. Unlike the candidate in the Dilbert cartoon, you will want to communicate that you can get along with others and are sensitive to diversity.

  - What did you do in college that helped you get along with others?
  - Were you a member, an officer, or president of an organization?

An effective interview reveals abilities beyond your technical qualifications.

- In regard to your organization, what did you accomplish? How did others perceive you? Were you a leader? How did your followers respond to your leadership style?
- Can you organize projects?

The extracurricular activities listed on your résumé give an indication of these traits, but how you talk about them in your interview helps. "I started as corresponding secretary and was subsequently elected to higher office for four semesters, eventually becoming president" is a statement that may prove your leadership qualities. If you can show your organization moved to greater heights, you will appear successful as well. You can also use questions about your extracurricular activities to show that you have broad, balanced interests rather than a single, time-consuming avocation that could lead to burnout and stress if carried to the job.

Critical Thinking

Is it possible for a candidate to interview too well?

What are other skills that graduating students need to succeed in a cross-cultural, interdependent workforce? While academic performance is weighted more heavily for some types of jobs than others, the ability to juggle a complicated schedule is weighed heavily by many employers as an important job-success factor. Additionally, a UNESCO report of employer views revealed certain skills to be essential for workers in today's business climate as shown in Figure 14-1.[12]

Consider these general job success traits and then use your knowledge of the job requirements and your own strengths to develop your "central selling features." These key points targeted to your audience is the central element of a winning argument: You are able and willing to add value to a company.

- ***Be prepared to answer standard interview questions.*** These questions are designed to show (a) why you want the job, (b) why you want to work for this organization, and (c) why the company should want you. Many of the career sites and printed sources discussed in Chapter 13 include lists of frequently asked interview questions; some sources

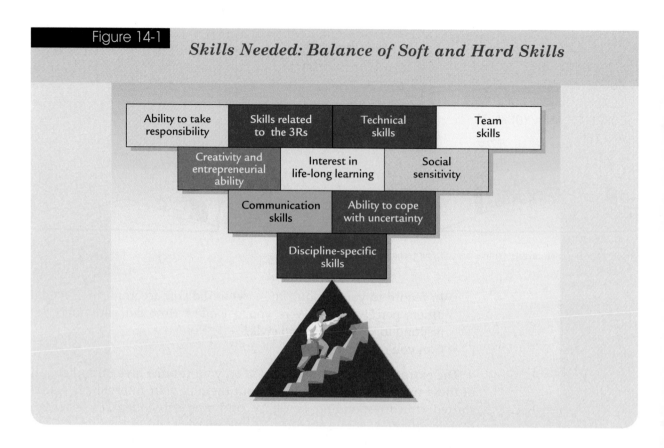

Figure 14-1

Skills Needed: Balance of Soft and Hard Skills

| Ability to take responsibility | Skills related to the 3Rs | Technical skills | Team skills |

| Creativity and entrepreneurial ability | Interest in life-long learning | Social sensitivity |

| Communication skills | Ability to cope with uncertainty |

| Discipline-specific skills |

provide suggested answers to the more difficult questions. Research these sites thoroughly, and visit the text support at http://lehman. swlearning.com for a sample of the types of questions you might expect to be asked.

Critical Thinking

What is involved in being your "best self" in an interview?

• **Be prepared to answer behavioral questions.** These questions are designed to challenge you to provide real evidence of your skills or the behaviors required to perform the job. Rather than asking applicants how they feel about certain things, interviewers are finding that asking potential employees for specific examples to illustrate their answers is a more objective way to evaluate applicants' skills. Behavioral questions include the following:

   • Describe a time when you (a) worked well under pressure, (b) worked effectively with others, (c) organized a major project, (d) motivated and led others, (e) solved a difficult problem, and (f) accepted constructive criticism.

   • What was the most difficult problem you had to overcome in your last job (or an academic or extracurricular activity)? How did you cope with it?

   • Tell me about a time you had difficulty working with a supervisor or coworker (professor, peer in a team in a class setting). How did you handle the situation?

   • Describe something you have done that shows initiative and willingness to work.

- How have your extracurricular activities, part-time work experience, or volunteer work prepared you for work in our company?
- Tell me about a time you hit a wall trying to push forward a great idea.

Critical Thinking

Select one of the listed behavioral questions and structure your personal response to it, using the STAR method. Share your response with a classmate.

To prepare for answering behavioral questions, brainstorm to identify stories that illustrate how your qualifications fit the job requirements. These stories should show you applying the skills needed on the job. Career counselors recommend using the STAR method (Situation or Task/Action/Result) as a consistent format to help you present a complete answer to these open-ended questions. You first describe a situation or task you were involved in, the action you took, and finally the result of your effort.[13] Even if the interviewer doesn't ask behavioral questions, you can use this approach when answering standard interview questions.

- *Be prepared to demonstrate logical thinking and creativity.* Many companies ask applicants to solve brain teasers and riddles, create art out of paper bags, solve complex business problems, and even spend a day acting as managers of fictitious companies. These techniques are used to gauge an applicant's ability to think quickly and creatively and observe an emotional response to an awkward situation.[14] You cannot anticipate this type of interview question, but you can familiarize yourself with mind teasers that have been used. Most importantly, however, recognize the interviewer's purpose; relax, and do your best to showcase your logical reasoning, creativity, or your courage to even try.
- *Display a professional attitude.* First, communicate your sincere interest in the company; show that you are strongly interested in the company and not just taking an interview for practice. Reveal your knowledge of the company gained through reading published information, and refer to the people you have talked with about the working conditions, company achievements, and career paths.

Second, focus on the satisfaction gained from contributing to a company rather than the benefits you will receive. What's important in a job goes beyond financial reward. All applicants are interested in a paycheck; any job satisfies that need—some will pay more, some less. Recognize that the paycheck is a part of the job and should not be your primary concern. Intrinsic rewards such as personal job satisfaction, the feeling of accomplishment, and making a contribution to society are ideas to discuss in the interview. You should like what you are doing and find a challenging job that will satisfy these needs.

Critical Thinking

What weakness do you have that you could share with an interviewer? How would you word your remarks?

Third, display humility. If you are being interviewed by a representative of a successful company, do not suggest that you can turn the company around. Similarly, telling an interviewer you have no weaknesses could make you sound shallow and deceptive. Instead, mention a weakness that can be perceived as a strength, preferably a "weakness" that a company wants. Indicate that you occasionally become overcommitted to extracurricular activities (assuming your résumé includes a high level of extracurricular participation *and* a strong academic record). If you're applying for a job that involves detail, confess that you are a perfectionist or that you are prone toward being a workaholic.

- *Be prepared to discuss salary and benefits.* For most entry-level positions, the beginning salary is fixed. However, if you have work experience, excellent scholarship records, or added maturity, you may be able to obtain a higher salary. The interviewer should initiate the salary topic. What you should know is the general range for candidates with your qualifications so that your response to a question about how much you would expect is reasonable. If your qualifications are about average for the job, you can indicate that you would expect to be paid the going rate or within the normal range. If you have added qualifications, you might say, "With my two years of work experience, I would expect to start at the upper end of the normal salary range."

  If you have other job offers, you are in a position to compare salaries, jobs, and companies. In this case, you may suggest to the interviewer that you would expect a competitive salary and that you have been offered X dollars by another firm. If salary has not been mentioned, and you really want to know about it, simply ask courteously how much the salary would be for someone with your qualifications. In any case, though, if you really believe the job offers the nonmonetary benefits you seek, do not attempt to make salary a major issue.

  Typically, an interviewer will introduce the subject of benefits without your asking about them. In some cases, a discussion of total salary and "perks" (perquisites) is reserved for a follow-up interview. If nothing has been said about certain benefits, you should take the liberty of asking, particularly when an item may be especially important to you. Health insurance, for example, may be very important when you have children. Retirement planning, however, is less appropriate for a new graduate to discuss.

- *Be knowledgeable of interview questions that might lead to discriminatory hiring practices.* Surveys indicate that more than one third of applicants have been asked an illegal interview question pertaining to race, age, marital status, religion, or ethnic background.[15] The types of illegal (or potentially illegal) interview questions and ways to handle them are described in the accompanying Strategic Forces feature, "Handling Illegal Interview Questions."

Objective **4**

Recognize and bypass illegal interview questions.

Legal & Ethical
Constraints

Asking Questions of the Interviewer

Both the interviewer and interviewee must know as much as possible about each other before making a commitment in order to increase the likelihood that the relationship will be lengthy and mutually beneficial. A good way to determine whether the job is right for you is to ask pertinent questions.

Good questions show the interviewer that you have initiative and are interested in making a well-informed decision. For that reason, be certain not to say, "I don't have any questions." Focus on questions that help you gain information about the company and the job that you could not learn from published sources or persons other than the interviewer. Do not waste the interviewer's time asking questions that show you are

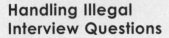

Handling Illegal Interview Questions

The Equal Employment Opportunity Commission (EEOC) and Fair Employment Practices Guidelines make it clear that an employer cannot legally discriminate against a job applicant on the basis of race, color, gender, age, religion, national origin, or disability. Interviewers must restrict questions to an applicant's ability to perform specific job-related functions essential to the job sought. Generally, the following topics should not be introduced during an interview or during the small talk that precedes or follows one:

- **National origin and religion.** "You have an unusual accent; where were you born?" "What religious holidays will require you to miss work?"

- **Age.** "I see you attended Metro High School; what year did you graduate?" "Could you provide a copy of your birth certificate?"

- **Disabilities, health conditions, and physical characteristics not reasonably related to the job.** "Do you have a disability that would interfere with your ability to perform the job? "Have you ever been injured on the job?" "Have you ever been treated by a psychiatrist?" "How much alcohol do you consume each week?" "What prescription drugs are you currently taking?"

- **Marital status, spouse's employment, or dependents.** "Are you married?" "Who is going to watch your children if you work for us?" "Do you plan to have children?" "Is your spouse employed?" Additionally, employers may not ask the names or relationships of people with whom you live.

- **Arrests or criminal convictions that are not related to the job.** "Have you ever been arrested other than for traffic violations? If so, explain." Keep in mind that the arrest/conviction record of a person applying for a job as a law enforcement officer or a teacher could be highly relevant to the job, but the same information could be illegal for a person applying for a job as an engineer.

Since interviewers may ask illegal questions either because of lack of training or an accidental slip, you must decide how to respond. You can refuse to answer and state that the question is improper, though you risk offending the interviewer. A second option is to answer the illegal question, knowing it is illegal and not related to the job requirements. A third approach for responding to an illegal question is to provide a low-key response such as "How does this question relate to how I will do my job?" or to answer the legitimate concern that probably prompted the question.

For example, an interviewer who asks, "Do you plan to have children?" is probably concerned about how long you might remain on the job. An answer to this concern would be "I plan to pursue a career regardless of whether I decide to raise a family." If you can see no legitimate concern in a question, such as "Do you own your home, rent, or live with parents?" answer, "I'm not sure how that question relates to the job. Can you explain?"[16]

Application

- In small groups discuss illegal interview questions that group members may have been asked. How did the group member handle the illegal question, and what were the consequences? Give suggestions for handling the questions effectively.

- Do you think managers ask illegal questions purposely or accidentally? What consequences does a company face when applicants believe illegal interview questions led to discriminatory hiring?

Just as a company must make the decision of whether to choose you as an employee, you must also decide whether to choose to work for the company. Salary is only one factor among many that may influence your satisfaction. Are the values of the company in keeping with your own? Does the company offer the type of work culture that will promote your comfort and sense of belonging? Will you have a reasonable opportunity for achieving your goals and aspirations?

© BOB DAEMMRICH/THE IMAGE WORKS

unprepared for the interview (for example, questions about the company's scope, products/services, job requirements, new developments). Having committed a block of uninterrupted time to talk to you, the interviewer will resent this blatant lack of commitment and respect for the company. Avoid questions about salary and benefits that imply you are interested more in money than in the contribution you can make.

To show further initiative, introduce questions throughout the interview whenever appropriate rather than waiting until you are asked whether you have questions. This approach will promote positive two-way interaction and should create a relaxed, unintimidating atmosphere. Just remember that the *interviewer* is in charge of the interview. Add your own questions to the typical interviewee questions that follow:

Critical Thinking

What are some other questions you would likely ask in a job interview?

- What is a typical day like in this job?
- What type of people would I be working with (peers) and for (supervisors)?
- Why do you need someone for this job (why can this job not be done by a current employee)?
- What circumstances led to the departure of the person I would be replacing? What is the turnover rate of people in this job? (or, How many people have held this job in the past five years?)

- Why do you continue to work for this company? (to an interviewer who has worked for the company for an extended time)
- Would you describe the initial training program for people in this position?
- What types of ongoing employee in-service training programs do you provide?
- How much value does your firm place on a master's degree?
- How do you feel this field has changed in the past ten years? How do you feel it will change in the next ten years?
- What advice do you wish you had been given when you were starting out?
- When do you expect to make your decision about the position?

The Closing

The interviewer will provide cues indicating that the interview is completed by rising or making a comment about the next step to be taken. At that point, do not prolong the interview needlessly. Simply rise, accept the handshake, thank the interviewer for the opportunity to meet, and close by saying you look forward to hearing from the company. The tact with which you close the interview may be almost as important as the first impression you made. Be enthusiastic. If you really want the job, you might ask for it.

Your ability to speak confidently and intelligently about your abilities will help you secure a desirable job. Effective interviewing skills will be just as valuable once you begin work. You will be involved in interviews with your supervisor for various reasons: to seek advice or information about your work and working conditions, to receive informal feedback about your progress, to receive a deserved promotion, and to discuss other personnel matters. In addition, your supervisor will likely conduct a performance appraisal interview to evaluate your performance. This formal interview typically occurs annually on the anniversary of your start of employment. Visit the text support site at http://lehman.swlearning.com to learn how you can make the most of the performance appraisal process.

Objective 5

Complete application forms accurately and write effective messages related to employment (follow-up, thank-you, job acceptance, job-refusal, resignation, and recommendation request).

Preparing Other Employment Messages

Preparing a winning résumé and application letter is an important first step in a job search. To expedite your job search, you may need to prepare other employment messages: complete an application form, send a follow-up message to a company that does not respond to your résumé, send a thank-you message after an interview, accept a job offer, reject other job offers, and communicate with references. A career change will require a carefully written resignation letter.

Application Forms

Critical Thinking

What types of job application forms have you been asked to complete? Did any of the items seem unusual?

Before going to work on a new job, you will almost certainly complete the employer's application and employment forms. Some application forms, especially for applicants who apply for jobs with a high level of responsibility, are very long. They may actually appear to be tests in which applicants give their answers to hypothetical questions and write defenses for their answers. Increasing numbers of companies are designing employment forms as mechanisms for getting information about a candidate that may not be included in the résumé. Application forms also ensure consistency in the information received from each candidate and can prevent decisions based on illegal topics which may be presented in a résumé. Review the following guidelines for completing application forms.

- *Read the entire form before you begin completing it.* This procedure will prevent you from making careless mistakes caused by not understanding the form. Preparing a rough draft on a photocopy of the form is an excellent idea.
- *Follow instructions.* If the form calls for last name first and you write your first name first, the damage could be fatal. If instructions clearly say "Print" and you write in cursive instead, you could be stereotyped immediately as a bungler. When the form has multiple copies, place the form on a hard surface and put enough pressure on the pen to make the last copy clear. If instructions say, "Do not fold," honor them.
- *Complete forms neatly.* If erasing is necessary, do it cleanly. Such techniques as marking through an original answer and squeezing another, or printing in all-capital letters in some blanks and in capital-and-lowercase letters in others may imply indecisiveness, carelessness, disrespect, or haste. Unless instructions or circumstances forbid, key your answers for a neat, legible document.
- *Answer all questions.* For any questions that do not apply, write "N/A" in the blank. If the form provides space for you to add additional information or make a comment, try to include something worthwhile. Applicants who leave such spaces blank may be perceived as employees who would habitually do no more than is required of them.
- *Answer accurately.* Carry information about courses taken, employment dates, and related experiences in a briefcase or portfolio and take it with you to employment offices and interviews. With a copy of your résumé and application letter in hand, you can make sure all factual statements are consistent with statements on the form. Providing false information would be unethical and impractical. It could result in your being hired for a job you cannot do well or termination in disgrace when the misrepresentation is discovered.
- *Keep a copy.* Save a copy of the application form for future reference.

Legal & Ethical Constraints

SPOTLIGHT COMMUNICATOR
Wanted: Diverse Team Players

GE's web site proclaims its firm commitment to diversity and team building: "We recognize the power of the mix, the strength that results from successful diversity. Our business and workforce diversity creates a limitless source of ideas and opportunities." As human resources manager for GE Asset Management, Marquette Wilson understands the importance of careful hiring decisions that promote the power of the mix. Because of the vital importance of teamwork, skill in this area is an important criterion for job selection. Wilson says, "During the interviewing process, I attempt to determine an applicant's ability to play different roles, to discuss input points that lead the group toward consensus, to be flexible, and to compromise one's ideas for the success of the team."

Wilson's own team experiences have taught her valuable lessons that apply to her hiring function.

She describes her experiences as a member of a quality team with the goal of redesigning the staffing process. Members from various areas of the company provide input to the hiring process, which allows human resources to become a strategic partner with the functional business areas. Wilson says that the reward of teamwork is not only rolling out a final product that adds value to the company but also gaining the opportunity to build relationships, brainstorm, and share ideas with other professionals who may become future resources for other projects and a referral source for other business professionals. "I was able to identify expert speakers for an event I was planning—all as a result of networks made during previous teambuilding sessions."

At GE Asset Management, successful implementation of teams begins with careful hiring decisions. Wilson recognizes the diverse nature of each individual and sees

COURTESY MARQUETTE L. WILSON

diversity as an untapped resource that has the ability to enrich the organization's mission and business strategies. "At the core of diversity is the goal that every employee feels valued and is provided the opportunity to excel. The success of business today is strengthened by diversity. When diversity is embraced as a vital part of the corporate culture, the result is a more productive workforce."

Applying What You Have Learned

1. How might Wilson assess an applicant's skills in teamwork?
2. Explain Wilson's perception of the relationship between effective teamwork and diversity.

Marquette L. Wilson, Human Resources Manager, GE Asset Management

http://www.ge.com

Refer to ShowCASE, Part 3 at the end of the chapter to expand your knowledge about GE's "America's Most Admired" awards.

If you complete the application form before the interview, reviewing it prior to the interview could be to your advantage.

Follow-Up Messages

When an application letter and résumé do not elicit a response, a follow-up message may bring results. Sent a few weeks after the original letter, it includes a reminder that an application for a certain job is on file, presents additional education or experience accumulated, points out its relationship to the job, and closes with a reference to desired action. In addition to conveying new information, follow-up messages indicate persistence (a quality that impresses some employers). Figure 14-2 shows a good example of a follow-up letter.

Thank-You Messages

Changing Technology

What purposes are served in sending a thank-you message, even though you expressed thanks in person after the interview or a discussion with a special employer at a career fair? After a job interview, a letter of appreciation is a professional courtesy and enhances your image within the organization. To be effective, it must be sent promptly. For maximum impact, send a thank-you message the day of the interview or the following day. Even if during the interview you decided you do not want the job or you and the interviewer mutually agreed that the job is not for you, a thank-you message is appropriate. As a matter of fact, if you've made a positive impression, interviewers may forward your résumé to others who are seeking qualified applicants.

The medium you choose for sending this message depends on the intended audience. If the company you've interviewed with prefers a traditional style, send a letter in complete business format on high quality paper that matches your résumé and application letter. If the company is technologically savvy and has communicated with you extensively by e-mail, follow the pattern and send a professional e-mail. Choosing to send an e-mail rather than slower mail delivery can give you a competitive edge over other candidates whose mailed letters arrive several days later than yours.

After an interview has gone well and you think a job offer is a possibility, include these ideas in the message of appreciation: express gratitude, identify the specific job applied for, refer to some point discussed in the interview (the strength of the interview), and close by making some reference to the expected call or message that conveys the employer's decision. The tone of this business message should remain professional regardless of the personal relationship you may have developed with the interviewer and the informality encouraged by e-mail. The message may be read by many others once it is placed in your personnel file as you complete annual appraisals and vie for promotions. Specific points to cover are outlined in Figure 14-3.

Figure 14-2

Example of a Follow-Up Letter

Jeanne Fulton | *89 Lincoln Street* | *San Antonio, TX 78285-9063*

October 23, 2004

Mr. Colin Franklin, Partner
Foster & Daniel, CPAs
1000 Plaza Court
Austin, TX 78710-1000

Dear Mr. Franklin:

> *States main idea and clearly identifies position being sought.*

Recently I applied for an audit staff position at Foster & Daniel and now have additional qualifications to report.

> *Refers to enclosed résumé; summarizes additional qualifications.*

The enclosed, updated résumé shows that I have passed the Auditing and Practice and Law sections of the CPA exam; I will take the final section at the next sitting. In addition, I have finished my last semester of cooperative education experience with Smith & Lewis, CPAs. This realistic work experience has added value to my formal education and confirmed my interest in working as an auditor.

> *Assures employer that Jeanne is still interested in the job.*

Mr. Franklin, I would welcome the opportunity to visit your office and talk more about the contributions I could make as an auditor for Foster & Daniel. Please write or call me at (512) 555-9823.

Sincerely,

Jeanne Fulton

Jeanne Fulton

Enclosure

Format Pointers

- Uses a template to design a professional personal letterhead and matching envelope.
- Formats as a formal business letter, but could have sent the message electronically if previous communication with the employer had been by e-mail.
- Prints letter and envelope with a laser printer on paper that matches the resume and application letter.

Figure 14-3

Example of a Thank-You Message

Deductive Outline for a Thank-You Message Following an Interview

1. Express appreciation for the interview; identify the interview date and the specific position.

2. Refer to some point discussed in the interview to personalize the message and to help the interviewer remember the particular interview. Ideally this point should reinforce a notable job-related skill.

3. Submit any information that may have been requested at the interview.

4. Close by referring to the expected call or message that conveys the interviewer's decision.

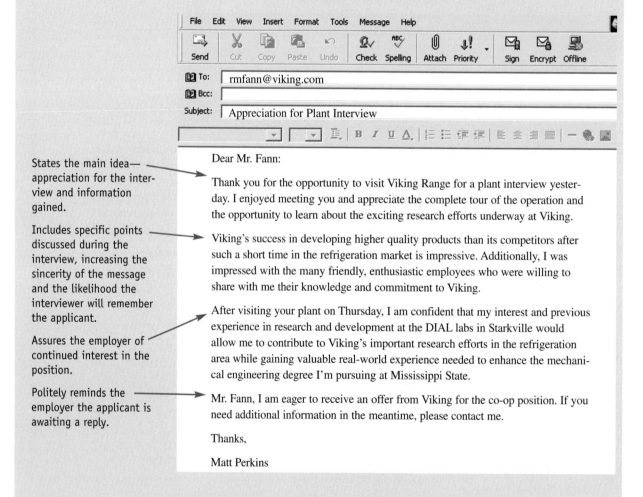

States the main idea—appreciation for the interview and information gained.

Includes specific points discussed during the interview, increasing the sincerity of the message and the likelihood the interviewer will remember the applicant.

Assures the employer of continued interest in the position.

Politely reminds the employer the applicant is awaiting a reply.

File   Edit   View   Insert   Format   Tools   Message   Help

Send   Cut   Copy   Paste   Undo   Check   Spelling   Attach   Priority   Sign   Encrypt   Offline

To: rmfann@viking.com
Bcc:
Subject: Appreciation for Plant Interview

Dear Mr. Fann:

Thank you for the opportunity to visit Viking Range for a plant interview yesterday. I enjoyed meeting you and appreciate the complete tour of the operation and the opportunity to learn about the exciting research efforts underway at Viking.

Viking's success in developing higher quality products than its competitors after such a short time in the refrigeration market is impressive. Additionally, I was impressed with the many friendly, enthusiastic employees who were willing to share with me their knowledge and commitment to Viking.

After visiting your plant on Thursday, I am confident that my interest and previous experience in research and development at the DIAL labs in Starkville would allow me to contribute to Viking's important research efforts in the refrigeration area while gaining valuable real-world experience needed to enhance the mechanical engineering degree I'm pursuing at Mississippi State.

Mr. Fann, I am eager to receive an offer from Viking for the co-op position. If you need additional information in the meantime, please contact me.

Thanks,

Matt Perkins

Format Pointer

• Prepared as an e-mail because all previous submissions have been completed by e-mail.

The résumé, application letter, and thank-you message should be stored in a computer file and adapted for submission to other firms when needed. Develop a database for keeping a record of the dates on which documents and résumés were sent to certain firms, and answers were received, names of people talked with, facts conveyed, and so on. When an interviewer calls, you can retrieve and view that company's record while you are talking with the interviewer.

Job-Acceptance Messages

A job offer may be extended either by telephone or in writing. If a job offer is extended over the telephone, request that the company send a written confirmation of the job offer. The confirmation should include the job title, salary, benefits, starting date, and anything else negotiated.

Often, companies require a written acceptance of a job offer. Note the deductive sequence of the letter shown in Figure 14-4: acceptance, details, and closing (confirms the report-for-work date).

Job-Refusal Messages

Like other messages that convey unpleasant news, job-refusal messages are written inductively: a beginning that reveals the nature of the subject, explanations that lead to a refusal, the refusal, and a pleasant ending. Of course, certain reasons (even though valid in your mind) are better left unsaid: questionable company goals or methods of operation, negative attitude of present employees, possible bankruptcy, unsatisfactory working conditions, and so on. The applicant who prefers not to be specific about the reason for turning down a job might write this explanation:

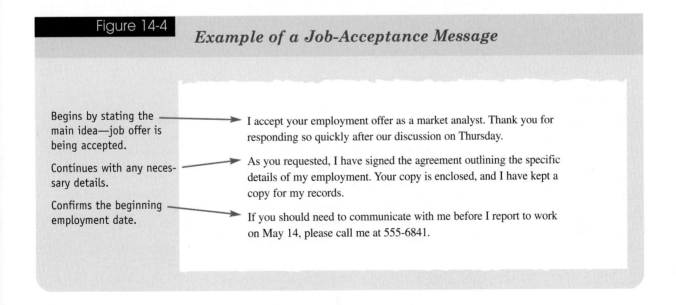

| Figure 14-4 | *Example of a Job-Acceptance Message* |

Begins by stating the main idea—job offer is being accepted.

I accept your employment offer as a market analyst. Thank you for responding so quickly after our discussion on Thursday.

Continues with any necessary details.

As you requested, I have signed the agreement outlining the specific details of my employment. Your copy is enclosed, and I have kept a copy for my records.

Confirms the beginning employment date.

If you should need to communicate with me before I report to work on May 14, please call me at 555-6841.

After thoughtfully considering job offers received this week, I have decided to accept a job in the actuarial department of an insurance company.

You may want to be more specific about your reasons for refusal when you have a positive attitude toward the company or believe you may want to reapply at some later date. The letter in Figure 14-5 includes the reasons for refusal.

Resignations

Resigning from a job requires effective communications skill. You may be allowed to "give your notice" in person or be required to write a formal resignation. Your supervisor will inform you of the company's policy. Regardless of whether the resignation is given orally or in writing, show empathy for your employer by giving enough time to allow the employer to find a replacement. Because your employer has had confidence in you, has benefited from your services, and will have to seek a replacement, your impending departure *is* bad news. As such, the message is written inductively. It calls attention to your job, gives your reasons for leaving it, conveys the resignation, and closes on a positive note. A written resignation is shown in Figure 14-6.

A resignation is not an appropriate instrument for telling managers how a business should be operated. Harshly worded statements could result in immediate termination or cause human relations problems during your remaining working days. If you can do so sincerely, recall positive experiences you had with the company. Doing so will leave a lasting record of your goodwill, making it likely that your supervisor will give you a good recommendation in the future.

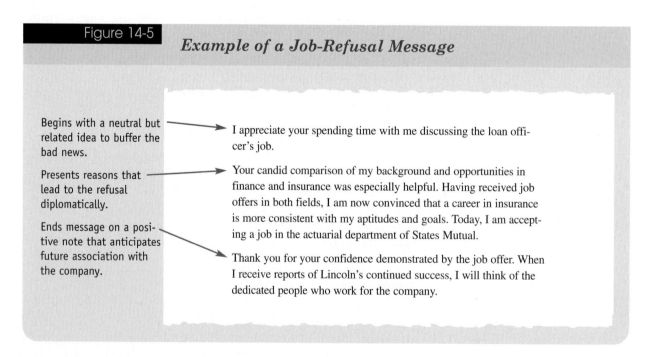

| Figure 14-5 | *Example of a Job-Refusal Message* |

Begins with a neutral but related idea to buffer the bad news.

I appreciate your spending time with me discussing the loan officer's job.

Presents reasons that lead to the refusal diplomatically.

Your candid comparison of my background and opportunities in finance and insurance was especially helpful. Having received job offers in both fields, I am now convinced that a career in insurance is more consistent with my aptitudes and goals. Today, I am accepting a job in the actuarial department of States Mutual.

Ends message on a positive note that anticipates future association with the company.

Thank you for your confidence demonstrated by the job offer. When I receive reports of Lincoln's continued success, I will think of the dedicated people who work for the company.

Figure 14-6

Example of a Resignation

SUBJECT: PLEASURE OF SERVING JARRETT STORES

Begins with appreciative comments about job to buffer the bad news. → My job as manager of Juniors' Apparel for the last two years has been a rewarding experience. It has taught me much about the marketing of clothing and changing preferences in style.

Presents reasons that lead to the main idea, the resignation. → Predicting public acceptance of certain styles has been fascinating. From the time I declared a major in fashion merchandising, I have wanted to become a buyer. Before I accepted my present job in manage-

States the resignation. Includes additional details. → ment, that goal was discussed. Now, it is becoming a reality, as I have accepted a job as a buyer for Belton beginning one month from today. If satisfactory with you, I would like May 31 to be my last day as manager here.

Conveys genuine appreciation for the experience gained at Jarrett and ends on a cordial note. → This job has allowed me to grow professionally. Thanks to you and others, I have had the privilege of trying new ideas and selecting sales personnel who get along well with one another and with customers. Thank you for the confidence you placed in me, your positive rapport with the sales staff, and your expressions of appreciation for my work. As I continue my career in fashion merchandising, I will always recall pleasant memories of my job at Jarrett.

Recommendations

When a former employee applies for a position with a new firm, the previous employer is frequently called upon to give a recommendation. Letters of recommendation are usually written in response to a request from either the applicant or the company to whom the applicant has applied.

Requesting and Acknowledging Recommendations

Critical Thinking

What individuals will you include as references for employment? What were the reasons for your selection?

Companies seek information from references at various stages. Some prefer talking with references prior to an interview, and others, after a successful interview. Specific actions on your part will ensure that your references are treated with common courtesy and that references are prepared for the employer's call.

- *Remind the reference that he/she had previously agreed to supply information about you.* Identify the job for which you are applying, give a complete address to which the letter is to be sent, and indicate a date by which the prospective employer needs the letter.

Sharing information about job requirements and reporting recent job-related experiences, you may assist the reference in writing an effective message. Indicate your gratitude, but do not apologize for making the request. The reference has already agreed to write such a letter and will likely take pleasure in assisting a deserving person.

- *Alert the reference of imminent requests for information, especially if considerable time has elapsed since the applicant and reference have last seen each other.* Enclosing a recent résumé and providing any other pertinent information (for example, name change) may enable the reference to write a letter that is specific and convincing. If the job search becomes longer than anticipated, a follow-up message to references explaining the delay and expressing gratitude for their efforts is appropriate.
- *Send a sincere, original thank-you message after a position has been accepted.* This thoughtful gesture will build a positive relationship with a person who may continue to be important to your career. The message in Figure 14-7 is brief and avoids clichés and exaggerated expressions of praise but instead gives specific examples of the importance of the reference's recommendation.

Objective 6

Write positive and negative recommendations that are legally defensible.

Writing Negative Recommendations

As an employer, you will be asked to provide recommendations for former employees or others you know in a professional capacity. Almost everyone who asks permission to use your name as a reference will expect your

| Figure 14-7 | *Example of a Thank-You Message to a Reference* |

States the main idea—appreciation for the recommendation. Informs reference of success in locating a job.

> Thank you so much for the letter of recommendation you prepared for my application to Tatum & Bayne. I learned today that I have been hired and will begin work next month.

Communicates sincere appreciation for reference's assistance; uses specific examples and avoids exaggeration.

> Because the position is in auditing, I believe your comments about my performance in your auditing and systems classes carried a great deal of weight. Mr. Gowan commented he was impressed with the wealth of evidence and examples you provided to support your statements, unlike the general recommendations he frequently receives.

Restates main idea and anticipates a continued relationship; is original and sincere.

> Dr. Dyess, I appreciate your helping me secure an excellent position in a highly competitive job market. Thanks for the recommendation and your outstanding instruction. I look forward to talking with you about how I am faring in the real world when I return to campus for fall homecoming.

Legal & Ethical
Constraints

recommendation to be favorable. For a person whom you could not favorably recommend, you have the following options:

1. *Saying "No" when asked for permission to use your name.* Refusing permission may be difficult; but, for you, it is easier than writing a negative recommendation. For the applicant, your refusing to serve as a reference may be preferable to your accepting and subsequently sending a negative message.

2. *Letting the request go unanswered.* Failure to answer a request for information is in effect a negative response, even though the employer does not know whether you received the request. Nonresponse is legal and requires no effort; but it does not reflect your responsibility to the applicant, the employer, and yourself.

3. *Responding with an objective appraisal.* Responding with an objective appraisal will give you the satisfaction of having exercised a responsibility to both the applicant and the employer. Because of your information, an employer may escape some difficulty encountered after hiring an unqualified person. Your message could spare an applicant the agony of going to work on a job that leads to failure. Figure 14-8 shows an example of a well-written negative recommendation.

4. *Responding in writing and inviting a telephone call.* Responding in writing and inviting a telephone call enable a reference to avoid putting negative ideas in writing. The message is short, positive, and easy to write as shown in the following example:

Critical Thinking

Which option would you likely choose when faced with providing a negative recommendation?

> Travis Kelley worked as a systems analyst for JEMCO from August 15, 2001, to December 30, 2004. The confidential information you requested will be provided by telephone: (601) 555-5432.

Recognizing the possibility of negatives, which the reference did not want to state in written form, the recipient might not call. In response to such a call, abide by the same precautions that apply to writing recommendations.

Because of the threat of possible litigation on the grounds of defamation, discrimination, or privacy violations, recommendations must be written carefully.[17] Suggested guidelines for writing a legally defensible recommendation are as follows:

- *Respond only to requests for specific information and indicate that your message is written in response to a request.* Verify only information that is provided by the employer making the request. Do not provide information that was not requested.

Critical Thinking

What is the advantage of labeling your recommendation letter "confidential" and reminding the reader that the information was requested?

- *Label your message as confidential.* Such precautions indicate that your intent was not to defame but to give an honest answer to a legitimate request for information. In addition, studies show that employers prefer confidential letters rather than open ones that allow the applicant access to the information. Employers perceive the message to be a more honest evaluation of the applicant's employability.[18]

Sorting fact from opinion is important when including negative information in a recommendation letter. Including only objective facts is the best safeguard against litigation and possible retaliation for losses caused by an employee's poor performance.

© MICHAEL NEWMAR/PHOTOEDIT, INC.

- *Provide only job-related information.* If you are not familiar with the requirements of the job applied for, ask the requester to send you a job description. Use this document to include information that is directly relevant to the future job and to eliminate irrelevant information that could be defamatory.
- *Avoid vague, general statements of the applicant's personal ability.* Instead, provide specific examples of performance and the situation in which the performance occurred.
- *Provide specific facts for any negative information.* For example, the number of workdays missed without prior communication with the supervisor is a verifiable fact. To label it as "a terrible record" or "irresponsible" is to pass judgment (which is best left to the reader). Avoid such defaming and judgmental words as *corrupt, crook, dishonest, hypocrite,* and *incompetent.*

Refer to the Internet Case for other legal implications of negative recommendations. Besides attending to legal issues in your response, realize that your writing techniques are also important factors in the overall message that you convey. Suggestions include the following:

Changing Technology

- *Include some positives, even if your overall recommendation is negative.* A balanced approach of positives and negatives will make the message appear more credible to the reader.
- *Use an inductive sequence and stylistic techniques of de-emphasis (unless your feelings are strong and you think emphasis of the negative is justified).* Typically, the inductive sequence with de-emphasis techniques will seem considerate.

Figure 14-8

Example of a Negative Recommendation

Identifies clearly the nature of the message in the subject line.

States the main idea—request for employment information.

Provides specific, objective information that can be verified easily.

Provides additional objective information; omits opinions or value judgments.

Describes Riley's past performance but does not project how he will perform on other jobs.

VANCE RILEY'S EMPLOYMENT RECORD

Osborn Grocery provides the confidential employment information about Vance Riley you requested in your June 1 letter.

Vance Riley worked from October 1 to December 13, 2003, as a courtesy clerk in our Greenwood store. He exhibited above-average skills at packing groceries, and he seemed to have good rapport with customers.

On three occasions (each on a Monday morning), he did not report to work as scheduled and had not given the shift supervisor any notice of his absence. He left the store at Osborn Grocery's request.

While he was on the job, his work was satisfactory.

Writing Positive Recommendations

Critical Thinking

How can strong adjectives in a positive recommendation be detrimental?

Fortunately, most people who invite you to write a recommendation are confident you will report positive information. Before requesting a recommendation, the employer has almost certainly seen the applicant's résumé, application letter, and (possibly) application forms. Although the effect of your message may be to *confirm* some of the information already submitted, do not devote all your space to *repeating* it. Instead, concentrate on presenting information the employer probably does not have. Your statements about proficiency and capacity to interact with others will be of special interest. Avoid unsupported superlatives and overly strong adjectives that may cause the employer to question your credibility. Regardless of whether a recommendation is for a promotion within the firm or for work in another firm, the same principles apply. Figure 14-9 shows a recommendation for an employee who is seeking a promotion within a company.

Figure 14-9

Example of a Positive Recommendation

Introduces the main idea. ⟶ Anne Payne would be an ideal senior loan officer. For the following reasons, I recommend her promotion:

Emphasizes each reason the promotion is deserved. Uses bullets with short sentences for high impact. ⟶

- She is efficient. Beginning with a $14 million loan portfolio, she now manages $25 million. In three years, the number of clients has grown from 16 to 26. Clients are astonished at the speed with which she completes paperwork.
- She stays informed. She spends time daily on the financial monitor and financial journals. Because of her knowledge, she has frequently made loans that would otherwise have gone to competitors.
- She works well with the staff. Colleagues communicate easily with her. Her friendly, positive disposition contributes to our pleasant office atmosphere.
- She helps maintain Southland's public image. Active in Kiwanis and in fund-raising for the needy, she has frequent contacts with clients, prospective clients, and competitors in social situations. To me, she is an ideal person for reflecting the bank's image.

Restates the main idea. ⟶ A promotion would reward Anne for the part she has played in expanding our loans and would help us to keep her on our team.

Summary

1. **Explain the nature of structured, unstructured, computer-assisted, group, and stress interviews.** Interviewers and interviewees can be considered as buyers and sellers: Interviewers want to know whether job candidates can meet the needs of their firms before making a "purchase"; interviewees want to sell themselves based on sound knowledge, good work skills, and desirable personal traits. Structured interviews follow a preset, highly structured format; unstructured interviews follow no standard format but explore for information. Computer-assisted interviews provide standard, reliable information on applicants during the preliminary interview stages. Group interviews involve various personnel within the organization in the candidate interview process. Stress interviews are designed to reveal how the candidate behaves in high-anxiety situations.

2. **Explain the steps in the interview process.** Successful job candidates plan appropriately for the interview so that they will know basic information about the company, arrive on time dressed appropriately for the interview, and present a polished first impression following appropriate protocol. During the interview, the candidate presents his or her qualifications favorably and obtains information about the company to aid in deciding whether to accept a possible job offer.

3. **Prepare effective answers to questions often asked in job interviews and questions that will communicate initiative to an interviewer.** The successful job candidate effectively discusses key qualifications and skillfully asks questions that show initiative and genuine interest in the company.

4. **Recognize and bypass illegal interview questions.** The successful job candidate recognizes issues that fall outside the bounds of legal questioning. Refusing to answer an illegal question could be detrimental to your chances to secure a job, but answering the question may compromise your ethical values. An effective technique is to answer the legitimate concern behind the illegal question rather than to give a direct answer.

5. **Complete application forms accurately and write effective messages related to employment (follow-up, thank-you, job-acceptance, job-refusal, resignation, and recommendation request).** Instructions on application forms should be followed carefully. Neatness, completeness, and accuracy are expected. A follow-up message is sent a few weeks after an applicant does not receive a response from an application. It includes a reminder that an application has been made, presents additional education or experience, and asks for action. A thank-you message following an interview is a professional courtesy and should be sent promptly. It expresses appreciation, refers to some point of discussion, and closes with an expectation of the employer's decision. Written deductively, job-acceptance messages include the acceptance, details, and a closing that confirms the date the employee will begin work. Job-refusal messages are written inductively and include a buffer beginning, reasons that lead to the refusal, and a goodwill closing. Resignation notices are typically required in writing;

they confirm that termination plans are definite. Assuming resignations are usually bad news for an employer, they are written inductively, with emphasis on positive aspects of the job.

6. **Write positive and negative recommendations that are legally defensible.** Requests for recommendations should include specific information about the job requirements and the applicant's qualifications to assist the reference in writing a convincing recommendation. Messages thanking a reference for a recommendation and providing an update on the status of a job search are a professional courtesy. For job seekers with good qualifications, recommendations are written deductively; otherwise, inductively. Because of the threat of possible litigation, special attention must be directed at writing legally defensible recommendations. General advice is to (1) provide only information that is requested; (2) indicate the information is confidential; (3) provide specific, job-related facts; and (4) avoid vague, general statements.

Chapter Review

1. What types of interviews are common in today's business environment? (Obj. 1)

2. How do team interviews differ from interviews with a single interviewer? (Obj. 1)

3. What information should you locate about a company with which you will interview? What means will you use to locate the information? (Obj. 2)

4. Write a brief statement that describes your unique value to an employer. Include information about your educational experiences, work experience, involvement in student organizations, and other pertinent information. (Obj. 2)

5. What nonverbal messages can an interviewee convey to favorably impress an interviewer? What negative nonverbal messages can be conveyed? (Obj. 2)

6. How do responses to direct and indirect interview questions differ? (Obj. 3)

7. What is a good strategy to use when you are asked about your major weakness? Provide a specific example you might use. (Obj. 3)

8. Discuss three ways an interviewee can handle an illegal interview question. What are the advantages and disadvantages of each? (Obj. 4)

9. What ideas are included in a follow-up letter? (Obj. 5)

10. In a thank-you letter, what is the advantage of referring to some point discussed in the interview? (Obj. 5)

11. How might an employer use the information you provide on an employment application?(Obj. 5)

12. Which would be written deductively: (a) an acceptance letter, (b) a refusal letter, or (c) a resignation? What ideas should be included in each of these letters? (Obj. 5)

13. Professor Ulmer agreed to serve as one of your employment references, but you have not talked with her for two years. Today, you listed her name on an application form. Should you contact her? Explain. (Obj. 5)

14. What guidelines should be followed in requesting a recommendation? (Obj. 5)

15. An employee whom you fired last year has given your name as a reference. Will you provide the reference? If yes, should you include positives and negatives? Discuss guidelines for writing a recommendation that you can legally defend. (Obj. 6)

Digging Deeper

1. How can a job applicant maximize the likelihood of accepting the "right" job?

2. Explain why communication skills are the universal job requirement.

To check your understanding of the chapter, take the practice quizzes at **http://lehman.swlearning.com** or your WebTutor course.

Coping with Technology's Downside

For all of its advantages, technology poses some negative aspects. Pessimists argue that online activities pull people away from real-world interactions, making them less concerned about individual relationships and their communities. Productivity gains for businesses are questioned in light of computer viruses, web surfing during work hours, and information overload. The Internet is charged with creating opportunities for invasion of privacy by commercial interests and the government. The following electronic activities will allow you to explore these complex issues and consider how to use technology to its best advantage:

 InfoTrac College Edition. Access http://www.infotrac.thomsonlearning.com to read about the curse of e-mail:

Graham, J. R. (2002, September). Who do we thank (and curse) for e-mail? *Supervision, 63*(9), 16(3).

The author of the article sums up his discussion with the following: "The genius of e-mail is primarily as an incredibly effective and efficient form of communication that deserves the same high standards as writing any thoughtful letter or memo. To abuse it is to abuse those who receive our e-mails." For each of the six negative aspects of e-mail that the author cites, develop a "commandment" for appropriate use.

 Text Support Web Site. Visit http://lehman.swlearning.com to learn more about appropriate online behavior that minimizes confusion, monotony, and negative attitudes. Refer to Chapter 14's Electronic Café activity that provides a link to an article on netiquette tips. Be prepared to discuss the value of the tips in class or follow your instructor's directions about how to use the information.

 WebTutor Advantage. Your instructor will give you directions about how to access an evaluation of your WebTutor course site.

 Professional Power Pak. Access your PPP CD for helpful tips for avoiding PowerPoint excesses.

Activities

1. **Subscribing to a Career Newsletter (Objs. 1–5)**

    Subscribe to the career newsletter at the following link or to one of your choosing: **http://www.quintcareers.com/QuintZine/subscribe.html**

    Create a career file that contains the following information about your selected career field:

    a. Outlook for job openings.

    b. Typical starting salaries by region.

    c. Minimum requirements.

    d. Desired skills and experience.

    e. Networking opportunities.

    f. Recommended interview strategies.

    g. Potential for advancement.

    Submit your file to your instructor for review or use it as directed.

    Visit the Interactive Study Center at **http://lehman.swlearning.com** for a downloadable version of this application.

2. **Preparing to Answer Interview Questions Effectively (Objs. 2–4)**

    Considering your career field, compose a list of potential questions you might be asked in a job interview. As directed by your instructor, complete one or more of the following:

    a. Divide into groups of three and discuss appropriate answers to the interview questions.

    b. Revise your answers, incorporating relevant feedback and being sure that the answers are truthful and reflect your individual personality.

    c. Conduct mock interviews, with one person portraying the interviewer, the second person portraying the interviewee, and the third person performing a critique of the interview. Discuss the results of the critique.

3. **Developing Appropriate Interview Questions (Objs. 2–4)**

    Bring a copy of your résumé to class and exchange it with another student. Assume you are an employer who has received the résumé, for one of the following positions:

INTERVIEWS

Planning Stage

- Learn as much as you can about the job requirements, range of salary and benefits, and the interviewer.
- Research the company with whom you are interviewing (products/services, financial condition, growth potential, etc.).
- Identify the *specific* qualifications for the job and other pertinent information about the company.
- Plan your appearance—clean, well groomed, and appropriate clothing.
- Arrive early with appropriate materials to communicate promptness and organization.
- Try to identify the type of interview you will have (structured, unstructured, computer-assisted, group, or stress).

Opening Formalities

- Greet the interviewer by name with a smile, direct eye contact, and a firm handshake.
- Wait for the interviewer to ask you to be seated.
- Sit erect and lean forward slightly to convey interest.

Body of the Interview

- Adapt your responses to the type of interview situation.
- Explain how your qualifications relate to the job requirements using multiple specific examples.
- Identify illegal interview questions; address the concern behind an illegal question or avoid answering the question tactfully.
- Ask pertinent questions that communicate intelligence and genuine interest in the company. Introduce questions throughout the interview where appropriate.
- Allow the interviewer to initiate a discussion of salary and benefits. Be prepared to provide a general salary range for applicants with your qualifications.

Closing the Interview

- Watch for cues the interview is ending; rise, accept the interviewer's handshake, and communicate enthusiasm.

- Express appreciation for the interview and say you are eager to hear from the company.

EMPLOYMENT MESSAGES

Application Forms

- Read the entire form before completing it and follow instructions precisely.
- Complete the form neatly and accurately.
- Respond to all questions; insert N/A for questions that do not apply.
- Retain a copy for your records.

Follow-Up Messages

- Remind the receiver that your application is on file and you are interested in the job.
- Present additional education or experience gained since previous correspondence; do not repeat information presented earlier.
- Close with a courteous request for an interview.

Thank-You Messages

- Express appreciation for the interview and mention the specific job for which you have applied.
- Refer to a specific point discussed in the interview.
- Close with a reference to an expected call or document conveying the interviewer's decision.

Job-Acceptance Messages

- Begin by accepting the job offer; specify position.
- Provide necessary details.
- Close with a courteous ending that confirms the date employment begins.

Job-Refusal Messages

- Begin with neutral, related idea that leads to the explanation for refusal.
- Present the reasons that lead to a diplomatic statement of the refusal.
- Close positively, anticipating future association with the company.

Resignation Messages

- Begin with positive statement about the job to cushion the bad news.

- Present explanation, state the resignation, and provide any details.
- Close with appreciative statement about experience with the company.

Recommendation Requests

- Begin with the request for the recommendation.
- Provide necessary details including reference to an enclosed résumé.
- End with an appreciative statement for the reference's willingness to aid in the job search.
- Send a follow-up letter explaining delays and expressing appreciation for extended job searches.

Thank-Yous for a Recommendation

- Begin with expression of thanks for the recommendation.
- Convey sincere tone by avoiding exaggerated comments and providing specific examples of the value of the recommendation.

- End courteously, indicating future association with the reference.

Negative Recommendations

- Begin by stating *confidential* information *requested* by the receiver is being provided.
- Provide *specific, objective* information that can be verified; omit opinions and value judgments. Invite receiver to telephone to avoid including negative statements in writing.
- End with a courteous statement.

Positive Recommendations

- Begin with a statement of recommendation.
- Provide *specific, objective* information that the interviewer likely has not received already.
- Avoid unsupported superlatives and overly strong adjectives and adverbs that destroy credibility.
- End by restating the positive recommendation.

---

a. A part-time job visiting high schools to sell seniors on the idea of attending your school.

b. A full-time summer job as a management intern in a local bank.

c. A campus job as an assistant in your school president's office.

Write several appropriate interview questions based on the résumé. With the other student, take turns playing the part of the interviewer and the interviewee. Critique each other's ability to answer the questions effectively.

4. **Responding to Challenging Interview Questions (Objs. 2–4)**

Your instructor will divide the class into pairs. One member will send an e-mail message; the other will respond. The sender will compose an e-mail message to the other

member asking for a thoughtful response to five tough interview questions. At least one of the questions should be sensitive in nature (possibly illegal or quite close). The team member receiving the message will e-mail answers to the five questions. Send your instructor a copy of the original message and the answers to the questions. The instructor may ask that you reverse roles so that each of you has experience composing and answering difficult interview questions.

5. **Critiquing a Job Application (Objs. 4–5)**

Obtain a copy of a job application and bring it to class. In small groups, critique each application, commenting on the appropriateness of items included. Discuss how you would respond to each item. Share with the class any items you felt were inappropriate or illegal and how you would respond.

Applications

| Read | Think | Write | Speak | Collaborate |

1. **Rebounding from a Termination (Objs. 1–6)**

Each year, many workers from every career field find themselves out of work. The process of becoming re-employed can be stressful, to say the least. Using InfoTrac College or another online database, locate the

following article that presents strategies for surviving a job termination and successfully becoming re-employed:

Harshbarger, C. (2003, May). You're out! (Job search, resume, and interview planning). *Strategic Finance*, 84(11), 46(4).

Using the information in the article, develop a checklist of strategies for locating and landing a desirable job. Add your own additional strategies. Submit your checklist to your instructor.

2. **Demonstrating Effective Verbal Skills in an Interview (Obj. 2)**

Using language effectively in an interview situation can give you the edge over another candidate. Locate the following article about language usage from an online database:

Riley, K. J. (2003, July). Watch your language! *Black Enterprise, 33*(12), 52.

Compose a list of rules for effective use of language in an interview. Expanding upon the information in the article, give several examples for each rule. In class, compare your list with those of others in the class. Develop a one-page plan of action for improving your own interviewing language skills.

Read	Think	Write	Speak	Collaborate

3. **Researching a Company and Asking Questions of an Interviewer (Objs. 2, 3)**

In small groups or individually, research a company of your choice. Use the chapter information in "Study the Company" as a guide for your research. Generate a list of ten questions to ask an interviewer from the company you researched. Your original questions should communicate initiative, intelligence, and genuine interest in the company and the job. Submit a memo to your instructor that summarizes important facts about the organization and shows the rationale for the selection of your ten questions.

4. **Learning to Play Mind Games to Win an Interview (Objs. 2–4)**

Locate five brain teasers that could be incorporated into a job interview to identify an applicant's ability to think logically and creatively. Choose your brain teasers from the numerous brain teaser books readily available in bookstores, or visit one of many brain teaser web sites (such as **http://amusingfacts.com/brain/**) or share brain teasers that you know have been used during actual job interviews. Write a two-page report on the importance of logical and creative thinking to your chosen career field. Include the brain teasers you have selected as examples of how critical thinking can be assessed in an interview.

Read	Think	Write	Speak	Collaborate

5. **Following Up on a Job Application (Obj. 5)**

Assume that you have applied for a position earlier in this current class term. Make the assumption you prefer about the position: You applied for (a) an immediate part-time job, (b) a full-time job for next summer, (c) a cooperative education assignment or internship, or (d) a full-time job immediately after your graduation. Assume you have now completed the current class term. Mentioning the courses you have taken this term, write a follow-up letter for the position for which you have applied.

6. **Saying "Thank-You" for an Interview (Obj. 5)**

Assume that you were interviewed for the job for which you applied in Application 5. Write a thank-you e-mail message to the interviewer; send it to your instructor or submit as directed.

7. **Accepting a Job Offer (Obj. 5)**

Write a letter of acceptance for the job (internship) for which you applied in Application 5. Assume you have been asked to start work in two weeks. Provide additional details concerning work arrangements, salary, etc. Supply an address.

8. **Refusing a Job Offer Diplomatically (Obj. 5)**

Assume that the job search identified in Application 5 was very successful; you were offered positions with two firms. Write a letter refusing one of the job offers. Because you want to maintain a positive relationship with the company for whom you are refusing to work, provide specific reasons for your decision. Supply an address.

9. **Resigning from a Job (Obj. 5)**

Write a letter resigning from your current job. If you are not currently employed, supply fictitious information.

10. **Requesting a Recommendation (Obj. 5)**

Write an e-mail message requesting a reference to provide information to prospective employers. Your reference could be a professor, past or present employer, or other appropriate person. Provide specific information about how your qualifications relate to the job requirements and include a résumé. Send the e-mail message to your instructor or submit as directed.

11. **Informing a Reference of an Extended Job Search (Obj. 5)**

Your job search is taking much longer than you had hoped. Because your references have been providing recommendations for six months now, you must write expressing your gratitude and updating them on the status of your job search. If your qualifications have changed, include an updated résumé. Compose an e-mail to one of your references. Send to your instructor or submit as directed.

12. Writing a Negative Recommendation (Obj. 6)

In your position as sales manager with V-Tech, you recently had to dismiss a sales trainee during her probationary employment period. While the trainee, Justine Simms, was pleasant and cooperative, her sales presentations were lackluster and unproductive. Ms. Simms has now applied for a similar position with Consolidated Technology, and they have contacted you for a written reference. Write a letter that is legally defensible, providing an appropriate address.

Read	Think	Write	**Speak**	Collaborate

13. Sending the Right Nonverbal Signals (Obj. 2)

While what you say in an interview will obviously be important, you will also have to be careful to send the right unspoken signals. Your numerous nonverbal messages will also be noted by a prospective employer. Locate the following articles about nonverbal communication in interviews through InfoTrac College or another online database:

Petrash, A. (2002, November 15). It's all in the body language. *The Bookseller,* 48.

Warfield, A. (2002, February). Your body speaks volume, but do you know what it is saying? *Business Credit,* 104(2), 20(2).

In teams of three or four, prepare a presentation on the topic of nonverbal communication in interviews; include demonstrations of appropriate and inappropriate nonverbal messages.

14. Investigating the Role of the Interviewer (Objs. 2–4)

An interviewer's role is to hire the ideal employee for the company—the person with the skills, experience, and demeanor required for the position. Getting the necessary information to make the right decision requires knowledge and skill. Using InfoTrac College or another online database, locate the following articles that provide advice to the interviewer for conducting a productive interview and avoiding legal liability:

Brune, C. (2003, April). The artful interviewer: Three experts offer a refresher course on the basics of conducting an interview. *Internal Auditor,* 60(2), 25(3).

Dubie, D. (1999, November 8). Asking the right questions. *Network World,* 16(45), 54.

Interviewer Advice: Steer clear of personal questions. (2001, November 16). *Long Island Business News,* p. 31A.

Prepare a short presentation on guidelines for interviewers. Include role playing that models appropriate interviewer behavior.

Read	Think	Write	Speak	**Collaborate**

15. Organizing an Employer Panel (Objs. 1–4)

Working with a small group, organize an employer panel for a class session on successful interviewing. Include the following elements in your panel activity:

a. Contact employers who would be willing to serve on the panel and share their views about successful job interviewing.

b. In advance of the panel presentation, prepare a list of questions to be asked of the panel.

c. Select a team member to serve as moderator for the panel discussion.

d. As part of the panel discussion, solicit questions from the class for response by the guest employers.

16. Conducting a Job Interview (Objs. 1–4)

Visit the text support site at **http://lehman.swlearning. com** for information about the types of questions typically asked in a job interview. Identify another student in your class with similar career goals, and together select a related job listing from a newspaper or web posting. Using that job listing, develop a set of questions for an employment interview. Stage an interview, with one of you portraying the role of the interviewer and one the interviewee. Submit your set of questions to your instructor. Be prepared to conduct your interview in a class session or follow your instructor's directions for recording it.

17. Conducting a Performance Appraisal Interview (Objs. 1–3)

Visit the text support site at **http://lehman.swlearning. com** for information about the performance appraisal process. In pairs, stage an effective mock performance interview. Videotape your interview and write a commentary that explains why the portrayed behaviors and dialogue are appropriate. Submit your tape and commentary to your instructor.

GE Earns Admiration and Applicants

General Electric has repeatedly appeared among the top ten of *Fortune* magazine's "America's Most Admired" designation. Studies of the ten most admired companies reveal that they attract far more applicants than they need, by an even greater ratio than *Fortune's* 100 Best Companies to Work For.[19] To find out why GE has repeatedly received the most admired designation, visit GE's career web site and link to the information about the award: **http://www.gecareers.com.**

1. What assessment factors are considered in determining the "America's Most Admired" award winners?

2. Using the assessment factors used in the award process as a guide, compose a list of questions that you might ask during an employment interview to determine the respectability of the company with which you are interviewing.

Part 4 of the GE ShowCASE focuses on how GE is responding to the issue of diversity.

http://www.ge.com

Visit the text support site at **http://lehman.swlearning. com** to complete Part 4 of the GE ShowCASE.

Internet Case

To Tell or Not to Tell: The Implications of Disclosing Potentially Damaging Information in an Employment Reference

Highly publicized and widespread business scandals have led to a significant increase in reference checking. While some firms do their own checking, others turn to the expertise of reference-checking services. Until recently, the rule for employers for responding to reference checks about their employees was fairly simple: The less said, the better. The risk of providing employment references to prospective employers is that former employees may sue if your references are unfavorable and lead to job rejection or if they constitute invasion of privacy. The employers may be liable to a former employee for defamation if the employer communicates to a prospective employer or other person a false statement that results in damage to the former employee's reputation. Defamation is commonly referred to as "slander" if the communication is verbal and as "libel" if the communication is written.

Employers have traditionally been cautioned about relating information that is not formally documented or for which no objective evidence exists. Thus, the more information provided, the greater the likelihood of a defamation or privacy invasion suit by the former employee. Awards in successful suits may include damages for lost earnings, mental anguish, pain and suffering, and even punitive damages.

Recent court decisions may have changed all of that or at least created confusion for employers about what to disclose. If an employer gives a positive reference for a fired employee, the employee could sue for wrongful termination. In situations where the employer knows that a former employee has a history of criminal violence or extremely aggressive behavior, the employer may have a legal obligation to provide such information to a prospective employer. Questions arise as to what to do if you are not sure that the information about the previous employee is true. The risk of remaining silent is that you could be sued for negligently failing to disclose the information if the former employee were to harm someone on the next job. On the other hand, you could be sued for defamation if you do disclose the information and the former employee can successfully establish that it is not true.[20]

Some attorneys recommend that companies have employees who are leaving the organization sign a form releasing the employer from any liability for responding truthfully during the course of giving references. All inquiries for references should be handled through an established point of contact, and only written requests for references should be considered. Only accurate and verifiable information should be reported.[21]

Visit the text support site at **http://lehman.swlearning.com** to link to web resources related to this topic. As directed by your instructor, complete one or more of the following.

1. Make a list of types of statements that a former employer should generally avoid making when giving employment references.

2. Write an organizational policy that addresses the appropriate guidelines for giving employee references. Include statements concerning appropriate content and the manner in which such information should be issued.

3. **GMAT** Formulate a legal argument that presents the conflict between the potential employer's right to know and the previous employer's right to avoid possible defamation charges. Present both sides in a short written report or presentation.

Video Case

Computer Directions: Interviewing for Success

Computer Directions, Dallas, Texas, opened in 1993 by Wanda Brice, is a staffing company that daily places anywhere from 50 to 100 programmers in as many as 20 different companies. The firm handles permanent and contract-to-hire placements as well as temporary placements primarily in their headquarter area of Dallas/Ft. Worth, but also in other locations around the United States. Many big companies depend on Computer Directions to keep their information systems current.

You'll gain some valuable insights from Wanda Brice about how hiring decisions are made during interviews based on how job candidates communicate what they have to offer the employer. Another way you can prepare for that all-important job interview is to practice answering typical questions you might be asked during an interview. Practicing before the real thing can result in increasing your confidence and helping you minimize—or even eliminate—clumsy and awkward responses to an interviewer's questions.

View the video segment about Computer Directions and related activities on WebTutor or your Professional Power Pak CD.

Discussion Questions

1. What three criteria does Wanda Brice use during the interview process to help her make hiring decisions?

2. What communication skills does Wanda Brice evaluate to determine whether a job candidate is a quick study?

3. Do you think Wanda's acid test for energy is reliable? Why or why not?

4. Why do you think it might be important to Wanda to hire only "nice" people?

Activities

1. Complete a virtual interview by following these instructions:

   a. Go to **http://interview.monster.com/**.

   b. Select the drop-down list next to "Virtual Interviews" and choose the position that most closely relates to the employment environment you would like to work in after you graduate.

   c. Respond to the interview questions that are typically asked of job candidates applying for the type of position you selected.

2. Write a three- to four-paragraph summary of the principles you learned from this interactive application that will be important for you to remember during a real interview.

Appendix

Document Format and Layout Guide

a

First impressions are lasting ones, and the receiver's first impression of your document is its appearance and format. This section presents techniques for producing an appealing document as well as standard letter, memo, and e-mail formats, punctuation styles, the standard and special parts of a letter, envelope-addressing formats, and report formats.

Appearance

To convey a positive, professional image, a document should be balanced attractively for visual appeal, proofread carefully, and, when appropriate, printed on high-quality paper. Other factors that affect the overall appearance of your document are justification of margins, spacing after punctuation, abbreviations, and word division. Review the following guidelines to ensure that your documents are accurate in these areas.

Proofreaders' Marks

Carefully proofread for three overall factors: (1) organization, content, and style; (2) grammatical errors; and (3) format errors. In addition, check your document with the electronic spellcheck. Refer to Chapter 4 for a detailed explanation of systematic proofreading procedures. Become familiar with the standard proofreaders' marks shown in Figure A-1.

Paper

The quality of paper reflects the professionalism of the company and allows a company to control communication costs effectively. Paper quality is measured by cotton-fiber content and weight. High-cotton bond

Standard Proofreaders' Marks

Proofreaders' Mark	Draft Copy	Final Copy
‖ Align type vertically	**Date:** May 21, 2004 **Subject:** International Assignments Available	**Date:** May 21, 2004 **Subject:** International Assignments Available
☰ Capitalize	*cap* The intern is enrolled in marketing research this term.	The intern is enrolled in Marketing Research this term.
◡ Close up	Staff meetings begin at 9 a. m.	Staff meetings begin at 9 a.m.
][Center	] Proofreading Procedures [	Proofreading Procedures
Change	*Supervised* ~~Responsible for~~ work crews of six-to-ten employees	Supervised work crews of six-to-ten employees . . . .
n ¶ Combine paragraphs	*n ¶* The manager approved	The manager approved . . . .
ℓ Delete	Presentation graphics software ~~available today~~ is capable	Presentation graphics software is capable . . . .
ⓓ Double-space copy	About two thirds of the consumers preferred to . . . . ⓓ	About two thirds of the consumers preferred to . . . .
=/ Hyphenate	Follow these easy to understand instructions.	Follow these easy-to-understand instructions.
∧ Insert	*m* This system can accommodate	This system can accommodate . . . .
∨ Insert apostrophe	The managers perspective	The manager's perspective . . . .
∧ Insert comma	Clear concise messages save time and money.	Clear, concise messages save time and money.
⋀ Insert em dash	Additional equipment--video camera and microphone-is needed	Additional equipment—video camera and microphone—is needed . . . .
∨ Insert quotation mark	Reread e-mail messages written in anger to avoid flaming.	Reread e-mail messages written in anger to avoid "flaming."
# Insert space	Managers address this problem everyday.	Managers address this problem every day.
⊙ Insert period	The agenda will be released on Friday	The agenda will be released on Friday.
⌐ Move left	[1. Use the default margins	1. Use the default margins . . . .
⌐ Move right	] Indent paragraphs in double-spaced text.	Indent paragraphs in double-spaced text.
/ Lowercase	Jill Cox, Assistant Manager of . . . . U.S. WORKFORCE	Jill Cox, assistant manager of . . . . U.S. Workforce

Standard Proofreaders' Marks

Proofreaders' Mark	Draft Copy	Final Copy
Move copy as indicated	Today your June payment was received	Your June payment was received today.
(SS) Single-space copy	About two thirds of the consumers preferred	(SS) About two thirds of the consumers preferred . . . .
Start a new line	Ms. Kelly Chen, Manager	Ms. Kelly Chen Manager
Start a new paragraph	Experts suggest students pursue electronic and traditional job search strategies.	Experts suggest students pursue electronic and traditional job search strategies.
Spell out	8 boxes of colored markers	Eight boxes of colored markers
Transpose	The Japanese beleive	The Japanese believe . . . .
Stet (let original text stand)	A memo template includes	A memo template includes . . . .
ital Use italics	Business Horizons *ital*	*Business Horizons*
bf Use boldface	Site Selection for New Plant *bf*	**Site Selection for New Plant**

Diversity Challenges

paper has a crisp crackle, is firm to the pencil touch, is difficult to tear, and ages without deterioration or chemical breakdown. The heavier the paper, the higher the quality.

Most business letters are produced on company letterhead printed on 16- or 20-pound bond paper. Extremely important external documents such as reports and proposals may be printed on 24-pound bond paper with 100-percent cotton content. Memorandums, business forms, and other intercompany documents may be printed on lighter-weight paper with lower cotton-fiber content. Envelopes and plain sheets to be used for second and successive pages of multiple-page documents should be of the same weight, cotton-fiber content, and color as the letterhead.

The standard paper size for business documents is 8½ by 11 inches in the United States, but this standard varies from country to country. For less formal messages, some U.S. businesspeople use executive-size (7¼ by 10½ inches) letterhead printed on 24-pound bond paper with 100-percent cotton content. However, this smaller size could easily be misfiled and may require special formatting that adds to the document cost.

Another characteristic of high-quality paper is the watermark, a design incorporated into the paper that can be seen clearly when held up to the light. The trademark of the company or the brand of paper is often used as the watermark. For a professional appearance, the watermark is positioned so that it can be read across the sheet in the same direction as the printing.

Justification of Margins

*Changing
Technology*

For a professional, personalized look, business documents are often printed using proportional fonts and unjustified margins. A ragged right margin opens up the space giving the document a friendly appearance rather than a computer-generated, form letter look. Other problems occur with justified right margins when monospaced fonts are used. Because all letters in a monospaced font are the same size, extra spaces must be added between words to end lines exactly at the right margin. These spaces are visually distracting, make the message more difficult to read, and reduce overall comprehension. Monospaced fonts also give the document an outdated look as you can see in the first sample paragraph displaying a monospaced font that resembles type produced by a typewriter.

Justified margins can give a highly professional appearance to formal documents when printed with proportional fonts (the size of the letters varies, and the extra space between words is minimized). These enhancements increase your ability to prepare professional newsletters, reports, and proposals. The following paragraphs illustrate the appearance of justified and unjustified margins using proportional and monospaced fonts.

Ineffective
Example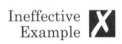

> **Justified Margins (Left and Right) Without Proportional Print**
> **ESSENTIAL COMPUTER SKILLS**
>
> Employees at all levels of our organization are using primary computer applications to increase their productivity and are eager to expand their knowledge to other more advanced areas. A primary need is to implement a telecommunications system that will allow our staff to transmit reports from the field to the home office.

> **Jagged Right Margin (Left Justified) with Proportional Print**
> **ESSENTIAL COMPUTER SKILLS**
>
> Employees at all levels of our organization are using primary computer applications to increase their productivity and are eager to expand their knowledge to other more advanced areas. A primary need is to implement a telecommunications system that will allow our staff to transmit reports from the field to the home office.

> **Justified Margins Using Proportional Print with Scalable Font**
> **ESSENTIAL COMPUTER SKILLS**
>
> Employees at all levels of our organization are using primary computer applications to increase their productivity and are eager to expand their knowledge to other more advanced areas. A primary need is to implement a telecommunications system that will allow our staff to transmit reports from the field to the home office.

Special Symbols

To give documents the appearance of a professionally typeset document, use the following special symbols in computer-generated material:

En dash	Use to separate words indicating a duration (May–June).
Em dash	Use instead of a dash (--) to indicate an abrupt change in thought (statement—that is,).
Hyphen	Use to indicate word division (nega-tive).
Quotation marks	Use instead of the inch (´´) and foot (´) symbols ("Today" or 'today').
Fractions	Create $\frac{1}{2}$ and $\frac{1}{4}$ rather than key 1/2 and 1/4. Special symbols are available for other common fractions.
Bullets	Use a variety of special symbols to highlight enumerated items (●, ❑, ■, *, ✗).
Other symbols	Learn the codes for printing symbols: ©, ®, ¢, £, %, ¶, and others.

Spacing

Proper spacing after punctuation is essential in preparing a professional document.

1. Space *once* after terminal punctuation (period, question mark, or exclamation point) when using a proportional font. The proportional font automatically adjusts the white space; therefore, adding an extra space to separate the sentences as traditionally done is not necessary. However, space *twice* after terminal punctuation if you use a mono-spaced font (a "typewriter-like" font with characters of *one* width) or a typewriter.

Proportional:	When will he arrive? Regardless of the time. . . .
Monospaced:	Step two was completed. Then. . . .

One space follows the terminal punctuation in the examples in this text. Because some writers advocate that extra space aids readability regardless of the font used, you should learn your instructor's preference before submitting documents.

2. Space twice after a colon except in the expression of time:

We have three questions: (1) When is . . . .

Please cancel my 9:15 a.m. meeting with Charlotte Gaines.

3. Space once after a comma or a semicolon.

> When the end of the month comes, we will be prepared.
>
> The operator left at three o'clock; he was ill.

4. Space once after a period following an initial and abbreviations.

> No. Co. Corp. Mr. Watson A. Reynolds

Word Division

Often word division is necessary to avoid extreme variations in line length. If the word processing software wraps a long word to the next line, the previous line will be extremely short (jagged right margin) or will have large spaces between words (justified right margin). In either case, the result is distracting. A divided word at the end of the line would be less distracting.

Changing Technology

Try to avoid dividing words at the ends of lines. If words must be divided, follow acceptable word-division rules. Word processing software can automatically hyphenate based on accepted word-division rules, or you can make the decisions manually. Apply the following word-division rules:

1. Divide words between syllables only. (Words with only one syllable cannot be divided: through, hearth, worked).
2. Avoid dividing a word containing six or fewer letters. (Lines on a printed page may vary as much as six or seven letters in length; therefore, dividing short words such as *letter* or *report* is pointless.)
3. Do not separate the following syllables from the remainder of a word:
   a. A syllable that does not include a vowel (e.g., contractions): *would/n't*.
   b. A first syllable that contains only one letter: *a/greement*.
   c. A last syllable that contains only one or two letters: *pneumoni/a, apolog/y, complete/ly*.
4. Divide a word between two single-letter syllables: *situ-ation, extenu-ate*.
5. Divide a word after a single-letter syllable except when the vowel is part of a suffix:

> **Single vowel:**   *clari-fication, congratu-lations.*
>
> **Suffix vowel:**   *accept-able, allow-able.*

6. Divide hyphenated words after the hyphen: *self-employed, semi-independent*.
7. Avoid dividing dates: *November 15, 2004*.

8. Do not divide proper names, abbreviations, or most numbers: *George Martin, AICPA, 3,189,400.*
9. Do not divide the last word in more than two consecutive lines.
10. Do not divide the last word on a page.

Letter Formats

Decisions about page format impact the effectiveness of the message. Many companies have policies that dictate the punctuation style, letter format, and other formatting issues. In the absence of company policy, make your format choices from among standard acceptable options.

Punctuation Styles

Two punctuation styles are customarily used in business letters: mixed and open. Letters using **mixed punctuation style** have a colon after the salutation and a comma after the complimentary close. Letters using **open punctuation style** omit a colon after the salutation and a comma after the complimentary close. Mixed punctuation is the traditional style; however, cost-conscious companies are increasingly adopting the open style (and other similar format changes), which eliminates unnecessary keystrokes.

Mixed Punctuation

June 12, 2004

Mr. Parker F. Baxter
1938 South Pines Avenue
Livingston, CA 95334-1938

Dear Mr. Baxter: ⟵ Includes a colon after the salutation

Sincerely, ⟵ Includes a comma after the complimentary close

Marla Vanderbilt

Marla Vanderbilt
Vice President

Open Punctuation

June 12, 2004

Mr. Parker F. Baxter
1938 South Pines Avenue
Livingston, CA 95334-1938

Dear Mr. Baxter ◄———————— Omits the colon after the salutation

Sincerely ◄——————— Omits the comma after
the complimentary close

Marla Vanderbilt

Marla Vanderbilt
Vice President

Letter Formats

The default margins set by word processing software typically reflect the standard line length to increase the efficiency of producing business correspondence. Letters are balanced on the page with approximately equal margins on all sides of the letter, a placement often referred to as fitting the letter into a picture frame. Generally, short letters (one or two paragraphs) are centered on the page; all other letters begin 2.2 inches from the top of the page. Edit the vertical alignment in the page setup menu to center a document, or insert blank lines until the status bar displays 2.2 inches. Be sure your document is displayed in print layout when making these changes and to evaluate the result. Side margins may be adjusted to improve the appearance of extremely short letters.

Three letter formats that are commonly accepted by business include block, modified block, and simplified block.

Block

Companies striving to reduce the cost of producing business documents adopt the easy-to-learn, efficient block format. All lines (including paragraphs) begin at the left margin; therefore, no time is lost setting tabs and positioning letter parts. Study carefully the letter in block format with open punctuation shown in Figure A-2.

Block Letter Format with Open Punctuation

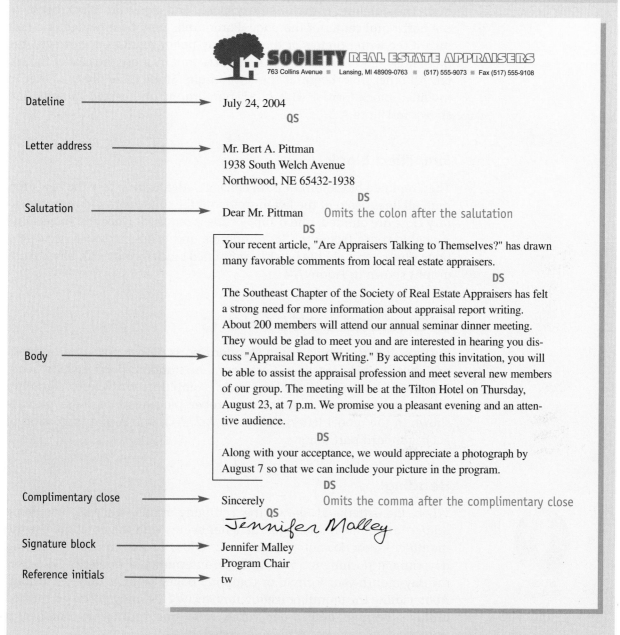

SOCIETY REAL ESTATE APPRAISERS
763 Collins Avenue ■ Lansing, MI 48909-0763 ■ (517) 555-9073 ■ Fax (517) 555-9108

Dateline → July 24, 2004
QS

Letter address → Mr. Bert A. Pittman
1938 South Welch Avenue
Northwood, NE 65432-1938
DS

Salutation → Dear Mr. Pittman   Omits the colon after the salutation
DS

Body → Your recent article, "Are Appraisers Talking to Themselves?" has drawn many favorable comments from local real estate appraisers.
DS

The Southeast Chapter of the Society of Real Estate Appraisers has felt a strong need for more information about appraisal report writing. About 200 members will attend our annual seminar dinner meeting. They would be glad to meet you and are interested in hearing you discuss "Appraisal Report Writing." By accepting this invitation, you will be able to assist the appraisal profession and meet several new members of our group. The meeting will be at the Tilton Hotel on Thursday, August 23, at 7 p.m. We promise you a pleasant evening and an attentive audience.
DS

Along with your acceptance, we would appreciate a photograph by August 7 so that we can include your picture in the program.
DS

Complimentary close → Sincerely   Omits the comma after the complimentary close
QS

Jennifer Malley

Signature block → Jennifer Malley
Program Chair

Reference initials → tw

Format Pointers

- All letter parts and paragraphs begin at the left margin in block letter format.
- Open punctuation omits the colon after the salutation and the comma after the complimentary close. Mixed punctuation style may be used with block letter format.
- Reference initials identify the person who keyed the document.

Modified Block

Modified block is the traditional letter format still used in many companies. The dateline, complimentary close, and signature block begin at the horizontal center of the page. Paragraphs may be indented one-half inch if the writer prefers or the company policy requires it; however, the indention creates unnecessary keystrokes that increase the cost of the letter. All other lines begin at the left margin. Study carefully the letter in modified block format with block paragraphs and mixed punctuation shown in Figure A-3.

Simplified Block

The simplified block format is an efficient letter format. Like the block format, all lines begin at the left margin; but the salutation and complimentary close are omitted, and a subject line is required. Place the subject line a double space below the letter address and a double space above the body. Study carefully the letter in simplified block format with block paragraphs shown in Figure A-4.

Standard Letter Parts

Business letters include seven standard parts. Other parts are optional and may be included when necessary. The standard parts include heading, letter address, salutation, body, complimentary close, signature block, and reference initials. The proper placement of these parts is shown in the model letters in Figures A-2, A-3, and A-4; a discussion of each standard part follows.

Heading

*Diversity
Challenges*

When the letterhead shows the company name, address, telephone and/or fax number, and logo, the letter begins with the dateline. Use the month-day-year format (September 2, 2004) unless you are preparing government documents, writing to an international audience who uses the day-month-year format, or company policy requires another format. Abbreviating the month or using numbers (9/2/04) may portray a hurried attitude. Because date order varies from one country to another, a numeric date can also be misinterpreted.

If a letter is prepared on plain paper, the writer's address must be included. Otherwise, the recipient may be unable to respond if the envelope is discarded. The writer's address can be keyed immediately above the dateline, creating a ***heading*** of three single-spaced lines: (1) the writer's street address; (2) the writer's city, two-letter postal abbreviation, and nine-digit zip code; and (3) the dateline. The writer's name is omitted because it appears in the signature block. Alternately, a personal letterhead can be

Modified Block Letter Format with Mixed Punctuation

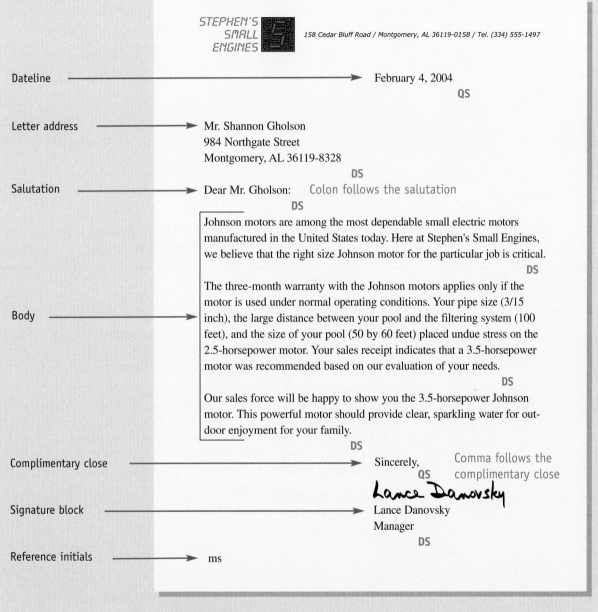

STEPHEN'S SMALL ENGINES
158 Cedar Bluff Road / Montgomery, AL 36119-0158 / Tel. (334) 555-1497

Dateline → February 4, 2004
QS

Letter address → Mr. Shannon Gholson
984 Northgate Street
Montgomery, AL 36119-8328
DS

Salutation → Dear Mr. Gholson: Colon follows the salutation
DS

Body → Johnson motors are among the most dependable small electric motors manufactured in the United States today. Here at Stephen's Small Engines, we believe that the right size Johnson motor for the particular job is critical.
DS

The three-month warranty with the Johnson motors applies only if the motor is used under normal operating conditions. Your pipe size (3/15 inch), the large distance between your pool and the filtering system (100 feet), and the size of your pool (50 by 60 feet) placed undue stress on the 2.5-horsepower motor. Your sales receipt indicates that a 3.5-horsepower motor was recommended based on our evaluation of your needs.
DS

Our sales force will be happy to show you the 3.5-horsepower Johnson motor. This powerful motor should provide clear, sparkling water for outdoor enjoyment for your family.
DS

Complimentary close → Sincerely,   Comma follows the complimentary close
QS

Lance Danovsky

Signature block → Lance Danovsky
Manager
DS

Reference initials → ms

Format Pointers

- The dateline, complimentary close, and signature begin at the horizontal center in modified block format.
- Paragraphs may be indented in modified block, but block paragraphs are recommended for efficiency.
- Mixed punctuation requires a colon after the salutation and a comma after the complimentary close. Open punctuation style may be used with modified block letter format.

Simplified Block Letter Format

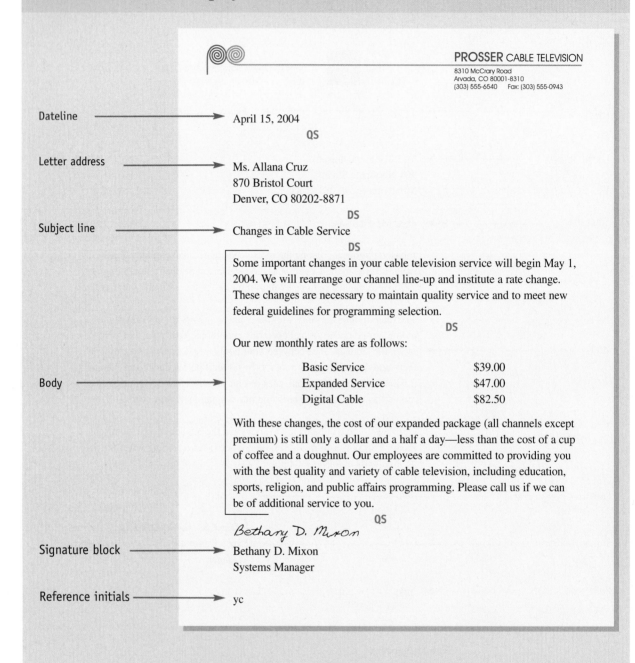

PROSSER CABLE TELEVISION
8310 McCrary Road
Arvada, CO 80001-8310
(303) 555-6540   Fax: (303) 555-0943

Dateline → April 15, 2004
QS

Letter address → Ms. Allana Cruz
870 Bristol Court
Denver, CO 80202-8871
DS

Subject line → Changes in Cable Service
DS

Body →

Some important changes in your cable television service will begin May 1, 2004. We will rearrange our channel line-up and institute a rate change. These changes are necessary to maintain quality service and to meet new federal guidelines for programming selection.
DS

Our new monthly rates are as follows:

Basic Service	$39.00
Expanded Service	$47.00
Digital Cable	$82.50

With these changes, the cost of our expanded package (all channels except premium) is still only a dollar and a half a day—less than the cost of a cup of coffee and a doughnut. Our employees are committed to providing you with the best quality and variety of cable television, including education, sports, religion, and public affairs programming. Please call us if we can be of additional service to you.
QS

Bethany D. Mixon

Signature block → Bethany D. Mixon
Systems Manager

Reference initials → yc

Format Pointers
- Subject line replaces the salutation. Complimentary close is omitted.
- All lines begin at the left margin.

designed using a word processing template or the graphic capabilities of word processing software as shown below. Note, the date is positioned at the left margin in block letter format and at the horizontal center in modified block format regardless of the paper type being used.

Heading printed on company letterhead (modified block format)

763 Collins Avenue ▪ Lansing, MI 48909-0763 ▪ (517) 555-9073 ▪ Fax (517) 555-9108

July 26, 2004   Date is the first line keyed on company letterhead

Ms. Donna Henson
Wyatt Enterprises
245 Southern Oaks Road
Corpus Christi, TX 78469-2988

Dear Ms. Henson:

Heading letterhead produced with a word processing template (block format)

PROSSER CABLE TELEVISION

8310 McCrary Road
Arvada, CO 80001-8310
(303) 555-6540   Fax: (303) 555-0943

July 26, 2004   Follow online prompts to create a letter with a template

[Click here and type recipient's address]

Dear Sir or Madam:

Type your letter here. For more details on modifying this letter template, double-click . To return to this letter, use the Window menu.

Dear Ms. Henson:

Heading printed on plain paper (block format)

1800 Brookdale Road
Albuquerque, NM 87102-1800
July 26, 2004   Key writer's address
above dateline

Ms. Donna Henson
Wyatt Enterprises
245 Southern Oaks Road
Corpus Christi, TX 78469-2988

Dear Ms. Henson:

Heading printed on letterhead created with word processing software (modified block format)

Stephen P. Donavon
1800 Brookdale Road
Albuquerque, NM 87102-1800
(505) 555-5765

July 26, 2004

Ms. Donna Henson
Wyatt Enterprises
245 Southern Oaks Road
Corpus Christi, TX 78469-2988

Dear Ms. Henson:

Letter Address

The *letter address* includes a personal or professional title (e.g., Mr., Ms., or Dr.), the name of the person and company to whom the letter is being sent, and the complete address. It begins a quadruple space after the dateline. Refer to Figure A-5 for appropriate formats for letter addresses.

Salutation

The *salutation* is the greeting that opens a letter and is placed a double space below the letter address. The salutation is omitted in the simplified block format shown in Figure A-4.

To show courtesy for the receiver, include a personal or professional title (for example, Mr., Ms., Dr., Senator). Refer to the *first line* of the letter address to determine an appropriate salutation. In the previous example,

Appropriate Formats for Letter Addresses and Salutations

Letter Address	Appropriate Salutation	Explanation
A Specific Person Mr. Chris Carlisle, President Merchant's Bank of Tampa P.O. Drawer 512 Tampa, FL 33630-9006	Dear Mr. Carlisle:	If the person is a business associate, use a courtesy title and the last name.
	Dear Chris:	If you know the person well, use the person's first name or the name you would use to greet the person face-to-face.
	Dear Chris Carlisle: Or use the simplified block format (Figure A-4) that omits the salutation.	If you aren't sure whether the person is male or female, use the whole name or omit the salutation in simplified block format to avoid offending the receiver.
A Company Merchant's Bank of Tampa P.O. Drawer 512 Tampa, FL 33630-9006	Ladies and Gentlemen: or use the simplified block format (Figure A-4) that omits the salutation.	This salutation recognizes the presence of men and women in management. Do *not* use "Dear Ladies and Gentlemen." You may use "Ladies" if you are sure management is all female or "Gentlemen" if you are sure management is all male.
A Company and Directed to a Specific Individual Merchant's Bank of Tampa Attention Mr. Chris Carlisle P.O. Drawer 512 Tampa, FL 33630-9006	Ladies and Gentlemen: or use the simplified block format (Figure A-4) that omits the salutation.	The letter is officially written to the company; therefore, "Dear Mr. Carlisle" is *not* acceptable. The salutation matches the second line of the letter address when you direct attention to a specific person.
A Specific Position Within a Business Purchasing Officer United Brokerage Firm 716 Jefferson Road Toledo, OH 43692-1645	Dear Purchasing Officer: or use the simplified block format (Figure A-4) that omits the salutation.	Because the name of the person is unknown, the simplified block format that replaces the salutation with a subject line would be useful.
A Group of People Institute of Public Accountants 2958 Central Avenue Baltimore, MD 21233-2958	Dear Accounting Professionals: Form letter to potential customers or policyholders (letter address may be omitted) Dear Customer:	When form letters are merged with databases, the letter is personalized by inserting the recipient's letter address and a specific salutation, such as "Dear Mr. Baxter." This automated process eliminates the need for less personal salutations.

Figure A-5

Appropriate Formats for Letter Addresses and Salutations, continued

Letter Address	Appropriate Salutation	Explanation
A Public Official Honorable (first and last name of U.S. Senator)	Dear Senator (last name):	
Honorable (first and last name of state U.S. Representative)	Dear Mr. or Ms. (last name):	This form is also used for senators and representatives.
Honorable (first and last name of state governor or lieutenant governor)	Dear Governor (last name): Dear Lt. Governor (last name):	

Refer to an up-to-date reference manual when writing other public officials.

"Dear Ms. Henson" is an appropriate salutation for this letter addressed to Ms. Donna Henson (first line of letter address). "Ladies and Gentlemen" is an appropriate salutation for a letter addressed to "Wyatt Enterprises," where the company name is keyed as the first line of the letter address. To avoid use of the impersonal salutation, "Ladies and Gentlemen," format the letter in simplified block format that omits the salutation. Use the examples shown in Figure A-5 as a guide when selecting an appropriate salutation.

Body

The **body** contains the message of the letter. It begins a double space below the salutation, and paragraphs are single-spaced with a double space between paragraphs. Because a double space separates the paragraphs, indenting paragraphs, which requires extra startup (setting tabs) and keying time, is not necessary. However, some companies may require paragraph indention as company policy. If so, the modified block block format (Figure A-3) with indented paragraphs is the appropriate choice.

Complimentary Close

The **complimentary close** is a phrase used to close a letter in the same way that you say good-bye at the end of a conversation. To create goodwill, choose a complimentary close that reflects the formality of your relationship with the receiver. Typical examples are "Sincerely," "Cordially," and "Respectfully." Using "yours" in the close has fallen out of popularity (as in "Sincerely yours" and "Very truly yours"). "Sincerely" is considered neutral and is thus appropriate in a majority of business situations. "Cordially" can be used for friendly messages, and "Respectfully" is appropriate when you are submitting information for the approval of another. Position the complimentary close a double space below the body. The complimentary close and the salutation are omitted in the simplified block format (Figure A-4).

Signature Block

The *signature block* consists of the writer's name keyed a quadruple space (three blank lines) below the complimentary close (or body in the simplified block format). The writer's name is signed legibly in the space provided. A woman may include a courtesy title to indicate her preference (e.g., Miss, Ms., Mrs.), and a woman or man may use a title to distinguish a name used by both men and women (e.g., Shane, Leslie, or Stacy) or initials (E. M. Goodman). A business or professional title may be placed on the same line with the writer's name or directly below it. Use the following examples as guides for balancing the writer's name and title in the signature block and the letter address:

Title on the Same Line	Title on the Next Line
Ms. Leslie Tatum, President	Ms. E. M. Goodman
	Assistant Manager
Perry Watson, Manager	Richard S. Templeton
Quality Control Division	Human Resources Director

Reference Initials

Legal & Ethical Constraints

The *reference initials* consist of the keyboard operator's initials keyed in lowercase a double space below the signature block. The reference initials and the signature block identify the persons involved in preparing a letter in the event of later questions. Reference initials are frequently omitted when a letter is keyed by the writer—a common practice now that many managers compose documents at computers from their offices and remote locations. However, company policy may require that the initials of all people involved in preparing a letter be placed in the reference initials line to identify accountability in the case of litigation. For example, the reference initials SF:LM:cd might be used to show the letter was signed by SF, actually written by LM, and keyboarded by cd. The reference line might also include department identification or other information as required by the organization.

Special Letter Parts

Other letter parts may be added to a letter depending on the particular situation. These parts include delivery and addressee notations, attention line, reference line, subject line, second-page heading, company name in the signature block, enclosure notation, copy notation, and postscript and computer file notation.

Delivery and Addressee Notations

A **delivery notation** provides a record of how a letter was sent. Examples include *Air Mail, Certified Mail, Express Mail, Federal Express, Registered Mail, Fax Transmission,* and *Messenger Delivery.* Addressee notations such as *Confidential* or *Personal* give instructions on how a letter should be handled. Key a delivery or addressee notation in all capitals at the left margin a double space below the dateline and a double space above the letter address.

Attention Line

An **attention line** is used for directing correspondence to an individual or department within an organization while still officially addressing the letter to the organization. The attention line directs a letter to a specific person (*Attention Ms. Laura Ritter*), position within a company (*Attention Human Resources Director*), or department (*Attention Purchasing Department*). Current practice is to place the attention line in the letter address on the line directly below the company name and use the same format for the envelope address. The appropriate salutation in a letter with an attention line is "Ladies or Gentlemen," or the simplified block format that omits the salutation may be used, as shown in Figure A-4.

Reference Line

A **reference line** (*Re: Contract No. 983-9873*) directs the receiver to source documents or to files. Key a reference line a double space below the letter address.

Subject Line

A **subject line** tells the receiver what a letter is about and sets the stage for the receiver to understand the message. The simplified block format requires a subject line; in other letter formats, the subject line is optional. Key the subject line a double space below the salutation as shown in Figure A-6. Use either initial capitals or all capitals for added emphasis. If modified block format is used, a subject line can be centered for added emphasis. To increase efficiency, the word *subject* is omitted because its position above the body clearly identifies its function. Note the difference between the subject line and the reference line that directs the receiver to source documents.

The delivery and addressee notation, attention line, reference line, and subject line are illustrated in Figure A-6.

Special Letter Parts

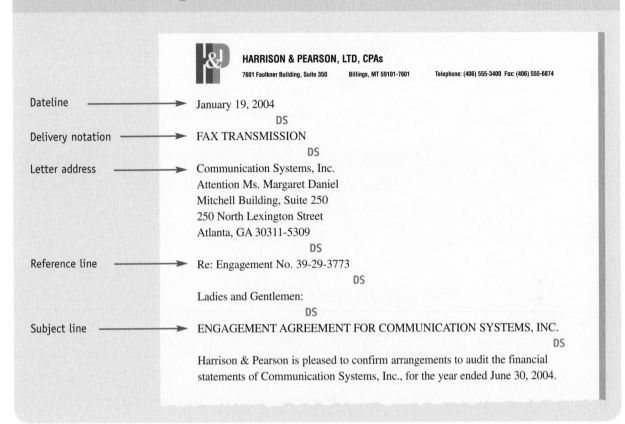

Dateline	January 19, 2004
	DS
Delivery notation	FAX TRANSMISSION
	DS
Letter address	Communication Systems, Inc.
	Attention Ms. Margaret Daniel
	Mitchell Building, Suite 250
	250 North Lexington Street
	Atlanta, GA 30311-5309
	DS
Reference line	Re: Engagement No. 39-29-3773
	DS
	Ladies and Gentlemen:
	DS
Subject line	ENGAGEMENT AGREEMENT FOR COMMUNICATION SYSTEMS, INC.
	DS

HARRISON & PEARSON, LTD, CPAs
7601 Faulkner Building, Suite 350   Billings, MT 59101-7601   Telephone: (406) 555-3400 Fax: (406) 555-6874

Harrison & Pearson is pleased to confirm arrangements to audit the financial statements of Communication Systems, Inc., for the year ended June 30, 2004.

Second-Page Heading

The second and successive pages of multiple-page letters and memorandums are keyed on plain paper of the same quality as the letterhead. A *second-page heading* is used on the second and successive pages to identify them as a continuation of the first page. A three-part heading includes (1) the name of the person or company to whom the message is sent (identical to the first line of the letter address), (2) the page number, and (3) the date.

Place the heading one inch from the top edge of the paper. Double-space after the heading to continue the body of the letter. Both vertical and horizontal formats are acceptable.

With all three lines beginning at the left margin, the vertical format is compatible with all letter formats. The horizontal format is more complex to prepare but looks attractive with the modified block format and is especially effective when using the vertical heading would force the letter or memorandum to additional pages.

Vertical Format

Communication Systems, Inc.
Page 2
January 19, 2004

DS

We at Harrison & Pearson look forward to providing these and other quality professional services to you.

Sincerely,

Patrick L. Numez

Patrick L. Numez
Audit Partner

Horizontal Format

Communication Systems, Inc.	2	January 19, 2004

DS

We at Harrison & Pearson look forward to providing these and other quality professional services to you.

Sincerely,

Patrick L. Numez

Patrick L. Numez
Audit Partner

Company Name in Signature Block

Some companies prefer to include the **company name** in the signature block, but often it is excluded because it appears in the letterhead. The company name is beneficial when the letter is prepared on plain paper or is more than one page (the second page of the letter is printed on plain paper). Including the company name also may be useful to the writer wishing to emphasize that the document is written on behalf of the company (e.g., an engagement letter establishing a contract with a newly acquired client). Key the company name in all capitals a double space below the complimentary close and a quadruple space (three blank lines) above the signature block as shown in Figure A-7.

Special Letter Parts

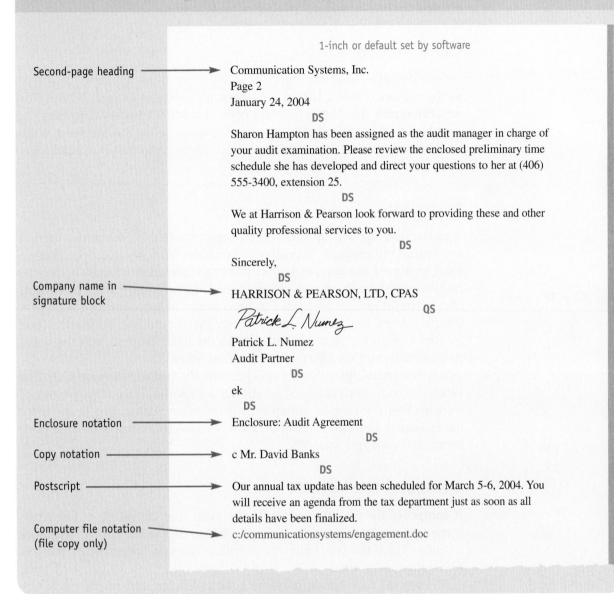

Second-page heading

1-inch or default set by software

Communication Systems, Inc.
Page 2
January 24, 2004
DS

Sharon Hampton has been assigned as the audit manager in charge of your audit examination. Please review the enclosed preliminary time schedule she has developed and direct your questions to her at (406) 555-3400, extension 25.
DS

We at Harrison & Pearson look forward to providing these and other quality professional services to you.
DS

Sincerely,
DS

Company name in signature block

HARRISON & PEARSON, LTD, CPAS
QS

Patrick L. Numez
Audit Partner
DS

ek
DS

Enclosure notation

Enclosure: Audit Agreement
DS

Copy notation

c Mr. David Banks
DS

Postscript

Our annual tax update has been scheduled for March 5-6, 2004. You will receive an agenda from the tax department just as soon as all details have been finalized.

Computer file notation (file copy only)

c:/communicationsystems/engagement.doc

Enclosure Notation

An ***enclosure notation*** indicates that additional items (brochure, price list, résumé) are included in the same envelope. Key "Enclosure" a double space below the reference initials (or the signature block if no reference initials appear) as shown in Figure A-7. Key the plural form (Enclosures) if more than one item is enclosed. You may identify the number of enclosures (Enclosures: 3) or the specific item enclosed (Enclosure: Bid Proposal). Avoid the temptation to abbreviate (Enc.) because abbreviations may give the impression that your work is hurried and careless and may show disrespect for the recipient. Some companies use the word "Attachment" on memorandums when the accompanying items may be stapled or clipped and not placed in an envelope.

Copy Notation

A *copy notation* indicates that a courtesy copy of the document was sent to the person(s) listed. Include the person's personal or professional title and full name, after keying "c" for copy or "cc" for courtesy copy. Key the copy notation at the left margin a double space below the enclosure notation, reference initials, or signature block (depending on the special letter parts used) as shown in Figure A-7.

Postscript

A *postscript*, appearing as the last item in a letter, is commonly used to emphasize information. A postscript in a sales letter, for example, is often used to restate the central selling point; for added emphasis, it may be handwritten or printed in a different color. Often handwritten postscripts of a personal nature are added as an attempt to keep in touch with people in today's high-tech society. Postscripts should not be used to add information inadvertently omitted from the letter. Instead, edit the document and reprint an effectively organized letter.

Key the postscript a double space below the last notation or signature block if no notations are used, as shown in Figure A-7. Treat the postscript as any other paragraph; indent only if the other paragraphs in the letter are indented. Because its position clearly labels this paragraph as a postscript, do not begin with "PS."

Computer File Notation

A *computer file notation* provides the path and file name of the letter. Some companies require this documentation on the file copy to facilitate revision. Place the computer file notation a single space below the last keyed line of the letter.

The second-page heading, reference initials, company name, enclosure notation, copy notation, postscript, and computer notation are illustrated in Figure A-7.

Envelopes

Changing Technology

The United States Postal Service (USPS) provides recommendations for addressing envelopes so that the address can be read accurately by optical character readers used to sort mail. Proper placement of the address on a large envelope (No. 10) is shown in Figure A-8. Additionally,

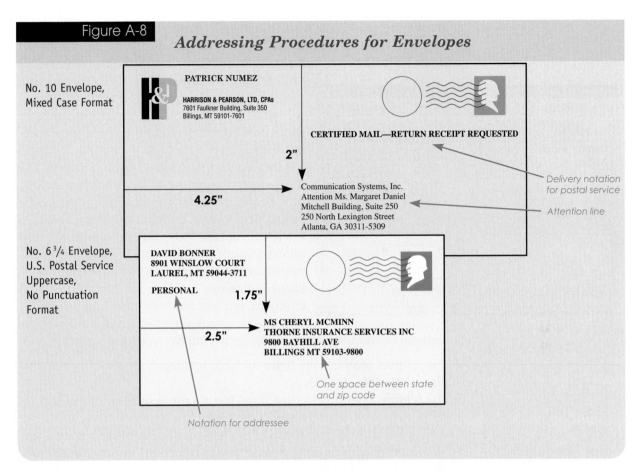

Figure A-8 — *Addressing Procedures for Envelopes*

No. 10 Envelope, Mixed Case Format

PATRICK NUMEZ

HARRISON & PEARSON, LTD, CPAs
7601 Faulkner Building, Suite 350
Billings, MT 59101-7601

CERTIFIED MAIL—RETURN RECEIPT REQUESTED

2"

4.25"

Communication Systems, Inc.
Attention Ms. Margaret Daniel
Mitchell Building, Suite 250
250 North Lexington Street
Atlanta, GA 30311-5309

Delivery notation for postal service

Attention line

No. 6 3/4 Envelope, U.S. Postal Service Uppercase, No Punctuation Format

DAVID BONNER
8901 WINSLOW COURT
LAUREL, MT 59044-3711

PERSONAL

1.75"

2.5"

MS CHERYL MCMINN
THORNE INSURANCE SERVICES INC
9800 BAYHILL AVE
BILLINGS MT 59103-9800

One space between state and zip code

Notation for addressee

to create a highly professional image, business communicators should fold letters to produce the fewest number of creases. The proper procedures for folding letters for large (No. 10) and small (6 3/4) and envelopes appear in Figure A-9.

Figure A-9 — *Folding and Insertion Procedures for Envelopes*

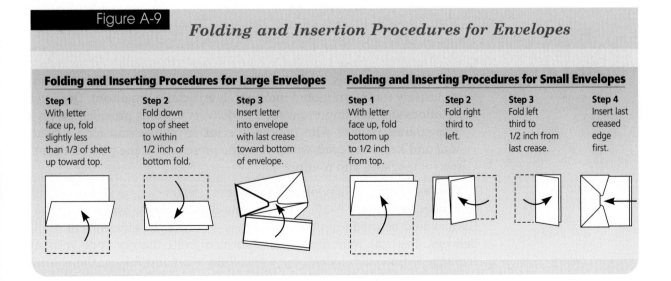

Folding and Inserting Procedures for Large Envelopes

Step 1 With letter face up, fold slightly less than 1/3 of sheet up toward top.

Step 2 Fold down top of sheet to within 1/2 inch of bottom fold.

Step 3 Insert letter into envelope with last crease toward bottom of envelope.

Folding and Inserting Procedures for Small Envelopes

Step 1 With letter face up, fold bottom up to 1/2 inch from top.

Step 2 Fold right third to left.

Step 3 Fold left third to 1/2 inch from last crease.

Step 4 Insert last creased edge first.

To prepare envelopes, use the envelope feature of your word processing program or templates available at the United States Postal Service (USPS) web site (http://www.usps.com/directmail/templates/welcome.htm). Adapt the default settings as needed for accurate placement of information. Note the efficiency of Microsoft's automated envelope function shown at the left, including options for changing the font.

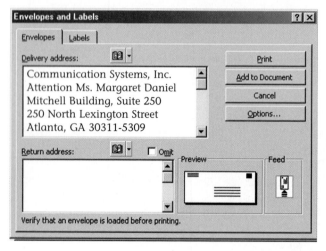

Most companies today do not follow the USPS recommendation to key the letter address in all capital letters with no punctuation. The mixed case format matches the format used in the letter address, looks more professional, and allows the writer to generate the envelope automatically without rekeying text. No mail handling efficiency is lost as today's optical character readers that sort mail can read both upper- and lowercase letters easily.

Note these specific points related to keying an envelope correctly:

- The address matches the letter address, including a personal or professional title (Mr., Ms., Dr.).
- The address contains at least three but no more than six lines.
- All lines of the return (writer's) address and the letter (receiver's) address are keyed in block form (flush at the left) and are single-spaced.
- The last line contains *only* three items of information: (1) city; (2) two-letter abbreviation for state, territory, or province; and (3) nine-digit zip code.
- One space appears between the two-letter abbreviation for state, territory, or province and the zip code.
- The writer's name is keyed in the half-inch of space above a preprinted company address.
- Addressee notations (*Confidential, Hold for Arrival,* or *Please Forward*) are placed a double space below the return address and keyed in all capitals. Delivery notations for postal authorities (*Air Mail, Certified Mail* or *Registered*) are placed a double space below the stamp position and keyed in all capitals. Including the *Air Mail* notation, which is used exclusively for international mailings, is especially important. Delivery notations are less important for fast-delivery options provided by private courier services who provide special envelopes and for *Certified Mail* and *Registered Mail,* which must be presented at the post office for special marking and routing.

Diversity Challenges

The two-letter abbreviations for states, territories, and Canadian provinces (see Figure A-10) and the nine-digit zip code assigned by the USPS should be used for all letters as they enhance the efficiency of mail delivery. The last four digits are separated from the zip code with a hyphen. To find a zip code or correct spelling of an address, use the online

USPS Official Abbreviations for States, Districts, and Provinces

State or Territory	Two-Letter Abbreviation	State or Territory	Two-Letter Abbreviation
Alabama	AL	North Dakota	ND
Alaska	AK	Ohio	OH
Arizona	AZ	Oklahoma	OK
Arkansas	AR	Oregon	OR
California	CA	Pennsylvania	PA
Canal Zone	CZ	Puerto Rico	PR
Colorado	CO	Rhode Island	RI
Connecticut	CT	South Carolina	SC
Delaware	DE	South Dakota	SD
District of Columbia	DC	Tennessee	TN
Florida	FL	Texas	TX
Georgia	GA	Utah	UT
Guam	GU	Vermont	VT
Hawaii	HI	Virginia	VA
Idaho	ID	Virgin Islands	VI
Illinois	IL	Washington	WA
Indiana	IN	West Virginia	WV
Iowa	IA	Wisconsin	WI
Kansas	KS	Wyoming	WY
Kentucky	KY		
Louisiana	LA	**Canadian Province**	**Two-Letter Abbreviation**
Maine	ME		
Maryland	MD	Alberta	AB
Massachusetts	MA	British Columbia	BC
Michigan	MI	Labrador	LB
Minnesota	MN	Manitoba	MB
Mississippi	MS	New Brunswick	NB
Missouri	MO	Newfoundland	NF
Montana	MT	Northwest Territories	NT
Nebraska	NE	Nova Scotia	NS
Nevada	NV	Ontario	ON
New Hampshire	NH	Prince Edward Island	PE
New Jersey	NJ	Quebec	PQ
New Mexico	NM	Saskatchewan	SK
New York	NY	Yukon Territory	YT
North Carolina	NC		

zip code locator at http://www.usps.com/zip4/. USPS official state abbreviations are available at http://www.usps.com/ncsc/lookups/abbreviations.html#states and Figure A-10.

Memorandum Formats

Changing Technology

To increase productivity of memorandums (memos), which are internal messages, companies use formats that are easy to input and will save time. Most companies use custom word processing memo templates. The form or the template contains the basic transmittal headings (TO, FROM, DATE, SUBJECT) to guide the writer in providing the needed transmittal information as illustrated in the memo template from Microsoft Word shown in Figure A-11. Needed notations are keyed after the body (e.g., enclosures or copy). Templates are also available for letters, fax cover sheets, and other frequently formatted documents. Memos may be printed on memo forms, plain paper, or letterhead depending on the preference of the company.

Regardless of whether the memo is created with a template or simply keyed in a word processing file, memos begin with a heading that contains the writer's name, recipient's name, date, and subject as illustrated in Figure A-12. When preparing the heading, follow these writing guidelines:

1. Omit personal and professional titles (Mr., Mrs., Dr.) on the *TO* and *FROM* lines because of the informality of this intercompany communication. Include job titles or department names.
2. Include a subject line in all memos to facilitate quick reading and filing. Key the subject line in all capitals for added emphasis or begin the first word and all other words except articles, prepositions, or conjunctions with capital letters.
3. Sign the writer's initials to the right of the writer's typed name.

Figure A-11

Memo Template in Microsoft Word

INTEROFFICE MEMORANDUM

Follow online prompts to create the heading and the message with a template.

TO: [CLICK **HERE** AND TYPE NAME]
FROM: [CLICK **HERE** AND TYPE NAME]
SUBJECT: [CLICK **HERE** AND TYPE SUBJECT]
DATE: 10/8/2004
CC: [CLICK **HERE** AND TYPE NAME]

HOW TO USE THIS MEMO TEMPLATE

Select text you would like to replace, and type your memo. Use styles such as Heading 1-3 and Body Text in the Style control on the Formatting toolbar. To save changes to this template for future use, choose Save As from the File menu. In the Save As Type box, choose Document Template. Next time you want to use it, choose New from the File menu, and then double-click your template.

Memo Printed on Company Letterhead

Litton Best Foods, Inc.
6285 Northwest Blvd.   Laurel, MS 77450
(800)734-5291 Fax: (713)555-9214

DS

Heading ———————————→

TO: Erin W. Lutzel, Vice President

FROM: Isako Kimura, Marketing Director *IK*

DATE: March 31, 2004

SUBJECT: Marketing Activity Report, June 2004
DS

The marketing division reports the following activities for June.
DS

Uses headings to divide ——→
message into easy-to-read
sections.

<u>Advertising</u>

Three meetings were held with representatives at the Bart and Dome agency to complete plans for the fall campaign for Fluffy Buns. The campaign will concentrate on the use of discount coupons published in the Thursday food section of sixty daily newspapers in the Pacific states. Coupons will be released on the second and fourth Thursdays in June and July.

Estimated cost of the program is $645,000. That amount includes 2.2 million redeemed coupons at 20 cents each ($440,000).

A point-of-sale advertising display, shown on the attached sheet, was developed for retail grocery outlets. Sales reps are pushing these in their regular and new calls. The display may be used to feature a different product from our line on a weekly basis.

<u>Sales Staff</u>

We have dropped one sales rep from the northern California section and divided the area between the southern Oregon and Sacramento reps.

Call me should you wish to discuss the information presented.

Enclosure notation ——————→   Attachment

Also, follow these general formatting guidelines when preparing the memo without a template:

1. Set one-inch margins or the default set by the word processing software.
2. Determine the starting line:
   Plain paper: $1^1/_2$ inches (add a triple space from the default top margin).
   Letterhead: A double space below the letterhead.
3. Single-space paragraphs and double-space between paragraphs. Do not indent paragraphs.
4. Handle reference initials, enclosure and copy notations, and postscripts just as in a letter.
5. Include a second-page heading on the second and successive pages of a memo just as in a multiple-page letter.

Memos are often distributed flat and are not enclosed in envelopes. If desired, place memos in special envelopes designated for intercompany mail or in plain envelopes. If you use plain envelopes, key COMPANY MAIL in the stamp position so that it will not be inadvertently stamped and mailed. Key the recipient's name and department in the address location and any other information required by company policy. Large companies may require use of office numbers or other mail designations to expedite intercompany deliveries.

E-Mail Format

Changing Technology

While certain e-mail formats are standard, some degree of flexibility exists in formatting e-mail messages. Primarily, be certain your message is easy to read and represents the standards of formality that your company has set. The following guidelines and the model e-mail illustrated in Figure A-13 will assist you in formatting professional e-mail messages:

- *Include an appropriate salutation and closing.* For example, you might write "Dear" and the person's name or simply the person's first name when messaging someone for the first time. Casual expressions such as "Hi" and "later" are appropriate for personal messages but not serious business e-mail. A closing of "sincerely" is considered too formal for e-mail messages; instead, a simple closing such as "regards" or "thank you" provides a courteous end to your message.
- *Include a signature file at the end of the message.* The signature file (known as a *.sig*) contains a few lines of text that include your full name and title, mailing address, telephone number, and any other information you want people to know about you. You might include a clever quote that you update frequently.
- *Format for easy readability.* Following these suggestions:
  - Limit each message to one screen to minimize scrolling to read multiple screens. If you need more space, consider a short e-mail message with a lengthier message attached as a word processing file. Be certain the recipient can receive and read the attachment.
  - Limit the line length to 60 characters so that the entire line is displayed on the monitor without scrolling.
  - Use short, unindented paragraphs. Separate paragraphs with a double space.
  - Use mixed case for easy reading. Typing in all capital letters is perceived as shouting in e-mail and considered rude online behavior.
  - Emphasize a word or phrase by surrounding it with quotation marks or keying in uppercase letters.
- *Use emoticons or e-mail abbreviations in moderation when you believe the receiver will understand and approve.* **Emoticons**, created by keying combinations of symbols to produce "sideways" faces,

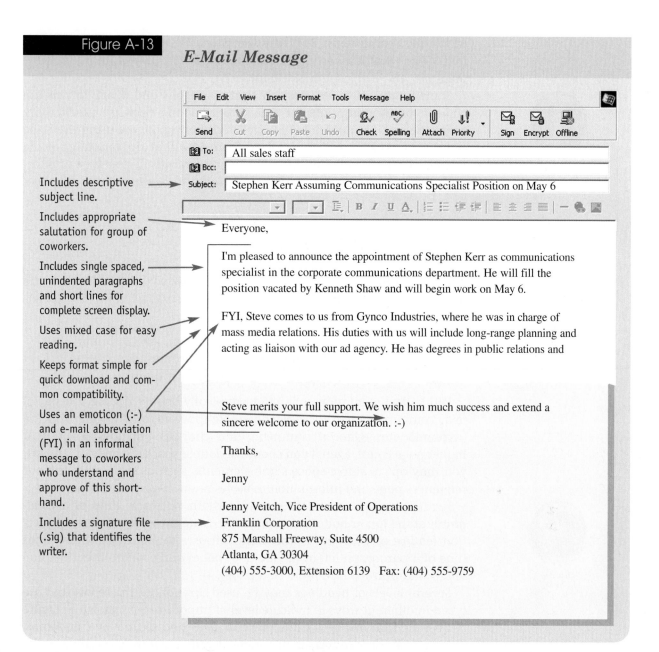

Figure A-13

E-Mail Message

Includes descriptive subject line.

Includes appropriate salutation for group of coworkers.

Includes single spaced, unindented paragraphs and short lines for complete screen display.

Uses mixed case for easy reading.

Keeps format simple for quick download and common compatibility.

Uses an emoticon (:-) and e-mail abbreviation (FYI) in an informal message to coworkers who understand and approve of this shorthand.

Includes a signature file (.sig) that identifies the writer.

File   Edit   View   Insert   Format   Tools   Message   Help

Send   Cut   Copy   Paste   Undo   Check   Spelling   Attach   Priority   Sign   Encrypt   Offline

To: All sales staff
Bcc:
Subject: Stephen Kerr Assuming Communications Specialist Position on May 6

Everyone,

I'm pleased to announce the appointment of Stephen Kerr as communications specialist in the corporate communications department. He will fill the position vacated by Kenneth Shaw and will begin work on May 6.

FYI, Steve comes to us from Gynco Industries, where he was in charge of mass media relations. His duties with us will include long-range planning and acting as liaison with our ad agency. He has degrees in public relations and

Steve merits your full support. We wish him much success and extend a sincere welcome to our organization. :-)

Thanks,

Jenny

Jenny Veitch, Vice President of Operations
Franklin Corporation
875 Marshall Freeway, Suite 4500
Atlanta, GA 30304
(404) 555-3000, Extension 6139   Fax: (404) 555-9759

are a shorthand way of lightening the mood, adding emotion to e-mail messages, and attempting to compensate for nonverbal cues lost in one-way communication:

:-) smiling, indicates humor or sarcasm   ;-) facetious statement
:-(frowning, indicates sadness or anger   %-(confused
:-/ wry face   :-0 surprised

Alternately, you might put a "g" (for grin) or "smile" in parentheses after something that is obviously meant as tongue-in-cheek to help carry the intended message to the receiver. Abbreviations for commonly used phrases save space and avoid unnecessary keying. Popular ones include

BCNU (be seeing you), BTW (by the way), FYI (for your information), FWIW (for what it's worth), HTH (hope this helps), IMHO (in my humble opinion), and LOL (laugh out loud).

Some e-mail users feel strongly that emoticons and abbreviations are childish or inappropriate for serious e-mail and decrease productivity when the receiver must take time for deciphering. Before using them, be certain the receiver will understand them and that the formality of the message and your relationship with the receiver justify this type of informal exchange. Then, use only in moderation to *punctuate* your message.

Diversity Challenges

Report Format

Page arrangement for reports varies somewhat, depending on the documentation style guide followed or individual company preferences. Typical margins are as follows:

Unbound: 1" for all margins (top, bottom, left, and right).
Leftbound: $1^1/_2$" left margin; 1" for other margins.
Topbound: $1^1/_2$" top margin; 1" for other margins.

While documentation style guides typically specify double spacing of text, company practice is often to single-space reports. Double spacing accommodates editorial comments and changes but does result in a higher page count. Even if you choose to double-space the body of a report, you may opt to single-space some elements, such as the entries in your references page and information in tables or other graphic components.

A muliple-page document should contain no single lines of a paragraph at the top or bottom of a page. Activate the widow-orphan protection feature of your word processing software to eliminate widow lines (line of a paragraph left at the top of a page) and orphan lines (first line of a paragraph left at bottom of a page).

Changing Technology

Several levels of headings may be used throughout the report and are typed in different ways to indicate level of importance, as shown in Figure A-14. Note that one blank line precedes first- and second-level headings. This method is not universal; therefore, identify the format specified by the documentation style you are using and follow it consistently. A further suggestion is to avoid placing two levels of headings consecutively without any intervening text. For example, always write something following a first-level heading and before the initial second-level heading.

You can develop fourth- and fifth-level headings simply by using boldface, underline, and varying fonts. In short reports, however, organization rarely goes beyond third-level headings.

Effective Heading Formats for Reports Divided into Three Levels

Centers and capitalizes all letters in the report title. ⟶ **REPORT TITLE**

DS

xxx xxxxxx xxxxxxxx xxxxx xxxxxxx xxxxxx xxxxxxx xxxxxx xxxx xxxxxx xxxxxxxxx xxx x xxxxx xxxx.

DS

Centers first-level headings and capitalizes initial letters. ⟶ **First-Level Heading**

DS

Includes intervening text between first and second-level headings. ⟶ xxxx xxxxxxxx xxxx xxxx xxxxxxx xxxxx xxxxx xxxxx xxxxxxx xxx xxxxxxxx xx xxxxxxx x xxxxxx xxxxx xxxxx xxxxx xxxxx xxxx.

DS

Places second-level subheadings at the left margin, underlines, and capitalizes initial letters. ⟶ **<u>Second-Level Subheading</u>**

DS

xxx xxxxxx xxxx xxx xxxxxxx xxxxx xx xxxx xxxxx xxxxxxx xxx x xxxx xxxxxx x xxxxxxxx xxxx x xxxxxx xxxxxxxxx xxxxxxx. xxxxxxxx.

DS

<u>Second-Level Subheading</u>

DS

x xxxx xxxxxxxxx xxxx xxxx xxxx xxxx xxxx xxxx xxx xxxxxx xxx xxx xxxxxx xxx xxxxxxx xxxxxx xxxxxxx xxxxxxxx xxxxxxxx xxxxx.

DS

Indents third-level subheadings as a part of the paragraph, underlines, and capitalizes first letter. ⟶ **<u>Third-level subheading.</u>** xxxxxx xx xxxx xxxxxxxx xxxxx xxx xxx x xxxxx xxx xxxx xxxxxx xxxx xxx xxxx xxxx xxxx.

DS

<u>Third-level subheading</u>. x xxxxxxx xxxxxxx xxx xxxxxx xxxxx xxxx xxxx xxx xxxxxxxx xxxxxxx xxx xxx xxxxxxxxx xxxxxxxx. xxxxxxx.

DS

First-Level Heading

DS

xxxxxxx xxxxxxxxx xxxx xxxxxx xxxxx xxxxxxx xxxxxxx xxxxx xxxxxxxx xxxx xxxxxx xxxxxx xxxxxx xxxxxxxxx xxxx xxxxxxx xxxxx.

Appendix

b

Referencing Styles

A number of widely used reference styles are available for documenting the sources of information used in report writing. Two of the more popular style manuals for business writing are as follows:

> *Publication Manual of the American Psychological Association*, 5th ed., Washington, DC: American Psychological Association, 2001.

> Joseph Gibaldi, *MLA Handbook for Writers of Research Papers*, 6th ed., New York: Modern Languages Association of America, 2003. MLA Handbook is designed for high school and undergraduate college students; the *MLA Style Manual and Guide to Scholarly Publishing*, 2nd ed. (1998) is designed for graduate students, scholars, and professional writers.

These sources, commonly referred to as the APA and MLA styles, provide general rules for referencing and give examples of the citation formats for various types of source materials. Occasionally, you may need to reference something for which no general example applies. Choose the example that is most like your source and follow that format. When in doubt, provide more information, not less. Remember that a major purpose for listing references is to enable readers to retrieve and use the sources. This appendix illustrates citation formats for some common types of information sources and refers you to various electronic sites that provide further detailed guidelines for preparing electronic citations.

In-Text Parenthetical Citations

The *APA Manual* and *MLA Handbook* support the use of **in-text citations**. Abbreviated information within parentheses in the text directs the reader to a list of sources at the end of a report. The list of sources at the end contains all bibliographic information on each source cited in a report. This list is arranged alphabetically by the author's last name or, if no author is provided, by the first word of the title.

The in-text citations contain minimal information needed to locate the source in the complete list. In-text citations prepared using the *APA Manual* include the author's last name and the date of publication; the page number is included only if referencing a direct quotation. The *MLA Handbook* includes the author's last name and the page number for both quotes and paraphrases, but not the date of publication. Note the following in-text parenthetical citations shown in APA and MLA styles.

One author not named in the text, direct quotation

APA: "A recent survey . . . shows that more and more companies plan to publish their annual reports on the Internet" (Prinn, 2002, p. 13). *Include page number only when referencing a direct quotation. Precede page numbers with p. (one page) or pp. (multiple pages).*

MLA: "A recent survey . . . shows that more and more companies plan to publish their annual reports on the Internet" (Prinn 13).

Direct quotation, no page number on source

APA: "Traditional college students have a perspective that is quite different from adult consumers" (James, 2001, Discussion and Conclusions section, ¶2).

MLA: "Traditional college students have a perspective that is quite different from adult consumers" (James). *Use par. 2 only if paragraphs are numbered in original text.*

Multiple authors for sources not named in the text wording

APA: Globalization is becoming a continuous challenge for managers . . . (Tang & Crofford, 2001).

MLA: Globalization is becoming a continuous challenge for managers . . . (Tang and Crofford 29).

APA: "For all its difficulty, teamwork is still essential . . ." (Nunamaker et al., 2001, p. 163).

MLA: "For all its difficulty, teamwork is still essential . . ." (Nunamaker et al. 163).

For works by six or more authors, use et al. after the last name of the first author. For works by fewer than six authors, cite all authors the first time the work is referenced; use the first author's last name and et al. for subsequent references. Do not underline or italicize et al.

For sources by more than three authors, use et al. after the last name of the first author or include all last names. Do not underline or italicize et al.

More than one source documenting the same idea

APA: . . . companies are turning to micromarketing (Heath, 2003; Roach, 2001).

MLA: . . . companies are turning to micromarketing (Heath 48; Roach 54).

More than one source by the same author documenting the same idea

APA: Past research (Taylor, 1995, 2001) shows . . .

MLA: Past research (Taylor, "Performance Appraisal" 6, "Frequent Absenteeism" 89) shows . . .

Reference to author(s) or date in the text wording

APA: Spalding and Price (2001) documented the results . . .

MLA: Kent Spalding and Brian Price documented the results . . .

APA: In 1999, West concluded . . . .

MLA: In 1999, West concluded . . . . (E2).
Omit a page number when citing a one-page article or nonprint sources.

No author provided

APA: . . . virtues of teamwork look obvious ("Teams Triumph," 2000).
Include first two or three words of title.

MLA: . . . virtues of teamwork look obvious ("Teams Triumph in Creative Solutions" 61).
Include full title or shortened version of it.

One of two or more works by the same author(s) in the same year

APA: Zuidema and Kleiner (1999a) advocated . . .
Assign a, b, c, etc. after year.

MLA: Zuidema and Kleiner ("New Developments in Self-Directed Work" 79) advocated . . .
Include full title of work.

References (or Works Cited)

The **references** or **works cited** page contains an alphabetized list of the sources used in preparing a report, with each entry containing publication information necessary for locating the source. In addition, the bibliographic entries give evidence of the nature of sources the author consulted. Bibliography (literally "description of books") is sometimes used to refer to this list.

A researcher often uses sources that provide information but do not result in citations. If you want to acknowledge that you have consulted these works and provide the reader with a comprehensive reading list, include these sources in the list of references. The APA and MLA styles use different terms to distinguish between these types of lists and those that list only the cited sources:

	APA	MLA
Includes only sources cited	References	Works Cited
Includes sources cited and consulted	Bibliography	Works Consulted

Your company guidelines or authoritative style manual may specify whether to list works cited only or works consulted. If you receive no definitive guidelines, use your own judgment. If in doubt, include all literature cited and read, and label the page with the appropriate title so that the reader clearly understands the nature of the list.

To aid the reader in locating sources in lengthy bibliographies, include several subheadings denoting the types of publications documented; for example, books, articles, unpublished documents and papers, government publications, and nonprint media. Check your reference manual to determine if subheadings are allowed.

Bibliographic styles for a variety of publications prepared using the APA style are shown in Figure B-1. The same entries prepared using the MLA style appear in Figure B-2. Note that the APA and MLA formats have several distinct variations:

Guide to Preparing References in APA (5th Edition) Style

A book reference with subtitle and two authors

Clark, B., & Crossland, R. (2002). *The leader's voice: How your communication can inspire action and get results.* New York: Select Books.

An edited book

Webster, S., & Connolly, F. W. (Eds.). (1999). *The ethics kit.* New York: McGraw Hill.

A chapter in a book or section within a reference book

Clark, J. L., & Clark, L. R. (2004). Electronic messaging. In *How 10: A handbook for professionals* (10th ed., pp. 285-300). Mason, OH: Thomson/South-Western.

Standard & Poor's. (2002). Unisys Corporation. In *Standard & Poor's standard corporation descriptions* (p. 439). New York: Author.

A report, brochure, or book from a private organization, corporate author

Wal-Mart Stores, Inc. (2003). *Annual report.* Bentonville, AR: Author.

Asahi Japan Collectibles. (2000). *Communication habits of Americans and Japanese.* [Brochure]. Kensington, CT: Author.

Note: When author and publisher are identical, use Author *as name of publisher.*

An article in a scholarly journal with separate pagination for each issue

Klein, L. R. (2003). Creating virtual product experiences: The role of telepresence. *Journal of Interactive Marketing, 17*(1), 41–55.

Note: 17(1) signifies volume 17, issue 1; volume number is italicized or underlined along with publication title.

An article in a scholarly journal with multiple authors and continuous pagination (page numbers do not start over with each issue)

Colquin, J. A., LePine, J. A., Hollenbeck, J. R., Ilgen, D. R., & Sheppard, L. (2002). Computer-assisted communication and team decision-making performance. *Journal of Applied Psychology, 87,* 402–411.

Note: After the sixth author's name, use et al. to indicate remaining authors. Issue number is omitted when page numbers continue across issues.

A periodical article without an author

Type it up. (2003, February 25). *PC Magazine, 22,* 25.

Note: For magazines, include volume number, but not issue.

An article in a newspaper

Amjadali, S. (2003, March 9). Taming your tongue. *Sunday Herald Sun (Melbourne),* p. 83.

Note: For newspapers, include p. or pp. with page number(s).

A government publication

U. S. Department of Education. (2002). *Federal student financial aid handbook.* (Report No. ED 1.45/4:998-99). Office of Student Financial Assistance. Washington, DC: Student Financial Assistance Programs.

U. S. Department of Homeland Security. (2003). *Preparing makes sense: Get ready now* [Brochure]. Washington, DC: U.S. Government Printing Office.

Note: Government documents available from the General Printing Office (GPO) should show GPO as the publisher.

Unpublished interviews, memos, and letters

Note: Do not include in reference list; cite in text only. Example: . . . internal communications at NASA have improved (J. D. Arceneaux, personal communication, July 9, 2003).

Computer software

Nero Mix (Version 1.3.1.6c) [Computer software]. (2002). Karlsbard, Germany: Ahead Software.

Note: Names of software, programs, or languages are not italicized.

Films, filmstrips, slide programs, and video recordings

Breaking the barriers: Improving communication skills [CD-ROM]. (2003). Princeton: Films for the Humanities and Sciences.

Guide to Preparing Works Cited in MLA (6th edition) Style

A book reference with sub-title and two authors

Clark, Boyd, and Ron Crossland. *The Leader's Voice: How Your Communication Can Inspire Action and Get Results*. New York: Select Books, 2002.
Note: For more than three authors, use et al. (meaning "and others") after the name of the first author or include the name of each author.

An edited book

Webster, Sally, and Frank W. Connolly, eds. *The Ethics Kit*. New York: McGraw Hill, 1999.

A chapter in a book or section within a reference book

Clark, James L., and Lyn R. Clark. "Electronic Messaging." *How 10: A Handbook for Professionals*. 10th ed. Mason, OH: Thomson/South-Western, 2004. 285–300.
"Unisys Corporation." *Standard & Poor's Standard Corporation Descriptions*. New York: Standard & Poor's, 2002. 439.

A report, brochure, or book from a private organization, corporate author

Wal-Mart Stores, Inc. *Annual Report*. Bentonville, AR: Wal-Mart Stores, 2003.
Asahi Japan Collectibles. *Communication Habits of Americans and Japanese*. Kensington, CT: Asahi Japan Collectibles, 2000.

An article in a scholarly journal with separate pagination in each issue

Klein, Lawrence R. "Creating Virtual Product Experiences: The Role of Telepresence." *Journal of Interactive Marketing* 17.1 (2003): 41–55.
Note: 17.1 signifies volume 17, issue 1.

An article in a scholarly journal with more than three authors and continuous pagination (page numbers do not start over with each issue)

Colquin, Jason A., et al. "Computer-assisted Communication and Team Decision-Making Performance: The Moderating Effect of Openness to Experience." *Journal of Applied Psychology* 87 (2002): 402–11.
Note: Issue number is omitted when page numbers continue across issues. For more than three authors, use et al. after the first author or include name of each author.

A periodical article without an author

"Type it up." *PC Magazine* 22 Feb. 2003: 25.
Note: For magazine articles, do not include volume and issue.

An article in a newspaper

Amjadali, Samantha. "Taming Your Tongue." *Sunday Herald Sun* (Melbourne), 9 Mar. 2003: 83.

A government publication

United States Dept. of Education. Office of Student Financial Assistance. *Federal Student Financial Aid Handbook*. Report No. ED 1.45/4:998-99. Washington, DC: Student Financial Assistance Programs, 2002.
United States Dept. of Homeland Security. *Preparing Makes Sense: Get Ready Now*. Washington: GPO, 2003.

Unpublished interviews, memos and letters

Arceneaux, Joshua D. Personal interview. 29 June 2003.
Note: For in-text citation, include only author name, as no page number applies.

Computer software

Nero Mix. Vers. 1.3.1.6c, CD-ROM. Karlsbard, Germany: Ahead Software, 2002.

Films, filmstrips, slide programs, and video recordings

Breaking the Barriers: Improving Communication Skills. DVD. Films for the Humanities and Sciences, 2003.

	APA	**MLA**
Indention and spacing	Begin first line of each entry at left margin and indent subsequent lines one-half inch. Alternately, paragraph indent is permitted. Double space within and between entries.	Begin first line of each entry at at left margin and indent subsequent lines one-half inch. Double space within and between entries.
Author names	List last names first for all authors. Use initials for first and middle names. Use an ampersand (&) before final author's last name.	List last name first for first author only. Use "and" before final author's name.
Date	Place date in parentheses after author name(s). Months are spelled out.	Place date at end of citation for books and after periodical title and volume for articles. Months are abbreviated.
Capitalization	In titles of book and articles, capitalize only first word of title, first word of subtitle, and proper names. All other words, begin with lowercase letters. In titles of periodicals, capitalize all significant words.	In titles of books, periodicals, and article titles, capitalize all main words.
Italicizing and quotation marks	Italicize titles of books, journals, and other periodicals, as well as periodical volume numbers. Do not use quotation marks around titles of articles.	Italicize titles of books, journals, and periodicals (or underline if directed). Place titles of articles within quotation marks.
Page notations	Use p. or pp. with page numbers for newspapers only.	Omit the use of p. or pp. on all citations.

Review the formal report in Chapter 11, Figure 11-4, prepared using APA documentation with annotations that conveniently highlight appropriate in-text citations and reference list entries. A model MLA report is available at the text support site (http://lehman.swlearning.com).

Electronic Citation Methods

Citing Internet and other electronic sources can be somewhat challenging, since electronic information and publication environments continue to evolve. The American Psychological Association offers an online update to its style manual that is amended regularly and provides guidelines for citing electronic sources. You may access this web site at http://www.apastyle.org/elecref.html.

The Modern Languages Association offers an online summary of its rules for citing electronic resources. This information is available at http://www.mla.org.

While the ordering of elements varies, the reference styles are fairly standardized as to the elements included when citing documents retrieved electronically. Include the following items:

1. Author (if given)
2. Date of publication
3. Title of article and/or name of publication
4. Electronic medium (such as online or CD-ROM)
5. Volume; series; page, section, or paragraph; and Internet address
6. Date you retrieved or accessed the resource

Examples of referencing formats for various electronically retrieved documents are illustrated in Figure B-3 (APA style) and Figure B-4 (MLA style).

A number of additional web sites are available that provide information about electronic citations in various style guides. Whenever you are not required to use a particular documentation style, choose a recognized one and follow it consistently. You will find that the formatting particulars become easier with repeated use.

Figure B-3

Guide to Preparing Electronic Citations in APA (5th edition) Style

Article from Internet site

Microsoft Corporation. (2001, October 25). Windows XP and Office XP: Collaborate in real time to perfect a presentation. Redmond, WA: Microsoft Corporation. Retrieved March 2, 2003, from http://www.microsoft.com/windowsxp/officexp/messenger.asp

Article from online periodical

Pirttiaho, L. (2003). Sound engineering practices and ethics in technology business. *Electronic Journal of Business Ethics and Organization Studies, 8*(1). Retrieved March 20, 2003, from http://ejbo.jyu.fi/index.cgi?page=articles/0701_3

Article from online database

Kryder, L. (2003, February). A better way to deliver bad news. *Technical Communication, 50*(1), 118. Retrieved March 20, 2003, from InfoTrac College database.

Article on CD-ROM

Microsoft Corporation. (2003). Fiber optics. *Encarta Encyclopedia Plus 2003* [CD-ROM]. Redmond, WA: Author.

Message posted to online forum or discussion group

Bridges, K. (2004, August 1). Top ten rules of international communication. Discussions on International Business Communication. [Msg 20]. Message posted to http://groups.yahoo.com/group/internationalcommunication/message/31

E-mail message

Note: E-mail is treated as a personal communication and, therefore, not cited in the reference list. The format in text is as follows: D. D. DuFrene (personal communication, January 23, 2004) said . . . .

Guide to Preparing Electronic Citations in MLA (6th edition) Style

Article from Internet site

"Windows XP and Office XP: Collaborate in Real Time to Perfect a Presentation." *Windows XP*. 25 October 2001. Microsoft Corporation. 2 March 2003 <http://www.microsoft.com/windowsxp/officexp/messenger.asp>.

Article from online periodical

Pirttiaho, Lauri. "Sound engineering practices and ethics in technology business." *Electronic Journal of Business Ethics and Organization Studies* 8.1 (2003). 20 Mar. 2003 <http://ejbo.jyu.fi/index.cgi?page=articles/0701_3>.

Article from online database

Kryder, LeeAnne. "A Better Way to Deliver Bad News." *Technical Communication* 50.1. 118. (Feb. 2003). *InfoTrac College*. 20 Mar. 2003 <http://web5.infotrac-college.com/wadsworth/session/270/11/34462304/3!xrn_3_0_A98055448>.

Article on CD-ROM

"Fiber Optics." *Encarta Encyclopedia Plus 2003*. CD-ROM. Redmond, WA: Microsoft Corporation, 2003.

Message posted to online forum or discussion group

Bridges, Keith. "Top Ten Rules of International Communication." Online posting. 1 Aug. 2004. International Communication Discussion Group. 27 Aug. 2004 <http://groups.yahoo.com/group/internationalcommunication/message/31>.

E-mail message

DuFrene, Debbie D. "Re: Netiquette Guidelines." E-mail to Carol M. Lehman. 23 Jan. 2004.

Appendix

Language Review and Exercises

C

Regardless of your ability, mastering specific language principles will aid you in preparing error-free documents that reflect positively on you and your company. Commit the time to complete this Language Review that focuses on common problems frequently encountered by business writers. You may choose to read the tutorials and complete the exercises printed in Appendix C or complete the Interactive Language Review accessible from your WebTutor course. Four interactive quizzes are also available at the text support site (http://lehman.swlearning.com) that assesses your (a) overall mastery, (b) language principles, (c) punctuation, and (d) word usage. For more thorough reviews, consult standard reference books on language usage.

Whether you're reviewing the printed copy in Appendix C or completing the Interactive Language Review, follow these procedures:

1. Complete the Precheck to assess your knowledge of basic language skills (grammar, punctuation, and word usage). Review the answers for immediate feedback on your progress.
2. Use the language tutorial to complete the topics in which additional review is needed. Take the short quiz available for each topic, and review the feedback provided in the Interactive Language Review or by your instructor.
3. Complete the Postcheck to assess your understanding of the principles you've reviewed. Check your answers for immediate feedback on your progress, and review areas that require further study.
4. Complete the Language Review Quiz and submit answers as directed by your instructor.

To measure your knowledge of grammar, spelling, and punctuation, follow these steps: Cover the answer that appears below each numbered sentence. Identify the grammatical error(s) in the numbered sentences. Then, slide the cover sheet down and check your answer against the correct sentence.

1. Only 1 of the applicants have completed the employment tests; but 3 have submitted résumés.

   Only <u>one</u> of the applicants <u>has</u> completed the employment tests, but <u>three</u> have submitted résumés.

2. Neither vice president Cox nor secretary Perez are ready to present their recommendations.

   Neither <u>Vice President </u>Cox nor <u>Secretary</u> Perez is ready to present _ recommendations.

3. One applicants' employment test was postponed for two hours, this may have effected the test score.

   One <u>applicant's</u> employment test was postponed for two <u>hours;</u> this <u>delay</u> may have <u>affected</u> the test score. (Nouns other than "delay" can be used.)

4. Stephen's grin and bear it attitude is his fundamental principal of survival.

   Stephen's <u>grin-and-bear-it</u> attitude is his fundamental <u>principle</u> of survival.

5. Supervisors discussed one criteria for promotion during annual performance interviews with full time personal.

   Supervisors discussed one <u>criterion</u> for promotion during annual performance interviews with <u>full-time</u> <u>personnel</u>.

6. I appreciate you writing a proposal, and sending it directly to the controller and I.

   I appreciate <u>your</u> writing a proposal_and sending it directly to the controller and <u>me</u>.

7. A short intensive review will be conducted on April 14, 2004 at 10:00 A.M.

   A short, intensive review will be conducted on April 14, 2004, at 10 <u>a.m.</u>

8. If you can complete the survey please proceed, otherwise ask the superintendent for a new set of questionnaires.

   If you can complete the survey<u>,</u> please proceed<u>;</u> otherwise<u>,</u> ask the superintendent for a new set of questionnaires.

9. Did the Controller really use the words "get out of my office?"

   Did the <u>controller</u> really use the words<u>,</u> "<u>Get</u> out of my office"<u>?</u>

10. Please try to quickly review these documents, it's to be returned before October 21st.

    Please try <u>to review</u> these documents <u>quickly;</u> <u>they</u> must be returned before October <u>21</u>.

Nouns

Nouns are words that name people, places, things, or ideas.

1. *Use specific nouns for most business writing because they let a receiver see exactly what is meant.* "The dean objected" gives a clearer picture than "An administrator objected"; "A 212-ton truck is missing" is clearer than "One vehicle is missing."

   Use general words when you do not want (or need) to convey a vivid mental picture. "I appreciated your letting me know about the accident" is less vivid (and better) than ". . . about your sprained ankle, your broken ribs, and the smashed-up car."

2. *Use concrete nouns as sentence subjects normally because they help to present ideas vividly.* "Joe explained the procedure" is more

vivid than "Explanations were given by Joe." Because "explanations" are harder to visualize than "Joe," the idea in the second sentence is more difficult to see. *Concrete* nouns are word labels for that which is solid—something that can be seen, touched, and so on. *Abstract* nouns are word labels for that which is not solid—something that cannot be seen, touched, and so on. *Tree* is a concrete noun. *Thought, confrontation,* and *willingness* are abstract nouns.

Use an abstract noun as the subject of a sentence if you do not want an idea to stand out vividly. "His weakness was well known" is less vivid than "He was known to be weak."

Exercise 1

Select the better sentence from each pair and provide a reason for your answer.

1. a. Mr. Phillips called me yesterday.
   b. A man called me yesterday.
2. a. Mallory was driving 40 mph in a 25-mph zone.
   b. Mallory was exceeding the speed limit.
3. a. We appreciate the explanation of your financial circumstances.
   b. We appreciate the information you gave about your losses from bad debts and your shrinking markets.
4. a. An explanation of the procedures was presented by Jim Lewis.
   b. Jim Lewis explained the procedures.
5. a. Authorization of payment is the responsibility of the controller.
   b. The controller authorizes all payments.

Pronouns

*P*ronouns (words used in place of nouns) enable us to make our writing smoother than it would be if no pronouns were used. For example, compare these versions of the same sentence:

Without pronouns: Mr. Smith had some difficulty with Mr. Smith's car, so Mr. Smith took Mr. Smith's car to the corner garage for repairs.

With pronouns: Mr. Smith had some difficulty with his car, so he took it to the corner garage for repairs.

1. *Make a pronoun agree in number with its* antecedent *(the specific noun for which a pronoun stands).*

   a. Use a plural pronoun when it represents two or more singular antecedents connected by *and.*

   The secretary <u>and</u> the treasurer will take <u>their</u> vacations.

   ["The" before "treasurer" indicates that the sentence is about two people.]

   The secretary <u>and</u> treasurer will take <u>his</u> vacation.

[Omitting "the" before "treasurer" indicates that the sentence is about one person who has two sets of responsibilities.]

b. Parenthetical remarks (remarks that can be omitted without destroying the basic meaning of the sentence) that appear between the pronoun and its antecedent have no effect on the form of the pronoun.

Daniel Brown, not the secretaries, is responsible for his correspondence.

[Because "his" refers to Daniel and not to "secretaries," "his" is used instead of "their."]

c. Use a singular pronoun with *each, everyone, no,* and their variations.

Each student and each teacher will carry his or her own equipment.

Everyone is responsible for her or his work.

d. Use a singular pronoun when two or more singular antecedents are connected by *or* or *nor.*

Neither David nor Brent can complete his work.

Ask either Mary or Sue about her in-service training.

e. Use a singular pronoun when a noun represents a *unit* composed of more than *one* person or thing.

The company stands behind its merchandise.

The group wants to retain its goals.

f. Use pronouns that agree in number with the intended meaning of collective nouns.

The accounting staff has been asked for its contributions.

["Staff" is thought of as a unit; the singular "its" is appropriate.]

The accounting staff have been asked for their contributions.

["Staff" is thought of as more than one individual; the plural "their" is appropriate.]

2. *Use the correct case of pronouns. Case* tells whether a pronoun is used as the subject of a sentence or as an object in it.

a. Use nominative-case pronouns (also known as subjective-case pronouns) (*I, he, she, they, we, you, it, who*) as subjects of a sentence or clause.

You and I must work together. ["You" and "I" are subjects of the verb "work."]

Those who work will be paid. ["Who" is the subject of the dependent clause "who work."]

b. Use objective-case pronouns (*me, him, her, them, us, you, it, whom*) as objects of verbs and prepositions.

Mrs. Kellum telephoned him. ["Him" is the object of the verb "telephoned."]

The increase in salary is for the manager and her. ["Her" is the object of the preposition "for."]

To whom should we send the report? ["Whom" is the object of the preposition "to."]

Tip: Restate a subordinate clause introduced by who or whom to determine the appropriate pronoun.

She is the type of manager whom we can promote. [Restating "whom we can promote" as "We can promote her (whom)" clarifies that "whom" is the object.]

She is the type of manager who can be promoted. [Restating "who can be promoted" as "She (who) can be promoted" clarifies that "who" is the subject.]

Tip: Change a question to a statement to determine the correct form of a pronoun.

Whom did you call? [You did call *whom*.]

Whom did you select for the position? [You did select *whom* for the position.]

c. Use the nominative case when forms of the linking verb *be* require a pronoun to complete the meaning.

It was he who received credit for the sale.

It is she who deserves the award.

["It was he" may to some people sound just as distracting as the incorrect "It was him." Express the ideas in a different way to avoid the error and an expletive beginning.]

He was the one who received credit for the sale.

She deserves the award.

d. Use the possessive form of a pronoun before a gerund (a verb used as a noun).

We were delighted at his (not *him*) taking the job.

["Taking the job" is used here as a noun. "His" in this sentence serves the same purpose it serves in "We are delighted at his success."]

3. *Place relative pronouns as near their antecedents as possible for clear understanding.* A *relative* pronoun joins a dependent clause to its antecedent.

Ambiguous	Clear
The members were given receipts who have paid.	The members who have paid were given receipts.
The agreement will enable you to pay whichever is lower, 6 percent or $50.	The agreement will enable you to pay 6 percent or $50, whichever is lower.

Restate a noun instead of risking a *vague* pronoun reference.

Vague

The officer captured the suspect even though he was unarmed.

Clear

The officer captured the suspect even though the officer was unarmed.

4. *Do not use a pronoun by itself to refer to a phrase, clause, sentence, or paragraph.* A pronoun should stand for a noun, and that noun should appear in the writing.

Incorrect

He expects to take all available accounting courses and obtain a position in a public accounting firm. This appeals to him.

Correct

He expects to take all available accounting courses and obtain a position in a public accounting firm. This plan appeals to him.

Exercise 2
Select the correct word.

1. The president and the chief executive officer reported (his, their) earnings to the employees.
2. Everyone was asked to share (his, their) opinion.
3. The production manager, not the controller, presented (his, their) strongly opposing views.
4. Stephen and Helen were recognized for (her, their) contribution.
5. Neither Stephen nor Helen was recognized for (her, their) contribution.
6. Our company is revising (their, its) statement of purpose.
7. The committee presented (its, their) recommendation to the president yesterday.
8. The instructor asked Dan and (I, me) to leave the room.
9. Stacey requested that proceeds be divided equally between Calvin and (her, she).
10. It was (she, her) who submitted the recommendation.
11. The speaker did not notice (me, my) leaving early.
12. (Who, Whom) is calling?
13. She is an employee in (who, whom) we have great confidence.
14. He is the one (who, whom) arrived twenty minutes late.
15. Mr. Pai forgot to retain his expense vouchers; (this, this oversight) caused a delay in reimbursement.

Verbs

*V*erbs present problems in number, person, tense, voice, and mood.

1. *Make subjects agree with verbs.*

a. Ignore intervening phrases that have no effect on the verb used.

Good material <u>and</u> fast delivery <u>are</u> (not *is*) essential.
<u>You</u>, not the carrier, <u>are</u> (not *is*) responsible for the damage. [Intervening phrase, "not the carrier," does not affect the verb used.]

The <u>attitude</u> of these customers <u>is</u> (not *are*) receptive. [The subject is "attitude"; "of these customers" is a phrase coming between the subject and the verb.]

<u>One</u> of the stock analysts <u>was</u> (not *were*) dismissed. ["One" is the subject.]

b. Use a verb that agrees with the noun closer to the verb when *or* or *nor* connects two subjects.

Only one or <u>two</u> questions <u>are</u> (not *is*) necessary.

Several paint brushes or one paint <u>roller</u> <u>is</u> (not *are*) necessary.

c. Use singular verbs with plural nouns that have a singular meaning.

The <u>news</u> <u>is</u> good.

<u>Economics</u> <u>is</u> a required course.

<u>Mathematics</u> <u>is</u> required for this major.

d. Use a singular verb with plural subjects that are thought of as singular units.

Twenty <u>dollars</u> <u>is</u> too much.

Ten <u>minutes</u> <u>is</u> sufficient time.

e. Use a singular verb for titles of articles, firm names, and slogans.

"Taming Your Tongue" <u>is</u> an interesting article.

Stein, Jones, and Baker <u>is</u> the oldest firm in the city.

"Eat Smart Play Hard" <u>is</u> a campaign slogan directed at better nutrition for children.

2. ***Choose verbs that agree in*** person ***with their subjects.*** *Person* indicates whether the subject is (1) speaking, (2) being spoken to, or (3) being spoken about.

First person:	I am, we are. [Writer or speaker]
Second person:	You are. [Receiver of message]
Third person:	He is, she is, they are. [Person being discussed]

<u>She</u> <u>doesn't</u> (not *don't*) attend class regularly.

<u>They</u> <u>don't</u> recognize the value of networking.

3. ***Use the appropriate verb tense.*** *Tense* indicates time. Tenses are both simple and compound.

Simple tenses:

Present:	I <u>see</u> you. [Tells what is happening now.]
Past:	I <u>saw</u> you. [Tells what has already happened.]
Future:	I <u>will</u> <u>see</u> you. [Tells what is yet to happen.]

Compound tenses:

Present perfect:	I <u>have</u> <u>seen</u> you. [Tells of past action that extends to the present.]
Past perfect:	I <u>had</u> <u>seen</u> you. [Tells of past action that was finished before another past action.]
Future perfect:	I <u>will</u> <u>have</u> <u>seen</u> you. [Tells of action that will be finished before a future time.]

a. Use present tense when something *was* and *still is* true.

The speaker reminded us that Rhode Island <u>is</u> (not *was*) smaller than Wisconsin.

The consultant's name <u>is</u> (not *was*) Ryan Abrams.

b. Avoid unnecessary shifts in tense.

The carrier <u>brought</u> (not *brings*) my package but <u>left</u> without asking me to sign for it.

Verbs that appear in the same sentence are not required to be in the same tense.

The contract that <u>was</u> <u>prepared</u> yesterday <u>will</u> <u>be</u> <u>signed</u> tomorrow.

4. *Use active voice for most business writing.* *Voice* is the term used to indicate whether a subject *acts* or whether it *is acted upon*. If the subject of a sentence acts, the verb used to describe that action is called an *active verb*.

The keyboard operator <u>made</u> an error.

The woman <u>asked</u> for an adjustment.

If the subject of the sentence is acted upon, the verb used to describe that action is called a *passive verb*.

An error <u>was</u> <u>made</u> by the help desk manager.

An adjustment <u>was</u> <u>asked</u> for by the customer.

Active voice is preferred for most business writing. Refer to Chapter 4 for a discussion of appropriate uses of passive voice.

5. *Use subjunctive mood when speaking of conditions that cannot or probably will not happen and conditions that are not true or are highly unlikely.*

a. Use *were* for the present tense of to be in the subjunctive mood.

I wish the story <u>were</u> (not *was*) true.

If I <u>were</u> (not *was*) you, I would try again.

b. Consider the subjunctive mood for communicating negative ideas in positive language.

I wish I <u>were</u>. [More tactful than "No, I am not."]

We <u>would</u> make a refund if the merchandise had been used in accordance with instructions. [Implies "we are *not* making a refund" but avoids negative words.]

Exercise 3
Select the correct word.

1. If he (was, were) over 18, he would have been hired.

2. Only one of the video clips (was, were) usable.

3. The typesetters, not the editor, (was, were) responsible for these errors.

4. Neither the manager nor the employees (was, were) aware of the policy change.

5. Both John and Steven (was, were) promoted.

6. The news from the rescue mission (is, are) encouraging.

7. *Ten Steps to Greatness* (has, have) been placed in the company library.

8. A child reminded me that the earth (rotates, rotated) on its axis.

9. Tim (don't, doesn't) ask for favors.

10. The president studied the page for a minute and (starts, started) asking questions.

Change each sentence from passive to active voice.

1. The brochure was designed by Susan Woodward.

2. The figures have been checked by our accountant.

3. Ms. Jackson was recommended for promotion by the supervisor.

4. The applications are being screened. (When revising, assume that a committee is doing the screening.)

5. Your request for a leave has been approved. (When revising, assume the manager did the approving.)

Adjectives and Adverbs

Adjectives modify nouns or pronouns. *Adverbs* modify verbs, adjectives, or other adverbs. Although most adverbs end in *ly*, some commonly used adverbs do not end in *ly*: *there, then, after, now,* and *very*. Most words that end in *ly* are adverbs, but common exceptions are *neighborly, timely, friendly, gentlemanly*. Some words are both adjective and adverb: *fast, late,* and *well*.

1. *Use an adjective to modify a noun or pronoun.*

   Doug developed an <u>impressive</u> slide show.

   I prefer the <u>conservative</u> presentation design template.

2. *Use an adjective after a linking verb when the modifier refers to the subject instead of to the verb.* (A linking verb connects a subject to the rest of the sentence. "He is old." "She seems sincere.")

   The applicant seemed <u>qualified</u>. [The adjective "qualified" refers to "applicant," not to "seemed."]

   The president looked <u>suspicious</u>. [The adjective "suspicious" refers to "president," not to "looked."]

3. *Use an adverb to modify a verb, an adjective, or another adverb.*

   The salesperson looked <u>enthusiastically</u> at the prospect. [The adverb "enthusiastically" modifies the verb "looked."]

   The committee was <u>really</u> active. [The adverb "really" modifies the adjective "active."]

Worker A progressed <u>relatively</u> <u>faster</u> than did Worker B. [The adverb "relatively" modifies the adverb "faster."]

4. *Use comparatives and superlatives carefully.*

She is the <u>faster</u> (not *fastest*) of the two workers.

He is the <u>better</u> (not *best*) writer of the two members of the public relations team.

Exclude a person or thing from a group with which that person or thing is being compared.

He is more observant than <u>anyone</u> <u>else</u> (not *anyone*) in his department. [As a member of his department, he cannot be more observant than himself.]

"The XD600 is newer than <u>any</u> <u>other</u> <u>machine</u> (not *any machine*) in the plant." [The XD600 cannot be newer than itself.]

Exercise 4
Select the correct word.

1. Our supply of parts is replenished (frequent, frequently).

2. Marcus looked (impatient, impatiently).

3. The server moved (quick, quickly) from table to table.

4. Of the two people who were interviewed, Jane made the (better, best) impression.

5. Benito is more creative than (any, any other) advertising agent in the company.

Sentence Structure

1. *State the subject of each sentence (unless the sentence is a command).*

<u>I</u> <u>received</u> (not *Received*) the supervisor's request today.

Return the forms to me. [The subject (*you*) is understood and can be omitted in this imperative sentence.]

2. *Rely mainly on sentences that follow the normal subject-verb-complement sequence.*

<u>Jennifer</u> and I <u>withdrew</u> for three <u>reasons</u>.
(subject)   (verb)   (complement)

People are accustomed to sentences stated in this sequence. Sentences that present the verb *before* revealing the subject (1) slow down the reading, (2) present less vivid pictures, and (3) use more words than would be required if the normal sequence were followed.

Original	Better
There are <u>two reasons</u> for our withdrawal.	<u>Two</u> <u>reasons</u> for our withdrawal are . . . .
	<u>Jennifer</u> <u>and</u> <u>I</u> withdrew for two reasons.
<u>It</u> is necessary that we withdraw.	<u>We</u> must withdraw.
<u>Here</u> is a copy of my résumé.	The enclosed <u>résumé</u> outlines . . .

There, it, and *here* are called *expletives*—filler words that have no real meaning in the sentence.

3. **Do not put unrelated ideas in the same sentence.**

The coffee break is at ten o'clock, and the company plans to purchase additional parking spaces. [These ideas have little relationship.]

4. **Put pronouns, adverbs, phrases, and clauses near the words they modify.**

Incorrect	**Correct**
Angie put a new type of <u>gel</u> on her hair, <u>which</u> she had just purchased.	Angie put a new type of <u>gel</u>, <u>which</u> she had just purchased, on her hair.
He <u>only</u> works in the electronics department for $8.50 an hour.	He works in the electronics department for for <u>only</u> $8.50 an hour.
The clerk stood beside the fax machine <u>wearing</u> <u>a</u> <u>denim</u> <u>skirt</u>.	The clerk <u>wearing</u> <u>a</u> <u>denim</u> <u>skirt</u> stood beside the fax machine.

5. **Do not separate subject and predicate unnecessarily.**

Incorrect	**Clear**
<u>He</u>, hoping to receive a bonus, <u>worked</u> rapidly.	Hoping to receive a bonus, <u>he</u> <u>worked</u> rapidly.

6. **Place an introductory phrase near the subject of the independent clause it modifies.** Otherwise, the phrase dangles. To correct the dangling phrase, change the subject of the independent clause, or make the phrase into a dependent clause by assigning it a subject.

Incorrect	**Correct**
<u>When</u> a little boy, <u>my mother</u> took me through a manufacturing plant.	<u>When</u> <u>I</u> <u>was a little boy</u>, my mother took me through a manufacturing plant.
[Implies that the mother was once a little boy.]	<u>When</u> a little boy, I was taken through a manufacturing plant by my mother.
<u>Working</u> at full speed every morning, <u>fatigue</u> overtakes me in the afternoon.	<u>Working</u> at full speed every morning, <u>I</u> become tired in the afternoon.
[Implies that "fatigue" was working at full speed.]	<u>Because</u> <u>I</u> <u>work</u> at full speed every morning, <u>fatigue</u> overtakes me in the afternoon.
<u>To</u> <u>function</u> properly, <u>you</u> must oil the machine every hour. [Implies that if "you" are "to function properly," the machine must be oiled hourly.]	<u>If</u> the <u>machine</u> is to function properly, <u>you</u> must oil it every hour.
	<u>To</u> <u>function</u> <u>properly</u>, the <u>machine</u> must be oiled every hour.

7. **Express related ideas in similar grammatical form (use parallel construction).**

Incorrect

The machine operator made three resolutions: (1) to be punctual, (2) following instructions carefully, and third, the reduction of waste.

The human resources manager is concerned with the selection of the right worker, providing appropriate orientation, and the worker's progress.

Correct

The machine operator made three resolutions: (1) to be punctual, (2) to follow instructions carefully, and (3) to reduce waste.

The human resources manager is concerned with selecting the right worker, providing appropriate orientation, and evaluating the worker's progress.

8. **Do not end a sentence with a needless preposition.**

Where is the plant to be located (not located at)?

The worker did not tell us where he was going (not going to).

End a sentence with a preposition if for some reason the preposition needs emphasis.

I am not concerned with what he is paying for. I am concerned with what he is paying with.

The prospect has everything—a goal to work toward, a house to live in, and an income to live on.

9. **Avoid split infinitives.** Two words are required to express an infinitive: *to* plus a *verb*. The two words belong together. An infinitive is split when another word is placed between the two.

Incorrect

The superintendent used to occasionally visit the offices.

I plan to briefly summarize the report.

Correct

The superintendent used to visit the offices occasionally.

I plan to summarize the report briefly.

Exercise 5

Identify the weakness in each sentence and write an improved version.

1. It is essential that you sign and return the enclosed form.

2. When a small girl, my brother taught me to play basketball.

3. I am submitting an article to Presentations, which I wrote last summer.

4. Almost all of my time is spent in planning, organizing, and the various aspects of control.

5. The work team wants to quickly bring the project to a conclusion.

6. To operate efficiently, you must perform periodic maintenance on your PC.

7. Protect your online privacy by use of effective password protection, clearing temporary menus regularly, and encryption of sensitive information.

Punctuation

Review basic rules for the use of the following punctuation marks in business writing.

Comma

1. *Use a comma*

   a. Between coordinate clauses joined by *and, but, for, or,* and *nor.*

   > He wanted to pay his bills on time, <u>but</u> he did not have the money.

   b. After introductory dependent clauses and certain phrases (participial, infinitive, or prepositional with five or more words). Sentences that begin with dependent clauses (often with words such as *if, as, since, because, although,* and *when*) almost always need a comma. Use a comma after prepositional phrases with fewer than five words if the comma is necessary for clarity.

Dependent clause:	<u>If you can meet us at the airport</u>, please plan to be there by six o'clock. [The comma separates the introductory dependent clause from the independent clause.]
Infinitive:	<u>To get the full benefit of our insurance plan</u>, just complete and return the enclosed card. [A verb preceded by "to" ("to get").]
Participial:	<u>Believing that her earnings would continue to increase</u>, she sought to borrow more money. [A verb form used as an adjective: "believing" modifies the dependent clause "she sought."]
Prepositional phrase:	<u>Within the next few days</u>, you will receive written confirmation of this transaction. [Comma needed because the phrase contains five words.]
	Under the circumstances we think you are justified. [Comma omitted because the phrase contains fewer than five words and the sentence is clear without the comma.]

   c. To separate words in a series.

   > You have a choice of <u>gray, green, purple, and white</u>.

   Without the comma after "purple," no one can tell for sure whether four choices are available, the last of which is "white," or whether three choices are available, the last of which is "purple and white."

   > You have a choice of <u>purple and white, gray, and green</u>. [Choice is restricted to three, the first of which is "purple and white."]

   d. Between two or more independent adjectives that modify the same noun.

New employees are given a <u>long, difficult</u> examination. [Both "long" and "difficult" modify "examination."]

We want <u>quick, factual</u> news. [Both "quick" and "factual" modify "news."]

Do not place a comma between two adjectives when the second adjective modifies the adjective and noun as a unit.

The supervisor is an <u>excellent public</u> speaker. ["Excellent" modifies the noun phrase "public speaker."]

e. To separate a nonrestrictive clause (a clause that is not essential to the basic meaning of the sentence) from the rest of the sentence.

Mr. Murray, <u>who is head of customer resource management</u>, has selected Century Consulting to oversee the rollout of a new software. [The parenthetical remark is not essential to the meaning of the sentence.]

The man <u>who is head of customer resource management</u> has selected Century Consulting to oversee the rollout of a new software. [Commas are not needed because "who is of customer resource management" is essential to the meaning of the sentence.]

f. To separate parenthetical expressions from the rest of the sentence.

Ms. Watson, <u>speaking in behalf of the entire department</u>, accepted the proposal.

g. Before and after the year in month-day-year format.

On <u>July 2, 2004</u>, Mr. Pearson made the final payment.

h. Before and after the name of a state when the name of a city precedes it.

I saw him in <u>Kansas City, Missouri</u>, on the 12th of October.

i. After a direct address.

<u>Jason</u>, I believe you have earned a vacation.

j. After the words *No* and *Yes* when they introduce a statement.

<u>Yes</u>, you can count on me.

<u>No</u>, I will have to decline.

k. To set off appositives when neutral emphasis is desired.

The group heard a speech from Mr. Kyle Welch, <u>a recruiting consultant</u>.

Arun Ramage, <u>former president of the Jackson Institute</u>, spoke to the group.

l. Between contrasted elements.

We need more money, <u>not less</u>.

The job requires experience, <u>not formal education</u>.

m. To show the omission of words that are understood.

Ms. Rent scored 96 percent on the employment examination; Mr. Mehrmann, 84 percent.

n. Before a question that solicits a confirmatory answer.

It's a reasonable price, <u>isn't it</u>?

Our bills have been paid, <u>haven't they</u>?

o. Between the printed name and the title on the same line beneath a signature or in a letter address.

Roy Murr, President

No comma is used if the title is on a separate line.

Cathryn W. Edwards
President of Academic Affairs

p. After an adverbial conjunction.

The check was for the right amount; <u>however,</u> it was not signed.

Exercise 6
Insert needed commas. Write "correct" if you find no errors.

1. The man who came in late has not been interviewed.

2. Emoticons which are created by keying combinations of symbols to produce "sideway faces" are a shorthand way to compensate for nonverbal cues lost in one-way communication.

3. Margie Harrison a new member of the board remained silent during the long bitter debate.

4. Primary qualifications for graduates seeking a first job are education work experience and activities.

5. We surveyed the entire population but three responses were unusable.

6. If you approve of the changes please place your initials in the space provided.

7. To qualify for the position applicants must have two years of work experience.

8. John was awarded $25; Bill $40.

9. We have lost our place in the production line haven't we?

10. We should be spending less money not more.

11. On November 20 2004 all related documents were submitted.

12. Yes I agree that the meeting in Oxford Tennessee should be scheduled in April.

Semicolon

2. Use a semicolon

a. To join the independent clauses in a compound sentence when a conjunction is omitted.

Our workers have been extraordinarily efficient this year; they are expecting a bonus.

b. To join the independent clauses in a compound-complex sentence.

As indicated earlier, we prefer delivery on Saturday morning at four o'clock; but Friday night at ten o'clock will be satisfactory.

We prefer delivery on Saturday morning at four o'clock; but, if the arrangement is more convenient for you, Friday night at ten o'clock will be satisfactory.

c. Before an adverbial conjunction.

Adverbial conjunction: The shipment arrived too late for our weekend sale; therefore, we are returning the shipment to you. Other frequently used adverbial conjunctions are *however, otherwise, consequently,* and *nevertheless.*

d. Before words used to introduce enumerations or explanations that follow an independent clause.

Enumeration with commas: Many factors affect the direction of the stock market; namely, interest rates, economic growth, and employment rates.

Explanation forming a complete thought: We have plans for improvement; for example, we intend. . . .

The engine has been "knocking"; that is, the gas in the cylinders explodes before the pistons complete their upward strokes.

Note the following exceptions that require a comma to introduce the enumeration or explanation:

Enumeration without commas: Several popular Internet browsers are available, for example, Netscape and Internet Explorer. [A comma, not a semicolon, is used because the enumeration contains no commas.]

Explanation forming an incomplete thought: Many companies have used nontraditional methods for recruiting applicants, for instance, soliciting résumé postings to company web sites. [A comma, not a semicolon, is used because the explanation is not a complete thought.]

e. In a series that contains commas.

Some of our workers have worked overtime this week: Smith, 6 hours; Hardin, 3; Cantrell, 10; and McGowan, 11.

Exercise 7
Insert a semicolon where needed.

1. Expense tickets were not included, otherwise, the request would have been honored.

2. The following agents received a bonus this month: Barnes, $400, Shelley, $450, and Jackson, $600.

3. The proposal was not considered it arrived two days late.

4. This paint does have some disadvantages for example a lengthy drying time.

5. Soon after the figures have been received, they will be processed, but a formal report cannot be prepared before June 15.

Colon

3. **Use a colon**

a. After a complete thought that introduces a list of items. Use a colon following both direct and indirect introductions of lists.

Direct introduction:	The following three factors influenced our decision: an expanded market, an inexpensive source of raw materials, and a ready source of labor. [The word "following" clearly introduces a list.]
Indirect introduction:	The carpet is available in three colors: green, burgundy, and blue.

Do not use a colon after an introductory statement that ends with a preposition or a verb (*are, is, were, include*). The list that follows the preposition or verb finishes the sentence.

Incomplete sentence:	We need to (1) expand our market, (2) locate an inexpensive source of materials, and (3) find a ready source of labor. [A colon does not follow "to" because the words preceding the list are not a complete sentence.]
	Examples of leading presentation graphics software include PowerPoint, Aldus Persuasion, and Apple Keynote. [A colon does not follow "include" because the words preceding the list are not a complete sentence.]

b. To stress an appositive (a noun that renames the preceding noun) at the end of a sentence.

His heart was set on one thing: promotion.

Our progress is due to the efforts of one person: Mr. Keating.

c. After the salutation of a letter when mixed punctuation is used.

Dear Dr. Gorga:

d. After a word or phrase followed by additional material in ads or signs.

No Parking: Reserved for executives

For Rent: Two-bedroom apartment

e. Between hours and minutes to express time in figures.

5:45 p.m.   11:05 a.m.

Exercise 8
Correct the use of colons. Write "correct" if you find no errors.

1. The program has one shortcoming: flexibility.

2. Our meetings are scheduled for: Monday, Tuesday, and Friday.

3. We liked this car because of: its price, durability, and appearance.

4. We liked three features of Ms. Cole's résumé: her experience, her education, and her attitude.

5. We are enthusiastic about the plan because: (1) it is least expensive, (2) its legality is unquestioned, and (3) it can be implemented quickly.

Apostrophe

4. *Use an apostrophe to form possessives.*

a. Add an apostrophe and *s* ('*s*) to form the possessive case of a singular noun or a plural noun that does not end with a pronounced *s*.

Singular noun:	Jenna's position	firm's assets
	employee's benefits	
Plural noun without a pronounced *s*:	men's clothing	children's games
	deer's antlers	

b. Add only an apostrophe to form the possessive of a singular or plural noun that ends with a pronounced *s*.

Singular noun with pronounced *s*:	Niagara Falls' site
	Ms. Jenkins' interview
Plural noun with pronounced *s*:	two managers' decision
	six months' wages

Exception: An apostrophe and *s* ('*s*) can be added to singular nouns ending in a pronounced *s* if an additional *s* sound is pronounced easily.

Singular noun with additional *s* sound:	boss's decision	class's party,
	Jones's invitation	

c. Use an apostrophe in an expression that indicates ownership. The apostrophe shows omission of a preposition.

Last year's reports. . . . (Reports of last year. . . .)

d. Use an apostrophe with the possessives of nouns that refer to time (minutes, hours, days, weeks, months, and years) or distance in a possessive manner.

eight hours' pay	today's schedule	a stone's throw
two weeks' notice	ten years' experience	a yard's length

e. Use an apostrophe in a possessive noun that precedes a gerund.

Ms. Bowen's receiving the promotion caused. . . .

The manager appreciated Mitzi's working overtime to complete the order.

f. Use an apostrophe to show whether ownership is joint or separate.

To indicate joint ownership, add an '*s* to the last name only.

Olsen and Howard's accounting firm.

To indicate separate ownership, add an 's to each name.

Olsen's and Howard's accounting firms.

5. *Do not use an apostrophe*

a. In the titles of some organizations. Use the name as the organization uses its name.

National Sales Executives Association

b. To form the possessive of a pronoun (most pronouns become possessive through a change in spelling; therefore, an apostrophe is not used).

yours [Not your's]

ours [Not our's]

Exercise 9
Correct the possessives.

1. This companies mission statement has been revised since it's recent merger.

2. The workers earned a bonus of three weeks wages for last months overtime.

3. The banks' had been negotiating a merger for several months time.

4. Two firms were cited: West and Johnson's.

5. The manager will appreciate you completing the review before the auditors arrive.

Hyphen

6. *Use a hyphen*

a. In compound words such as *father-in-law* and *attorney-by-law*, words beginning with *ex* (ex-mayor), and *self* (self-analysis).

b. Between the words in a compound adjective. (A *compound adjective* is a group of adjectives appearing together and used as a single word to describe a noun.) Hyphenate compound adjectives that appear before the nouns or pronouns they describe.

An attention-getting device

A hard-to-follow lecture

A two-thirds interest

Do not hyphenate a compound adjective in the following cases:

(1) When the compound adjective follows a noun.
A device that is attention getting.
A lecture that was hard to follow.

Note: Some compound adjectives are hyphenated when they follow a noun.

The report was up-to-date.
The speaker is well-known.
For jobs that are part-time, ...

(2) An expression made up of an adverb that ends in *ly* and an adjective is not a compound adjective and does not require a hyphen.

commonly accepted principle

widely quoted authority

(3) A simple fraction and a percentage.

Simple fraction: Two thirds of the respondents
Percentage: 15 percent sales increase

c. To prevent misinterpretation.

A <u>small-business executive</u> [An executive who operates a small business]

A <u>small business executive</u> [An executive who is small]

<u>Recover</u> a chair [To obtain possession of a chair once more]

<u>Re-cover</u> a chair [To cover a chair again]

<u>Eight inch</u> blades [Eight blades, each of which is an inch long]

<u>Eight-inch</u> blades [Blades eight inches long]

d. When spelling out compound numbers from 21 to 99.

Thirty-one   Ninety-seven

e. To avoid repetition of a word in a series of hyphenated adjectives that has a common ending.

<u>Short-, medium-, and long-range</u> missiles

"Short-range, medium-range, and long-range missiles" have the same meaning; but repetition of "range" is not necessary. The hyphens after "short" and "medium" show that these words are connected to another word that will appear at the end of the series (called *suspending hyphens*).

f. To divide words at the end of a line. (See the discussion of word division in Appendix A.)

g. In a nine-digit zip code.

83475-1247

Exercise 10
Add necessary hyphens. Write "correct" if you find no errors.

1. The employee's self confidence was damaged by the manager's harsh reprimand.
2. State of the art computers provide us quick access to accurate information needed to manage our business effectively.
3. Surveys indicate that a majority of today's consumers are convenience driven.
4. A two thirds majority is needed to pass the 5 percent increase in employee wages.
5. Sixty five of the respondents were female; nearly one half were highly educated professionals.
6. Print résumés and cover letters on 8½ by 11 inch bond paper.

Quotation Marks and Italics

7. *Use quotation marks*

    a. To enclose direct quotations.

Single-sentence quotation:	The supervisor said, "We will make progress."
Interrupted quotation:	"We will make progress," the supervisor said, "even though we have to work overtime."
Multiple-sentence quotation:	The president said, "Have a seat, gentlemen. I'm dictating a letter. I should be through in about five minutes. Please wait." [Place quotation marks before the first word and after the last word of a multiple-sentence quotation.]
Quotation within quotation:	The budget director said, "Believe me when I say 'A penny saved is a penny earned' is the best advice I ever had." [Use single quotation marks to enclose a quotation that appears with a quotation.]

Note: Periods and commas appear within the quotation marks. Other punctuation marks appear outside—unless the punctuation mark is part of the quotation.

"Take your time," she said, "and the work will be easier." [Periods and commas *inside* the quotation marks.]

The manager said, "That's fine"; his facial expression conveyed an entirely different message. [Semicolon *outside* quotation marks.]

The contractor asked, "When will we begin?" [Question marks *inside* quotation marks when the question is within the quotation.]

Did the contractor say, "We will begin today"? [Place question marks *outside* quotation marks when the question is not within the quotation.]

    b. To enclose titles of songs, magazine and newspaper articles, lecture titles, and themes within text.

"Candle in the Wind"

"Progress in Cancer Research"

The chapter, "E-mail Protocol," . . .

    c. To enclose a definition of a defined term. Italicize the defined word.

The term *downsizing* is used to refer to "the planned reduction in the number of employees."

    d. To enclose words used in humor, a word used when a different word would be more appropriate, slang expressions that need to be emphasized or clarified for the reader, or nicknames. These words can also be shown in italics.

Humor/ Different Word:	Our "football" team. . . . [Hints that the team appears to be playing something other than football.]
	Our football "team" . . . . [Hints that "collection of individual players" would be more descriptive than "team."]
	. . . out for "lunch." [Hints that the reason for being out is something other than lunch.]
Slang:	With negotiations entering the final week, it's time "to play hardball."
Nicknames:	And now for some comments by Robert "Bob" Johnson.

8. *Use italics* (Underscore is not used in computer-generated copy.)

   a. To indicate words, letters, numbers, and phrases used as words.

   The word *effective* was used in describing his presentation.

   He had difficulty learning to spell *recommendation*.

   b. To emphasize a word that is not sufficiently emphasized by other means.

   Our goal is to hire the *right* person, not necessarily the most experienced candidate.

   c. To indicate the titles of books, magazines, and newspapers.

   Managing for Quality   *The New York Times*   *Reader's Digest*

   Underscore or italicize the titles of books, magazines, and newspapers within text. Refer to documentation style manuals for correct treatment of these titles in citations and bibliographic references.

Exercise 11
Add necessary quotation marks and italics.

1. Goleman presents an interesting theory of intelligence in his book Emotional Intelligence.

2. The article Editing Like a Pro appeared in the July 2003 issue of Presentations.

3. His *accomplishments* are summarized on the attached page. [Indicate that a word other than accomplishments may be a more appropriate word.]

4. Nick said the firm plans to establish a sinking fund. [direct quotation]

5. The term flame is online jargon for a heated, sarcastic, sometimes abusive message or posting to a discussion group.

6. Read each e-mail message carefully before you send it to avoid flaming.

Dash, Parentheses, Brackets, Ellipses, and Period

9. *Use a dash*

   a. To place emphasis on appositives.

   His answer—the correct answer—was based on years of experience.

   Compare the price—$125—with the cost of a single repair job.

b. When appositives contain commas.

> Their scores—Mary, 21; Sally, 20; and Jo, 19—were the highest in a group of 300.

c. When a parenthetical remark consists of an abrupt change in thought.

> The committee decided—you may think it's a joke, but it isn't—that the resolution should be adopted.

> *Note*: Use an em dash (not two hyphens) to form a dash in computer-generated copy.

10. *Use parentheses*

   a. For explanatory material that could be left out.

   > Three of our employees (Sam Bachman, Lyn Russo, and Mark Wilds) took their vacations in August.

   > All our employees (believe it or not) have perfect attendance records. [Note a parenthetical statement within a sentence neither begins with a capital letter nor ends with a period.]

   > Use commas before and after parenthetical material for neutral emphasis; use dashes for added emphasis.

   b. For accuracy in writing figures.

   > For the sum of three thousand five hundred dollars ($3,500). . . .

   c. To enclose numbers or letters used to enumerate lists of items within a sentence.

Incorrect	Correct
. . . authority to 1) issue passes and 2) collect fees.	. . . authority to (1) issue passes and (2) collect fees.

   d. *After* a period when an entire sentence is parenthetical; *before* a period when only the last part of a sentence is parenthetical.

   > The board met for three hours. (The usual time is one hour.)

   > Success can be attributed to one person (Earl Knott).

11. *Use brackets*

   a. To enclose words that are inserted between words or sentences of quoted material.

   > "How long will the delay be? No longer than this: [At this point, the speaker tapped the lectern three times.] That means no delay at all."

   b. As required in certain mathematical formulas.

   c. To enclose parenthetical material within parentheses.

   > The motion passed. (The vote [17 for and 4 against] was not taken until midnight.)

   d. To explain, clarify, or correct words of the writer you quote.

   > "To [accounting] professionals, the ability to express themselves well is more than a hallmark of educated persons," was quoted from a study conducted by the American Institute of Certified Public Accountants.

12. *Use an ellipsis to indicate words have been omitted from a quotation or to add emphasis in advertising material.* Insert a space between the three periods. Use four periods in ellipses at the end of a quotation; one period indicates the end of the sentence.

Omission: Mr. Thomas said, "We believe...our objectives will be accomplished."

Mr. Thomas reported, "The time has come when we must provide our employees with in-service training. . . . "

Emphasis: Don't be left out in the cold . . . order your cost-efficient Premier gas logs today.

13. *Use a period after declarative and imperative sentences and courteous requests.*

We will attend. [Declarative sentence.]

Complete this report. [Imperative sentence.]

Will you please complete the report today. [Courteous request is a question but does not require a verbal answer with requested action.]

Exercise 12
Add necessary dashes, parentheses, brackets, ellipses, or periods.

1. Our accountant said, "Such expenses are not justified." [Show that words have been omitted in the middle of the sentence.]

2. Our accountant said, "Such expenses are not justified." [Show that words have been omitted at the end of the sentence.]

3. Additional consultants, programmers and analysts, were hired to complete the computer conversion. [Emphasize the appositive.]

4. The dividend will be raised to 15 cents a share approved by the Board of Directors on December 1, 2004. [Deemphasize the approval.]

5. The following conclusions were presented for the plan: 1) it is least expensive, 2) its legality is unquestioned, and 3) it can be implemented quickly.

Numbers

Businesspeople use quantitative data often, so numbers appear frequently in business writing. Accuracy is exceedingly important. The most frequent problem in expressing numbers is whether to write them as figures or spell them out as words.

1. *Use figures*

   a. In most business writing because (1) figures should get deserved emphasis, (2) figures are easy for readers to locate if they need to reread for critical points, and (3) figures can be keyed faster and in less space than spelled-out words.

Regardless of whether a number has one digit or many, use figures to express dates, sums of money, mixed numbers and decimals, distance, dimension, cubic capacity, percentage, weights, temperatures, and chapter and page numbers.

May 10, 2004	165 pounds
$9 million	Chapter 3, page 29
5 percent (use % in a table)	
over 200 applicants (or two hundred) [an approximation]	

b. With ordinals (*th, st, rd, nd*) only when the number precedes the month.

The meeting is to be held on June 21.

The meeting is to be held on the 21st of June.

c. With ciphers but without decimals when presenting even-dollar figures, even if the figure appears in a sentence with another figure that includes dollars and cents.

He paid $30 for the cabinet.

He paid $31.75 for the table and $30 for the cabinet.

d. Numbers that represent time when a.m. or p.m. is used. Words or figures may be used with o'clock.

Meet me at 10:15 p.m.

Please be there at ten o'clock (or 10 o'clock).

Omit the colon when expressing times of day that include hours but not minutes, even if the time appears in a sentence with another time that includes minutes.

The reception began at 7 p.m.

The award program began at 6:30 p.m. with a reception at 7 p.m.

2. *Spell out*

a. Numbers if they are used as the first word of a sentence.

Thirty-two people attended.

b. Numbers one through ten if no larger number appears in the same sentence.

Only three people were present.

We need ten machines.

Send 5 officers and 37 members.

c. The first number in two consecutive numbers that act as adjectives modifying the same noun; write the second number in figures. If the first number cannot be expressed in one or two words, place it in figures also.

The package required four 37-cent stamps. [A hyphen joins the second number with the word that follows it, thus forming a compound adjective that describes the noun "stamps."]

We shipped 250 180-horsepower engines today. [Figures are used because neither number can be expressed in one or two words.]

Legal & Ethical Constraints

d. Numbers in legal documents, following them with figures enclosed in parentheses.

For the sum of Five Thousand Four Hundred Ninety-five Dollars ($5,495), . . .

3. *Use symbols*

For convenience in completing forms such as invoices and statements, but not in letters and reports. The dollar sign ($), in contrast with such symbols as %, ¢, @, and #, should be used in letters and reports.

Spell out terms rather than use symbols in sentences of letters and reports.

31 percent (not "31%")

80 cents a foot (not "80¢ a foot")

21 cases at $4 a case (not "21 cases @ $4 a case")

Policy No. 468571 (not "Policy #468571")

Exercise 13
Correct the number usage in the following sentences taken from a letter or a report.

1. The question was answered by sixty-one percent of the respondents.
2. The meeting is scheduled for 10:00 a.m. on February 21st.
3. These 3 figures appeared on the expense account: $21.95, $30.00, and $35.14.
4. Approximately 100 respondents requested a copy of the results.
5. We ordered five sixteen-ounce hammers.
6. The MIS manager ordered 150 80-GB hard drives.
7. 21 members voted in favor of the motion.
8. The cost will be approximately $8,000,000.00.
9. Mix two quarts of white with 13 quarts of brown.
10. Examine the diagram on page seven.

Abbreviations

Avoid abbreviations because they are visually distracting to the reader, are difficult to understand, and may send the mistaken message that you are too hurried to do a complete job. Follow these guidelines when abbreviating is appropriate:

1. *Abbreviate*

a. Titles that come before and after proper names and academic degrees

Dr., Mr., Mrs., Ms.
M.B.A., Esq., Jr., M.D., Ph.D., R.N., Sr.

[Periods are not used in the abbreviations of CPA (Certified Public Accountant), CPS (Certified Professional Secretary), and CLU (Chartered Life Underwriter).]

b. Commonly known government agencies, organizations or businesses, and institutions.

Government agencies: SEC, FBI, FDA, FDIC, FCC, FHA, SBA, USDA, VA

Business and educational organizations: GE, IBM, TWA, UPS, MIT

Other organizations: AMA, BBB, NBC, WLOX, YMCA, UN, NASDAQ

c. Commonly used business expressions:

ATM, EDP, COD/c.o.d, FIFO or LIFO, FOB/f.o.b., CD-ROM, CEO, CFO, MHz, LAN, RSVP, TQM, VCR, WWW, time zones (EST, CDT), a.m., p.m.
Note: Use a.m. and p.m. only when a specific time is mentioned. Small letters—a.m. and p.m.—are preferred.

Come to the office at 10:15 a.m. (not this a.m.)

d. The words *Co., Corp., Inc., Ltd.,* and *Mfg.* in the names of businesses when their own letterheads contain abbreviations:

JCPenney Company, Inc.   S & A Restaurant Corp.

Microsoft Corporation   C. Thames & Co.

e. The word *number* when a numeral directly follows the term unless the term begins the sentence.

Ship a gross of No. 10 envelopes.

Refer to Policy No. 384862.

Number 89-9-1 bolts will be replaced with an improved part on March 1.

f. The word extension (*Ext.*) when it appears with a telephone number.

Please call our regional sales rep at (404) 555-9620, Ext. 139.

g. The names of states when they appear as parts of envelope addresses or letter addresses. Use the two-letter abbreviations recommended by the U.S. Postal Service shown in Appendix A, page A-25.

2. *Do not abbreviate*

a. The names of cities, states (except in an envelope and letter address), months, and days of the week. They may be abbreviated in lists, tables, graphs, charts, illustrations, or other visuals where space is limited.

b. Points on the compass.

Tom has lived in the West for seven years.

Go east one block and turn south; then continue to 650 North Cypress Street.

Capitalization

Capitalize

1. *Proper nouns (words that name a particular person, place, or thing) and adjectives derived from proper nouns.* Capitalize the names of persons, places, geographic areas, days of the week, months of the year, holidays, deities, specific events, and other specific names.

Proper nouns	Common nouns
Lynn Claxton	An applicant for the management position
Bonita Lakes	A land development
Centre Park Mall	A new shopping center
Veteran's Day	A federal holiday
Information Age	A period of time

Proper adjectives: Irish potatoes, Roman shades, Swiss army knife, Chinese executives, British accent, Southern dialect

Do not capitalize the name of the seasons unless they are personified.

Old Man Winter

2. *The principal words in the titles of books, magazines, newspapers, articles, compact disks, movies, plays, television series, songs, and poems.*

Seven Habits of Highly Effective People [Book]

"Add Dimension to Presentations with a Document Camera" [Article]

Video Producer [Magazine]

Encarta 2003 Encyclopedia [Compact disk]

3. *The names of academic courses that are numbered, are specific course titles, or contain proper nouns.* Capitalize degrees used after a person's name and specific academic sessions.

Thomas Malone is enrolled in classes in <u>French</u>, <u>mathematics</u>, <u>science</u>, and <u>English</u>.

Students entering the MBA program must complete <u>Accounting 6093</u> and <u>Finance 5133</u>.

Ms. Sheila O'Donnell, M.S., will teach <u>Principles of Management</u> during <u>Spring Semester</u> 2004.

Ms. O'Donnell earned a <u>master's</u> degree in business from Harvard.

4. *Titles that precede a name.*

Mr. Ronald Smith	Editor Franklin	Uncle Fred
Dr. Sarah Hobbs	President Lopez	Professor Senter

Do not capitalize titles appearing alone or following a name unless they appear in addresses.

The <u>manager</u> approved the proposal submitted by the <u>editorial assistant</u>.

Susan Morris, <u>executive vice president</u>, is responsible for that account.

Dean has taken the position formerly held by his <u>father</u>.

Address all correspondence to Colonel Michael Anderson, <u>Department Head</u>, 109 Crescent Avenue, Baltimore, MD 21208.

5. *The main words in a division or department name if the official or specific name is known or the name is used in a return address, a letter address, or a signature block.*

Official or specific name known:	Return the completed questionnaire to the <u>Public Relations Department</u> by March 15.
Official or specific name unknown:	Employees in your <u>information systems division</u> are invited . . .
Return or letter address, signature block:	Mr. Owen Rowan, <u>Manager</u>, <u>Public Relations Department</u> . . .

6. *Most nouns followed by numbers (except in page, paragraph, line, size, and verse references).*

Policy No. 8746826	Exhibit A	Chapter 7
page 97, paragraph 2	Figure 3-5	Model L-379
Flight 340, Gate 22	size 8, Style 319 jacket	

7. *The first word of a direct quotation.*

The sales representative said, "<u>We</u> leave tomorrow."

Do not capitalize the first word in the last part of an interrupted quotation or the first word in an indirect quotation.

"<u>We</u> will proceed," he said, "<u>with</u> the utmost caution." [Interrupted quotation]

He said that the report must be submitted by the end of the week. [Indirect quotation]

8. *The first word following a colon when a formal statement or question follows.*

Here is an important rule for report writers: <u>Plan</u> your work and work your plan.

Each sales representative should ask this question: <u>Do</u> I really look like a representative of my firm?

Exercise 14
Copy each of the following sentences, making essential changes in abbreviation and capitalization.

1. The first question asked of me during interviewing 101 was "why do you want to work for us?"

2. The summer season is much slower than the rest of the year according to the Sales Manager.

3. We paid for *Awaken the Giant Within* with check no. 627 on Dec. 10.

4. The N.C.A.A. meeting, moderated by president Marla Stanton, will be held in N.Y.

5. A retirement ceremony is being planned for president Sims at 9 P.M. E.S.T.

6. Inform the marketing department of the temporary shortage of Model Y-139.

7. We recently purchased corel stock music gallery, an excellent source of copyright-free music clips.

8. Bill Gates, President of Microsoft, was interviewed on a national television program last week.

Words Frequently Misused

1. *Accept, except.* *Accept* means "to receive willingly," "to give admittance or approval," "to make a favorable response." *Except* means "to exclude" or "with the exclusion of."

   I <u>accept</u> your offer.

   All columns have been added <u>except</u> one.

2. *Advice, advise.* *Advice* is a noun meaning "suggestions or recommendations about a course of action." *Advise* is a verb meaning "to give advice; to caution or warn."

   The supervisor's <u>advice</u> to John was to abide by safety rules.

   Supervisors <u>advise</u> employees of the consequences of safety rules violations.

3. *Affect, effect.* *Affect* is a verb meaning "to influence." *Effect* is a noun meaning "result"; *effect* is also a verb meaning "to bring about."

   The change does not <u>affect</u> his pay.

   What <u>effect</u> will the change have?

   The manager wants to <u>effect</u> a change in the schedule.

4. *Among, between.* Use *among* to discuss three or more. Use *between* to discuss two.

   Divide the earnings <u>among</u> the six workers.

   Divide the earnings <u>between</u> the two workers.

5. *Amount, number.* Use *amount* when speaking of money or of things that cannot be counted. Use *number* when speaking of things that can be counted.

   The <u>amount</u> of grumbling has been troublesome to the supervisors.

   The <u>number</u> of workers has been increased.

6. *Capital, capitol.* *Capital* is money, property, or a city in which state or national government is located. A *capitol* is a building in which the government meets.

   One business partner provided the <u>capital</u>; the other provided the expertise.

   The <u>capitol</u> is at the intersection of Jefferson Street and Tenth Avenue.

7. ***Cite, sight, site.*** *Cite* means to quote or mention. *Sight* refers to the sense of seeing, the process of seeing, or a view. *Site* is a location.

Marianne <u>cited</u> several authorities in her report.

Working at the computer is affecting her <u>sight</u>.

Market Avenue is the <u>site</u> of the new store.

8. ***Complement, compliment.*** *Complement* means "to complete" or "that which completes or suits another." *Compliment* means "words of praise."

This shipment is a <u>complement</u> to our latest series of orders.

The clerk deserved the manager's <u>compliment</u>.

9. ***Continual, continuous.*** If an action is *continual* it will have planned-for breaks in continuity. If an action is *continuous*, it will be constant, without breaks.

The mechanism for raising and lowering the garage door has given <u>continual</u> service for four years.

The clock has run <u>continuously</u> for four years.

10. ***Council, counsel.*** *Council* means "an advisory group." *Counsel* means "advice," "one who gives advice," or "to advise."

<u>Council</u> members will meet today.

First, seek legal <u>counsel</u>.

The defendant and his <u>counsel</u> were excused.

An attorney will <u>counsel</u> the suspect.

11. ***Credible, creditable.*** *Credible* means "believable." *Creditable* means "praiseworthy" or "worthy of commercial credit."

The explanations were <u>credible</u>.

Mr. Fulton did a <u>creditable</u> job for us.

12. ***Criteria, criterion.*** A *criterion* is a standard for judging, a yardstick by which something is measured. The plural form is *criteria*.

The most important <u>criterion</u> was cost.

Three <u>criteria</u> were developed.

13. ***Data, datum.*** *Datum* is a singular noun meaning "fact," "proposition," "condition," or "quantity" from which other facts, and so forth, may be deduced. *Data* is the plural form.

This <u>datum</u> suggests . . .

These <u>data</u> suggest . . .

Use of *data* as a singular form is gaining some degree of acceptance. Some people use the word in the same way they use *group*. Although composed of more than one, *group* is singular. [The group has decided.] Until *data* becomes generally accepted as singular, the word should be used carefully. Instead of "This data is" or "These data are" such expressions as "This *set* of data is" or "These facts are" can be used to avoid the risk of alienating certain readers or listeners.

14. ***Different from, different than.*** *Different from* is correct. *Different than* is to be avoided.

That machine is <u>different from</u> mine.

15. ***Each other, one another.*** Use *each other* when referring to two people. Use *one another* when referring to more than two.

The two employees competed with <u>each other</u>.

The members of the group helped <u>one another</u>.

16. ***Eminent, imminent.*** *Eminent* means "well known." *Imminent* means "about to happen."

An <u>eminent</u> scientist will address the group.

A merger seems <u>imminent</u>.

17. ***Envelop, envelope.*** *Envelop* is a verb meaning "to surround" or "to hide." *Envelope* is a noun referring to a cover for a letter.

A fog was about to <u>envelop</u> the island.

Just use the enclosed <u>envelope</u> for your reply.

18. ***Farther, further.*** Use *farther* when referring to distance. Use *further* when referring to extent or degree.

Let's go one mile <u>farther</u>.

Let's pursue the thought <u>further</u>.

19. ***Fewer, less.*** Use *fewer* with items that can be counted. Use *less* with items that cannot be counted.

<u>Fewer</u> than half the employers approved the proposed pay plan.

Maria spent <u>less</u> time writing the report than Michael because she had spent more time organizing her data.

20. ***Formally, formerly.*** Use *formally* when discussing that which is ceremonious or done according to an established method. Use *formerly* in discussing that which has preceded in time.

The award will be <u>formally</u> presented at tomorrow's convocation.

Tom <u>formerly</u> worked for the department of revenue.

21. ***Infer, imply.*** *Infer* means "to draw a conclusion"; readers or listeners infer. *Imply* means "to hint" or "to set forth vaguely"; speakers and writers imply.

I <u>infer</u> from your letter that conditions have improved.

Do you mean to <u>imply</u> that conditions have improved?

22. *Insure, ensure.* To *insure* is to contract for payment of a certain sum in the event of damage or loss. To *ensure* is to make certain that a specified event or result will occur.

We plan to <u>insure</u> the house for $80,000.

To <u>ensure</u> a passing score, study systematically.

23. *Irregardless.* Avoid using this word, which is a double negative. Use *regardless* instead.

24. *Its, it's. Its* is a possessive pronoun. *It's* is a contraction for "it is."

The phrase has lost <u>its</u> meaning.

<u>It's</u> time to quit.

25. *Lead, led. Lead* is a noun or an adjective referring to a metallic element. *Led* is the past tense of the verb *lead* meaning to guide or go through.

<u>Lead</u> paints were removed from the market when scientific evidence proved they were harmful.

The speech coach <u>led</u> the participants in practicing several voice strengthening exercises.

26. *Lend, loan. Lend* is a verb meaning to let another use something temporarily. *Loan* is a noun referring to the thing given for the borrower's temporary use.

The bank has agreed to <u>lend</u> us the money.

The bank has approved our <u>loan</u>.

27. *Lose, loose. Lose* means "to fail to keep." *Loose* means "not tight."

Don't <u>lose</u> the moneybag.

The cap on the fountain pen is <u>loose</u>.

28. *Media, medium.* A *medium* is a means for transmitting a message. Letter, e-mail, telephone, radio, and newspaper are examples. The plural form is *media.*

The best <u>medium</u> for advertising this product is the radio.

The news <u>media</u> are very objective in their coverage.

29. *Personal, personnel. Personal* means "concerned with a person" or "private." *Personnel* means "people" or "employees."

Omit the questions about family background and musical preference; they're too <u>personal</u>.

All advertising <u>personnel</u> are invited to participate in the workshop.

30. *Principal, principle. Principal* means "a person in a leading position," "main," or "primary." *Principle* means "rule" or "law."

The <u>principal</u> scheduled an all-day faculty meeting.

The <u>principal</u> purpose is to gain speed.

The <u>principal</u> plus interest is due in thirty days.

The theory is based on sound <u>principles</u>.

31. ***Reason is because.*** *Because* means "for the reason next presented"; therefore *reason is because* is a redundancy.

   Not: The <u>reason is because</u> losses from bad debts tripled.

   But: The <u>reason is</u> that losses from bad debts tripled.

   Or: Profits decreased because losses from bad debts tripled.

32. ***Stationary, stationery.*** *Stationary* means "without movement" or "remaining in one place." *Stationery* is writing paper.

   The machine is to remain <u>stationary</u>.

   Order another box of <u>stationery</u>.

33. ***That, which.*** Use *that* when a dependent clause is essential in conveying the basic meaning of the sentence. Use *which* when a dependent clause is not essential in conveying the basic meaning of the sentence.

   The books <u>that</u> were on the bottom shelf have been sent to the bindery. [The clause identifies certain books sent to the bindery; therefore, it is essential].

   Multigrade oil, <u>which</u> is only slightly more expensive than one-grade oil, will serve your purpose better. [Purpose of sentence is to convey the superiority of multigrade oil; therefore, "which is only slightly more expensive than one-grade oil" is not essential.]

34. ***Their, there, they're.*** *Their* is the possessive form of "they." *There* refers to "at that place" or "at that point." *They're* is a contraction for "they are."

   The president accepted <u>their</u> proposal immediately.

   The final copy must be <u>there</u> by May 1.

   <u>They're</u> eager to complete the renovation in time for the spring selling season.

35. ***To, too, two.*** *To* is a preposition or the beginning of an infinitive. *Too* is an adverb meaning "also" or "excessive." *Two* is a number.

   José organized the campaign <u>to</u> initiate flexible scheduling.

   Twenty percent overtime is <u>too</u> demanding.

   The entire department shares the <u>two</u> laser printers.

Exercise 15
Select the correct word.

1. All questionnaires were returned (<u>accept</u>, except) one.

2. Exactly how will the change (affect, <u>effect</u>) us?

3. The consultants' (<u>advice</u>, advise) is to downsize the organization.

4. The commission is to be divided equally (among, between) the three sales agents.

5. We were astonished by the (amount, number) of complaints.

6. The (cite, sight, site) of Jim's receiving the service award was exhilarating.

---

7. I consider that remark a (compliment, complement).

8. Because the suspect's statements were (credible, creditable), no charges were filed.

9. The three panelists were constantly interrupting (each other, one another).

10. The issue will be discussed (further, farther) at our next meeting.

11. Limit your discussion to five or (fewer, less) points.

12. From his statements to the press, I (infer, imply) that he is optimistic about the proposal.

13. (Irregardless, Regardless) of weather conditions, we should proceed.

14. The storm seems to be losing (its, it's) force.

15. The chemical engineer (lead, led) the research team's investigation to eliminate (lead, led) from gas emissions.

16. Please, (lend, loan) me a copy of today's *The Wall Street Journal*.

17. Employees are entitled to examine their (personal, personnel) folders.

18. The system's (principal, principle) advantage is monetary.

19. (Their, There, They're) planning to complete (their, there, they're) strategic plan this week.

20. The supervisor expects us (to, too, two) complete (to, too, two) many unnecessary reports.

Complete the "Postcheck" and the "Language Review Quiz" to test your understanding of grammar, spelling, and punctuation principles.

Cover the answer that appears below each numbered sentence. Identify the error(s) in a sentence; then, slide the cover sheet down and check your answer against the correct sentence. Refer to the pages listed in parentheses to review the reasons for each correction. The first number is a page number in Appendix C; the second number or letter identifies a certain place on the page.

1. Although Jan's request for promotion had been denied 3 times her self esteem was high.

   Although Jan's request for promotion had been denied <u>three</u> times<u>,</u> her <u>self-esteem</u> was high.

   (25, 2b) (13, 1b) (19, 6a)

2. I will appreciate you sending next months report too my home address, 9 S. Maple St.

   I will appreciate <u>your</u> sending next <u>month's</u> report <u>to</u> my home address, <u>Nine</u> <u>South</u> Maple <u>Street</u>.

   (6, 2d) (18, 4a) (33) (25, 2b) (27, 1) (27, 2b)

3. Only one of the participant's were willing to ask what do you think? [**direct quote**]

   Only one of the <u>participants</u> <u>was</u> willing to ask, <u>"What</u> do you think?<u>"</u> (18, 4) (7, 1a) (20, 7a; 28, 8) (20, 7a)

4. On March 1st, 2004 we moved to a five room suite, it was formally occupied by Woodson Travel Agency.

   On March <u>1, 2004</u>, we moved to a <u>five-room</u> suite<u>;</u> it was <u>formerly</u> occupied by Woodson Travel Agency.

   On March <u>1, 2004</u>, we moved to a <u>five-room</u> suite<u>,</u> <u>which</u> was <u>formerly</u> occupied by Woodson Travel Agency. (14, 1g) (19, 6a) (15, 2a; 14, e) (32,20)

5. The box, which was in room 12, has been prepared for mailing, all other boxes are to be wrapped with heavy paper and returned to room 5.

   The box <u>that</u> was in <u>Room</u> 12 has been prepared for mailing<u>;</u> all other boxes are to be wrapped with heavy paper and returned to <u>Room</u> 5.

   [**for . . . mailing<u>,</u> but . . . .**] (14, e) (28, 6) (15, 2a) (28, 6)

6. I am willing to complete this long complicated questionnaire but I lack the required experience.

   I am willing to complete this long<u>,</u> complicated questionnaire<u>;</u> but I lack the required experience. (14, d) (16, b)

7. Although the company has lost their first place position the next six months predictions are promising.

   Although the company has lost <u>its</u> <u>first-place</u> position<u>,</u> the next six <u>months'</u> predictions are promising. (32, 34) (19, 6a) (18, 4b)

8. That price seems reasonable for you and I, however, it probably seems very high for a recently-hired assistant.

   That price seems reasonable for you and <u>me;</u> <u>however</u>, it probably seems very high for a <u>recently</u> <u>hired</u> assistant. (5, 2b) (16, 2c) (19, 6b2)

9. The spellcheck was not able to detect all errors, for example, derive was keyed incorrectly as drive.

   The spellcheck was not able to detect all errors<u>;</u> for example, <u>derive</u> was keyed incorrectly as <u>drive</u>. (16, 2c) (21, 8a) (21, 8a)

10. The following employees have worked 7 hours of overtime this week; Welch, 4, Redford, 6, and Woods, 11.

    The following employees have worked <u>seven</u> hours of overtime this week<u>:</u> Welch, 4<u>;</u> Redford, 6<u>;</u> and Woods, 11. (25, 2b) (17, 3a) (16, 2e)

11. Helen made a higher score than any one in her work unit but her promotion was denied because of habitual tardiness.

    Helen made a higher score than <u>anyone</u> else in her work unit<u>,</u> but her promotion was denied because of habitual tardiness. (10, 4) (13, 1a)

12. Spamming is considered improper online behavior by most netiquette experts.

    <u>*Spamming*</u> is considered improper online behavior by most netiquette experts. (21, 8a)

To test your understanding of the grammar, spelling, and punctuation principles presented in Appendix C, identify the error(s) in each sentence.

1. Less than 25% of the questionnaires mailed on June 21st have been returned.

2. George was once in charge of security at the capital building, he is not impressed with our firms security system.

3. Lin Daniel, President of Haneman Industries has written an article that will appear in "Newsweek".

4. Will you please find out whether first and second year students are eligible too receive that scholarship.

5. Although the committee agreed with the plant managers' conclusions; several members raised serious questions about the survey instrument.

6. John has submitted more suggestions than anyone in his department but he has yet to receive an award.

7. The procedure has been highly successful; however, is not popular in the advertising department.

8. The man, who came late to the meeting, is the new Sales Manager for the southwest region.

9. The 3 applicants were waiting to interview for the same job, therefore they had little to say to each other.

10. Only one of my recommendations were considered, this was very disappointing to the supervisor and I.

11. Most of the discussion was devoted to personal policy but that topic has not been listed on the agenda.

12. After you have completed your Management class, write to me, we have some highly-important matters to discuss.

13. When you rewrite the final draft please change the word charge to debit.

14. Each of our assistants are required to take a short intensive Internet course.

15. 13 respondents thought the company was loosing site of it's objectives.

16. One June 3, 2003 the Carlisle Pennsylvania location was officially approved.

17. John insisted on us listening to his play by play recap of the game.

18. No the bicycle comes in these styles only, 1) road, 2) mountain and 3) Y-frame.

19. The sight for the new plant is 5 blocks East of N. Lampkin St.

20. While presenting the proposed change in distribution, an emergency call required the manager to leave abruptly.

Appendix

d

Grading Symbols and Proofreaders' Marks

Your instructor may use the following grading symbols and the proofreaders' marks in Figure A-1, pages A-2–A-3 to note corrections on your writing assignments. Use this feedback to continue to review specific language principles and to improve your writing on each assignment.

Content

appeal	Incorporate primary appeal (central selling point).
cite	Add a citation to a direct quotation or paraphrased idea from a supporting source.
eth	Use ethical, honest language that abides by legal requirements.
explain	Provide sufficient detail to develop the main idea.
facts	Verify accuracy of names, places, amounts, and other data.
spec action	Identify specific action to be taken.

Organization

c-p	Include a counterproposal to regain lost or damaged goodwill.
close	Use a closing sentence that is courteous and indicates a continuing relationship with the receiver.

d-order	Use deductive organizational pattern for message (place main idea in the first paragraph).
i-order	Use inductive organizational pattern for message (position details or explanation before the main idea).
log seq	Present supporting details in a logical sequence to improve organization.
r/sp	Include resale or sales promotion.

Style

act	Use active voice.
awk	Revise awkward expression to make smoother and more readable.
bf	Use bias-free language.
choppy	Use longer sentences to avoid choppiness. Vary sentence structure.
clr	Improve clarity so that message is easily understood.
coh	Develop coherence between ideas. Repeat key ideas or add transitional expression to avoid abrupt changes in thought.
con	State ideas concisely; include only essential ideas.
emp	Emphasize this significant thought.
obv	Eliminate obvious statement.
r-vp	State from reader's viewpoint.
redun	Eliminate redundancy.
tone	Use conversational and positive tone.
you	Emphasize the "you" viewpoint.
vague	Revise to eliminate vagueness.
var	Vary sentence length and structure and paragraph length.
wordy	Revise to tighten sentence structure.
wc	Improve word choice by providing word with precise meaning or eliminating cliché, outdated, or overally casual expression.
// or par	Use parallel expressions in a list of related items.

Mechanics

abv	Use correct abbreviation or do not abbreviate.
cap	Correct capitalization error.
cs	Revise comma splice by separating independent clauses with a semicolon or comma.
dm	Correct misplaced or dangling modifier by moving modifier closer to the word it describes.
exp	Eliminate expletives (*there are, here is, it is*).
frg	Revise sentence fragment to express a complete thought.
num	Express numbers in correct word or figure form.
pro agr	Make each pronoun agree in number with its antecedent.
pro case	Choose correct subjective, objective, or possessive case for each pronoun.
ref	Correct ambiguous pronoun reference; avoid pronoun referring to a phrase, clause, sentence, or paragraph.
ro	Revise run-on or fused sentence by adding a comma or a semicolon to separate the independent clauses.
s/v agr	Make each subject and verb agree.
sp	Correct spelling.
v-shift	Correct unnecessary shifts in verb.
ww	Correct wrong word (e.g., *your* for *you're*).

Format

cen ↔ or ↕	Center document horizontally (↔) or vertically (↕).
bl or nl	Add bulleted or numbered list for added emphasis.
ss, ds, or qs	Insert single, double, or quadruple space.
mar	Revise margins to fit document attractively on the page.

References

Chapter 1

[1]Baer, S. (2002, July 3). Anthrax response leader to head CDC; AIDS expert became chief spokeswoman after agency came under fire. *The Baltimore Sun*, p. 1A.

[2]McKenna, M. A. J. (2002, July 4). Q & A with Dr. Julie Gerberding: "We have the opportunity to transform public health." *The Atlanta Journal and Constitution*, p. 12A.

[3]The challenges facing workers in the future. (1999, August). *HR Focus*, 6.

[4]Roth, D. (2000, January 10). My job at The Container Store. *Fortune*, 74–78.

[5]Hunt, V. D. (1993). *Managing for quality: Integrating quality and business strategy*. Homewood, IL: Business One Irwin. [p. 37].

[6]Garvey, M. (2002, July 3). First woman likely to be named to head CDC. *Los Angeles Times*, p. 1A18.

[7]McKenna, M.A.J. (2002, July 4). Q & A with Dr. Julie Gerberding: We have the opportunity to transform public health. *The Atlanta Journal and Constitution*, p. 12A.

[8]Bayer, J. A. (2002, August 12). Fall from grace. *BusinessWeek, 50*(7).

[9]A critical mass of disgust? (2002, September 7). *Economist*, 57+.

[10]Slayton, M. (1980). *Common sense & everyday ethics*. Washington, DC: Ethics Resource Center.

[11]Slayton, M. (1991, May–June). Perspectives. *Ethics Journal*. Washington, DC: Ethics Resource Center.

[12]When something is rotten. (2002, July 27). *Economist*, 53+.

[13]A gift or a bribe? (2002, September). *State Legislatures, 2*(8), 9.

[14]Mathison, D. L. (1988). Business ethics cases and decision models: A call for relevancy in the classroom. *Journal of Business Ethics, 10*, 781.

[15]McGarry, M. J. (1994, June 9). Short cuts. *Newsday*, p. A50.

[16]Allen, M. (1996). NAFTA can't undo mistakes: Small businesses still find it hard to sell into Mexico, sidestep goofs. *Dallas Business Journal*, p. 1.

[17]Francese, P. (2002, February). The American workforce. *American Demographics*. Retrieved December 30, 2002, from Lexis-Nexis database.

[18]Marshall-Mims, P. (1999, July 26). Aging work force creates new challenges for restaurant industry. *Nation's Restaurant News, 33*(30), 82.

[19]Bisio J. (1999. February). The age boom. *Risk Management, 46*(2), 22–27.

[20]Grant, G. (1996). Emerging platforms for commerce over the Internet. In Cronin, M. J. (Ed.), *The Internet strategy handbook*. (1996) Boston: Harvard Business School Press.

[21]Green, D. J., & Scott, J. C. (1996). The status of international business communication courses in schools accredited by the American Assembly of Collegiate Schools of Business. *The Delta Pi Epsilon Journal, 39*(1), 43–62.

[22]Marquardt, M. J., & Engel, D. W. (1993). HRD competencies for a shrinking world. *Training & Development, 47*(5), 59–64.

[23]Shannon, J. H., & Rosenthal, D. A. (1993). Electronic mail and privacy: Can the conflicts be resolved? *Business Forum, 18*(12), 31–34.

[24]Mason, R. O. (1986). Four ethical issues of the information age. In Dejoie, R., Fowler, G., & Paradice, D. (1991). *Ethical issues in information systems* (pp. 46–55). Boston: Boyd & Fraser.

[25]Felts, C. (1995). Taking the mystery out of self-directed work teams. *Industrial Management, 37*(2), 21–26.

[26]Miller, B. K., & Butler, J. B. (1996, November/December). Teams in the workplace. *New Accountant*, 18–24.

[27]Ray, D., & Bronstein, H. (1995). *Teaming up*. New York: McGraw Hill.

[28]The trouble with teams. (1995, January 14). *Economist*, 61.

[29]Equifax report on consumers in the information age, a national survey. (1992). In Laudon, K. C., & Laudon, J. P. (1994). *Management information systems: Organization and technology*, (3rd ed.). New York: MacMillan.

[30]Orwell, G. (1949). *1984*. New York: Signet Classics. [6–7].

[31]Brown, W. S. (1996). Technology, workplace privacy, and personhood. *Journal of Business Ethics, 15*, 1237–1248.

[32]Frohman, M. A. (1995, April 3). Do teams . . . but do them right. *IndustryWeek*, 21–24.

[33]Zuidema, K. R., & Kleiner, B. H. (1994). New developments in developing self-directed work groups. *Management Decision, 32*(8), 57–63.

[34]Barry, D. (1991). Managing the baseless team: Lessons in distributed leadership. *Organizational Dynamics, 20*(1), 31–47.

[35]Cushing, K. (2002, July 18). Instant benefits. *Computer Weekly*, p. 24.

[36]McKenna, M.A.J. (2002, July 4). Q & A with Dr. Julie Gerberding: "We have the opportunity to transform public health." *The Atlanta Journal and Constitution*, p. 12A.

[37]Pounds, M. H. (1996, April 12). New breed of executive is ruthless, highly paid. *Sun-Sentinel* (Fort Lauderdale), p. 1F.

Chapter 2

[1]Stone, B. (2002, May 20). The Carly way. *Newsweek*, 50.

[2]Galpin, T. (1995, April). Pruning the grapevine. *Training & Development, 49*(4), 28+.

[3]Chellam, R. (1999, October 29). Fiorina's fun formula for success. *Business Times* (Singapore), p. 30.

[4]Zesiger, S. (1999, August 16). Fortune cover girls storm valley. *Fortune*, 29.

[5]Chellam, R. (1999, October 29). Fiorina's fun formula for success. *Business Times* (Singapore), p. 30.

[6]Hersey, P., & Blanchard, K. H. (1982). *Management of organizational behavior: Utilizing human resources*, (4th ed.) Englewood Cliffs, NJ: Prentice-Hall.

[7]Felts, C. (1995). Taking the mystery out of self-directed work teams. *Industrial Management, 37*(2), 21–26.

[8]Mehrabian, A. (1971). *Silent messages*. Belmont, CA: Wadsworth.

[9]Axtell, R. E. (1997, April). Watch what you say: Hand gestures mean different things to different people. *Reader's Digest*, 71–72.

[10]Flannigan, T. (1990). Successful negotiating with the Japanese. *Small Business Reports, 15*(6), 47–52.

[11]Briggs, W. (1998, December). Next for communicators: Global negotiation. *Communication World, 16*(1), 12+.

[12]Hillkirk, J. (1993, November 9). More companies reengineering: Challenging status quo now in vogue. *USA Today*, p. 1b.

[13]Zuidema, K. R., & Kleiner, B. H. (1994, October). Self-directed work groups gain popularity. *Business Credit*, 21–26.

[14]Hunt, V. D. (1993). *Managing for quality: Integrating quality and business strategy*. Homewood, IL: Business One Irwin. [p. 121].

[15]Chaney, L. H., & Lyden, J. A. (1998, May). Managing meetings to manage your image. *Supervision, 59*(5), 13–15.

[16]Munter, M. (1998, June). Meeting technology: From low-tech to high-tech. *Business Communication Quarterly, 61*(2), 80–87.

[17]Munter, M. (1998, June). Meeting technology: From low-tech to high-tech. *Business Communication Quarterly, 61*(2), 80–87.

[18]Stuart, C. (1994, February). Why can't a woman be more like a man? *Training Tomorrow*, 22–24.

[19]Kaser, J. S. (1985). Count me in: Guidelines for enhancing participation in mixed-gender groups. Su. Doc.#FD.1.310/2:29Y996. Washington D.C.: U.S. Government Printing Office.

[20]Savicki. V., & Kelley, M. (2000, October). Computer mediated communication: Gender and group communication. *CyberPsychology & Behavior,* 3, 817+.

[21]McCafferty, D. (2002, August 5). Keeping e-mail secure. *VARbusiness,* p. NA. Retrieved September 26, 2002, from http://infotrac.thomsonlearning.com database.

[22]Marchetti, M. (1999, September). A sales pro tries to energize HP. *Sales & Marketing Management,* 151(9), 15.

[23]Salopek, J. J. (1999, September). Is anyone listening? *Training & Development, 53*(9), 58+.

Chapter 3

[1]Dennett, J. T. (1988). Not to say is better than to say: How rhetorical structure reflects cultural context in Japanese-English technical writing, 16-1998. In Subbiah, M. (1992). Adding a new dimension to the teaching of audience analysis: Cultural awareness. *IEEE, 35*(1), 14–17.

[2]Farren, C. (1999, June). How to eliminate the generation gap in today's work team. *Employee Benefit News,* 34.

[3]Heselbarth, R. (1999). Good managers must cross millennial generation gap. *Contractor, 46*(7), 10.

[4]Coolidge, S. (1999, August 9). Generations apart. *Christian Science Monitor,* 11.

[5]Accounting industry likely to see more skeptics in positions of oversight. (2002, November 11), *Chicago Tribune,* Retrieved November 14, 2002, from EBSCOhost database.

[6]Reinemund, S. S. (1992). Today's ethics and tomorrow's work place. *Business Forum, 17*(2), 6–9.

[7]Telushkin, J. (1997). Avoid words that hurt. *USA Today,* p. 74.

[8]Horton, T. R. (1990, January). Eschew obfuscation. *Security Management, 34*(1), 22+.

[9]Mckenna, J. F. (1990, March 19). Tales from the circular file. *IndustryWeek,* 38.

[10]Husted, B. (1999, November 28). Cyberscene; E-cards perfect for the forgetful. *Atlanta Constitution,* p. 3H.

[11]Cole-Gomolski, B. (1998, December 29, 1997–January 5). IS casts wary eye on digital greeting. *Computerworld, 32*(1), 2.

[12]Rodenbough, D. T., & Rodgers, V. L. (2001, June). *Using communication to transform culture—A case study from Hallmark Cards, Inc.* Paper presented at IABC International Conference. Retrieved November 8, 2002, from Academic Search Premier database.

[13]Shi, D. (1997, March 17). "We regret you'll be unbearable." *Christian Science Monitor,* 18.

[14]Corbitt, T. (1994, December). A leap over the language barrier. *Accountancy,* 62.

[15]Machine translating (2002, March 16). Tongues on the web. *Economist, 362,* 26+.

[16]Nobel, C. (2002, September 23). Industry capsule: Translator runs on pocket PCs. *EWeek,* 18.

Chapter 4

[1]Prudential, MetLife are first to speak clients' language (1999, July). *Best's Review, 100*(3), 93.

[2]Stucker, H. (1999). Annuity issuers hustling to speak 'plain English.' *National Underwriter, 103*(14), 7, 22.

[3]Barry, J., Wolffe, R., Brant, M., Klaidman, D., & Joseph, N. (2002, December 160). The quiet power of Condi Rice, *Newsweek,* 24–34.

[4]Fontaine, V. (2002, October). Receiving loud and clear: While it may appear that speech language technologies have not had the impact that many initially predicted, Vincent Fontaine, CEO of Babel Technologies, argues that recent developments are now starting to bear fruit. *Communicate.* Retrieved January 3, 2003, from the InfoTrac College Edition database.

[5]Rindegard, J. (1999). Use clear writing to show you mean business. *InfoWorld, 21*(47), 78.

[6]Gunning, R. (1968). *The technique of clear writing.* New York: McGraw-Hill.

[7]Dyrud, M. A. (1996). Teaching by example: Suggestions for assignment design. *Business Communication Quarterly, 59*(3), 67–70.

[8]Wrong number. (1995). *Central New Jersey Business, 8(*13), 3.

[9]Neuwirth, R. (1998). Error message: To err is human, but darn expensive. *Editor & Publisher, 131*(29), 4.

[10]Armstrong again proves strong. (1996, May 7). *The Fresno Bee*, p. C3.

[11]Charlton, J. (Ed.) (1985). *The writer's quotation book*. Stamford, CT: Ray Freeman.

[12]Sullivan, M. (2002, September 16). Collaboration. *Forbes*, 7.

[13]Downing, C. E., & Clark, A. S. (1999). Groupware in practice. *Information Systems Management, 16*(2), 25.

[14]Newing, R. (1997, January). Benefits of groupware. *Management Accounting*, 56–57.

[15]Weintraub, A. (2002, December 23). Privacy rights—In plain English. *BusinessWeek*, 10.

[16]Plain English Campaign. (2003). Retrieved January 4, 2003, from http://www.plainenglish.co.uk

Chapter 5

[1]American Resort Development Association. (2003). A consumer's guide to vacation ownership. Retrieved January 14, 2003, from http://www.arda.org/industry/arda/public/guide/guide.htm#growth

[2]What the futurists see. (1999, September). *Communication World, 16*(8), 40–41.

[3]McCune, J. C. (1997). E-mail etiquette. *Management Review, 4*(86), 14.

[4]Letters: E-mail etiquette. (1996, July 26). *Information Week*, 6.

[5]Mohan, S. (1998, June 29). New technology makes communication harder. *InfoWorld*. Retrieved July 13, 2000, from http:// archive.infoworld.com/cgi-bin/displayStat.pl?/careers/980629comm.htm

[6]Gerlitz, E. (1999). The facts about computer 'e-mail viruses.' Retrieved July 12, 2000, from http://www.gerlitz.com/virushoax

[7]Cushing, K. (2002, July 18). Instant benefits. *Computer Weekly*, 24.

[8]Electronic Privacy Information Center. (2002). BusinessWeek/Harris Poll: A growing threat. Report in *BusinessWeek Online*. Retrieved January 25, 2003, from http://www.epic.org/privacy/survey

[9]Greenlaw, P. S. (1997). The impact of federal legislation to limit electronic monitoring. *Public Personnel Management, 26*, 227–244.

[10]McLaren, B. J. (1999). *The Internet*. Cincinnati: South-Western Educational Publishing.

[11]Pretzer, M. (1998, September/October). Common sense web page design: Cleaning out the cob webs. *Rural Telecommunications, 17*(5), 40–46.

[12]Ackermann, E., & Hartman, K. (1999). *Internet today!* Wilsonville, OR: Franklin, Beedle & Associates.

[13]McAlpine, R. (2001). *Web word wizardry: A guide to writing for the Web and intranet*. Berkeley, Ten Speed Press.

[14]Chase, N. (1999, April). Quality data on the Internet. *Quality, 38*(5), 122–126.

[15]Dvorak, P. (1999, July 22). Automatic project web pages keep teams informed. *Machine Design, 71*(14), 88.

[16]Fichter, D. (2001, November/December). Zooming in: Writing content for intranets. *Online, 25*(6), 80+

[17]How to get the most out of voice mail (2000, February). *The CPA Journal, 70*(2), 11.

[18]Leland, K., & Bailey, K. (1999). *Customer service for dummies* (2nd ed.). New York: Wiley.

[19]Berkley, S. (2003, July). Help stamp out bad voicemail! *The Voice Coach Newsletter*. Retrieved July 25, 2003 from http://www.greatvoice.com/archive)_vc/archiveindex_vc.html

[20]McCarthy, M. L. (1999, October). E-mail, voice-mail and the Internet: How employers can avoid getting cut by the double-edged sword of technology. *Business Credit, 100*(9), 44+.

[21]Cell phone etiquette (2001, March). *Office Solutions, 18*(3), 13.

[22]Emerging trends in technology. (2002, January–February). *Financial Executive, 18*(1), 12.

[23]Mason, R. O. (1986). Four ethical issues of the information age. In Dejoie, R., Fowler, G., & Paradice, D. (1991). *Ethical issues in information systems* (pp. 46–55). Boston: Boyd & Fraser.

[24]Laudon, K. C., & Laudon, J. P. (1994). *Management information systems: Organization and technology*, 3rd ed., New York: Macmillan.

Chapter 6

[1]The new college try. (2000, May). *Brandmarketing 7*(5) 11.

[2]Brown, S. S. (1998, August 27). The backpack: For 40 million teens, it's the bag of choice. *Denver Rocky Mountain News*, p. 3D.

[3]Hugenberg, L. W., LaCivita, R. M., Lubanovic, A. M. (1996). International business and training: Preparing for the global economy. *Journal of Business Communication, 33*(2), 205–222.

[4]Oblander, P., & Daniels, E. (1997). International communication and the U.S.-Japan lumber trade: An exploratory study. *Forest Products Journal, 47*(3), 38–44.

[5]Varner, I. I. (1987). Internationalizing business communication courses. *Bulletin of the Association for Business Communication, 50*(4), 11+.

[6]Stern, A. (2001, July 22). New president of Appleton, Wis.-area backpack firm keeps youthful perspective. *The Post-Crescent*. Retrieved February 11, 2003, from LexisNexis database.

[7]Buss, D. (1999, November). Teen nation. *Brandmarketing, 6*(11), 16

[8]Keizer, G. (1992, August). Press one for Gregg. *Compute!, 17*(7), 73–75.

[9]Kaye, S. (1999, March). Attitude adjustments. *Quality Progress, 32*(3), 28–33.

[10]Discarded hard drives prove a trove of personal info. (2003, January 16). *The Daily Sentinel*, 7A.

Chapter 7

[1]Suriano, R. (2003, August 28). NASA chief vows to make changes set out in report; O'Keefe says he'll correct flaws in culture blamed for Columbia disaster. *The Baltimore Sun*, p. 3A.

[2]Sussman, S. W., & Sproull, L. (1999). Straight talk: Delivering bad news through electonic communication. *Information Systems Research, 10*(2), 150+. Retrieved April 13, 2003, from Business Source Premier database.

[3]Weaver, J. (2003, March 20). Ads retreat amid Iraq war coverage. MSNBC. Retrieved April 1, 2003, from http://www.msnbc.com/news/888117.asp

[4]Federal Trade Commission. (2003)). *Fair Credit Reporting Act*. Retrieved April 14, 2003, from the World Wide Web: http://www.ftc.gov/os/statutes/fcrajump.htm

[5]Tolson, M. (2003, February 9). Dittemore's church prepared him for crisis, friends say. *Houston Chronicle*, p. 20A.

[6]Carreau, M. (2003, April 29). Lame duck Dittemore 'accountable' to team. *Houston Chronicle*, p. A1.

[7]Malnic, E. (2003, February 6). Hot seat makes a good fit for NASA's shuttle manager: Ron Dittemore gets high marks for his candid replies to probing questions. *Los Angeles Times*, p. 20.

[8]Morris, J. (2003, May 12). NASA names Stennis director new shuttle program manager. *Aerospace Daily*, p. 4.

[9]Advice from the pros on the best way to deliver bad news. (2003, February). IOMA's Report on Customer Relationship Management, 5–6.

[10]Makeever, J. J. (1996, October 3). Privacy and anonymity in cyberspace. A law of cyberspace? Retrieved November 25, 1997 from the World Wide Web: http://host1.jmlx.edu/cyber/1996/r-priv.html

Chapter 8

[1]Bradley, P., Gooley, T., & Cooke, J. A. (2000, February). FedEx re-brands units, launches home delivery service. *Logistics Management & Distribution Report, 39*(2), 25.

[2]Thompson, R., & Howard, S. (2000, January 21). Evolving FDX Corp. retools for higher place on e-chain. *The Plain Dealer*, p. 2C.

[3]Shook, D. (2002, April 30). FedEx keeps delivering. *BusinessWeek Online*. Retrieved May 27, 2003, from EBSCOhost database.

[4]FedEx Corporation. (2000). About FedEx Corporation. Retrieved July 10, 2000, from the World Wide Web: http://www.fedex.com

[5]Iwata, E. (2000, August 1). Gateway goes to extremes to empathize. *USA Today*, p. 3B.

[6]Cody, S. (1906). *Success in letter writing: Business and social*. Chicago: A. C. McClurg. [pp. 122–126].

[7]Cooper, T., & Kelleher, T. (2001). Better mousetrap? Of Emerson, ethics, and postmillennium persuasion. *Journal of Mass Media Ethics, 16*(2/3), 176+.

[8]Neuborne, E., & Kerwin, K. (1999, February 15). Generation Y: Today's teens—the biggest bulge since the boomers—may force marketers to toss their old tricks. *BusinessWeek Online*. Retrieved May 14, 2003, from http://www.businessweek.com

[9]Beauprez, J. (2003, April 13). Despite their unpopularity, Web pop-up ads adept at selling products. *The Denver Post*. Retrieved May 28, 2003, from InfoTrac database.

[10]Nelson, E. (1993). WordPerfect 6.0: 10 new things it does for you. *WordPerfect Magazine, 5*(7), 36–38, 40, 42–43. [p. 37].

[11]Sweeney, T. (2000, May). E-mail marketing set to take off. *Credit Union Management*, 8.

[12]Bell, J. D. (1994). Motivate, educate, and add realism to business communication using the claim letter. *Business Education Forum, 48*(2), 42–43.

[13]Liu, B. (2002, January 15). Branching out helps FedEx to deliver success. *Financial Times*, p. 24.

[14]Liu, B. (2002, January 15). Branching out helps FedEx to deliver success. *Financial Times*, p. 24.

[15]Krause, K. S. (2000, January 24). Unleashing FedEx. *Traffic World, 261*(4), 11–12.

[16]Steak and Ale. (1997). *Signature style at Steak and Ale*. Dallas, TX: Steak and Ale.

[17]Do-it-yourself: Stop junk mail, email and phone calls. (1998). Evergreen Industries. Retrieved May 27, 2003 from http://www.obviously.com/junkmail

[18]Federal Trade Commission. (2003, March). You make the call: The FTC's new telemarketing sales rule. Retrieved May 27, 2003, from http://www.ftc.gov/bcp/conline/pubs/tmarkg/donotcall.htm

[19]Walker, W. (2000, May 9). Junk mail, telemarketers, catalogs: How to get off the list. *Family Circle*, 40–43.

[20]Wal-Mart annual report 2002. Retrieved February 25, 2003, from http://walmartstores.com/Files/2002_annualreport.pdf, 7.

Chapter 9

[1]Leonhardt, D. (2000, June 9). Procter & Gamble shake-up follows poor profit outlook. *The New York Times*, p. C1.

[2]Neff, J. (2003, February 24). New area. *Advertising Age, 74*(8), 6.

[3]Wound healing discovery leads to antiaging cosmetics. (2003, April 25). *Drug Week*, 34.

[4]Grimes, B. (2003, May 6). Fooling Google. *PC Magazine, 22*(8), 74.

[5]Syllabus of Supreme Court Opinion for 96-511(1997). Reno, Attorney General of the United States, *et al.* v. American Civil Liberties Union *et al.* Retrieved February 27, 1998, from the World Wide Web: http://supct.law.cornell.edu/supct/html/96-511.ZS.html

[6]Adams, D. (2000). Literacy, learning, and media. *Technos: Quarterly for Education and Technology*. Retrieved December 4, 2001, from the World Wide Web: http://www.findarticles.com

[7]Rosencrance, L. (2000, April 3). BetaSphere delivers FedEx some customer feedback. *Computerworld*, 36.

[8]Tomkins, R., & Voyle, S. (2000, June 12). Revenge of the proctoids: The ousting of Durk Jager as Procter & Gamble's mould-breaking chief executive may end a period of turmoil but not solve the company's problems. *Financial Times* (London), p. 22.

[9]Procter & Gamble's renovator-in-chief. (2002, December 12). *BusinessWeek Online*. Retrieved May 12, 2003, from EBSCOhost database.

[10]Reece, D. (2000, June 14). Procter & Gamble calls on an exorcist. *Ottawa Citizen*, p. D6.

[11]Rowling wins Potter plagiaism case (2002, September 19). BBCI. Retrieved May 14, 2003, from http://news.bbc.co.uk/1/hi/entertainment/arts/2268024.stm

[12]Bruner, K. F. (2001). *The publication manual of the American Psychological Association*, (5th ed.). Washington, DC: American Psychological Association [p. 216].

[13]Kinzer, S. (1994, August 22). Germany upholds tax on fast-food restaurants. *The New York Times*, p. 2.

[14]Kets de Vries, M. F. R. (1994). Toppling the cultural tower of Babel. *Chief Executive, 94*, 68.

[15]Heath, R. P. (1996, October). Think globally. *American Demographics*, 48–54.

[16]Sandoval, G. (2002, June 13). The tech success that Ivory built. *News.com*: http://news.com.com/1200-1120-975484.html

[17]Alfvin, C. B. (1997, May). Information please!...or not. *Once a Year Magazine*. Retrieved December 16, 1997, from the World Wide Web: http://www.tefnet.org/oay97/overload.html

[18]Stanley, T. L. (2003, March). Information overload: Conquer the chaos. *Supervision, 64*(3), 10–12.

[19]E-mail contributes to "Information Overload, claim UK managers (2003, February). *Information Systems Auditor*, 8.

[20]Alfvin, C. B. (1997, May). Information please!...or not. *Once a Year Magazine*. Retrieved December 16, 1997, from the World Wide Web: http://www.tefnet.org/oay97/overload.html

[21]Johnson, M. (1997, April/May). Battling information overload. *Communication World*, 26-27.

Chapter 10

[1]Stone, B. (2003, February 24). Yahoo's pony tricks. *Newsweek, 141*(8). Retrieved April 17, 2003, from EBSCOhost database.

[2]Walker, L. (2002, January 16). New to Yahoo: Home-page improvement. *The Washington Post*, p. H07.

[3]Martin, M. H. (1997, November 27). The man who makes sense of numbers. *Fortune*, 273–275.

[4]Wright, P., & Jansen, C. (1998). How to limit clinical errors in interpretation of data. *Lancet, 352*(9139), 1539–1543.

[5]Kienzler, D. S. (1997). Visual ethics. *The Journal of Business Communication, 34*(2), 171–187. [p. 17].

[6]Borden, M. (2000, January 10). Keeping Yahoo! simple—and fast. *Fortune*, 167.

[7]Benezra, K. (2003, January 20). The game. *Brandweek*. Retrieved May 6, 2003, from Lexis-Nexis Academic database.

[8]Hewitt, M. (1997, March 13). Armed to present. *Marketing*, 33–36. [p. 3].

Chapter 11

[1]AFLAC's annual report ranked first in Chief Executive magazine's listing of 10 Best (1999, November 17). *PR Newswire, Financial News*.

[2]AFLAC's annual report ranked first in Chief Executive magazine's listing of 10 Best (1999, November 17). *PR Newswire, Financial News*.

[3]Osundiya, G. (1997, March). Making the annual report more relevant. *Management Accounting*—London, 58.

[4]Get ready for international financial statements you can work with! (2003, March). *Managing Credit, Receivables and Collections*, 8.

[5]Moyer, L. (1999, December 2). Ads libs: Annual report guru ranks those that measure up, or don't. *The American Banker*, 4.

[6]Critic of annual report hails Manitowoc Co. for readability, information. (1999, October 11). *Milwaukee Journal Sentinel*, p. 4.

[7]Nunnemaker, J. F., Jr., & Briggs, R. O., Mittleman, D. D., Vogel, D. R., Balthazard, P. A. (1996/1997). Lessons from a dozen years of group support systems research: A discussion of lab and field findings. *Journal of Management Information Systems, 13*(3), 163–207.

[8]Emling, S. (2003, June 13). Patriot Act stirs concerns. *The Daily Sentinel* (Nacogdoches, TX), p. 4B.

[9]Dart, B. (1997). Internet copyright treaty: The stakes are high. Cox News Service. Retrieved December 19, 1997, from the World Wide Web: http://nytsyn.com/live/Latest/237_082597_094213_1037.html

[10]Wallack, T. (1997, January 20). Copyright protection now your job. *Network World*, 1, 14.

Chapter 12

[1]Out on the edges with Java. (2003, May 29). *Apple eNews*. Electronic newsletter, Apple Computer, Inc.

[2]Glinert, S. (1999, December). Presenting on the Web. *Home Office Computing*, 114.

[3]Axtell, R. E. (1992). *Do's and taboos of public speaking: How to get those butterflies flying in formation*. New York: John Wiley.

[4]Britz, J. D. (1999, October). You can't catch a marlin with a meatball. *Presentations, 13*(10), A1–22.

[5]Hughes, M. (1990). Tricks of the speechwriter's trade. *Management Review, 9*(11), 56–58.

[6]Hughes, M. (1990). Tricks of the speechwriter's trade. *Management Review, 9*(11), 56–58.

[7]Axtell, R. E. (1992). *Do's and taboos of public speaking: How to get those butterflies flying in formation.* New York: John Wiley.

[8]Mayer, K. R. (1998). *Well spoken oral communication for business.* New York: Dryden.

[9]Decker, B. (1992). *You've got to be believed to be heard.* New York: St. Martin's Press.

[10]Jayaraman, M. S. (1999, September 15). No point in power presentations. *Computer Today*, 7.

[11]Ganzel, R. (2000, February). Power pointless. *Presentations, 14*(2), 53–58.

[12]Holzberg, C. S. (1999, December). When you wish upon a star. *Home Office Computing*, 32.

[13]U. S. Copyright Office. (2000, September). What is copyright? Retrieved June 20, 2003, from http://www.copyright.gov/circs/circ1.html#wci

[14]Zielinski, D. (2001, July). Stop! Thief! The great web copyright crackdown. *Presentations, 15*(7), 50(9).

[15]University of Texas System. Using materials from the Internet: What are the rules? Retrieved June 20, 2003, from http://www.templetons.com/brad/copymyths.html

[16]Newcombe, P. J. (1991). *Voice and diction,* (2nd ed.). Raleigh, NC: Contemporary Publishing Company.

[17]Axtell, R. E. (1992). *Do's and taboos of public speaking: How to get those butterflies flying in formation.* New York: John Wiley.

[18]Decker, B. (1992). *You've got to be believed to be heard.* New York: St. Martin's Press. [p. 137].

[19]Kincaid, P., & Stees, Y. (1992). Learning to use simplified English: A preliminary study. *Technical Communication, 39*(1), 69(5).

[20]Hanke, J. (1998, January). Presenting as a team. *Presentations, 12*(1), 74–82.

[21]Hanke, J. (1998, January). Presenting as a team. *Presentations, 12*(1), 74–82.

[22]Hanke, J. (1998, January). Presenting as a team. *Presentations, 12*(1), 74–82.

[23]Flett, N. (1998, March). Ensure you're on the same team. *Management*, 14.

[24]Hanke, J. (1998, January). Presenting as a team. *Presentations, 12*(1), 74–82.

[25]Davids, M. (1999). Smiling for the camera. *Journal of Business Strategy, 20*(3), 20–24.

[26]Turner, C. (1998, February). Become a web presenter! (Really it's not that hard). *Presentations, 12*(2), 26–27.

[27]Nicholaus B., & Lowrie P. (1996). *The conversation piece: Creative questions to tickle the mind.* New York: Ballantine Books.

[28]DeShields, O. W., Kara, A., & Kaynak, E. (1996). Source effects in purchase decisions: The impact of physical attractiveness and accent of salesperson. *International Journal of Research in Marketing, 13*(1), 89–101.

[29]Stern, D. A. (1996). Speaking without an accent. Dialect Accent Specialists, Inc. Retrieved May 10, 2000, from http://www.bypass.com/~dasinc/

Chapter 13

[1]Hein, K. (2003, April). Talking heads: Practical advice from 10 top companies. *Incentive, 177*(4), 21–22.

[2]Container Store's CEO: People are most valued asset. (2003, January 13). *Business and Management Practices*, 18.

[3]Roth, D. (2000, January 10). My job at The Container Store. *Fortune*, 74–78.

[4]Jackson, T. (2003). Find a job you love and success will follow. *Career Journal (The Wall Street Journal).* Retrieved July 1, 2003, from http://www.careerjournal.com/jobhunting/strategies/20030415-jackson.html

[5]Riley, M. F. *The Riley guide: Employment opportunities and job resources on the Internet.* Retrieved May 17, 2000, from the World Wide Web: http://www.dbm.com/jobguide/

[6]Wilson, K. C. (2003). The new rules for hunting on the net. *Career Journal* from *The Wall Street Journal.* Retrieved July 3, 2003, from http://www.careerjournal.com/jobhunting/usingnet/19990817-wilson.html

[7]Marcus, J. (2003). How to prompt employers to read your résumé. *Career Journal* from *The Wall Street Journal*. Retrieved July 3, 2003, from http://www.careerjournal.com/jobhunting/resumes/20020130-marcus.html

[8]McGarvey, R. (2003, April 15). Lies, damned lies and résumés: Background checks get more vigilant. *Electronic Business, 29*(5), 17.

[9]McGarvey, R. (2003, April 15). Lies, damned lies and résumés: Background checks get more vigilant. *Electronic Business, 29*(5), 17.

[10]Ireland. S. (2002, July–August). A résumé that works. *Searcher, 10*(7), 98(12).

[11]Leonard, B. (2003, February). Study suggests bias against 'black' names on résumés. *HR Magazine, 48*(2), 29–30.

[12]Leslie, L. M. (2002, September 9). Muslims, Arabs say September 11 backlash has changed: Physical and verbal harassment have been replaced by subtle discrimination, related to jobs, for example. *Star Tribune (Minneapolis)*, p. 8A.

[13]Seifert, M. W. (2001, July 20). Appearances count to the point of bias? *Austin Business Journal, 21*(18), 21.

[14]Bowers, P. (2001, October 19). Bridging the gender gap vital part of networking. *The Business Journal-Milwaukee, 19*(4), 13.

[15]Harshbarger, C. (2003). You're out! *Strategic Finance, 84*(11), 46(4).

[16]Hutchinson, K. L., & Brefka, D. S. (1997). Personnel administrators' preferences for résumé content; ten years after. *Business Communication Quarterly, 60*(2), 67.

[17]Crosby, O. (1999, Summer). Résumés, applications, and cover letters. *Occupational Outlook Quarterly,* 2–14.

[18]Kennedy, J. L., & Morrow, T. J. (1994). *Electronic résumé revolution: Create a winning résumé for the new world of job seeking.* New York: John Wiley.

[19]Kennedy, J. L., & Morrow, T. J. (1994). *Electronic résumé revolution: Create a winning résumé for the new world of job seeking.* New York: John Wiley.

[20]Kennedy, J. L., & Morrow, T. J. (1994). *Electronic résumé revolution: Create a winning résumé for the new world of job seeking.* New York: John Wiley.

[21]Young, J. (2002). 'E-portfolios' could give students a new sense of their accomplishments. *Chronicle of Higher Education, 48*(26), 31(2)

[22]King, J. (1997, July 28). Point-and-click career service: Recruitingware does more than track résumés. *Computerworld*, p. 37.

[23]Murray, F. (2000, May). Associates keep score at The Container Store. *Chain Store Age, 76*(5), 18.

[24]Roth, D. (2000, January 10). My job at The Container Store. *Fortune*, 74–78.

[25]Container Store's CEO: People are most valued asset. (2003, January 13). Business and Management Practices, 18.

[26]Research demonstrates the success of Internet recruiting. (2003, April). *HR Focus, 80*(4), 7.

[27]EEOC addresses online recruiting. (2002, September 15). *Employee Benefit News*. Retrieved June 25, 2003, from InfoTrac database.

Chapter 14

[1]General Electric Company. (2003). About GE Asset Management. Retrieved June 26, 2003, from http://www.geassetmanagement.com/us/about/history.html

[2]General Electric Company. (2003). GE Careers. Retrieved June 26, 2003, from: http://www.gecareers.com

[3]Washington, T. (1997). Are you prepared for interviewers' new techniques? Retrieved September 20, 2000, http://www.occ.com/occNBEW/InterviewerTechniques.html

[4]Marion, L. C. (1997, January 11). Companies tap keyboards to interview applicants. *The News and Observer*, p. B5.

[5]Bhasin, R. (1997, January). The group interview: A new selection process. *Pulp and Paper*, 47.

[6]Vicers, M. (1997, April 14). Video interviews cut recruiting costs for many firms. *International Herald Tribune*, p. 15.

[7]Vicers, M. (1997, April 14). Video interviews cut recruiting costs for many firms. *International Herald Tribune*, p. 15.

[8]Mueller, S. (1996). What skills will graduating students need to make it in the business world? *Business Journal–San Jose, 14*(8), 8.

[9]Lai, P., & Wong, I. (2000). The clash of cultures in the job interview. *Journal of Language for International Business, 11*(1), 31–40.

[10]Austin, N. K. (1996, March). The new job interview. *Working Woman,* 23–24.

[11]Kennedy, J. L., & Morrow, T. J. (1994). *Electronic résumé revolution: Create a winning résumé for the new world of job seeking.* New York: John Wiley.

[12]Kleiman, P. (2003, May). Armed for a multitude of tasks. *The Times Higher Education Supplement,* p. 4.

[13]Eng, S. (1997, June 1). Handling "behavioral interviews." *The Des Moines Register,* p. 1.

[14]Munk, N., & Oliver, S. (1997, March 24). Think fast! *Forbes,* 146–151.

[15]Clarke, R. D. (1999). None of their business. *Black Enterprise, 30*(2), 65.

[16]Smith, K. S. (1996, March 24). Interviewing tips for job seekers, managers. *Rocky Mountain News,* p. 6W.

[17]Gill, B. (1998). Establishing job reference policies. *American Printer, 220*(4), 66.

[18]Knouse, S. B. (1987). Confidentiality and the letter of recommendation: A new approach. *Bulletin of the Association for Business Communication, 50*(3), 6–8.

[19]Fortune. (2000). America's most admired companies. Retrieved June 15, 2000, http://www.fortune.com/fortune/mostadmired/gat.html

[20]Zimmerman, E. (2003, April). A subtle reference trap for unaware employers. *Workforce, 82*(4), 22.

[21]Smith, S. (2003, March 17). Rethinking your reference policy. *Westchester County Business Journal,* p. 4.

Index

N

O

P

Index to Web Enrichment

Expanded content available at the text support site is seamlessly integrated into the chapter and the end-of-chapter activities.